D1387147

John Bayley is the author of *Alice, The Queer Captain, George's Lair* and *The Red Hat* as well as the bestselling memoirs *Iris, Iris and the Friends* and *Widower's House*. He was Warton Professor of English at the University of Oxford and is a fellow of St Catherine's College.

THE IRIS TRILOGY

Iris: A Memoir of Iris Murdoch

Iris and the Friends: A Year of Memories

Widower's House

JOHN BAYLEY

Iris:

A Memoir of Iris Murdoch

For Peter Conradi and James O'Neill

PART I

THEN

1

A hot day. Stagnant, humid. By normal English standards really hot, insufferably hot. Not that England has standards about such things any more. Global warming no doubt. But it's a commonplace about growing old that there seem to be no standards any more. The Dog Days. With everything gone to the dogs.

Cheerless thoughts to be having on a pleasure jaunt, or what used to be one. For years now we've usually managed a treat for ourselves on really hot days, at home in the summer. We take the car along the bypass road from Oxford, for a mile or two, and twist abruptly off on to the verge – quite a tricky feat with fast moving traffic just behind. Sometimes there are hoots and shouts from passing cars who have had to brake at speed, but by that time we have jolted to a stop on the tussocky grass, locked the car, and crept through a gap in the hedge.

I remember the first time we did it, nearly forty-five years ago. We were on bicycles then, and there was little traffic on the unimproved road. Nor did we know where the river was exactly: we just thought it must be somewhere there. And with the ardour of comparative youth we wormed our way through the rank grass and sedge until we almost fell into it, or at least a branch of it. Crouching in the shelter of the reeds we tore our clothes off and slipped in like water-rats. A kingfisher flashed past our noses as we lay soundlessly in the dark sluggish current. A moment after we had crawled out and were drying ourselves on Iris's waist-slip a big pleasure boat chugged past within a few feet of the bank.

The steersman, wearing a white cap, gazed intently ahead. Tobacco smoke mingled with the watery smell at the roots of the tall reeds.

I still have the waist-slip, I rediscovered it the other day, bunched up at the back of a drawer, stiff with powdery traces of dry mud. It is faded to a yellowish colour, with a wrinkled ribbon, once blue, decorating the hem. Could someone, later my wife, have indeed once worn such a garment? It looks like something preserved from the wardrobe of Marie Antoinette. I never gave it back to Iris after that occasion, and I think she forgot all about it.

In any case we were having a busy day, that day. We had a lunch-time engagement to get back to. By the time we had cycled back into Oxford, and down the Woodstock Road, we were as hot as we had been earlier that morning, before we had crawled through the dense green undergrowth and discovered the river. Still dripping with sweat, and making vague efforts to tidy our hair and clothes, we rang the bell of a flat in Belsyre Court. As we waited we looked at each other expressionlessly, then burst at the same moment into a soundless fit of giggles.

Our host, who had been getting lunch, was quite a time coming to the door. He was a brilliant young doctor with green eyes called Maurice Charlton. When even younger he had been a classics don at Hertford College, and considered one of the best in the university. So good indeed that he gave it up after three years and turned to medicine. He now held a research appointment at the Radcliffe Hospital. He was supposedly rather in love with Iris. That was why he had asked her to lunch. She had told him she was spending the morning with me – we were going to cycle out together to see Cassington Church – and so could I come too?

He took it like a man. He had prepared a delicious lunch. The flat was not his own but belonged to a rich older don at Balliol, with whom he may or may not have had an ambiguous relationship. He seemed to be able to borrow the flat any time, for his friend lived mostly in college when he wasn't away in Italy or Greece.

Fifty or so years ago life in the university was more constricted and formal, but at the same time more comfortable and relaxed. For us, in those days, there was no paradox involved. We maintained public standards and conventions almost without being conscious of them, while leading our own private lives. We worked very hard, at least Iris did: I was more naturally indolent.

Maurice Charlton probably worked harder than both of us together. But he was totally relaxed, his green eyes sparkling, and with a delightful air – as soon as he saw us – of collusion in something or other: what he had been doing, what we had been doing. This intimate feel, as if we could become naughty children together any moment, was enhanced by the sombre dignity of the flat: full of rare books, good furniture, glass. I still remember the longstemmed green and white wineglasses, out of which we drank a great deal of very cold hock. I think it was the white wine people usually drank in those days.

I feel admiration now for the way Charlton must have apprehended that we had been up to something together, and not only took it in his stride but encouraged us in some way to enjoy it with him. We had never got to Cassington Church, we said. It had been far too hot. We had cycled back in an exhausted state, and it was wonderful to be here in the cool, drinking the wine. We both said something like this without looking at each other. Iris jumped to her feet to go over and kiss Maurice Charlton, and it seemed just the right and spontaneous act, making us all three laugh: we two men laughing both at and with Iris as she gazed delightedly round the dark and as it seemed rather mysteriously grand flat, as if she were Alice in Wonderland on the threshold of a new series of adventures.

As we sat laughing and eating – I remember lobster and the delicious garlic mayonnaise our host had made – I was conscious of my soaking trouser-pocket, where Iris's undergarment reposed, rolled up. I hoped the wet wouldn't get on the dining-room chair, which was covered in some sort of damask. As lunch went hilariously on we seemed more and more like a family. Through a bewitching miasma of hock I was conscious of Iris as a kind sister, fond of both her brothers, equally close to them. Maurice had the air of a brother, but also looked like a sort of patriarch as he sat grinning benignly at the top of the table.

Maurice Charlton died young, of cancer I believe, more than twenty years ago. My impression is that he never married, but I may be wrong about that. He certainly looked at Iris with his green eyes as if he liked her very much. It was possible he had borrowed the flat and prepared the lunch with a purpose, and that my presence had thwarted his plans for the afternoon. In that case I admire his behaviour all the more, at this distance in time. He carried off perfectly what might well have been for him a frustrating situation.

I mention the lunch with Maurice Charlton, and that enchanted Sunday morning when Iris and I had our first swim together, because I remember it all very vividly, not because it had any great importance in itself. Although I had met Charlton a few times, and admired him, that lunch was probably our only social occasion together. He continued to work in Oxford but we lost touch, which is why I don't know what happened to him later, except that he was a distinguished man when he died. It was typical of my relations with Iris at that time that I had very little idea of the other people in her life, or what they might mean to her. That was probably due to the ecstatic egoism of falling in love for the first time. For me it was the first time, though I was not exactly young. Iris was thirty-four, Maurice Charlton about the same age. I was twenty-eight. Difference in age, which means a good deal at school and not much in later years, was only a part of the atmosphere of that lunch party, because we seemed for the moment like a family. And a family takes such differences in age for granted.

But, as I say, I still had very little idea of the other people in Iris's life, or what they meant to her. That was instinctive on her part, I think, rather than deliberate. There was a lot of privacy about in those days. An 'open' society is what we aim for now, or say we aim for, as an enhancement of our all being more classless and democratic. We were not consciously undemocratic, I think, in the fifties, but we took private life for granted. That was particularly true in Oxford, still a scholastic society in which one could be on good terms with a large number of people, meeting them most days in college, at dinner in hall or in lecture rooms and laboratories, without having any idea of how they were situated domestically, or socially, or sexually. Other peoples' lives might seem intriguing, which was part of the fun of privacy, but they remained what was on the whole an accepted and comfortable blank.

By some emotional paradox being in love made me, at least at first, not less but more incurious about this. Iris existed for me as a wonderful and solitary being, first seen about six months before, bicycling slowly and rather laboriously past the window in St Antony's College, where I was living. Trying to work, and gazing idly out at the passing scene on the Woodstock Road, now intolerably full of traffic but then a comparatively quiet thoroughfare, I noted the lady on the bicycle (she seemed at once to me more of a lady than a girl) and wondered who she was and whether I would ever meet her. Perhaps I fell in love. Certainly it was in the innocence of love that I indulged the momentary fantasy that nothing had ever happened to her: that she was simply bicycling about, waiting for me to arrive. She was not a woman with a past, and an unknown present.

She was looking both absent and displeased. Maybe because of the weather, which was damp and drizzly.

Maybe because her bicycle was old and creaky and hard to propel. Maybe because she hadn't yet met me? Her head was down, as if she were driving on thoughtfully towards some goal, whether emotional or intellectual. I remember a friend saying playfully, perhaps a little maliciously, after she first met Iris: 'She is like a little bull.'

It's true in a way, although I have never seen it, because of course I have never seen her objectively. But if each of us resembles some sort of animal or bird, as our personalised bestiary emblem, then I can see that Iris could indeed be a small bull. Not unfriendly, but both resolute and unpredictable, looking reflectively out from under lowered brows as it walks with head down towards you.

In her first published novel, *Under the Net*, it is remarked of the leading female character that she never lets on to any one of her friends just how closely bound she is to all the rest of them. Few of them even know each other. That was true of Iris. Naturally enough it made quite a difference to the heroine of the novel, but it has never made any difference for Iris. She always used to write back to fans who had written to her. Careful long intelligent letters, directed to a person, not just to a fan. They were real letters, even though she had never met, and probably never would meet, the real person to whom she was writing. I have to try to write letters back to her fans now, and naturally enough I can't do it like that; although from their letters, and their attitude towards their adored author, I see why one of them at once replied, after Iris had written to him, that he felt now they had become 'pals for life'.

Like so much to do with our emotions the egoism of love has something absurd about it, though something touching as well. It was certainly absurd that I should have taken for granted in those days that Iris was, so to speak, pure spirit, devoted to philosophy and to her job, leading a nun-like existence in her little room in college, devoid of all the dissimulations and wonderings and plottings and plannings that I took for granted in myself. She was a superior being, and I knew that superior beings just did not have the kind of mind that I had.

Besides there had been something almost supernatural about the way I had actually met her, after I had seen her riding past the window on her bicycle. The following day I had encountered Miss Griffiths in the street, outside the Examination School where university lectures were given. A diminutive figure, she was just taking off her billowing black gown, preparatory to mounting her own bicycle and cycling home to St Anne's College. She had been lecturing on Beowulf. Miss Griffiths had had a soft spot for me ever since my Viva (the face to face oral exam), when she had congratulated me on my essay on Chaucer's *Knight's Tale*, but caught me out on a minor question of Anglo-Saxon syntax. After I had obtained my degree she had followed my career, such as it was, with benevolent interest, and now she seized me by the arm as I walked past and enquired how things were going. Things in fact were barely going at all, as I had no proper job, and stayed on sufferance in the newly-founded St Antony's College, where I was supposed to act as a tutor and guide to a few ebullient Frenchmen and Americans who had come to study science or politics there.

St Antony's at that time was a study in itself, but its principal interest for me now, and in memory, was its proximity to St Anne's College, a foundation designed at the time solely for women students, although like most other colleges it has since become bisexual. Out of the deference I felt for an older and senior member of the English faculty I walked a few yards that morning beside Miss Griffiths, who showed no immediate disposition to mount her bicycle and be off. I think she wanted to enjoy reminiscing for a moment about the exam and the Viva – like most dons she was vain of her examination exploits and technique – and to recall with the pleasure of generosity her discernment about the good points of my Chaucer essay, as well as to remind me, with the pleasure of superior knowledge, about my errors in Old English grammar. Having done those things she suddenly asked me if I would care to come to her college room for a drink that evening. I was happy to accept.

Although it was just across the road from St Antony's I had never been into St Anne's, which I regarded as an all-feminine province, likely to be virtually out of bounds to males and male students. I wasn't wholly wrong about this. Incredible as it may seem today, there were then fairly strict rules governing the conduct of men who had the nerve and temerity to go visiting in these female strongholds. They had to remain in the public parts of the college, and the girls were not allowed to receive them in their rooms. The matter was in any case of little or no interest to me. Students like myself, who had been in the army at the end of the war, were older than the new gen-eration of undergraduates, whom they were sometimes employed temporarily to instruct, owing to the post-war shortage of teachers. Oxford at the time seemed to me like a school; apart from having to teach a few of them I took no account of its younger denizens. The cinema was my resort for relaxation and refuge, and cinemas were cinemas in those days. In the afternoon they were church-like spaces dense with tobacco smoke, inhabited by couples, or by solitary worshippers motionless in the darkness, illuminated from time to time by the glowing tip of a cigarette.

The idea of a drink with funny wizened little Miss Griffiths – I imagine she was only a year or two over forty, but if I thought of it at all I thought of her as having passed the boundaries of age – was a decidedly agreeable one. Drinks were drinks in those days, just as cinemas were cinemas, and I had heard that Miss Griffiths – 'Elaine' as I afterwards came to know her – liked a good strong drop of gin. Besides it could only be a good thing to be on social terms with a senior member of the English Faculty, to which I aspired in time to belong.

All such prudential considerations vanished when I presented myself at six o'clock that evening. Miss Griffiths was just finishing a tutorial, and as I knocked on the door a young girl in a scholar's gown came out, dropping her eyes demurely at the sight of a man standing there. I barely glanced at her, for through the open doorway I had caught sight of the person on the bicycle – the woman? the girl? the lady? – standing and talking to some unseen character, with a well-filled glass in her hand.

She looked different from the bicycle lady, naturally enough. This was a social scene and she was not wearing an old macintosh. Her short fairish hair, unkempt and roughly fringed on the forehead, looked both healthy and greasy, as it still does. Later on I was to cut and shampoo it for her now and then: at that distant time she hardly bothered. Indeed I have the feeling that women then – certainly academic women – were nothing like so attentive to appearances as they are today, when girls may look like scarecrows, but only of set purpose. Slovenliness in those days was next to seriousness, at least in university circles. It was rare, however, for women in those circles to wear trousers. Iris had on a worn and grubby tweed skirt, rather overlong and ungainly. I noticed her legs were short and robust, clad in brown cotton stockings. Nylons were still uncommon in the early fifties.

This woman certainly had a serious look, and it dawned on me that my bicycle lady, who this clearly was, must be an academic of some sort. That gave me an immediate feeling of despondency. Just as my fantasy when I first saw her was that she had neither a past with others nor a future without me, so now I was reluctant to feel that she could be anything so commonplace as a university don. It placed her; and I disliked the idea that she should be placed, even by myself. At the same time I was heartened by her general

appearance, and its total absence of anything that for me
in those days constituted sex-appeal. There was nothing so
conventional as that about this woman. She was not 'a girl',
and she had no girlish attractions. That made the fact that I
was in love with her much more exciting; and it also seemed
highly satisfactory, for what, as I instantly realised, was a
rather ignoble reason. Since she had no obvious female
charms she was not likely to appeal to other men.

Why I was so convinced at first that there was nothing
sexually attractive about Iris is a complete mystery. Other
people, of both sexes, certainly didn't think so. It was my
naive and now inexplicable assumption that she could only
appeal to me, and to no one else, that stopped me seeing
how fearfully, how almost diabolically attractive everyone
else found her. They knew more about such things, I
suppose.

'Ah there you are, John. I may call you John, mayn't I?'
Miss Griffiths gave a characteristic small giggle. 'Meet Miss
Ady, and Miss Murdoch. Iris, this is one of the more promising young ones in the English School. Very good results
in Finals. I caught him out over Old English grammar, his
weaker side I fear, but he did a beautiful piece on the
Knight's Tale.'

That bloody *Knight's Tale*. Was I never going to hear
the end of it? Iris Murdoch gave me a kindly look, said
'Hullo', and continued talking to Miss Ady. Miss Griffiths
handed me a glass, from which I at once took a desperate
swig. I coughed, and felt myself going scarlet in the face.
It was a strong gin and french, the English equivalent of an
American martini – no ice in those days of course. Although
I had become accustomed to strong drink in the army I had
barely touched it during my student days. I had lost the
taste, and besides it was too expensive. Iris and her friends
drank a lot of it, and for me that was the first of many.

I resented Miss Griffiths referring to me as one of the
'young ones' in the English School. I was not particularly

young. Were these women so much older? – for I now saw, and with a certain satisfaction in spite of my embarrassed state, that I was the only man in the room. There were four or five women at the party, and as a result of my confusion and fit of coughing they were all looking at me in a kindly way. Obviously they took it for granted that I was a clueless young creature, and that it behoved them, as sophisticated women of the university world, to be nice to me.

But they all seemed to want to talk to Iris. I was left with Miss Griffiths, who was herself looking at Iris with a wistful expression which even at that awkward moment surprised me.

What I had not the slightest idea of was that St Anne's, at that time, was a hotbed of emotion. The dons in general were not, so to speak, professional lesbians. Many were, or had been, married: they led domestic as well as academic lives. They were nice clever donnish women, hard-working and conscientious, but a lot of feelings ran beneath the surface, and I had the impression later on that they seemed to catch such emotional intensities from each other, like germs or fashions. Some time afterwards I heard the novelist Elizabeth Bowen, who had become a great friend of Iris's, describe an acquaintance as 'an oldfashioned lesbian of the highest type'. Elizabeth Bowen's inimitable stutter on the 'L' made this sound both grand and comic. The ladies of St Anne's were not grand exactly, but their type, I'm sure, was both high-minded and sound. Whatever they felt among themselves was never communicated to their pupils, nor were their pupils ever roped in. I had Iris's word for that, much later on. Any suggestion that one of their girl charges had been made advances to, or encouraged in a crush for one of them, would have been universally frowned upon.

In any case I had simplistic ideas about sex at that time, supposing that everybody must be either one thing or the other. When it dawned on me, a short time after the party, that they had all seemed to be in love with Iris, I had a sensation of despair. If they all felt like that about her, didn't it follow that she must feel the same about them? – at least about one or two of them? Iris was, as I realised later, much too kind to discourage affection, even yearning affection, but she was apt to draw a line if a woman expressed it too physically. She never went to bed with any of her colleagues, or indeed with any other woman, although the novelist Brigid Brophy tried very hard indeed to persuade her. That was both before and after we were married.

Miss Griffiths seized her colleague in the English department, a lady with a resounding Polish surname, introduced me to her, and made thankfully off to join the little group around Iris. I saw the dashing Miss Ady, dark-haired and with beautiful eyes, tap Iris playfully on the wrist while emphasising some point to her, perhaps about their teaching: for Miss Ady, as I afterwards discovered, taught politics and economics, while Iris handled the philosophy. The Polish-sounding lady, who wore a black coat with a scarlet lining and seemed to me equally dashing, departed from the party's air of cheerful frivolity by asking in an intense and as I thought foreign tone a serious question about my 'research'. My reply failed to carry conviction to myself, or, it seemed, to her. Her gaze was forgiving but also I felt a little reproachful.

Instead of talking to the person I had fallen in love with, or even meeting her properly, I seemed destined as a result of Miss Griffiths' heaven-sent invitation only to make a decidedly mediocre impression on another of my senior faculty teachers. I discovered afterwards that Miss Griffiths' colleague was well known for her air of severity among pupils and colleagues alike, but that she was in fact a kind as well as a devoted teacher, married to a Polish officer during the war. She was herself from Yorkshire and bore some sturdy name like Sidebotham, but preferred to retain the more romantic patronymic she had acquired from a husband, now absconded.

I never managed to talk to Iris at that party, although at a later stage, and after two or three other men had arrived, I hovered vainly near her, seeming to exchange words with every other person present. After a few of those gins and frenches I felt I could have made a good impression, but no opportunity arose, and Iris excused herself and departed well before the gathering dispersed, amid much conviviality.

The god of chance seemed however to be in a long-suffering mood. After seeing me fail to make anything of the unexpected coincidence he had arranged, he patiently set to work yet again. Asked to supper three weeks later by a couple who knew a friend I had not seen for years, I discovered that Iris was my sole fellow-guest. But I soon felt that I was failing again. Although friendly and not at all shy Iris was not a helpful conversationalist. I offered openings and raised points in what I hoped was an interesting way, but she smiled kindly and did not respond. Like many philosophers in Oxford she had the habit of considering what was said in a silence that was judicious, almost sibylline. She turned my poor little point over as if asking 'What exactly does this mean?' and if she decided it indeed meant very little she was too polite to say so. Mutual enthusiasm failed wholly to take fire. I was comforted to observe that our host, a lively law fellow who was clearly hoping to pump Iris about the fashions and topics of contemporary philosophy, fared no better than I did. At the same time I resented his air of knowing her so well that he could often appeal to jokes or thoughts they had in common, or jolly times she had shared with him and his family. My solitary bicyclist, I felt, should not have been happy to go on holiday with these people. I became prey to the retrospective jealousy I was often to suffer from in the months to come. I began to see that there was a lot that Iris had done   must have done, during the long years I had not known her – which I could not approve of, which was not suited to the image my fancy had officiously formed of her.

Quite abruptly, and early, Iris said she must go home. Our hosts looked disappointed. For the first time I managed to seize the moment, and I said regretfully that I must go too. Our hosts looked more philosophical about that: it was Iris they had wanted, and almost greedily, to stay; and I was surprised by this, because as a guest she had seemed to take very little trouble, if any, even though she had disseminated around her what seemed an involuntary aura of beneficence and good will. But she had not risen at all to the law fellow's blandishments, his attempts to interest her in his ideas and persuade her to set forth her own. To have observed this gave me some satisfaction.

Goodnights being said and the front door closed we unlocked our bicycles and set out together into the damp mild Oxfordshire night. My lights were in order; her front one dimmed and wavered on the verge of final extinction, and I respectfully urged her to bicycle on the inside, and to keep as close as possible to my own illumination. Then we rode in silence, and I assumed it was to break it that she asked me in her friendly way if I had ever thought of writing a novel. It was a wholly unexpected question, but for once I had an answer ready. Yes, I had: indeed I was writing one, or trying to write one, at that moment.

This was not strictly true. It was nearly true, and I determined on the spot and as we rode to make it true that very night. The wife of my professor, a sweet tremulous woman whose father had been a well-known critic, had asked me the same question about a month before. I had given her much the same disingenuous reply; and by way of encouragement she had suggested with a gentle smile that we should both try to write one – she wouldn't mind having a go herself. With some laughter we had made a pact to see who could finish first. I had since attempted to have a few ideas, and I had thought of an opening for the first chapter, but I had done nothing.

But why should Miss Murdoch ask me about novels? It must be to indulge me and get me to talk about myself, for clearly she, a philosopher, could have no interest in the matter. She probably never read them; far too busy with higher things. I made some deprecating comment to this effect, and the next moment could hardly believe my ears. Miss Murdoch said that she herself had written a novel, which was shortly to be published.

I felt overwhelmed with awe and admiration. So this extraordinary creature had thrown off a novel, as if negligently, in the intervals of a busy life of teaching and doing philosophy. What could it be about? I ventured to ask. 'You mustn't tell anyone,' she said, stopping her bicycle and putting a foot to the ground. She looked straight at me, speaking lightly but also very seriously. 'I don't want anyone to know.'

I gave a fervent undertaking. I would not reveal her secret to a soul. I was overwhelmed with joy that she could have confided this secret to me. She must for some extraordinary reason not only have complete trust and confidence in me, although we had scarcely met each other, but with swift and masterful decision have concluded that I was just the right person – the one who ought to know. Why? I could only marvel, and be aware that my heart was bounding with gratitude and joy. As well as with love of course. I really felt as we stood there in the dark road, half on and half off our bicycles, that this wonderfully intuitive and perspicuous being had seen right down inside me, liked what she saw, judged it worthy of her fullest trust. Perhaps even loved what she saw? Could she have known that I had fallen in love with her, and had decided like a philosopher, on a ground of reason and good sense, that she was also in love with me?

As I came to know her it soon occurred to me to wonder if

she had not in fact revealed this secret of her novel to quite a number of people. Maurice Charlton seemed to know about it: so did the Johnsons – the law fellow and his wife. Most of her many friends in London must have known about it too. What is more some of them had even read it – in manuscript, in Iris's own handwriting. The Johnsons had read it, as they took good care to let me know when they saw that I was becoming friendly with Iris, and met her at other places than their own house. For of course there is something highly displeasing about one of our friends getting to know our other friends without telling us, as La Rochefoucauld might have said.

Iris's instinct here was essentially a kindly one. She wanted to have her friends, each of them, for themselves; she wanted them to know her in the same pristine way. No groups, no sets. No comparing of notes between two about a third. This desire that each of her relationships should be special and separate, as innocent as in the garden of Eden, was of great significance with Iris. Since what she felt about each of them was totally genuine and without guile it could have no relation to any other person. There was no graduation among her friendships, no comparisons made. Each was whole in itself.

I had, in fact, misunderstood her. No doubt because I was in love with her. Like all lovers, I suppose, I wished to be a special case in quite the wrong sense. To be 'the one'. By telling me she didn't want anyone to know of the novel's existence I felt she was singling me out. But it was a routine precaution, almost a formula. Her friends could know, should know. But she didn't want the matter talked about, either among them or in a wider context.

Naturally enough the precaution functioned only on the higher level: as a practical measure it was ineffective. That was brought home to me when I realised that many people who knew Iris were talking about her novel. I did not resent the fact, nor did I feel in the least disillusioned. I was so much in love (or so I told myself) that I saw clearly and without dismay that Iris was not in the least in love with me. She had told me about her novel as an act of kindness, seeing that I was interested in such matters. She had told me precisely because she was not in love with me; not because she was, or was beginning to be. We had become friends: that was all.

Friendship meant a great deal to her. It was a sign of how much she valued her friends that she kept them so separate. To me it meant nothing, or at least very little. For me friendship was a question of contextual bonding, as I believe psychologists call it. I had met people at school and in the army whose company was agreeable at that time and in that place; it did not occur to me to ask whether or how much I valued them as friends. When the situation changed, so did my acquaintance, so that I retained nobody who could be called 'an old friend'. The idea of Iris wishing, or at least being prepared, to regard me as one of her friends did not appeal to me in the least.

None the less that was the way it had to be. We met about once a fortnight. We both disliked the telephone – that was something about her I found out early on – so communicated by note. Such notes were exchanged via the college messenger, by what was known as pigeon post. I disliked pubs, but there was no alternative to suggesting we should meet in a pub. Iris liked them and had her favourites among them, as I soon found out. I also disliked eating out, which in Oxford at that time was expensive, at least in terms of my slender income, and usually bad. We sometimes ate at cafés or in bars. I became a gloomy connoisseur of their shortcomings.

I suppose we got to know each other, and talked a good deal, but I don't remember what about. I know there was never anything so electrifying as the pause on our bicycles had been, when we confronted one another in the darkness and she told me not to mention the existence of her novel.

After we remounted and rode slowly on I enquired diffidently about the content of this work. What was it about?
How had she come to write it? She made no direct reply,
but much more excitingly she said with emphasis how
important it was for any narration to have something for
everybody, as she put it. This was a discovery she had
made. I was surprised but also impressed by the simplicity
of the idea, and the force with which she spoke of it, slowly
and reflectively.

'A bit like Shakespeare,' I suggested.

'Well perhaps, yes.'

I have often pondered that moment, and whether her
words really meant anything very much, or were they for
me part of the unmeaning electricity of falling in love?
Falling in love on my side, that is. For her, it was obvious,
and still is; the words were grave, sober, and true. She
wanted, in her novels, to reach all possible readers, in
different ways and by different means: by the excitement
of her story, its pace and its comedy, through its ideas
and its philosophical implications, through the numinous
atmosphere of her own original and created world: the
world she must have glimpsed as she considered and
planned her first steps in the art of fiction.

In the early summer St Antony's College gave a modest
dance, a much simpler affair than the big college dances
– 'commem balls' as they are called – which are held after
the end of the summer term and go on all night long. A
double ticket for such an elaborate affair might then cost
as much as thirty pounds, and nowadays is of course far
more expensive. The St Antony's hop was not much more
than a couple of guineas. Although I was not by training or
by temperament a dancing man I determined to go none the
less, and to ask Iris if she would come with me. I bought the
tickets, with the reflection that I could probably resell them
if I had to. But to my astonishment, and not altogether to

my delight, Iris accepted the invitation with alacrity. This caused a further range of complications in my heart. There were also practical problems which might well follow. Other people, my colleagues at St Antony's, would ask her to dance, and suppose one of them were to fall in love with her, or she with him? (It did not then occur to me that she might equally well become attached to one of the girls who would be present.)

There were other and even more pressing practical considerations. Where would I take her to dine before the dance, which was a simple nine to midnight affair. I had no money to spare, but I felt it must be somewhere reasonably 'good', not just a pub or a café. In the end I chose the Regency Restaurant, which advertised itself in the *Oxford Mail* as serving 'probably the best food in Oxfordshire'. This Delphic pronouncement could hardly be discredited, if one came to think about it, but naturally enough I did not think about it. At half-past six I went to collect Iris in her college room, waiting outside the door after I had knocked, and a voice from within had requested me to hang on a minute. While waiting I speculated on what she would look like, what she would be wearing. I assumed and rather hoped it would be something dark, preferably black, suited to the person of mature years and sober disposition which I still assumed and hoped her to be. Was it not these imagined qualities in her which had attracted me so strongly when I first saw her on her bicycle?

The door opened. An apparition in what seemed a sort of flame-coloured brocade stood before me. I felt in some way scandalised: dazzled but appalled at the same time. All my daydreams, my illusions and preconceptions about the woman – the girl? the lady? – of the bicycle seemed to have torn away and vanished back into a past which I would still very much have preferred to be inhabiting, given the choice. But I had no choice. The person before me was exactly the same as the one riding the bicycle. I still

thought her face homely and kindly, not in any conventional
sense pretty or attractive, even if it was a strong face in its
own blunt-featured snub-nosed way; and for me it was
always mysterious too. But now I was seeing it as other
people saw it. Although it was in no way conventional
itself its trappings, so to speak, were now conventional.
Their appearance disappointed me sadly. They seemed the
sort of things that any girl would wear; a silly girl who had
not the taste to choose her clothes carefully.

Well, there was nothing to be done about that. Iris seemed
preoccupied. Perhaps about her face, which she now dabbed
with powder, or her hair, or some hitch in her underwear.
She wriggled and pulled her dress about uneasily, as if
she were unfamiliar with whatever lay underneath it, and
uncomfortable in consequence. Or perhaps she was preoccupied with the thought of what she might be doing
somewhere else, with some other friends. She seemed preoccupied with anything and everything except me, about
whom she appeared as unconscious as she had been when
she rode past under my window. She didn't look at me, but
she did take my hand in an absent way as we went out to
the entrance of the St Anne's house where she lived; and
that cheered me as much as the awkward movements she
had made, as if she were wearing something thoroughly
unfamiliar and uncomfortable. A corset probably.

The restaurant was a disaster. I can't remember what we
ate, but it was very nasty, and the waiter was both gloomy
and supercilious. He seemed preoccupied with quite other
things than us, just as Iris had seemed to be preoccupied
with other things than with me when I met her at the door
of her room. Even the bottle of red wine which we drank
was tasteless and bad. But as the dreadful dinner went
on – there were very few other people in the restaurant
– our spirits for some reason appeared to rise amazingly.
We began to giggle and to talk in whispers about the few
other sepulchral-looking diners. At the end of it Iris excused

herself and went out to the Ladies, leaving me to pay the bill. I did this and added an enormous tip, which the waiter paid no attention to when he came to collect the money. I felt discouraged by this, because I was hoping in some way for a friendly word, and perhaps a benevolent query about where we were going. The saturnine waiter simply took up the money and departed, as absent and intent on other matters as ever. Perhaps his wife had just left him. If the Regency Restaurant had 'probably' the best food in Oxfordshire it had certainly the worst service.

I was left to contemplate the green and white stripes of the wallpaper, a kind of wallpaper then very much in the fashion which I have hated ever since. Iris was away for an age. When she finally came out of the Ladies she was transformed again. Now she looked like a doll, a Watteau china doll with incongruously schoolgirl hair. She had lathered her mouth with lipstick, which she now proceeded in an amateurish way to kiss at with a scrap of paper taken from her bag. I noticed handwriting on this paper, and wondered if it could be a love letter, an urgent note from some admirer. But at least she did not put it back in her bag but crumpled it up and left it on the table.

It was drizzling outside. By the time I had managed to find a taxi it was well after half-past nine. The dance was in full swing when we got to St Antony's.

I felt in a resigned way now that I was taking some quite different girl to the dance: one with bright red lips, covered inexpertly with a substance which made them look thick and unattractive: not that I had ever noticed them particularly in the first place. This strange girl would no doubt appeal to my St Antony colleagues and their friends. That would be something anyway, I thought, because I had no wish myself to spend the evening dancing with her. My one wish now was that the whole thing should be over as soon as possible, and I was extremely glad that the dance did not propose to prolong itself past midnight. Most sincerely I hoped it would not.

St Antony's was a former Anglican convent, built around 1870. A steep flight of stone steps led down to the crypt below the nuns' chapel, now the library, in which the dance was to be held. As we went down Iris trod on her long dress, slipped, and slid inelegantly down a few steps on her behind. People descending before and after us rushed to help me help her get up. I found myself entertaining the unworthy thought that she might have sprained her ankle; not badly, but enough to incapacitate her for the evening. She would not wish to stay on the sidelines, and I could take her home. Perhaps we could go on talking in her room.

But Iris was not hurt at all. She got up and smiled while the others brushed her down, amid laughter and joking. The ice was already broken as far as fellow-dancers were concerned. We moved on to the floor among a crowd, who all seemed to be chatting to us and to each other. I made a few introductions. She seemed already to have made new friends. Her manner was no longer quiet and withdrawn. I made unconfident gestures indicative of asking her to dance, and we assumed the appropriate semi-embrace.

My dancing was indeed unconfident. I had sometimes enjoyed it at hops in the nightclubs or weekends in the army, when already more than a little drunk. Now, when we moved, there seemed no correlation between the different parts of us. Iris smiled at me encouragingly, but soon relinquished me and began to execute arm-twirlings and arabesques on her own. She looked ungainly and rather affected, but touchingly naive at the same time. It seemed clear that she knew no more about dancing *à deux* than I did; but when we brushed accidentally against a dancing couple a few seconds later, and the man turned with a smile and seized hold of her, she melted into him at once, and the pair swung off together in perfect unison. The girl whom the man had been with did not look best pleased, but she too had no choice but to smile at me as we began to revolve in some sort of way. I felt the dance was already going against me, and that success, whatever it might have consisted in, had already gone beyond recall.

The band gave a flourish, and stopped. Iris came back to me at once, looking happy and relaxed. She asked about my room in the college, which she had not yet seen. I asked if she would like to go up there for a minute, thinking of the bottle of champagne I had bought that morning, and put in my cupboard along with two glasses. She said she would like to very much. I took her arm as we mounted the stone steps, in case she had another fall. My room was small and spartan: a bed, cupboard, table and wooden chair. But there was a gas fire, which I now turned on. I got the bottle and glasses out of the cupboard. As I put them down on the table we fell into each other's arms.

It seemed as natural as it had been to take her arm when coming up the stairs, or for her to take my hand for a minute when we had left her own room in St Anne's. We never returned to the dance floor but sat in my room until two in the morning. We talked without stopping. I had no idea I could talk like that, and I am sure she never knew she could, either. It was endless, childish chatter, putting our faces together as we talked. I think Iris was accustomed only to talk properly, as it were: considering, pausing, modifying, weighing her words. To talk like a philosopher and a teacher. Now she babbled like a child. So did I. With arms around each other, kissing and rubbing noses (I said how much I loved her snub nose) we rambled on and on, seeming to invent on the spot, and as we talked, a whole infantile language of our own. She put her head back and laughed at me incredulously from time to time, and I think we both felt incredulous. She seemed to be giving way to some deep need of which she had been wholly unconscious: the need to throw away not only the manoeuvres and rivalries of intellect, but the emotional fears and fascinations, the power struggles and surrenders of adult loving.

She asked me endlessly about my childhood, and told me about her own. She had been a happy child, attached equally to both her parents. I saw that they had doted on her, but it seemed in a very sensible way. Her father, who came from Belfast, was a minor civil servant, now on the verge of retirement. His salary had always been extremely modest, and he could never have afforded to send her to a good school, even with a scholarship, if he hadn't borrowed money. A cautious and prudent man, he had been as brave as a lion about this, and tears came into her eyes as she told me about the sacrifices her parents had made. But our talk was too happy and silly to stay long on the actualities of childhood. It was the atmosphere of it that we suddenly seemed to be breathing together, having rediscovered it mutually and miraculously in each other's presence. The dance and the dancing, the dinner we had eaten and all that, seemed like ludicrous adult activities which we had put behind us.

I had a wish to rub my nose and lips along her bare arms. She made me take off my dinner jacket so that she could do the same to me.

'If we were married we could do this all the time,' I said, rather absurdly.

'We shall be doing it nearly all the time,' she answered.

'Yes, but if—.'

She stopped that by starting to kiss me properly. We remained locked together for a long time. The bottle of champagne remained unopened on the table.

Long long afterwards I was having to look through her manuscripts and papers to find some stuff requested by the publisher. In the back of an exercise book containing notes for a novel were what seemed to be a few entries, some dated, others random observations, comments on books, philosophers, people she knew, denoted only by initial.

Some notes on pupils too, and on points that had struck her in their work. One entry, dated June 3 1954, read: 'St Antony's Dance. Fell down the steps, and seem to have fallen in love with J. We didn't dance much.'

2

We trailed slowly over the long field towards the river. The heat seemed worse than ever, although the sun, overcast, did not beat down as fiercely as it had done earlier in the day. The hay had been carried away some time before, and the brownish surface of the field was baked hard and covered incongruously with molehills. The earth in them was like grey powder, and I wondered how the moles ever managed to find any sustenance as they tunnelled within it. A pair of crows flapped lazily away as we approached the river bank. Crows are said to live a long time, and I wondered idly if they were the same birds we had seen there on our bathing visits for many years past.

I wished we had managed to come earlier, before the hay was cut, and when wild flowers – scabious, white archangel, oxeye daisies – stretched over the whole field among the grass. It was not a lush river field, probably because a bed of gravel lay just below the surface. There were big gravel ponds not far away, by the main road, but this field was a protected area, a plant and bird sanctuary of some kind. Not a fish sanctuary however: there were sometimes a few fishermen about, who kept themselves to themselves and remained almost invisible among the reeds.

Our own little nook was seldom occupied however, and it was empty as usual today. Once we would have got our clothes off as soon as possible and slid silently into the water, as we had done on that first occasion. Now I had quite a struggle getting Iris's clothes off: I had managed to put her bathing dress on at home, before we started.

Her instinct nowadays seems to be to take her clothes off as little as possible. Even in this horribly hot weather it is hard to persuade her to remove trousers and jersey before getting into bed.

She protested, gently though vigorously, as I levered off the outer layers. In her shabby old one-piece swimsuit (actually two-piece, with a separate skirt and tunic top) she was an awkward and anxious figure, her socks trailing round her ankles. She was obstinate about not taking these off, and I gave up the struggle. A pleasure barge chugged slowly past, an elegant girl in a bikini sunning herself on the deck, a young man in white shorts at the steering-wheel. Both turned to look at us with a slight air of incredulity. I should not have been surprised if they had burst into guffaws of ill-mannered laughter, for we must have presented a comic spectacle – an elderly man struggling to remove the garments from an old lady, still with white skin and incongruously fair hair.

Alzheimer sufferers are not always gentle: I know that. But Iris remains her old self in many ways. The power of concentration has gone, along with the ability to form coherent sentences, and to remember where she is, or has been. She does not know she has written twenty-seven remarkable novels, as well as her books on philosophy; received honorary doctorates from the major universities; become a Dame of the British Empire . . . If an admirer or friend asks her to sign a copy of one of her novels she looks at it with pleasure and surprise before laboriously writing her name and, if she can, theirs. 'For Georgina Smith. For Dear Reggie . . .' It takes her some time, but the letters are still formed with care, and resemble, in a surreal way, her old handwriting. She is always anxious to oblige. And the old gentleness remains.

Once in the water Iris cheers up a bit. It is almost too warm, hardly refreshing But its old brown slow-flowing deliciousness remains, and we smile happily at each other

as we paddle quietly to and fro. Water-lily leaves, with an
occasional fat yellow flower, rock gently at the passage
of a pleasure boat. Small bright blue dragonflies hover
motionless above them. The water is deep, and cooler as
we move out from the bank, but we do not go out far.
Looking down I can see her muddy feet, still in their socks,
moving in the brown depths. Tiny fish are inquisitively
investigating her, and I can see and feel them round me
too, gently palpating the bare skin.

Once, if there had been little river traffic about, we would
have swum at once the hundred yards or so across the river
and back. Now it is too much trouble, and a possible producer of that endless omnipresent anxiety of Alzheimer's,
which spreads to the one who looks after the sufferer. Not
that it would be dangerous; Iris still swims as naturally
as a fish. Since we first entered the water here together,
forty-four years ago now, we have swum in the sea, in
lakes and rivers, pools and ponds, whenever we could and
wherever we happened to be.

I recalled now a moment in Perth, Australia, when we
managed to get into the Swan River, scrambling down
a shelving concrete slope from a busy arterial road. The
famous Swan brewery was just up at the broad river's
next bend, and the water flowing past us was peculiar,
to say the least, but we enjoyed our swim. We saw the
faces of motorists going past up above, staring at us with
surprise, and, presumably, disapproval. In fact there was a
swimming-pool at the hotel the University had put us into,
but that would not have been the same thing. It was always
fringed with strapping Australian girls sunning themselves.
We never used it: I think we felt too shy.

Iris was never keen on swimming as such. She never
swam fast and noisily or did fancy strokes. It was being
in the water she loved. Twice she came quite close to
drowning. I thought of that, with the anxiety that had now
invaded both our lives, as we approached the bank again,

to scramble out. This had always been a more difficult and inelegant operation than slipping into the river, but it had never bothered us in the past. The river was as deep near the bank as in midstream, the bank itself undercut by the water's flow. It shelved a little in our own corner, the soft clay occasionally imprinted by the hooves of drinking cattle. I pulled myself out first and turned to help Iris. As she took my hands her face contracted into that look of child-like dread which so often came over it now, filling me too with worry and fear. Suppose her arm muscles failed her and she slipped back into deep water, forgetting how to swim, and letting water pour into her mouth as she opened it in a soundless appeal to me? I knew on the spot that we must never come to bathe here again.

The panic moment passed, but it had never existed for either of us at a moment when, ten or fifteen years before, we had swum with a friend, the artist Reynolds Stone, off the Chesil Bank in Dorset. The Stones lived a few miles inland, and in summer we used to go down to the sea, to the great inshore curve that sweeps all the way from Portland Bill to Bridport and Lyme Regis. The tides have left there a massive embankment of grey shingle, graduated as if by hand from huge smooth pebbles at the Portland end to fine gravel twelve miles further west. When a sea is running it is a dangerous place, and even in calm weather the swell and the suction of the undertow make it a tricky beach to go in from. Fearlessly gentle and absent-minded, Reynolds Stone never mentioned any danger nor was apparently aware of it. In we always went together, laughing and talking, and on one occasion Iris missed the pulse of the wave that carried us back on to the shingle, and was sucked out again as it ebbed. Speaking of Piero or Cézanne, two of the artists he most admired, Reynolds noticed nothing; nor did I. Listening to him as we trod gingerly over the stones to where our clothes lay, I turned back to include Iris in what he was saying. She was not there. But in a moment she was, and I helped her over the shingle while Reynolds stood gently and imperturbably conversing.

Only afterwards did she tell me of her moment of incredulous surprise and terror as she felt herself drawn back under the smooth sea. It was deep over her head, but she kept her mouth tight shut by instinct, and in another moment the next wave had brought her ashore. Had she panicked and swallowed water the next swell of the insidious undertow might well have carried her farther out and down; and then, easy swimmer as she was, she could have drowned in a few seconds.

She said nothing until we were in bed that night, and then she was not frightened but full of curiosity, and an excitement she wanted to share with me. 'I'll put it in my next novel,' she said. And she did.

After she had become well-known she never mentioned the novel she was working on in public; nor, I think, to her friends; scarcely to me either. She would say something about it if I asked, but I soon had no habit of asking. One of the truest pleasures of marriage is solitude. Also the most deeply reassuring. I continued to do my own job, teaching English in the university, writing the odd critical study. Iris soon gave up St Anne's – the emotional pressures in that community may have had something to do with it – and entered her own marvellous world of creation and intellectual drama, penetrating reflection, sheer literary excitement. Something for everybody in fact: just as she had said as we first stood there that late evening, beside our bicycles.

Occasionally she used to ask me about some technical detail she wanted for a novel. Once she enquired about automatic pistols – old army training made it easy to answer that one – sometimes about cars, or wine, or what would be a suitable thing for a certain character to eat. The hero of *The Sea! The Sea!* required, so to speak, a very special diet, and I had fun suggesting all sorts of unlikely combinations to which he might be partial: oat bran and boiled onions, fried garlic and sardines, tinned mango and stilton cheese. Some of these found their way into the novel; and when it won the coveted Booker Prize one of the judges, who happened to be the distinguished philosopher A.J. Ayer, remarked in his prizegiving speech that he had much enjoyed everything in the novel 'except for the food'.

Only to one of Iris's novels, and that was a long time ago, did I contribute a small section myself. It was in her fourth published novel, *The Bell*. For a reason I now forget she asked me to read the first chapter, which has one of her most sibylline epigrammatic openings. She never used a typewriter, and in her first handwritten version it read: 'Dora Greenfield left her husband because she was afraid of him. A year later she returned to him for the same reason.' I was thrilled by this instant concision, as many a subsequent reader must have been, for the sentence remained substantially as quoted here. But as I read on I began to feel an immediate inquisitiveness about young Dora Greenfield and her husband Paul which the early pages did not satisfy. So arresting were they, as characters, that I wanted to know a little more of them at once, to be given a hint by which to glimpse their potential. I said something of the sort to Iris, who said 'OK then, you write something for me.' I think she may already have felt herself something of what I, as reader, was now feeling: our sympathy and intuition automatically intermingled.

At the time I was trying to write a study later titled *The Characters of Love*. I was bewitched by Henry James, who observed to a friend about one of the ladies in the novel he was writing that he could already take 'a stiff examination' about her. Concerning such a personality, he had remarked, the author needs to supply a forewarning, 'an early intimation of perspective'. With this in mind, and highly flattered by Iris's suggestion, I set out to produce some idea of what *might* have happened to Dora and her

husband, even if it was to have no part in the book, whose
story as yet I did not know.

My idea was that he as a husband deeply needed and
wanted children, even if he was not necessarily conscious
of the fact, while she – much younger than her husband –
did not. I suggested that she had it in her none the less to
become 'a prompt and opinionated mother', and that this
would be her only means in their marriage of standing
up to Paul. As it was she was highly alarmed at the
prospect of 'becoming two people', though in her passive
manner she had done nothing to inhibit conception. Indeed
she had come back to her husband like an apprehensive
sleepwalker, still unconsciously depending on the ability of
her fears to 'whisk her instantly away, like a small animal'.
At the same time she wanted him because she feared him,
and because she knew he had it in him to allay her fears.

I produced something to this effect, and the results are on
page ten of the novel as first printed, in a longish paragraph.
It reads a bit too much in the Jamesian style, rather than
merging into Iris's own inimitable originality; but it does
none the less perhaps have the function of suggesting
alternatives and open spaces, which the scope and intent
of the novel will not necessarily want to occupy. The novel's
theme is the desire and pursuit, whether in true or false
ways, of the spiritual life; and I had nothing to contribute to
Iris's own marvellous feeling for what some people hunger
for, and how in consequence they behave. Indeed I have
very little understanding of the spiritual life; but that has
never stopped me having a passionate appetite for Iris's
novels, which I have usually read only after publication.
The Bell, or at least the first piece of it, was an exception.

This sympathy for what was or might be going on in
Iris's mind, together with my inability to understand or
enter into it, must have developed quite early on. The
sympathy alone was what was needed in the case of our
communing together over the beginning of *The Bell*, and I

remember vividly my then unexpected sense of it. Normally it was something which by then I took for granted in our marriage, like air or water. Already we were beginning that strange and beneficent process in marriage by which a couple can, in the words of A.D. Hope the Australian poet, 'move closer and closer apart'. The apartness is a part of the closeness, perhaps a recognition of it: certainly a pledge of complete understanding. There is nothing threatening or supervisory about such an understanding, nothing of what couples really mean when they say (or are alleged to say) to confidants or counsellors, 'the trouble is that my wife/husband doesn't understand me'. This usually means that the couple, or one of them, understands the other all too well, and doesn't rejoice in the experience.

Still less is such apartness at all like what the French call *solitude à deux*, the inward self-isolation of a couple from anything outside their marriage. The solitude I have enjoyed in marriage, and I think Iris too, is a little like having a walk by oneself, and knowing that tomorrow, or soon, one will be sharing it with the other, or equally perhaps again having it alone. It is a solitude, too, that precludes nothing outside the marriage, and sharpens the sense of possible intimacy with things or people in the outside world.

Such sympathy in apartness takes time to grow, however, as well as being quite different by nature from that intoxicating sense of the strangeness of another being which accompanies the excitements of falling in love. The more I got to 'know' Iris, in the normal sense, during the early days of our relationship, the less I understood her. Indeed I soon began not to want to understand her. I was far too preoccupied at the time to think of such parallels, but it was like living in a fairy story – the kind with sinister overtones and a not always happy ending – in which a young man loves a beautiful maiden who returns his love but is always disappearing into some unknown and mysterious world, about which she will reveal nothing. Eventually he makes some dire mistake and she disappears for good. At this distance in time that comparison seems more or less true, if a bit fanciful. Iris *was* always disappearing, to 'see' her friends (I began to wonder and to dread, early on, what the word 'see' might involve) about whom, unlike the girl in the fairytale, she was always quite open. I knew their names; I imagined them; I never met them.

And there seemed to be so many of them. Persons who were in a sense in my own position. Iris seemed deeply and privately attached to them all. No doubt in all sorts of different ways. I could only hope that she did not talk to any of the others in quite the way that she talked to me, chattered childishly with me, kissed me. This Iris was so different from the grave being I had seen on the bicycle, or at a party in the public domain, that I sometimes wondered what had become of the woman I had fallen in love with, as I then supposed. Absurdly, I had imagined our future together as somehow equally grave, a wonderfully serious matter, and only the pair of us of course, for no one else in the world was or would be in the least interested in either of us. We would simply be made for each other, and exist on that basis.

The happy childlike girl or woman she had now turned into when she was with me was delightful, but also – as I sometimes could not stop myself wistfully thinking – fundamentally unreal, like the girl in the fairy story. This could not be the real Iris. But with the hindsight that also saw a parallel with the fairy story I can now feel that I was giving Iris without knowing it the alternative being that she required: the irresponsible, even escapist persona ('escapist' was a word often used in those days, accompanied by a disapproving headshake) which she had no idea that she wanted or needed. Neither did I have any idea that I was supplying it. I felt I was in love, indeed I was sure of it; and I was innocently sure, too, that it must be the most important thing for both of us, although Iris never gave

any indication that she thought so too. The Iris with whom
I talked nonsense and gambolled about, the woman who
entered with such joy into those frolics, was delightful; and
yet I could not but feel that she was not the same woman
I had first seen and marked out: nor was she the 'real'
Iris Murdoch, the serious hard-working responsible being
observed and admired by other people.

After our relationship became itself more serious, and
as we became aware that we were travelling inevitably
towards a separation or a solution we couldn't anticipate
or foresee, Iris once or twice mentioned the myth of Proteus.
It was in reply to my despairing comment that I couldn't
understand her, or the different person she became for the
many others with whom she seemed, in my view, helplessly
entangled. 'Remember Proteus,' she used to say. 'Just keep
tight hold of me and it will be all right.' Proteus had the
power of changing himself into any shape he wished – lion,
serpent, monster, fish – but when Hercules held tightly on to
him throughout all these transformations he was compelled
in the end to surrender, and to resume his proper shape as
the man he was.

I used to reply gloomily that I was not Hercules, lacking
that hero's resources of musclepower and concentration.
Then we would laugh and become our old secret and
childish selves again for the moment. As we did when we
first crawled through the undergrowth and slipped secretly
into the river.

That occasion for me marked a turning-point in our
relations, although it was one I didn't grasp at the time,
nor could I have defined it until much later. The fact was
that on that day she had let me for the first time into another
of her friendships, by asking Maurice Charlton if I might be
included in the lunch he had planned for the pair of them.
I had no idea of this, nor, as I said, of the admirable good
nature which Charlton himself must have displayed. If he
was disappointed he gave no hint of it at all. Because I

was there with them both I was not conscious of him as a rival, nor did I mind at all the way in which he seemed spontaneously included in the relations between Iris and myself. All fitted in, and seemed beautifully natural.

I never asked Iris how I had come to be included in that party. It would not have occurred to me to ask. Now, of course, it is too late. Iris does not remember the lunch party, nor the bicycle ride, nor the morning swim, nor Maurice Charlton himself. I have sometimes mentioned that occasion, without evoking any response beyond a usual and touchingly anxious interest in what I am talking about. And yet I think she would recognise Maurice Charlton, or other friends from those days, were they to appear suddenly before her in the flesh. Memory may have wholly lost its mind function, but it retains some hidden principle of identification, even after the Alzheimer's has long taken hold.

A woman I sometimes meet, whose husband is also an Alzheimer sufferer, once invited me to share in a brisk exchange of experiences. 'Like being chained to a corpse, isn't it?' she remarked cheerfully. I hastened to agree with her in the same jocular spirit, feeling reluctant none the less to pursue that particular metaphor. 'Oh, a much-loved corpse naturally,' she amended, giving me a slightly roguish glance, as if suggesting I might be thankful to abandon in her presence the usual proprieties that went with our situation.

But I was not at all thankful. I was repelled – I couldn't help it – by the suggestion that Iris's affliction could have anything in common with that of this jolly woman's husband. She was a heroine no doubt, but let her be a heroine in her own style. How could our cases be compared. Iris was Iris.

Troubles do not necessarily bring people together. I felt no togetherness at all. This lady wanted – needed – to dramatise her situation and claim me as a fellow actor.

I felt I could not cooperate in the spirit, though out of politeness I made a show of doing so. My own situation, I felt, was quite different from hers. It's not an uncommon reaction, as I've come to realise, among Alzheimer partners. One needs very much to feel that the unique individuality of one's spouse has not been lost in the common symptoms of a clinical condition.

But the woman's figure of speech did not lose its power to haunt me. Her image of the corpse and the chain still lingered. There is a story by Thomas Hardy called 'On the Western Circuit', one of those soberly ironic tales the author obviously enjoyed writing, in which a young barrister meets a country girl while accompanying the rounds of the circuit judge. They fall in love and he makes her pregnant. She implores the sympathetic married lady in whose house she works as a maid to write letters for her to the young man, she being illiterate. Her mistress does so, and as a result of their correspondence begins to fall for the young man herself, while he, instead of escaping from his predicament as he had first intended, is so charmed by the girl's sensible and loving little letters that he determines to marry her. The outcome, though predictable and characteristic of Hardy, is none the less moving for that. The marriage takes place in London, and the sole meeting between the young man and the girl's employer, before she returns to her own lonely and barren married life in Wessex, reveals to him how their involuntary intimacy has taken place. The love letters she has written have made him love her, not the girl. The poor girl is distracted by her husband's discovery of the deceit – he had asked her to write a little note of thanks to one of the guests – and he is left to face the future fettered to an unchosen partner, like two slaves chained in a galley. Hardy's grim metaphor no doubt seemed wholly appropriate both to him and to his young hero.

I remembered the story while the woman was speaking.

Our own situations were not the same, it was to be presumed, as those of the young man and girl. Fate had not deceived us. We had known our partners as equals over many years, told and listened and communed together, until communication had dwindled and faltered and all but ceased. No more letters, no more words. An Alzheimer sufferer begins many sentences, usually with an anxious repetitive query, but they remain unfinished, the want unexpressed. Usually it is predictable and easily satisfied, but Iris produces every day many such queries, involving 'you know, that person', or simply 'that', which take time and effort to unravel. Often they remain totally enigmatic, related to some unidentifiable man or woman in the past who has swum up to the surface of her mind as if encountered yesterday. At such times I feel my own mind and memory faltering, as if required to perform a function too far outside their own beat and practice.

The continuity of joking can very often rescue such moments. Humour seems to survive anything. A burst of laughter, snatches of doggerel, song, teasing nonsense rituals once lovingly exchanged, awake an abruptly happy response, and a sudden beaming smile that must resemble those moments in the past between explorers and savages, when some sort of clowning pantomime on the part of the former seems often to have evoked instant comprehension and amusement. At cheerful moments, over drinks or in the car, Iris sometimes twitters away incomprehensibly but self-confidently, happily convinced that an animated exchange is taking place. At such moments I find myself producing my own stream of consciousness, silly sentences or mashed-up quotations. 'The tyrant of the Chersonese was freedom's best and bravest friend', I assure her, giving her a solemnly meaningful look. At which she nods her head gravely, and seems to act a conspiring smile, as if the ringing confidence of Byron's line in 'The Isles of Greece' meant a lot to her too.

Our mode of communication seems like underwater sonar, each bouncing pulsations off the other, and listening for an echo. The baffling moments at which I cannot understand what Iris is saying, or about whom or what – moments which can produce tears and anxieties, though never, thank goodness, the raging frustration typical of many Alzheimer sufferers – can sometimes be dispelled by embarking on a joky parody of helplessness, and trying to make it mutual. Both of us at a loss for words.

At happy moments she seems to find them more easily than I do. Like the swallows when we lived in the country. Sitting on the telephone wire outside our bedroom window a row of swallows would converse animatedly with one another, always, it seemed, signing off each burst of twittering speech with a word that sounded like 'Weatherby', a common call-sign delivered on a rising note. We used to call them 'Weatherbys'. Now I tease her by saying 'You're just like a Weatherby, chattering away.' She loves to be teased, but when I make the tease a tender one by adding 'I love listening to you', her face clouds over. She can always tell the difference between the irresponsibility of a joke, or a straight tease, and the note of 'caring' or of 'loving care', which however earnest and true always sounds inauthentic.

All this sounds quite merry, but most days are in fact for her a sort of despair, although despair suggests a conscious and positive state and this is a vacancy which frightens her by its lack of dimension. She mutters 'I'm a fool' or 'Why didn't I' or 'I must . . .' and I try to seem to explain the trouble while rapidly suggesting we must post a letter, walk round the block, go shopping in the car. Something urgent, practical, giving the illusion of sense and routine. The Reverend Sydney Smith, a benevolent clergyman of Jane Austen's time, used to urge parishioners in the grip of depression who appealed to him for help, to 'take short views of human life – never further than dinner or tea'. I used to quote this to Iris, when troubles began, as if I was recommending a real policy, which could intelligibly be followed. Now I repeat it sometimes as an incantation or joke, which can raise a laugh if it is accompanied by some horsing around, a live pantomime of 'short views' being taken. It is not now intended to be rationally received, but it gets a smile anyway.

That is something to be tried for all the time. It transforms her face, bringing it back to what it was, and with an added glow that can seem almost supernatural. The Alzheimer face has been clinically described as the 'lion face'. An apparently odd comparison but in fact a very apt one. The features settle into a leonine impassivity which does remind one of the King of Beasts, and the way his broad expressionless mask is represented in painting and sculpture. The Alzheimer face is neither tragic nor comic, as a face can appear in other forms of dementia: that would suggest humanity and emotion in their most distorted guise. The Alzheimer face indicates only an absence: it is a mask in the most literal sense.

That is why the sudden appearance of a smile is so extraordinary. The lion face becomes the face of the Virgin Mary, tranquil in sculpture and painting with a gravity that gives such a smile its deepest meaning. Only a joke survives, the last thing that finds its way into consciousness when the brain is atrophied. And the Virgin Mary, after all, presides over the greatest joke of the lot, the wonderful fable made up, elaborated, repeated all over the world. No wonder she is smiling.

The latest smile on Iris's face seems to come from association with another Mary. Trying to cheer her up one day I thought of an inane childhood rhyme, forgotten for years.

> Mary had a little bear
> So loving and so kind
> And everywhere that Mary went
> You saw her bear behind.

Iris not only smiled – her face looked cunning and concentrated. Somewhere in the deserted areas of the brain old contacts and impulses became activated, wires joined up. A significance had revealed itself, and it seems only to work with jokes, particularly silly jokes, which in the days of sanity would have been received with smiling but slightly embarrassed forbearance. Iris always mildly disliked and avoided what used to be called vulgar or risqué jokes. Maybe the innocence of the bear rhyme pleased her – who can say what subtle feelings and distinctions from the past can be summoned back to her mind by something as childish – but perhaps as touching too – as the bear rhyme? My own memory had retained it despite my conscious wishes, which is something that often happens. I could recall now the small boy at school – I secretly thought him rather repulsive but was too polite to say so – who told me the rhyme with a knowing air of complacency, sure that it would be a hit with me. I resolved on the spot to forget it at once, but here it was back again.

When I quoted Byron's certainly very memorable line about the old Greek hero Miltiades, Tyrant of the Chersonese and victor at the Battle of Marathon, I thought involuntarily again of Maurice Charlton, and the enchanted lunch on that hot summer day. He had been this fabulous young Greek scholar, before he had become a medical doctor. No doubt Iris had admired him, as she had admired all high skill and learning. And had he been going to attempt seduction that warm afternoon, a project thwarted by his own courtesy in acceding to her suggestion that I should come along too? I had no idea, and still have none. Clueless as I still was I did know by then that Iris had several lovers, often apparently at the same time. I also intuited – quite how I don't know but it turned out to be correct enough – that she usually gave her favours out of admiration and respect: for, so to speak, the godlike rather than the conventionally attractive or sexual attributes in the men who pursued her. Men who were like gods for her were also for her erotic beings, but sex was something she regarded as rather marginal, not an end in itself.

3

I had no illusions about being godlike. I realised that she loved to be with me as if we were children again, and was tender when she saw with what childlike eagerness I had come to desire her. She sensed I had next to no knowledge of lovemaking (how absurdly oldfashioned it all seems today!) A little while before our own swimming expedition on that hot morning she had remarked with brisk indulgence 'Perhaps it's time we made love,' and she had shown me how, although as I had no condom with me (they were known as French letters in those days and a good deal of guilt and secrecy hung about their supply and use) she did not permit me to get very far. We had done better once or twice after that, but in a genial and wholly unserious way that did not in the least mar for me the unfamiliar magic of the proceedings: doing this odd and comical thing with someone whom one really loved. The paradox was itself comical, though not at all depressing.

What was a trifle depressing was the growing knowledge that I was far from being the only one with whom she was doing it – probably only on occasion: she was much too busy and interested in other things to make a habit of it, so to speak. But to me in those days she seemed at the negligent disposition of these unknown and godlike older men, whom she went humbly to 'see' at times when it suited them. Here, I began dimly to perceive, was where her creative imagination lay, and it was to feed it – almost, it seemed, to propitiate it – that she would make what appeared to me these masochistic journeys to London; and chiefly to Hampstead, for me the abode and headquarters of the evil gods.

As my own feelings became closely involved I saw all such matters in an absurdly lurid light. In reality the people Iris went to see were not gods or demons but intellectuals, writers, artists, civil servants, mostly Jewish, mainly refugees, who knew one another and formed a loose-knit circle, with its own rivalries, jealousies and power struggles. They loved Iris and accepted her as one of themselves, although she remained inevitably an outsider, living and teaching as she did in humdrum academic circles, away from their own focus of attention. In time I met most of them and got on with them well, surprised and in later days amused when I looked back at the storm of fears and emotions they had once aroused in me. It was Iris's own imagination which had in a sense created them, and continued to create and nurture them as the strange and unique characters of her wonderful novels. It was the second of these, *The Flight from the Enchanter* in 1955, which first showed me how the genius of Iris's imagination did its own work, in its own way. And all the teeming complex variety of her later novels continued in its own mysterious fashion to be distilled from the alembic of those original obsessions and enchantments.

But Maurice Charlton was quite different: a sunlit character whose spiritual home was that hot but never oppressive Oxford summer, even though he lived for the moment, as if himself the beneficiary of some enchantment, in that gloomy exotic flat, surrounded as it seemed to me by heavy glittering cutlery and tall green Venetian wineglasses. When first in love one feels attended on all sides, almost jostled, by such unexpected and incongruous symbols of romance. That morning marked a turning-point, however little I realised it at the time, in the way in which Iris behaved towards me. The lunch party and the river made me too bemused and delighted to see it, but she was not only including me in another part of her social life: she was also indicating to a third person that I played a role in that life which had begun to possess a public continuity, and was not something to be privately taken up between us and discarded from moment to moment. I was far from becoming her official 'swain', in the quaint old sense, but in the eyes of the world I had come to have some kind of status beyond the sphere of mere acquaintanceship.

With the perception that made him an excellent doctor as well as a brilliant classical scholar Maurice Charlton may well have been aware in some sense of all this, while his green eyes went on surveying us in their merrily convivial but impassive way. He reminded me in some way of the great Professor Fraenkel, whom I had seen once or twice at the time, a venerable almost gnome-like figure, shuffling up the High Street after giving some class or lecture, surveying the world with a disconcertingly bright and youthful eye. A Jewish refugee from Germany, he arrived in Oxford at the time Iris became a student, and such was his reputation that he soon acquired a Chair, even though Oxford had by then a glut of distinguished refugees. He had given Iris tutorials, and she attended his famous Agamemnon class. I had been a mere schoolboy then, and so for that matter had been Maurice Charlton himself, though an older one. But his green glance had much the same light in it as Fraenkel's black twinkle. Perhaps that resemblance was what had attracted Iris to him.

She had already told me how fond she had been of Fraenkel, both fond and reverential. In those days there had seemed to her nothing odd or alarming when he caressed her affectionately as they sat side by side over a text, sometimes half an hour over the exact interpretation of a word, sounding its associations in the Greek world as he explored them, as lovingly keen on them as he seemed to be on her. She had been pleased it was so, and revelled in the sense of intellectual comradeship she felt. That there was anything dangerous or degrading in his behaviour, which would nowadays constitute a shocking example of sexual harassment, never occurred to her. In fact her tutor at Somerville College, Isobel Henderson, had said with a smile when she sent Iris along to the professor, 'I expect he'll paw you about a bit,' as if no sensible girl, aware of the honour of being taught personally by the great man, would be silly enough to object to that.

Nobody did, so far as Iris knew. She sometimes spoke to me of the excitement of the textual world Fraenkel revealed to her, and mentioned in an amused way how he had stroked her arms and held her hand. Few girl students had any sexual experience at that time, and Iris was in any case unusually virginal. We sometimes laughed together over her memories of the one 'bad' girl in Somerville, a dark-haired beauty who used to climb back into the college late at night, assisted by her boyfriend. Professor Fraenkel was devoted to his wife, and had told a close friend that when she died he would follow her. He did, taking an overdose the same night.

My ancient Greek is virtually non-existent; and Iris's, once extensive, of course has gone completely. I used to try reading the *Agamemnon* and other Greek plays to her in a translation, but it was not a success. Nor was any other attempt at reading aloud. It all seemed and felt unnatural. I did several chapters of the *Lord of the Rings* and *The Tale of Genji*, two of Iris's old favourites, before I realised this. For someone who had been accustomed not so much to read books as to slip into their world as effortlessly as she slipped into a river or the sea, this laborious procession of words clumping into her consciousness must have seemed a tedious irrelevance, although she recognised and reacted to them, even knowing, as they appeared before her, the people and events described. But the relation of such rec-ognition to true memory is clearly a painful one. Tolkien and Lady Murasaki had been inhabitants of her mind, denizens as native to its world as were the events and people who so mysteriously came to her in her own process of creation. To meet them again in this way, and awkwardly to recognise them, was an embarrassment.

On the other hand she was always roused to the point of animation if I managed to turn some matter from reading into our own sort of joke. Then we would stop at once and I would embroider the idea into a mini-fantasy, as I did when attempting to interest her again in a translation of the *Odyssey*. The Lestrygonian giants had just sunk eleven of Odysseus's twelve ships and devoured their crews. I imagined him calling an office meeting in the surviving flagship next morning, and starting the proceedings by saying, 'Gentlemen, we shall have to do better than this.' She thought that quite funny, and always seemed to remember it if I said to her when she had arranged dead leaves and bits of rubbish from the street in patterns round the house, 'Come gentlemen, we shall have to do better than this.' I was unconsciously copying the phrase from some other context half-remembered – possibly the moment in *Pride and Prejudice* when Mr Bennet remarks to his younger daughter who has been playing her instrument before the company: 'Come Mary, you have delighted us long enough.' (The unfortunate Mary is the only one among Jane Austen's characters who never gets a fair deal from the author at all, any more than she does from her father.)

I think this attempt at reading and being read to is also a reminder of the loss of identity; although reminder is hardly the word, for an Alzheimer patient is not usually conscious in any definable way of what has happened. If it were otherwise the process, however irreversible it becomes in the end, would have developed along different lines, in a different form. Some sufferers do remain conscious of their state, paradoxical as this seems. The torment of knowing that you cannot speak or think what you want must be intolerable, and I have met patients in whom such a torment is clearly visible. But when Iris talks to me the result seems normal to her and to me surprisingly fluent, provided I do not listen to what is being said but apprehend it in a matrimonial way, as the voice of familiarity, and thus of recognition.

Time constitutes an anxiety because its conventional shape and progression have gone, leaving only a perpetual query. There are some days when 'When are we leaving?' never stops, though it is repeated without agitation. Indeed there can seem something quite peaceful about it, as if it hardly mattered when we went, or where, and to stay at home might in any case be preferable. In Faulkner's novel *Soldier's Pay* the blinded airman keeps saying to his friend, 'When are they going to let me out?' That makes one flinch: the writer has contrived unerringly to put the reader in the blind man's place. Iris's query does not in itself suggest desire for change or release into a former state of being; nor does she want to know when we are getting in the car and going out to lunch. The journey on which we are leaving may for her mean the final one; or, if that sounds too portentous, simply some sort of disappearance from the daily life which, without her work, must itself have lost all sense and identity.

Iris once told me that the question of identity had always puzzled her. She thought she herself hardly possessed such a thing, whatever it was. I said that she must know what it was like to be oneself, even to revel in the consciousness of oneself, as a secret and separate person – a person unknown to any other. She smiled, was amused, looked uncomprehending. It was not something she bothered about. 'Then you live in your work? Like Keats and Shakespeare and all that?' She disclaimed any such comparison; and she did not seem particularly interested when I went on to speak (I was after all in the Eng. Lit. business) of the well-known Romantic distinction, fascinating to Coleridge, between the great egocentric writers, Wordsworth and Milton, whose

sense of self was so overpowering that it included everything else, and these identity-free spirits for whom being
is not what they are, but what they live in and reveal. As
a philosopher I suspect that she found all such distinctions
very crude ones. Perhaps one has to be very much aware of
oneself as a person in order to find them at all meaningful
or interesting. Nobody less narcissistic than Iris can well be
imagined.

Conceivably it is the persons who hug their identity
most closely to themselves for whom the condition of
Alzheimer's is most dreadful. Iris's own lack of a sense
of identity seemed to float her more gently into its world of
preoccupied emptiness. Placidly every night she insists on
laying out quantities of her clothing on my side of the bed,
and when I quietly remove them, back they come again.
She wants to look after me? Is that it? It may be a simpler
sort of confusion, for when we go to bed she often asks me
which side she should be on. Or is it something deeper
and fuller, less conscious and less 'caring' than that far too
self-conscious adjective suggests. She has never wanted to
look after me in the past, thank goodness; indeed one of the
pleasures of living with Iris was her serenely benevolent
unawareness of one's daily welfare. So restful. Having a
busy personality, I made a great thing to myself about
looking after her: she never needed to tell herself to look
after me. But when I broke my leg once in the snow at
Christmas, and had to lie up for a few days in Banbury
hospital, a dozen miles off, she came and stayed in a bed
and breakfast hotel outside the hospital gate. I besought
her to remain at home and work, instead of wasting her
time. There was nothing she could do. But no. She stayed
there until I was fit enough to come home with her.

Philosophers once used to argue the question of whether
I could have a pain in your foot. Iris certainly could not.
Presumably the point of the argument, if it has any, is
to investigate the possibilities of physical sympathy. 'She

may not understand you, but she always feels with you,'
remarked Coleridge fondly of his ideal woman. One doesn't
need to be a feminist to find this nonsense. Either sex may
or may not be able to feel the pleasure or pain of other
persons, just as either sex can possess or lack a sense of
smell. Iris, as it happens, has no sense of smell, and her
awareness of others is transcendental rather than physical.
She communes with their higher being, as an angel might,
and is unconcerned with their physical existence, their
sweaty selves. I have often been struck by the brilliant
accuracy with which she can notice details about the lives of
the characters in her novels, their faces and bodies, without
any instinctive sense of how those characters function in
themselves, on the humbler level.

But of course she was instantly aware of emotion, and
quick to respond to it. Misery or mere sadness in her friends
she intuited at once, and was always able to help it, often
by letting it put on for her some dramatic appearance,
gently encouraging it to assume some form gratifying or
reassuring to its owner. She never participated in the drama
of themselves put on by others, but she could feel intensely
herself emotions of love, jealousy, adoration, even rage. I
never saw them myself but I knew they were there. In my
own case she could always take jealousy away simply by
being with me. In early days I always thought it would be
vulgar – as well as not my place – to give any indications
of jealousy: but she knew when it was there, and soothed it
just by being the self she always was with me, which I soon
knew to be wholly and entirely different from any way that
she was with other people.

In those early days as I now think of them, about a year or
eighteen months after we first met, she was engaged every
Saturday evening with a Jewish Italian professor, another
wartime refugee, from London University. He loved her
deeply, an affection she sweetly and reverently returned. He
was a gentle little man, neat and elderly, and they did not go

to bed together (I believed that) but sat talking all evening about the ancient world while he kissed her sometimes and held her hand. He had a wife and grown-up daughter in London, whom Iris knew well and was greatly attached to. His wife accepted their relationship with complete understanding. Punctually at half-past eleven the professor would leave her room – she was then living not in college but on a top floor in Beaumont Street, close to the centre of Oxford – and walk to his small hotel in the Banbury Road. I knew, because I was usually there. Sometimes I would follow him back – he never guessed my presence: he did not know about me – or sometimes I continued to stand in the street looking up at her lighted window.

There was nothing obviously god-like about this quiet little professor of Ancient History, although he was probably the most distinguished man in his field at the time. In a respectful way I felt quite fond of him, even proud of him. With the other master-figure in Iris's life, a *Dichter* of legendary reputation among people who knew, it was another matter. This man held court, as I thought of it, secretly and almost modestly in Hampstead, and Iris was very much under his sway. He had several mistresses whom Iris knew, and she seemed to revere them almost as much as the great man himself. His wife too she revered. Sometimes Iris spoke to me of this woman, her sweet face and air of patient welcoming reserve, who was sometimes present in the flat when the *Dichter* made love to Iris, possessing her as if he were a god. This she told me later, before we got married, when her close relationship with the man had come to an end, and he had given us his blessing, as she put it. She continued to see him from time to time and her creative imagination continued to be enthralled by him, even though, as she told me, by writing about him in her own way she got him out of her system, and finally in a sense out of her novels too

The *Dichter* was a *Dichter* in the German sense, not

actually a poet but a master-spirit of literature. He had been a friend of another German Jewish writer, a real poet, with whom Iris had been very much in love. She would possibly have married him had he lived, but he had a serious heart ailment, and knew that he could not live long. He died a year before I met her. She grieved for him deeply. He sounded a delightful man, gentle (like all Iris's close friends, as opposed to her 'gods') and humorous. The gods were not funny, I suspect; perhaps it was beneath the dignity of godship. The poet was also in the anthropology department at Oxford, although he was never strong enough to go 'into the field', as they called it. At the time he gave his weekly lecture, he told Iris, he invariably found himself confronting a blank page on which he had written 'As I was saying in my last lecture.' During the week he had never managed to get any farther, and on the morning of the lecture he always found himself confronting the page. It had been a joke between them, and it became a joke between Iris and me. It still is. She always understands it, and when it comes up I always speak of her dead poet by name, though I am never sure if she remembers him. Only the joke remains alive.

Iris's seriousness – a friend once seriously annoyed her, she told me, by implying that her air of gravity was too great for her ever to be imagined as having fun – could, it was true, take disconcerting forms. Greatly to my anguish there was never an actual moment when she told me she had decided to marry me – the matter remained still unsettled a few weeks before it occurred – but there was one occasion when she sat me down in her room and said she had better tell me something of the people in her past. I was reminded of her originally remarking that perhaps it was time to make love. I was startled by her almost portentous air. Had I not heard all about them, the people of her past and present, at one time or another during the period of our own intimacy?

It appeared that I had not. Unknown figures arose before me like the procession of kings in *Macbeth*, seeming to regard me with grave curiosity as they passed by. There was so-and-so with whom she had first been to bed, and so-and-so and so-and-so who had wanted to marry her. There was a friend and fellow-student, whose advances she had resisted in her virginal days (she did not of course put it quite like that). At the beginning of the war he had joined the army and asked her half-jokingly to marry him, pointing out that he was sure to be killed before the war was over and she would be able to draw a widow's pension. Iris's seriousness broke down in smiles at this point, and also in tears.

She had said she still did not want to marry him but she would go to bed with him before he went overseas. He was killed in action later in the war, when she was working at an office in Whitehall.

Incongruous as the memory was at that moment I found myself back for a moment at my first school, when the headmaster gave us each a few moments alone in his study, to tell us about 'the facts of life'; and here were the 'facts' of Iris's life, in grave procession. Suppressing the impulse to recall this for Iris's amusement, I found myself telling her instead that even an officer's widow received only a very small annual sum. I knew, because some of my own contemporaries and fellow-soldiers had been killed before the war was over. It was a feeble attempt to assert myself, and my own meagre experience in the face of what seemed a rich and stately litany of other days, joys, faces, which I would never share. It felt graceless too as I said it, but I could not think of anything else to say.

It broke the mood anyway. Iris laughed and kissed me. 'After all that, isn't it time for me to have a kind word?' I said, and then we both laughed. Getting 'a kind word' had become a regular plea on my part, and a part of our amative speech. It still is, and the phrase continues always to mean something to her. To me at that time, of course, it was wholly different from what I had guessed of her behaviour with others. No doubt it really was different. I could not imagine the god in Hampstead getting a kind word, or giving one. Not even the quiet professor of ancient history, whom I had followed in a dog-like manner back to his hotel. Kind words, in Iris's style to me, were not for them. That was a kind of consolation. Yet I divined already how good she was at the real business of cheering other people's troubles. She had present and former pupils some of whom – often the sad-faced ones – I had seen gazing at her with looks of heartfelt gratitude as well as adoration. But that again was quite different from anything she said or did with me in response to my plea for a kind word.

None the less I was really very cast down by everything she had just been telling me. There seemed so many of them, these fortunate persons, and to my amazement I had just learned that some, as I thought of them, quite ordinary people, acquaintances and even colleagues of my own, had at some time or other in the past been recipients of Iris's kindness. They had desired her, and not been rejected. However different that 'kindness' was, and however unimaginable in terms of what I asked and received, it had nevertheless been given.

Looking back from the standpoint of today, it seems all very unreal, and so oldfashioned. But a woman with a past was different in those days, just as the past itself is always different, and always a foreign country. Today even caring about the past seems an emotion or indulgence that belongs to the past itself, not to the present or future, to the place where we live today. That talk we once had – the way Iris delivered it, and the way in which deep inside me I received it – now seems to me almost mediaeval.

Could we really have thought and behaved like that?

It seems that we did. And now, nearly fifty years later, we

remain for ourselves the same couple, even though a sort of incredulity comes over me in remembering what we seem to have been like, the ways in which we behaved. Looking back, I separate us with difficulty. We seem always to have been together. But memory draws a sharp divide, none the less. The person I was at that age now seems odd to myself – could I have *really* been in love? Could I have felt, at least some of the time, all that jealousy, ecstasy, misery, longing, unhopefulness, mingled with a fever of possibility and joy? I can hardly believe it. But where Iris is concerned my own memory, like a snug-fitting garment, seems to have zipped itself up to the present second. As I work in bed early in the morning, typing on my old portable with Iris quietly asleep beside me, her presence as she now is seems as it always was, and as it always should be. I know she must once have been different, but I have no true memory of a different person.

Waking up for a peaceful second or two she looks vaguely at the 'Tropical Olivetti' lying on my knees, cushioned by one of her jerseys. Not long ago, when I asked if it disturbed her, she said she liked to hear that funny noise in the morning. She must be used to it, although a couple of years ago she would have been getting up herself at this time – seven o'clock – and preparing to start her own day. Nowadays she lies quietly asleep, sometimes giving a little grunt or murmur, often sleeping well past nine, when I rouse and dress her. This ability to sleep like a cat, at all hours of the day and night, must be one of the great blessings that sometimes go with Alzheimer's, converse of the anxiety state that comes on in wakefulness and finds worried words like 'When are we leaving?'

Dressing most days is a reasonably happy and comic business. I am myself still far from sure which way round her underpants are supposed to go: we usually decide between us that it doesn't matter. Trousers are simpler: hers have a grubby white label on the inside at the back. I ought to give her a bath, or rather a wash of some sort since baths are tricky, but I tend to postpone it from day to day. For some reason it is easier to do the job in cold blood, as it were, at an idle moment later in the day. Iris never objects to this; she seems in a curious way to accept it as both quite normal and wholly exceptional, as if the two concepts had become identified for her. Perhaps that is why she seems to accept her daily state as if none other had ever existed: assuming too that no one else would find her changed in any way; just as my own memory only works with her now as she is, and so, as my memory seems to assume, must always have been.

It seems normal that the old routines of washing and dressing have vanished as if they too had never existed. If she remembered them, which she doesn't, I can imagine her saying to herself, did one really go through all those unnecessary rituals every day? My own memory, after all, can hardly believe that I once went through all those other rituals of falling in love and becoming agitated, ecstatic, distracted . . .

At the same time Iris's social reflexes are in a weird way still very much in place. If someone comes to the door – the postman, the man to read the gas meter – and I am for the moment occupied elsewhere, she receives him with her social smile, and calls for me in those unhurried slightly 'gracious' tones which married couples automatically use on each other in the presence of a stranger. 'Oh I think it is the man who has come to read the meter, darling.' In the same way she deals instinctively with more complex social situations; seeming to follow the conversation and smiling, prepared to bridge a silence by asking a question. Usually the same question: 'Where do you come from?' or 'What are you doing now?' – questions that get repeated many times in the course of a social event. Other people, visitors or friends, adjust themselves well to these repetitions as soon as they grasp what is happening and what motivates them:

they usually manage to adopt the same social part that she is playing.

I find myself making use of the behavioural instincts that survive. In the old days I would sometimes produce what in childhood used to be called 'a tantrum', if something had gone wrong or not been done properly, something for which, rightly or wrongly, I held Iris responsible. She would then become calm, reassuring, almost maternal, not as if deliberately, but with some deep unconscious female response that normally had no need to come to the surface, as it would have had to do on an almost daily basis with a young family. Iris in general was never 'female' at all, a fact for which I sometimes remembered to be grateful. Nowadays I have learnt to make on occasions a deliberate use of this buried reflex. If she has been following me all day, like Mary's bear, interrupting tiresome business or letter-writing (very often letters to her own fans), I erupt in what can seem even to me an uncontrolled fit of exasperation, stamping on the floor and throwing the papers and letters on it, waving my hands in the air. It always works. Iris says 'Sorry . . . sorry . . .' and pats me before going quietly away. She will be back soon, but that doesn't matter. My tantrum has reassured her as no amount of my own caring, or my calming efforts to reply to her rationally, could have done.

The lady who told me in her own deliberately jolly way that living with an Alzheimer victim was like being chained to a corpse, went on to an even greater access of desperate facetiousness. 'And, as you and I know, it's a corpse that complains all the time.'

I don't know it. In spite of her anxious and perpetual queries Iris seems not to know how to complain. She never has. Alzheimer's, which can accentuate personality traits to the point of demonic parody, has only been able to exaggerate a natural goodness in her.

On a good day her need for a loving presence, mutual

pattings and murmurs, has something angelic about it; she seems herself the presence found in an icon. It is more important for her still on days of silent tears, a grief seemingly unaware of that mysterious world of creation she has lost, and yet aware that something is missing. The 'little bull' aspect of her, putting her head down, and herself moving determinedly ahead, used once to be emphasised when she got up in the morning and headed for the bathroom. Dressed, she would visit me, still working in bed, and then go down to open the garden door and see what was going on in the morning. The weather and the birds, the look and sound of things, were sometimes jotted in her diary as she settled down to work. She never had breakfast then, although if I was at home I brought her coffee and a chocolate biscuit later in the morning.

Now that once good morning time has become the worst time. Like 'stand-to' in the trenches for soldiers in the two world wars. Trench humour is the natural response, even if one can only crack the dark joke inside oneself; it would be heartless at that once hopeful hour to try to share it with the victim. While trying to think of ways of getting through the day I feel all the more comradely at this time, with the woman who had found some relief – at least I hoped so – in being facetious about herself and her Alzheimer husband. Although I hadn't felt inclined to join very heartily in the joke, it was better, far better, than having to sympathise, in a caring po-faced way, from a similar position. In any case those in the same boat have a natural desire to compare notes. A spruce grey-haired man whom I had once known, when we were both eighteen-year-olds and in the army, wrote to me to commiserate. Aside from his job as a stockbroker his chief interests had been girls and vintage cars. When his wife, younger than he, developed the condition and deteriorated rapidly, he looked after her with exemplary devotion. He liked reporting progress, or the reverse, in terms of effective notes. Once he wrote: 'I used to view the female form divine in a rather different light. Now I just find myself hosing it down every morning.'

I do it much less often. But I giggle internally if that jest comes into my head when washing between her legs and working over the contours of Iris's 'female form divine'. From where had my old army acquaintance obtained that unexpected specimen of Edwardian archness, a comic but also rather lyrical cliché that had also appealed once to James Joyce? No use trying to share this joke with Iris. Not that she would object, but the bounderish absurdity of the idiom has passed beyond her critical faculty. I recently came across a collection of palindromes somebody sent us years ago – ingenious and surreal sentences, appropriately illustrated. One of them, which had amused us as much by the illustration as by the telegraphic simplicity of the palindrome, was 'Sex at noon taxes.' Recently I showed this and other one-time favourites to Iris, and she laughed and smiled a bit, out of the wish to share them with me, but I knew that they were not getting through. At the same time she will watch the animated cartoons on children's TV with something approaching glee. They can be a great stand-by at ten or so – the trickiest time – till eleven in the morning. I usually watch the Teletubbies with her, and become absorbed myself in their odd little sunlit world, peopled with real rabbits, real sky, real grass. Or so it seems. Is some human agency inside the creatures, some actual and cunning little mannikin? It certainly looks like it, and the illusion, if such it is, continues to hold both our attentions.

We have only had television a few months – it never occurred to us before. Now I listen for its noise from the kitchen and hope it will remain switched on. If there is silence I know that Iris has switched it off and is sitting there without moving. Attention-span does not seem to be the trouble. She will watch with absorption a football game, cricket, bowls, tennis, without knowing the play or the scores, but immersed in the feel of the thing. My woman friend chained to the corpse told her husband every evening, 'There's a snooker programme on.' Then she played an old one on the video. It was always a new one for him, she said.

Unfortunately, not having a handy six-year-old child about, I have never managed to programme the video. In any case Iris turns the thing off not because she is bored with it – boredom doesn't seem with her a possible state of mind – but out of an instinct to get away, the one that makes her say 'When are we leaving?' or 'Must do go'. She leaves offered and attempted occupations – all now tacitly given up – for the same reason. When are they going to let us out?

Neither of us ever attempted, from our earliest married days, to do much about the house. A routine of chores never existed. Neither of us felt any need to keep it clean, and we were bothered by the notion of somebody coming in to do it for us. Now I suppose the house has reached what seems a comfortable point of no return. Once nothing seemed to need to be done, or so we took it all for granted, and now nothing can be done. If friends notice the state the place is in – a perfectly cosy one really – they don't say anything. None the less I feel from time to time that if we had ever developed a habit of working together on the chores we might be able to continue with it now. Self-discipline. And a way of passing the time. But somehow, as the tramp more or less says in *Waiting for Godot*, the time seems to pass anyway.

We don't exactly keep a dust museum, like Dickens's Miss Havisham. If undisturbed it seems to fade easily into the general background. Like the clothes, books, old newspapers, letters and cardboard boxes. Some of them might be useful some time. In any case Iris has never been able to bear throwing anything away. She has always felt a tenderness for the feelings of torn open envelopes, or capless plastic bottles, which has now become obsessive. Old leaves are rescued, sticks, even cigarette ends smoked not very furtively in the street by the girls at the High School near by. Smoking in our time has become an outdoor activity. Quite a wholesome one I sometimes think.

It is wonderfully peaceful to sit in bed with Iris reassuringly asleep and gently snoring. Half asleep again myself I have a feeling of floating down the river, and watching all the rubbish from the house and from our lives – the good as well as the bad – sinking slowly down through the dark water until it is lost in the depths. Iris is floating or swimming quietly beside me. Weeds and larger leaves sway and stretch themselves beneath the surface. Blue dragonflies dart and hover to and fro by the river bank. And suddenly a kingfisher flashes past.

4

Rivers featured on our honeymoon.

We were married nearly three years after we first met. I once worked out the number of days that had gone by since the morning I had seen Iris bicycling slowly past the window; but I have forgotten the number now and it would take me too long to work it out again. We were married at the Registrar's office in St Giles, a broad street which runs between the Martyrs' Memorial at its south end and the War Memorial at the north end, at the junction of the Woodstock and Banbury roads. Opposite the Registrar's office, now disappeared or moved elsewhere, is the Judge's House, a fine Palladian building which is supposed to have given Henry James his idea for the house in his novel *The Spoils of Poynton*.

I talk like a guidebook now because in a way I felt like one that morning. I gazed at these familiar landmarks as if I had never seen them before. In a sense I never had seen them before, because I had always hurried along, going somewhere, late for something, preoccupied with my own affairs, taking no notice. Now I found myself looking round as I waited on a corner near the office, seeing everything very clearly and as if for the first or the last time. I remember that the painter David, who sketched Marie Antoinette in the tumbril on her way to execution, noticed that she kept glancing all round her with vacant curiosity, as if she had never seen these streets and squares of Paris before. I felt rather like that I think. I was also preoccupied, as every bridegroom is supposed to be, with the question of the ring, which I had amongst various other things in my right-hand trouser pocket. It was obviously an unsatisfactory place to keep it, but I could not think of a better one. I was wearing a dark suit, with which I had been issued on demobilisation from the army, nine years previously. It had no waistcoat, or perhaps the waistcoat, a necessary attribute of gents' suiting in those days, had become mislaid. I had selected the suit from among others lighter in colour, and it had been quite a good choice because I had scarcely ever worn it, except on rare occasions of this kind. Weddings, christenings, funerals.

I had bought the ring the day before at a pawnbroker's. It was a solid job, plain and oldfashioned, possibly disposed of by a widower in needy circumstances. It had been my idea. Iris had never mentioned it. She never wore a ring, and I had never thought of giving her one, since we had never been engaged. I had no idea whether this ring would fit, and I was anxious about that. Fortunately it was a beautiful fit, and still is, though it has now worn down from its old robust self into being the slimmest of gold bands.

After the operation – one could hardly call it a ceremony – which lasted about three minutes, the wife of my senior colleague – they were a very nice couple – said in her rather fussy way 'I must go and look after Mrs Bayley'. She meant my mother, but her husband said to her with what Iris later described as 'a grim laugh', 'Every woman here is called Mrs Bayley, except you.' It was true. My mother and sister-in-law, also a Mrs Bayley, were present: no other ladies. Iris said that this was the ghastliest moment of what was for her an extremely gruesome occasion. She was now lumped among a lot of Mrs Bayleys. Her own mother, incidentally, had managed to miss the train from Paddington to Oxford. After the business was over we went down to the station to meet the next train, found her, and cheered up a good deal over a drink at a nearby pub.

This was not a very good start; but it was not exactly

a start in any case. It seemed more of an anticlimax, the world we knew ending not with a bang but a whimper. At the same time this feeling of *détente* was very welcome. All tensions, queries and uncertainties, all the things that for months and years seemed to have made up the drama of living, were now over. That was a real source of satisfaction to both of us. At least I knew it was for me; and when Iris squeezed my hand at the station, and said how nice and settled and yet unfamiliar it felt now to be together, it reassured me that all was well. Reassurance was probably what was wanted.

In another sense it seemed to be there already, in the mere fact of marriage. In his memoirs the novelist Anthony Powell observes that marriage does not resemble in the smallest degree any other comparable human experience. You can live with someone for years and not feel in the least married. Alternatively you could finally take the step, as Iris and I had done, and at once feel you have moved into a wholly different sphere of sensation and behaviour. As Powell puts it, in order to know what it is like you have to experience the thing itself. 'Nothing else will do.'

The meeting with Iris's mother was also reassuring. She was a quite exceptionally nice woman, who looked rather younger than her daughter. She had been only nineteen when Iris was born. She was a Dublin girl, and a young man from Belfast, recently joined up in the army, had fallen in love with her. This was in 1917. Iris was proud of the fact that her father, who had been brought up on a farm, was in a Yeomanry Cavalry Regiment, King Edward's Horse. That probably saved his life, as the cavalry were rarely able to get into action during trench warfare battles. Iris's mother, who had been an amateur soprano of considerable promise, gave up her singing when she got married. Iris inherited her singing voice in some degree, and was always sorry that her mother had never gone on with a serious musical career.

Instead she had Iris, with a difficult birth, following which she had taken a silent decision to have no more children. Iris told me later that she knew this by instinct, although her mother had never said anything about it. I had pointed out that if more children had been born, a son among them, her own life would have been drastically different. As it was she had lived on the happiest terms of equality with her mother and father, who had adored her. After the Irish troubles the small family had moved to England, where her father had obtained a modest job in a branch of the civil service. Iris's childhood was spent in a small semi-detached house in Chiswick. She went first to a Froebel day school in the same district. Then she was sent to Badminton, an excellent private boarding school for girls near Bristol. Her father's sacrifices for her education, including the borrowing of money, were something altogether against the instincts of a frugal and godly Belfast upbringing, although by that time neither parent had any interest in religion, or affiliations with any church. Iris's childhood was happily godless.

Her appetite for the spiritual developed in her Oxford days, nurtured by Plato and by her studies in philosophy. It was part of the inner world of her imagination and never appeared on the surface. The way she fell in love when young, and the people she fell in love with, resembled in some degree the search for wisdom, authority, belief, which a lot of people feel the need to embark on at some point, whether young or old. At the same time I suspect there was always something both tough and elusive about Iris, perhaps the circumspectness of her Northern Irish ancestors. Falling in love with people who represented for her spiritual authority, wisdom, beneficence, even a force that might seem darkly ambiguous and enigmatic, was an adventure in the soul's progress and experience; she craved it, needed it, but she was far too sensible ever to become enslaved. Like silly young Dora Greenfield in her novel *The*

Bell, she could get away when she wanted: common sense was the final arbiter of her emotional impulses.

Her sunny adolescence, happiness at school, happy relations with her parents, may well have played their part in giving her this nèed, as she grew up, for strongly contrasting kinds of experience. But with her parents she always seemed to return, as I felt she did with me, to the cheerful and enterprising innocence which seemed to have been her natural character when young. She behaved with her mother with complete naturalness as if they were sisters, herself the elder. Her father at that time, newly retired, was already an invalid, and died of cancer the next year. (He had always smoked his sixty a day, but so had her mother.) Iris was deeply attached to him, and she grieved for and missed him greatly, while instinctively taking over the role he had played in her mother's life. I still wish there had been time for me to know him better.

When the three of us got back from the station that day, my mother had a moment's hesitation when introduced to Mrs Murdoch and her daughter. Which of them had her son just married? The instant of confusion was pardonable; and I attempted, perhaps not very wisely, to make a joke of it. How this went down I don't know, because we were immediately plunged into the business of the party, modest as were the numbers attending it. It was given in a small reception room in my college; and the college butler, a genial patriarch, had suggested to me that he serve some champagne from the college cellars which was already many years past its sell-by date. He wanted to use it up. 'I don't mind telling you, sir, that it's not entirely reliable,' he warned me, 'but I can let you have it cheap.'

In the event every bottle proved delicious, deep gold in colour and without much fizz, but giving just the right amount of conviviality to the few guests, and valuable support to the wedding couple. I can still remember the romantic name of the *marque*: it was called Duc de Marne.

The Duke still seemed to be giving us his benevolent support as we got through the other trials of the day, culminating in a debacle at the posh hotel, The Compleat Angler at Marlowe, where we had been going to spend the night. The name had seemed propitious; and when we had been in to book a room we saw the river Thames pouring itself over a weir outside the windows. The sound of that weir at night would have been a delightful epithalamion.

When we turned up there, however, the hotel staff were polite but puzzled. They were full up. Had we booked a room? Yes, we had – I had been there in person a week before. (In those days the telephone seemed, at least to me, a not entirely trustworthy instrument to make so vital a reservation.) The young women at the reception desk exchanged a swift look. 'That must have been when Camilla was on,' murmured one. I gathered at once and despairingly that Camilla was a delinquent girl, since sacked no doubt, who had forgotten to record the booking. In those days fashionable country hotels prided themselves on the attractive amateur débutantes they employed as part-time staff. Camilla had no doubt been attractive, but not, it appeared, reliable. Profuse in their apologies the hotel booked us by phone into a solid old-world establishment in the main square of neighbouring Henley. It was called The Catherine Wheel.

Our mothers had hit it off pretty well at the wedding party, and continued doing so on the basis of not seeing much of each other until both were old, when they became closer friends. Iris's mother seemed to take it for granted that we would not want to have children. I suspect she had not wanted them herself, although Iris as she grew up had become her joy and pride. How such a conclusion could have been reached by me as an outside party is difficult to say; but Mrs Murdoch certainly seems to have assumed from the start that the three of us would form a harmoniously self-sufficient triangle, similar to the one she had shared with her daughter and husband. Nor was she wrong, although her own presence in the relationship was happy but hardly noticeable. She continued to live in London; she never bothered us.

Although no more intrusive in the affairs of her son and daughter-in-law, my own mother would, I knew, have liked grandchildren. She had three sons and only one produced an heir. But she had too much sense and tact to voice this hope. After some initial uneasiness – she had barely met Iris before the wedding – my mother became very deeply attached to her increasingly famous daughter-in-law, and continued to be so until she died, not so very long ago, in her late eighties. By then Iris's mother, herself a victim of Alzheimer's, was also dead.

It had never for a moment occurred to either of us that the disease, or the gene that brought it about, could be hereditary. Indeed apart from the blanket term 'senile dementia' the condition had then no specific name, nor did the specialists we consulted about her mother's case prove in the least helpful, beyond suggesting various physiological explanations and attempting to treat them. Mrs Murdoch's own doctor, a hardbitten London GP, merely hinted at a fondness for the gin bottle, a suggestion that upset Iris very much, although it was obvious to me that her mother had for some time been putting away a good deal. Why not? She was never lonely, because we had subsidised an old friend of hers, a sterling character, to live with and look after her, but age and its problems are surely entitled to any aids they can find. Alcohol undoubtedly exacerbates the symptoms of Alzheimer's in many of those who suffer from it, but where would they have been without the stuff? Iris drinks wine nowadays as she has always done, but in diminished quantity, which for her seems natural. Other bottles of various kinds lie about the house, but she ignores them.

As regards children, more than forty years ago, her

attitude seemed equally natural. We hardly spoke of the question, because I suppose we knew we both understood it. Iris's attitude to procreation, as to sex, was not dismissive: it was detachedly and benevolently indifferent. She herself had other things to do. How many women feel the same, but feel also that it is unnatural to do so, as if motherhood were an achievement they could not let themselves do without? Stevie Smith, the poet, whom Iris knew and liked, used to say in her rather deliberately elfin way, 'My poems are my kiddo.' Iris would never have spoken of her novels as her children: she would never have said anything about the matter at all. Her reserve was deep, and as natural to her as it was deep.

D.H. Lawrence worship was getting into its stride in the mid-fifties, reaching a sort of climax in 1963, the year in which the failure of an Old Bailey court case against Penguin Books licensed *Lady Chatterley's Lover* for unlimited printing; the year in which, according to a sardonic poem of Philip Larkin, 'sexual intercourse began'. There was a sense in which this was true for England, where the matter had not previously been much discussed, or thought suitable for discussion. And so to the post-war generation Lawrence appealed less as a writer than as a cult figure, like the newly famous Beatles, a symbol of enlightenment and modernity. For Iris it was only as a writer that he mattered. I remember hearing a philosophical colleague complaining to her about Lawrence's 'half-baked religiosity' in matters of sex. Iris mildly demurred, saying she thought he was such a marvellous writer it didn't matter what he wrote about, or how. But sex certainly did become one of the new religions of the sixties and seventies; and when disillusionment set in it was succeeded by a crudely Faustian view: sex as a performance sport, for ever striving after new records, new achievements in the state of the art. All this passed by us, and our own cosy and quietistic approach to the matter.

There have been moments when I found myself wondering how Iris got on in bed with lovers whose approach was more ambitious or more demanding than my own; and on one occasion I accidentally received an unexpected hint from an acquaintance who had, as I knew, been for a brief period a successful admirer. I did not greatly care for this character, a highly distinguished figure in his own sphere, with a weakness for keeping his friends a trifle overinformed about a current love affair, and how painful or ecstatic or both it was turning out to be. On this occasion he made some remark about how important it was to get the girl proficient at what you wanted to do yourself, indicating that if she was gone on you enough she would – whatever it was. 'Nothing more discouraging than a partner who won't enter into the spirit of the thing,' he observed sagely, and then gave me a sudden guilty look as if he might have given something away. It was unlikely that he knew I was aware of his one time walk-out with Iris, but that brief hangdog look gave me a strong suggestion that he was thinking of her and her shortcomings in bed, thoughts which he realised were now not best communicated to the husband.

Certainly our bedroom habits (the deep deep peace of the double bed after the hurly-burly on the chaise longue, as Mrs Pat Campbell noted) were always peaceful and unbothered by considerations of better, or more. The lady in Iris's novel *A Severed Head* who complained that her marriage 'wasn't getting anywhere' would probably have made the same observation about her sex life. We expected neither sex nor marriage to get anywhere: we were happy for them to jog on just as they were.

Although Iris remained quite untroubled by any wish to have a family life of her own she had a touching desire to join in any family activities that might be going on around her. As an only child she greatly welcomed the prospect of having two brothers-in-law, although neither of them showed much interest in her. She bore this patiently, and was rewarded in the course of time by the increasing regard, almost devotion, given her by my middle brother Michael, a bachelor and brigadier in the army, now retired. He had a distinguished military record, but his occupation since retirement has been the repair of monuments in churches derelict and no longer in use: some of them magnificent buildings, mainly in East Anglia. Nothing seemed to give him more pleasure than to take us on tour and to show Iris round any work he had been doing, commenting on the finer points of alabaster restoration – his speciality – and proudly showing off any neglected statue or cherub's head he had unearthed in the course of his work.

The now restored church of Lydiard Tregoze in Wiltshire was a special showpiece of his. A frugal person and careful with his pension – he made almost nothing out of restoration work – he used to sleep in his campbed in the churches where he worked, however remote or desolate they might be. I once asked him if this wasn't a shade spooky at times. He pooh-poohed the idea; but added, after a pause for reflection, that he had once felt a little uneasy on waking up in the night in a private chapel on the Harewood estate in Yorkshire. We inquired whether any explanation for this had manifested itself. Not exactly, he said, and yet he had been beset with the sense that something flat and dark, of considerable size, was in motion on the floor in the half-light, slowly coming closer to his bed. Rather tactlessly I mentioned M.R. James's ghost story, 'The Treasure of Abbot Thomas', in which a creature resembling a damp leather bag has been set in mediaeval times by some satanic cleric to guard a treasure concealed under a church's nave. He had not read it, he said shortly. In fact, as he occasionally remarked, almost the only book he had read since his schooldays was *A Month in the Country*, not Turgenev's play but a brief romance about a young man engaged like himself in the work of church restoration. I cannot recall the name of the author, but about this book my brother was prepared to be enthusiastic.

I don't think he ever read any of Iris's novels, but in his own way he greatly respected her achievement. Perhaps because he saw her in a sense as a dedicated fellow-soldier: one who had been prepared, as a good commander should be, to devote herself singlemindedly to the job of winning the battle. Certainly there was an unspoken accord between them, notwithstanding his extreme reserve, which was perhaps in secret sympathy with her own. Undoubtedly they felt close to each other, although only meeting on rare occasions, family Christmases and the like. Since Iris developed Alzheimer's he has expressed, most uncharacteristically for him, a wish to come and see us at fairly frequent intervals, driving down from London on Sundays for lunch. Although she doesn't remember him beforehand, or grasp who it is that is coming, these visits always have a cheering effect on Iris.

My own feelings are more mixed as I have to produce something in the way of lunch instead of our vague little everyday picnic. When at home or on a job my brother lives on sardines and tomatoes, a healthy diet although he's not concerned with that. But he unconsciously expects his younger brother to take trouble for him. There is something I enjoy in this fraternal manifestation – essentially one of kindness, unspoken protectiveness – even though it is a bit irksome, practically speaking, to go along with it. He is punctilious about not drinking when he drives, bringing his own bottle of alcohol-free beer with some military name like 'Caliber'.

I used sometimes to tease Iris by telling her that she possessed, in mild form, a 'Lawrence of Arabia complex'. She smiled but did not deny it. I have always held the opinion that T.E. Lawrence was a bogus figure. *The Seven Pillars of Wisdom*, once worshipped as a cult book among upper-class homosexuals and academics pining for action, seemed to me so turgidly written as to be almost unreadable. I still think this is true, but Iris always remained quietly loyal to her affection for the book and its author. She had read it at school, 'soon after my Rafael Sabatini period', as she once told me. (Sabatini, author of *Captain Blood* and *The Black Swan*, was a prolific swash and buckle performer of popular literature.) This willingness to be unserious about *The Seven Pillars* went with its much deeper and more serious romantic influence, strongly discernible in many of her own novels. Transmuted as they are, and as is the world she gives them to inhabit, her characters frequently have for the addicted reader the same sort of powerful fascination that the Lawrence legend and personality once exerted. My brother himself has a shadowy presence in some of her novels, appearing in *An Unofficial Rose* as a character called Felix. I doubt if he would be recognised in the role, by himself or by anybody else, and I never commented on the point to Iris. She always hated to think her characters were in any sense identifiable, least of all by her own family. She had made them up: they were completely her own and belonged to her own world, which in its own way was certainly true.

At the time we got married she had written three successful novels and had begun on her fourth. An unforgettable scene in her third, *The Sandcastle*, has a green Riley car undergoing a complex underwater adventure. I was proud of knowing where the original of the Riley, as a character in the book, had come from, because I had found the car for Iris after a diligent study of the advertisements in the *Oxford Mail*. This had itself followed a mildly unfortunate incident involving a car – her car. It was a pale blue Hillman Minx, and it had been bought out of the proceeds of the preceding novel, *The Flight from the Enchanter*. During the fine summer of 1955 I had acted as driving instructor. I had an old Morris car I had bought cheap from my parents when they had acquired a more respectable vehicle, and

Iris quickly learnt to drive, and to drive very well. It would be presumptuous to say I taught her, but I sat beside her and made suggestions. My old car was known to us by its number EKL, which, as I pointed out, indicated the German word *ekelhaft* – disgusting – but we were fond of it none the less. Iris took her test in it and passed first time. I was hovering in the background when she met the test official – in those days even driving tests were more informal than they are now – and I was relieved to see her make a conspicuous point of adjusting the driving mirror before moving off, as I had advised her.

After this sage display of advice and instruction on my part it was I who managed to crash the poor Minx on an icy road in December. I had borrowed the car to go to a party outside Oxford. No one has ever taken a piece of bad news better than Iris did when I broke it to her. She loved her Minx, and its life had been a sadly short one. But looking back I think that was the moment at which our life together really began, even though there was still nothing said about marriage, and I had long since given up even hinting at it. But on its own minor scale this was the kind of domestic disaster which tests a relationship, and shows whether or not it is going to work. Iris was so relieved I wasn't hurt that she didn't mind too much about the Minx. The accident had shown my importance to her more effectively than any loving deeds on my part could have done. Moreover the insurance company paid up, and the green Riley, though impractical in many ways, was a far more romantic and beautiful car. It was a 1947 model, nearly ten years old, and its dark green chassis, recently and rather amateurishly repainted, was set off by elegant black wings and the graceful curl of the marque's radiator, with the name enamelled in blue. No one could have been less fickle than Iris, but in her excitement over the Riley the Minx was soon out of mind, if not forgotten.

Not forgotten until now, that is. That memory has passed

beyond her mind, but when I mention the Riley, and describe it to her, there is still a very faint flicker of recognition. She even smiles when I go on to remind her of its bad habits and its bad brakes. It would be a valuable car today if it still exists. We kept it in honoured retirement for more than twenty years, until we could no longer afford garage space and so let it go for a few pounds.

Rivers, as I said, featured in our honeymoon, although not by intention. Our idea had been to take a cultural tour in a leisurely manner, down through France and over the Alps into north Italy, keeping clear of famous places like Florence and Venice, which we would leave for another time, staying instead at Urbino, San Gimignano and Arezzo, places earnestly recommended to Iris by a couple whom I thought of as her 'art friends' – Brigid Brophy and her husband Michael, who was later to become director of the National Gallery. Brigid had chided Iris for allowing herself to do anything so banal as to get married, but her sarcasms were weakened by the fact that she had, however reluctantly, taken the same step herself. She wanted the experience of having a child, and single mothers in those days had not yet acquired the glamour they would achieve later on.

Wisely we were not going in the Riley, but in a very small Austin van, which I had recently bought new for a modest sum. It was all the cheaper because being a 'commercial vehicle' it was exempt from what was then called Purchase Tax. The same Elaine Griffiths who had asked me to the party at St Anne's where I met Iris, had recently acquired one of these, and being a crafty lady had caused a garage to remove the metal side panels at the back, substituting neat glass windows. The vehicle now became officially a saloon car, and as such was not subject to the 30 mile an hour speed limit imposed in those days on all trucks and vans. She recommended this device, but after consideration we rejected it, unwisely as it turned out, because I was soon stopped and fined by an unsporting policeman for doing nearly forty miles an hour.

Notwithstanding this setback I clung to my idea that it would be better for the van to remain as it was, because then we should be able to sleep in it, at a pinch, when on our travels. In fact we only did this once, and that was a few years later, in the west of Ireland. We had been to see the famous black granite cliffs of Moher, and a large farmer, whom we christened the Moher giant, had conscripted ourselves and the van to help him get in the hay from a field almost on the edge of the abyss. He even offered to buy the van, enquiring with interest 'what price would it be now' in England. Escaping at last in a state of exhaustion we found a fishing hotel who could give us a 'high tea' of grilled trout, but had no room for the night. So we drove to a quiet beach, fried a further supper of bacon and eggs in a rugged iron frying pan bought in Belfast market, and settled down for the night. We slept soundly, roused early by the scream of the gulls meeting the scallop boats as they chugged into the next cove. We then returned to the hotel and had bacon and scallops for breakfast, the favourite morning dish, as I recalled, of good Queen Elizabeth the First, who used to wash it down with a pint of small beer. We had Irish coffee instead.

It was on this trip, during which we explored the rocky coast of County Clare and the strange stony waste of 'the Burren', that Iris conceived the idea of her haunting novel set in Ireland, *The Unicorn*, and found the landscape that embodied the feel of it. With its fantasy of a woman immured in a kind of sexual cloister near the wild coast, *The Unicorn* has always been for me the most purely Irish of all her novels, more so even than *The Red and the Green*, her novel featuring the Easter Rebellion of 1916.

It was on this trip that I made the discovery of how to swim comfortably in cold water. Or rather not to swim but to hang suspended in a narrow bay, observing the flora of the seabed with a pipe and mask. The underwater scene off a rocky northern shore is far more magical than anything in the tropics. Fronds of seaweed, dark red and amethyst, undulate quietly over vast smooth stones, polished by the storms of the winter. Green crabs as big as dinnerplates limp away sideways. Fish are rare, but a plaice like a freckled partridge lay half hidden on the white sand and looked up at me obliquely. Enthralled, I was unaware of the cold, but when I came out I shook and shivered uncontrollably. Iris rubbed some feeling into me, clucking like a disapproving parent, but when I handed her the rubber pipe and mask she became as enraptured as I had been, nor did she feel the cold. She remained in the water for what seemed hours, while with trembling hands I lit a driftwood fire and crouched beside it, taking swigs from our whiskey bottle. Later I tried going into the sea in all my clothes, and a macintosh, and that worked well, although removing the saturated garments that clung like an icy shirt of Nessus was far from easy. Hercules had been set on fire by his fatal shirt, and at those moments I quite envied him.

Having acquired the habit I usually kept a vest on when swimming, even in warm water. Once in Pisa harbour, in a drizzle of rain, I was examining the fishes, numerous and even colourful, who congregated by the side of the harbour breakwater, where one or two anglers were fishing. Iris, who had decided not to follow me into the water, was standing there under an umbrella; and she later reported seeing one of the fishermen give a start of surprise and peer down intently into the harbour. The reason for this was not clear until I reappeared under my snorkel, clad in an ancient vest. 'I saw the fishermen peering down and trying to read the label on your neck,' chortled Iris. 'I really did.' The episode much amused her, particularly the moment – sometimes mimed by her in later years – when the incredulous Italian fishermen had craned their heads sideways, so as to keep in view the apparition slowly progressing below them in the harbour.

Half a century ago the roads of France were empty. Long straight poplar-bordered roads, still full of '*déformations*' as a result of war-time neglect, but wonderfully relaxing to buzz happily down in a reverie *à deux*. No trouble going through towns. A helpful sign promised '*Toutes Directions*'; a bored gendarme blew his whistle unnecessarily; small restaurants advertised their *repas* with a sign on the pavement. France existed not for the tourist nor for its own people (where were they? who were they?) but for honeymoon couples like us, without much money, listening together to each poplar saying 'hush' as we drove past, as regularly as the telegraph wires of those days used to rise and fall beside the train. Then we would stop at one of the little restaurants, three-quarters empty, and have *charcuterie* and *entrecôte aux endives*, with unlimited quantities of red wine which never had to be uncorked or bought by the bottle. Cramped little hotels (*de la Poste* or *du Gare*) had scrubbed floors that smelt of garlic and gauloise cigarettes. Natives were taciturn, speech formalised and distant; but I noticed that the severest French person (and to me all their faces looked austere, like those of monks and nuns) responded to Iris's smile.

Of course she knew France already – another France, inhabited entirely, in my eyes, by writers and intellectuals who sat in cafés and wrote books between drinks. It was not so long since Iris had been under the spell of Sartre's novel *La Nausée* and Raymond Queneau's *Pierrot Mon Ami*. She had met Queneau in Brussels cafés at the end of the war, and through him had heard of Samuel Beckett's pre-war novel *Murphy*. *La Nausée* had interested her philosophically, and *Murphy* had bequeathed to her own first novel *Under the Net* a notional spirit of Bohemia. Along with existentialism, and perhaps partly in response to it, there went at that time with Iris something less *engagé* and more irresponsible, something that made me think of the young person in

Boswell's Johnson who wished to study philosophy, but 'cheerfulness kept breaking in'.

Our own cheerfulness found a perfect foil in quiet empty unresponsive France, which fed us so deliciously and so cheaply, and sent us on our way down endless roads on which one seemed to cover hundreds if not thousands of kilometres without any effort at all.

Our first swim was in a river of the pas de Calais, a deep placid tributary of the Somme. Perhaps the place of the poem by Wilfred Owen, where hospital barges had been moored during those futile offensives of the First World War. The next was much further south, in a steep and wild wooded valley, with pine and chestnut growing up the mountains. The water was warm, and the stream so secluded that we slipped in with nothing on. Usually cautious, Iris may have felt that now we were in France Anglo-Saxon inhibition could be discarded. It was in this remote spot that my feet encountered a smooth round object in the shallows. It was half buried in the ooze, but I fished it up without difficulty and found an object like a Greek or Roman amphora, earth-coloured and cracked in one or two places. It was clearly not ancient – we found a trade name stamped on the base – and I was about to let it sink back into its underwater home when Iris, treading water beside me, vigorously demurred. Even at that date she wanted to keep everything she found. Wrapped in French newspapers it reposed in the bottom of the little van and lived on for years in a corner of our garden back home, until its cracks were found out by the frost and it came to pieces.

After setting it down on the bank we slipped in again for another swim. Iris seemed dreamy and absent. 'Suppose we had found a great old bell,' she said as we dried ourselves. I pointed out that this would hardly be likely in such a wild spot, far from any town or village. But her imagination was equal to that one.

'It could have been stolen from a belfry and buried in

the river until they could dispose of it. People at home are stealing lead from country churches all the time, aren't they? Then the thieves here never came back.'

'Quite a recent event? Nothing legendary about it?'

'No, wait . . . The church was desecrated at the reformation by those – what did they call them in France?' she appealed as she stood beside me, an earnest figure streaked all over with river mud, which she was vaguely spreading over herself with the towel.

'Huguenots?'

'That's it. The Huguenots got down the bell and wanted to break it up or melt it or something, but some devoted worshippers of the old church managed to steal it away and bring it here for safe keeping.'

Although she had done ancient history in her exams, Iris was a scholar who had done her best papers in philosophy. So she had often told me; and her sense of the historical was certainly rather sketchy. But as her novels show, her imagination possessed its own brand of sometimes almost pedantic accuracy.

The most striking episode in her next novel *The Bell* certainly came out of that river. A great bell is found in an old abbey, now the centre of a modern religious community. The symbol of the bell is enigmatic: not so the penetrating and perceptive account of characters who wish to try to lead the religious life.

Next day we were in a mountain region, nearing the frontier. In order to make an early start for crossing the Alps we decided to stop the night at a small town with a railway junction. In the dead of night our bedroom door was suddenly flung open and a voice proclaimed in dramatic tones *'Georges! C'est l'heure.'* The unshaded light over the bed dazzled us, and when he saw how things were the young railwayman who had come to rouse his comrade hastened to switch it off again, muttering in a more subdued way, *'Ah – Madame, mille pardons.'*

As we negotiated the hairpins next day I could talk of nothing but Hannibal. I remembered the story told by Livy. Confronted in the pass with a wall of solid rock, perhaps the result of a landslide, Hannibal had great fires lighted and attempted to crack open the obstacle by pouring vinegar on it as the stone cooled. 'But where could he have got enough vinegar,' demanded Iris, 'and in any case would it work? Has any one tried it?' Her scepticism was an instance of the meticulous way she always planned the more outlandish episodes in her fiction, testing them in her mind with careful commonsense to make sure they really worked. *The Bell* itself was an example. I always felt there was something wonderfully literal about the discovery of the great bell, which reminded me of *Alice in Wonderland*, one of Iris's own favourite books.

We contined to debate the logistics of Hannibal's campaign, and the difficulties his quartermasters must have had with the vinegar supply. As we drove higher we came into mist, and there was a sound of cowbells. We had a bottle of sparkling burgundy with us in the van, bought with this ceremony in mind. At the top of the pass we drank it, and laid the bottle to rest under a stone beside the road. I marked the place carefully, as I thought, for our idea was to retrieve the bottle on our return journey. When it came to the point, Iris did not like to think of the bottle we had shared being left there. On our return we repeated the ceremony with a bottle of Asti Spumanti, from its home town, but try as I might, and I was sure I had the right place, I could not find the other bottle. So we put the Italian one in a similar place, Iris hoping they would keep one another company.

The life of inanimate things was always close to her. I used to tease her about Wordsworth's flower, which the poet was confident must 'enjoy the air it breathes'. 'Never mind about flowers,' Iris would say, impatiently and somewhat mysteriously, 'There are other things that matter much more.' Though good about it at the time, she also felt real sadness for the abandoned bottles, and I think of it now when she stoops like an old tramp to pick up scraps of candy paper or cigarette ends from the pavement. She feels at one with them, and will find them a home if she can.

Intellectuals, I have noticed, are apt to dislike in her novels what they regard as such signs of whimsy, even of sentimentality. They misunderstand, or do not bother to be aware of, the unobtrusive seriousness with which she treats such things, and the way she feels about them. I think of it as her Buddhist side. She has always had a strong regard for that religion, which, as its enlightened practitioners will tell you, is not really a religion at all. One of the most enlightened is our friend Professor Peter Conradi, who is writing a biography of Iris, and whose devotion to her novels is certainly connected with his practice of Buddhism. One does not of course 'believe' in Buddhism, or even in the sacredness of the Buddha. 'If you meet the Buddha on the road, kill him.' Peter sometimes repeats to us the ancient proverb, with a smile that is far from being whimsical. There seems no doubt that Iris's own private devotion to things finds a response in some of the tenets of Buddhism.

Safe down from the Alps, in Susa, we ate our first Italian spaghetti. It was sunny now, after the grey Alps, and hot, even though we were still high up. As we left Susa, full of spaghetti and red wine, a stout grocer, who had been standing at the door of his shop, stepped out in the road and held up his hand. Did we perhaps require any supplies? Wine? He could let us have jars of very good wine – his own. Lowering his voice he said we could have it all free in exchange for a few petrol coupons – *coupone*. Petrol was scarce in Italy and extremely expensive. Supplied by the travel agent at home with these coupons for the journey, the tourist motoring on the continent found himself a popular figure.

We would have liked to oblige, but we would be needing the coupons ourselves – how many we could not yet say. The friendly grocer appreciated the dilemma. If there were coupons over when we returned, then we would do business. A fortnight or so later we did so. Massive salamis a yard long were pressed upon us, and huge bottles of wine. When we stopped again on the way over the alpine pass Iris unearthed a vast smooth stone – perhaps it had been dislodged by Hannibal's experiment with the vinegar? She longed to take it home, so I heaved it on top of all the other rubbish that by now cluttered the floor of the van. It must have landed on top of one of the big wine bottles. Unknowing we descended into France with a gallon or so of red wine trickling through on to the road. Much remained behind. I still have an old vest, marbled, despite occasional washings over the years, in a delicate patterning of pink and tuscan red.

Our appetite for *spaghetti pomodoro* was insatiable. We seemed to eat or want to eat nothing else on that honeymoon. And eating it very often in the open air, under what Shelley calls 'the roof of blue Italian weather'. In the afternoons we slept deeply after several lunch-time carafes of cold white wine, Chianti too. The white wine came in carafes beaded with condensation and with a little leaden seal on one side, certifying a *mezzolitro*. We persuaded the friendly maternal waitress of a *trattoria* to sell us one of them.

Our search for rivers continued, and the afternoon we left Susa for the south we found another one. As I later discovered from the map, it was the Tanaro, a branch of the Ticino, where Hannibal's Numidians had soundly beaten the Roman cavalry. In contrast to our last swim this now idyllic stream ran through the open sun-filled plain, reached after bumping for a mile along on a sandy track which instinct told me must lead to a river. No one was about: we had the whole landscape and the hot afternoon to ourselves.

Or so we thought. We were about to come out of the water when Iris gave a warning cry. The bank was lined with people – Italian farmers, a uniformed policeman. Some child must have spotted us and called his elders to come and see what these strange foreigners were up to. Conversing animatedly they gazed on us with friendly smiles, teeth flashing in their brown faces and under the policeman's fine black moustache. It was a frieze from a painting, perhaps the Baptism of Christ. But there we were in the water with nothing on and somehow we had to get out and get to our clothes. And without shocking any local susceptibilities.

Suddenly the policeman seemed to appreciate the problem. How did he do so? – it may have been the look on our faces. With authoritative gestures he drove the farmers and children – there were no women present – along the river bank and back to the road. When they were gone he remained where he was, just beside our belongings and bedraggled towel, and seemed to smile invitingly. There was nothing else for it. We emerged with what dignity we could, bowing our thanks and smiling graciously as if we were fully clad.

A day or so later we were in Volterra, the 'lordly Volterra' of Macaulay's *Lays*,

> Where scowls the far-famed hold,
> Piled by the hands of giants
> For god-like kings of old.

The mountains were full of marble quarries and there were shops selling alabaster. We used to sit at a café in the square where the waiter looked exactly like photographs of the young Kafka. Iris took a great interest in him. Unlike most Italian waiters he moved with diffidence, as if uncertain of what he was carrying or where to put it. He seemed to like us, but his smile was distrait, a little tormented, as if he were planning some work he knew he would never finish. His head was always surrounded by wasps which he made no attempt to brush away, as if they were visible embodiments of the angst within him. 'Perhaps he will put us both in one of his stories,' said Iris.

It was while asking poor Kafka and his attendant wasps for *Punt e Mes*, the delicious slightly bitter Italian vermouth we had both taken a fancy to, that I realised a difference, suddenly seeming to me very important, between our sense of him and his interior troubles, and our growing sense of each other. If Kafka were really a troubled soul, and not just worried about the football results, there was nothing we could do about it, no way we could establish contact with him. His sadness, if it existed, was that of an unknown life, a part of life we were familiar with back home and took for granted, but which here had no existence we could enter into. Sitting at the sunlit table, the desolation of things, the tears of things of which Virgil's Aeneas was reminded in passing, seemed all around us, but in an inaccessible almost surreal form, that of young Kafka wandering in and out of the café carrying glasses of *Punt e Mes* and the tiny cups of espresso.

Iris seemed to be in a reverie too. I took her hand and it pressed mine. What was she thinking? I had no idea, any more than I had in the case of Kafka, and I knew very well there was no way to find out. But this realisation reassured me deeply: it made me as happy as the hypothetical woes of Kafka had made me feel sad. Such ignorance, such solitude! – they suddenly seemed the best part of love and marriage. We were together because we were comforted and reassured by the solitariness each saw and was aware of in the other.

The hotel we found in a back street was old and shabby; our room with its furniture and its dusty red velvet hangings might have been in a decaying palazzo. It gave no meals, and in the morning we returned to the square, where Kafka brought us coffee and buns. It was in Volterra, I think, that we began to feel really married, as if something in the old grand forbidding little town had reminded us of both good and bad fortune, of short time, and the long wearisomeness of history. It was in Volterra, too, that Iris's life of secret creation became a reality for me. I felt her at work, with no idea of what she was doing or how, and that gave me the same feel of safe and yet distant closeness. I think she realised then how much I was beginning to enjoy this, and would come to depend on it.

At a comically lower level we both of us realised then that we daydreamed about the people we encountered together, in my case girls and women, in hers, men. It was another aspect of our closeness, another safe and reassuring one, and in this case an amused one too. And we did then, in fact still do, sometimes show our amusement about it to each other. I think Iris may have dreamed a little about Kafka, and what it would be like to mother him, to encourage him, perhaps have an affair with him.

I don't know whether she dreamed about the policeman by the river bank but that too seems quite possible, for he had been in his own way a memorable figure. We had done our best to ignore him when we came out of the river. Iris seized the towel and wrapped it round herself. But our policeman, I noticed, had turned away, and with his hands behind him was gazing into the distance. He combined boldness with delicacy. When we were dressed he had turned with his friendly smile and inquired if we had enjoyed our swim. 'Non troppo fresco?' Iris had spent one or two holidays by herself in Rome and Florence and her Italian was considerably better than mine. She engaged him in conversation, and it soon turned out that he would like a lift to the neighbouring town. He had come to see relatives on the farm near the river which, like most buildings in such an Italian landscape, blended in so well that it was hardly visible. I was rather relieved to find that despite his grey uniform and military cap he was not on duty, and was not going to accuse us of violating the civic code of public decency. As he talked his face ceased to look like that of a modern functionary and took on that withdrawn dignified air which portraits and faces possess in Quattrocento painting.

Were we going to stay in Orbessano? If so he could recommend a hotel kept by friends of his aunt. By this time we were bumping back towards the road, with Iris sitting on the policeman's lap. The van only had its two front seats and the back of it was thoroughly encumbered. We parted on the best of terms. I thought of the policeman on the way back home, when on a very hot afternoon in Padua we were trying vainly to find somewhere to stay. There were a lot of young conscripts in uniform about, and Iris asked one of them, a scholarly-looking weedy boy wearing spectacles, if he knew of any hotel. He seemed surprised but politely beckoned her to follow him, I trailing behind with the bags. An officer was passing, and he appeared to ask the young soldier rather severely what he thought he was doing. Iris later reported that the young soldier replied with dignity, 'Sir, I am taking this lady to a hotel.' The officer smiled, unbent, and uttered what was presumably the Italian equivalent of 'Vive le sport!'

The policeman by the river bank entered, I know, into Iris's imagination. In some of her novels he, or someone very like him, is a ghostly presence, transmuted into a flux of different types and personalities. Such persons are accompanied by water, as if it were their native environment: the story of their spirits seems to arise from sea or river and return to them. Iris never cared for the novels of George Eliot, but her own wholly different plots and beings sometimes remind me of Maggie Tulliver in The Mill on the Floss saying 'I am in love with moistness.' Maggie lives by the river, and in rather contrived circumstances – much more contrived than any comparable scenario in Iris's work – eventually drowns in it.

A few years ago a writer called Charles Sprawson sent Iris his remarkable book with the odd title *Haunts of the Black Masseur*, a title inspired by a story the author had read when young about such a negro massage expert. The tale mingled in his mind with a film he had thought marvellous called *The Creature from the Black Lagoon*, and became for him a symbol of the whole swimming mystique. Iris had no such mystique, only one about water, but we both liked the book very much and I reviewed it under her name.

Black masseurs and lagoons were a far cry from sun-filled Italian landscapes, and the green rivers full of rushes and golden sandbars that meandered past hills resembling those in the background of Bellini's pictures, or Perugino's. The sea in Italy was by contrast the greatest possible disappointment to us. In most cases it was shut off into holiday camps by barbed wire, and impossible to get at. When we once managed to do so, near Pesaro, we had hardly got into the water before an immense caterpillar of holidaying toddlers came crawling over the beach, engulfing our possessions and undulating onwards as we rushed out to rescue them. By contrast with France, Italy and the Italian seaside were distinctly overcrowded.

Rivers and pictures were our holiday ideals. We have never been greatly drawn to spectacular or picturesque tourist attractions, but picture galleries are another matter. We visited Borgo San Sepolcro, a small place in those days quite difficult to get at, situated, as I recall, in the heart of Umbria. In a bleak room of its town hall one was suddenly face to face with the Resurrection, the masterpiece of Piero della Francesca. In an essay with that title Aldous Huxley refers to it quite simply as 'the finest picture in the world'. What awed and amazed us, and must indeed be the first impression the picture makes on the ordinary viewer, is the immense difference between the figure of Christ Piero represents, and that found in any other religious painting. It is a fresco, and was for years concealed under a layer of whitewash, conceivably even because of this startling and almost alarming singularity. When finally brought back to light it was in excellent condition, just as it must have been when first painted.

Huxley's essay is by far the best thing ever written about it. He does not emphasise unduly the originality of Piero's statuesque figures, a product of the painter's interest in geometry and linear mathematics. Technicians of the art world dwell on this unusual interest, and it might well be that Piero's impassive geometry was what suddenly brought him into such outstanding favour with the modernists, for whom romanticism meant emotional indulgence and, as T.E. Hulme put it, 'spilt religion'. No religion is being spilt in Piero's painting, no human impulses emotionally indulged. We can see why the painter was disregarded in the nineteenth century, as in the later renaissance. The figure in the great fresco that seems to hoist itself effortlessly out of the tomb, one muscular leg poised on its stone coping, is not the Christ of medieval or Catholic Christianity, nor the liberal humanitarian Christ who took over a new human role at the end of the age of faith. He is, as Huxley says, a masterful even an insolent figure, his expressionless eyes fixed on no goal that religion would recognise or aspire to. Huxley calls him the embodiment of the classical ideal, the superb image of man as self-sufficient, immortalised by his own sense of art and form.

However that may be the picture is not only supremely satisfying but electrifying. It inspires awe. We ate our spaghetti that morning with a sense of high achievement, for who can see a great picture or read a great book without taking some of the credit for it himself? – but also in sober mood. The restaurant was almost empty; there seemed to be no other tourists in the sleepy little town. Things are different today: there are phalanxes of buses bearing German and Japanese tourists. The section of the town hall housing the picture has been turned into an arty art gallery;

the picture itself lit up, set off, protected. I am glad we saw it before these transformations took place. The picture would have been even more inaccessible when Huxley first saw it, arriving at Borgo San Sepolcro after a laborious train journey. Piero has now become a major tourist attraction.

The picture fascinated Iris. We talked of it a lot, but however much we talked of it I knew the real impression it had made on her lay below the level of speech, like the iceberg below the water. The god whose own physical strength and dark force of being seemed to be impelling him out of the tomb would inspire in the future many visions and creations of her own. She once said to me when I commented on the importance of the role, visible and invisible, that pictures played in her novels, 'You're right. They're all just pictures really.'

'Well, I wouldn't say "just pictures". But I've often thought that what some of your readers find spiritual and uplifting in your novels is, unknown to them, a silent fellowship with great art of other kinds. You are the only novelist I know who can make the whole world of art come into your novels without being laborious about it, or making it seem fancy.'

Iris smiled. 'Well thanks very much. I don't like to think about what happens when I do it. You're the critic, not me.'

Almost any picture could inspire her in these invisible ways. Once we were in Lille, the big bustling industrial town in the north of France, a sort of Pittsburgh or Manchester one would think where the fine arts were concerned. We were going to do our usual thing, a joint discussion and a question and answer session. The occasion was a festival, boosting the cultural life of the university and town. We always enjoyed such outings. Iris loved meeting new people; and although she never wanted to give a proper lecture she was always immensely popular as a speaker because of her candidly unofficial approach and the warmth with which she talked to everyone she encountered. Lille was no exception: but what was surprising in those days was the unexpectedly magnificent bookshop, called 'le Furet' – the Ferret – and the equally grand and well-filled art gallery. We had trouble in finding it – a long walk – but there was a small picture by a lesser Dutch master which absorbed Iris's silent attention while I wandered on among enormous late-Empire canvases by Bouguereau and his friends – ample naked ladies expanding like balloons into a sky full of sickly-tinted flowers. No doubt they had once been popular with the burghers of Lille, but Iris had found a small gem (I still cannot recall the name of the painter) which showed no more than a narrow white road ascending through broom bushes over a hill, and disappearing. As with the Italian policeman, and Piero's mysterious and saturnine Christ, that picture has a ghostly presence among the landscapes and characters of many of her later novels.

There were other pictures. The one by Balthus of the girl with the slyly indulgent smile playing cards with a flamboyant opponent who holds a card or two behind his back. Perhaps a retarded youth from the locality, to whom in her own self-possessed way she is being kind? Perhaps a younger brother? Having seen it in the catalogue Iris and I chased that picture through the many galleries and corridors of the Thyssen-Bornemisza Art Collection in Madrid. This emanation, as the poet Blake would have said, is there transmogrified in her next novel, as are the Beckmanns we were to see in the St Louis Art Gallery.

But the painting which had the deepest and at the same time the most visible effect on her work was the very late Titian, the faun Marsyas flayed by Apollo, which lives in a remote monastery in Moravia and was lent a few years ago to a Royal Academy exhibition in London. Iris went to see it countless times, and never said a word. To be mute about pictures was her way of paying them homage. Once when we were in the gallery together, and almost to tease her, I remarked that the martyred faun was like Piero's Christ in reverse, and that the terrible smile – of agony? of ecstasy? – on his upside-down features reminded me in some way of the terrifying detachment of Christ's face as it rises indifferently above what is happening lower down in the picture. She looked at me, thought, and smiled to herself, but said nothing. The Titian became her most 'public' picture however, the one whose effect on her was most apparent and acknowledged. It features as a background icon, dusky but unmistakable, in the portrait of her done by the London artist Tom Phillips, which hangs in the National Portrait Gallery.

So married life began. And the joys of solitude. No contradiction was involved. The one went perfectly with the other. To feel oneself held and cherished and accompanied, and yet to be alone. To be closely and physically entwined, and yet feel solitude's friendly presence, as warm and undesolating as contiguity itself.

5

I never 'missed' Iris, and I don't think in that sense she ever missed me. Apartness, when it happened, was itself a kind of closeness. In those early days, when televisions were all black and white and we never possessed or wanted one, there was an advertisement we saw on the flickering screen sometimes when we visited her mother. It showed a young man on a genteel urban street corner with an English drizzle gently falling. He is turning up his hat brim against the rain (hats were still quite normal then) and lighting a cigarette. Along the road some young people have emerged laughing from a lighted house and are getting into a car. Our young man surveys them with a self-satisfied and slightly pitying amusement, and puffs on his cigarette. The caption was: 'You're never alone with a Strand.'

We had often seen the Strand advertisement together on her mother's TV, and laughed over it. And so TV advertisements as well as great pictures entered the emerging world of her novels. More important for me, the advertisement symbolised the satisfactions of our own kind of solitude in closeness.

The Strand was one of the most unsuccessful brands of cigarette ever marketed. I remember later hearing from a young man, an ex-pupil who worked in advertising, that in those circles it was mentioned in the same breath as Craven A. Craven A, though it continued to be a popular smoke, once nearly ruined itself with the advertisement: 'Craven A – does not affect your throat.' Smokers had at once put their hand to their throats and thought God, I'd better cut them out. The young man in the Strand advertisement had the same effect on the smoking public. He was so clearly going to be alone for a long long time. But I took the same satisfaction in the advertisement that I did in our new way of life.

It was very different from the life we live today. It was like being alone, and yet we were not alone. I never travelled in the spirit after Iris when she was away for a brief period – in London or teaching – or once when she had a half semester's fellowship at Yale – and I don't think she ever needed or wanted to rush back to me. We were separate but never separated. I never looked at a photograph of her either. It seemed to have no connection with her as she was.

Now we are together for the first time. We have actually become, as is often said of a happy married couple, inseparable, in a way like Ovid's Baucis and Philemon, to whom the gods gave the gift of growing old together like entwined trees. It is a way of life that is unfamiliar. The closeness of apartness has necessarily become the closeness of closeness. And we know nothing of it; we have never had any practice.

Not that we ever practised the opposite: the way of life, not uncommon in academe, to define which a philosophical friend of Iris's coined the word *telegamy*. Telegamy, marriage at a distance, works well for some people, who prefer to remain an independent part of an item. It may sharpen their satisfaction in time spent together, as well as being of practical convenience if careers are to be pursued in places far apart. But it is not, as noted by Anthony Powell, the same thing as being married. Apartness in marriage is a state of love; and not a function of distance, or preference, or practicality.

A goose which cannot find other geese will attach itself to some object – another animal, even a stone or a post – and never lose sight of it. This terror of being alone, of being cut off for even a few seconds from the familiar object, is a feature of Alzheimer's. If Iris could climb inside my skin now, or enter me as if I had a pouch like a kangaroo, she would do so. She has no awareness of what I am doing, only an awareness of what I am. The words and gestures of love still come naturally, but they cannot be accompanied by that wordless communication which depends on the ability to use words. In any case she has forgotten public language, although not our private one, which cannot now get us far.

I sit at the kitchen table, and make desperate efforts to keep it as my own preserve, as it has always been. Iris seems to understand this, and when prompted goes obediently into the sitting-room where the TV is switched on. In less than a minute she is back again.

Before we got married we had found a house to live in. Visiting houses round Oxford, in the Riley, armed by the Agent with a sheaf of particulars and prices, was more like a game than the real thing. (Perhaps we were never the real thing, in that serious sense, the sense intended by Iris's character in A Severed Head who complained that her marriage was not going anywhere.) We looked at these houses in an atmosphere of frivolity. One, at Bampton, fascinated Iris because it had a powder closet next to one of the bedrooms. Another had a sizable pond in the garden, perhaps big enough to swim in. A third, rather far out, possessed a real swimming pool, even though a small one and obviously neglected. But man-made pools had little appeal for us. In those days there was a rich variety of country houses for sale, mostly old ones, going cheap. We got as far as saying to one another: 'This could be your work-room' or 'The kitchen fire-place would be nice to sit in front of', but we had no idea about heating, cooking, drains, bathrooms (though we admired one all-tiled number done in peacock blue).

Iris fell in love with a house in the village of Taynton, near Burford. The place itself, near the river Windrush, was very beautiful. This was the house she must have. Even though she was still not at all sure she wanted to get married. She could always live there on her own, I said craftily, and as if in the most rational way. I would come and visit her. 'But what about the badgers,' she said smiling. The badger joke had already become well established. How would she cope with them when they broke in if I didn't return from work every evening? 'But you would be working in Oxford too – the badgers would have to look after themselves.' We laughed, and never decided anything, except about this house.

It was June 1956. Iris was going over to Ireland to stay with the novelist Elizabeth Bowen, with whom she had recently become very friendly. I was left in charge of making a bid for the house, arranging a down payment, all that sort of thing. I did so, and everything seemed satisfactory. Then the Agent rang to say the owner had changed his mind. He would sell the house not to the buyer who offered the asking price, but to anyone who made an offer, unspecified, above it. No doubt he had heard that several potential buyers were interested. I knew how much Iris wanted the place, wanted to marry it more than she wanted to marry me. Perhaps I was jealous. I was certainly innocent about property selling and its techniques, and I was cross with the owner, who I felt had deceived us, although the Agent seemed to regard his procedure as perfectly normal. I told the Agent we would stand on the offer we had made. Next day he rang to tell me we had lost the bid: the house had gone to another purchaser.

The day after that Iris arrived back from Ireland. On the phone she was unusually expansive and confiding, telling me of the great time she had had at Bowen's Court, the gaunt house in County Cork, where she and the owner had sat chatting and drinking Guinness and brandy. Iris disliked telephoning, using it only for the briefest of practical messages, and I was both touched and disturbed by her ebullience about the Irish visit. I dreaded having to tell her she had lost the Taynton house. But when I nerved myself to do so she was as calm and understanding as she had been on the occasion when I had crashed the Hillman Minx. She was generously philosophical: she told me not to worry – it couldn't be helped. I have sometimes wondered at odd moments whether those two accidents did more to make her feel she would like to be married than any amount of faithful and supportive attention on my part could have done. Misfortunes suffered together, even before the normal misfortunes of married life, can no doubt have such an effect.

There might have been something else as well. She told me a good deal later, after we were married and when we were going to see Elizabeth Bowen who was by then living in Oxford, that Elizabeth had shown a good deal of quizzical Irish curiosity about her younger guest's emotional life. Perhaps under the influence of the Guinness, or the brandy, Iris had most uncharacteristically confided in her hostess. Alone together in the big house, apart from the 'outside man' and a young girl who cooked, the pair had several heart-to-hearts together. Elizabeth told Iris of the happiness of her own marriage, which many of her intellectual friends had regarded as incongruous, even incomprehensible: her husband a worthy man but painfully dull. She and her husband had agreed together not to have children. She had wanted above all things to write; her husband had been through the war on the western front, and sincerely felt the modern world too awful to justify bringing a new life into it. Unlike Iris, Elizabeth had some regrets in later life about this decision, as her last novels touchingly though fleetingly reveal. Her husband's death must have increased her sense of loneliness and lack of family life, for her own mother and father died before she was twelve.

I find it touching myself to think of the two women, normally of an almost masculine reserve, confiding in each other during those quiet damp days in an Irish country house. In the mornings they remained apart and got on with their own work – each was writing a novel. After lunch they walked or went out in the car, then more work after tea. Claret flowed freely at both meals, but for Elizabeth the high spot of the day, well documented in her late novel *The Little Girls*, was the drinking time at six, the happy hour as she used sardonically to refer to it, for she loved America and the Americans. For the fellowship of this hour she had always depended on what she called a 'boon companion', and it so happened that Iris's visit filled a gap between the departure from Doneraile of two of Elizabeth's old friends, and her own sudden decision to sell the family house and leave Ireland. This too she had confided to Iris, and insensibly they had got on to the question of how one decided things in life. For Elizabeth the business of leaving Ireland, with no husband to support her and to confer with, was going to be agonising. 'I couldn't buy a pair of shoes without Alan,' she told Iris, and the most terrible moment in her life had come when she woke up in the night at Bowen's Court and found him dead beside her.

I think Iris was much moved by the helplessness revealed to her by this strong sardonic reserved woman, whose work she admired without being at all familiar with it, and whose friendship at that moment she so greatly valued. No doubt she had been unusually confiding in her own turn, and she told me later that Elizabeth had impressed upon her almost with urgency the advantages of the married state. Before she left she had said something about me, and about her idea of a house in the country. Elizabeth, whom I had not met at that time, sent her best wishes to me, and for the house.

And now I had to tell Iris that the house had fallen through. I did not tell her that it had been through my own caution, or lack of enterprise and financial spirit. The truth was that apart from possible feelings of jealousy I had never believed in that house. There was something fishy about it. Iris, carried away by its undoubted charm and the beauty of village and countryside, perhaps also its proximity to the river Windrush, had been indifferent to all else. As it happened the house agent rang me again a few weeks later to report that the other sale had gone off and that we could have the house on the old terms. This information too I suppressed, for by that time, fortunately for me, another house had turned up, and it engaged all Iris's attention.

I had never met Elizabeth, but I had read everything she had written and had lived in the world of her novels and stories with immense pleasure, almost with passion. *The Death of the Heart* was my favourite. I once made the mistake of telling Elizabeth that, and she looked displeased. She had never cared for *The Death of the Heart*, or its success; she preferred her fans to find whatever was her latest book her most intriguing, challenging, unexpected. Those things were certainly true of her last two novels, *The Little Girls* and *Eva Trout*, but what I had specially liked about them was her return to the magic place she had made her own, the seaside country of Romney Marsh and the little town of Hythe. She had lived there as a girl before her mother died, and after trying Oxford she bought a little house on the hill in Hythe. No doubt she knew well that it is usually a mistake to return to live in a place in which one has been happy, and about which she had incidentally created so vivid a comedy world. Or perhaps she didn't know it: she was very simple and uncalculating in some ways. She never spoke of it, but I had the feeling on our visits to her that the experiment of living in Hythe had not been entirely a success, although she had no trouble there in finding 'boon companions' and being at home in a wholly unliterary and unintellectual world, rather like that of *The Little Girls* and of the Heccomb family in *The Death of the Heart*.

She was far from well when she decided to come back to Oxford, to settle in a couple of rooms in an annexe of the Bear Hotel at Woodstock. She had throat cancer – always a sixty-a-day smoker, she liked to puff on a cigarette between mouthfuls at lunch and dinner – but she made a good recovery after the operation and often came to visit us. Once I was doing a class on Jane Austen, and to my great concern she asked if she could come along. I felt overwhelmed at first by her powerful presence, but she could not have been nicer or more quietly helpful, silent most of the time, but now and again injecting a shrewd query or making some encouraging comment on a point raised by one of the young graduates. Quite unacademic by nature, she was of course well-read, a sharp and droll natural critic. About this time she had great success as a visiting teacher on campus in America, where the students viewed her queenly presence with delight and awe.

There could indeed be something peremptory, almost alarming, about her. Lord David Cecil, who was a very old friend, told me that he had once asked her to a small dinner party with a carefully chosen and congenial company, which he was sure she would enjoy. But the party was not a success. Elizabeth could never be silent, but she remained uncooperative and on her dignity all evening. Afterwards she said to her host severely, 'David, I think you should know me well enough by now to realise that I want to see you either on your own, or at a large party.' There was no answer to that one. She could be jealously possessive of her close friends, and hostile to their wives or husbands; and she could be fiercely loyal to an institution or person, even if she disapproved of what they stood for.

Her own family was Protestant – 'Ascendancy' as it used to be called in Ireland – and she would have attended the Church of Ireland service as a part of her position and lifestyle, but she never forgave her fellow-novelist Honor Tracy for investigating a financial scandal which had occurred among the local Roman Catholic clergy, and denouncing it in an article which appeared in the *Sunday Times*. Honor was a Roman Catholic herself, but that was neither here nor there. The point was the indecency, as Elizabeth saw it – and here all her Irish and local instincts were atavistically at work – of being disloyal to neighbours. By seeking to uncover its scandals Honor Tracy as journalist was guilty of treachery to a hallowed Irish institution, the Roman Catholic Church.

Elizabeth knew very well that the clergyman involved was a crook, as she privately put it, and she also greatly disliked the role played by the Catholic Church in Irish society; but she would never have said so in public, nor been disloyal to a man of the district which she loved and lived in.

Honor Tracy was also a great friend of Iris's. She was a fearlessly independent woman with flaming red hair, flamboyant in manner, unrestrained in the expression of her opinions and prejudices. She came from an older family than Elizabeth's, the Norman De Tracys, who helped to conquer England and then took part in the conquest of southern Ireland in the twelfth century. The Bowens arrived much later: Colonel Bowen had been one of Cromwell's trusted officers, presented with the estate and land on which he had begun to build Bowen's Court. Irish history counted for a good deal in the background of both ladies, and each was redoubtable in her own style. None the less Honor Tracy, as she once told Iris, shook in her shoes at the thought of Elizabeth Bowen's displeasure.

Elizabeth, oddly enough, was not really at her best as a novelist when writing about Ireland. Perhaps its sorrows, and her own responsibilities there, inhibited her sense of fun. Her own best novels, including the one she was working on at the time of her death and which survives only as a fascinating fragment, were comedies – sometimes tragi-comedies – of English life and manners. She had been most at home in wartime London: Hitler's blitz on the city helped produce one of her finest novels, *The Heat of the Day*, as well as some brilliant short stories. The unearthly light of what was then called a 'bomber's moon' transfigures *Mysterious Kor*, a story about bombed-out wartime London, which a girl working there sees as the ghost city of a poem she has once read.

> Not in the waste beyond the swamps and sand
> The fever-haunted forest and lagoon,
> Mysterious Kor, thy walls forsaken stand,
> Thy lonely towers beneath a lonely moon.

I always meant to ask Elizabeth where she had read the poem, but I never got around to it. Years after her death her story was our subject at a class I was giving, and when one of the students asked who had written the lines I had to admit I had no idea. Bowen had perhaps written them herself? My curious student – now a doctor and don at Glasgow University – did not leave the matter there, but investigated in the Bodleian library until he found the answer. The poem turned out to be the work of a minor Edwardian poet and man of letters called Andrew Lang, who had written it to his friend Rider Haggard, explorer and author of many best-selling romantic tales, including *King Solomon's Mines*. Most of the poem is poor stuff, but Elizabeth when a young girl had no doubt come across it in some long-forgotten anthology of the period, and it had returned to haunt her imagination in maturity, and create her story.

Iris's own creative mind worked the same way. Her novels are full of buried quotations remembered from child-hood, or once quoted and discussed between us. (One of them is 'the ouzel cock so black of hue' from *A Midsummer Night's Dream*, which surfaces in *A Severed Head* and refers obliquely to a cuckolding which takes place in the novel. We used to chant it, together with other catches, when driving in the car.)

Both Honor and Elizabeth sometimes stayed with us at Steeple Aston after we had settled in the house there. Honor liked to rest between quite gruelling bouts of investigative reporting, and she usually left us to stay at The Bell at Aston Clinton, a pub where she knew the landlord and where she used to stand us marvellously alcoholic lunches and dinners. After giving up working journalism she lived in a small cottage on Achill Island in the West of Ireland, where she wrote her lively comedies of Irish life. The best of these, *The Straight and Narrow Path*, concerns an Irish priest who once exhorted his flock 'always to follow the straight and narrow path between virtue and wrongdoing'. It was a true tale: Honor had heard the sermon herself; but though the Irish can be totally irreverent in private and among themselves, they do not care to be publicly teased. Honor's delightful novels were not read on her native soil, nor were they obtainable. It is a shame, too, that they never seem to have been reprinted, either in England or America. The peculiar powers of Irish censorship, once paramount in the island itself, are still to be reckoned with elsewhere.

It turned out to be a blessing that we viewed the house at Steeple Aston, because it at once drove all longings for poetical and rivery Taynton out of Iris's head. Neither house nor village were as pretty as those she had first fallen in love with, but both were old and solid and friendly. A farmhouse had been built on to in the early nineteenth century, and turned into a gentleman's residence not far from the church. The grounds were large, almost two acres, and sloped sharply downhill to a stream that ran through the valley. On our side of this were ancient ponds, possibly medieval fishponds. These appealed to Iris at once. So did the sheer impracticality of the place, from the point of view of two teachers working in Oxford, fifteen miles away. That did not daunt her at all: she did not even consider disadvantages. The equal impracticality of Bowen's Court may have influenced her. Cedar Lodge, as the house was rather primly called, was cheap to buy – startlingly cheap – but we discovered later that it was in bad condition, however solid it looked. Mr Palmer, a veteran builder with very bright blue eyes, was soon in constant attendance. He used to gaze wonderingly at Iris as she sat and wrote in an upstairs room, through the ceiling of which water from an undiscoverable source was apt to drip.

Apart from Mr Palmer, who constituted no sort of social burden, we had the place to ourselves. The previous owner was going to live on the island of Guernsey, in a small modern bungalow her son had bought for her. She was an old lady who had lived long in the village, and she recommended various persons who might come to help or 'do' for us. We both felt disinclined to be done for. For the thirty years and more we lived at Cedar Lodge we had no help in the house or garden, and both were presently in a state in which help of any kind would have come too late. That seemed to suit us, or at least to suit Iris: I was less sure of the benefits of what the authoress Rose Macaulay – Iris met her once or twice – used to call 'letting things go to the devil and seeing what happens when they have gone there.'

At first I made strenuous efforts to assert the will – my will – over the place. I cleaned, mowed, chopped, painted, tried to repair the electricity. But I soon gave up. Iris always helped me, and seemed herself to enjoy the idea of doing all the things women do in houses, but it was a dream occupation, a part of her imagined world, of the worlds she was creating in her novels as she sat in her dusty sunlit room upstairs, submerged by old letters, papers, broken ornaments, stones she had picked up, or which had been given her by friends. It grieved me then, and still does, that these stones, once so naturally clean and beautiful from continual lustration in a stream, or by the tides of the seashore, should have become as dusty and dead-looking as everything else in the house. But this never seemed to bother Iris in the slightest. The stones for her were Platonic objects, living in some absolute world of Forms, untouched by their contingent existence as a part of the actual and very grubby still life that surrounded us.

Stones were not the only Platonic objects in our daily life, or – so close that it came to the same thing – in Iris's imagination. Cooking pots, never properly cleaned in practice, had the same status. So, I felt, did those imaginary badgers which she had invoked once when I had tried to suggest to her what the rewards of married life might be like. 'Yes,' she had replied with a sort of wistfulness which gave me a sudden hope that she might be prepared to take the idea of marriage seriously. 'I do like to imagine your coming home, and me meeting you, and saying "Darling, the badgers have broken in".' Her ancient badger fantasy, with its image of a cosy domestic drama, has probably been forgotten, but she used sometimes to say with a smile to friends, or even to interviewers, that she originally had every intention of doing the cooking after we got married. 'But after a few days John suggested it might go better if he took over.' The image of herself as cook and apron-wearer stayed in her mind less long than the to me delightful and hopeful one of herself as wife rushing down to greet her husband with a kiss, and with the mock-horror news that the badgers had broken in.

And yet her intention of becoming the cook was no idle boast. Iris could cook – could have cooked – magnificently, just as she could have done all sorts of other practical things. While working at the treasury, the most prestigious branch of the civil service, she had made herself an expert during the war years on a tricky concept known as 'notional promotion *in absentia*', which involved assessing pay-rises and promotions which would have accrued, had they remained in their old jobs, to functionaries called up at that time into the armed forces. Senior colleagues consulted her on this question and accepted without demur what she told them. Had she concentrated on any of those careers she could have become a doctor, an archaeologist, a motor mechanic. It used to be thought at one time that Shakespeare might have started off as a horse-holder outside the theatre. A nineteenth-century scholar had observed that, if so, one could be sure that the Bard had held his horses better than anyone else. A really great artist can concentrate and succeed at almost anything, and Iris would have been no exception. If she had borne a child she would have looked after it better and more conscientiously than most mothers, and no doubt would have brought it up better too. But in that case she would not have written the books that she did write.

I can't recall myself saying that I would be the cook. To me it just happened, and in any case it was not really cooking. The point was that Iris was working – properly working – and I was determined she should not be distracted from this. Getting something to eat was easy, and we often used to go to a pub on the main road where a good plain dinner could be had cheap. That was long before the present situation in England, when cooking has at last become an art to be treated seriously – overseriously. There was no fiddly *nouvelle cuisine* forty years ago.

Yet there had been one occasion when Iris took as many pains as any acolyte in the media-haunted kitchens of today. Well before we were married, and when I really thought she never would marry me, she decided to entertain to supper the same pair – the academic lawyer and his wife – at whose table we had eaten our first meal together. She had another guest too, and made no apology for not including me in the party. She was living in her Beaumont Street flat at the time, on the top floor. There was no dining-room and her attic kitchen was barely a room at all. I had been a little hurt, none the less, and had suggested that if she must entertain the Johnsons, couldn't she take them to a restaurant? She'd said pacifically she didn't want to do that: they'd asked her to supper so many times, and she felt the least she could do was to make a special effort of her own. Iris, as I saw then a little gloomily, could be very conscientious about such things.

She took immense trouble. First of all she bought herself at great expense a red enamel casserole, a boat-shaped one with a close-fitting lid. It weighed about a ton. I think it was the first time either of us had seen such a thing. I gazed at it in awe: Iris with all the pride of new possession. A culinary-minded friend of hers who was partly Greek had told her this was what she needed to prepare the very special Attic dish called *stephados*. He had told her that if properly done, which only very rarely happened, it was the most delicious dish in the world. He was a philosopher, a follower of Plato, but his real interest was in cooking and telephones. Since he was the inspiration of the dish Iris proposed to prepare it was natural that he should be one of the three guests invited.

Iris took two days to prepare that dish. I cannot recall exactly what was in it, as neither she nor I ever attempted to prepare it again, but there was a lot of high-quality beef from the market, and olive oil and aubergines and spices and herbs and tomato purée. It was, of course, a colossal success. She allowed me to finish it with her, cold, the following day, and I honestly don't think I have ever eaten anything more delicious in my life.

So Iris could cook, and to perfection, just as she might have done all sorts of other things superlatively well. But as I sat eating it with her the following day – and to my great satisfaction she admitted it was even better cold than hot – I had not been able to avoid a feeling of disappointment. Somehow it was not like Iris to have done such a thing, to have pulled off a culinary coup that must have staggered the Johnsons, accustomed as they were to thinking Iris an odd but lovable and unworldly person, a philosopher, a hopeful writer of novels, whom they had got the measure of, whom they could patronise in their own fashion. Was that why she had done it? If so, I could not escape a fellow-feeling with the Johnsons. Friends, who fill their own allotted place in your life, should not behave wholly uncharacteristically. Still less so if you are in love with such a friend, as I was.

Perhaps Iris knew this too: perhaps that is why it was such a one-off occasion? It surprised me none the less, and continues to do so, trivial as the occasion might now seem. My memory of it could be the difficulty I now feel in writing about Iris as she was. Is it that I can only think of her as she now is, which is for me the same as she has always been? In any case no description of anybody, however loving, can seem to do anything but veer away from the person concerned, not because it distorts their 'reality', whatever that may be, but because the describer himself begins to lose all confidence in the picture of the person he is creating. The Iris of my words cannot, I know, be any Iris who existed. In writing about the *stephados* (or should it be *stefados*?) episode I can no longer believe in my own account of the Iris who willed it, who so uncharacteristically made it happen.

The words in which to talk about it are in any case becoming muddled in my mind, because Iris is stirring out of her doze beside me, making me attentive to her, and not to what I am trying to write. And this is the Iris I now know, the unique one as it seems: the one who has been here always: thus the only one I have ever known.

As for the expensive red casserole boat, it was never used again. Or hardly ever. Maybe it was cooked in by me once or twice, without conviction and without much success. I may have made a few stews eaten without comment by our guests, or perhaps with some kindly routine commendation by one of the women present. Like so many other things in the house it is lost now, undiscoverable, although I remember that the last time I saw it, covered with cobwebs at the bottom of a cupboard, it looked as if worn out, terribly old and tired, with rust patches coming through the red enamel from the iron underneath. But when new it once housed the most perfect dish in the world, made by the person who then seemed, and in a sense was, the least likely person to make it.

I could record one other cooking experience in Iris's life, and one I still find quite upsetting to remember. It must have taken place about the time I first met her, or perhaps before I met her. Two friends of hers, the strong-minded female philosopher who practised 'telegamy', and a mathematical logician of international standing who was a bachelor, had asked to borrow her room for a day while she was absent. The room she then lived in had a gas-ring and wash-basin but not much else, and they required it not for secret sexual congress but because the mathematician wanted to indulge himself in a culinary experiment. Why they should have required Iris's room for this purpose I still cannot fathom, except that the room was handy and they knew they could presume on her discretion and her unbounded good nature. (They were right of course, but I still grind my teeth when I think of it, even though they are not my own teeth any more but false ones, a denture.) The experiment was in the manufacture of herring soup, which the mathematician, Viennese but possibly with Baltic origins, swore he was on the verge of perfecting. The philosopher affected not to believe him, and swore in her turn – she was a lady with a strong streak of puckish humour – that she could never be induced under any circumstances to partake of such a dish, however exquisitely prepared. The very idea of it was repellent to her. So they made what amounted to a bet.

The mathematician won the bet. The soup was a triumph: the philosopher capitulated and said that it was so. Indeed she consumed it with relish. When Iris returned a few days later it was to find her room in the most gruesome possible disorder, smelling strongly of fish, and her landlady furious. Other tenants had complained of the noise and the smell. Miss Murdoch's reputation, once immaculate, was now in ruins. In the eyes of the landlady she was, and remained, a fallen woman: one who allowed the most unspeakable orgies to take place in her room, and no doubt participated in them herself. Iris left the house not long after, although its position and amenities had suited her very well. But that was not what upset me when Iris told me the tale, which she did in a tolerant amused way, without a trace of resentment.

Indeed she remained, and still does, on the best possible terms with both parties, even though neither attempted an apology for what had taken place, or even seemed to think one might be appropriate. It annoys me intensely that she should still revere them, none the less. But what upset me even more, and for some reason can still go through me like a spear, was that Iris found one of her most treasured possessions lying on the floor of the room, hideously violated. It was a blue silk chiffon scarf which her mother had given her as a special birthday present. Its state when discovered was so repulsive that Iris had no choice but to take it straight out to the dustbin, holding her nose while she did so. The logician had required the finest possible sieve to strain the end product of his masterpiece, and the philosopher, casually opening a drawer, had handed him the scarf.

I can still see and imagine the pair, wringing out the last drop. I have only met either of them a few times, but when I do I find it difficult to be more than barely civil.

It is too late to remind Iris of the story now, but if I were able to do so I am sure that she would reveal the same Christ-like qualities of tolerance, amusement and good nature – forgiveness would not even be in question – which she must have felt as she gazed on that fearful scene. Or perhaps it only became fearful in the telling? – more specifically, in the way she told it to me? All my instincts, or so I still feel, would have led me into some wild counter-excess. I should have gone after the pair, murdered one or both of them, or at the very least cut as many of their possessions as I could find into ribbons, with a sharp knife. And yet here I was, when Iris told me the story, longing to share my life with a woman who could behave as angelically as she seemed to have done.

I think that was what really upset me most of all. It seemed so unnatural. As it still does. I can upset myself still more if I am not careful by wondering whether Iris really behaved so angelically after all? Did something in her secretly long to be violated in this way by the pair? Did she in some sense invite this wanton exercise of power over her? Was she submitting to these gods of logic and philosophy as she submitted to the godmonster of Hampstead? Was she, almost as if in one of her own novels, the absent victim of a sacrifice in which she would have participated as a willing victim, had she been present?

The idea still makes me shiver a bit. Have I really been sharing my life with someone like that? But if I have it has never seemed to matter much, even though the idea of having behaved in a way so unlike myself can give me the occasional shock of incredulity. One thing remains certain: Iris has always disliked fish, and particularly abominated the whole herring tribe. That may well have been true before the episode: it has certainly been the case ever since.

Why should someone who loves water so much have so little desire for the creatures that live in it? Or is it that she feels in unconscious fellowship, and so would not dream of eating them? As a strict matter of fact, however, she *will* eat my sardine paté, heavily flavoured with curry powder. Perhaps she doesn't recognise it as fish at all? But there must have been no doubt about what caused the appalling smell that came from her scarf, when she picked up the poor bedraggled thing. My instinct, none the less, would have been to try to wash it out, to rescue and cherish it. But Iris was not like that. She sacrificed the scarf cheerfully; and seemingly at least on the wholesome altar of friendship.

6

'The house and premises known as Cedar Lodge', as the old deeds described them, were neither warm nor dry. There were the remains of a huge cedar near the front gate, just a vast plate of rotten wood nearly flush with the earth. Perhaps they had chopped this great tree down and burnt it indoors in a vain attempt to keep warm? We ourselves tried various ways of doing the same thing. An old Rayburn stove my mother gave us, night storage heaters, electric fires, an expensive affair in the front hall, with a beautifully fluted stainless steel front, which burned anthracite nuggets as expensive as itself. Nothing seemed to do any good. When we at last installed some partial central heating, after one of Iris's novels had been turned into a film, that failed to work properly too. Something about gravity, the position of the oil tank, the installation of pipes . . . Our dear Mr Palmer was dead by then, and his son put it in.

But we never minded the cold and the damp; indeed I think we rather enjoyed them. We were always warm in bed, and in retrospect I seem to spend most of my time in bed: I very soon developed the habit of working there. I remember coming home on a snowy evening, and uttering wild cries as we rushed about the garden together hand in hand, watching our feet make holes in the printless snow. It often snowed at Steeple Aston, which is several hundred feet higher than Oxford, where it seldom or never does. Our bed, too, was the one place from which to me the house felt safe and natural. The bed was home, even if unknown creatures might be living at the other end of the long house, perhaps unaware of our existence?

It was when Iris was away for a day or two that I realised that the existence of such beings was not just fantasy. We had never heard anything, but as I came from the garden and went up the dark rather narrow staircase I saw something going up ahead of me. It was a large rat. It reached the top, looked around unhurriedly, and dived with a plop into a wide crack between the oak boards. It had come home.

Those rats were gentlemen. Until that moment we had no idea of their existence. Nor did their presence, once defined, cause us at first any bother. They led their lives and we led ours. But since we knew they were there, and they knew we knew they were there, our relations could never feel quite the same. For one thing their behaviour ceased to be so considerate. Now we often heard them moving about in their own solid subterranean world beneath the floorboards. Although the house was in bad condition it had been built in the solid style of its period, and there must have been plenty of room in that other world, and plenty of massive woodwork to gnaw upon. Those rats took to gnawing it as a night-time occupation, and sometimes, as it seemed out of sheer *joie de vivre*, they charged up and down those long invisible corridors at one or two in the morning. They must have been in residence for many generations, and the arrangements they had made must by now have suited them perfectly.

It seemed clear that something had to be done. From the rural chemist I obtained large quantities of a substance alleged not only to destroy rats without pain but to be positively enjoyed by them in the process. We spooned it lavishly through the cracks: soon we could hear the rats enjoying it. Now there were not only cavorting noises in the night but squeals of ecstasy as well. Iris began to look worried, in fact anguished. Didn't I think we ought to stop, while there might still be time? I began to waver, but fortunately the rats solved the problem for us. The sounds ceased quite abruptly, as if the animals had decided that if we would not play the game, neither would they – they would rather leave home. Iris looked more anguished than ever: I was concerned about the probable smell of unburied rat bodies. But the cold old house remained odour-free. It really looked as if they had staged a final feast and moved out.

And indeed something like that may have happened. I think mutual awareness of each others' presence may have unsettled them, inclined them to change their habits. Previously they had seemed to accommodate us by leaving to work in the outside world by night, and sleeping in the house by day. That had caused no problems, and I daresay the previous owner, the kindly old widow Blanche Tankerville-Chamberlayne (her real and fabulous name) had never bothered them, nor they her. Perhaps she never knew they were there.

And now of course we missed them. Iris ceased to look so agonised, and we never mentioned the rats, but I think we sometimes listened for them, perhaps a little wistfully, if we woke up in the night. I can feel and hear their almost sympathetic company in some of Iris's novels, written at her table just above their heads; for after we first realised their presence she used to say she had become aware of it in the day-time as well as by night, and found it congenial, even stimulating. In summertime it blended with sounds from the garden, the song of blackbirds and the twittering of the swallows – 'the Weatherbys' – on the telephone wire outside the window.

After she had given up her teaching post at St Anne's Iris used to write every morning, from about nine to one o'clock. If I was away in Oxford she listened to the news, had something to eat, and then went into the garden. She didn't actually do much gardening, if any, but she liked to find places to put things. It was the time when the new fashion for the old shrub roses was coming in. They had wonderful names: Duc de Guise, Captain John Ingram, *Cuisse de Nymphe*, and *Cuisse de Nymphe Emue*. They had tissue-like petals and smelt of wine. The white petals looked as transparent as ice, with a vivid green centre ('muddled centres', as the book called them, became a favourite phrase with Iris). The deep mauve ones like Captain Ingram faded almost into black.

We bought them at a rose garden at the weekends and I put them in inexpertly. Iris soon had her rose walk, and in a sense they were all Unofficial Roses, of the sort her heroine Fanny Peronet would have approved. (Her title *An Unofficial Rose* comes from a poem by Rupert Brooke which Iris had always been fond of.) But we had no idea how to look after them, and roses need a lot of looking after. Quite soon they began to look sickly, and the leaves became covered with black spots. A friend when he saw them teased Iris by remarking that she seemed to be keeping a concentration camp for flowers. The pleasantry was not in good taste, nor was it taken in good part. For a short while at least Iris's behaviour towards the friend cooled distinctly. She could be quite touchy, but never for long, and the friend was soon received back into favour. I don't think he put her off the roses, but somehow they had their day – most of them – and ceased to be, without either of us getting distressed about it. One only, I remember, continued to survive and flourish without appearing to need care or attention at all. It had thick luxurious foliage deeply furrowed and indented like a tropic plant, and its crimson hips were as big and glossy as a tropical fruit. It was called, I think, the Queen of Denmark.

Possibly as a result of all the effort that I felt I should – and indeed wanted – to put into the place, I fell ill with the glandular fever after we had been there less than a year. Like a Victorian illness, it makes the patient weak, as if fading painlessly away. It also keeps recurring at intervals. After the first recovery I used to totter down beside Iris through the tall grass to the pond, where she swam or rather paddled about, stirring up the dark mud. I felt I should be there, but had she got into difficulties I should have been far too weak to do anything about it. Of course she didn't, and in my enfeebled state I was greatly cheered by the sight of her face smiling blissfully up at me from under the willow shadows. Then I climbed thankfully and laboriously back into bed.

It was the sort of bed you do have to climb into, or on to, a wide high Victorian bed with a carved oak frame and a great soft almost soggy mattress. We had attended an auction in Oxford at the time we moved, and we got the bed for a pound. No one else seemed to want it, and when I got up the courage and offered a bid the auctioneer gave me a pained look. 'That's a bad bid, Sir,' he remarked, 'a very bad bid, but in the absence of another offer I shall have to accept it.' That summer the bed became my home, as the house itself never seemed to do. I read in it, ate and drank in it, wrote reviews in it, for I was still doing the novels for the *Spectator*, and the bed was always covered with them.

Up inside the bed, secure and, as it seemed, protected from the world, I could feel that this was marriage, the true nirvana of the wedded state. One of the books I reviewed in that dreamy time was by Pamela Hansford Johnson, a very capable novelist of the fifties, wife of the scientist and PR man C.P. Snow, who also wrote novels. Power was his chief interest: *The Masters*, concerning the power struggle to be the head of a Cambridge college, an early and original specimen of the campus novel.

Snow's wife had what for me were more subtle interests, and I enjoyed her novel, the last of a trilogy. An earlier one, advertised on the jacket and which I had not read, had its title borrowed from a poem of Donne's: *This Bed Thy Centre*. I felt that was a good omen, though I discovered later that the authoress had intended it satirically. The novel was an early feminist outcry against the sexual and domestic subordination of women. For me domestication on and in the bed was sheer bliss.

Certainly Iris did not at all regard the great bed as her centre, and the knowledge of that seemed perfectly harmonious to me too. Our marriage was shared, but the bed was mine. Iris would sit beside it, after bringing me barley water and orange jelly, the only things that the ulcerated glands in my throat would tolerate. As I got better we seemed to live mostly on poached eggs. Iris developed a skill in doing these which I have since envied. I have never been able to master it as she did: I regard skill in poaching an egg as the ultimate cooking test.

What I most appreciated too was Iris's complete indifference to the womanly image of a helpmate. She was not in the least a Florence Nightingale. She just looked after me, and as she did so I could see from her face that her mind was far away, pursuing the plot of the story she was engaged on. She found no bother at all in getting on with it while I was ill, and indeed told me later that she owed the genesis of that particular tale to the quiet time my illness had brought us both. That gave me such satisfaction that I at once fell ill again.

The second bout was worse than the first, and our doctor, an elderly dapper little man who always wore a rose in his buttonhole, looked a little worried, I thought, under his professionally jovial manner, just as one of his Victorian predecessors might have done. I was gratified by this, and also because Iris paid no attention. She knew in some way that there was nothing to worry about, although she politely shared the doctor's pleasure when he looked in later after making a blood test to announce that it had shown 'the Paul Bunnell effect', which meant that the trouble was indeed glandular fever, and not something worse. A charming and probably an extremely competent doctor, he used to look from one to the other of us with his bright old eyes, as if incredulous that two such absurd if engaging creatures could be living in this house, pretending to be husband and wife. While I was ill he came over every day from Bladon, a good many miles distant. It was in the early days of the National Health Service, and Dr Bevan – his name coincidentally the same as that of the minister who had just done the most to plan the service – took no private patients; but he always behaved as if we were the only people he had to look after, and that it was never any trouble to do so.

The comfortable feel of space, distance and separation which seemed to me to confirm the pleasures of the married state, in spite of Dr Bevan's incredulous and amused glances at what he appeared to regard as two quaint children rather than a married couple, was greatly enhanced by that summer of illness. When the term began I had to get sick leave. I luxuriated in the business of Iris working and me being ill. She was working away at her novel, now nearly finished. Bed had inspired me too, after a fashion. I had the idea for a book that became *The Characters of Love*, a study in detail of three texts – a poem, a play, and a novel – which seemed to me to exemplify in one way or another the understanding about love which I had picked up in the course of my relationship with Iris. It was a very naive idea, although some of the comments that I made about Chaucer's long narrative poem *Troilus and Criseyde*, Shakespeare's *Othello*, and Henry James's *The Golden Bowl*, still seem to me quite sophisticated if I re-read them. Critical books of that sort were in fashion at the time, and *The Characters of Love* did quite well, although I can't now imagine anyone trained on literary theory in the new schools of English Literature wanting to read it, or indeed being able to do so. Its vocabulary of appreciation and technique of appraisal are too different from anything currently in vogue.

The real satisfaction I got from it at the time was Iris's

wish to read it as it slowly proceeded, and what was for me the unexpected warmth of her reaction. This was not just automatic loyalty and a simulated interest in what hubby was up to, any more than her care of me when I was ill had been an imitation of wifely behaviour. She was really interested. We talked about it a lot, although as always without any attempt to have rational and serious discussion of the kind she would have engaged in with her pupils, or with friends and colleagues. We had already got to the stage of a relationship which Tolstoy writes about in *War and Peace*, where Pierre and Natasha, as husband and wife, understand each other and grasp each other's viewpoint without having to make sense or needing to be coherent. I was fascinated in my turn when I found later how much of what we had felt and spoken together had gone into Iris's landmark seminal essays. *Against Dryness* and *The Sovereignty of Good* are not in the least incoherent. They are not 'muddled centres' but lucid dewdrops, pearls of distilled wisdom, and yet I recognise in them the things we used to talk about in our own way, of which we had become conscious together by our own private and collective means.

Iris is without question the most genuinely modest person I have ever met, or if it comes to that, could ever imagine. Modesty is apt to be something acted, by each individual in his or her own way, part of the armoury with which people half-consciously build up the persona they wish others to become aware of, and with which they intend to confront the world. Iris has no pride in being modest: I don't think she even knows she is. The normal anxieties and preoccupations of a successful writer about status and the future – whether, to put it crudely, they can keep it up – were with her completely absent. Now that she has forgotten all about it anyway I am struck by the almost eerie resemblance between the amnesia of the present and the tranquil indifference of the past. She went on then secretly quietly doing her work, never wishing to talk about it, never needing to compare or discuss or contrast, never reading reviews or wanting to hear about them, never needing the continual reassurance from friends or public or the media which most writers require, in order to go on being sure that they are writers.

This normal need for status and reassurance, for feeling at however a humble a level 'a published writer', can have its endearing side. It often goes with real modesty, and with an accurate self-assessment of what the writer concerned can and cannot do. This would be true of a writer like Barbara Pym, whose novels I have always enjoyed and re-read, together with those of Raymond Chandler, C.S. Forester, Anthony Powell, one or two others. I can read them over and over, as if indulging in a private and comforting vice.

I recommended Pym's novels to Iris, and put them in her way, but I don't think she read them. She hardly ever read a contemporary novel, except when a friend or the friend of a friend had written one, and asked if she could bear to give an opinion, whereupon she would read every word of it conscientiously. Having done so she was very often enthusiastic, sometimes it seemed to me, if I also read the work submitted, disproportionately so. I think this came not only from the warmth and loyalty of friendship but from a kind of innocence: she had no experience of what novels today were like, and was impressed by what I could have told her was just the current way of doing it, a mere imitation of contemporary modes and fashions. I had the feeling that in the past, and before I met her, she had not so much read as absorbed the great classic novels, and in our early days she used to read and re-read Dostoevsky or Dickens, sometimes Proust. We got in the habit of reading at lunch-time, each with a book, and she read them with something of my own absorbed addict's pleasure, though she never minded my interrupting her with something I was reading myself, and which had entertained me.

She always shared in these moments of entertainment, and during my most addicted Pym period she liked me to read out comic scenes to her, at which she laughed with real amusement, though I think partly because I was laughing so much myself as I read, and she liked that. Having comic passages read to one – by P.G. Wodehouse say – can be exhausting: there is the need to simulate a hilarity which on the spur of the moment it may not be easy to feel. But Pym, like Austen, does lend herself particularly well to the sharing of short passages. We met her only once, with a young friend of hers who had been a pupil of mine. We liked her and her sister very much, within the limitations of a short meeting and the usual English awkwardness. She was a very tall woman, and when her diaries were posthumously published I was amused to find from a letter of hers to Philip Larkin that she felt she had 'seemed to tower above Iris (though only in height, of course).'

Barbara Pym was as modest as she was satirical about herself, and in both those modes of being, as one sees in her Diaries, wholly different from Iris. Iris had no need for consciousness of herself as an author; but there is an endearing moment in the Pym diaries when she imagines herself – as it is clear she frequently did, as most of us do – being looked at by persons who might have heard of her, and one of them saying 'There is Barbara Pym, the writer.'

There is the kind of literary personality, of the sort the Germans refer to reverently as a *Dichter*, who is organised on so impressive and heroic a scale that questions of modesty, image, attitudinising, can hardly be said to arise. One such was the writer already referred to, whom I thought of in early days, when I first knew Iris, as the Hampstead Monster (one of his female disciples wrote a novel on the subject of such monsters). This impressive figure had finally won, in old age, a Nobel prize. He had come to be revered, particularly in Germany (he wrote in German), although he had lived when young near Manchester and spent much of his life in London.

I encountered the Dichter on few occasions, and only once, at a literary party, had any conversation with him. He asked me what I thought about *King Lear*. This is never an easy question to answer. My experience of attempting to 'teach' the play to Oxford students was no help at all at that moment. I made some sort of reply none the less, to which he listened with flattering attention. 'What do *you* think?' I asked, after submitting in silence for some moments to his penetrating stare.

He continued to be silent for what seemed a long time. Finally he spoke. 'Friends tell me that my book is unbearable,' he said. Fortunately I knew this to be a reference to his long novel *Die Blendung*, and I nodded my head gravely. There was a further silence. '*King Lear* is also unbearable,' he pronounced at last.

I bowed my head. Shakespeare and his masterpiece would never be paid a greater compliment than this. The Mage was certainly mesmeric. The solemn atmosphere of our conclave was itself becoming unbearable, and it was a relief when we were interrupted by a bumptious but rather engaging young man, who was on the crest of a wave of self-esteem. His survey of contemporary *angst* had itself been hailed as a masterpiece, and had become an unexpected best-seller.

'What did you think of my book, sir?' he now asked in breezy tones, clearly confident that the great man could not have missed this experience.

The Dichter's appearance was always impressive. Squat, almost dwarfish, with a massive head and thick black hair, he looked like a giant cut short at the waist, what the Germans call a *Sitzriese*. Gazing up with an air of mild benevolence at the young man, he seemed none the less not fully to understand his question, not to have grasped the point at all, even though English was virtually his first language and he used it as masterfully as he did German. There was a long pause. The young man appeared to wait with growing expectation, but also a growing embarrassment.

The Dichter spoke at last, in a wondering way and without any inflection of emphasis or irony. 'You are asking me – me – whether I have read your book?' His sole reason for repeating the pronoun seemed to be to clear up a possible misunderstanding. Perhaps the young man thought he was addressing some ordinary mortal? There was another long pause while he continued to smile at the young man in friendly fashion. At last, murmuring something apologetic, the young man slipped away.

I felt torn between involuntary admiration and strong dislike. Dislike won, as it did on other occasions when I encountered the monster, or Mage. And yet he could exhibit not only an apparent warmth of manner but a shy almost diffident charm which he seemed to keep, as it were, solely for you. No wonder he was worshipped. Certainly I was fascinated myself on that occasion, and I longed to see how he would continue to behave. He did so by ignoring the existence of all the writers, intellectuals, and important people present, seeming to compel them also to ignore him. After that first encounter he moved about by himself with perfect ease, avoided by all, with no one venturing to address him. They might have decided deliberately to snub him, and if so he found that amusing and highly satisfactory. I watched him talk to another young man, who stood on the edges of the party, clearly knowing no one there. Soon they were laughing together and deep in conversation. I could not resist approaching them, and as I did so recognised this man, who at close quarters had a comically villainous appearance, as an actor I had often seen in gangster B movies, to which I was at that time addicted. As this was a talking-point I told him I had often enjoyed his screen performances. He seemed pleased, but said he had never yet had the role of chief gangster, only a subordinate one. Hailed now by a fellow actor who had just arrived he moved off, and the Dichter, who seemed greatly taken with him, enquired from me what he did. 'The only one here worth talking to,' he added smiling.

Feeling myself included in this judgement I sought to escape. At that moment our hostess fortunately claimed the Dichter, and the young actor returned to where I was standing. He asked me who the funny-looking cove was. 'What a really *marvellous* guy!' he said. 'Really interesting. He liked me,' he added, dramatising in a stage manner his own enthusiasm. 'We talked about fishing. I'm mad about it – my real hobby. I don't know how he knew that, but he seemed to . . .'

A potent Oxford figure, Isaiah Berlin, was different from the mage-like Dichter in almost every way – for one thing he was truly and unselfconsciously benevolent – but he shared the ability to charm anyone by the interest he took in them. He once told me he liked bores, and was never bored by them. That was probably true, and certainly he made himself familiar, in a warm-hearted spontaneous Russian way, to everyone he met – shy academic wives, worldly hostesses, scientists and intellectuals, philosophers and music-lovers. He had the common touch, and some people spoke patronisingly of him for that reason, implying that his fame and reputation were almost entirely due to his extraordinary powers of getting on socially, rather than to any real originality or achievement of his own.

Isaiah Berlin's favourite authors were Herzen, the Russian memoirist whose works were his bible, and the novelist Turgenev. In style and gusto and personality both resembled himself, though he would never have said so. The Dichter's bookishness was far more mysterious, no doubt deliberately. He would indicate to his followers that a certain text was the thing, the *real* right thing, without inviting discussion of the matter, or giving any reason why it should be so. In this sibylline manner he once urged on his disciples perusal of the *P'ing Ching Mei*, a long and complex Chinese novel of the seventeenth century. Everyone, including Iris, hastened to read it, but none of them seemed able to fathom what was so remarkable about it. Was it some sort of key to understanding, like Henry James's 'Figure in the Carpet' – perhaps, indeed, the key to an understanding of the Dichter's true greatness? Herzen and Turgenev are as open, as brilliant, as palpably fascinating, as Isaiah Berlin himself; but what was the secret of the *P'ing Ching Mei*, or any other work to which the Dichter gave the seal of his approval or, come to that, himself composed? There seemed no answer to that one. Mystery always remains the hallmark of the Mage.

Iris's works, at least to me, are genuinely mysterious, like Shakespeare's. About her greatness as a novelist I have no doubts at all, although she has never by nature needed, possessed or tried to cultivate the charisma which is the most vital element in the success of a sage, or mage. Her books create a new world, which is also in an inspired sense an ordinary one. They have no axe to grind; they are devoid of intellectual pretension, or the need to be different. They are not part of a personality which fascinates and mesmerises its admirers. Although any of her readers might say or feel that a person or an event in her fiction could only occur in a Murdoch novel, and nowhere else, this does not mean that the personality of the writer herself is in any obvious sense remarkable.

Her humility in this respect seems itself so unpretentious, unlike most humility. She had no wish to dwell apart, but took people and what they told her on trust, at their face value. I was often surprised by how easily she could be, as I saw it, taken in. She never needed to be 'knowing', to see through people, to discover their weak spot. Reflecting on Napoleon's comment that no man is a hero to his valet, Hegel remarked this was true; not, however because the hero was no hero, but because the valet was a valet. For Iris everyone she met was, so to speak, a hero, until they gave very definite signs or proof to the contrary. I have never met anyone less naturally critical or censorious. Her private judgements – if they were even made – remained her own and were never voiced publicly.

This is so rare in academic and intellectual circles that I suspect many more naturally animated and gossipy persons may actually have found conversation with her rather dull, while continuing very much to respect her. Religious people, like her pupils, took to her immediately and instinctively. But she never seemed to discuss religion or belief with them, nor they with her. In some way the 'spiritual', as I suppose it has to be called, seemed to hover in the air, its presence taken for granted. When W.H. Auden, whom she had once met when he was giving a talk at her school, came to live for part of the year in Oxford, they met on various casual occasions. 'He likes to talk about prayer,' she reported with a smile. I asked if they had exchanged views on how it should be done. 'Oh no, neither of us do it,' said Iris. 'But he jokes about how he would do it if he did.'

Although Iris was a scholar of Platonic philosophy, and it is so much a part of the atmosphere in many of her novels, it had no importance in her life that I could see, any more than did any kind of organised religion. This was true even of Buddhism, which she has come to know a good deal about, chiefly through her great friends Peter Conradi and James O'Neill, both of whom are practising Buddhists. I gather that such a description is in fact irrelevant, just as it would be to speak of a 'devout' or 'serious' Buddhist. (I have sometimes been struck by the analogy with Iris as a writer: there would be no point in describing her as a practising novelist, or even a 'serious' one. The Shakespearean comparison again comes to mind: in what sense was he a 'serious' dramatist?) I do not think Iris would ever have taken up meditation, as done in their own way by Peter and Jim. Her sense of things worked differently and in its own way; but she at once fell in love – and that was some years ago now – with their Welsh sheepdog Cloudy, a beautiful animal with a grey and white coat and blue eyes. It appears in her penultimate novel, *The Green Knight*, as the dog Anax.

Iris is and was *anima naturaliter Christiana* – religious without religion. She has never made a religion of art, and yet pictures have certainly meant more to her than any other product of the spirit, not excluding literature and philosophy. I mentioned Piero, and our experience of his Resurrection at Borgo San Sepolcro: and by coincidence we were to meet in Canada, five or six years after that honeymoon time, the painter Alex Colville, who had himself been deeply influenced by Piero's art. It was the first time we had been to the New World together; although a year or so after we were married Iris visited Yale on a month's Fellowship, travelling alone and reluctantly, but enjoying it when she got there. Until very recently going to America was always a problem, thanks to an Act vigorously restricting the issue of a visa to any former member of the Communist Party. Iris had been briefly a Young Communist while still an undergraduate at Oxford, leaving the Party before the outbreak of war, but her scrupulousness barred her from conveniently forgetting this fact, as many of her Oxford political friends had done, when filling out the visa form. She was duly restricted to single visits, for strictly academic purposes.

This proved to be inconvenient when we were in Canada, where no sort of restriction applied. Our hosts at McMaster University had planned to take us to the Buffalo Art Gallery and to see Niagara from the US side. These pleasures she had to forgo, since we planned to visit Chicago on the way home, where Iris was to give a philosophy paper. She also longed to visit the Chicago Art Gallery – she had managed to visit the Washington Gallery while on her visit to Yale.

Such an expedition could only be made if we did not use up her precious single visa on a Buffalo visit. She insisted the rest of the party should go as arranged, and stayed on the Canadian side herself until we returned. There was a compensation next day when we were to go to Stratford for the Shakespeare Festival; it had been arranged that I should give a talk there on the plays to be performed. We made a detour to Lake Huron, and plunged into waves which were uncannily like those of the ocean but had no salt savour about them.

Stratford was memorable less for Shakespeare than for a performance of *The Mikado*, the best that could be imagined. But the real revelation of our Canadian visit was the pictures of Alex Colville. This quiet reclusive artist, who lived at St John's in New Brunswick, was then painting one or at most two canvases a year. His art is meticulous in detail, taking infinite pains over extreme niceties of composition, and this precision contrasts with the statuesque solidity of his human figures, as massive and mysterious as Piero's, and yet wholly absorbed in the commonplace activities of contemporary life. Iris was spellbound by them. She and Colville took to each other at once, and he showed her all the portfolios he had brought with him: he had been coaxed over to take part in one of those symposia on 'Whither the Arts?' which are cosy routine for so many writers and academics. It was pleasant enough in the insipid way such events are; but Colville's presence and the ease we both found in talking with him, gave the days a sudden individuality. It was almost as if we had been unexpectedly received into one of his own pictures, where a husband stands naked and pondering, studying a refrigerator's contents by the dim light from within: or a woman, as massively inscrutable as any in Piero's paintings, holds the car door open for her children to enter.

We should much like to have seen more of Alex Colville, and talked to him, but he comes to Europe only rarely.

On one such occasion we managed a meeting in London, when he was en route for The Hague to repaint a tiny damaged area in the corner of one of his pictures, called 'Stop for Cows'. The paint in this corner had been minutely scratched in the course of handling by the museum, and the authorities there had been prepared to pay for Alex to come all the way over and put it right. They must have thought highly of the picture, as well they might. A big girl with plump cheeks and buttocks is raising one majestic arm as she turns to confront an invisible motorist. In front of her are the massive backsides and tails of black and white alderneys, and a wide sky suggests the sea not far away. In one way the picture is reassuringly Dutch, robustly, even humorously physical. But it also contrives to be full of a magic strangeness in complete contrast with appearances. How Colville does this, and plans or imagines compositions that reveal it, remains a mystery; and one that I know Iris at once found familiar and friendly with her own. With her own outlook on art, too. She used once to sit and study her volume of Colville reproductions by the hour. She has lost her interest in painting now that her powers of concentration have gone, but if I root out the album of Colvilles and put them in front of her she still shows for a brief time something of her old fascination.

Part of Colville's appeal for her undoubtedly lay in his complete lack of modishness. No other modern painter is so unconscious of the fashion, and so indifferent to what's new in the art world. Like the woodland watercolours of our old friend Reynolds Stone, Colville's paintings have no urge whatever to get on in society, the smart society of the in-group. Nor had Iris. She never had any instinct for what constituted the Where It's At of social or artistic success. If a criticism can be made of the social scene in her books it might be that her sense of it is not so much innocent as non-existent. Her world lacks any true sense of worldliness. In her grasp of how actual people behave her novels can be both shrewd and sharply observant, but there is no indication in them of knowingness, of having, as it were, got even her own world on a lead. Her feeling for things is far from being streetwise in the manner of Kingsley Amis, whom she knew and liked, and his brilliant son Martin.

This unworldliness is not common among writers and novelists. Tolstoy retained to the end his involuntary fascination with high society. His zest for finding out what dances were being danced and what the girls were wearing persisted long after he had supposedly renounced all fleshly temptation. Among writers the lofty moralists, the politically and socially correct, usually turn out in their private lives to be as pushy as Proust's Madam Verdurin. Social snobbery in the crude old sense is probably on the way out today, but the need to be in the swim is as strong as ever, itself a product of democratic hypocrisy; the need to oppose fox-hunting now as much the form as fox-hunting itself once was. Many of Iris's friends and fellow-writers were censorious when she was made a Dame of the British Empire. They maintained such an honour to be unacceptable on democratic or political grounds: but I suspect they really saw it as out of fashion – things like that were simply not done nowadays. Iris didn't care whether it was the done thing or not. It pleased her mother and her real friends, and that was what mattered to her.

Colville must have been happy in Canada, for nobody bothered about him there, or took him up, and yet he sold his paintings internationally for what seemed to us large sums. 'I like being a provincial,' he remarked once to Iris in his dry way. 'And you don't mind my saying, do you, that I loved your books and now you for the same reason. No striving towards Mayfair, if you see what I mean.' He looked so droll saying this that I could not help smiling, and I teased him by saying that of course only provincials exhibited at the Fisher Art Gallery and stayed at Brown's

Hotel, as he had already told us he was in the habit of doing when he came to London.

Iris and he were in fact the least upwardly mobile people one could imagine. Neither of them was in the least socially conscious, nor did they have any aptitude for making a good thing out of it. Colville's remark about provincialism was an unusual spurt of self-satire, prompted by the behaviour at the conference of a smart New Yorker and his even smarter wife, both art critics, who had been laying down the law at the discussion that morning. After it Colville remarked to us in a conspiratorial whisper that he was becoming 'a mite stir-crazy', so we got a lift into Hamilton that evening and had some drinks in a bar.

And yet I never knew Iris to disapprove of anyone on account of their pretensions, or the way they behaved. J.B. Priestley would show off to her outrageously, which she enjoyed in her benign way, without trying to enter into the spirit of things when he made efforts both crafty and elephantine to draw her out on the subject of Plato or religion, politics or feminism. He called her 'Ducky', which she also enjoyed, and he affected robust irritation at the sensible and rational answers she gave him. Had he lived a generation earlier, he used to boast to her, before successful writers had their entire income removed by the government's tax policies, he would have funded an expedition to Antarctica, or set up a Research Institute in Oxford or Cambridge. 'Cambridge wouldn't have thanked you for it,' his wife Jacquetta Hawkes would say dryly, 'I can tell you that, Jack.'

They made a most engagingly incongruous pair, and their happy relationship always used to remind me of Queen Titania and Bottom in *A Midsummer Night's Dream*. Iris was deeply fond of them both. I got along well with Jack and was somewhat in awe of Jacquetta, who always made me think of an old don's remark that they'll smile in your face in Oxford and stab you in the back, whereas in Cambridge they might do you a good turn, but with a disapproving face. Jacquetta did not exactly disapprove, but her smile, though friendly, was always a little frosty too. Her father had been the eminent Cambridge biologist who discovered vitamins, and she had a way of making unexpected confidences with a sort of scientific calm. She once told me she had jumped out of a window in Cambridge to impress a bumptious boyfriend and had seriously damaged her womb. 'You have charm,' she said another time, making it seem like something one's best friends didn't tell one about. That discomposed me a lot, but she made up for it by remarking on another occasion in an equally detached way that Iris was the only woman of whom she was never jealous where Jack was concerned. That made Titania sound quite vulnerable and human.

Jack's robust tones concealed the same vulnerability. He once asked me with a wistful look if I knew anyone in the British Academy: how could he become a member? I had no idea, but he must have thought that as an academic I should have known the answer. He also said he would once have given anything to have lived in the smart world, like Evelyn Waugh. In a weird way he made being in 'the smart world' sound the same thing as having the right views on England or politics or feminism. He could manage those all right, and they had put him on the map, but to be really on the map one should have been in the smart world as well. Such remarks fascinated me but also made me feel uncomfortable, and I think Iris too, although she never showed it. Her way of dealing with Jack was to ask him about his life; and I was reminded of the time a newspaper interviewer told Iris she had found out all about herself, while she had found out nothing about Iris. Iris's fondness for Jack Priestley was almost like that of a daughter, and she missed him greatly when he died.

Her fondness for Jack grew with time, but she was equally good at making instant friends. And in a sense still is.

The other day a caller rang up from an Irish monastery. He had long admired her work and had written to her, a correspondence I had had to take over. He asked if he could look in briefly on his way from Limerick to pick up a fellow monk from a sister foundation. He was immensely tall, dark-suited, urbane, with that indefinable air many monks have of moving in a distinctly smart world. (I thought of Tolstoy, Jack Priestley, Evelyn Waugh!) He told us the Duchess of Abercorn had sent her love; it seemed she had once met us in connection with a Pushkin Festival.

All this was momentarily discomposing, but when the tall monk and Iris sat down together, things changed at once. They became extraordinarily animated – she starting sentences, or ending them – he appearing to know at once what she wanted to ask, and filling the words they were failing to make with a professional abundance of loving kindness. And yet his face looked really transfigured: so, a few moments later, did hers. They were soon on about his childhood, why he joined the order, most of all about his plans to make discussion of her works a regular thing at Glenstal Abbey. He assured us that two of her novels, *The Book and the Brotherhood* and *The Good Apprentice*, could be said to have inspired the recent setting-up of the monastery, and the way they wanted it to go. For the first time Iris looked blank. Perhaps she had detected a note of Irish hyperbole; perhaps she was simply puzzled about the names of her novels. What were they? From whom? But she didn't enquire, only asking for the third or fourth time. Where living? Where born? – and did he know Dublin?

Transfiguration doesn't last. His enthusiasms soon began to seem no more out of the ordinary than those of most religious people: Iris's own animation faded into her lost look; she seemed bewildered now by the presence of the tall handsome monk in his incongruous city clothing. Practised in such matters, fully aware that the good minute was going, he rose swiftly, blessed her, and was out of the

door. The little van in which he had driven all the way
from Limerick to Holyhead, and across Wales to Oxford,
was waiting at the kerb. I remarked that we had ourselves
once driven about Ireland in such a van, but he was not
interested. I felt he had taken my measure, not because he
was a clever man but because experience had taught him
much about the stupidity of intellectuals, their obtuseness
about the things that really mattered. He was off now to
pick up his Benedictine colleague, and as a parting shot I
remarked that I had heard that the Benedictines were the
most learned order. 'Don't you believe it,' he replied with a
great laugh, and a look of contempt which I felt I had fully
deserved.

Inside the house Iris had regained her animation and was
full of pleasure in the visit. She grasped that the caller had
been Irish, but that was about all. I tried to remind her
of the time, some years before, when she had gone to
lecture at Maynooth, the big Roman Catholic seminary
outside Dublin. It had been at the height of the troubles
in northern Ireland, and her host had made some reference
to the IRA detainees there, 'the men behind the wire' as
they were known in the south. 'Aren't we all with the
men behind the wire?' he had observed rhetorically, and
his fellow-priests had nodded their heads in approval. Iris
had been incandescent with fury. She told me later that she
had been hardly able to contain herself and maintain her
usual civil and smiling demeanour. I am sure the priests
would have had no idea of the passion they had unwittingly
unleashed, assuming in their bland way that Iris, like all
London intellectuals, would have the fashionably correct
attitude towards Irish unity. She did not. It was the one
political topic on which the presbyterian atavism of her
Northern Irish ancestors completely took over.

I used sometimes to tease her by reminding her of the
misprint a typist had made in one of her essays. Uncertain
of Iris's writing she had substituted 'Pearson' whenever the

word 'reason' appeared in the text, thinking that this was
some philosopher Iris frequently referred to. This produced
a number of sentences beginning 'Pearson requires' or 'as
Pearson indicates', and Pearson became ever after a familiar
figure in our private language. But Pearson certainly had
no place where Iris was concerned if any discussion arose
among her friends about the future of Northern Ireland.
She used to keep silent if she could but often burst out
in the end. She once silenced me when I attempted some
facetious reference to Pearson in this context by reminding
me sharply of Hume's pronouncement that 'Reason is, and
ought only to be, the servant of the passions.' It was not a
view she held in any other context.

Iris's longhand was usually clear, was indeed an excellent
and wholly distinctive handwriting with no resemblance to
anyone else's. Bringing her a cup of coffee in the morning
at Steeple Aston I sometimes used to stop and watch as
her pen travelled across page after page of looseleaf paper.
Occasionally it raced, and then her writing did become
hard for the typist to decipher. The business of typing her
MS was always arranged by Norah Smallwood at Chatto,
an admirable managing director who had the reputation
of being close-fisted, but who always treated Iris with
maternal firmness and kindness – a favoured but rather
unpredictable daughter. Norah, who had no children of her
own, behaved like a tyrant to her young female employees,
except when they were in trouble, or if she found them in
tears as a consequence of her severity.

Iris was always happy to stop for a chat, never minded
being interrupted, whereas if I was trying to type something
in bed I used to find interruptions fatally dismantled whatever insecure pile of syntax my mind was endeavouring to
set up. If it collapsed like a house of cards I had trouble
starting over again, or remembering what I had been trying
to say. But Iris, good-natured as ever, never minded my
snarling at her briefly if she put her head round the door

to ask some question about the day's activities. She would murmur something pacific and withdraw. Nowadays I remember those occasions when she comes anxiously after me in the house, or if I look up from a book and see her peering at me in the doorway.

Once when I was standing by her side while she wrote I saw a fox strolling about on the lawn and pointed it out to Iris, who was always glad to see the creature, even though our foxes were a well-known family, as much in residence in a corner of the wild garden as the rats had once been in the house. Our neighbour's cats were also frequent visitors. A cat was crossing the lawn when we heard, a few moments later, a tremendous sound of screeching and spitting. A fox was dancing round the cat, which revolved itself to face it, making these noises. Impossible at first to say whether the fox had intended to attack and perhaps even to eat the cat, or if it was all in play, an idea suggested by the way the fox would lie down between its leaps and manoeuvres and put its muzzle between its front paws. Finally it seemed to weary of the game, if such it was, and strolled off, leaving the cat to its own devices. While the confrontation was going on I had the greatest trouble to dissuade Iris from tearing downstairs and rushing between them, like the Sabine women between their embattled Roman husbands and their Sabine relatives. Fascinated, I had longed to see how the situation would end, even though Iris kept distractedly saying, 'Oh we must separate them – we must.'

Her instincts were always pacific, and she hated the idea of animals harming each other as much as she did human beings doing so. When the local hunt killed a fox in the neighbouring field she was up in arms at once, remonstrating with a civil and perplexed huntsman who sat on his horse with an apologetic air saying, 'Oh I'm so sorry, Miss Murdoch, I understood you were a supporter.' This was perfectly true, but there was a difference between being mildly in favour of country sports and hearing one of her own foxes, as she supposed it must be, despatched close by, especially as she might well have known the creature when it was a cub. If we walked very quietly to that secluded corner of our garden by the drystone wall, where bramble-bushes and elder flourished, and mounds of earth had been mysteriously raised, we would often see a small face with myopic pale-blue eyes peering out at us. The vixen usually raised five or six young there each year.

Iris felt the foxes were part of her household. To me they were signs, as the rats had been, that the place didn't belong to us, that we were there on sufferance. This didn't trouble Iris at all. She was often away, seeing her mother and her friends in London. Possessions sat lightly upon her; she once said to me that she was no more concerned with their existence than she was with her own. I saw what she meant, and yet it was not really true. She was jealous of her things, like her stones, roses and pictures, and yet it never occurred to her to nourish or to visit them, to clean them as real householders clean silver or china, and to give them loving attention. They must never be got rid of or moved, and that was all. So the house always had a look of dereliction, as did the very small pad or perch we acquired later in South Kensington, at the time we found someone to live with Iris's mother in her London flat and look after her.

I myself felt no more at home in this London pad of ours than I did in the house at Steeple Aston, although oddly enough I settled down at Steeple Aston much more readily on the days when Iris was away. When in 1980 or so she had her visit to China (going with quite a highpowered delegation and meeting Deng Shao Ping the Chairman) I found myself making serious efforts to clean the house up. It was during the vacation, no teaching in Oxford, and I used to work on Shakespeare in the morning and clean and tidy in the afternoons. I got into quite a bachelor routine, all the more readily from knowing it wouldn't last.

Iris was greatly impressed when she got home, and

touched too. I think she felt, with a momentary pang, that this was the way I had always wanted things. Not true: I had no idea what I wanted in this or any other respect provided she was there; and her own lack of identity with self or place precluded me from feeling at home there except when she wasn't. Her novels, and her ceaseless invention, from day to day and month to month, were where she lived. And so, after my tidy interlude as a bachelor householder, married demoralisation swiftly and comfortably returned.

None the less she loved the place in her own way, far more than I did. Apart from her refusal to go back there, a visit in which I would have felt retrospective fascination and morbid enjoyment, Cedar Lodge was the Camelot where she had the original comforting future in her head: her vision of the badgers breaking in, and herself rushing out to tell me about it when I got home. Perhaps that was her sole wifely vision; and after the vision dissolved and departed with the sale of the house she never wanted to see either again. I once teased her by saying it was the foxes who in fact had broken in, not the badgers, but, as she pointed out, that wasn't the same thing at all. Oddly enough I did once see a real badger there, though in a wholly inconclusive manner. It was a shabby elderly creature, but unmistakably a badger, who once shuffled past when I was sitting in the long grass down the slope, looking as if he had lost his way and didn't want attention drawn to himself while he tried to find it. In general they are exclusively nocturnal creatures.

I told Iris about him, but she was not really interested. I suppose it was the Platonic idea that counted with her, not the real example. When UFOs became the fashion she claimed to believe in their existence at once. And she was convinced of the reality of the Loch Ness monster, a fabulous creature adored and probably invented by the British Press, reputed to live in the unfathomable depths, surfacing at intervals to be sighted by local ghillies and lucky tourists. When we visited friends in the Highlands, John and Patsy

Grigg, Iris could not be dissuaded from sitting for hours in the heather above the loch, staring down hopefully. I don't think she was ever disappointed when nothing happened.

Since a child I had myself taken pleasure in submarines and aeroplanes, without becoming seriously interested in them, and Iris ordered for me a magazine series about the two world wars which lavishly featured the various types. She never wanted to study them herself, but she liked to see me looking at my 'aeroplane books', as we called them, and she liked me to tell her about them. She herself was devoted at that time to the adventures of Tintin, the perky young Belgian 'boy reporter' invented by Hergé, whose comic strip stories are illustrated with an inspired contemporary detail, reminiscent of some of the old Flemish masters. Iris was introduced to these by the same Greek friend who had once told her how to cook the legendary *stefados*. Both of us became hooked at once; I think partly because of the French dialogue, which is extraordinarily witty and apt, and does not come over at all into English. I have learnt a lot of French from the Tintin books, mostly idioms now outdated, which we used to repeat to each other on suitable occasions. There was a moment when the villains had hired a diver to go down and attach a limpet mine to the good characters' ship. Just as he is fixing it the anchor happens to be released from up above, banging him on the head and knocking him and his mine down into the depths. '*Fichu métier!*' he remarks philosophically into his diving helmet. A comment whose pithiness is as untranslatable as poetry.

Iris wrote Hergé a fan letter, and thanking her in reply he mentioned that he would be signing copies in Hamley's toyshop, halfway up Regent Street. We were in the shop on the day, and Iris had a long chat with the great man, telling him about her time in Brussels with the relief organisation UNRRA, just after the war ended. She never spoke of this to anyone else. He was a big gangling sandy-haired man, like a scoutmaster as we agreed afterwards, and he spoke excellent English. Iris's fondness for the boy reporter, and his moderately alcoholic older friend Captain Haddock, had made her suppose that their creator was very likely homosexual. I think she hoped he was, for she had an odd streak of romanticism about gay men, and was apt sometimes to be naive in her assessment of who was what. I doubted she was right about the author of Tintin, and by chance happened to see lately in the paper what was I think an obituary article, mentioning a long and happy marriage, and hinting that he had also been something of a womaniser.

I recall the day we met him because it was the day we bought a gramophone. We had no TV of course, and it was some years before we even acquired a radio. Our first LP was Mussorgsky's 'Pictures from an Exhibition', which was quite new to us; and I can never listen to it now on the radio – the gramophone and LP have long since vanished – without remembering hearing it raptly with Iris that first evening, and how the Great Gate of Kiev seemed to resound in harmony with the spaghetti we were eating, and the red wine. Food and music are very contextual in that way. Later we became fond of song albums, chiefly Scottish and Irish airs, the early Beatles too, and we used to chant together an imaginary pop song whose words had somehow come into existence between us. In its early version it ran something like

> Waterbird, waterbird, I love you
> Waterbird, waterbird hoo hoo hoo.

I think it may have been suggested by the low clucking call of the moorhens down on our pond. Iris later tidied it up (the song not the pond) and put it into one of her novels.

When we had a radio we used to listen to the Archers, a long-running soap which came on at twenty to two, during our lunch-time. We put down our books to listen to it.

We then discussed the characters and their adventures, or lack of them. I was all for romance: Iris preferred the villains, who always had BBC accents while the honest folk conversed in various sorts of rustic dialect. The Archers is still going, but I have lost interest in it now that Iris can no longer listen with me, to make out who the persons are and what they are up to. The high spot of her radio life was long ago, in the days when the Home Service, as it was then called, used to run a lengthy serial tale between five and six in the evening. Her favourite, featuring the slim dark-haired young heroine Mary McCaskabell, was called 'Dark House of Fear'. The heroine's name perhaps reminded her of the north of Ireland, and she became totally gripped every evening by the lurid development of the tale. I loved watching her as she listened.

I was always intrigued by the ways in which Iris's creative mind seemed to work, never bothering itself much with 'highbrow' literature, however much she might herself enjoy reading Dickens, Dostoevsky, Kafka, and so forth, but latching on to unexpectedly simple and straightforward stories with a popular appeal. These her unconscious mind could always make something of, although she never read them in book form but only heard them on the radio. I was reminded of Dostoevsky's own interest in lurid newspaper stories, which often found their way into his novels.

7

In some way, or so I felt, the house itself let us know when it was time to depart. That was nearly fifteen years ago. Our most ambitious project had been to remove an inner wall and turn round the lower steps of the dark narrow staircase, making a wide and rather too obviously spacious descent into what now became a hall. Young Mr Palmer and his helper had stood precariously on ladders, manoeuvring a gigantic steel girder into position on top of the new brick piers. Owing to some elementary miscalculation this RSJ ('rolled steel joist') however massive in appearance, was barely long enough to span the gap, and one of its ends only just rested on the brickwork. After it had been shrouded over with paint and plaster I used sometimes to give it a glance of apprehension as I descended the stairs, wondering if it would come crashing down on top of us, as on the day when Samson pulled down the temple on the Philistines.

The girder is still there and the house still stands, so I suppose that young Mr Palmer's reassurances to me at the time have been justified. But I felt none the less that the venerable spirit of Cedar Lodge resisted this radical alteration. For one thing the house did not, as we hoped and expected, feel at once roomier and more compact. It merely felt colder, the wide open spaces of the new hall more difficult to heat. Our successors have made more drastic alterations, transforming the old house at some expense into a mansion that has even figured in the magazine *House and Garden*. But houses, like people, can lose their old character without gaining a new one. Iris's instinct never to return is probably justified.

Wanting very much to give her a small pool in which she could swim at all seasons, or at least splash about in, I plotted with young Mr Palmer to make one in the derelict greenhouse. It was only a few feet square but nearly five deep, so that a few strokes were possible in any direction. The place was roofed in a simple fashion with polystyrene, and once filled the pool was kept topped up with rainwater from the roof. The water became brown and clear, with the authentic river smell, the concrete sides deliciously silky and slimy to the touch. The rainwater had a softness not to be found in ordinary swimming pools and remained surprisingly pure; I never needed to put in chemicals. I put in a few small fish, green tench and carp, who seemed happy enough in the dark depths. Surrounded by the delicate greenery which sprouts in abandoned greenhouses it was most agreeable in high summer, a paradisal plunge pool known to some of our friends as 'Iris's Wallow'.

My ambition was to make it possible to swim there all the year round, and I devised a method which would have been an electrician's nightmare had I allowed any electrician to become involved. The place was wired for some old electric heating pipes; and as the power point seemed in reasonably good condition I installed a couple of immersion heater elements, intended for use in a domestic heating system. They lay on the bottom, and when switched on sent a cloud of bubbles up through the brown water. I was careful to put a notice beside the pool, advising, with the aid of a skull and crossbones, that the power must be switched off before entry into the pool. Even this elementary precaution seemed barely necessary; one does not after all electrocute oneself by dipping a finger in the electric kettle, and these heating elements were designed to operate when immersed. The cables could have caused trouble however, and I did not like the idea of finding Iris floating and insensible, although she herself remained blissfully unaware of any hazard involved, and I was always careful to be present when the pool was being used in its heated state.

Like so many brilliant and inventive ideas this one was not destined to be a long-running success. It worked beautifully, but Iris's arthritis was getting worse (today it is inexplicably much better) and a walk in the cold, even to the now heated pool, became uninviting. It was in any case destined to be my final attempt to impose innovation and improvement on Cedar Lodge. After it I relapsed into quietism, and the house seemed to approve of that. Iris had always been pleased for me whenever I had planned anything, but not greatly concerned about it herself. The house and its garden never featured in any of her books. Perhaps in her own way she was too intimate with it, and too close for it to become involved in her own imaginative life.

The grass of the former lawns grew longer and longer and more tussocky; I never attempted to mow them now. The box hedges, neat and trim when we moved in, had climbed to giant size and height, almost obscuring the front of the house, which faced north and was in any case on the sombre side; the southern 'aspect', from which one went down into the garden, was much more sunny and attractive. Letting things go, a principle which we had once followed almost unconsciously, was now asserting itself as a positive force. The house seemed waiting, with benevolence and without haste or regrets, for its next occupant. It had always made clear in some way that we were not the kind of people who should be living in it. We had not been county people, or even country people, nor did we properly belong to the new race of enterprising commuters who left the village to their jobs in London or Birmingham, returning to improve their properties at the weekend.

There were still many good moments. A family of kingfishers was reared somewhere by the pond, and I went down one day to find small apparitions in vivid turquoise and red exploding among the willow-trees and uttering thin piercing cries. They must have just crawled out of the fishbone-lined tunnel where they had been born, and they could barely fly. Another time, on a day in February which was as warm and humid as summer, we watched black and white woodpeckers drilling holes for their nest. The tree on which they operated was only a few yards from the drawing-room window.

And yet, for all these favouring distractions, the moment seemed to have come. I remembered Mary Queen of Scots, just before her execution, telling her ladies in waiting that it was time to go. Anachronistic fancy might imagine her raising a black-sleeved arm and looking at a watch. Mustn't keep Queen Elizabeth and her executioner waiting. For us too it was time to go, but we didn't know where. Should we try to find another place in the country? That seemed pointless – nothing could be so good as what we had. To Oxford then? Yes, that seemed the obvious choice. I still had my job: Iris was deep into what proved in the end to be the most lengthy arduous project she had yet undertaken – the Gifford Lectures, to be delivered in the Faculty of Theology and Philosophy at the University of Edinburgh. Later she was to incorporate them in her book *Metaphysics as a Guide to Morals*.

In retrospect we seem to have become absentees about this time, like the *rentiers* in *The Cherry Orchard* who spend their time in German resorts while feeling a real and profound nostalgia for their estates back in Russia. Cedar Lodge was still very much home, but we seemed less and less to be there. Almost unconsciously we came to spend more and more time with hospitable friends, who themselves appeared to take for granted that we had become permanent waifs and strays, needing a home now rather than a home from home. We spent weeks in this way at Cranborne with my old tutor and colleague David Cecil, whose wife Rachel, to whom I had dedicated my first novel, had recently died.

He was often visited for tea in the afternoon by Janet Stone, herself now a widow, living in a small house in an old street on the riverbank, just outside the close in Salisbury. We could bathe there in the river from her tiny garden, in the shadow of the ancient stone bridge which had once taken the high road over Salisbury Plain past the cathedral and down to the coast. I was never much impressed by the cathedral, but it always made me think of Thomas Hardy and that haunting tale of Salisbury 'On the Western Circuit', the story of which I was to be reminded in sadder circumstances after Iris had developed Alzheimer's.

From Janet Stone's drawing-room window, opening on the river, we fed the Avon's busy population of coots and mallards and swans. Janet would stand there to watch us bathing, her gravely beautiful face always sad in repose. She had never got over the sudden death of her husband Reynolds; nor, I think, the move from Litton Cheney, the magic vicarage under a Dorset hill where they had lived for years. A wonderful hostess, also an outstandingly good photographer, she seemed made to live among a lot of people, caring for them, amusing them. Widowhood did not suit her at all. She loved visitors; she taught Iris grospoint embroidery, a simple skill but one to which Alzheimer's, alas, swiftly put a stop. When she died at last, quietly in her big four-poster bed, she looked like a medieval saint stretched on a tomb.

We had also taken to going abroad again, not on our own as we used to do when younger, but shepherded and looked after by a pair of great friends, Borys and Audi Villers, the dedicatees of one of Iris's novels. Audi, a Norwegian – Borys was Russian Jewish Polish – had formerly been a travel courier. She suffered from severe asthma, which was why they had built themselves a charming little house in the interior of the Canary Island of Lanzarote, where the volcanic air – that at least is what it feels like – is particularly pure and dry. Their house, high up, is surrounded by black hills and fields of lava, growing the tenderest and mildest garlic and onions in the world. This seems inexplicable, as it never rains, and the only other vegetation is an occasional withered looking fig or palm tree. Lanzarote is a nice place if you avoid the beaches, which are black not only with lava but with German and British tourists. Audi used to take us to swim in the small harbour where the steamer left for the next island. The fish population there was considerable; an extremely handsome purple fish who sometimes appeared in the dark blue depths was my undoing. In my excitement at the sight of him through the glass mask I took in water, and inadvertently spat out with it my lower plate of teeth. For the remainder of that stay I had to give up eating delicious crisp *tapas* and crustacea. Even a mild Canary onion was too much for me. It was like trying to cut with one half of a pair of scissors. Ironically my dentist was himself on a Canary holiday when we got home, but on his return he regaled me with warning stories. Watch out for your dog if you are a denture wearer, he told me: the airedale belonging to one of his patients had once found and eaten his master's set. He also tried to cheer me up by pointing out the timelessness of tooth acrylic: it is the last thing to go in the crematorium. My teeth, uncorrupted, would lie five fathom in the harbour ooze for evermore.

But some lessons are, as it were, too improbable to be learnt. I forgot this one when swimming in Lake Como a couple of years later. We were guests at some academic conference; I contrived to repeat the accident. This time it was a school of perch, cruising sprucely striped among the lake weeds, who were my undoing. Italian doctors of philosophy were charmed by what they regarded as a peculiarly English misfortune. Hearing of my accident the waitress in the villa dining-room trilled with mirth like a stage soprano. *Niente al dente per il professore inglese*! she would cry merrily. Only Iris remained firmly sympathetic, and did her best, wearing my mask and up-ended like a duck, to probe the shallows where the teeth had vanished. No luck of course.

Borys and Audi loved to visit Italy and often took us with them. Since they were also picture lovers we saw again the Piero Resurrection, and we became knowledgable about frescoes, and the isolated churches that cherish a single masterpiece. Audi had once taken her flock on guided tours of Capri and the Amalfi peninsula, and one year she decided to revisit. My instinct was to shun such picturesque places, but 'Just you wait,' said Audi, with a smile like the goddess Freya's, and she was right as usual. Iris fell specially for Sorrento; I think the old-fashioned seafront reminded her of Dublin, the Kingstown harbour of her childhood and the saltwater baths where her father taught her to swim.

The bathers down below our hotel room windows were all deeply bronzed, but on our first morning there suddenly appeared a tall woman – she must have been well over six feet – with black hair and a very white skin. Wearing a deep purple bikini she looked immensely dignified but also rather sinister, like the goddess of death herself, come to claim a victim. I was fascinated, and pointed her out to Iris, whose less romantic view was that she must be a female drug-dealer. I knew better than to try to nudge Iris's inspiration, which rarely or never began with an incident from real life, but I hoped none the less that the scene below might alchemise at some time into one of her plots. To my surprise however, she nodded down at the woman and said 'Why don't *you* write a story about her.'

From their balcony Borys and Audi had also glimpsed the apparition, which made a little fantasy for us to laugh about at breakfast-time. Encouraged by them all I dreamed up a possible scenario which ended as a novel, *Alice*, the first I had tried to write for nearly forty years. *Alice* produced a sequel, *The Queer Captain*, and eventually the third of a trilogy, *George's Lair*.

Although it was not until two or three years later that

the Alzheimer symptoms became fully apparent, I have sometimes wondered if Iris knew that her own career as a novelist was nearly over. Was she encouraging me to start again? Sorrento was somehow a sad place, in spite of its charms. It was also, alas, Borys's last holiday. He died a few months later and Audi missed him terribly. She went on living in Lanzarote, and we went on seeing a great deal of her. For me too one of her holiday schemes was again a source of inspiration. She took us to The Hague for the Vermeer exhibition. The crowds made it difficult to see the actual pictures, but the 'Girl Wearing A Red Hat' was reproduced on posters and tickets. A story suggested itself. I told it to Audi and Iris as we sat in a peculiar little restaurant which itself began to take part in the plot.

I arranged for the novel to end in a locale we knew well. Stephen and Natasha Spender had acquired the ruin of an old stone farmhouse in Provence, which Natasha had skilfully rebuilt over the years. It was very isolated, up in the limestone Alpilles district near St Rémy, and at first there was no water. Iris and I enjoyed fetching cans from the well in the nearest village. In the great heat of July we used to plunge into the ice-cold 'agricultural', an old irrigation canal that wound through the steep contours of the hills, running swiftly among the dense thickets of green canes and rosemary and cypress that bordered abandoned apricot and olive groves. They seemed to have reverted to a wild state. Nightingales sang there in June, even in July. A gripping sequence in Iris's novel *Nuns and Soldiers* was inspired by our discovery of a tunnel in the *maquis*-covered hillside. We could see light at the end of it and ventured to wade through. The hero of the novel had a more exciting adventure in a subterranean stream. But the magic place, the overpowering heat of midday, and the grey alpine water rushing on its mysterious course through the abandoned country – these were just as Iris described them.

Once a dowser came to try for water on the Spenders'

small property. He was a polite man, forthcoming about his craft, and it was uncanny to hold his willow switch in both hands and feel it stir and tremble. Iris stood motionless and enthralled for minutes, until the dowser eventually had to remove it from her hands with a courteous '*S'il vous plaît, Madame.*' He found water all right, but it was far down, the well that was at last built over a hundred feet deep. It solved the problem of a domestic water supply, but Iris and I always rather missed the need to visit the well in the village square – it was a chore we could perform together like Jack and Jill – and going to 'wash' at noon in the agricultural.

In the evening at Mas St Jerome we used to play Scrabble, Stephen and Natasha being great experts. Outside in the warm night treefrogs made a soft soporific din. Stephen had an innocently cunning smile which was delightful to watch as he coaxed improbable words on to the Scrabble board. Picking up my seven letters once I found they made the word 'Bunfish', which I attempted to pass off as an authentic marine species. The others weren't having any, but the word found its way into our language, and that of the Spenders too. 'Doing a bunfish' became quite an expressive term for trying to get away with something.

Back in Oxford we drove about, looking at 'For Sale' signs. I loved now the idea of a small house. Iris was sorry to see that there didn't seem to be any big ones, not at least For Sale. With a rush of warmth and relief we decided mutually to abandon the whole idea, only to go home and find the house expectant in some way, but not of our return. It was waiting for us to go away, and for all the accumulated dirt and debris of our long sojourn to go with us. It gave me a slight feeling of horror, and we looked at each other. We were becoming too anthropomorphic by far. The house was just a house after all, and couldn't order us about.

And yet it did. Or it seemed to. Iris went to London. I went to Oxford, and after my day of a lecture and classes

visited a house agent and was equipped with the prospectus
for a number of desirable residences. I drove to the first, up
a long straight street in Summertown, a leafy suburb of
north Oxford. There it was on the corner, a pleasant little
brick house. My heart warmed to it at once. I felt we would
really own that house. No more living on sufferance in a
place that had always been the haunt and the property of
other beings.

Without bothering to look at other houses whose particulars he had supplied I rushed back to the estate agent.
I was in a fever to buy that little house before it should be
snapped up by someone else. I knew that all the residences
in this part of Oxford were extremely sought after. I all
but besought the agent to let me pay for the house straight
away. He pointed out that he would first have to consult the
owner, but he was kind enough to accept a deposit. I don't
suppose so naive a purchaser had ever come into his hands
and he played my enthusiasm craftily, regretting that so
many other candidates were in the market, some of whom
were only awaiting a bridging loan before they established
their right to number 54 Hartley Road. The thought of
these effective and determined purchasers made me more
agitated than ever.

Early next morning, with Iris still in London, I went to
view the house. The owners had gone to work. Their young
daughter, eating her breakfast before setting off for school,
appeared baffled by the purpose of my visit but raised no
objection to my wandering about. She seemed herself a
delightful emblem of urban pastoral. The clean sunlit little
rooms had a fresh and fragrant smell. A canary sang in its
cage; a cat lay asleep on the dresser. A whole new mode
of existence, original, unsampled, never even encountered
in married life before, seemed to offer itself, seductively
yet modestly. I felt sure that the poet John Betjeman, who
sang of the joys of suburban life, would have approved that
house and its occupants. I saw myself sitting reading by the

gasfire while Iris worked upstairs. Presently we would stroll down to the shops to make some simple purchase for our supper. There were no shops to speak of in Steeple Aston, and nowhere much to stroll to either, outside our own wild garden.

Iris took it wonderfully well. I think she saw at once that it was no use arguing with me in my besotted state. The power of a new daydream had overwhelmed me. Nor was it, as fantasies go, at all an ambitious one. It was commensurate, as no previous lifestyle of ours had been, with my own instincts for living; and those instincts had apparently been lying in wait for years. I think Iris saw that, and even felt a kind of guilt about it. Although a stricken look rapidly crossed her face when she saw my dream house she threw herself into the dream like a Roman matron putting her hand into the fire. She acted as if her enthusiasm matched my own.

I saw that it didn't of course. But I was obdurate – why shouldn't I be obdurate for once? And yet the dream faded even before the new house was bought and the old one sold. I realised – we realised – what a mistake we were making, but it seemed as if such a mistake was inevitable, was all we could do in return for all those years – more than thirty of them – spent together in the country in the happy shadow of Iris's own original daydream. Those badgers of hers had, so to speak, come home at last. The old house was in a terrible state and we left it like that, still full of every kind of rubbish. But much of the rubbish, including all the old dusty stones, had to be taken to the new establishment. Poor Iris had been so good that I could not even try to prevent that happening.

The house in Hartley Road was a predictable disaster, but I continued to feel a dogged loyalty to it, even when the children round about screamed all day, and the neighbourhood burglars payed us routine visits at night. We stuck it for three years, longing to go, and finally found a quieter and more suitable small house which a colleague of mine was preparing to sell. Oddly enough Iris had done some of her best work at Hartley Road, including the Gifford Lectures. She had driven her pen there day after day, and all the more determinedly because the place was, as I well knew, so uncongenial to her. Needless to say we never seemed to stroll together down to the shops; nor, so far as I recall, did I ever sit cosily with a book in front of the gasfire, 'like a picture of somebody reading', as Keats chortles in one of his letters.

The colleague who was selling us her house (she taught economic history) enquired if we would be wanting Mrs Shostakovich, two days a week. As a cleaning lady she could be highly recommended, and she was familiar with the house. Mrs Shostakovich, married to a Polish ex-serviceman of that name, turned out to be a genial rather bossy Irish-woman who saw through us in the first seconds of our meeting. We were not serious householders. She could start on Monday, she told us, implying not unkindly that by the time she had finished that day we would know what was what so far as our own domestic duties were concerned. We behaved in a craven fashion. We thanked Mrs Shostakovich effusively, and then told my colleague that we would be making our own arrangements. We had not come through thirty-three years of home life together to be bullied by a cleaning lady who would regard our house as her own property.

Our own arrangements were easily made, and we heaved a sigh of deep relief at having escaped the Irish dominatrix. Spick and span at the time of our arrival in August 1989, Number 30 Charlbury Road soon found itself joining the seedy but, as I privately hoped, not undistinguished club of our former residences. All the miscellaneous rubbish arrived, and the books, and the armchairs grey in our service, impregnated with the dust of four decades. Perhaps the house welcomed them with a secret relief. There were little flecks and blobs of blutack on the walls, relics of posters and drawings stuck on by my colleague's little boy, and Mrs Shostakovich had spared these. I started to get some of them off as I hung our own pictures but Iris soon stopped me. They belonged to the house, as our own things would soon do.

Number 30 has not much in the front garden beyond two tall trees which almost wholly conceal the front of the house. Iris fell in love with these when she saw them. In 1925, when the house was built, they must have been intended as rather unusual miniature ornamentals. Nobody seems to have known then that this new import, *Metasequoia glyptostroboides*, the Chinese Dawn Redwood, was a serious conifer that would grow to a hundred feet, even though not aspiring to quite the height and girth of its majestic cousin, the true sequoia. Now when the wind blows lithe reddish twigs and bigger branches rain down incessantly, creating a sort of shadowy Tannenburg below which a Russian caller, come to ask Iris questions for a thesis on her novels, eyed with some respect. '*Diky sad,*' she murmured. 'A wild garden.' I think she began to look instinctively, as a good Russian would, for forest mushrooms poking their heads through the mat of brown needles.

The back garden is also full of trees, including three gnarled and ancient Japanese prunus which in summer form a deep bower of foliage, amethystine in spring with white blossoms like English wind-flowers, turning in summer and autumn to a dusky red. Beneath them in May shoots up a wilderness of bluebells and cowparsley – Queen Anne's Lace – so that the small garden seems to recede into the endless enchanted wood of *A Midsummer Night's Dream*. When we arrived I put a heavy teak garden-chair out for Iris to sit at, and for the first time she started on fine days to write outdoors. I feel now it was a sign that things were beginning to slow down; and when I looked at her through the window and saw her sitting tranquilly, with the pen idle in her hand, I felt a slight qualm. It was scarcely to be called a premonition, but Iris was enjoying the garden, as she still does, in a way that she never seemed to do at Steeple Aston, where it would not be glanced at while work was in progress. On the wall at the back is a fine fig-tree, with leaves large enough to make biblical loincloths. The college gardener told me that one must never feed a fig-tree, otherwise it will produce a mass of foliage but no fruit. I had given it bonemeal conscientiously, until it was too dark in summer to see out of the windows: our drawing-room concealed its dust and dirt and became a shadowy bower of deepest green. After the gardener's wise words I hastily stopped the bonemeal treatment and the next year figs abounded. Blackbirds as tame as cats reposed in a gorged state among them, taking an occasional languid peck. They left plenty for us. The leaves remained huge too, the drawing-room as umbrageous as ever.

At the foot of the fig-tree I put the bronze bust of Iris, done in 1963 by Tolkien's daughter-in-law. The birds did not respect it, but Iris's serene features remained unperturbed. Faith Tolkien also did an excellent head of her father-in-law, looking like the Lord of the Rings himself, which broods benevolently on a plinth in the Oxford English Faculty Library.

8

In 1994 we were invited by the University of the Negev in Israel, to take part in an international gathering whose purpose was to celebrate, I think, the University's coming of age. I was to read a paper on 'Aspects of the Novel' or 'The Novel Today', one of those comfortably vague prospectuses which make few demands on either speaker or audience. Iris asked not to give a paper, but said she would rather take part in a discussion in which she would answer questions on her novels or philosophical writings. She had often done this before, and it was always a success, because while never holding the floor she had the knack of taking seriously anything that was put forward by a questioner, and investigating its potential in a friendly and sympathetic way which was both flattering and rewarding for the audience.

This time it all went wrong. The chairman was sympathetic, but soon baffled and made uncomfortable by Iris's inability to bring out the words she seemed to want. Her delivery had always been slow and thoughtful and a little hesitant, and at first I was not perturbed, sure that she would recover in a few minutes as she got the feel of the gathering. It was hard to say how conscious she was of her own difficulty, but the effect soon became paralysing, for the listener as well as for herself. The audience was polite, but the liveliness and curiosity in their faces was gone: they began to look concerned and embarrassed. Israelis are straightforward in their reactions. Several people simply got up and left the conference room.

I thought she would tell me afterwards how awful it had been, and that for some reason she simply hadn't felt up to it, but that did not happen. She seemed unaware and to shrug the incident off, together with my cautious solicitude: I tried to avoid giving any impression that a fiasco had taken place. The chairman and one or two others came up to her afterwards and she talked to them and laughed in her natural way. One asked about her last novel, *The Green Knight*, and produced a copy for her to sign. It was at that moment I remembered being surprised at her telling me, several months before, that she was in trouble over her current novel, the one that appeared the following year as *Jackson's Dilemma*. Often before, if I asked her, or sometimes if I didn't, she would complain she was stuck, she couldn't get on with the current novel, and in any case that it was no good at all. I used to make reassuring noises, knowing this would pass, and that in a few days she would suddenly seize pencil and paper while we sat eating or drinking at the kitchen table and write something down. I would say 'Better?' and she would reply 'I think so.'

But this time it was quite different. 'It's this man Jackson,' she had said to me one day with a sort of worried detachment. 'I can't make out who he is, or what he's doing.' I was interested, because she hardly ever spoke of the people in a novel she was writing. 'Perhaps he'll turn out to be a woman,' I said. Iris was always indulgent to a joke from me, even a feeble one, but now she looked serious, even solemn, and puzzled. 'I don't think he's been born yet,' she said.

Inside marriage one ceases to be observant because observation has become so automatic, its object at once absorbing and taken for granted. The mysteriousness of Iris's remark seemed to me at the time quite normal. 'Don't worry – I expect he'll be born any day now,' I said absently, but she continued to look worried and upset. 'I shan't do it, and shall never do another,' she said, still in that quiet detached tone. She had often said such things before, though not quite like that. I had known before the mood would pass; and this one, though much odder, would too – I could not imagine anything else. But suddenly, standing blinking in the dry dusty sunlight of the Negev, I realised for the first time that something might be seriously wrong.

I 'realised' it, but without any feeling of alarm, because I was somehow sure that everything would carry on just as usual. In a sense I was right. When the Alzheimer patient loses touch with time, time seems to lose both its prospective and its retrospective significance. For the partner, that is. Knowing that Iris would always be the same, I felt that the tiny disturbing eccentricity I had noticed then, when we talked about 'Jackson', must always have been present, and would go on undisturbed into the future. Nothing that Iris could do, and nothing that could happen to her, could possibly make her any different. As we stood in the Negev sunshine the matter simply drifted out of my mind. The eeriness of Alzheimer's beginnings is also its reassurance. Part of me knew that I ought to be seriously worried about the future; part knew that neither future nor past was of any consequence. The shortest possible view, even shorter than the kind the Reverend Sydney Smith recommended . . .

None the less the disquiet returned in full force when the extremely nice Israeli novelist Amos Oz came up to speak to me next day. He said nothing about Iris, but from the way he looked at me I was suddenly aware that he, so to speak, knew all. Perhaps as a fellow novelist, perhaps just because he was an extremely shrewd, observant and knowledgeable man. He said casually that he lived in the Negev desert not far away, and would love us to come and stay with him. Any time, for as long as you want, it would be no bother. I could not make out whether this was pure kindness on his part, whether he meant it, whether he was lonely, whether he had taken a fancy to Iris, or wanted to study a fellow-novelist who had gone off the beam, or was going off it. Oz's handsome and youthful face, which reminded me a little of Lawrence of Arabia, seemed none the less far too natural and too much on its own to be concerned with any of these motives. Or so it seemed. And I think it was equally natural for him to say, and to want, what he suggested. I have sometimes wished that we could have gone, but it seems much too late now to take someone up, even this seraphic man, on such an offer. I have always enjoyed his novels. He might – looking back – have been a kind of angel of the desert, like the one who appeared to Jacob.

That was in the spring of 1994. Jerusalem, 'city of light, of copper and of gold', was looking marvellously beautiful. In the autumn, by coincidence, we received another exotic invitation, as if such things had begun to arrive – for one reason or another it was years since we had been abroad in this way – at a time when Iris's ability to respond to them, and to do a good job, had begun to falter. It was to Bangkok, to take part in the ceremony of awards at the South-East Asian Writers' Conference. All went well. Possibly the writers from Thailand, Singapore, Malaya and the Philippines were not sufficiently in fine tune with their European colleagues to detect when a novelist like Iris, who happened to be the only writer from the West present, was in trouble with what had begun to amount to speaker's, as well as writer's, block.

Writers are not usually behindhand in talking about themselves, their projects and methods of work, and Iris's backwardness in this respect may have seemed at this voluble oriental gathering a becoming sort of modesty. Or perhaps they were too polite to notice. Even when the Crown Prince awarded the prizes, and we had each to make a little speech, Iris acquitted herself well. I had rehearsed her, and written out a suggested version of what she should say, in block capitals. Each writer who attended the ceremony was required, on reaching the podium, to present a sample of his or her work to the Crown Prince.

Iris duly presented a Penguin *Under the Net*. This the Prince accepted and passed behind him without looking round. A courtier received it at the crouch, at once passing it to another official behind him, as in a game of rugby football. The book eventually reached the end of the scrum and disappeared through a doorway. I wondered what happened to the books at the end of the day: whether they were preserved in the royal library or quietly incinerated in some remote compound.

I was the more reassured during this visit because an extremely pleasant Englishman who worked on the *South China Times* sought us out whenever his duties permitted, and himself seemed to find Iris's company and conversation reassuring. He told us he often felt extremely lonely and depressed out there. That didn't seem surprising. We ourselves felt weighed down by a sort of Far Eastern melancholy, not wholly attributable to the monsoon weather, for the monotonous rain and soft overpowering warmth was something to be enjoyed, at least for a time. The broad river spilled over the hotel frontage like tea brimming over a saucer, and we used to stand watching it, fascinated by the huge branches wreathed in green creepers that floated past at high speed, level with our eyes. They did nothing to intimidate the drivers of the slender craft that buzzed about the river, propelled by a sort of eggwhisk at the end of a powerful engine that roared and echoed down the *klongs* like an express train. It was a special relief to stand outside in the warm rain because the hotel rooms, heavily air-conditioned, felt icy. Our suite, furnished in ornate colonial style, advertised itself as the favourite stopping-place of Somerset Maugham on his Far Eastern trips. His chilly presence certainly seemed to pervade it.

Jackson had been finished at last, and named *Jackson's Dilemma*. Iris was gloomy about it, but so she was about any novel she had done with, and I did not feel unduly perturbed. For the first time I took to enquiring about her ideas for a next novel. She had ideas she said, but they wouldn't come together. She was trying to catch something by its tail, and it always eluded her. She sounded resigned. Hoping against hope now I worried and importuned her every day. Any luck? Is anything happening? You must go on trying. If I went on too long she would start crying, and then I stopped quickly and tried to console her. After the Far Eastern trip the sardonic face of Somerset Maugham, smiling from signed photos all round the hotel room, still haunted me at moments when I was telling Iris that all writers at some time suffered from writer's block. 'I never had writer's block,' he seemed to be saying, with an air of contempt.

Nor did Iris have it. That soon became clear. Alzheimer's is in fact like an insidious fog, barely noticeable until everything around has disappeared. After that it is no longer possible to believe that a world outside fog exists. First we saw our own friendly harassed GP, who asked Iris who the Prime Minister was. She had no idea but said to him with a smile that it surely didn't matter. He arranged an appointment at the big hospital with a specialist in geriatrics. Brain scans followed; and after an article appeared about this famous novelist's current difficulties the Cambridge Research Unit of the Medical Council took a special interest, giving her a number of exhaustive tests in memory and language which she underwent politely, seeming both to humour the researchers and to enjoy working with them. *Jackson's Dilemma* came out and got exceptionally good reviews. I read these reviews to Iris, a thing I had never done before because she had never before wanted to listen. Now she listened politely but without understanding.

The irony did not bother her or even occur to her. Nor did I tell her that there had also been a number of letters about the reviews, pointing out small errors and inconsistencies in the narrative of *Jackson's Dilemma*. It was clear that these points were mostly made by fans, fondly indicating that the writer they admired so much could sometimes nod. Meanwhile I was anxiously canvassing medical opinion about the possibility of ameliorative drugs. An old friend and fan, a Swedish expert on autism, sent some pills to try, a mild stimulant of the intellectual processes. The new experimental drugs were not recommended, and no doubt wisely, for they have since been shown to be all too temporary in their effect, and apt, during a brief period of possible effectiveness, to confuse and even horrify the recipient. The friendly fog suddenly disperses, revealing a precipice before the feet.

When writing about the onset of Alzheimer's it is difficult to remember a sequence of events; what happened when, in what order. The condition seems to get into the narrative, producing repetition and preoccupied query, miming its own state. I remarked on this to Peter Conradi, Iris's future biographer, who had already become a pillar of close friendship, support and encouragement. He and his friend and partner Jim O'Neill were longstanding friends of Iris's, who had in former times often visited them in Clapham. He is a passionate admirer of her books and knows them inside out. Even more important, he loves her and the atmosphere in which she lives and moves. He knows her thought; and he responds to her own knowledge with deep feeling. The same goes for Jim, whose sense of Iris's being gives her a unique kind of comfort. He too is widely read in her novels, and a shrewd and practical critic.

Iris loved seeing their blue-eyed sheepdog Cloudy, and she loved talking to this extraordinarily dedicated and relaxing couple about books and philosophy and Buddhism. Both somehow fit a routine of meditation, retreats, hospitality to visiting dignitaries from Tibet or Bhutan, into their own working lives: Jim a psychotherapist, Peter a professor of literature. In now distant days Iris used to return to Steeple Aston or Hartley Road full of her visit to them, and of what they had told her about their Welsh cottage, a converted schoolhouse. They told her of the pool they had built in the field beneath it, the kingfishers and otters who came to visit there.

They were always pressing us to come and stay. When we managed it at last Iris already needed all the support this great pair could give her. *Jackson* came out in 1995: Iris's condition has deteriorated steadily over the past eighteen months. Like someone who knows he cannot for much longer avoid going out into the cold I still shrink from the need for professional care – helpers, the friendly callers of Age Concern, even the efforts of kind friends. All that is to come, but let us postpone it while we can: Iris becomes troubled as well as embarrassed if she feels a visit is to keep her company, or to look after her if I have to be absent. In fact I am never absent, so helpers are not now needed. We are lucky to be able to go on living in the state to which we have always been accustomed; Iris can still go out to lunch alone with such an old friend as Philippa Foot.

And Peter and Jim make all this still easier. They do not bother about the dirt in the carpet or the stains on the glasses, although their own home is kept like a new pin and so is the Welsh cottage. They pick us up as often as it can be done, and carry us off there.

> When life fails
> What's the good of going to Wales?

We proclaim Auden's lines joyously together sometimes, sitting in the back of the car. It's a joke, for we know better. So it seems does Cloudy, who sleeps during the journey with her head in Iris's lap, but who opens her muzzle to smile, while her blue eyes shine with anticipation.

PART II

NOW

1997

Didn't Margaret Thatcher, at mention of whose name Cloudy always starts barking, use to say there was no such thing as 'society'? She didn't put it in inverted commas of course: she knew what she meant. But her point wouldn't have been so obviously untrue if she had said there is no such thing as the 'people', a word that today only achieves some sort of meaning if placed, whether accidentally or deliberately, in a given context. It made sense afterwards to say that Diana Princess of Wales was 'the people's princess', because when she died everybody grieved, publicly and together. But 'the people' are a fictitious body, invoked by politicians in the interest of democratic emotionalism, whereas 'society' is still a neutrally descriptive term, making sense in any context. The only way 'the people' can be contextualised is as 'ordinary people', another purely emotive phrase which has just been used by the Archbishop of Canterbury in his New Year's speech on TV. Every 'ordinary' person is in fact extraordinary, often grotesquely so, and in every sort of way.

Pondered such matters while making Iris her drink, after the Archbishop's speech. Important to make a routine of this. Around twelve o'clock or a little before. The drink itself slightly dishonest: a little drop of white wine, a dash of angostura bitters, orangeade, a good deal of water. Iris likes it, and it has a soothing effect, making her sit watching TV for longer periods. Otherwise she is apt to get up and stand with her back to the TV, fiddling incessantly with her small *objets trouvés* – twigs and pebbles, bits of dirt, scraps of silver foil, even dead worms rescued from the pavement

on our short walks. She also puts water – sometimes her
drink – on the potted plants by the window, which are now
wilting under the treatment. But she never does this with a
real drink, an alcoholic one. Sensible girl, her old fondness
for bars still stands her in good stead.

20 February 1997

Teletubbies. They are part of the morning ritual, as I try
to make it. I have to insist a bit, as Alzheimer's now
seems to have grown inimical to routines. Perhaps we
all know by instinct that an adopted routine preserves
sanity?

Just after ten, as part of the BBC 2 children's programme,
the Teletubbies come on. One of the few things we can
really watch together, in the same spirit. 'There are the
rabbits!' I say quite excitedly. One of the charms of this
extraordinary programme is the virtual reality landscape
supplied. An area of sunlit grass – natural – dotted with
artificial flowers beside which the real rabbits hop about.
The sky looks authentic as well, just the right sort of
blue with small white clouds. The Teletubbies have their
underground house, neatly roofed with grass. A periscope
sticks out of it. A real baby's face appears in the sky, at
which I make a face myself, but Iris always returns its
beaming smile.

The creatures emerge, four of them, in different coloured
playsuits. How are they animated, what is inside their
plump cloth bodies? The way they trot about and smile
is almost obscenely natural, as are their grown-up male
voices. Twiggy or something, Winky, Poo . . . They trot
about, not doing anything much, but while they are there
Iris looks happy, even concentrated.

This form of childishness is itself like virtual reality. We
used to have a more genuine spontaneous kind. It began,
just before we were married, with a postcard of a very
clueless-looking kitten putting its nose wonderingly round

a door. Appropriately labelled 'Ginger'. Iris sent it to me, making a balloon on the front and writing in it 'Just coming'. She became Ginger, and then Gunga.

'Haunted by Gungas', I teased her the other day, will be the title of the first section of my autobiography. She laughs and is pleased to be talked to that way, but I don't think she recognises the word any more.

Something about the Teletubbies reminds me of going to see the bluebells in Wytham Wood. Since living in Oxford and finding out about this amenity we have been to see them every year. Coming on them if the sun is shining has something of the beautiful dubiousness of Teletubby land. Can they be real? Do they really exist? They live in a thick and distant part of the wood, under dark conifers which stretch away downhill, and as they recede into darkness they light up into their most intense colour. They vanish as if into a strange land where an endless dark blue lake begins. Close at hand they look much more ordinary. Greyish, purplish.

We stand and look at them. For the first time last May Iris seemed not to take them in at all.

On the way there are real trees. Two gigantic syca-mores, overpowering as a cathedral. But Iris has now a great fear of trees and I hurry her past them. I thought: this had better be the last time we go. And that was last year.

As we got in the car I said to her reassuringly, 'Soon be back in Teletubby land.' But I don't think she remembered what Teletubbies were. I would quite like to be able to forget them myself.

The sense of someone's mind. Only now an awareness of it; other minds are usually taken for granted. I wonder sometimes if Iris is secretly thinking: How can I escape? What am I to do? Has nothing replaced the play of her mind when she was writing, cogitating, living in her mind? I find myself devoutly hoping not.

1 March 1997

When Iris's mother was taken to the mental hospital we did not tell her where she was going. I had doped her but the drive seemed interminable. As the nurse took her away she looked back at us with a lost unreproachful look.

The same look on Iris's face when I manage to leave her for an hour with a friend.

Like school. Being left there. Probably such moments would not be so painful now if they hadn't started all those years ago at school, inside one's own ego.

I knew where I was going when I was taken to school. But being left there felt the same as the look on Iris's face, and her mother's. In fact we retrieved her mother after she had been a few weeks in the asylum. Back again later. So it was like school.

Associations of that look. Seeing it I remember the first little boy I met at the school, after being left there. He was wizened, like a little old man, with a pale leprous skin. I shrank from him, all the more because he was extremely friendly. Confidential. He said: 'Shall I tell you what my father told me? My father said it was the most important thing there was. He said: "There is no difference at all between men and women. *Absolutely none at all.*"'

I regarded the little boy with horror and fear. It all seemed part of this nightmarish new world of school. At the time it seemed the worst thing I had ever heard, or was ever likely to hear.

Long piece in *London Review* on Iris's essay collection *Existentialists and Mystics*. The critic made a great thing of the contrast between Iris's views on the novel, the importance in it of free and independent individuals, character creations etc., and her own practices in writing fiction, which instead of giving her characters 'a free and realised life make them as unfree as pampered convicts'. This has always interested me too. In one way it is an obviously true point: in a more important sense it is irrelevant. For Iris makes a free world in her novels, which carries total conviction because it is like no other, and like no one else's. That is what matters, and that is why this world has such mesmeric appeal for all sorts of different people.

It is bound to be a tautology to talk about 'freedom' in a novel, in which only the author is free to do as he likes. Pushkin, and Tolstoy following him, liked to emphasise that their characters 'took charge', and that they were surprised by what they did, and by what happened to them. Once again there is a kind of truth in that, but it won't really do. It is a cliché which novelists invent or repeat. What matters is whether the world created is both convincing and wholly *sui generis*, and here of course Pushkin and Tolstoy pass with top marks. So does Iris in her own way.

I remember that time, years ago, when I was working on a study of Tolstoy, and we used endlessly to discuss the sort of perplexing questions that arise in the case of great novelists. I used to make the point that Tolstoy's greatest and least visible strength, or 'freedom', was the cunning way he blended many different novel tactics when creating a character. At one moment they behave, as if deliberately, like 'people in a novel'; at the next they are suddenly like people we know, as inconsequential as people in life. They seem entirely themselves, as created characters, but the next moment they are behaving just as we might do, so that one can feel in a rather eerie and disquieting way, 'How does this writer know what I am like?'

Tolstoy's people are both completely particular and completely general. At this point in my argument (such as it was) Iris used to look thoughtful. As a philosopher she wanted to get things more clear than that; and I used to think that perhaps there was a real incompatibility between the philosophic mind and the simple undifferentiated muddle in which free characters and creation must move. Tolstoy, I felt, was not clear-headed at all; he merely picked up one thing and dropped another. Plato wouldn't have cared for that, or for Tolstoy, or for the novel generally?

Your characters, I used to tell her, have contingent aspects because you know that there are so many contingent things in life, and therefore the novel must have them too. But contingency in some novels is not like that; it is glorious in itself and has no other purpose than to be itself. It's always funny, like the dog in *Two Gentlemen of Verona*.

'Is there a dog in *Two Gentlemen of Verona*?'

'I think so. I hope so, but I may have got the play wrong. Anyway you see what I mean?'

Iris always, and as if indulgently, did see what I meant, though it didn't necessarily mean anything to her. We loved those conversations, usually over food or wine. Only for a few moments or minutes did they bother to last, with the gramophone playing in the background. It all seemed funny too. But I was surprised how much of what we touched on, all clarified and sharpened, is there in the essays collected in *Existentialists and Mystics*, now superbly edited by Peter Conradi. Peter pointed out a lot of things to me, which he said were like things in *The Characters of Love* and *Tolstoy and the Novel*. It hadn't struck me before, because those words between us, now vanished, just seem part of us both, although how that can be when our minds were so different – hers clear, mine muddled – remains a mystery.

We can still talk as we did then, but it doesn't make sense any more, on either side. I can't reply in the way I used to do then but only in the way she speaks to me now. I reply with the jokes or nonsense that still makes her laugh. So we are still part of each other.

30 March 1997

The horrid wish, almost a compulsion at some moments, to show the other how bad things are. Force her to share the knowledge, relieve what seems my isolation.

I make a savage comment today about the grimness of

our outlook. Iris looks relieved and intelligent. She says: 'But I love you.'

Iris surprised me when the radio was on and we were having lunch – toast, cheese, beetroot and lettuce salad – by asking, 'Why does he keep saying "education?"' She sounded anxious. Anxiety and agitation are so much a part of her speech now, like the unending query, 'When are we going?' But lunch and supper are usually quite peaceful times. Trying to make everything as much a reassuring routine as possible. But now something on the radio has very much unreassured her. Government ministers say 'education' so often. It ought to be a soothing word, even if a comparatively meaningless one.

It occurs to me that Iris is worried that it might mean something different now, which she has failed to grasp. In a sense of course that is true. It refers to skills with computers and such, which we know nothing about. But I think it is the frequency of the word in political speech that bothers her. It becomes almost like her own queries.

I try to say something about the importance of education, and everyone getting enough of it. Iris still looks anxious. 'Do they read books?' I wonder whether education now chiefly means reading books, as it did when she was at school and college. Her coherence perturbs me. Normally now sentences trail off, become deadlocked – start again in another place. Only anxiety queries complete themselves, and this seems to be one. I remember the kindly specialist at the hospital advising that another word suggested from outside can as it were clear the circuit, temporarily allay the language anxiety. 'It's a question of learning, I suppose. As we used to.' Her face does clear a little. Learning is not a word one hears much now, and certainly not 'book learning'. 'Education' has taken over. But learning is, or used to be, the more specific term.

When land is sold and money spent,
Then learning is most excellent.

The old rhyming proverb returns to my head – is it borne on the same mysterious circuitry that has failed in Iris's case?

'When are we going?'
  'I'll tell you when we go.'
  Iris always responds to a jokey tone. But it is sometimes hard to maintain. Violent irritation possesses me and I shout out before I can stop myself, 'Don't keep asking me when we are going!' Only a short time ago, as it seems, this would have registered as a 'tantrum', and the circuit would have visibly adjusted itself and responded with that mixture of amusement and forbearance, complete understanding, which survived as an automatic but infinitely welcome response. One notices that a lot of women respond to snappish husbands in public, and no doubt in private too, with what Milton, describing Eve, tellingly refers to as 'sweet austere composure'. The opposite of understanding. Eve was the first to rail herself off in sex disapproval.

  Iris never did that. She never got cross herself, and never does now: but when I did so in the past she would soothe me by a particular sort of reassurance, implying that I was most lovable and close to her when I was being angry, silly, or tiresome.

  Now her face just crumples into tears. I hasten to comfort her and she always responds to comfort. We kiss and embrace now much more than we used to.

Often something that Iris says now, or a word she repeats, starts me off too on some more or less dotty train of association. I remember her mother with early Alzheimer's – not diagnosed or labelled then – used to repeat a word in a touching way, as if it were a talisman or portent. If somebody said 'journey' or 'Baron's Court', where she lived, she would go on repeating it at intervals, and the same if the word happened to be 'shandy' or 'ham and cheese'. Once the mind attends to this involuntary habit it becomes a conscious one. I become aware that the word 'learning' has been popping up at intervals in my mind, and so play with it idly.

Significant, perhaps, that it is in some way a competitive word. A learned man stands out from his fellows: an educated man does not especially do so. Hence education is a more OK word, something we can all have if the government goes about it the right way. It used to be normal to try to shine, to have read some book or books that others had not, to be able to quote. Lord Birkenhead or someone like that proclaimed in the 30s – was it in Oxford? – that there were still 'plenty of glittering prizes for the sharp sword'. The comment was adapted, ironically, by Auden in his poem 'Oxford', so attitudes to that sort of thing must already have been changing. If prizes are given now they must be given to all. In theory at least.

It's a relief in a way that things have changed. The atmosphere of 'learning' is always tiresome, can be oppressive. Even my dear Barbara Pym, whose novels I am so fond of, must have been awful when she was young, and all her set too, because they were always trying to dazzle with clever remarks, or by neatly capping quotations. Innocent enough, and rather charming in her early novels, but it must have been fatiguing in life. Socially speaking, people thought they had to *try* in those days.

Iris is a great contrast with all that. When young she was already formidably learned, but I'm sure it never showed. Perhaps considered unsuitable for serious women to show it? Male dons certainly vied with each other, and I remember disliking it while trying to keep up with it. Nowadays Common Room conversation is blessedly untaxing. But does 'learning' require some sort of overt display, like a bird's feathers, to show how important it still is, or should be? It would have been thought odd if Prime Minister Blair had proclaimed his new government's policy to have been 'Learning, learning, learning', instead of 'Education, education, education'. In spite of its competitive nature learning is ideally an end in itself, and no government particularly wants to encourage that, or to pay for it either.

15 April 1997

Moving from stage to stage. How many are there? How many will there be? I used to dread her moment of waking, because the situation seemed to strike her then in full force, at least for a minute or two. Reassuring noises, so far as possible, and then she would go back to sleep, and I would sit beside her reading or typing. The sound of it seemed to help as reassurance. Iris's greed for sleep had something desperate about it, and yet she slept, and still sleeps, so easily and so long in the morning that it was a great mutual comfort. Lying beside me she is like an athlete who has passed on the torch to a back-up member of the relay. I couldn't do what she had done, but I was doing something.

Not a good metaphor though. It would be truer to say that I myself was reassured by her unawareness of anything that I might be doing on my own. It would have been unbearable if she had shown her old friendly interest. Where work was concerned we had always left each other alone, so that being cut off now about such things was positively welcome. The simpler and more primitive our needs and emotions now, like those of babies to mothers, the more absolute they feel. The exasperation of being followed about the house now by Iris is as strong and genuine as is my absolute need for it. Were she to avoid me, or 'tactfully' leave me alone, I would pursue her as anxiously, if not quite so obsessively, as she now pursues me. I don't feel any particular pleasure or emotion when her whole face lights up at the sight of me, when I come back to the car after ten minutes shopping. But

I remember it if I wake up in the night, and then reach out to her. The 'lion face' of Alzheimer's used to be transformed in that way when her mother saw daughter Iris. Not that Iris's face has grown as expressionless as her mother's used to be. Sitting waiting for me in the car she looks quite alert and amiable, and passing strangers smile at her.

But thank goodness the stage of that old despair on waking seems to be over. Now she makes a soft chuckling sound and looks at me like the Teletubby baby in the blue sky on TV. No anxious queries. We exchange a few of the old nonsense words before she goes to sleep again. As the condition gets worse it also gets better. It seems to compensate each new impoverishment. Should be more thankful for that.

The agony of travel nowadays. Iris has always loved travelling, and craves it now more compulsively than ever. I have always detested the business of leaving home, and was so thankful in the old days to drive her to the station and wave her goodbye. Now I have a fever of travel angst – taxis, tickets, train-times. Iris never worried about all that. She used to arrive at the station like a Russian peasant and wait for the first train to arrive.

The worst of both worlds. Although Iris is compulsively eager to be 'going' – somewhere, anywhere – she is in as much of a flap in her own way as I am. At the station she keeps repeating, 'Why didn't you tell me we were going?' I had told her many many times. Now I tell her again sharply, and with her own degree of querulous repetition. People look round at us. I am fumbling in my wallet, checking the tickets. They are hard to separate, and after shuffling them wildly again and again I can still find only one return ticket. The whole system is absurd; why must they give us four separate tickets when two would do? It's definitely not there. I rush to the ticket office, where a queue is made to unwind in serpentine fashion between rope barriers. My ticket man has drawn his little curtain and gone off. The customer at the other guichet seemed to want a round the world ticket, and to be in no hurry about getting it. He and the ticket clerk canvass the possibilities in leisurely fashion. Iris clutches me anxiously, urging us to run to a train which has just come in, the wrong train I hope. At last the ticket man is free. I produce the receipt and the delinquent tickets. No, he can do nothing – it wasn't his sale. I turn away in despair. Why can't we just go home?

Iris has not understood the problem and keeps urging me towards the wrong train. At that moment a man comes up to us and holds out a ticket. It is the original ticket man himself, strangely naked and unrecognisable now he's not behind the counter. He doesn't explain what happened but gives me a small collusive smile and walks rapidly back to his place of work.

On the train I keep counting the tickets. The elderly couple opposite look sympathetically at Iris. I am clearly the one who's become a problem.

Utterly exhausted and drenched in sweat. Vague heart sensations too. And the whole thing so trivial. Alzheimer's obviously has me in its grip, and the ticket man too. As well as Iris, and probably everyone else.

Does the carer involuntarily mimic the Alzheimer condition? I'm sure I do.

Sitting exhaustedly in the train I suddenly recall a droll moment at the time when Iris seemed more or less to have decided to marry me. She was going down to her old school – to give the prizes or something – and suggested I should come along. After her business there was over she wanted to call on the retired headmistress, a famous old white-haired lady, who lived in a flat on the school premises. In her bleak way she had been very kind, regarding schoolgirl Iris as the jewel in her crown. I was introduced, and after a few minutes managed to slip away, leaving the pair of them together. When Iris came out she was looking much amused. 'Do you want to know what BMB thought about you?' she asked. I expressed a natural curiosity. 'Well,' said Iris, 'she just said: "He doesn't look very strong."'

I didn't bother about being strong in those days. Now I have to try, but I'm sure the attempt wouldn't deceive BMB.

Kind friends up our street are giving a Sunday morning drinks party. I used to enjoy the quiet of Sunday mornings, the Sunday paper, leisurely breakfast with Iris working upstairs, absence of morning anxiety about what I had to do that day. In those days I should have made some excuse, Iris acquiescing. She wouldn't have minded going, but knew I wouldn't want to. Now it offers a welcome distraction. I say nothing about it until 11. If I did she would panic, demand why I hadn't told her sooner. She does not distinguish now between what she wants to do and what is happening.

'Are we going to London?'

'No, just up the street. You'll know them when we get there. They're very nice. You'll like it.'

I know this is true, but it produces a 'trouser grimace' as I now call it in my mind. Every evening we have the battle of the trousers. She wants to go to bed in them, and everything else she is wearing too. My resistance to this is half-hearted, compared with the determination she shows on the issue. Sometimes I win, more or less dragging them off. Iris gives up the struggle, but produces a frightful grimace, an expression wholly new and different from anything her face ever did in the past. It always unnerves me, and is becoming more frequent in other situations.

Not that I care about her trousers. Our habits have never been exactly hygienic; and yet distinguishing day from night now seems vital to our saving routines. Twice in the day, at ten in the morning and five in the evening, panic and emptiness descend, not because there is something we have to do but because there isn't. Routine has no suggestions to make. All I can do then is to promise the next thing soon. A drink. Lunch, or supper.

Iris's fear of other people if I'm not there is so piteous that I cannot bring myself to arrange for carers to 'keep her company', or to take her to the age therapy unit. All that will have to come. Meanwhile I am ruthless about getting her ready for the party, confident that she will enjoy it when she gets there, as they used to tell us in childhood.

She does. It is a nice party. I marvel, as I have often done before, at the way in which guests enjoy being guests. Standing opposite someone and keeping going, holding eye contact in the same practised precarious way that one holds glass and canapé. Like a naval battle in Nelson's times: ship to ship, yardarm to yardarm. Sometimes another ship looms up through the noise of battle. Should I switch targets, or redouble broadsides against the present opponent? There is something remorseless about the concentration required. No one wants to be drifting aimlessly through the battle, guns silent, disengaged . . .

The extraordinary thing is that Iris can, as it were, serve her guns and return fire just like everybody else. I shouldn't have brought her if I hadn't known it would be so. Her face becomes animated – no trace of trouser grimace; she is playing her part just like the rest of us. Mustn't this be good therapy? I should like to think so, but exercise in that sense would imply improvement, recovery. This happy distraction can only be for the moment. I close cautiously on the stern (still automatically Nelsonian) of the guest who is talking to Iris. He is giving a tremendous impression of being good at his work, and happy at it. Half listening, while at the same time engaging my own opponent closely, I overhear a lively account of the way things are done in an Insurance Adjustment office. Smiling Iris listens closely – her attention must be flattering. Then I hear her say: 'What do you do?' From the face opposite her it is evident that the question has been repeated several times in the last few minutes. Undiscouraged he begins all over again.

Some people might actually find it more restful at a party to talk to someone more or less with Iris's condition. I think I should myself. Apart from making you feel you are performing a service to the community it is also in the short run less demanding and taxing than the conventional art of party intercourse.

Coming up to me the hostess says: 'Isn't Iris wonderful?' She sounds surprised, perhaps thankful that there is no squeaking or gibbering going on. I am conscious of a base sense of annoyance, even exasperation. People who see Iris on such occasions assume there must be nothing much to worry about. Suppose I were to say to our hostess, 'You should see how things are at home.' Thank goodness one cannot or does not say things like that at parties.

When we get home I try to keep Iris interested in the party, saying how much people had liked seeing her. In retrospect the party does seem to have been a happy time, I am already looking back on it with nostalgia. But it is not remembered. Iris begins to say anxiously, 'When do we go?' I wonder how many times she asked the insurance man what it was that he did.

10 May 1997

Continually surprised by the way in which the most un-expected people look a little embarrassed if I make some flippant remark about the caring services, the welfare ethic, even 'lone' mothers (previously single mothers). Can it be that nice people don't mock such things, even as a joke? No one needs to be nice about sex any more, or religion. But the modern feeling about social or state 'compassion' is uncannily like the old silence about sex, or the reverence about religious beliefs. It's puritanical too, blasphemy not now recognised as a part of faith, as it was in the older religions.

'Niceness' is always with us, and a good thing too, but it shifts its ground, even though still clinging precariously on to its ambiguities of meaning. Iris's novel *The Nice and the Good* implied these in a masterly way, with as much humour as precision. Does that novel, her others too, none the less demonstrate in some way the inescapability of innocence, perhaps arising from a secure and happy childhood? Iris was both a nice child and a good one, and her parents were the same. None of the three had religion; all were, in the theological sense, naturally Christian souls. Like many philosophers Iris is impatient of wickedness, its commonplaceness, its knowing conceit.

The bad despise the good: confident, and with some justification, that the hapless good may think they 'understand' the bad, but in fact can have no true awareness of them. In the characters of her novels Iris substitutes the desire for power, which fascinates her, for commonplace disgusting wickedness, which she is neither fascinated by nor understands. To understand wickedness you must resemble it, possess some at least of its knowing conceit and its inherent dullness. You must be, as Isaiah Berlin said of Dostoevsky, 'not a very nice man'.

An argument with Iris once about that, or rather about the good man, Alyosha Karamazov. A projection of the author's will, I said, whereas Dostoevsky's Underground Man slides effortlessly and absolutely into existence. Why? Because Dostoevsky was as boringly familiar with his Underground Man as he was with himself, while Alyosha is basically an idea, a good idea of course. Iris objected that great novelists were explorers as well as natural knowers. Wasn't Dostoevsky going to send Alyosha into the pit of hell in a later volume, make him commit all the sins of man? Not real sins I objected, because they wouldn't have been dull enough, nor conceited enough. Not *natural*. They would have been sins in the author's will, not in the book's reality.

I said this, as it made a reasonably smart point, but I knew my position was undermined by Iris's quiet good sense, by her niceness in fact. I was point-scoring, something she never did in her novels, nor in her daily life. At the same time I think one reason we fell in love, and got on so well, is that both of us have always been naive and innocent, at some deep healing level. Finding it in each other, but not saying so, or even knowing so. Iris is good. I'm not good inside, but I can get by on being nice. A wit remarked of Cyril Connolly, from whose features amiability did not exactly shine, that he was 'not so nice as he looked'. Iris is just as nice as she looks; indeed in her case the feeble though necessary little word acquires an almost transcendental meaning, a different and higher meaning than any of its common and more or less ambiguous ones.

Knowingness. Have got it in my head today, instead of 'learning'. Peter Conradi told me that the French word for it is *déniaiserie*.

And that awkward word, which I can hardly believe really exists, reminds me in some Proustian way of a disgustingly knowing boy at school. Haven't thought about him for years, if at all. One Sunday his eye lit up with malicious glee when the lesson was read in school chapel. I couldn't help being curious, and he was delighted to tell me why. It was the story of the woman who anointed Jesus's feet with a precious ointment. 'Jesus was awfully pleased with himself. When they said the ointment should have been sold and the money given to the poor, he said "Bugger that for a lark – I'm the one who matters, not the poor." I'm going to take the piss out of God Clark about that.'

'God' Clark was the chaplain. When I enquired how, as I was meant to, he said he'd do it in the Divinity Essay we had to write at half-term. He did too. But he failed to get a rise out of the chaplain. Himself all too knowing about the ways of boys, the chaplain returned the essay without comment, merely congratulating the crestfallen youth on the fact that it was 'well-written'.

'God' Clark, a saintly looking old fellow with white hair, had a dark-haired young assistant chaplain with saturnine good looks, who was known as 'Jesus' Steed.

Now why should I have remembered that? Having done so, I would once have rushed to tell Iris, sure that the story would amuse her. Now it wouldn't, alas. I can see her face if I told her, with its bothered and confused look.

We can still have jokes, but only very simple ones. Not anecdotes. Least of all anecdotes about 'knowingness'.

Iris once told me she had no 'stream of consciousness'. She did not talk to herself. She did not say to herself (I had said that I did): 'I am doing this – and then I must do that. Sainsburys – the clouds – the trees are looking nice.'

No trivial play with the inner words? Did all at once go into the world of creation, which lived inside her?

They say people with a strong sense of identity become the worst Alzheimer patients. They cannot share with others what they still formulate inside themselves. Does Iris speak, inside herself, of what is happening? How can I know? What is left is the terrible expectancy. 'When?' and 'I want . . .'.

Is she still saying inside herself, like the blind man in Faulkner's novel, 'When are they going to let me out?'

Escape. The word hovers, though she never utters it.

Home is the worst place. As if something should happen here for her, which never does. Anxiety pushing behind at every second. Picking up things, as if to ward it off. Holding them in her hands like words. Wild wish to shout in her ear: 'It's worse for me. *It's much worse!*'

This after the TV breaks down. It is I who miss it more obviously than Iris does, but in its absence she becomes increasingly restless. The recommended sedative seems not to help.

When are they going to let *me* out?

4 June 1997

Nightmare recollection of a day in the hot summer last year, just before or after our swim in the Thames. What provoked it, apart from the heat, and a drink or two I had at lunch (when I normally try not to drink: Iris has her few drops of white wine with orangeade)? I must have been feeling unusually low. Rows like that are unpredictable, blowing up like squalls out of nowhere and subsiding as quickly. Then the sun is out, the water calm: one can even forget it is going to happen again. Quite soon.

The cause though? The reason? There must be one. I remember being struck once, when reading Tolstoy, by his description of anger and emotion, which resembles the one theorised about by William James, the novelist's philosopher brother. According to James, at least as I recall, the anger or fear or pity is itself its own cause. I doubt this means much, but in Tolstoy the notion becomes extra-ordinarily graphic: as when the movement of the wrinkled tiny fingers of Anna's baby are imitated involuntarily by Karenin's own fingers and face. His pity, even love, for this child of another man by his unfaithful wife existed purely in physical terms.

Was it for me some memory of the smell of Iris's mother when she was daft and elderly, nosed now from Iris herself in the muggy heat, which expressed itself not in love and pity but in repulsion and disgust? Smell, as Proust knew, can certainly coincide with pleasure and relaxa-tion, and become identified with those things. Or with their opposites? Iris is not responsive to subtle smells, I have a very acute sense of them. Perhaps that divides us? I like almost all smells that one becomes conscious of, without having to sniff at them, or recoil from them. All our houses have had their different smells, neither good nor bad in the obvious sense but characteristic – that of Hartley Road, ironically enough, was especially memorable and attractive.

To me the smell of Iris's mother's flat, though quite faint, was appalling. I had to nerve myself to enter; but Jack, who for quite a while looked after the old lady, never seemed to notice it, and nor did Iris herself. The ghost of that smell certainly comes now from Iris from time to time: a family odour and a haunting of mortality. But it wasn't that which caused the row I made, although if William James was anything like right, physical causes are too wrapped up in their emotional results to be disentangled.

The trouble was, or seemed to be, my rage over the indoor plants. There are several of these along the drawing-room window-sill – cyclamen, spider-plant, tigerplant as we called a spotty one – to which I had become rather attached. I cared for them and watered them at the right intervals. Unfortunately they had also entered the orbit of Iris's obsession with her small objects, things she has picked up in the street and brought into the house. She began to water them compulsively. I was continually finding her with a jug in her hand, and the window-sill and the floor below it slopping over with stagnant water. I urged her repeatedly not to do it, pointing out – which was certainly true – that the plants, the cyclamen in particular, were beginning to wilt and die under this treatment. She seemed to grasp the point, but I soon found her again with a jug or glass in her hand, pouring her water. Like those sad daughters in Greek mythology, condemned for ever to pour their pitchers into vessels full of holes.

I was not put out at the time: I was fascinated. I took to coming very quietly through the door to try to surprise Iris in the act, and I frequently did. Once when her great friend and fellow-philosopher Philippa Foot came to see her, I found them both leaning thoughtfully over the plants, Iris performing her hopeless destructive ritual, Philippa looking on with her quizzically precise polite attention, as if assessing what moral or ethical problem might be supposed by this task. I was reminded of their colleague

Elizabeth Anscombe, absently bringing up her immense brood of children, and once amusing her audience at some philosophical gathering with a sentence to illustrate some subtle linguistic distinction. 'If you break that plate I shall give you a tin one.'

Whether or not the fate of the plants, or the ghost of an odour, had anything to do with it, that day I went suddenly berserk. Astonishing how rage produces another person, who repels one, from whom one turns away in incredulous disgust, at the very moment one has become him and is speaking with his voice. The rage was instant and total, seeming to come out of nowhere. 'I told you not to! *I told you not to!*' In those moments of savagery neither of us has the slightest idea to what I am referring. But the person who is speaking soon becomes more coherent. Cold too, and deadly. 'You're mad. You're dotty. You don't know anything, remember anything, care about anything.' This accompanied by furious aggressive gestures. Iris trembling violently. 'Well—' she says, that banal prelude to an apparently reasoned comment. Often heard in that tone on BBC discussions, usually followed by some disingenuous patter that does not answer the question. Iris's 'Well' relapses into something about 'when he comes' and 'Must for other person do it now.' 'Dropping good to borrow when . . .' I find myself looking in a mirror at the man who has been speaking. A horrid face, plum colour.

While I go on acting horrible things, as if kicking a child or a lamb, I suddenly think of the Bursar of St Catherine's College, a charming scholarly man, a financial wizard, a Parsee, who was telling me about his little son Minoo, a year or two old. 'He's very tiresome. He's always breaking things. But it's not possible to be angry with him.'

The Bursar looked surprised and interested by his own reaction. I wonder briefly, if we'd had a child, would I have learnt not to be angry with it? In which case would I not be angry with Iris now?

20 November 1997

Anger sometimes seems now to be a way of still refusing to admit that there is anything wrong. Like a sincere compliment. You are just the same as ever, bless you (or curse you) and so shall I be. I wouldn't insult you by pretending otherwise.

A happy stay with our friend Audi in her little house in the middle of Lanzarote. Getting there is an ordeal, the charter flight always packed to the doors with holidaymakers. Reminded of the old joke about Géricault's painting, 'The Raft of the Medusa', with stricken castaways clinging on at all angles in the last stages of exposure and thirst. Reproduced with a Holiday Brochure caption: 'Getting there is half the fun.' But Peter and Jim come with us and look after us, so the whole ordeal is almost pleasurable.

Return a fortnight later. I have a heavy cold and feel unnaturally tired, although journey could not have been easier. Peter puts us on the bus for Oxford. Sink back thankfully. Nearly home. Bus cruises steadily on through the dark, seeming to shrug off the rush-hour traffic on either side of it. The few passengers are asleep. But we have no sooner started than Iris is jumping up and down in agitation. Where are we going? Where is the bus taking us? She won't sit still but rushes to the front and looks out anxiously ahead. I manage to get her sitting down. I say: 'We're going back to Oxford. Back home.' 'No! No home. Why travelling like this. He doesn't know.'

Before I can stop her she is speaking agitatedly to the bus driver. She has caught hold of one of the bags, which begins to spill things on the gangway. I pick them up, push her into a seat opposite a sleeping woman. I apologise to the driver, who remains ominously silent. When I get back the woman, a nice-looking person, is awake, and distraught, desperately trying to regain the handbag and other possessions which had been on the seat beside her. I take them from Iris and put them back, apologising again in a whisper. Iris says, 'So sorry', gives the woman her beautiful smile. I get Iris into a seat and give her a violent surreptitious punch on the arm by which I am holding her.

Gatwick to Oxford in the late Friday rush-hour is a long way. Every second of it occupied by tormented squirrel-like movements and mutterings. She grips the seat in front and stares ahead. A feeling of general distraction and unease eddies along the calm of the bus darkness. I can see faces now alert and fixed resentfully. As the bus at last nears Oxford I try to show things she might recognise, but the agitation gets worse.

Clumsy escape from the stares of the passengers. Only one ancient taxi left, driven by a villainous looking Indian with a gentle cultured voice. He starts to go the wrong way half-way up Banbury Road, and I distractedly put him right. He says, 'Oh no I should know better really. Very sorry about that.' I give him a ten pound note through the wire grille and get very little change, but I can't be bothered about that. I give some of it back as a tip and he says nothing. Open the door. Get inside the gate. The house feels deathly cold. I find Iris looking at me in a wonderful way, just as she used to do when we came home together from some trying outing. I ignore her look, rush to the central heating switch. Then I come back and say in a cold furious voice, 'You behaved disgracefully on the bus. I felt ashamed of you.'

She looks surprised, but then reassured, as if recalling an old cue. She would just be defending her corner by the kind old method – that is to say, not defending it. Leaving me to work out my nastiness as if I were a child. 'Well,' she says. Her equivalent now of what might once have been a soothing 'So sorry.' I have lost my voice, can't hear, and am drowning in a cold that seems more ominous than an ordinary cold, as the bus driver's silence seemed more ominous than words. My chest hurts when I cough. After a few more ugly words I say I've probably got pneumonia.

Hasn't she noticed I'm ill? She looks uncomprehending
again. The moment of realisation and reassurance has gone
with my own fit of cold fury that brought them on. My
appeal for sympathy leaves her lost and bewildered.

What will she do if I die? If I'm ill and have to go to
hospital. If I have to stay in bed – what will she do then?
Still exasperated by the bus business I make these demands
with increasing hostility and violence. I am furious to see
my words are getting nowhere, and yet relieved too by this,
so that I can continue to indulge my fury. She knows none of
these things can or will happen. While I am still screaming
at her she says, 'Let's go. There now. Bed.' She says this
quite coherently. We squeeze together up the stairs, huddle
under the cold duvet, and clutch each other into warmth.
In the morning I feel a lot better.

Iris, I think, has never felt bad. She didn't catch the cold,
as if the Alzheimer's is a charm against mere mundane
and quotidian ailments. Jim washed and cut her hair in
Lanzarote; Audi gave her a shower and a bath. She said to
Audi as they stood together in the shower, 'I see an angel.
I think it's you.' Having caught the cold the poor angel was
in fact suffering from asthma and a serious chest infection
for which she had to start taking tetracycline, fortunately
available over the counter in Spain. How sensible, because
Audi has never found a proper doctor there, though she has
lived on the island on and off for years. Her temperature
went up to nearly 103, but then came down quickly, much
to our relief. I think we were all grateful in some way that
Iris knew nothing about it. She reassured us by not knowing
of troubles, and the tears of things.

Or rather they touch her heart in invisible and mysterious
ways. To Audi's cats, which she was once very fond of, she
now seems almost indifferent. She strokes them absently.
Peter and Jim's dog Cloudy, whom she loved once to
make much of, now seems to have for her the distance and
impersonality of an angel. When she sheds tears, softly and

for short periods, she hides them with an embarrassment which she no longer feels about any other physical side of herself.

In old days she used to weep quite openly, as if it were a form of demonstrable and demonstrated warmth and kindness. Now I find her doing it as if ashamedly, stopping as soon as she sees I have noticed. This is so unlike the past; but disturbing too in another way. It makes me feel she is secretly but fully conscious of what has happened to her, and wants to conceal it from me. Can she want to protect me from it? I remember as a child finding my mother crying, and she stopped hastily and looked annoyed. In Proust the grandmother has a slight stroke while taking little Marcel for a walk in the park, and she turns her face away so that he should not see it all puckered and distorted.

There are so many doubts and illusions and concealments in any close relationship. Even in our present situation they can come as an unexpected shock. Her tears sometimes seem to signify a whole inner world which Iris is determined to keep from me and shield me from. There is something ghastly in the feeling of relief that this can't be so: and yet the illusion of such an inner world still there – if it is an illusion – can't help haunting me from time to time. There are moments when I almost welcome it. Iris has always had – must have had – so vast and rich and complex an inner world, which it used to give me immense pleasure *not* to know anything about. Like looking at a map of South America as a child, and wondering about the sources of the Amazon, and what unknown cities might be hidden there in the jungle. Have any of those hidden places survived in her?

Showing me a tracing from the most elaborate of the brain scans Iris underwent a year or so ago, the doctor indicated the area of atrophy at the top. The doctors were pleased by the clearness of the indication. I thought then – the old foolish romantic idea of the Amazon – that her brainworld had lost its unknown mysteries, all the hidden life that had gone on in it. It had been there, physically and geographically *there*. And now it was proved to be empty. The grey substance that sustained its mysteries had ceased to function, whatever a 'function', in there, can possibly mean.

Twice Iris has said to Peter Conradi that she feels now that she is 'sailing into the darkness'. It was when he asked her, gently, about her writing. Such a phrase might be said to indicate the sort of inner knowledge that I had in mind. It seems to convey a terrible lucidity about what is going on. But can one be lucid in such a way without possessing the consciousness that can produce such language? And if consciousness can go on producing such words, why not many more, equally lucid?

Were I an expert on the brain I should find it hard to believe in such flashes of lucidity revealing, as it were, a whole silent but conscious and watching world. It would be as if – to use a clumsy analogy from my hidden city in the jungle – a flash of lightning were to reveal its existence, and then the explorers found that it didn't exist after all. The words which Iris used with such naturalness and brilliance cannot be stacked there silently, sending out an occasional signal. Or can they? I notice that the eerie felicities which Iris has sometimes produced, like 'sailing into the darkness' or 'I see an angel', seem to come, so to speak, with a little help from her friends. They are like the things a young child suddenly comes out with, to the delight and amusement of parents and friends. But it was the friends or parents who unconsciously did the suggesting. Must have been.

Iris has heard nothing from a great friend, a novelist whom she had once befriended and inspired, counselled and consoled. Had this now famous friend left her, abandoned in her silence? Was it in resignation or in bitterness of spirit that she spoke those words? Sailing alone into the dark . . .

In my own daily intercourse with Iris words don't seem to be necessary, hardly appear to be uttered. Because we don't talk coherently, and because we talk without seeming to ourselves to be talking, nothing meaningful gets said. The clear things Iris does sometimes come out with are intended for public consumption. They are social statements. They have the air of last remarks before all the lights go out.

1 December 1997 (I think, a Sunday anyway.)
I always liked a Sunday morning. Iris never noticed them. She still doesn't, but now I find TV a great help. Looking in on her as I potter about I am relieved to see her sitting intently, like a good child, watching the Sunday morning service. Later she is still there; the service has changed to an animated cartoon featuring bible history, Roman soldiers etc., in which she is equally engrossed. Thank goodness for Sunday morning TV.

There are occasions when I have such a strong wish to remind Iris of something we did or saw that I find myself describing it hopefully, in great detail. I don't say, 'You probably don't remember, but—.' Instead I now have the feeling that she is trying to follow something I am myself creating for her. Spring is more vivid when you talk about it in winter, and I find myself telling her about one of our visits with Peter and Jim to Cascob in Wales, at the end of last May. The small school house, where twenty or thirty children were once taught, lies on a rising knoll at the end of a steep and narrow valley. It is an old place, a single large high-roofed room, with the schoolmistress's house, one up and one down, almost touching but separate. The friends have joined the two, and made some alterations, but left the structure intact. The crown of the hillock on which it stands slopes sharply down to their pond, with a little island in the middle, thick with alder and willow and with flowers in summer. Just beside the school is an extremely old church, half buried in green turf nearly up to the window openings

on one side, so that the sheep could look in. An immense
yew tree, much older even than the church, makes a kind
of jungle beside it, dark red with shadows.

On that visit to this enchanting place we soon found
a special routine. A pair of redstarts were nesting just
above the back doorway. If we sat motionless in the little
courtyard, or looked out of the schoolhouse window we
could see them come and go: small flame-like birds, looking
much too exotic to be seen in England. The breast and tail
(*steort* means tail in Old English) are bright cinnamon red,
the head jetblack, with a white ring on the neck. When they
hovered near the nest-hole, wary of a possible watcher, they
were as jewel-like as hummingbirds.

After watching the redstarts our ritual was to go round
to the churchyard, where we could have quite a different
experience, though of the same kind. Jim had fixed a nesting
box on a great ash tree where the graveyard bordered their
copse. He told us a pair of pied flycatchers were nesting
there. This is a little bird even more rare and local than the
redstart, a migrant who now only comes back to the borders
of south and central Wales. We stood by a gravestone,
watching. Nothing happened for a long time. Suddenly and
soundlessly a neat little apparition, in black and pure white,
appeared by the nest-hole. It was motionless for a moment
and then vanished inside. We looked at each other, hardly
believing we had really seen it. It seemed like a pure speck
of antiquity, robed in the hues of the old religion, almost as
if a ghostly emanation from the church itself.

After this we could not keep away from the gravemound
by the edge of the copse, the vantage point only a few feet
away from the nest on the ash tree. The little birds seemed
unaware of us, just as ghosts would have been. Their busy
movements had a soft spirit-like silentness. Peter and Jim
told us they did have a small song, but we never heard
them make a sound. Although we saw both birds, and
identified the male and the female, we could not really

believe in their physical existence at all. Like the ghosts in *Macbeth* they came like shadows, so departed.

In the winter I find myself telling all this to Iris, and she listens with a kind of bemused pleasure and toleration, as if I were making up a fairy-story. She doesn't believe it, but she likes to hear it. I found myself that these bird memories, and the whole memory pattern of summer sunshine and green leaves, was becoming subtly different from what it had been like at the time. It really was as if I had made the whole thing up.

I remembered that Kilvert, the Victorian parson who had lived not far off in the same part of Wales, and had so much loved writing his Diary about his days, his walks and his priestly duties, had once confided to it that what he wrote down was more real to him than what he had actually seen that day or the one before, and was now writing about. Only memory holds reality. At least this seems to have been his experience, and that of a lot of other writers too – romantic souls who, like Wordsworth (worshipped by Kilvert), made the discovery that for them to remember and to write was to make their lives, and their sense of living things. The actual experience was nothing beside it, a mere blur always on the move, always disappearing. Proust or D.H. Lawrence must have felt the same, however much Lawrence himself might protest about 'Life – *Life*' being the great thing. Wordsworth only *really* saw his daffodils when he lay on his couch and viewed them with his inward eye.

Iris's genius as a writer is rather different, I think, more comprehensive. Nor does one think of Shakespeare as creating this wonderful vision, after the event. It seems to be a romantic discovery, this sense that all depends on memory. But like all such generalisations that can't be more than a little bit true: writers and artists (Vermeer for instance) have done it and known it for ages, but without bothering to make a song and dance about it.

As I create, or recreate, those birds for Iris I wonder what is going on in her head. Is she cognisant of an invention, a fairy-tale, instead of a memory? For a writer of her scale and depth the power of creation seems so much more important than memory, almost as if it could now continue independent of it. And yet the one seems to depend on the other. So what are we remembering when we invent?

The main thing is she likes to hear me talk about the birds. They must be just a part, a coming-and-going part, of the me she is always with. Once I was right away outside her, a reality quite separate from herself, her mind, her powers of being and creating. Not now.

Now I feel us fused together. It appals me sometimes, but it also seems comforting and reassuring and normal.

Reminded of my novel *The Red Hat*, and the Vermeer portrait that for me haunted our short happy stay at the Hague. When we were there I at once began to have that fantasy about it, which I told to Audi and Iris, separately I think. For Audi I wanted it to be comic, a comical adventure fantasy, with sinister overtones, which we could laugh at together. Could it be that for Iris I instinctively tried to make it sound a bit like something in her own novels? As if I were trying to remind or inspire, or even carry on the torch by a kind of imitation? However that was, the story I wrote about it does not sound in the least like Iris, except perhaps to me. It came out much more like the fantasy I told Audi, who kindly said she enjoyed it when the book appeared a year later.

Life is no longer bringing the pair of us 'closer and closer apart', in the poet's tenderly ambiguous words. Every day we move closer and closer together. We could not do otherwise. There is a certain comic irony – happily not darkly comic – that after more than forty years of taking marriage for granted, marriage has decided it is tired of this, and is taking a hand in the game. Purposefully, persistently, involuntarily, our marriage is now getting somewhere. It is giving us no choice: and I am glad of that.

Every day we are physically closer; and Iris's little 'mouse cry', as I think of it, signifying loneliness in the next room, the wish to be back beside me, seems less and less forlorn, more simple, more natural. She is not sailing into the dark: the voyage is over, and under the dark escort of Alzheimer's she has arrived somewhere. So have I.

This new marriage has designed itself, as Darwin once speculated that fish perhaps designed their own eyes, to bring to an end her fearful anxieties of apartness – that happy apartness which marriage had once taken wholly for granted. This new marriage needs us absolutely, just as we need it. To that extent it is still a question of 'taking for granted'.

The phrase was in my head because I had just received a letter from the Japanese psychologist Takeo Doi. Admiring her novels, he had once corresponded with Iris, and his ideas had interested her. As pen friends they had got on, and the three of us had once met in Tokyo. He had read a piece of mine on 'marriage' which had been commissioned by *The Times*. The paper had naturally wanted it to be about Iris's Alzheimer's, but I had also made our old point about taking marriage for granted, quoting Iris's character in *A Severed Head* who had lamented that her marriage 'wasn't getting anywhere'. This had struck the distinguished psychologist, the explorer of *amae*, the taken-for-granted bond which supplies the social cohesion of the Japanese people, and he had titled the essay which he now sent me 'Taking for Granted'. Japanese husbands and wives, he said, do not make a fuss about marriage, in the western style, but take it for granted. I wrote thanking him for the piece, and remarked that marriage was now taking us for granted rather than we, it.

As in old days nothing needs to be done. Helplessness is all. Yet it's amusing to contemplate 'new marriage'. Like New Labour, the New Deal etc? Not quite like that. Hard, though, to contemplate one's arrangements without their becoming, at least to oneself, a private form of public relations. I need our closeness now as much as Iris does, but don't feel I need cherish it. It has simply arrived, like the Alzheimer's. The best as well as the fullest consciousness of it comes in the early morning, when I am beside Iris in bed tapping on my typewriter, and feel her hearing it in her doze, and being reassured by it.

In the old days she would have been up and in her study, in her own world. I am in mine, but it seems hers too, because of proximity. She murmurs, more or less asleep, and her hand comes out from under the quilt. I put mine on it and stroke her fingernails for a moment, noticing how long they are, and how dirty. I must cut them and clean them again this morning. They seem to grow faster by the month, and I suppose mine do the same.

14 December 1997

As I am sitting in the kitchen, trying to read something, Iris makes her mouse noise at the door. She is carrying a Coca Cola tin picked up in the street, a rusty spanner – where on earth did she get that? – a single shoe.

Single shoes lie about the house as if deposited by a flash flood. Never a matching pair. Things in odd corners; old newspapers, bottles covered in dust. A mound of clothing on the floor of the room upstairs where she used to write. Dried-out capless plastic pens crunch underfoot. A piece of paper in her handwriting of several years ago with 'Dear Penny' on it.

Rubbish becomes relaxing if there is no will to disturb it. It will see out our time. I think of the autumn in Keats's poem 'Hyperion'. 'But where the dead leaf fell, there did it rest.'

An odd parallel between the rubbish on the floor and the words that fly about the house all day. Words the equivalent of that single shoe.

Tone is what matters. All is OK with a child or cat or gunga exclamation. 'The bad cat – what *are* we going to do with her?' I stroke her back or pull her backwards and forwards till she starts laughing. I imitate the fond way her father used to say (she told me this long ago) 'Have you got no sense at *all*?' In his mock-exasperated Belfast accent. Iris's face always softens if I mention her father in this way. Instead of crying she starts to smile.

I rely on the bad child ploy, which can easily sustain some degree of frenzy. 'You *bad* animal! Can't you leave me alone *just for one minute*!' Or sometimes I sound to myself like Hedda Gabler needling her lover. But if I give it the tone of our child talk Iris always beams back at me.

She never showed any interest in children before. Now she loves them, on television or in real life. It seems almost too appropriate. I tell her she is nearly four years old now – isn't that wonderful?

The Christmas business. It's all come round again. Iris has always enjoyed Christmas, and the socialising that goes with it. The festive season always makes me feel glum, though I go through the motions. Why not get away from it all? In the old days Iris wouldn't have liked that. Now I am not so sure. Change in one sense means little to her, yet a different scene of any sort can cause her to look around in astonished wonder, like the Sleeping Beauty when she stirred among the cobwebs and saw – must have seen surely? – spiders and rats and mice running away in alarm. (I am assuming that the Prince who woke her would have stepped tactfully back into the shadows.)

Wonder on the edge of fear. That shows in Iris's face if we go anywhere unfamiliar to her. A momentary relief from the daily pucker of blank anxiety. A change only relieves that anxiety for a few minutes, often only seconds. Then anxiety returns with new vigour. The calmness of routine has more to recommend it. But no choice really – Hobson's Choice. Routine needs a change, and change finds some relief again in routine, like the people in Dante's hell who kept being hustled from fire into the ice bucket, and back again.

Well, not as bad as that. The point about Christmas could be that it combines a change with a routine, a routine of custom and ceremony that has at least the merit of a special occasion, of coming but once a year. Years ago Brigid Brophy and her husband decided to go to Istanbul for Christmas. 'To eat our turkey in Turkey' as they explained. Iris then laughed politely but she was not really amused. Indeed I am not sure she was not really rather shocked. Christmas to her was not exactly holy, but it meant something more important than the opportunity for a witticism about turkey in Turkey.

I think she welcomed at that time the idea of inevitability – something that has to happen. Mary and Joseph in the stable could do nothing about it – why should we need to?

Now I must encourage that instinct towards passivity, taking refuge in blest, or at least time-honoured, routines. No point in getting away from it all, nowhere to get away to. Alzheimer's will meet you there, like death at Samarra.

So we'll go to London as usual, visit my brother Michael, have Christmas dinner with him. We'll do all the usual things.

25 December 1997

And it's Christmas morning. And we are doing all the usual things. Routine is a substitute for memory. Iris is not asking the usual anxious questions – 'Where are we? What are we doing? Who is coming?'

Someone, or something, is coming. The silence it brings makes no demands. London is uncannily silent on Christmas morning. Nobody seems to be about. If there are church-goers and church bells we see none, hear none. The silence and the emptiness seem all the better.

We walk to Kensington Gardens up the deserted street, between the tall stucco façades falling into Edwardian decay, but still handsome. Henry James lived on the left here; Browning further up on the right. We pass their blue plaques, set in the white wall. A few yards back we passed the great gloomy red-brick mansions where T.S. Eliot had a flat for many years. His widow must be in church now.

Our route on Christmas morning is always the same. We have been doing this for years. As we pass their spectral houses I now utter a little bit of patter like a guide. Henry James, Robert Browning, T.S. Eliot. On former mornings like these we used to gaze up at their windows, talk a bit about them . . . Now I just mention the names. Does Iris remember them? She smiles a little. They are still familiar, those names, as familiar as this unique morning silence. Just for this morning those writers have laid their pens down, as Iris herself has done, and are taking a well-earned rest, looking forward to their dinners. Thackeray, the gourmet, whose house is just round the corner, would have looked forward to his with special keenness.

Now we can see the Park, and beyond it the handsome Williamite façade of Kensington Palace. When Princess Diana died the whole green here was a mass of cellophane, wrapping withered flowers. And the crowds were silent too. As quiet, the media said in an awed way, as it is in this morning's calm. The grievers were like good children at bed-time, folding their hands in ritual prayer. It was a tranquil ceremony, like our Christmas, as we wander now vaguely over the deserted road, usually a mass of traffic, and up the expanse of the Broad Walk.

A few dogs here, unimpressed by Christmas, but seeming merrier than usual in contrast with the silence. There is one bell now, tolling somewhere on a sweet high note. Up in the sky the jet trails move serenely on, seeming more noiseless than usual, their murmur fainter when it comes. Christmas morning in London is always calm and mild and bright. I can only remember one time when it rained, even snowed a bit. I ask Iris if she can remember that Christmas. She smiles. No need to remember, as this ritual that has replaced memory goes on.

The Round Pond. Canada geese standing meditatively, for once making no demands. The same path as usual, downwards, to the Serpentine. Nobody round the Peter Pan statue. Not even a Japanese couple with a camera. One Christmas we met two middle-aged ladies from New Zealand here, who told us this statue was the one thing they really wanted to see in London.

Young Pan himself, bronze fingers delicately crooked, his double pipe to his lips, has the sublimely sinister indifference of childhood. Captain Hook, his great enemy, was always made nervous by that pose. He considered Peter to have Good Form without knowing it, which is of course the best Form of all. Poor Hook was in despair about this. It made Iris laugh when I told her, years ago, before we were married. I read a bit of the book to her (the book is much better, and funnier, than the pantomime play). Iris, I recall, was so amused that she later put the Good Form business into one of her own novels.

Iris's amusement may even have been shared, in a quiet way, by the sculptor himself, who covered the base of the group with elves and rabbits and snails in the Victorian fairytale tradition, but at the top put the elegant figure of a much more worldly young woman, scrambling determinedly over the plinth to proposition Peter, giving the bystander an agreeable view of her polished bronze derrière. It is clad in a modishly draped and close-fitting Edwardian skirt, and she looks much too old for Peter anyway. Could it be that Sir George Frampton, as well as being an excellent artist and sculptor, had a sense of humour about these matters? It certainly looks like it, on such a quiet sunny Christmas morning, with real squirrels hopping about all round the statue, vainly soliciting the nuts which the fat little beasts have no trouble in getting from tourists, on ordinary busier days.

As we walk round and admire I tell Iris that my mother assured me that if I looked hard enough over the railings, into the private dells where the bluebells and daffodils come up in spring, I might see fairies, perhaps even Peter Pan himself. I believed her. I could almost believe her now, with the tranquil sunshine in the Park making a midwinter spring, full of the illusion of flowers and fairies as well as real birdsong.

Iris is listening, which she rarely does, and smiling too. There have been no anxious pleas this morning, no tears, none of those broken sentences whose only meaning is the dread in her voice and the demand for reassurance. Something or someone this morning has reassured her, given for an hour or two what the prayerbook calls 'that peace which the world cannot give'.

Perhaps it is the Christmas ritual. It is going somewhere, but it is also a routine, even though a rare one. It is both. And now it will go on. We shall return to my brother, who has attended matins this morning at Chelsea Old Church, where Sir Thomas More used once to worship. We shall eat sardines and sausages and scrambled egg together, with a bottle or two of Bulgarian red wine which goes with anything. The sort of Christmas dinner we all three enjoy, and the only time of the year Michael permits a little cookery to be done in his immaculate and sterile little kitchen. The sardines are routine for him, but the eggs and sausages represent a real concession. I shall do them, with Iris standing beside me, and we shall bring the wine.

A snooze then. Iris will sleep deeply. Later we listen to carols and Christmas music. I have the illusion now, which fortunate Alzheimer partners must feel at such times, that life is just the same, has never changed. I cannot now imagine Iris any different. Her loss of memory becomes, in a sense, my own. In a muzzy way – the Bulgarian wine no doubt – I find myself thinking of the Christmas birth, and also of Wittgenstein's comment, once quoted to me by

Iris, that death is not a human experience. We are born to live only from day to day. 'Take short views of human life – never further than dinner or tea.' The Reverend Sydney Smith's advice is most easily taken during these ritualised days. The ancient saving routine of Christmas, which for us has today been twice blessed.

Iris and the Friends:

A Year of Memories

PART I

MEMORY

1

I can hardly believe it's all over. At the end it happened so quickly. My diary says that Iris and I were still together, struggling along together, in the peculiar way that an Alzheimer patient and carer do, less than three weeks ago.

And then between one day and the next it became all but impossible to get her to eat and drink. I coaxed her in every way I could think of, but she seemed abruptly to have given up being a good if sometimes difficult child, and became a sadly but politely determined adult. Politely and smilingly she declined to open her mouth to have a teaspoon or the edge of a cup put in. As if she had decided it was no longer worthwhile.

With the brain gone can the body take over the power of decision? It looked like it. What Pascal said of the heart may be true of the body too? Like the heart it has its own reasons, which reason knows nothing about? If no one interferes, it knows how to do the right thing at the right moment?

And that is surely very comforting? For whom do I mean? For the onlooker of course, the carer. The patient is already far off. In a dark country where they have their own ways of knowing things. And doing things.

One night some months ago, in the autumn of '98 it must have been, I had woken up suddenly with the feeling that something was wrong. I switched on my pencil torch and found it was two o'clock. I'd been asleep two hours. I felt bemused, but at the same time intensely wakeful. For there was a subdued noise somewhere in the house. The sound of voices.

Was it burglars? But why should burglars be talking? Did they think the house was empty? I reached over to the other side of the bed. There was nothing there. Iris had gone.

She's always such a good sleeper! That was my first thought. In its earlier stages Alzheimer's Disease actually seems to confer minor physical compensations. The sufferers may sleep soundly, look well, never get a cold. Iris liked to go to bed early and slept almost without stirring until eight or nine in the morning. So what had gone wrong?

And whom was she talking to? Surprising how eerie her voice sounded, in the silence of the night, coming up muffled from somewhere downstairs. No words to recognise. There wouldn't, in any case, be intelligible words: and no doubt that's why it sounded like two or three people, conversing together, voices merging.

Who were these new friends of Iris, with whom she was chatting as if they were already old friends?

My heart sank inside me as I realised that the disease must have entered another phase. Sometimes in the early morning Iris has got up to go to the loo. As I might do: as anyone might do. But wandering round the house and chatting to herself at two in the morning was a new development.

For a moment I thought I heard the voice of Macbeth, the most terrifyingly intimate of all Shakespeare's tragic characters. 'Methought I heard a voice cry "Sleep no more!"' One is apt to get such dramatic visions of despair into one's head at two in the morning.

It passed. Daylight came. A bit of sleep for both of us. And a little later that morning I had a visitation. Perhaps it was one of Iris's nocturnal friends? Or perhaps it was Dr Alzheimer's very particular, very special intimate, who in time would become the friend of us both . . .

*   *   *

Doctor Alois Alzheimer, a native of Alsace, wrote a treatise in 1907 on the disease or condition that is named after him. He had observed it in patients who were in their fifties as well as in older people, and he had concluded that this type of dementia differed from more generalised aspects of senility. The condition was also marked by a regular progression, which might be either rapid or slow; but he found no cases of remission or recovery.

A bleak outlook, which left not much room for lightness of heart in the sufferer, or for those who attended the sufferer? Not necessarily. There may be rewards and alleviations on the way, for all parties. As well as anxiety in the patient there may be a kind of merciful indifference, even lightness of heart, a shrugging off of responsibility for the things most of us feel we have to do every day – washing, dressing, keeping up appearances.

Even the good doctor's name, ill-omened as it might seem, can possess a droll freedom of association. Remove it into other circumstances and it could signify other and more cheerful things, more comical things even. 'The Alzheimer', a potent vintage racing car which in its time even challenged the Bugatti? A gambling club, a select restaurant? Or a youthful hostess might candidly admit, when a guest praised the pâté, that she had got it at Alzheimer's . . .

Bad situations survive on jokes. That was the point of trench humour. If they are in close contact with one another carer and patient can even share such things. I will tell my thoughts, such as they are, to Iris; and she will smile at me when she sees from my face that I am wandering off into some sort of fantasy.

It is possible for both of us to have friends in common with Dr Alzheimer, who certainly does have his friends. And now it's as if my own memories were becoming Iris's friends too.

On that morning last winter I was fully conscious that Iris's affliction had suddenly entered a new and ominous phase. I did not know it would be all but the final one. At the time I was more aware of what I now think of as a visitation.

Perhaps it started in my head as a kind of joke? Perhaps I came to associate the joke later not with Dr Alzheimer himself but with a delightful and humorous man, a real doctor from the Warneford Hospital, who although he was immensely busy came regularly to call during the final stages of Iris's illness. A true scholar and healer, as well as the kindest of men. It was he who saw when the time had come, the moment when we had to get Iris into a home as soon as possible.

But on that morning, after her night out downstairs, Iris was peacefully asleep. I went down to the kitchen and made myself a mug of green tea. 'Gunpowder' tea. Each curly dark-green leaf expands to unexpected size in the boiling water, like a Japanese paper flower. In its dry unexpanded state it must have looked to those early tea merchants like a grain of gunpowder.

I've become partial to it in the early morning. Should be made weak, when it's mild and delicious. Said to be good for the heart. Good for the memory perhaps too.

Coming up from the kitchen with my mug of tea I caught the tail of my vest on the arm of a kitchen chair. Over the years the vest has become ragged, with a sizeable hole at the back. I pulled at it like a dog pulling at the lead, but this did not help. I put the tea down, wriggled around, and managed at last to unhook the vest from the arm of the windsor chair – a chair polished by more than forty years of me sitting in it.

We bought the chair cheap at a junkshop in 1957, the year after we were married. The proprietor had showed us its wormholes with a great appearance of candour, and went on to sell us a little can of some chemical treatment, with a tube and nozzle which had to be inserted into each wormhole in turn.

Iris did this conscientiously for more than a week, like the priestess of some strange cult. And the chair still hangs together, so perhaps her labours were not in vain.

Such a visit was indeed more like a visitation. Even an annunciation. When I got back upstairs with my tea Iris was still peacefully asleep. I looked at her quiet face, remembering that ancient time, and the zeal with which she had manipulated her little can of chemical. And there was something else too, trying to get into my mind. What was it?

Proust was quite right about the onset of memory, although his theory of it soon begins to sound rather too portentous. But it is sudden, and it is unexpected. It is also a source of joy.

Back in bed beside Iris I lay and thought of that moment when I had freed the tail of my vest from the arm of the windsor chair. The moment was bringing something back to me. But what was it? I looked for inspiration at the dear creature asleep beside me, but it was nothing to do with her . . .

And then I remembered. Sleeping and at peace at last as she was, she had brought me this visitation. Even though it came from a much earlier time, a time long before she knew me.

Lying back, relaxed now and sipping, I found I was on the golf course of my childhood. The golf course of Littlestone-on-Sea. But I was not trying to play golf. It was the family game, but I had always managed to avoid it. I had other things to do on the golf course.

At that moment I was slinking furtively through the thick seaside grass – 'the rough' – at the side of the course. I was making for an old and derelict brick cottage, which lay in the no-man's-land between the golf course and the fields and dykes of Romney Marsh.

Perhaps it had once been a smugglers' lair? Perhaps it still was? I had been reading about their exploits. The book was *Dr Syn*, by Russell Thorndike, brother, as I later discovered, of the famous actress, Sybil Thorndike. *Dr Syn* must have appeared in 1931, when I was six. Perhaps 1932.

But I was not much interested in smugglers as such. It was the place itself, its nearness and its otherness. It was close to the links, where dedicated golfers in plus-fours selected and swung their clubs, but it seemed all the more remote and strange for that, in a world of its own.

And what preoccupied me at that moment was something quite different from smugglers or golfers. It was mantraps. I knew that these diabolical contrivances had once been set among long grass to catch poachers, and why not to catch smugglers too? I knew it, because one rainy morning I had opened a book on the shelves of our seaside house. I hardly registered the title at the time, but it must have been Hardy's novel, *The Woodlanders*.

It opened at the page on which the heroine, skimming lightly along a woodland path, just escapes the jaws of a mantrap. Her foot touches the plate and sets off the trap, but so swift and lissom is she that her ankles evade the clash of the serrated iron jaws as they spring together. Not so her trailing skirts however. Pulled down by them, she finds herself helpless in the monster's grasp. Unable to move, she is compelled at length to abandon decorum and contrive to slip out of her silk dress and her petticoats. The scene then shifted to her estranged husband, awaiting her in the midnight gloom at their agreed rendezvous.

But distraught wives and estranged husbands were not an exciting topic. Having established the heroine's safety I lost interest and put the book back in its place. *Dr Syn*, which I had already twice devoured, fascinated me much more. Not only was one of the miniature engines on the Romney Hythe and Dymchurch Light Railway called after him, but in the book he was a local parson, admired by his flock, who had been a pirate and was now secretly a smuggler. I could appreciate that. I loved the deceit of it, and the enigmatic figure of Dr Syn himself. Perhaps the ruined cottage would turn out to be his private lair?

It was twenty years or so before I actually read *The Wood-landers*. Had I been six or seven years older when I found it in our seaside cottage I might have been more intrigued by the heroine's predicament, as she sped on agitatedly to her rendezvous, clad only in her vest and drawers. It must have given her husband a thrill, and no doubt assisted in their subsequent reconciliation. Hardy was very well aware of the graphic and dramatic possibilities of female underwear in his plots. For a Victorian he sailed quite close to the wind on this occasion, and on another too: in his early novel *A Pair of Blue Eyes*, he has the heroine remove all her underclothing to make a rope to rescue her fiancé, who is clinging precariously to the edge of a cliff.

But at the age of eight, even though I was nearly nine, female underwear had no special charms. Mantraps were the thing. They equally thrilled and alarmed my imagination. And so I approached the ruined cottage with exaggerated care. Who knew what might lie concealed in the thick marsh grass around it? Partly in the story I was telling myself inside my head, partly in sober reality, I was relieved to reach the crumbling brick wall of the cottage unscathed, untrapped. I could now see a sort of hatch in the wall like a miniature barn door, not very high up. I gave the side of it a tentative pull, and with a creak it swung open. I was mentally prepared for smugglers, but not for the apparition now confronting me. Two foot in front of my face sat a large living creature. It had a snowy white breast and huge dark eyes. We stared at each other. Then it swept over my head and flew across the marsh, a soundless brown shadow.

It had all come from the moment when I had freed the tail of my vest from the arm of the windsor chair. I had wriggled out of the trap, like Hardy's heroine.

Iris was still peacefully asleep, lying on her back, giving an occasional little snore or grunt. Beside her I sipped my tea, and abandoned myself to thoughts of that summertime at Littlestone, the ruined cottage, Dr Syn, the great barn owl . . .

Consciously and greedily I gave myself up to these memories. The habit of memory has become a real solace now. Almost, one might say, a fix. Especially in the early morning. With Iris still sweetly and childishly asleep, still unafflicted with the compulsions of Alzheimer's, which will cause her on bad mornings, and most mornings are bad, to shed silent miserable tears, or to utter small anxious cries and queries on waking.

'Where is? We going? Then go? Where this?' I shall stroke her, soothe her down. With luck she may go to sleep again. If she does I shall plunge back into the flow of memory, as if I were slipping down the bank and into a cool river, on a hot day.

Later on I shall be able to attend to Iris with one part of my mind while continuing to meander about in my own thoughts. But they will not then be so vivid or so complete, so almost sensually satisfying as they can be at this early hour. It reminds me of one of the devils in *Paradise Lost*, who while his more heroic companions are planning a hazardous vengeance upon God, only wants to be left safe to think his own thoughts. Milton speaks on his behalf with great eloquence.

> For who would lose
> Though full of pain, this intellectual being,
> These thoughts that wander through eternity? . . .

Never mind eternity: I am quite content to wander back to actual years and months, actual places. But when Iris wakes up they will have to vanish, at least for the moment. I cannot make the right noises, and deliver reassurance, while they are going on. Something in what's left of Iris's mind would know that her anxieties were not being paid full attention to; and they would increase.

Alzheimer's is implacable: it grows worse all the time, but insensibly. It is only by thinking back a few months, or looking in my diary, that I can register the changes. But as the condition grows worse, and its successive stages more difficult to cope with, compensations multiply.

It is these I think of as the friends. Iris's and mine. Dr A's too. Some are mutual. Today we can still cuddle together; we still enjoy lucid jokey moments, small bouts of pleasure in each other, at each other. But many more now have to be solitary, unshareable. It is no use trying to tell Iris about these memories as I would once have done, no use trying out an idea or a thought on her. It upsets her; a bothered look can come over her face, but usually there is only vacancy and, with luck, a smile.

Last year, 1997, I wrote a book about Iris, our past life and our present one. Worse as the condition now is, we can still go along living alone together. The certainty of things getting worse is our most unexpected friend; yet undoubtedly he is one. And I suppose it is the friend who sharpens an appetite for living in the past, gives the process a kind of connoisseurship. Someone with cancer once told me of the relief he felt when he refused further therapy, although doctors urged him to stick with it. The future had ceased to concern him. He was free to think only of the past.

Iris is awake. Her endless fidgets and queries begin to empty my mind. I must summon up logic and language, and reply properly. At this time of day she relies – paradoxically – on what seem to be real answers: jokes and nonsense – old chums as they are – won't do.

I sometimes say, 'Don't worry, darling, we shall soon be

dead.' This makes a silence, but not exactly a restful one. Is Iris thinking about it? Does the word still mean something? I have no way to find out.

I do not regard suicide or euthanasia as Iris's friends, or as friends of Dr A. Belial, that unheroic devil in *Paradise Lost*, would not have approved of them either. He deprecated his fellow devils' heroic wish to immolate themselves in the destruction of heaven and earth. He was for life, at any price; he knew that as things get worse the life of the mind can seem ever more and more worth having.

And yet I have had frequent thoughts of doing ourselves in together, if there were a nice safe reliable way.

The writer Arthur Koestler and his wife did that. He was ailing and had cancer: she was young and in good health, but she wanted to go with him. Hard to understand, and yet there it was. Would she have had second thoughts the next day, if there had been a next day? Like impulse buys in the supermarket, most suicides only seemed a good idea at the time, for the time?

In a sense it has all happened before. Iris's mother succumbed in her eighties to what was then called senile dementia. No reason to suppose it hereditary; no fear then it might affect her daughter too. But as Iris's mother began to go round the bend, her minder Jack amassed on her behalf a collection of sleeping pills. Barbiturates: the real thing. A host of blood-red capsules. After her death I found and appropriated them, thinking they might come in handy one day. If they still worked. They must be somewhere in the house, but in this house, or any house we've ever lived in, I would be most unlikely to find them.

We used to have a phrase for it: 'Gone to Pieland.' Once we had bought a pork pie, a very fine pie indeed, from some superior delicatessen. We put it on the table to eat for supper, and when the moment came the pie had gone. It has not been seen since.

Resolving itself back into its contingent ingredients the

pie seemed to have gone to a happier place. Perhaps to the 'Valley of Lost Things', once visited by the hero of Ariosto's mock-heroic epic, *Orlando Furioso*. Thank goodness that does not apply to those memories of the distant past which now keep me going.

Iris is awake, and mental life must be suspended. I give a last wistful glimpse back at the barn owl, the ruined cottage on the links, the mantrap fantasy . . . What took place in my head when I hooked my tail on the chair seemed involuntary, a sensation too immediate for pleasure. Only afterwards, when I got back to bed, did I begin to enjoy it.

Proust must have been the same. He dramatises the joy he received from that sudden flooding back of the past, its recapture through the cake in the tea (how disgusting that combination sounds!) and the way he knocked his foot against an irregular piece of pavement. But I feel sure that he had to arrange such things quietly in his mind before he began really to enjoy them. Proust never saw a television set but the process seems to me now a little like sitting down in front of one's own private television screen, and turning it on. Total recall at my age seems a very deliberate process.

And Belial, that insinuating devil, was surely right?

But never mind the present; it is saying goodbye to one's life in the past that would make one think twice about suicide, however simple and easy its process. Leaving the present would be nothing: it has no shadow and no substance, no memory power either. When addressing an envelope the other day I came to a sudden stop. The letter was to somebody I knew well, and I'd written his first name.

What's the other? It's gone. It will be back in a few minutes but in the meantime I want to post the damned letter and be rid of it. The life of the present is full of such exasperations, riddled too with angst, alienation, fear of contemporary life. Fifty, even forty years ago, everything was so much better?

Well, naturally. If we had grandchildren the present time might not seem so repulsive, so vulgar, so swiftly decaying, so full of daily dread and dislike. I can't imagine having had a family, but I suppose what they say must be true. We are born to reproduce, and to find satisfaction when old in the thought of those others' future. Though I avoid children, even I can see that they cannot help finding this world a wonderful place, and some of that continuing wonder must, as it were, rub off on their grandparents?

How would Iris feel about it, if she did feel nowadays? Even in the midst of the poor darling's endless agitations – banging on the front windows to alert passers-by, jerking endlessly at the locked front door, carrying clothes and cutlery round the house – there does seem to remain a core of serenity, in her smile, in the response to a tease, which I can't find anywhere in myself.

Illusion? Or is that still centre, from around which everything else has departed, another of the friends, come to drop in on us at this stage of Iris's dark journey? Nearly five years now since the first symptoms declared themselves.

They are trying to find out, so a doctor told me, what it is that Alzheimer patients actually die of. Physically they can appear in good health; but they do die, usually within seven or eight years of diagnosis, and seemingly of nothing in particular, although pneumonia steps in at the end. The last of the friends.

So what about hastening the process? Couldn't we do it together, as I said? I may forget names when addressing envelopes, but there are two names as firmly in my head as any steadfast memory of childhood. Dr Alzheimer of course: he is in my mind every day, as the badge of the society called after him is in my buttonhole. But there is another name too.

Dr Kevorkian. A strange, saturnine name. Dr Kevorkian, death's angel, often pops up in newspaper features, showing off his polythene apparatus, teaching his fragile willing victims to do it themselves. Surely too he must be a boon and companion of our old pal Dr A? That might seem suitable?

But no: on reflection he certainly isn't a friend – very much the opposite. Dr A's rewards and compensations, even the most unexpected ones, are concerned with being alive; finding out not only how much there is in being alive, but what surprising *new* things there turn out to be: freedoms, and pleasures in constraint, which we would never have imagined or thought of, never even have considered possible.

'Sweet are the uses of adversity.' The commonest, sanest Shakespearean wisdom. And yet it doesn't seem like adversity exactly. Just the way things are, or have become. That ever present need to escape, Dr A's most elusive friend, can only be implemented in the mind.

If I had a stroke or broke an arm I should be frantic to get back to Iris. If Iris were 'taken away' I would hardly know what to do. This is obvious, but it is less easy to grasp the inner point: that I have been embarked on a way of life, and could hardly find another one now. What would become of the mind, the memories I cling to now, if I were free to do as I wanted? Free to go anywhere and do anything?

I cannot imagine Iris without me. Just as I cannot imagine myself without her. She is always there, and so am I: she cannot do without me. Now I tell her I am going to the loo or into the kitchen, and she gazes at me anxiously, and tries to come. When I evade her she stands very close, fretting and peering. The objects she is usually carrying have the look of empty space, no longer having a purpose. Even if they are ordinary cups or knives and forks.

As her condition worsened, and our imprisonment became more complete, the compensations mounted up – they had to. For her as well as for me? I can hope so, at least. We both still have our small pleasures, which have become happily and mutually important: more and more important, not only because they are all we have left but because we can still share them.

When Beau Brummell, once the law-giver of high society's dress and behaviour, lost all his money and began to go mad, he took pleasure in walking on the beach at Boulogne, where he had fled to escape his creditors. He picked up seashells, carried them home to his lodgings, and experimented in restoring their brightness by painting them with vinegar.

As I watch Iris absorbed in the twigs and bits of paper she has picked up on our walks, I enter more and more into what she seems to be feeling. I look serious with her as she does it. We bend our heads together over what she has found.

2

Littlestone-on-Sea. The flat bright wastes of shore; the huge pale sky above the marsh. Our holiday home was behind the sea-wall, a curved concrete embankment above the sand and shingle. When the tide was up the sea was above our heads as we stood in the garden. Tamarisk and Euonymus bushes grew there, but not much else. Holes and small flags had been inserted in the sparse lawn to make a miniature putting green, which we despised. There was a proper one outside the club buildings by the golf course.

My brothers were both keen golfers. (In those days some of the more elderly members of the club used to pronounce the word as 'goffers'.) During our summer holidays two eighteen-hole rounds, morning and afternoon, were nothing to Michael and David; and they talked golfing technicalities at mealtimes with my father, a less dedicated performer who was none the less glad to see his sons devoting their energies so singlemindedly to the game.

But family toleration extended itself to me in the role of non-performer. It was somehow tacitly accepted that I need not seriously take part, all the more so as I was perfectly serious in paying lip homage to the game and listening with pleasure to their discussions. I also enjoyed 'walking round', as it was called; holding their clubs while they played a shot, and meanwhile daydreaming about my own concerns, such as the ruined cottage which I saw every morning as we processed along the fairway.

I was born in India in 1925, probably something of an

afterthought. (My father was working for an oil company which never found any oil.) I felt different from the rest of the family, and they regarded me, but quite philosophically, as different too. At any date my brothers always seemed to me grown-up, whereas I was permanently childish.

My second brother Michael, nearly three years older, was easy both to admire and to get on with. I was very fond of him without knowing it, nor did he give signs of fondness for me. In our family, in any case, any demonstrations of affection were not so much disapproved of as assumed to be unnecessary and out of place. Michael tolerated my private world, and condescended at times to share in some of my secret fantasies and stratagems, although I would never have confided to him my most private ones, such as Dr Syn or the mantraps, or my ideas about the ruined cottage.

I never told him of my undercover visit there, nor of my unexpected confrontation with the great snowy-breasted owl. But in a good mood he was prepared to lay aside his bag of clubs on a fine evening, and indulge me in a stalking game. For this I took my sixpenny repeating cap pistols, a passable imitation of the Browning automatic. I know that now, after seeing the real thing in the army, and I can feel retrospective surprise at how comparatively well-made these little toy guns were, even to the 'blueing' on the metal; and how cheap too, even by the deflationary standards of the thirties.

Michael, I accepted, was of an age to regard cap pistols as for the children. He had bought them for me at the village shop, where they also sold pingpong balls and fishing nets and buckets and spades, with his own pocket money. Naturally and properly he had more of it than I did, but it was a kind thing to do none the less. We kept the existence of these toy guns a secret from my parents, who would have strongly disapproved, my father particularly.

He had been through the 1914–18 war, ending up as a major and battery commander in the field artillery. Like many ex-soldiers at the time he deplored warlike attitudes or national aggressiveness, although he was not in the least a pacifist. He would also have frowned upon his sons' showing what would have seemed to him a frivolous interest in the weapons of modern warfare.

Of course when the next war arrived he made passionate efforts to get back into the army and was highly upset that age and rheumatics stopped him. I think he secretly grudged his three sons' being in the army and he a civilian, although he was as devoutly grateful as my mother that all three survived; the eldest, David, becoming a prisoner of war in 1944, while Michael was wounded a few months later.

But such things were still what now seems to me a long way off, and in another world. What matters in my memories is that Michael bought me the cap pistols, and I was thrilled. I kept them well hidden and caressed them in secret. So much of childhood seems to have been spent in secret, and most of its pleasures came from this. Most of the memories I have of it too.

I already considered life to be far from wonderful; something, indeed, to be avoided as much as one could, like school or games or children's parties. Life, real life, was like a picture that frightened me seriously. It was represented for me on the cover of a magazine that I had read avidly, many times over. The magazine was called *Wings*, and consisted mostly of tales of aerial combat and reminiscences by pilots who had flown and fought in the Great War.

My eldest brother had managed to buy it surreptitiously on Ashford station, and it had come down to me after the pair of them had finished with it. They were rather superior about it but I was not. I was both frightened and fascinated. And my parents would have disapproved. I had been warned by both brothers to keep its existence a secret.

The coloured cover illustration showed not a 'Hun' Fokker or Albatros but an English SE 5, very meticulously drawn, going earthward in a slow slant, the pilot slumped forward over the controls. His leather helmet and sightless goggles haunted me, as did the streak of blood on the outside of the cockpit, where the dead arm rested. I associated that cover picture with the wax model of a dog, strapped down and stuck full of needles, which lolled realistically in the window of the Anti-Vivisection Society's premises, just off Trafalgar Square. Both, I knew, represented what life, real life, was about.

In fact these two things did not so much frighten me as produce a dire and settled kind of hopelessness in the pit of my stomach. How different they were from the evening game with Michael, when we pretended to stalk and shoot each other on the deserted links. The Germans never won at those times and there were no shadows in the long evening sunlight. The turf of the fairway smelt of thyme, and in the immense arc of the sky, just beginning to glow a deeper blue, a lark or two was still singing. Here was romance and excitement, with no damage done. I knew it was all make-believe, and so much preferred it to the real thing.

I always lost the game, and really preferred losing it, without admitting this to myself, or of course to Michael. My usual idea was to lie on the brow of a big bunker, one of the few eminences on the links. I would be hidden in the tussocks of marram grass, able to see out, and all around. Or so I thought. In choosing this place I showed a touching ignorance of one of the cardinal points of military strategy: never do what the enemy expects you to do.

Lying there in the sunny evening I happily awaited the moment at which my unsuspecting brother should by rights appear, somewhere in front of me. In fact he usually managed to stalk me from behind, crawling silently until he was in range, and then startling me with a volley of gunfire, so that I surrendered on the spot. The shock and the surrender were equally delicious. At such moments he had a kind yet weary air, never seeming pleased with his victory or contemptuous of my own shortcomings as a tactician.

Once when he was slow in finding me, and I lay still a long time, a lark, still singing, dropped to its nest a few feet away. Their nests are so simply but effectively camouflaged – the brown speckled eggs nestled into a twist of matching grass – that they are impossible to find except by accident. From my lair I marked the spot, and when I had been duly flushed out and our stalking game was over, I found the nest and proudly showed it to Michael, who permitted himself to be interested in his kindly negligent way. We took none of the eggs – it would have seemed unsporting to both of us – but I was not above removing the occasional egg from a thrush's or linnet's nest that I found elsewhere. I never 'blew' the eggs, although in theory I knew how to. Their delicate round weight was part of their appeal to me, but my private egg collection, also concealed from my parents, was not an extensive or a methodical one.

Our house being a few feet from the sea we used to bathe in summer, always at high tide. My brothers could be lofty about this to them childish practice, alleging that it 'put the eye out', for golf. Both were in fact good swimmers, and sometimes Michael let me ride on his back to a raft which was moored for the summer some distance offshore. My father, who never bathed himself, was impatient at the way I kept in my depth with a toe safely on or near the sea bed, and offered me a pound note if I would swim back from the raft after Michael had carried me there. Although ashamed that I could not swim properly I never dared attempt to win the pound, although with my brothers giving me close escort back to the shore I knew I could easily have done so.

My father struck me as a melancholy man, although with the uninterested detachment of the age I then was I could not see why he should be. He had my mother after all, who loved him – I could see that, though again it did not interest me – and he had three fine sons. That was how it struck me one day, as we paraded, washed and combed, before some social event or other. I noticed how my father, in his dark blue summer jacket with brass buttons, eyed us in what seemed to me a surprisingly unenthusiastic way. Why should he think so little of his offspring? It did not occur to me that the reason might be that we were all boys, and he would have liked a girl, particularly as the youngest. Or perhaps there was some other reason. But that seems to me now the most probable one. Perhaps he did not know it himself. Perhaps he did not know he was a melancholy man? But I was sure of it.

My father certainly went out of his way not to spoil us – so did my mother – and to discourage me in particular from acting in any but a manly way. Once I remarked that a little dog we had seen was sweet. He made a face, and said that I must not use that word: I should say 'nice'. I was duly careful to say 'nice' in future but I thought him unnecessarily censorious. On another occasion he found me reading my mother's copy of *The Queen*, a fashion magazine, and told me that at my age I should be reading about pirates. I thought this highly unfair. I was all for pirates, but why shouldn't I enjoy looking at the elegant ladies in *The Queen* as well?

There was no sandy beach at Littlestone, which meant we had the foreshore at low tide largely to ourselves, if we wanted it. There were sometimes a couple of bait diggers trudging over the flat bright wastes in the far distance. They wore dark thigh boots which as a child I rather envied, as an asset to the personality rather than a practical measure against the black sticky mud. I liked the mud and its marine smell; in summer I used to wander through it barefooted for miles, occasionally disturbing the small flat fish who lay waiting in the ooze for the sea to return. I was not aware of the weaver-fish, with its highly poisonous spines whose poison can cause acute agony, even death when untreated. The wife of Field Marshal Montgomery is thought to have died in this way, after paddling with her children off the east coast. The victor of Alamein was then an unknown major. He is reported never to have mentioned her name again, and never looked at another woman.

I was fortunately ignorant of the weaver-fish and of Montgomery too, naturally enough, although I was devoted to Hannibal, whom I read about in Warne's *Encyclopedia of Pictorial Knowledge*. A vigorous drawing showed him surveying Italy from the Alps, his famished men beside him with their short swords drawn. At Cannae in another picture Roman legionnaires were desperately defending themselves against the Carthaginian troopers pressing down on them. I was bitterly disappointed when Hannibal lost the war, but by the time I was seven and a half I had left behind both the Carthaginians and the pleasures of our muddy foreshore. I struck off inland, to the golf links and the mysteries of the marsh. And to Dr Syn of course.

The links was not only a haunt of mystery and romance, where smugglers and owls made their homes in deserted cottages. It was also a social setting, a place of sophistication, and fascinating new enigmas. From its edges I could observe the local gentry at play, recognising some as neighbours and acquaintances, and speculating to myself about those whom I could not identify. Breasting the bright skyline with their golfbags, sometimes with a caddie or two in attendance, they had a heroic look which I took for granted: it was their promise of sophistication which intrigued me more. Most of them wore plus-fours and suede leather jackets.

Our family had these too; even I had one, a present from

my mother on my last birthday. But it had only buttons down the front, not a zip. Zips, less common then than now, were for me an essential mark of sophistication and maturity. My brothers had them; so did my mother, whose golf jacket would have suited Papagena in *The Magic Flute*, Maid Marian on a romp with Robin Hood. Its soft, very dark green suede had a woollen edge of the same hue, and the zip fastener was ornamented with a spray of dark green leather tassels. I loved it, studied and relished its every detail, and felt proud of my mother when she was wearing it. I felt she was the equal of any lady on the course, even the dashing Mrs Bruce, whose family lived in a great red castle of a house further down the sea-wall, and who had written a novel which my mother had taken out of Boots' library. It was called *Duck's Back*.

My mother explained to me how clever the title was. 'Like water off a duck's back', she told me, was a proverb. It meant something one could take in one's stride, as the heroine of the novel did when she fell in love. I felt sure that this heroine was none other than Mrs Bruce herself, but in spite of my new devotion to the sophisticated world I felt no urge to read *Duck's Back*. I opened it but found the sentences incomprehensible and unseductive. My mother said loyally that it was clever, but I felt something was missing none the less. I plunged thankfully back into the world of *Dr Syn*.

Familiar and unfamiliar figures on the links could be watched from the top of the sea-wall, where the concrete curve and the line of houses behind it came to an end. It was here, where tall plumy reeds made a jungle between the drainage dykes, that it occurred to me to make a secret lair for myself, from which I could survey all that took place on the links.

I decided it should be tunnelled into the marram grass and sandhills like a large rabbit burrow. It does not seem to have occurred to me that once inside my burrow I should not have been able to see anything at all. Perhaps that was the real point: perhaps I really preferred not to see anything, and only supposed, in a notional way, that it would be a fine idea to watch the traffic on the links.

The first morning I managed to make only a feeble scrape in the sand. Then it occurred to me to confide in Michael. At first he was only amused and superior, but when I showed him the place he began, as I hoped, to view the project as a challenge, and he determined to make it a practical proposition. With me keeping guard and watching admiringly he soon disappeared underground. I crept in after him to help remove the excavated sand, and by lunch-time we were both invisible.

It was dark and cramped in the tunnel. After the first thrill there seemed nothing much to do, and I began to wonder if all romantic prospects ended in this sort of monotony, even though there were moments of undoubted excitement when we heard almost over our heads the voices of passing golfers, sounding muffled and hollow.

Having completed his work Michael lost interest. He had the good sense to order me never to go underground by myself, but he need hardly have bothered. I had enjoyed the enterprise in his company, but it had had the effect of inhibiting my own daydreams. The best place for the tunnel was in bed at night, when I drew up my plans in my mind, full of secret store rooms lined with tins of sardines and kegs of spirit (whatever they were: they featured lavishly in *Dr Syn*). I installed a ventilation shaft or two. In the daytime I attempted to draw a cross-section of the workings, ornamented with grass on the top and a lark up in the sky. Michael smiled wearily when I showed it to him, and indeed it was a disappointing affair compared to my daydreams in bed, when I had magnified the golfers' voices into the guttural conversation of German officers – the villains from whom we were escaping.

I disobeyed Michael's orders a day or two later, just

to confirm that the real thing bore little relation to what I had been dreaming about. I was too timid to do more than just submerge, and as I returned to the surface a voice addressed me. 'Good evening,' it said, as if I were a fellow grown-up encountered at the club.

The speaker was Major Bucknall, a gaunt, courteous relic of the war, who lived by himself in one of the coastguard cottages. Like some solitary nocturnal bird he only appeared on the links in the evening, playing a few holes by himself, the holes that were furthest away on the course. I often saw him in the far distance, stalking quietly along in the golden evening light. There was something comforting and inspiring about his distant figure, but he was also an intimation to me of that unknown excitement in the lives of others, the people of the links, indeed all the denizens of Littlestone, except ourselves.

And here he was, actually addressing me. Overcome by my stammer I could manage only a faint gargling sound in reply. But waving his hand in courteous farewell the major was already striding away over the dusky turf.

Something in me determined on the spot to be more sociable in the future. I would dig no more lairs for myself, even with Michael's help. And when I passed close to people, on the links or elsewhere, I would incline my head a little and say to them, 'Good morning,' or 'Good evening,' as the case might be.

The chance was soon given to me to put this resolve into practice. Adjacent to the main links was a nine-hole course for ladies. My brothers despised it, but my mother was not above putting in an occasional practice round, with me carrying her slender bag of clubs.

On these occasions she would urge me gently to try a few shots myself. I was nearly nine now, and if I were to play golf – and she hoped I would, because there was a lot of fun to be got out of it – I ought to start as soon as possible. To this well-meant encouragement I returned an evasive reply. I knew I would much rather take part in the game as a spectator only, an enthusiastic auxiliary. Once I began to try to hit the ball everything would be different, and I would be vulnerable to all sorts of criticism and advice which, however well-meaning, would destroy my pleasure in the links itself, and what went on there. I think my mother understood this feeling in her own way, because she never bothered me for long. She went on playing in her own quiet absorbed style – she was not very good at it – while I marked her card at the end of every hole, and fulsomely praised her occasional good shots.

Although one was discouraged from doing either, it was much easier for a small boy to wander by himself on the ladies' course – naturally keeping well away from the fairways – than among the spacious and intimidating perspectives where men strove to shorten the long ninth with a really good drive, or carry the cross bunker at the famous fourteenth. Even my brothers could not yet manage some of these things, though they were in a fair way to do so. Apart from the indignant cries of 'Fore' which would have greeted any trespassing into the path of the players on the main course, I was frightened of the balls themselves, which could suddenly appear out of the wide sky to pitch soundlessly along the turf. To be in the line of fire would be to court disaster.

When on my own, therefore, I was careful only to potter warily in the distant rough of the 'Ladies', with the excuse if I was ever challenged of looking for a lost ball, perhaps one my mother had failed to find a day or two previously. I became good at finding lost balls. It was rare to discover a nearly new one, and if I did I presented it jointly to my brothers, with all the pleasure of a generous donor.

It gave me intense satisfaction when they acknowledged the gift with real pleasure; new golf balls were expensive things, and a find in premier condition was well worth having. Old ones a good deal cut about I quietly reserved for myself, for no very good reason except the pleasure of having a secret hoard. I hid a clutch of them in the warm sand among the dunes, like crocodiles' eggs as I imagined, remembering also the she-cobra guarding her eggs in the *Jungle Book*.

I had another reason for exploring the distant rough on the 'Ladies'. My ruined cottage was itself not far away, but nearer at hand were one or two deep dark pools, lying at the extreme edge of the rough. No life seemed to stir in those stagnant salty depths, probably linked with the sluices that ran into the sea. But there was a copy of Wordsworth's poems at home, and leafing through its totally uninteresting and barren pages I found some lines about a pool frequented by leeches. Interest was at once aroused. What were leeches? There were sometimes 'leech-haunted swamps' in the adventure stories I had read, but that these creatures – whatever they were – should actually be discoverable in England gave me a new idea.

I had often lain on my stomach looking down into the black salty water of the little pools, and now I could do so with a new interest. I probed their depths with an old wooden club Michael had outgrown and casually bestowed on me. I loved it. The dark hickory shaft was beautifully stippled by frequent oilings, and I greatly preferred such clubs to the steel-shafted ones now in favour, shiny and elegant as these might look in the display cases of the Professional's shop.

I was doing this one day, still disappointed of any sign of the sleek black and sticky creatures I supposed leeches to be, when the head of my ancient club struck something round and solid. The pool was deep, but I patiently manoeuvred the object, until I could reach in an arm well above the elbow and secure it. Disappointment. Not a leech or the skeleton of a leech, as I hoped it might be. Only a golf ball – but a perfect one. It was a Dunlop 65, the best brand and, as I saw when I had dried it on my handkerchief, totally unmarked. Its first shot into the air must have been its last. Wildly mis-hit, no doubt by some eccentric but powerful lady, it must have soared out above the lefthand rough – a truly heroic case of 'slicing' – and plunged, as it must have seemed for ever, into the dark depths of my pool. I put it in my pocket, well satisfied.

As I rolled over to get up I found I was not alone. A tall young man was gazing down at me. To me, lying on my back and dazzled by the sun, he seemed a giant whose shape blocked out the entire skyline. How long had he been there? I devoutly hoped he had not seen me find and pocket the brand-new golf ball.

Here was the chance to practise my new social ideas. I remembered the 'Good evening' which Major Bucknall had so effortlessly uttered when he happened to surprise me emerging from my sandy underground lair. Suppose, before rising to my feet, I were to give this apparition a cool but cordial 'Good morning'? An excellent idea, except that I could not find my tongue, or any way of getting out the words. Instead I scrambled to my feet with undignified haste. The person confronting me was not so enormously tall after all when I was at the same level. He looked about my eldest brother's age.

But there was something indefinably different about him. For one thing he wore no suede jacket, no stockings and plus-fours. In spite of his apparent age he had on a pair of sandy-coloured shorts and a faded pink blazer with a badge on the pocket. To wear one's school blazer in the 'hols' would in our circles be considered a solecism too gross even for overt sneers. This young person would be simply ignored, not visible. It was in the light of this knowledge that I suddenly felt quite at home with him, although my natural instinct was to shrink away from anyone of my own age and kind who looked in my direction.

Whistling to himself he peered down into the pond, in which nothing now revealed itself beyond muddied water.

Contrary to all my resolutions I was still speechless. But he broke the social ice with an unexpected remark.

'Have you ever seen a heron's skull?' he asked. 'I've got one at home.'

Looking into the water he seemed again to muse, unaware of me.

'A heron's skull,' I murmured, lost in the contemplation of what such an object must be like. Leeches were nothing to this. I saw the huge delicate eye-sockets (I knew from my bird book that the eyes of a predator could be as much as a fifth of its total weight), the long straight yellow beak, like a spear . . .

'I could show it to you, if you like,' he went on with the same abstracted manner as before, as if he hardly knew what he was saying. But I noticed his eyes were now focused on mine, and as sharp as I imagined the heron's to be.

Suddenly I remembered a phrase from a book, a historical romance, which had caught my fancy for some reason. Probably one by the then popular author, Stanley J. Weymer. A cunning old gentleman, encountering the stalwart young hero at an inn, had inquired coyly: 'If it be a proper question, who are you?' The words were the author's, not mine, and this seemed an appropriate moment to try them out.

'Excuse me,' I observed, 'coyly' I hoped, although I was not quite sure what the word meant. 'If it be a proper question, who are you?'

For a moment the blue eyes looked amazed, absolutely astounded. The boy clearly could not believe what he had just heard. I was in a bit of a panic myself. Perhaps the phrase I had used was incorrect today? Out of place? Or just downright rude?

Suddenly he burst out laughing. 'If it be a proper question?' he repeated incredulously. No doubt it was the use of the subjunctive that struck him as comic, though at the time I had no idea what the subjunctive was.

His amusement greatly relieved me. Indeed I began to feel rather pleased with myself, as children do when they succeed in making the grown-ups laugh. For part of my relief was the sudden realisation that here was not a boy at all, whether of my brothers' age or older. Here was not a boy at all but a man; and I much preferred men, grown-ups of any kind, to boys.

He seemed to realise that the game was up. That was a conclusion that I reached years later on, naturally; but even at the time I had the exhilarating sense of having won something: a game, a competition.

'If it be a proper question?' he repeated again. 'Well, I don't know whether it is or not, but my name is Peter Russell.' He made no further reference to herons' skulls, or showing his particular specimen to me.

'Peter Russell.' The name had at once had for me a singular enchantment. Somehow none of my acquaintances had a name in the least like that. And I repeated it aloud in fascination, just as he had repeated my own question.

The man was looking at me quizzically. But at the same time he seemed to have lost interest.

I'm sure that he did have a heron's skull, and that he would have shown it to me. What else might have happened I of course had no idea at the time. In those days children – children at least of our class and background – were not warned against the possible consequences of speaking to strangers.

'Perhaps we may meet again,' he said, but not at all hopefully, as if such a further encounter were now extremely unlikely to take place.

To this I enthusiastically assented, and was going on to ask more questions and volunteer further information, since I felt that the social ice had now been well and truly broken. But to my disappointment he was already walking swiftly away, not in the direction of the golf course and clubhouse, but across the marsh towards the distant village. I gazed after him, but not with any undue sense of loss, or of being abruptly abandoned. I felt that I now possessed him in some way. He was Peter Russell, and I said the words over to myself as I walked slowly home, with the new golf ball in my pocket.

The other day I found myself wondering if it had been his real name. He might have been a local man, or possibly a schoolmaster on holiday, staying in the village. I never mentioned his existence to my parents or brothers. I felt instinctively that they would disapprove, but apart from that I wanted to keep this Peter Russell person to myself, among my other secret possessions.

The new golf ball was definitely not one of these. As I made my usual slightly furtive way home I was already anticipating the moment when I would present it to Michael and David. Its extreme newness and beauty would excite even their admiration, although I knew from experience that their thanks and praise would be more or less perfunctory. They would probably not even bother to inquire where I had found it, and that would be a good thing, as I had no wish to reveal the existence of my pool, or the heron's skull, or of course Peter Russell.

Children with my background – the upper class as it then thought itself – at that time developed a class sense very early. I had known at once that Peter Russell was in some sense a 'gent' – one of us – even though he did not easily fit into any of the categories of our neighbours by the sea. If he was a schoolmaster, which I incline to believe, he may well have known all about the subjunctive. But why should its unexpected use by me have dissuaded him from whatever project he had in mind: possibly a not so very alarming or repellent one? Perhaps just because it was so unexpected? Having, so to speak, got to know me in this way, he could no longer regard me as a mere object of desire, as he may have done when he saw me lying on my stomach by the pool. He may have thought I was a village boy, or 'oik' as my brothers used to refer to them. I would have been distinctly flattered if he had, for although I automatically subscribed to all the class conventions in which I had been brought up, I also longed to be different. In any way, even a class way.

I never expected to see Peter Russell again, though I thought about him and his name with pleasure for some days afterwards.

Everyone at Littlestone – that is to say all the 'gents' and their ladies – played golf; and that to me was a reassurance and a comfort, even though I had no wish to do it myself. I loved so much everything that went with the game; and in late June and July that included the wild flowers growing on the edges of the links. I found out their names from Edward Step's three-volume work, which I had asked for as the present on my eighth birthday. I think my mother was in two minds about this request but she bought the book for me anyway. Cinquefoil, Ladies' Bedstraw, Houndstongue, the tall spiky blue Viper's Bugloss, which grew in the remote rough into which even golfers whose handicap was 'scratch' occasionally hooked or sliced their shots.

I had no interest in gathering specimens, examining or cataloguing them. I liked their names. The later use of herbicides means that few if any survive today, possibly only the beautiful and indestructible Evening Primrose, which grew in a stony gully by the sea, and on the sandhills where we had made the tunnel. I had occasionally picked one or two and given them to my mother, but the pale yellow that was so right in the corners of the bleached links looked washed-out and faded in her bedroom water jug; and the thin petals only seemed to last indoors for an hour or two.

In addition to all these auxiliary and concomitant things I loved Golf, the Platonic Form or idea of it. This almost religious devotion, coupled with an unwillingness to participate in practical worship, must have baffled my parents. But by the family standards of that age and culture both my mother and father were tolerant: they wisely preferred not to encourage any lack of conformity by commenting on it, although my father did occasionally grumble, as he had done at my reluctance to earn his pound note by struggling to shore from the raft.

After finishing their morning game the golfing community used to foregather in the Mixed Room, a modern extension of a clubhouse built in Edwardian times. There was also a smaller clubhouse for ladies, set modestly beside their nine-hole course, but it was seldom used. The Mixed Room, where both sexes could congregate, was a few steps from the Pro's shop, where members kept their clubs and other belongings, with no precautions against theft in those days. At the back of the Pro's shop the caddies themselves foregathered, like labourers at a Victorian hiring fair, waiting for a job. I was rather fearful of the caddies, although they always seemed pleasant when my parents laughed and joked with them in a man-to-man sort of way. Most of them 'moonlighted', with different part-time jobs in the locality, and their sons were often boy caddies, who could be hired by ladies at half price to carry their lighter bags. Some of them were quite small and probably not much older than I was; but they were already professionals, who would give grave advice on what club to select, and take a genuine interest in their employers' game. The dashing Mrs Bruce was especially attached to one gnome-like little caddie who seemed equally devoted to her: a relationship which provoked smiles and amused comment among the other ladies.

I was more apprehensive of the boy caddies than of their fathers. The latter's movements were predictable: in the late summer evenings when the course was empty they played golf among themselves, in a serious and orderly fashion; but their children might be encountered at any hour, lurking about the course as I did myself. In such conditions they were not at all well-behaved, shouting and quarrelling among themselves and yelling derisively after me if I happened to encounter them near any of my secret haunts. Among the sand-dunes they were like wild animals who had escaped from domestic employment, and the sight of them always caused me to beat a hasty retreat.

Rather surprisingly children were permitted in the Mixed Room, or at least no questions were asked if they did not draw attention to themselves. I discreetly followed my mother in when she finished her round and was allowed a gingerbeer, which I enjoyed because I regarded it as a sophisticated drink. I sat in a corner and watched the room fill up with returning golfers until the discussion of their morning fortunes reached a crescendo. The room had a delicious indefinable smell; not just of cigarettes (mostly Turkish of course) and cocktails. It was not like the smell of any hotel or bar I have since been into. Facepowder must have come into it, and Cologne, and suede leather which had spent the morning in close proximity to energetic women wearers. All mingled with the salty fragrance of sand and sea.

It was always known as the Mixed Room, but its chief appeal for me was the women and their loud though never raucous voices, and the unrecognised scent of femininity. Diana was there with all her nymphs, and their extensive hunting equipment, their leather golfbags brown or green, some with hoods and with gaudy close-furled umbrellas clipped on to them. These things lay easily about among all the easy chairs. I sat with my gingerbeer on an upright one in the corner of the room, listening to my mother talking to Mrs Alan or another of her friends.

While waiting for my father and brothers to appear I pondered the status of Littlestone among the other courses of the Kentish coast, which I knew about only from the cards and notices of competitions displayed in the main clubhouse. Was Littlestone on a par with Rye or Deal, where friendly foursomes were sometimes played between us and them? I knew we could scarcely compete with the Royal St Mark's at Sandwich, but that, as I had often heard my father and brothers say, was in a class by itself.

I enjoyed every minute in the Mixed Room; I hoped my father and brothers would be some time coming. I might even be stood another gingerbeer by Mrs Alan, whom I greatly admired. She was not dashing like Mrs Bruce, but she was tall and dark, and kind in an anxious almost excessive way. My mother, the elder by ten years or so, was fond of Mrs Alan, but also, as I now suspect, slightly patronised her: her extreme desire to please obviously lent itself to a touch of patronage.

We called her Mrs Alan because she had a son with that Christian name. Even my parents had taken to using it because her real married name was not mentioned. Her husband was in China, having deserted his family. Commonplace enough today, but in our circles at that time it was most unusual and fairly scandalous. Mrs Alan must have lived on handouts from relatives, but seemed, at least to me, as well-off as the rest of us. I had seen my father shake his head and refer to her delinquent spouse as 'no good'; and Mrs Alan's position, still officially married as she was, and with a nearly grown-up son, was clearly an anomalous one. Alan and my brothers played golf and tennis together. Although he was quite a bit older they contrived themselves to patronise him a little: I could grasp the process much more clearly in their company than I could in the case of my mother, with whom patronage took the form of kindness as careful and thoughtful as Mrs Alan's own.

Since my mother gently refused Mrs Alan's offer of another drink and would not let her buy me one either, we awaited in enforced dryness the arrival of the rest of the family. I loved the Mixed Room so much that I did not mind the absence of gingerbeer. I remembered Hannibal, and wondered what Peter Russell would look like, were he to walk in like a general about to address his troops. He would of course be wearing the helmet and armour illustrated in my book; but I had the feeling that he would none the less not go down well. The troops would not spring up as Hannibal's had done, and clash their weapons in acclamation, vowing to follow him anywhere. If the mysterious Peter Russell were not fully equipped in Carthaginian style his bare brown legs and faded blazer would cause positive embarrassment, especially when the Mixed Room saw, as I had done, that contrary to appearances he was not a boy at all but a man.

Never mind; I still felt proud of having met him, and of what I had said to him. 'If it be a proper question, who are you?' He had told me who he was, and that was all there was to it, and I should never see him again; but it gave me a secret pleasure that he was a part of my life that no one else would ever know about. Being secretly pleased with oneself is a childhood compensation for bruises to the ego almost if not quite involuntarily inflicted in the give and take of family life; and now I felt I had another private talisman to protect me from them.

The Mixed Room was filling up. The scent of drink steadily intensified, as did the hubbub of Standard English voices (except that no one then seemed to know about Standard English, or the alternatives in vogue today). I watched the barman prepare pink gins for newcomers, taking a slice of lemon peel, bruising it in his fingers and asperging it over a measure of Gordon's. In a rising scent of lemony spirit he took up the angostura bottle, shook a few drops into each glass, stirred them with a little chromium stick, and carried the tray to the seated ladies.

Most of the gentlemen preferred to get their drinks at the bar. My father and brothers had come in. They must have been playing a foursome with Alan, who accompanied them. I wondered how they had 'split up'. I suspected my father had paired off with Michael, the son with whom he felt most at home, and who although the youngest was the most competent golfer of the three. I had a bet with myself that they had won, and I hoped so, for it would have put my father – melancholy man as I thought him – in a good humour.

Sitting listening to my mother and Mrs Alan still chatting together, and watching the backs of Bayleys at the bar with young Alan, I saw with what seemed a sudden triumphant clairvoyance that Peter Russell was literally not of this world. He was not a boy like us or a man like my father, or even something betwixt and between. He belonged exclusively to myself, and to that moment at the side of the dark pool.

I felt exultant, perhaps slightly intoxicated by the fumes of pink gin. My mother and father preferred 'gimlets' – gin and lime – which I had heard my father call a 'clean drink', but at that moment nothing could have seemed cleaner than the pink scent reaching my nostrils as the ladies at the low table nearby called out 'Cheers' to one another.

Two days later I saw Peter Russell coming out of the ironmonger's shop in New Romney. It was quite a shock. So much for moments of vision. It was him in person all right, and yet of course it wasn't. Turning rapidly away I expelled his name from my mind as I had seen boys – village boys – spit out a gob of exhausted chewing gum.

That glimpse I had really did make me forget him, and it was only a day or two ago, lying in bed beside Iris, that I thought of him again. Why, I have no idea. But Littlestone and childhood, together with Iris as she now was, all seemed to dissolve and come together in the wanderings of memory.

I leaned over and kissed her, wondering with a now

wholly detached amusement whether Peter Russell had
wanted to kiss or caress me, that morning long ago beside
the links.

3

It was time to go home to lunch. I wondered what there would be. At that time we had a Danish cook, Gerda, a surly shapeless girl to whom I was greatly attached. Gudrun, the pretty parlour-maid who wore a cherry-coloured uniform with frilled collar and apron in *café au lait*, I did not for some reason much care for, although she was always nice to me. I think Gudrun looked down on Gerda, who came from some outlandish part of Denmark while she herself was a Copenhagerin.

When Gudrun was out or otherwise engaged I enjoyed sitting with Gerda in the kitchen. Gerda's English, unlike Gudrun's, was extremely limited, although she could understand what was required in the house; possibly her command of Danish was not much better. I was fascinated by the words and pictures on the lurid covers of the magazines she had brought with her from home, all now tattered and dog-eared as if she had been spelling them out for years. I sometimes asked her to explain the story to me. She seemed to enjoy attempting this and grew quite animated. The man in one story had murdered the son of his best friend, why I could not make out. I felt the Danes must be more sinister than we were, as well as more grown-up in some way. I felt more respect as well as more fear for what went on in Gerda's awful magazines than I did even for Dr Syn and his activities.

My mother was pleased with Gudrun and the pretty way she had of changing the plates and waiting at table. I knew my mother did not care for Gerda and was surprised by the trouble she took to be nice to her. I suppose both girls had come to England to learn, and I remember my mother saying with satisfaction that they were much cheaper than English equivalents would have been. I think Gerda was fond of me in a gloomy way, and when she returned home she sent me a postcard of some dark urban building in the rain. I sent her a postcard of Buckingham Palace in return, with a message that began 'Dearest Gerda'. My father happened to see this when it lay on the hall table ready to be posted, and took me to task over it, brusquely pointing out that only my mother should be addressed as 'Dearest'. I attempted to argue that Gerda was just the dearest of possible Gerdas, but he dismissed the quibble.

He had a soft spot for Gerda's cuisine, none the less. She made a kind of Danish fish pie which my mother thought too rich, complaining of Gerda's extravagance. My father pronounced his own verdict one lunch-time. 'Say what you like about Gerda,' he remarked, 'but her fish soufflé is out of this world.' I had never heard the word soufflé before, and was much impressed by my father's style of utterance, as well as by his knowledgeability.

I was more impressed by him at such moments than fond of him. He was part of the general harassment of life, like school and other children. I wished he would give up trying to persuade me to play golf and tennis. Cricket and football I was starting to have to play at school anyway: both were just a part of the travail of that establishment, equally unpleasant and unavoidable.

My father suffered from an unplacid temperament. He enjoyed work, and in his job he now had little or no work to do. He was intensely loyal to the big concern he had been with since before the war, and never breathed a word against them when he was passed over for promotion. I think in those more upright business days the firm felt equally loyal – at any rate they never got rid of him. He had gone to the war in 1914 and married my mother in the course of it: she had been engaged to an officer who was killed. He used to say that he would have liked to stay in the army, but the company had asked for him back, and he went willingly. That was when they sent him to India to help look for oil. I was born there, as I said, but no oil was ever discovered. His employers could find no more work for him to do, so he sat on in an office in Whitehall waiting – had he but known it – for the big moment in his career, when at the outbreak of the Second World War he was put in charge of the whole London office, all the high-ups preferring to evacuate themselves to the country.

In the days before the war my father went up to London one or two days a week. Every Sunday at Littlestone, after my brothers were at boarding-school, I hoped against hope that tomorrow might be one of the days when he felt he should go to the office. It rarely was, but when he did decide to go he was much more cheerful. More usually Monday was a bad day, with my father departing sombrely after breakfast for a round of golf.

I had no pleasure from his absence because I knew he would have liked me to go with him. I knew my mother would have wanted it too, but nothing was said: it had to be my own voluntary decision. So I was silent until he had set out, and then spent the morning loitering in the sea-bare garden, pretending that the berberis which grew on the side of the house was 'Wait-a-bit' thorn. I had read how explorers in Africa had to cut their way step by step through miles of this terrifying growth, which tore their clothes and equipment to pieces. Forlornly I imitated their arduous progress in my mind, half aware that such fantasies were no longer quite suited to my age.

I would see my mother looking at me from the drawing-room window. Her resigned air caused me to move as if purposefully in the direction of the garage, where the family car lay as if moored. It was a faded old open Rolls, which my father had got for a song, as he said. If it still exists it must be worth today any number of thousands of pounds. But none of us thought much of it, not even my father. And my mother complained of the draught that blew through the celluloid side-curtains when the hood was put up in winter.

Neither the Rolls nor the big engine which made electric light appealed to me as material for the stories I could make up and tell myself. But twice a week Tom Mills the gardener came in the early morning to start the engine before doing his day in the garden. Tuesdays and Thursdays I thought of as rosy or crimson – happy days. Not only would my father have gone to London but Tom Mills – Mr Mills to me – would be there as company as soon as I had finished breakfast. I never saw him start the engine, nor did I wish to – I felt it would be a frightening experience – but I loved watching him intently measuring the level of the acid in each massive accumulator. At least he said it was acid and I believed him, although I was surprised the first time I watched him fill up the level from a big bottle marked 'Distilled Water'. I was too polite to point out the apparent discrepancy; and I was in any case highly respectful of acid because Mr Mills had said that if you touched it accidentally it would burn right through you.

The Rolls had gone and I was glad of that. My father had driven it to Ashford station where he caught the London train. He would be back at six, but meanwhile I had the whole day in the company of Mr Mills, or of Gerda in the kitchen. My mother tolerated this arrangement. She would be playing golf in the morning with Mrs Alan, and they would probably make up a four at bridge in the afternoon. The idea of bridge gave me almost as much satisfaction as that of golf. I was usually allowed to sit in a corner of the room where it was going on. I decided that if I were playing I would ask to be 'dummy' the whole time. The fortunate person in that position could enjoy the game without the appalling intellectual strain of deciding what to bid and how to accommodate a partner. Though surprised and rather shocked by it I was familiar with the uninhibited sharpness with which persons always smooth and polite in normal society were privileged by the game to turn on a partner who had apparently let them down.

My father disliked bridge, and yet had no choice but to play if he were needed. He would say 'no bid' in a testy apprehensive tone, his eyes glued to the cards he held in his hand. I was intensely proud of my mother's skill at the game, and of the fact that she sometimes won as much as half a crown at one of her bridge sessions. If not present I looked forward to asking her how she had got on. I was aware of the superiority of 'contract' bridge over the old fashioned 'auction'; and I concluded that some neighbours along the sea-wall were not up to much when I heard my mother say they only played auction. My father, to whom she made the remark, merely raised his eyebrows in a quizzical way as if auction would be quite good enough for him, if he had to play at all.

All this was during an idyllic interlude. Childhood ailments, which I no doubt unconsciously welcomed, had got me off going to school, a day-school near our flat in Queen's Gate. After the flat had been sold during one of my parents' bursts of economy (Gudrun disappeared at the same time and I imagine for the same reason) I was allowed to stay at Littlestone until the winter term should begin at the school which had swallowed up my brothers. David had left it for public school and Michael was about to follow. Strangers to me now – even Michael was more or less a stranger – they reappeared at the beginning of the holidays in their grey tweed suits, and showed no sign of becoming themselves again during the short weeks of the old familiarity which followed.

I did not mind. I had regressed into an earlier and solitary phase of childhood in which I went back to throwing pebbles on the beach at forts constructed of seaweed and driftwood. I trotted about after the godlike Mr Mills whom I still never addressed as 'Tom', as my father and brothers did; and on Millsless days I explored imaginary jungles in the garden, among the meagre tamarisks and euonymus stunted by the salt spray of winter gales.

Even Gerda may have noticed that I was growing backwards – I must have seemed a more precocious child when she arrived – and if so she connived in the process in her own stolid and secretive way. It may have comforted her to have a fellow-creature in a foreign country with whom she could feel on equal terms. Mrs Mills, who sometimes appeared in the kitchen and bossed Gerda around, as I imagine she must also have bossed her husband, was a person I did not care for at all.

But there was another bond between Gerda and me, although we never spoke of it, and I myself never even thought about it at the time, at least not in the way that I had once brooded for a couple of days over the phenomenon of Peter Russell. Gerda had a bleak room at the top of the house, which during this period I used to visit in the daytime. She sat there when she wasn't in the kitchen, sometimes poring over one of her dog-eared magazines but more often looking dully out over the links – her room faced away from the sea – and at the small figures scattered over its sunlit expanse.

Once, to my surprise, I found her in bed. Grown-ups never went to bed in the daytime, although it was one of my own pleasures when I was ill, or pretending to be ill, and I gazed at her with a new respect as she lay passive, staring at the ceiling. She was fully dressed as usual, in her slatternly green overall, which had made such a contrast with Gudrun's spick and span uniform of cherry serge.

Abruptly she raised her suety arms as if in invitation, and I saw tears glistening at the edges of her eyes, which looked half buried in the fat of her cheeks. I was not at all bothered by her crying, though I had been deeply embarrassed once when I came on my mother shedding a few tears in the drawing-room. My mother had hastily blown her nose and spoken to me in an irritated way – a rare thing for her. I knew she knew she should not have been doing it – such demonstrations either of grief or happiness were not the thing at all – and so I was not upset by her crossness, feeling that we had been, as it were, caught out together, and that we must both do better in future. But Danes were obviously a different matter. Being foreigners they were allowed to do what they liked, at least in the context of the emotions.

Intrigued none the less by Gerda's tears I approached the bed and was not at all startled to find myself enfolded in her arms. Indeed I was rather gratified by being given the honour of participating in this unusual Danish practice, so different from anything we did ourselves. I soon got tired of the feel of the embrace however, and Gerda was decidedly niffy under the arms. To children all grown-ups smell, or at least did in those days – either fascinatingly or disagreeably. Women smelt of scent and face-powder, men of tobacco, even if there were no other odours around.

When I wriggled away as politely as I could Gerda dropped her arms apathetically and seemed to feel that nothing of interest had happened – which pleased me too. Denmark-wise, tears and embraces were obviously just routine stuff, like watching her roll pastry in the kitchen, or listening to her stumbling translation of one of her magazines.

Going up to Gerda's room was a positive pleasure now, none the less, and I took to running up there in my pyjamas when I was supposed to be asleep. I knew by instinct that my parents would disapprove, and I always made sure they were still safely in the drawing-room, my mother knitting and my father reading *The Times* and smoking his pipe. Gerda would be sitting on the wooden chair in her bedroom, sometimes brushing her hair but more often just gazing apathetically out of the window. She never drew the curtains, perhaps because punctually every minute there was a swift rhythmic lightening in the dark sky, from the beam of the lighthouse on Dungeness.

It seemed to hypnotise Gerda, who sat on in a sort of trance, as if the fact of being alive was a puzzle she had never even begun to understand. She would be wearing a long shapeless garment with a floral pattern, but it never occurred to me that this was what she went to bed in. I did not think of her or Gudrun as going to bed at all, in the sense that I and my family did: taking off our shoes and clothes, washing (or not, mostly, in my case), donning our pyjamas. The Danish maids were just there, day by day, like two dolls of very different appearance, and always in their dolls' costume.

One evening, after I had been pottering around her room like a small rodent, Gerda suddenly said in her flat thick voice, 'I want to feel what man be in bed. Come in bed here.' She said this with the same apathy and lack of interest with which she let me flour the pastry dough (my father was partial to pastry) or asked me by gestures to turn the handle while she fed the mincing machine. I received her suggestion in the same spirit. She held back the sheet, gestured me to get in, and followed. She lay on her back, staring at the ceiling; she didn't look at me or show awareness of my presence. We were a close fit and I was crammed against the wall as if in a game of sardines. I might have been lying beside a big dead fish, a whale or crocodile.

It soon began to feel very uncomfortable; but I was resolved to endure it for the sake of politeness, and showing that I could be as good as a Dane in carrying out this to us unusual practice. But I did think how very boring it was, and how unlike my usual pleasure at being in my bed and reading a book or *Wings* magazine. Perhaps Gerda found it boring and uncomfortable too, because to my relief she soon rolled out and released me. I said good-night and crept down to my own bed, a delightful place by contrast.

Going to real school seemed the end of the world. It certainly was the end of that last childish period, into which I had gone thankfully backwards into the past, in the knowledge that the future was none the less certain to come. When at last it came, and I was going off to school next day, there was no question of keeping, as I knew I ought to do, a stiff upper lip.

The full horror of it came over me when I went to bed, curling up small and as it felt for the last time. I had no heart to read a book. I slept at last but then I woke, and started helplessly to cry. Almost at once my mother came in: I think she must have been expecting it. It seemed a dreadful omen of what must be coming that there were no reproaches, no tacit disapproval. All such conventions seemed beside the point, as if I was to be hanged tomorrow. My mother took me in her arms, cradled and shushed me. I stopped crying at once, appalled at this disquieting kindness, and embarrassed by it too. I found she was saying, 'You must see the new moon, darling, but not through glass. I'll put the window wide. And then you must kiss your hand to it seven times and wish.'

With her arm round me I stood at the window, still snuffling back tears, and obediently went through this unfamiliar ritual, as outlandish as the Danish habit of going to bed in the daytime. She had never mentioned it before, just as I could not remember her ever calling me 'Darling' before. It occurred to me that there must be modes of behaviour even in England which were still unknown to me. Rather like those unusual things that were done among the Danes.

'Have you wished?' said my mother. I hadn't, but I nodded dumbly. 'Then back to bed and go fast asleep,' she said, with a return to something like her usual briskness, 'and in the morning it will be quite all right.'

Next day came, naturally enough, and my mother wasn't far wrong. I found it easy, when the moment came, to seem composed, and to be properly indifferent. I was lucky too. My brother Michael, who had just finished his last term at the school, had volunteered to escort me on the train journey and show me where things were and what to do. As an illustrious old boy his commanding presence would lend me, as a new boy, the glamour of the connection: I would not begin entirely raw and unknown, with a personality to make out of nothing. I should be Bayley *Mi* or *Min*, the direct heir of the distinguished couple who had gone before me.

I was sensible, too, of the sacrifice Michael was making on my behalf, and guilty about it, for it was his last day before going off to his new school, and he would otherwise have spent it in some preferred favourite activity, probably at least two rounds of golf. But nothing was said of this sacrifice, and in face of such silent generosity I could only do the decent thing myself, departing in the comfort of his company with as near an imitation of the Spartan boy as I could manage.

This precluded any leavetaking of Gerda, and fortunately it was not one of Mills's days. I was conscious that if I went into the kitchen I should break down, and once the bonds of stoicism were snapped anything might happen. It was the thought of leaving Gerda and the kitchen that had most oppressed me in the night, and it did not strike me that for Gerda herself my going away might be a matter of complete indifference. In fact as I passed the kitchen door on my way to what I thought of as execution I caught a glimpse of Gerda doing something at the table and waved what I hoped was a nonchalant hand. She did not look up or seem aware of me and this in some odd way cheered me very much. By the time we were in the car, my mother driving, and going to the station, I felt ready for anything, and began questioning Michael with animation about how to comport myself at school. He looked surprised; for he had already taken trouble to initiate me in what and what not to do, but like everyone else, as it seemed, that morning, he made no comment.

I never saw Gerda again. When I came home at the end of term she was gone, and I asked no questions. With her went my childhood. Littlestone itself never felt quite the same.

4

This feast of memory seems never to have existed for me, before these days when Iris has lost her own memory. Or so it seems to me today, when I lie in bed and luxuriate in thoughts about Gerda and Littlestone and times past, memories which have been brought to me, as if with the flourish of a *maître d'hotel*, by one of Dr A's closest friends and allies. The friend who ministers to her, as she lies beside me, is not recollection but unconsciousness, the tranquil shallow doze in which she will lie, I hope, for two hours yet, murmuring and crooning a little at intervals.

Might she herself be soothed at these times of the day by some obscure knowledge of the compensatory pleasures which memory, let loose now like a horse in a meadow, is bringing me? It seems possible: or do I just like to think it might be so? Remembering for love of doing it – a comfort food – is bound to be selfish. But selfishness can itself help the very person who might seem cut off by it. The comfort I give Iris depends on my ability to lead this inner life, whose vividness ironically depends on Iris not being present in it. It is all pre-Iris; all done and gone long before our own life together.

So I return to Gerda, as if stretching out my own arms this time. Permissible to feel that Gerda, if she still exists, could only be pleased by being the focus of such recollection. At least I should like to think that someone of that time, whom I hardly remember, might none the less be remembering me. I think – I almost hope indeed – that Gerda may have forgotten me utterly. That would give greater intensity to my own present sense of her.

Would it be perverse to say we only want to remain alive in the memories of those we have ourselves forgotten? But if Gerda is married, and a grandmother, living in a small Danish town, shrunken and white-haired perhaps, or still fat and uncouth, I do not want to know about it – to think about it rather. Perhaps she became a girl of the streets in Copenhagen (yet I feel that I know, in some way, that she would never be anything less than respectable). Perhaps a sodden *plongeuse* in some seedy provincial hotel? Or perhaps she returned to England, her conquest of the language miraculously complete, and settled down here? A much valued cook-housekeeper, in some family that loved her and her fish soufflé, and continued to cherish her when she was old and grey?

But all this means nothing. Gerda is not there. Only in my mind. The mind that is helped and solaced by the same demons, the same friends, who have destroyed the mind of an Iris who is close to me now, closer to me than ever, and yet far away.

Walking in a dream, with Iris beside me. And thinking of Gerda and the kitchen, the links in the distant sea air, the figures far away on it, trudging purposefully along.

They come and go on these walks. I can't hold them long in my mind. Perhaps because Iris, on our slow routine walk, is herself a soothing presence. In the house she is a constant source of anxiety, for herself and for me. But once out, and moving slowly along, we become a couple in harmony, like the nearly blind lady whom we sometimes meet, and her guide dog. The dog, a plump placid retriever, ambles quietly at his mistress's pace, and seems happiest to do this, though his own native instinct must be to tear about at top speed, investigating this and that, sniffing lamp-posts and excreta. I too should like to walk at top speed – I couldn't run now – anywhere, as far away as possible.

Well, so would Iris. When I have forgotten to lock the door and she has got out she can cover the ground very quickly at her determined shuffle. Her impulse then is not exactly to escape, only to get away. We share it. And that makes it all the easier to amble along together, comforting each other by our presences. Iris starts to speak, does not get very far, but it does not seem to worry her out here, in the deadly familiarity of the North Oxford street. I too start to say things to her which do not get very far. They glide gently underground, or into the air, and are lost in our mutual vacancy, and in that growing familiarity of my conscious being with childhood's daydream world. Second childhood? A parallel to the world of poor Iris?

There is no desperation now in either of us, though we have plenty of it at home. It was probably in my mind the other day when I found myself starting to hum some Schubert. *Winterreise* had been on the radio a day or two before, and the singer had given great vigour to my favourite lines.

> *Nun weiter denn, nur weiter,*
> *Mein treuer Wanderstab! . . .*

I am not mad about *Winterreise*, really preferring the more comfortable sentimentality of *Die Schöne Müllerin*. I don't go for the old *Leiermann* at the end, the *Wunderlicher Alter* who seems to be about to act the part of a Holy Fool to the mad and distracted young man. My favourite bit is the wild triumphant strain of *Nun weiter denn, nur weiter*, as he gives way to his impulse to go on, go farther, anywhere, anywhere to escape the madness in his mind. This must be why Iris stands at the front door, rattling the handle. Anywhere, anywhere, to get out of it all.

As we wander along, 'intellectual being' begins to play

with ways of translating the lines. 'Further now, still further, my good walking stick'? Doesn't sound the same somehow, naturally enough. 'My trusty *wanderstaff*'? There's a touch of the German magic in that perhaps, although it's magic of a comical kind.

Anything will do to think about, to wonder about. Anything at all. Sometimes I babble out such a fantasy to Iris, as if in response to the anxiety-fed beginnings she seems to be telling to me. But there is no sign of recognition now. There used to be the ghost of a polite smile. He is saying something silly, bless him. I don't get it, but I shall humour him by pretending to do so. That's what it looked like once, but not any longer.

Is it the absence of any such goings-on now in Iris's mind which stimulates the production of them in my own? As if my own brain chemistry were responding to a deficiency in another brain, involuntarily seeking to compensate? All such ways of looking at it are probably equally misleading: anything looked at in the mind vanishes by the act of looking? A kind of Heisenberg effect?

These little walks round the block together. Without them now I don't know what I should do, and I never want them to end, and to have to go inside again with Iris. I know she feels the same reluctance, but she doesn't seem to know what it is, what causes it. For me it is like two prisoners going back to their cell after a permitted period of exercise together.

After the *Winterreise* hero and his walking stick I start to think this morning about Jackson, the mysterious hero of Iris's last novel. Perhaps because of what was about to happen she was much more forthcoming to me about this novel than she usually was about work in progress. In fact I remember that her forthcomingness made me vaguely uneasy. A bad sign? She only thought of calling it *Jackson's Dilemma* when it was virtually finished; before that it had been just *Jackson*.

His dilemma may be the plot of the book, but who was Jackson? She said she didn't know: she was puzzled by him. It seems obvious today – perhaps too obvious? – that in one sense at least he was what was coming. The dark foreshadow of her present disease.

Heard the owl hooting this morning, before six, when it was still quite dark and we lay in bed together. I was propped up and beginning to type: Iris not quite asleep but drowsing. She used to say she liked the sound of the typewriter in the early morning. She had never used one herself, nor did she ever try to write at this hour.

Like the owl I have become a nocturnal creature. Now the hateful summer is over at last and blessed autumn properly begun, I feel at home in the early morning darkness. As I do in the late evenings, between nine and midnight. No 'work' then. If there is any sort of thriller on – an American not a British one – I am watching the television. Iris is asleep, and will sleep without a sound until I crawl into bed at one or two in the morning. Then she makes little noises, stretches, sometimes gets up. This is her good time too. Often in the next few hours she wakes me by humming. I reach over to her then and we stroke each other. If she talks much or wanders round the house it is harder to go back to sleep.

Not much sleep in the night, but I prefer it that way. I still manage to sleep deeply for an hour in the afternoon. Iris will drowse beside me then too, if she is not in one of her wanderfits, now increasingly frequent, when she carries clothes or sticks and stones about the house, or pulls again and again at the locked front door. Since I know it is locked – I sometimes used to forget when we came in from the walk round the block but now I check it carefully – I try to pay no attention. I *will* myself to sleep. But it is impossible. I lie listening to the sounds, muffled exclamations as if from the bottom of a well. '*Going – going*' sometimes, or '*Soon – help.*'

There is a story by Walter de la Mare in which an old gentleman in his country house wanders about at night saying, 'Coming, coming.' His voice is querulous but there is a dreadful patience in it. He has convinced himself – or maybe it is true? – that the house is aswarm with ghosts, who summon him all night long from every corner.

No use trying to nap away this afternoon. I get up and go down to make tea. Teatime, though it is too early for it: any appearance of routine can sometimes have a calming effect.

Iris still picks up whatever she can find on our walks round the block. Old sweet wrappings, matchsticks, cigarette-ends. She has a sharp eye, sharper than mine, but I am gazing with my own sort of fascinated attention at what is going on among the trees and in the sky. Autumn at last. And then winter. Thank goodness for both of them. The misty rain and the yellowing chestnut trees are what I seem to need. They are like the dusk and the dawn which are my hunting hours. The owl's too.

Suddenly feel happy and skip along, with Iris responding, as she always does to a jovial atmosphere. Autumn and winter are certainly good friends of ours. Does her good angel promise her that these are the last she will have to see?

Now I pat Iris vigorously on the bottom and she smiles like an angel's friend. I often tease her about being like a water-buffalo, a big creature lumbering out of the pond, always getting in the way. And it's true that at home she not so much clings to as nudges me, always just in front of me when I am trying to do something in the kitchen, or just behind if I turn round to go to get something. I think she understands the pantomime of the water-buffalo, though it seems unlikely that the word itself is still there. But she used to love the idea of water-buffalo, or pictures of them.

But the old paradox remains; indeed becomes more paradoxical than ever. I must be there; she wants me there every
minute; if I am in the loo she stands outside the door. Her
little mouse-cry comes up or down the stairs. And yet the
wild urge to escape, *nun weiter denn, nur weiter*, seems at
moments to be equally strong. When she stands by the front
door rattling the latch she is quite indifferent to where I am
or what I am doing.

Water-buffaloes. Nice animals. The way she moves just in
front, or accidentally nudges me, seems very like an animal.
Eating is becoming rather like that too. She eats best if I put
the spoon to her mouth: otherwise hardly anything gets
done. 'What a silly animal it is!' We laugh, and I have
no trouble getting another spoonful in. Baked beans or
ice-cream. Iris wouldn't mind if both came together; she
might even prefer it. She eats so little now and yet she
looks so well. When she is asleep I eat and drink wildly
– all sorts of unsuitable things – and they make me feel as
if I am wilting and vanishing, disintegrating and coming
to pieces.

Sex is not exactly a friend of Dr A. It seems in any case to
have more or less given us up. Iris never bothered with it
very much: now not at all, and that seems natural. Only
a short while ago I used to think: I don't mind sex going
in fact, if it doesn't go in fancy. I used to spend long and
happy hours pondering and dreaming about it.

My daydreams now are not about sex but about the
women in my childhood, which seems quite a different
thing. Even if it isn't.

Animals. What have they got to do with Dr A, or with
his friends? Actually quite a lot. When I can see us, feel
us, as two animals pushing about together, nudging and
grooming each other, grunting together as they bask in a
mutual doze. Our animal togetherness is better than sex,
and makes me forget Iris's night conversations downstairs.

I don't feel haunted any more. I don't feel like the old gentleman in the de la Mare story, in thrall to a pack of ghosts, trudging up and down flights of stairs in the small hours and calling out querulously, 'Coming – coming.'

5

The only ghosts are safely in the past. Good, good ghosts, from far away and long ago. And they were liberated by a very animal-like experience – the feel of tugging at my vest to free it from the arm of the windsor chair. I might have been pushing at Iris to get her out of the way. My fellow-animal always beside me while memory disports itself, courtesy of Dr Alzheimer.

Iris blessedly back in sleep: she has hardly woken. I am free to drowse beside her and 'think about things'. Distant things. Is it because of our present animal closeness that no memories seem to come back of the times the two of us have spent together? Later perhaps. Does true memory require distance, space in which to uncoil itself, like a genie coming out of a bottle?

Alzheimer, the dark doctor, seems to have got hold of all memories of our life together before his time. He has wiped them, or whatever it's called, from his computer. Or he doles them out at unpredictable intervals. But he has given handsome compensation, a really lavish pay-off in terms of the pre-Iris memories which now for me enchant our walks together, our early mornings in bed.

I think of my mother shushing and cradling me, to my extreme surprise and no little embarrassment, that night before I went to boarding-school for the first time. Even in my misery and apprehension I felt embarrassed, and she must have felt me stiffen. She relinquished me and became brisk, I remember that. Did she feel any regret that she had brought us up to be so unresponsive, so wary of her physical comfort? I ponder the matter now, when it doesn't in the least matter, and I enjoy nothing but the memory itself, devoid of regret or guilt or any emotion. And yet I am so pleased she did it; and that she once showed me the new moon.

Recall cannot be much bothered with the people at the school. Of course I can remember them, but it is hardly any fun to do so, just as there was hardly any fun in being at school. Just getting through the days. Waiting to get back to Littlestone. Our house had been sold after I had been at school for less than a year – another burst of parental economy – and from then on we led a nomadic existence, never leaving the seaside but moving progressively further down the front, from one rented flat or bungalow to another. We ended up at the point furthest from the links and nearest to Greatstone-on-Sea, a bungalow town of decidedly inferior social standing. I didn't mind that, because I had discovered an absorbing new holiday activity. Sailing my boat.

It was a crude little model of a Breton fishing lugger, with a red sail. It belonged to a boy at school called Michel, who must have been partly French though he seemed perfectly normal and indeed rather dull. I fell in love with the boat at first sight. Although I was by then familiar with the technique of swapping I felt there was no hope of acquiring such a precious object as that little boat. It must be a prestige object. So no doubt it once was, but as Michel had risen further up the school the prestige had worn off. Not, I suspect, a sensitive lad, he had none the less received intimations from his contemporaries that such things were only suitable for little boys.

To my delight and astonishment he seemed more than open to offers for his boat; although when he grasped the degree of my interest, which I found impossible to conceal, he prepared openly to drive a hard bargain. Precious as it was to him he might part with the boat, but what had I to offer? My only asset was a large quantity of 'tuck' – doled out to us twice a week under the matron's supervision. Michel was, fortunately for me, a greedy boy; and by handing over all the supplies of chocolate, 'crunchies', lollipops and sherbet which I had saved up, and even mortgaging future rations for that term and the next, I persuaded him to part with the boat at last.

From his look of satisfaction I could see he felt he had got a bargain, but my heart was filled with delirious joy. For the rest of term I hid the boat carefully in my tuck box and showed it to nobody. Then I took it home, to our latest rented accommodation, which was not far from the point where the shingly wastes of Dungeness began, a deadflat area dotted with salt pools and tracts of marsh.

My parents were tacitly apologetic, at least to my brothers, about the way we had come down in the world. They considered our gimcrack bungalow and its surroundings a dreary hole, but I loved them as much as I had once loved the links and the houses at the 'good' end of Littlestone. My brothers had other interests now, and were only fleetingly at home in the holidays. So it was by myself that I explored my new domain, and soon found a lonely lagoon which seemed perfectly adapted for the purpose of sailing my boat.

So it was, although the boat itself was not co-operative. For me she was beautiful, with her bluff bows and transom stern carved out of a single chunk of wood. During an earlier period of interests I had managed to collect most of a Player's cigarette card series called 'Curious Beaks'. I now christened my boat *Toucan*, because she looked like the big contoured beak of that tropical bird. She was a poor sailor, proceeding a trifle crabwise, but she was none the less a fine sight as she stood out from the shore with a ripple round her bluff bows. When the breeze took her in mid-pond she was apt to keel ignominiously over.

I did not mind; wrecked or upright she was always

beautiful for me, and I loved her. The desolate little lagoon where I sailed her was now a place of even greater romance than the golf-links had been, or the ruined cottage. And one day, as I waited for *Toucan* to drift ashore, the scene made me remember a poem I had been fascinated by in what I already thought of as the old days, before I had been sent to boarding-school. It had been read to us by Miss Jocelyn, one of the mistresses at the day-school in Queen's Gate. I had not thought her beautiful, but she was tall, dark and mysterious, with a deep thrilling voice. The poem, 'Overheard on a Saltmarsh', was a dialogue between a goblin and a nymph who possesses a string of green glass beads. He covets them and begs her for them, but she refuses to give them up.

He had nothing to offer the nymph in exchange, I reflected, whereas to obtain *Toucan* I had fortunately possessed a whole lockerful of goodies. I had been sorry for the goblin, none the less, and thought the nymph hard-hearted, which must have been one of the perquisites of being a nymph. Saying the poem to myself brought back all its old allure, and with it came a sudden stab of real homesickness. It was my first realisation that the past is the thing, never the present, and it would be by no means my last. I thought of Miss Jocelyn, and her dark hair and thrilling voice, and the dark green velvet jacket she always seemed to be wearing. That brought back thoughts of Gerda, and how comforting her surly presence had once been. Standing by the shore, watching the capsized *Toucan* borne steadily away from me on the stiff seabreeze, I had my first true experience of nostalgia, and all its rich self-indulgent solitude.

It comes back much richer and with keener force today, as I lie in bed beside Iris and give myself up to it. Have I been given, as a kind of bonus or legacy, the memories that in her brain have been wiped away, if indeed for her such self-indulgent memories ever existed? Difficult not to feel it now as a part of a new and as it were emergency mode of consciousness. It connects with those 'short views of human life – never further than dinner or tea' which the Reverend Sydney Smith always recommended to parishioners bereaved, or in the grip of depression. I notice now that there is a positive pleasure in feeling we are getting through the time *somehow*: anyhow, as if time existed for no other purpose than to be got through.

Always something to look forward to: the coming of night and the evening drink: the time before dawn when I can give myself up to a frank enjoyment of all that's past. Anything that comes along.

An orgy of 'Wandering through eternity', as dear old Belial put it. He put it not only beautifully but accurately, for consciousness – whatever goes on inside our own head – is surely all that eternity can mean to us?

What an admirable fellow Belial sounds. Even if he wasn't very good at being a devil.

Still dreaming idly about Miss Jocelyn and my memory of her. How old would she be now – about a hundred? Less probably. She was ageless to us, but I should guess now not much over thirty. She read poetry without a poetry voice – just made it sound good. And thrilling. She did 'The Pied Piper of Hamelin' very well, but 'Overheard on a Saltmarsh' is the one I particularly remember. She sounded amused by it, and yet excited too.

Long afterwards I came on it in an anthology, and found it was by Harold Monro, a Georgian poet. He and his wife ran The Poetry Bookshop. They had tea-parties there for fellow Georgians. As a poet he had his felicitous moments, as the saltmarsh poem shows. In private he seems to have been a haunted man, a secret homosexual, with a possibly all too understanding wife. It must have been a common enough situation in those days.

Sailing my little boat slowly down the stream of memories

Life does seem but a dream when I can lie in bed like this, with Iris unconscious beside me, or sometimes briefly awake and making quiet little cooing or humming sounds. However bad night may have been early morning is usually a good time. At such moments we seem together, although I am feeding only on memories from the deep past long before we were married. Yet again I wonder: why am I not remembering now things we have done together? Of course there is a sense in which I do remember them; but I suppose I don't want to think about them, as I think about what happened to me, years and years ago. Will I get nauseated by such memories in time, as if by eating too many chocolates?

The present flow was certainly started by that moment when I stood trouserless in the kitchen, trying to wriggle the tail of my vest off the windsor chair. That was a kind of involuntary shock, bringing back the mantrap, the ruined cottage, the owl . . . The recall of everything else has just been deliberate self-indulgence: Gerda and the golf course, my mother showing me the new moon, the boat *Toucan*.

Had Iris been with me in the kitchen when I caught my vest on the chair I should not have had this sudden flood of memory. I should have been too conscious of her, too bothered by my own sense of her anxieties. These childhood memories are a way of escape.

We had yet another repetition of the incident this morning. Getting out of the front door is a difficulty, because Iris, in her water-buffalo guise, crowds up against me, and will hardly wait for the door to be unlocked before she is pushing through it. I have no room to shut the door, and when I do get it shut I find that the back of my coat has got stuck as it closed. I am more seriously trapped this time. When I manage to get the key back into the Yale lock it will not turn, and held fast as I am I cannot exercise any pressure. I shall have to wriggle out of the coat, like the heroine caught in the mantrap wriggling out of her dress. But no sooner is the expedient in my mind than the lock suddenly yields, the key turns and the door opens.

Iris might have escaped, leaving me standing there helpless. But no, of course she hasn't. She is herself standing vacantly, like a good water-buffalo, as if waiting for me to be beside her again, and direct her.

These repetitions, absurd as they are, give me no pleasure. Not like the first time, which unlocked memory. Once we would have joked about them together. It is a sort of joke to me now, not a specially funny one, but in the old days Iris and I would both have burst out laughing. Of course we would. Iris has in fact been watching the incident, but without any reaction. She seems to think it just something that happens every day. And I take it in the same spirit. Gravely we link arms and set out on one of our little walks. Round the block and back home.

As we go I remember a similar repetition. I once lost the lower half of my denture swimming with a pipe and mask at Lanzarote. A year or so later I did just the same thing in Lake Como. It was such an improbable misfortune that everybody laughed – our friend Audi Villers who lives on Lanzarote, Drue Heinz with whom we were staying on Lake Como. They were sympathetic too of course, but on neither occasion did Iris laugh: she was much too concerned for me and my welfare, and she made valiant underwater efforts herself to locate the teeth. Quite hopeless in both cases. They were much too far down.

I think of her goodness about that now as we walk along. It gives me a sudden lift, and I put my arms around her, hug her, kiss her on the cheek.

As a 'carer' I am sometimes conscious of the way one ought to behave: the way, that is, in which a professional would behave. Never losing the temper, never raising the voice. Persuading and controlling in that firm wheedling tone which carers come to have. As if talking to an imbecile child. Whatever exasperations they may sometimes feel, they hide it. I don't, I can't. Hardly a day goes by without my flying into a brief frenzy, shouting at Iris, or saying in level tones something like: 'I don't know *what* to do with you – you exhaust me so much.' Or sometimes saying, with a reassuring smile, 'Have you any idea how much I hate you?'

It sounds then as if I am making a reasonable point, and she seems to receive it in the same spirit. She knows me, she wants me. She knows the violence that is in me at moments and is just controlled, but only just. When I have been struggling for minutes at a time to get arms through sleeves or heels into shoes, she can feel that surge of ungentleness very close to the surface. Once she put her hands over her head and whimpered, 'Don't hit me.' She knew better than I did what might happen.

At one level I felt horribly shocked: at another I simply accepted the possibility of what she was saying. I did want to hit her. Parents do too, I'm sure. If I'd been a parent would I have learnt more control? So useful later on, if the wife, or the husband, becomes a child again.

I could feel that Iris wasn't in the least resentful of the wish she intuited in me. Something inside her accepted it, as if it were a part of loving me and being loved. One of those tedious 'social' questions presents itself. Would a child, or a senile adult, prefer to be looked after by a parent or partner who both loved it and knocked it about? Rather than go into some sort of state care?

Depends on the degree of knocking about I suppose. The opposite of those violent impulses when I am trying to get Iris into shoes or clothes is the pleasure I find in feeding her. She hardly eats now unless I spoon it gently into her mouth. Baked beans, ice-cream. She makes crooning and glugging noises then. Highly satisfactory for both of us. No need whatever to find words and be coherent. But there was nothing in the least incoherent when she cowered, and said,

'Don't hit me.' The nearness of violence brought stark sense back into her speech.

I muse now, as we walk along, on the reasons for my reluctance to undress Iris at night. I know I ought to: it should be part of our routine. But it is such a relief to go along with her simple wish to get into bed in all her clothes, shoes included. Then I shan't have to dress her in the morning, and shan't get in such a temper with elbows and feet. The other night as she got under the duvet I said, 'You're like the Burial of Sir John Moore at Corunna, darling.

> 'He lay like a warrior taking his rest,
> With his martial cloak around him.'

Iris appeared delighted by that. Not only did she seem to remember the reference (I used to quote the poem some- times in the old days) but she seemed pleased to think of herself as Sir John Moore, not enclosed in a 'useless coffin', but lying there in his soldier's cloak, fully dressed and ready for action, as he always slept when on campaign.

Something to think about, to amuse oneself with. And it definitely amused Iris too. We could share it. But on these little walks thoughts are usually solitary. And I no longer wonder what, if anything, is going through Iris's head. Instead I find myself coming back, full circle, like the familiar houses we shall be walking round, to the moment when I closed the front door and trapped the tail of my coat.

It was like *The Woodlanders*, the Hardy novel I now start consciously to think about. The point was, I recall, that the husband was a philanderer, as no doubt Hardy himself would secretly have liked to be. He seduces the wife of the village woodcutter – isn't she called Sukey? – as he has seduced other and grander women in the neighbourhood; and his wife finds out all about it and leaves him. The woodcutter finds out about it too, and murderous with jealousy fixes a mantrap on the woodland path the seducer (he's a doctor) uses when he goes on his professional visits.

It so happens that the doctor has just begged his wife to come back to him, and she had promised to meet him in the evening on that very path, for a discussion. Hence she is the one who sets off the trap and is nearly caught in it. In the dark the doctor finds her abandoned clothes in the jaws of the monster, and is distraught. What has happened? Is she dead?

It occurs to me now that Hardy had an unconscious recollection of *A Midsummer Night's Dream* – the play within the play. Pyramus finds Thisbe's clothes, bloodied by the lion, and kills himself. The seducer doctor of course does no such thing. The danger and escape, to say nothing of his wife in her undies, brings them back together and reconciles them. Like the wonderful and ambiguous ending of *A Midsummer Night's Dream*. Play and novel have the same woodland pastoral atmosphere. Beautiful, but disturbing.

The old Eng. Lit. again. I taught it for nearly fifty years and feel detached from it now. Glad to be so. But old habits die hard. Thinking about *The Woodlanders* has seen me through another little walk. But I really prefer my own memories.

Or do I? Those morning memories, lying in bed, are so pleasant that I took it for granted that memory could never be dull or desolate or boring. But perhaps it can? Suppose I was blind, and in a home or hospital day after day. Would memory be as good there as it is now – as comforting, as reliable? I rather think not.

Hastily think of something else. Where was I? The little boat *Toucan*. She survived at least until the end of the war, and then must have disappeared on my parents' final move into Kent. I was still in the army in Germany at the time. But

before she went to limbo, or to 'Pieland', *Toucan* made one
final appearance on water.

It was after I was called up into the army, in 1943. I was on
leave. Probably my first leave. We were up in London, my
mother and I, and I was due to return to barracks the next
day. I very much wanted to sail *Toucan* on the Round Pond
in Kensington Gardens, before I went back. My mother was
doubtful, but she agreed. We had *Toucan* with us in a bag.
It was a fine day, nice breeze. I was just bending down in
my cap, tunic and army boots to put her in the water when
my mother gave a warning cry. An officer was just about
to walk past us. We were supposed to salute officers. I left
Toucan to her own devices. She sailed merrily away into
the pond. I stood up and saluted. As smartly as I could.

The officer returned the salute in the normal way, and
then looked at me, and saw the boat. He hesitated a moment
in his stride; his expression seemed unbelieving, incredulous. He glanced towards my mother, who gave him an
inviting smile. That did the trick. As if it had checked any
need he may have felt to stop and investigate this unmilitary
scene he looked once more from my mother to me, and then
he walked on.

I breathed a sigh of relief. My mother had a fit of uncontrollable giggles. *Toucan*, having gallantly and precariously
reached the middle of the pond under sail, now capsized.
It would be some time before she floated in, but I knew
she would come. She was the only boat on the pond that
wartime day in bombed-out London. My mother and I stood
waiting for her in the spring sunshine, my mother still going
into a fit of giggles from time to time as she remembered the
officer's face. I felt it had been a lucky escape, although I
don't suppose the officer would really have put me on a
charge. Presumably for slovenly behaviour while wearing
His Majesty's uniform?

My father was not told of the incident. My mother and
I were staying in a hotel in London that night, as a final

treat for my leave before I had to go back to barracks the next day.

I wish I could tell Iris about *Toucan*. In fact I must have told her in the old days, perhaps when we visited Littlestone together. Everything now reminds me of that childhood idyll, even small things as we walk round the block together. A house under extensive repair is having metal-framed windows taken out and replaced with timber ones. Apart from the more select residences, like the one we originally had, all the seafront houses at Littlestone had 'metal casements', as John Betjeman called them. Metal was much used on smart little houses in the '30s. 'Oh the metal lantern and the white enamelled door!' Our present house has both, which I take pride in, as I do in adjacent Belbroughton Road, one section of our little walk, and celebrated by John Betjeman in his poem 'Spring in North Oxford'.

> Belbroughton Road is bonny, when pinkly bursts
> the spray
> Of prunus and forsythia across the public way . . .

Rachel Cecil, wife of my old friend and teacher, always used to giggle when we chanted together her own favourite lines.

> And a constant sound of flushing runneth from the
> windows where
> The toothbrush too is airing in this new North
> Oxford air . . .

Street and houses were new when they must have given the ebullient Betjeman his impulse to dash off the poem. Around 1927? – two years after I was born. A feeling of hope and expectation of the future at that time? I suppose it was created by reaction against the war, by the new Garden Cities, by modernity itself? All that sort of thing.

*   *   *

Excitement this morning. Iris escaped. After the postman came and I had to sign for something I was flurried and forgot to relock the door. A few minutes later I realised the silence. Called again and again but no reply. Overwhelming sense of being alone. But no time to think of that – rush out of the front door, look up and down the street. Nothing. Sometimes she has gone into a neighbouring garden – not hiding exactly, just out of sight.

After scouting vainly about I get out the car, drive concentrically round the neighbouring streets. No sign of her. I ring the police. A policeman in a car comes round, a nice elderly man, and says he will put out a search for her. Having taken the particulars in a leisurely way he thinks he had better just look round the house. This has happened before, so I don't point out that I have already done so. He gazes impassively at the heaps of this and that in every room. 'Most admired disorder'! – doesn't Hamlet's mother say that about the state of her son? Gertrude in the play must have meant it was something to be wondered at. But the policeman gives no sign of either wonder or admiration.

'You never know, sir,' he says. A conclusion for all occasions. Perhaps a person reported missing is sometimes found concealed and dead? Have I done in Iris and stowed her away somewhere? Why would I call the police in that case? Well, you never know.

Hours seem to pass, though actually not much more than two. The policeman sensibly advises me to stay at home. Impossible to do anything.

A loud knock on the door. I rush, and scrabble to open it. I have locked it on the inside – too late now – and for the moment can't find the key. Must have left it on the kitchen table. Run to get it, thinking distractedly of stable doors. When I've got it open there stands Iris. Expectant, sly but triumphant, enormously refreshed. She looks a bit like a schoolgirl who has won the record for running away from school the longest time. And indeed she has: she has never been away so long before.

A seraphic smile for me, and an even bigger one for the man who stands just behind her. I start to thank the man, and ask where she was found. He happened to see her – nearly at the top of the Woodstock Road. He turns to go. I thank him effusively. I am too flustered to ask how he knew it was Iris, but I manage to stutter out, 'Do just tell me your name!'

He looks amazed. 'Why I'm Valentine Cunningham, John. Your old colleague. It was just a bit of luck I happened to spot her. I'm late for a pupil – I must be going now.'

Amidst all the anxiety and relief I hadn't recognised him. My own mind must be going. I call out after him, 'I'm so sorry, Val,' and he turns and gives a wave and a smile as he gets into his car.

Iris still looks well and happy, as if basking in her achievement. How did she manage to get so far? No point in asking. I put my arms round her. We sit at the kitchen table and presently have a cup of coffee, but she hardly drinks any.

If it's warm the house cats of the area lie out on the pavement, giving an impression of the bright young people of the '20s, gossiping and showing off. Obliging animals, they always rise to have their backs stroked and rub themselves against Iris's old trousers. I point them out as we round the corner, and Iris makes little mewing noises of recognition.

In Linton Road, outside the Linton Lodge Hotel, there are always a number of interesting cars. Like all children I once loved admiring cars. There was a Hispano-Suiza at Littlestone with a windscreen which screwed up and down, and an open Mercedes with three shiny and scaly pipes coming out from its bonnet. I asked David, my eldest brother, what was the function of these pipes. 'Superchargers of course,' he said, dismissing my ignorance with kindly impatience. I had a feeling that he might not know what a supercharger was, or what function it performed, and so was careful not to ask him, although I would have liked to find out more.

Today I have none of my old interest left in the insides of cars; I don't keep up; but as part of recent life's little compensations I like looking at them again, especially the sleek oriental ones, with peacock logos on their gleaming bonnets, in dark blue or purple enamel. I have the impression that these eastern cars are washed and cleaned with special zeal by their owners.

Our old Fiat Panda has green mould round the windows, and pigeon droppings from the trees in the front garden under which it stands. Some delicate-looking little seedlings – wild geranium perhaps? – are growing in the crevice where the bonnet opens. I feel I want to cherish them, like indoor plants.

As we shuffle along together I go on dreaming about cars. The old Rolls at Littlestone sitting in its garage. In the first days of our honeymoon in 1956 we visited Littlestone on the way to Dover. We had a little green Austin van which I had bought (it was very cheap – no purchase tax) just before we were married, and in it we were going to drive through France, over the Alps and into northern Italy.

But I wanted to show Littlestone to Iris and she was keen to see it.

The visit was not exactly a success. It was a grey day – the weather had been awful all summer – with none of that golden light from the wide pale-blue sky which I remembered. The tide was far out but Iris was keen to swim, so we trudged out for half a mile across the rippled sand and mud flats. Although she waded out an immense distance Iris could only immerse herself a foot or two. I stood in the grey featureless expanse, guarding her clothes (there wasn't a soul for miles of course) and her new wedding ring which she had entrusted to me in case it should come off and be lost in the sea.

She emerged eventually, black to the knees as if she were wearing a pair of mud stockings. While she was away, becoming a small featureless figure in the grey shallows that seemed to stretch all the way to France, I had experienced a failure of nerve. Littlestone meant nothing to me now, and what else did? For the moment marriage seemed as unpromising a prospect as this mud and sky and sea. With acute nostalgia I remembered the green waves washing on the shingle and round the seaweedy groynes. It was high tide in childhood, just as the sun always shone.

I could not then share Littlestone with Iris, just as I cannot do so today, while we walk hand in hand round our unending little block. I think of it myself, as it was, and the thought inevitably separates me from her, as she now is. I loved, almost worshipped, the loneliness of childhood, the immense pleasure one felt in being alone. But that, like our marriage, was being alone among invisible but watchful angels. This is the real thing. Iris can comfort me by her presence but she cannot watch over me any more. In memory and daydream there is nothing but solitude. The friend I have come to depend on.

6

And a friend, I'm glad to say, who could well have been an enemy.

My awareness of solitude today brings back that visit to the small town of Rye, not far from Littlestone, which we made together only a few years ago. Landlocked now but once a 'Cinque Port' with the sea at its gates. The picturesque streets were garlanded for a Festival.

In his first published novel, a wonderful farrago of rusticity and melodrama called *Desperate Remedies*, the youthful Hardy observes that small towns holding 'Festivals' are the dullest things in creation. His example he calls Hocbridge, which is the real Banbury, not far from Oxford, where the proceedings are only enlivened by the heroine's father, an architect like young Hardy himself, falling to his death from the summit of the church tower.

No such excitement occurred when we were in Rye, but for me it was a memorable visit none the less. Iris, although more than willing to take part in the Festival, had excused herself from giving a talk. I would do what I could, I said, offering something on Henry James and ghost stories. From a cultural point of view James, who lived there for many years, is still patron spirit of the town of Rye.

As the easiest way of making up a little talk I brought in the other James too. This is M.R. James, sometime Provost of Eton and of King's College, Cambridge, legendary scholar and author of *Ghost Stories of an Antiquary*. One of the best of these is 'Oh Whistle and I'll Come to You, My Lad'. I had no difficulty in concocting a little 'theory' about it, which I hoped might amuse the festival-minded ladies of Rye.

The terrifying phantom of this tale, brought back to life by the note of an antique whistle, sits up suddenly in the darkness of a hotel room, feeling around, with outstretched arms of crumpled linen, for the scholarly victim in the bed. He has accidentally summoned the ghost by unearthing on the local golf course this ancient whistle or pipe and rashly blowing it.

Surely, I suggested to the Rye ladies, this apparition must be the implacable goddess of the linen cupboard, an embodiment for the author of threatening femininity? And what an appalling experience for a misogynistic bachelor, however amiable – and Monty James was certainly that – to imagine himself going snugly and safely to bed in his favourite little seaside hotel: only to wake up in the night and see a sheeted woman sit up beside him!

There were a few uncertain titters from the audience, but my little idea, such as it was, had not really struck a chord. Never mind. We were to be put up in Lamb House, Henry James's very own residence, and our kindly host and hostess, Guardians of the National Trust, gave us excellent drinks and supper. We retired to bed in good spirits – in the Master's very own bedroom.

What an honour! As we got into the comfortable double bed I wondered aloud to Iris if this was the Master's bed as well as his bedroom. Did he like to sleep in a big bed or a narrow one? Did any of the detailed and exhaustive biographies have anything to say about the matter? Iris grunted, already half asleep, and in a few seconds I was asleep too, having made a mental note to ask our host and hostess about the bed in the morning.

It must have been between three and four when I woke abruptly. There was faint daylight already in the room. Something was wrong. What was it? Indigestion, heart attack? No, I felt quite normal. Then what was the trouble?

Suddenly I realised. I felt full of an overwhelming depression, as if the day to come was to offer nothing but utter emptiness and loneliness, boredom, the knowledge of all that was lacking in life, all that had been missed.

It was so overwhelming that I could not stay in bed. I got up and went over to the window. I drew aside a corner of the thick curtain and peeped out. There, in the still grey light of dawn, was the view, unchanged, that James must have seen every morning on rising. An almost too perfect English vista of cobbled street, comfortably huddled old houses, the little church beyond. Wasn't it called Watchbell Street, an almost too perfect English name?

How reassuring it might have been for James, to look out on such a view when he got up in the morning! But somehow it did not look now as if the view had reassured him. On the contrary it had a look about it of desolation, as if it were faithfully reproducing what was in the mind and soul of the man who had gazed out. Had it brought home that all his years had passed him by? With nothing truly suffered and enjoyed, with nothing loved?

In later years James suffered from insomnia – I remembered reading that. How many times had he looked out on that view in the summer dawn with the sensation of loneliness that I was now mysteriously experiencing? But mine had no apparent cause. On the contrary.

I crept back into bed beside Iris (James had no Iris), fell asleep at once and woke at eight feeling quite cheerful and ready for breakfast. I told Iris what I had felt when I woke in the night, or rather in the early dawn. She was sympathetic, but smiled at my suggestion that Henry James had been with us in the night. I felt sure he had. Had he been aware, or not aware, of the couple from the future who had officiously installed themselves in his chaste bedroom? There had been many others like ourselves after all, including the writer E.F. Benson who had lived in the house for many years after James's death, and who had even become the Mayor of Rye, a position James would have evaded with polished modesty and elaborate self-depreciation.

I forgot to ask our host and hostess about the bed. None the less I was privately convinced that the strange shock of waking, and then of looking out on James's motionless street, had been the only paranormal experience I have ever had. Not exactly of the occult, but of what James himself had referred to in the title of one of his last novels, *The Sense of the Past*. It had happened to be a highly uncomfortable sense. But the very acuteness of that depression made me convinced of its authenticity – it must have come from somewhere.

It was easy after the event to start fitting the pieces together, as it were. I had talked about the other James's ghost story; and amused myself, if not my small audience, with notions of bachelors, fearful of women, waking at night to see the sheets sit up in the bed, ripple into hostile form, and seek with blind malice to envelop the helpless male. Such a nightmare might have befallen either of the Jameses, but of course it could not have happened to me.

For them it was a case of things not happening, of things which afterwards they might have longed to happen – love, passion, fulfilment. Not, in the case of both Jameses, with a vengeful woman from the linen cupboard, but with the boy or young man of their dreams.

Fanciful no doubt. But there is no doubt too that ghost stories can tell the truth, in their own peculiar kind of way. In *The Turn of the Screw* James's real *donnée*, as he would have termed it, is not the haunting of the children but the children's own secret and inscrutable self-sufficiency. They are of their very nature remote from the adult world, living in a universe of their own; and James perceives this with all the more force because for him too the 'adult' world – love and marriage and all its casual intimacies – were things unknown, things guessed at, intuited, sometimes envied, never experienced.

And had I for a few seconds or minutes been inside James's head, or his mind, when he woke in the morning to a feeling of his life's emptiness and loneliness? Perhaps it was presumptuous of me to feel I had; but I did feel it none the less. Perhaps if there is anything at all in the idea of 'haunting', or being haunted, it is in this sense of being slipped, involuntarily or unwillingly, into someone else's mind, someone in the past or the present.

I remembered then that other ghost story, the one by Walter de la Mare, in which the solitary old gentleman who craves for company wanders about the stairs in the middle of the night, calling out, 'Coming, coming.'

In that story the young man whom he has virtually kidnapped and forced to stay the night and be entertained at supper, wakes as I had, and finds the bedroom looking inexplicably different: looking the way a room might look to someone who was intensely afraid. The young man is not afraid; there does not at that moment seem anything to be afraid of. But then as he gets out of bed he hears voices sounding plaintively and distantly, all over the house.

I don't feel in the least depressed now as I get cautiously back into bed beside sleeping Iris, snuggle down and begin to drink my cup of tea. Freeing my tail from that windsor chair has certainly released the flood of memory. But it is easy enough to find memories when one depends on them and courts them all the time. I am conscious once more of how much they have become a way of escape; even, it must be said, a way of escape from the loved one who lies at my side. So long as I can be free to remember I can still need to be physically with her, still depend entirely on her being there.

Strange that I seemed to find myself, that time in Rye, in Henry James's mind, the mind of a man who has been dead for so many years, when I can't today imagine what it's like to be inside Iris's poor distracted head. Of course we can communicate, are in a touch so close that we both take it for granted. But it is far easier to experience, or at least to imagine, what Henry James may have felt than what Iris is, or is not, feeling.

Even while thinking that, I find myself escaping again. I am back in the Mixed Room, with the pale blue sea light flooding in, and the lemony scent of gin mingling with the suede and leather odours of coats and golfbags. Had these people really been as nice, I now wonder, as I used to be sure they were at that time, when I was seven, eight or nine years old? For me they were romance and mystery as well as casual niceness: I contemplated without envy, and without much curiosity, what unknown things they might be doing when they were not in here, or on the golf course, what dashing events and excitements filled their days. That was all a part of the idyll of the place, its space and air and wide sky.

I knew that some, in their other lives, were stockbrokers, whatever that was. I had no wish to find out. I was not anxious to know about any of these people, because I was obscurely aware that knowledge could only compromise the charming mystery of their lives, lives which were a part of houses I had never been into, seeing only their sea-bleached cotton curtains blowing in the sunshine.

The Spicers (he was 'in paper') had the grandest house on the sea-wall, but I had heard my father remarking that Glucksteen could have bought out the lot of them. Why Nancy Glucksteen's father, always chuckling and chatting away in the Mixed Room, should have wanted to do such a thing I had no idea; and Nancy herself, a year or so younger than me, gave no impression of affluence. She was a nice plump little girl to whom I felt rather attached, although I did not want anyone to be aware of it, least of all Nancy herself. We sometimes watched the tennis on the courts near the clubhouse, and once as we were walking home together she said how romantic everything looked in the twilight, rolling her little black eyes at me. I thought this a silly remark but was rather touched too: vanity suggested this might be Nancy's way of saying she was fond of me.

Apart from the general fact that she belonged to the world of Littlestone there was nothing romantic about Nancy for me. I reserved such feelings for older girls, like Patricia Terry. Moving as she did in a world of sports cars and young men who wore silk scarves, Patricia scarcely noticed me, and I much preferred things that way; but once she came up to me in the Mixed Room and said, 'You read such a lot, don't you? Shall we two start a society called "The Readers"?' I fervently assented to this proposition, not grasping that she was teasing me, though in quite a kind way. Sunburned and handsome, a good tennis-player, she must have been nearly ten years older than I was.

Nancy Glucksteen's parents were over by the bar, in loud and hearty conversation with Mr Oberlander – Herr O as he was known. It was a nickname he encouraged. He was famous for his putting, which he took very seriously. When he sank a long putt on the eighteenth green he would perform a little dance of triumph, waving his club in the air and chanting,

> 'Said the old Obadiah to the young Obadiah
> I am dry, Obadiah, I am dry.
> Said the young Obadiah to the old Obadiah
> So am I, Obadiah, so am I.'

The Glucksteens lived in the next house to Herr O and obviously got on with him very well. This would have been in 1933 or '34. The Glucksteens were certainly Jewish: Herr O very much a self-declared German. How did they really get on, and what did they think of each other? The strange thing is that both these families, as I now feel looking back, were, at least temporarily, innocent. Perhaps unconsciously they regarded the Littlestone world as a holiday and a refuge, something quite separated from whatever was going on in politics and public affairs.

The other possibility is that Littlestone was not innocent at all, any more than anywhere else at the time, or at any other time; and that the usual dislikes, envies and resentments were festering below the surface; the usual amounts, too, of marital misery, jealousies, affairs and intrigues, money worries . . . No doubt. But I still feel I was not entirely naïve in taking the idyllic nature of that little society for granted. It still seems so, even after all the things that have happened since, to myself and to the rest of the world. I have no idea what became of Herr O – was he interned? Did he see the signs in time and go back to Germany? – or what happened to the Glucksteens.

They live in the past. Patricia Terry is vanishing up the New Romney road in a sports car. On the eighteenth green Herr O is for ever singing his little song; Nancy is rolling her little black eyes at me and saying the twilight was romantic . . .

7

In 1943 I was called up into the army, from which I didn't escape until 1947, two years after the war ended. I dreaded the army just as I had dreaded school, but to my amazement I found it quite different, and infinitely preferable. The sheer relief of this discovery made the experience itself seem almost delightful. Soldiers were not a bit like the schoolboys whom I had so much disliked. There was no team spirit, no rivalry or censoriousness, and very little attempt at organisation.

My fellow soldiers or recruits were big and clumsy, unworldly and uncouth, kindly and fearful. Unlike the correct public schoolboys I was accustomed to they made no attempt to hide their feelings, and their apprehension and misery at finding themselves away from home for the first time. They were helpless; they missed their mothers dreadfully: in the adjacent bunks of the crowded barrack-room I could hear some of them weeping in the night.

It was a most comforting sound. I wished I could console them. No stiff upper lips here: they were openly and pathetically grateful for my sympathy, or anyone else's. Sometimes two of them would huddle together, and hold one another, as I had seen women do on the wartime railway stations. All this was deeply reassuring. Previously I had led my own life, inside my own solitary concerns. Now, and for the first time, I felt wholly at home with other people. I felt I could do everything the army expected of me – which was not much as it seemed – and do it as well as or even better than the others.

I even did my best at 'Physical Training', and the savage corporal with a curiously fluty voice who swore at us as we tried to negotiate rope nets and wooden horses at least recognised how hard I was trying. At weapon-training I earned the commendation of the sergeant for remembering the names of the many parts of the Bren machine-gun. When he covered my hand with his big brown fist as he taught me to pull back the bolt of my rifle and take the first pressure, I felt absurdly gratified by his saying reminiscently that it reminded him of the hand of a girl he once knew.

Soldiers in my experience could say such things without sounding either soppy or as if they were making a sexual advance. In fact I neither learned nor saw anything of homosexuality in the army, although I knew all about it theoretically from school, where my instinct had in any case been to keep away from everyone. Now a physical contact like the sergeant's hand, or a fellow-recruit putting an arm round my neck, merely seemed pleasurable and humane. I relished the camaraderie which in a very few days began to grow up between us all in the barrack-room. No more books and private dreams: all such things now seemed equally and entirely out of place.

Great then was my dismay when I was told one morning to report to the Orderly Room. Although I had been only two months in the army I was already quite familiar with its little ways, and this could only mean trouble in some form. Nor was I wrong. I received instructions to report to the OCTU (Officer Cadet Training Unit) at Aldershot. I was also given seven days' leave. My kindly comrades commiserated with me. They crowed a little too. 'Cor, you'll catch it now, Johnny. They'll turn you into a fucking officer.' The only thing they envied me was the week's leave, a pearl beyond price.

I was warmed by their sympathy, but their frank amusement very much depressed me. It was going to be all right for them. I wanted only to stay with them in the snug barrack-room, with the undemanding routines and the total absence of responsibilities. I already disliked the officer types: they seemed much the same as boys at school. Without knowing it I had discovered, as many middle-class boys had done at that time and in those circumstances, the romance of the proletariat. It features in the poetry of the period – Auden and Spender – and in the outlook of the intelligentsia. It comes in Orwell, most obviously in *1984*. Romance is the right word for it. The lower classes were wonderful. Exploited and downtrodden as they were they remained the salt of the earth, the whisper of love, the hope of the future. Their mysterious culture was to be admired and emulated. It all seems very old-fashioned today.

I went on leave in a rather low state. It seemed an anti-climax. I knew that being at home would seem empty and meaningless now, just as Littlestone itself had seemed long ago, back for the holidays for the first time from school.

And so it proved. At the beginning of the war we had been living in a small London flat, which was bombed during the blitz in 1940. Something else had to be found, and my parents had been offered a small house at Gerrards Cross, to rent for the duration. There I had soon become just as attached to the woods and wild places round about as I had been to the open skies and the sunlit links of Littlestone.

The woodlands near which we lived at Gerrards Cross are now bisected with the motorway and dotted all over with desirable residences. But during the war years all was peace and rural quiet and stagnation. Grass already sprouted through the newly madeup drives and roads; no hiker or tripper walked in the wild glades, full of golden beechleaf drifts and Rose Bay Willowherb. Rare White Admirals, one of the most beautiful and least gaudy of all butterflies, flitted ghostlike along the lush damp woodland rides. I had private holes and lairs among the Macrocarpa and Lawson's cypress where I lay reading, or attempting to write poems. Dreams of fair women, imagined but never encountered, mingled with the sights and smells of the woodland, and the resinous odour of the conifers on hot days.

This period too was now over and past. Home on leave I saw that all too well. In my last schooldays at Gerrards Cross I had been fond of Katherine Mansfield's Journal, and had marked the passage where she says, 'I shall not walk with bare feet in wet woods again.' She must have been just developing the tuberculosis which eventually killed her. Now I felt, or felt I felt, the same. For me too the woods were over, just as the dunes and links of Littlestone had been. I would have to stop going backwards instead of forwards. The future had come upon me, as the curse came upon the Lady of Shalott in Tennyson's poem.

But just for the moment I welcomed it. I did not in the least worry about the war, the army, all the unknown life that was to be. I recognised that I was in limbo, and the sooner I got back among my fellow-soldiers the better. I remember being surprised at the sheer unusualness, in me, of this state of mind.

But in 1943 everything seemed to be on the move. Even my parents appeared to have caught the prevailing mood and to be as preoccupied with getting on with their job, or the war, as everybody else was. My mother worked long hours in a soldiers' canteen; my father, having made desperate but unavailing attempts to get back into something military, had got himself temporarily into the aircraft business. My brothers were both in the army. I scarcely saw either of them during the war. One was to be captured by the Germans during the advance north of Rome; the other was seriously wounded in 1945 at the Rhine crossing.

Lying in bed with Iris beside me I think about those comparatively recent years, as they now seem to be. What was she doing then, in those years before I met her? She had been a grown-up person during the war, and I had scarcely been that. She had finished 'Greats' at Oxford – the demanding four-year course in classical literature, history and philosophy which only the best and most intellectual students could tackle – and she had at once been drafted for the duration into the Treasury, the top flight of the civil service. After working there a short time she became the acknowledged expert on one of the trickiest fiscal concepts which had arisen during the emergency period. This was 'National Promotion in Absentia', and it related to the complex problem of pay ratio. What might a functionary have been earning, what status in the hierarchy might he have achieved, had he not been called to the colours on the outbreak of war to serve his country in a more warlike capacity?

There is always something intriguing about the hypothetical. Imagining Iris at her desk in Whitehall (she showed me the window once, quite close to the Parliament buildings) I imagine too the life she was living there, and the far from notional steps and decisions she might have taken in her private life – happenings which would have ensured that I never met her. Her brilliant and creative mind, preoccupied for many hours a day with the niceties of bureaucratic business, contrived to function none the less in other fields, notably in a hunger for the kinship of her kind: people with whom she could argue about the arts and discuss literature, people with whom she could fall in love.

Wartime London was in many ways far more active intellectually and artistically – emotionally too no doubt – than it has ever been since. Those were the great days of magazines like *Horizon* and *Poetry London*, for whose cultural offerings there was an extraordinary appetite among both civilians and the armed forces. Cyril Connolly's highbrow *Horizon* would actually be passed from hand to hand in barracks and mess rooms, the troops appreciating its bland refusal to concern itself with any sort of wartime propaganda.

Iris met Cyril Connolly, Stephen Spender, and Arthur Koestler (whom she instantly disliked, a rare thing for her) and she became a friend of Tambimuttu, the charming and eccentric little Sri Lankan editor of *Poetry London*. Her more serious contacts dated back to her time in Oxford, where all the young men had adored her. She had probably been closest emotionally to Frank Thompson, the brilliant elder brother of our contemporary historian E.P. Thompson.

Frank had joined the special forces in 1944, fighting undercover in Greece and the Balkans. Captured by the Bulgarian army after a misdirected parachute drop he was shot along with the other partisans. Iris told me that she and he had not been in love exactly – they had been so full of their own work and their own play – but the waste of his death seemed an almost mortal blow to her own powers of living, and one from which they took many months to recover. Recover in a sense she did, to fall in love with other men, men as remarkable in their own way as the hero who had died in the Balkans. Destiny might, as I later felt, have promoted any one of them. But Iris remained like a star, shining and single in the middle of her constellations. And neither of us knew of the other's existence.

For me the army had become like a womb. Birth into a terrifying world of military realities could not be far away and yet gestation continued to prolong itself. For months I was sent here and there, on this 'course' or that; all designed, as it seemed, to further my military education; and yet there were no exams to pass, and no special penalties for poor performance. The army seemed to value good manners above dedication and high achievement. Once, after I had returned to the home counties from distant Catterick, where I had been instructed in the art of the Four Point Two Inch Mortar, the Adjutant of our unit sent for me. He was gazing thoughtfully at a sheet of paper. Standing to attention I saluted but he did not look up at me. It seemed to take him a very long time to read the page on the desk before him, and I wondered haplessly what horrors it could contain.

Had I done so badly that he was about to invite me to leave His Majesty's Service? Would I be sent down a coalmine instead, or on board a destroyer? The Adjutant, a gangling kindly man with weak eyes and an always immaculate tunic and Sam Browne belt, hardly knew how to put the worst into words.

Finally he looked up and said, 'It's an interesting report, Bayley. Very interesting. Does you credit on the whole. It seems you set a good example. Always tried to do your best. Various mishaps. It seems you had difficulty getting the hang of it. But you always managed to cheer them up. That's what it says.'

He looked puzzled for a moment, as if finding it hard to grasp how I might have accomplished this feat. Then his face broke into the kindest of smiles. 'So it all seems eminently satisfactory,' he said. 'Very good. Keep up the good work.' And he dismissed me with a courteous little gesture.

The irony of the 'report', good-humoured as it was, seemed to have been lost on the Adjutant's own impenetrable courtesy. In view of some of the things that had taken place while I had been put in charge of the Four Point Twos while on exercises, I felt greatly relieved. The instructor, a saturnine captain with three wound stripes on his arm, had shown no sign whatever at the time of being cheered up by whatever errors and miscalculations I had been responsible for. Indeed they had caused him at times to indulge in fits of hysterical rage, obscenities flowing freely from a mouth horribly deformed by the wound inflicted by a German 88 in North Africa.

But it seemed that he had not held these incidents against me. Perhaps they had indeed helped to cheer him up after the event, distracting the inner traumas from which he was all too evidently suffering? In any case when it came to writing that report he had behaved, as it now seemed, like a gentleman.

As a result I was put in charge of the Three Inch Mortar Platoon, smaller weapons than the big Four Point Twos and requiring less expertise in their operation. It was hinted that my custodianship might only be temporary, until a more suitable permanent appointment could be made. I did not mind that. As a Second Lieutenant, the most disposable and unconsidered rank in the army, I was accustomed to look no further than whatever stroke of fortune might befall. 'De minimis non curat exercitus', to adapt the old legal proverb: for good or ill one was too low to be much bothered about.

More to the point perhaps, it was in expectation of a bloodbath, after the Second Front and the serious fighting should begin, that the army had created too many junior officers. The army was expecting something like the first day of the Somme, in 1916, and fortunately nothing quite so bad as that was to take place. Some of my contemporaries were promoted and sent overseas; some were wounded or killed; but a sizeable surplus, of which I continued to be one, remained.

Such calculations seemed far from anyone's mind at the time, and I looked forward to taking out the Three Inch Mortar Platoon on exercises, well away from the supervision of authority. Our tube-like weapons were carried in tracked vehicles, like a miniature open-decked tank, and in these we could roam the deserted wartime roads at will, seeking suitable sites to set up our apparatus and practise a leisurely shoot. Sometimes these were practice affairs – 'going through the motions' as it was known in the military vernacular. Sometimes our voyages took us to a regular firing range, where the crews would vie with each other to feed the mortar Moloch at top speed like jugglers, and see how many of its projectiles could be kept in the air at the same time.

At first I was secretly frightened of the creatures, and of my turn as a member of the crew who stood by the uptilted gaping muzzle and slid the finned bomb swiftly into it – the right way round of course. There had been accidents when some clumsy soldier had put the bomb in fuse-end downwards, and it had exploded at the bottom of the tube. It had also been known for the hand or hands of the crewman to be taken off by the emerging bomb, if he were not smart enough in removing them from the muzzle. It could even happen that an over-adroit and over-zealous handler might get another bomb down the spout before the previous one had time to emerge.

All these possibilities received a mention during our early training period, retailed in various styles of military humour. They were vividly present to my imagination when we first practised with live mortar bombs, but what was the use of worrying, as the troops used to sing in the first war. I soon got used to ladling the bombs down the spout with the same careless ease as the rest of the platoon. The big Four Point Two on which I started training was a more sober weapon, fired by a lanyard pulled well back from the mortar, and its rate of fire was nothing like so frenetic as its sprightly junior, whose bomb simply hit a spike at the bottom of the tube and was instantly ejected with an ear-splitting crack. I used to surreptitiously stuff my ears with bits of paper, concealing this timorous practice from the rest of the platoon with the straps of my steel helmet.

I had two particular friends and allies on these expeditions. One was Sergeant Eastwood, the oldest man in the platoon, who actually came from Eastwood, the midland town near Nottingham where D.H. Lawrence was born. Invalided home from active service in Italy he was strongly in favour of a quietistic approach to the routine of our daily training. In this I found him supportive, though he was an NCO of few words and his manner towards a very junior officer like myself carried a degree of patronage as well as a mild edge of contempt.

Though I did not make any such comparison at the time, Sergeant Eastwood was a bit like the Gerda of my childhood, those distant days at Littlestone-on-Sea. His surly silent company was distinctly soothing of an evening, when if we were out on an exercise we sometimes sat in a pub together, drinking weak wartime beer. I did not like beer, but I supposed it was the sort of thing one should drink. Once Sergeant Eastwood offered to stand me a whisky. He had become friendly with a landlord who kept a supply under the counter. Taking this hint I was prompt afterwards to ply him with spirits when we could get them, on the grounds that we had had a hard day. He preferred brandy to whisky, having acquired a taste for it overseas, and we discovered one pub which still possessed a good supply. For the first time I discovered the pleasures of becoming soberly drunk, and when we returned late in the evening to the barn where we slept on such outings the sergeant sometimes laid a guiding hand on my shoulder.

My other friend and companion on these excursions was our driver and mechanic, a lance-corporal always known to the platoon as Curly. In the army the nickname is usually given to soldiers with heads unusually flat and straight, or to elderly-looking storekeepers with hardly any hair at all. Curly was an exception. His curls were indeed spectacular: arranged in symmetrical waves, which sprang out intact and erect whenever he took off his military cap.

Naturally I never used his nickname, always referring to him correctly as Corporal Perivale. He himself came from that part of London; but strange as it now seems the remarkable coincidence that Sergeant Eastwood came from Eastwood and Corporal Perivale from Perivale never then occurred to me. Nor, I think, to any other member of the platoon. Part of the fatalism of the Forces is that oddities of all kinds were taken for granted, and accepted without comment or surprise.

Although an expert mechanic Curly had been a window-dresser at Selfridges in civilian life, and he was a great one for the girls. I had reason to know this because he once approached me confidentially and enquired whether there was any chance of our taking a 'recce' – reconnaissance – by ourselves. Did I perhaps wish to investigate a new and interesting training area while the rest of the platoon were on routine exercise? I was naturally curious about Curly's motives, but he said no more at the time and I did not enquire further. A few days later some occasion did arise when we could go off by ourselves and I remarked as much to Curly, who looked jubilant.

We set off, traversing Chiltern beech wood country with which we were both familiar, until he halted the mortar carrier on a village green where, as far as I could remember, I had not been before. But it seemed that Curly had. With a hurried word of apology he climbed out of the vehicle and disappeared through the back door of a sizeable house. Minutes passed. The sun was warm, the village green peaceful. Dozing contentedly, as one often did during the idle moments in the army, I waited for quite a long time.

At last I felt this had gone on long enough. Should I go and see what had happened to Curly? I felt it might be bad manners to do so. At that moment a lady carrying a shopping basket came out of the front door. She saw the carrier, with me sitting in it, and looked a little surprised. She was about to walk on to do her shopping or whatever it was, but then, seeming to change her mind, approached the carrier.

I sprang up, but the vehicle was not easily quitted for the purposes of an introduction. When I scrambled clear at last she looked amused. 'Would you like some tea?' she said. Women everywhere in those days were accustomed to giving tea to soldiers, who were known to have an insatiable thirst for it. My undignified exit from the carrier and the smile on her face made me wish to keep our acquaintance as short as possible, so I made some noise of polite deprecation, indicating that I did not want to interrupt her morning's shopping.

'Oh, that's all right,' she said. 'Done any time. Who are you? I didn't know we had any troops round here.'

She spoke rather as if with the royal 'We', and her blunt 'Who are you?' seemed less interested in me personally than in the nature of the military organisation I represented. Taking it in the latter sense I told her, but she seemed scarcely to hear. We were through the front door by this time and into a large room filled with books in shelves and on chairs and tables, and decorated in a dashingly flamboyant manner which in some way both excited and intimidated me. *Horizon, Penguin New Writing* and Walter de la Mare's new anthology *Love*, with its stylish but romantic cover, were strewn over a wide elegant marble table with a raised bronze edge.

This was clearly no ordinary country lady. Though I felt shyer with her every moment my excitement continued to rise as well. After so many months in the army the sight of books, and all the latest and most in vogue books, had an intoxicating effect on me.

'Do sit down,' she said, and I did so reluctantly, on an upright chair by the table. I would much rather have been allowed to wander round and have a look at everything. But good manners hardly permitted that.

No more was said about tea, and the silence grew rather awkward, though it did not seem to worry my hostess who continued to look at me in a quizzical way, almost, I thought, as if wondering what kind of use could be made of me. She was a big tall woman with fair hair and a strikingly large face and long neck. Much later I was to hear Lord David Cecil, my professor at Oxford, remark that she seemed to loom over you like a ship's figurehead. So indeed she did.

Feeling a bit confused I looked down at the table and saw

some proof sheets corrected boldly in red. At the top of the page was a title 'Happy Holidays', and a name, 'Rosamond Lehmann'. I stared unbelievingly. Could this really be the woman whose novels I had read with such an intensity of pleasure, whose stories I had devoured in *Penguin New Writing* just before the army called me up? Surely there must be some mistake? This big, overpowering, and as I thought rather tiresomely upper-class woman could not be the unimaginably remote and sensitive and understanding person (rather like myself I had thought) who had written those novels and stories? I had yet to learn that writers when you meet them seldom seem in the least like their books.

Rosamond Lehmann, if indeed it was she, was looking at me now in an even more quizzical way, but with a complacent glance which somehow touched me. Probably my face had given me away. But how to make matters clear, in a mannerly and tactful fashion? She saved me the trouble. 'I see you know my writing,' she said, with a regal forward swoop of the head that brought her big features quite close to my face. She smelt strongly but most alluringly of some very grand scent or face-powder.

From then on it was easy. I chattered away about how much *Dusty Answer* and *The Weather in the Streets* had meant to me. For days they had bemused me into a thrilling grown-up world, but I did not use the word 'grown-up'. 'What do you think would have happened to them all,' I ventured, 'after the book was over?'

She looked kind and pitying for a moment, as if to a literary and worldly innocent. But she looked seriously gratified too. I was promising material, I would learn: and in the meantime I had paid her a compliment. 'Ah,' she said, adopting a slightly histrionic manner (many of her family were or had been on the stage) –

> 'What a dusty answer gets the soul
> When hot for certainties in this our life . . .'

Some time later, after we had talked a good deal about hers and other books she started laughing. 'Here am I keeping you from your duties,' she said. I thought wistfully how proper it was that she seemed to have none of her own. I liked the idea of such a distinguished idleness in wartime.

'Let's go into the kitchen,' she said. 'My cook must have some cake she could give you, and perhaps tea is on too.'

She led me across the passage and opened a door. There sat Curly with his arm, and indeed his leg too, around the cook, an attractive woman built on the same heroic scale as her mistress. They disentangled themselves, looking pink and rather dishevelled, the cook especially so.

'Oh, never mind us,' said Rosamond Lehmann, shutting the door and leading me back into the drawing-room. She made no further reference to what we had seen, but took a book from amongst many of the same kind on a shelf and scribbled her name in large letters on the flyleaf. It was *The Weather in the Streets*, but I have a recollection that her latest book, *The Ballad and the Source*, was just about to come out.

She gave me the book with a smile, and then plucking it back demanded my name. My stammer overcame me and I could hardly get it out. 'John will do fine,' she said writing it. 'My brother's name too.' And she dismissed me with great ease, saying, 'Come again.'

I knew as I walked exultantly back to the carrier that I had been wiped instantly off her mind, but that was only proper and it did not depress my spirits in the least. More pleasing still was the earlier glance that seemed to want to make something out of me. I did not then interpret her interest as the one some writers can assume as painters do, summing up the human material in front of them in terms of composition.

I thought perhaps I might find myself figuring in one of her *New Writing* stories: perhaps a young officer, rather sweet really, who appeared from nowhere one morning? . . .

Lost in the daydream I felt caught up into heaven, like Jacob in the Bible.

Curly was sitting very upright in the driving-seat of the carrier, with the air of a patient chauffeur. I climbed in beside him and we started off without a word. With their steel tracks and exposed Ford V8 engine, carriers made a frightful din and were not suited for conversation. I sat rapt in a dream, hugging my book to me and thinking of writing; and the immense good fortune of having met a great writer, one whom I so much admired.

I am not sure now that Rosamond Lehmann is a great or even a very good writer, although she has a force and a flavour of her own, and her earlier books survive pretty well. Elizabeth Bowen, whom I knew later when she had become a friend of Iris, used to say that Rosamond was a loose cannon, always charging into other people's lives and having her own life knocked about in consequence. The poor woman was certainly knocked about, losing the poet Cecil Day Lewis, the great love of her life, to Jill Balcon the actress, who was later to become a friend of ours; and her much loved young daughter to polio in Singapore. That became the subject of a late novel, *The Swan in the Evening*.

When I encountered her by chance on that village green in the Chilterns she had, at least to my innocent eye, an air of inviolability, as if none of the mean and commonplace woes of life, with which I felt myself already familiar, could come anywhere near her. Her books of course show the opposite. There is a strong odour of unhopefulness about them, more realistic and chilling I now feel, than in, say, Hardy's novels. Other odours too. Rachel, David Cecil's wife and daughter of the literary critic Desmond McCarthy, used to say that Rosamond's novels reminded her of a very grand Ladies' Cloakroom. Scent and toilet-water and face-powder, and under it all a hint of things not so pleasant.

After we had driven a few miles on our homeward

road Curly turned the roaring carrier off into the yard of a transport café where we had often been accustomed – sometimes just the pair of us, sometimes the whole platoon – to refresh ourselves with 'tea and a wad' – the soldiers' equivalent of the office coffee break. I had supposed Curly to be sufficiently refreshed already, but I suspected he wanted the chance of a little private chat about what had just taken place.

I was determined to ask no questions myself. I was more than happy with the book I had acquired, which I brought in with me in case it should be removed from the open carrier (books were surprisingly valuable objects at all levels of wartime society), and also with my memory of the meeting.

''Course I can see you read a lot, Sir,' Curly began in a kindly way, eyeing the book in my hand, and as if to demonstrate a preliminary magnanimity about such habits, which he would soon have to be telling me, none the less, could go on if unchecked to be the cause of impotence or blindness.

I felt slightly nettled by Curly's line, since I felt he had some explaining if not apologising to do himself, having kept me waiting outside in the carrier while he had caroused over limitless tea and cake in the kitchen, astride the majestic cook. But since I had had my own windfall, in the shape of a meeting with the fabulous Rosamond Lehmann, it would only be fair to be magnanimous myself.

'Have you known her long?' I asked, wishing out of politeness to seem warm and interested in Curly's lovelife. I supposed it would follow what I took to be the normal if to me still inconceivable progress of amorous ritual: dalliance, engagement, followed after a short or a longer interval by marriage. Sentimentally I supposed they had been seeing each other at weekends in the teashops of Henley or Reading, and exchanging tender epistles. Curly would no doubt have sought to devise other ways of meeting his lady-love, and to use the carrier for this purpose must have seemed a heaven-sent opportunity.

I enjoyed imagining the strange but touching ways in which other people behaved, and was glad now to show fellow-feeling with what I decided must be Curly's programme.

A look of utter incredulity passed rapidly over Curly's mobile features, to be succeeded by a kindly smirk. It was plain that the full depth of my unworldliness, the product no doubt of books, and the result of reading them, had been revealed to him in a sudden flash.

'Herb in Signals told me there were a couple of nice bits of stuff over at that village place,' he explained. 'So I thought it might be worth our while, Sir, to have a bit of a recce.'

I tried not to appear as discomfited as I felt. For a moment I even wondered if Herb in Signals, that unknown philanthropist, might not have set the whole thing up. Two nice bits of stuff, each of ample size, domiciled together? What a treat for his friend Curly and Curly's officer, since they had the carrier at their disposal!

But the philanthropy of Herb in Signals could hardly have extended that far. With a rapid feat of adjustment which I still feel to be rather creditable, considering how innocent I was, I now managed to favour Curly with a slight leer of admiration and fellow-feeling. Should I pretend that some sort of amorous passage had indeed taken place in the drawing-room, while he and the cook were locked together in the kitchen?

But I realised at once that the new book lying on the table would in itself at once belie such a claim. As if to confirm my thought Curly picked it up a moment and gazed incuriously at the picture on the jacket. An upper-class-looking couple, drinks in their hands, were just emerging through French windows into a garden. Curly put the book down again.

'She's a smasher, Sir,' he said solemnly. 'A real smasher.

But I wouldn't want to go again. Bit too demanding, if you see what I mean.'

Curly smiled reminiscently, clearly confident, none the less, that I wouldn't have the slightest hope of seeing what he meant. He stuffed a large piece of the 'wad' into his mouth, as if to restore his primal vigour, taxed by his recent encounter with the cook. On his feet he made a mildly histrionic gesture, indicating extremes of exhaustion. It was time to go.

That was the Golden Age of my army service. The war was raging; the Second Front had begun, but routine and training went on in the same old comfortable way, with plenty of cosy incidents and a few memorable ones, like the encounter with Rosamond Lehmann. Sometimes the Three Inch Mortar Platoon went on longer training forays, extending over a couple of days and nights, as on the early occasion when Sergeant Eastwood and I had found the pub which possessed a supply of brandy.

In my spare time, and for reasons which my powers of recall cannot now fathom, I had taken to learning the descant recorder, having managed to buy one at the Dolmetsch shop in London when I was on leave. I must have been fascinated by the pure reedy sounds, and by the revelation of simple musical notes, which I mastered from the children's handbook supplied. The names of the little airs – 'Greensleeves', 'Go to Joan Glover', 'Sellinger's Round' – seemed in themselves a pure element of escape. Escape into the past, to a happier world. 'Escapist' was a word of those days, used rather disapprovingly, but with a hint of yearning none the less.

I was shy of trying to play the thing in barracks, except when the two other officers who shared the room were absent. But on exercises I could remove myself to a little distance and laboriously pipe an air or two, in slow time and with frequent pauses. Once Sergeant Eastwood heard me at it, and listened for a moment or two as if in incredulous resignation. What would these so-called officers get up to next?

'I should swing it a bit, Sir, if I were you,' was his only comment as he stumped off to attend to some needful military chore.

The most ambitious of these expeditions was also to be the last. Nemesis was lying in wait, as is usual during a Golden Age. We were to go down to a large training area near Minehead in Somerset, the haunt of serious armoured vehicles, Churchill and Cromwell tanks. They had presumably all vanished away in ships across the Channel to the Second Front, and we had the large wild area by Exmoor to ourselves.

I was impressed by the beauty of the countryside, but as often happened in the army it was not possible to do much more than feel tantalised by beautiful places – military training never seemed to take place in ugly ones – which there was no way of appreciating. I felt I *did* appreciate them, but only as if I were a quite different person, not the same me who had haunted the links and shore of Littlestone and the woods of Gerrards Cross. I might have said with Coleridge in his 'Dejection Ode', 'I see, not feel, how beautiful they are.' I had not read the poem then, but I knew that Coleridge had lived at Nether Stowey, and I was thrilled when our carriers went clanking through the village, and I saw a dovecot on a high wall which I thought looked very Coleridgean.

No time to stop of course, even if I could have thought of a reason for doing so. Besides I had other things to preoccupy me – real worries. They came from the very fact which had made the whole idea of the expedition so delightful. We were supposed officially to have gone by train, with the carriers transported on flat cars. The necessary Movement Order had been issued. Then at the last moment Corporal Perivale observed insinuatingly that it would be much more fun to drive. I think he fancied the idea of rampaging with his beloved carriers for hundreds of miles, instead of on the short routine trips to which they were accustomed.

I too saw the powerful charm of the idea, and I allowed myself to be tempted. Sergeant Eastwood, when consulted, merely smiled his sardonic smile and gave no opinion either way. If trouble came later he was not to be part of it.

On my own dubious authority I cancelled the Movement Order, and when the day came we set out by road, chattering like a bunch of schoolboys. The maximum speed of a mortar carrier was under forty miles an hour, and Curly Perivale saw to it that the four vehicles vied with each other in a race along the almost empty wartime roads. There was next to no civilian traffic; all we met was an occasional convoy of army trucks. Road signs had been removed since the invasion scare of 1940, and my simple task was to read the map. Between doing that I could stand up in the leading carrier, with the March wind blowing me about, and feel like Alexander at the head of his army.

Disaster struck somewhere near Shepton Mallet. The carrier behind me lost speed, started smoking, and finally came to a halt. We all stopped. Curly got to work and looked grave. 'Big end, Sir,' he reported. I had no idea what a big end was but I could see that it seriously mattered. We left the vehicle in a farmyard and drove on, crowded into the surviving three. Not many miles later another gave out. I forget what was wrong this time, but to my surprise and relief Curly now looked positively cheerful. He explained that we should return to the stricken carrier and cannibalise it. That would do the trick. Hours later he and his mate triumphantly reported success. We set off again, towing the casualty, at Sergeant Eastwood's suggestion. He said nothing more, but I think he had the canny idea that authority might be less displeased if we at least arrived with all our military gear, instead of abandoning some of it on the way.

Our convoy was now very slow, and night began to fall. I was becoming more and more conscious of the unwisdom of cancelling that Movement Order. But then we had a stroke of luck. We passed a large camp, full of American soldiers. On an impulse I stopped at the gate and asked the sentry if we could come in. With that American friendliness and casualness which seemed to us so delightful during the war he raised no objection. The irrepressible Curly admired his Winchester carbine, an exotic weapon quite unknown to the British Army, and the sentry obligingly let him examine it. The Commandant was obliging too when I explained our predicament and asked if we might spend the night with him. 'Sure, boys, sure. Make yourselves at home.' We did; feasting in the mess room on unheard-of quantities of ham and eggs, blueberry muffins, pecan pie . . . And we slept between sheets – a great luxury – in a vacant hut.

I was a little uncertain of our reception when we arrived at the Minehead camp next day, but the CO there seemed not to have heard of our change of plan and was sympathetic about the breakdown. We covered ourselves with glory too, as it happened, by our part in a set-piece infantry attack in which we were allotted the task of giving covering fire. Real fire. We plastered the hillside where the enemy was supposed to be with our mortar bombs, and after the exercise the plywood targets were brought in for inspection. They were gratifyingly riddled with shrapnel holes and I told the platoon I was proud of them. This was an error, to remember which makes me grow hot and cold with embarrassment to this day. Sergeant Eastwood looked disgusted, the rest of the platoon merely uncomfortable.

But all was forgotten and forgiven when we set out next day for an exercise on our own, crammed into the surviving carriers. We roamed over Exmoor and found an idyllic campsite by a moorland stream. Our only accident that day had been the refusal of one of the mortar bombs to go off when it landed. This was a rare eventuality and there was a drill for dealing with it. The officer in charge – it had to be the officer – approached the unexploded bomb with circumspection and laid beside it a fused cone of plastic explosive which smelled of marzipan and gave one a headache if handled too long. The fuse was then lit with a special match and the officer proceeded at a dignified pace under cover. I knew the drill though I had never had to perform the operation before. I set out across the heather with my apparatus, and happening to glance back became aware of Sergeant Eastwood behind me.

I stopped. This was most irregular. Only one person, and he an officer, was supposed to do the job. I pointed this out to the sergeant. He looked unconcerned but obstinate, and I had no choice but to let him follow me. The bomb was easily found – it had a scarlet band round its bulbous middle – and I knelt down to perform the task, very conscious of the watching sergeant. When the fuse was lit both of us walked 'without haste', as the drill prescribed, to a big boulder we must have marked independently, and got well behind it. The sergeant winked at me – the only comment he made throughout – and after the successful explosion we walked in silence back to the platoon.

The sergeant had rum with him, and he gave me a tot that evening as we lay on the green bank of the stream. The rest of the platoon was larking about by the water, some distance off. Presently the balmy evening silence, with a single curlew calling somewhere, was disturbed by a muffled explosion. Agreeably muzzy with rum I wondered without much concern whether one or more of the men had managed to blow themselves up. We lay smoking peacefully, and soon there was another explosion. This time I felt a shade alarmed and glanced over at the sergeant who merely winked at me, for the second time that day. Soon there were cries of enthusiasm from downstream and the soldiers came tumbling back to us, their hands full of things that glistened and wriggled.

Fried in our mess-tins and eaten with hunks of army bread and mugs of strong sweet tea those moorland trout were delicious. I felt a little upset about the fate of the trout, blasted unconscious in their beautiful native element by plastic explosive which I, as the officer, was alone allowed to handle, and of which I was supposed to be the careful custodian. Naturally I never enquired how the soldiers had got hold of it. Sergeant Eastwood was obviously implicated in the conspiracy, if not its prime mover, his task to keep me happily occupied while the dirty work went on.

I ate the trout none the less. There were plenty to go round, since many in the platoon turned up their noses at the idea of eating fish, or at least fishes that had never been properly exposed for sale on a fishmonger's slab. Sport, rather than gastronomy, had been their motive. 'Some of the lads have got a proper headache this morning, Sir,' said Sergeant Eastwood next day with his sardonic grin. That came from too much handling of the plastic explosive.

The early March weather was unusually fine and warm, and we basked in it. But there was a day of reckoning still to come, for Curly and for Sergeant Eastwood as well as for me. The carriers' caterpillar tracks and sturdy bodies had got mired in the bogs of Exmoor; and on Sunday afternoon, with nothing much else to do, Curly must have decided to take them across the firm sand and shingle and into the sea, to give them a good wash. He was very proud of the carriers, and zealous about their smart appearance. All had gone well apparently until the drivers attempted to reverse them from the shallow water in which they and their steeds had, as it were, been paddling. Then it was found that the sand was not so firm after all: the carriers were immovable. With Herculean efforts the men managed to drag one out by brute force; the other two stayed stuck.

By this time I had got the news and was on the scene, but there was nothing to be done. The tide was coming in. With set pale face Curly went from one to the other of his stricken monsters, removing carburettors and other of the more delicate pieces of mechanism from their insides. Presently nothing was visible of the carriers above the waves but the tops of their steel sides.

A Court of Enquiry was held. I was myself of course responsible, but the Commandant knew quite well how things were when it came to the causes of such an accident. Both Curly and Sergeant Eastwood were put on a charge. I was reserved for higher judgement and sent back alone to our parent unit. The cancellation of the Movement Order, the breakdown of the carriers on the road, and their final immolation in salt water – a crane had had to be ordered to pull them out – all lay heavily against me.

The Adjutant was as courteous as ever, but I was posted overseas, to war-torn Holland on the borders of the *Reich*, with the next draft, about a fortnight later. This might have happened anyway in the course of routine, and no suggestion of punishment was hinted at. The army showed all its remarkable powers of tolerance, and toleration. I still marvel today at the way these seem to have been exercised during the war.

I never saw Curly and Sergeant Eastwood and the platoon again. I did not miss them or they, I'm sure, me. But in memory we seem to have had a jolly time together for a while, in the way that such things sometimes happened in the army, at least in my later – much later – recollection. That, for all of us, was perhaps something to be thankful for.

8

Memory has a much larger appetite for small things than for anything on a scale not easily managed. The last days of the war, the last days of German resistance in their own backyard, are for me now only a blur.

Perhaps because of what had taken place in the Three Inch Mortar Platoon when I was in charge I had no further acquaintance with these weapons but became a supplementary Infantry Platoon Commander, waiting for whatever officer was in charge of a platoon to become a casualty. When someone did I was posted to a front line company, and for the few remaining days the war continued I saw what the languid officer meant whose only comment on warfare is alleged to have been, 'My dear! – the noise, and the people.'

Noise and people are in any case not friendly to the habitat of the 'intellectual being', and the memories that wander through eternity in the early morning, as I lie waiting for another day of caring and looking-after to begin.

I know there is a law of the conservation of energy, although I'm not sure how to define it. There is certainly a law of the conservation of trouble, the troubles we must all undergo in this vale of tears. If some are taken away, by God or the government or scientific discovery, we can be sure not only that the ones which remain will seem more burdensome than before but that quite new and unexpected ones will appear. Cancer may be cured; we may all live longer and healthier lives. But a new disease will be discovered: we shall find fresh cause for boredom, dissatisfaction and misery in the longer time we have to experience them.

Fortunately there is also a law of the conservation of pleasure. In bed in the morning, waiting for the day to begin, I comfort myself with this knowledge. Thank goodness for it. As troubles get worse, small satisfactions increase, both in intensity and in expectation. I look forward with passion to the moment after I put Iris to bed. I come down, pour myself a drink, and while enjoying it read a page or two of a book, some old favourite that is lying near the kitchen table. Nothing new – never a newspaper or periodical – but nothing old and famous either, and nothing demanding. Something I have read many many times before. It might be a Barbara Pym or a James Bond novel, or Anthony Powell's *A Dance to the Music of Time*, or a travel book by Ian Fleming's brother Peter, or a history of the Hundred Years War, or Alan Clark's *Barbarossa*. All these lie about within easy reach.

But Belial's method is best of all. Just letting the thoughts wander. I should never have supposed before that there could be so much positive pleasure in remembering things.

I cling to this pleasure grimly, as if I were holding on to the side of a lifeboat. The pleasure boat. But remembering is one thing – an innocent involuntary thing like Shelley's Spirit of Delight. Writing it down is another. There creeps into recollection the complacency which is also a part of memory. I am pleased with myself not only for remembering but for having recorded it in the mind with such precision. Most memoirs and autobiography have a 'clever little me' feel about them somewhere.

Thank goodness too that the summer is over – the hateful end of summer, which I dislike more and more the older I grow. A wonderful autumn has come at last, much more hopeful and reassuring than the spring. Down the road a tall Ginkgo tree, it must be the tallest in North Oxford, has turned pure Chinese yellow. The English beeches more bronze every day; chestnuts shedding leaves in all shades of pink and gold.

Our daily walks round the block are a real pleasure now. I would rather keep quiet about the trees, and enjoy them more that way, but I must try to enjoy them with Iris, and I keep pointing them out to her, not knowing it is the last time she will see the tints of autumn. She doesn't seem to respond. Does Alzheimer's take away the faculty of visual enjoyment, as well as of sense and coherence in the brain? I have a horrid feeling that I enjoy such things more and more now, because Iris does not, cannot, do so herself. It is not as if I was enjoying them for her, or trying to share my pleasure. More as if her inner desolation had stimulated my own receptivity, my own private powers of response.

It's depressing to see all this biologically. *The Woodlanders* again: Hardy's vision of the beautiful trees battening on one another, helpless not to profit from their neighbours' wounds and death. If the tree close beside me dies I have that much more light and air.

If I do it properly, with the proper degree of routine, Iris does at least still enjoy her supper. Lunch not. Perhaps there is invisible fellow-feeling between us there? One has to eat something about then, but one cannot be bothered with it. It is just a stage in the process of getting through the day. But supper is another matter – the day's crown and consolation.

Iris likes me to feed her then. I stand beside her like a serving-man in the Middle Ages and put each spoonful in her mouth – baked beans, tomato, bottled mayonnaise, a bit of Skipper's sardine. Then ice-cream and banana. Iris makes furry happy noises through all this. I feel happy too – my own drink and book and supper are not far away – and I can feel happy with her. No separation now, as when out on the walk, watching the trees. Now I can feel that Iris is aware of my happiness with her, perhaps she can even

feel pleased that I am looking forward to my own solitary
evening to come.

After the war in Europe was over we had all dreaded being
sent off to the Far East, to fight the Japanese. But then that
war was over too, and so I remained in Germany with the
occupying forces. Demobilisation was not yet in sight – the
earliest to be called up were the first to be let out – but there
was not much now for the troops to do. With no looming
conflict in prospect training tended to languish.

I was eventually found a 'job' in T force – army abbrevi-
ation for Target Force – who were supposed to be removing
useful bits and pieces from German factories. This was for
the benefit of equivalent English firms who might wish to
profit from examples of Teutonic expertise. In practice, as
we heard later, the bits and pieces did not fit in England, or
were worn out, or already obsolete. Our cunning opponents
had seen to that, and in due course their own factories
started up again with all the benefits of modernisation,
and brand new equipment paid for at least partly by the
British taxpayer.

Our good-natured commander, a silent smiling brigadier
who liked his gin, had liberated one of the Volkswagen
factories at the end of the war, so the unit had a good
number of early Beetle models, which the more enterprising officers among us delighted to drive. They required a
lot of gear-changing and double-declutching, like a vintage
racing car, but they were exhilarating to travel in and had
a marvellous heating system, well-suited to the German
winter and a joy after the draughty trucks. I never aspired
to drive a Beetle – I was too junior anyway – but I enjoyed
riding in one with the Brigadier or the dashing captain who
was his assistant, and listening to their tales of being put
in charge of the moribund VW factory. Higher authority
had offered it lock stock and barrel to Morris Motors, but
Lord Nuffield swore he wouldn't touch a Beetle with a

bargepole – he was in the business of building respectable motor cars.

I was thought for some reason to know German, which was why I got the job. I had little to do, but I learned German feverishly in order to make some pretence of doing it. When a blueprint or a piece of machinery had been commandeered, my task was to pay a visit to the factory and make sure they were delivering the goods as bespoke. In practice these visits were fairly infrequent, and I also had the services of a German interpreter, but it had been decreed that an authentic British officer was required to make sure that nothing underhand went on between this interpreter and the factory officials whom we met. It was not clear how I was to ensure that there was none of such potential monkey-business, but at least I constituted a token presence, a warning against any attempt at cheating.

Herr Braatz, our mild-mannered interpreter, had lost an eye on the Eastern Front when attempting to clear a Russian minefield. His eye-socket wept copiously as if for Germany's sins, which of course we never spoke of. We sat companionably beside the driver in the front of the icy truck, and conversed as we could about education and children and moral welfare, subjects of exquisite boredom when expounded in Herr Braatz's pedantic English; but I found his company soothing and congenial none the less.

In spite of the easy work and driving about with Herr Braatz there were days when I felt quite homesick for my comrades of the old Three Inch Mortar Platoon, and I missed Curly invariably remarking 'end of another perfect day', as we drove back past the barrack square in the evenings.

Such nostalgia was dissipated one morning when I was sitting in the office surreptitiously trying to read Goethe's novel about the Sorrows of Young Werther while pretending to be engaged in unit correspondence. A young woman was shown in. She was plump and rosy, very German in appearance but in an artless way, as if she were an English schoolgirl pretending to look like a German. She wore short white socks and a black skirt. It was part of the uniform, as I subsequently discovered, of the *Bund deutscher Mädchen*, female component of the Hitler Youth.

Addressing me respectfully in halting English she said she had been sent from the Autobahn office, where she worked as secretary. They hoped we would excuse the road repairs and alterations that were going on as a result of the wartime bombing. They trusted we would not be unduly inconvenienced? It was typical of the Germans to gently rub in the fact that we had been bombing them, while naturally saying nothing about what they had done to other people.

I made some suitable reply, speaking in my new German. It was the conceit of showing that I could do it, and the girl switched to her own language with an air of submission. For my benefit she spoke slowly and carefully, as if she were still speaking English. When I made a joke of sorts she laughed conscientiously.

I visited Hannelore very discreetly. We were not supposed to fraternise with the Germans. I always took a tin of corned beef or a packet of cigarettes. In practice the non-fraternising regulation was not taken very seriously, although it was applied more strictly in the case of officers than men, and if my visits became known I was well aware that the army would once more show its powers of toleration by removing me without comment to a worse job, probably supernumerary platoon commander in some training unit.

So I was careful. And the cigarettes and the bully beef always ensured my welcome. The mark had no value. Everything was done by barter. Ten cigarettes were like the single dollars in Russia which became the accepted currency after the collapse of the Soviet empire. I bought what

seemed a good Adler typewriter from a senior colleague
of Hannelore for twenty Player's. The man was delighted
and Hannelore was happy to arrange the deal. She wanted
perhaps to pay me back for the good things I had lavished
on herself and her family: the Autobahn official did not
know that they got much more from me *gratis* every week
than I had given him for his typewriter.

But he had the last laugh. I had dreamed of learning to
type and becoming a writer later on in Civvy Street. I did
learn to type, after a fashion, but the Adler turned out to
be rather like those bits and pieces we were removing from
the German factories. It held together more or less until I
returned to England, and then it broke down. There was
something radically wrong with it; and no spare parts were
available at home even if they had been in Germany.

My relations with Hannelore were not what might have
been expected, or what I thought I would have liked them
to be. I thought naturally, as any romantic twenty-year-old
might, that I wanted her as a mistress. Whether I really did
I now rather doubt. If she had done all the work, as it were,
then I suppose I would have had no choice, but she had
no idea, apparently, that the idea might be in my mind. It
was certainly not in hers. No doubt she was a genuinely
virtuous girl; in any case she took our relations for granted
just as they were: a jolly friendship sprung up between me
and her family.

That was really what suited me too. It would be a
good idea to improve my German in her company and
Hannelore loved to talk, to chatter away endlessly in her
own language about anything and everything. We kissed
a good deal – Hannelore received and returned them like
someone playing ping-pong – but we never got warmed up.
One clear sparkling night when we had gone out to admire
the stars after drinking some home-brewed alcohol of her
father's, I put my hands under her skirt as we embraced and
attempted something more robust in the way of a clinch. She

pushed my hands away, wriggling and giggling, and when we went in – her parents had gone to bed – she apologised for her brusque behaviour and said it was better for girls to keep such goings-on until after they got married.

She sounded quite confident about this, but the mention of marriage alarmed me. Could that be what she was thinking of? She looked at me in an embarrassingly unfamiliar and even loving way as she said it. When I kissed her and said I understood she seized me impulsively in her arms. Her breath smelt of the strong sickly homebrew, and her features resembled what the young German in the ballad calls a *Bild von Milch und Blut*. Hannelore really did look then as if her plump engaging face had been made of blood and milk. Picturesque in a way – no doubt Goethe would have enjoyed the effect – but somehow at that moment too biological. It would have been like making love to a young heifer.

My ardour was the more easily quenched because Hannelore, disentangling herself from me, began to talk with enthusiasm about the summer holiday she was hoping to have on the North Sea island of Nordeney. Wouldn't it be *wunderschön* if I could meet her there? I said it would be, but the idea did not greatly appeal. For one thing it would be taking fraternisation a trifle too far; for another, there was no indication that Hannelore proposed to share a room and bed with me: indeed it seemed likely that such an idea had not even occurred to her. Such things were kept for after marriage, even when on a holiday on Nordeney.

In any case my demob papers came through a little earlier than expected. But as we said goodbye, after a last lavish presentation to her family of cigarettes and chocolate, the idea of Nordeney and our possible reunion still lingered. I would come to her there from England? I didn't of course; but we corresponded now and again over the next couple of years. My own affairs kept me from having any curiosity about hers, but it seemed she just went on living with her parents and working in the Autobahn office.

Six years later on, it must have been in 1953, my brother Michael, now a Lieutenant-Colonel, was stationed in Germany, somewhere near Düsseldorf. This was quite close to Kamen, the small town where I had been stationed and where Hannelore lived. On the impulse I asked if I might pay him a visit. He was acquiescent if not particularly enthusiastic. But as it happened he would be away on an exercise for a month or so, and if I liked I might borrow his car.

After a tedious train and boat journey from England I picked it up at the barracks. A fatherly mechanic in uniform handed it over, and told me to watch out for the overdrive. The car was a lordly creature, an open Mercedes of pre-war vintage. I drove it with caution, not using the perilous overdrive, and was soon in an area which I recognised. I had written to Hannelore, who had replied with great vigour and excitement. And so my brother was now *Berufsoldat*, an *Oberst*, and he was nearby in Germany! Could I not bring him with me for a visit? I had just time to reply that he was away at the moment – well away I hoped – but that I had borrowed his car, and would appear on Sunday morning. The times had worked out quite conveniently.

Hannelore's excitement about my brother was rather damping to the spirits, but while driving along I was able none the less to indulge a daydream. I had the romantic car – why shouldn't we drive down the Isar, or the Moselle valley, stop at a friendly *Gasthaus*, have a two- or three-day romance? It was a nice idea, even though I was well aware that daydreams seldom or never materialised, not at least in the form in which one has indulged them. Still, Hannelore's ideas might have changed a bit in the last five years?

The dilapidated house on Jahnstrasse looked just the

same, though all around the *Wirtschaftswunder* was performing its miracle of reconstruction, and spreading abroad a new post-war German prosperity. Hannelore was out at church when I arrived, but her mother was there to greet me.

Frau Jenker was an admirable woman, as was her husband, the gentle creature who sold beer at the local *Stube*. Frau Jenker seemed excited about something other than my arrival, although she was obviously pleased to see me, and proud of the Mercedes outside the door, shedding lustre and prestige on the house.

In the early days of our acquaintance she had confided to me that in the first alarming weeks of the British Army's occupation she had seriously considered arranging for Hannelore to be temporarily walled up – '*aufgemauert*' – to protect her from the brutal and licentious soldiery. In the Russian zone this simple expedient would hardly have sufficed. Even after the end of hostilities the Russians were in the habit of firing their sub-machine-guns into the walls of a house, to flush out any girls they suspected might be lurking there.

I remembered too that I had seen a girl raped by a Russian soldier when I had been sent to Berlin on T force business; and that was three or four months after the end of the war. We had permission from the Russian *Kommandatura* to enter their zone to retrieve some escaped scientist's furniture. Perhaps it was not furniture only – I never found out about that – but negotiations with the Russian authorities, in which I had had no part, had been protracted though apparently quite cordial.

Gazing now into Frau Jenker's ruddy and seemingly guileless countenance I remembered watching in surreptitious fascination as the soldier had worked on the girl in a sort of slow motion, like a spider giving its quietus to a fly. Like the fly the girl had seemed in some sense resigned to the soldier's methodical activities. It was impossible to tell how far, if at all, she was willing. Perhaps it had been a purely commercial transaction? I had, after all, brought those cigarettes and tins of corned beef to the Jenker household.

The corned beef and cigarettes must originally have made a difference, but this sterling woman had natural good manners and a kind heart. She had always seemed to take for granted my relations with her daughter, an only child with whom she was on close terms. No doubt she had sized me up effectively, and yet she seemed fond of me in an artless way, this foreign young thing in uniform – officer's uniform, could it be possible? – who had appeared laden with gifts in that grim period after the war, and who had now suddenly reappeared, driving a grand Mercedes car.

In her old innocently inquisitive way she fingered my grey flannel trousers and worn tweed jacket, clearly finding these garments something of a comedown after my military gear. And so my brother was now *Oberst?* A fine man he must be she was certain! – they would love so much to meet him.

At that moment Hannelore arrived, and her mother glowed at her while pointing me out. With her rosy cheeks shining like freshly scrubbed apples Hannelore looked just the same, except that she now seemed mildly embarrassed about something – perhaps the same thing – quite apart from my arrival – which her mother had seemed excited about?

I could not make out what this was, and the two women did not enlighten me. We had a lavish snack of hardboiled eggs and pickled gherkins, together with every sort of salami and German sausage. A spread which was startlingly different from the post-war years, though I forbore to comment on the change.

Frau Jenker seemed the one who was to reveal whatever was in the air. But she didn't – she started to wonder at the Mercedes instead, and then remarked how *wunderschön* it would be if she and Hannelore could have a ride in it. Of course I said yes, they must, how splendid! *'Ach Mutti,'* protested Hannelore, looking embarrassed again, but her mother overruled her, and in a few minutes I found myself back in the Mercedes, with Frau Jenker beside me and her daughter behind.

This was not at all how I had imagined things going, but there was nothing to be done about it. I felt I was the victim of some sort of conspiracy, hatched at short notice by Frau Jenker. What could they have in mind for me, beyond free transport for a shopping expedition? Was I to be married on the spot to Hannelore?

It was suddenly alarming to be in the power of these two unknown women, as they now seemed to me, and I began to regret my impulse to return to Germany and seek out Hannelore again.

The little industrial towns of the Ruhr are all close together, like the pottery towns of Staffordshire, and presently we were in the streets of one not far from Kamen, which I remembered driving through in army days. I was bidden to stop by a house very like the one in Jahnstrasse. Hannelore and her mother disappeared inside. I remained sitting in the car under the curious gaze of one or two local residents. It was a sunny autumn day, and I wondered what Michael, the *Oberst*, was doing on his army manoeuvres. Could it be Michael himself who these two women were now after? In this new Germany there seemed to be all sorts of new and sinister developments and spells. It was the same, and yet wholly different; and I began to feel nostalgic for the abject country in which T Force had cruised around with casual lordliness.

The door of the house burst open and its denizens came rushing out in a babel of chatter, Hannelore and her mother in the midst of them. They surrounded the car like a mob who might drag me out of it and string me up to the nearest lamp-post, although their shining faces were all wreathed in smiles. One of them was a tall young man with a mop of dark hair.

I now realised, with mixed feelings, that no one was paying any attention to me at all. This young man was the focus of interest. Amidst the babel of speech my understanding of the language seemed to have totally deserted me, but at last I made out that here was Hannelore's fiancé, and that he was just returned from Russia, where he had been a prisoner of war for nearly ten years. Neither Hannelore nor her parents had ever said a word about him. She had merely been waiting for him to reappear.

It is all hard to imagine in an age when counselling is offered for every minor misfortune. But after the war the Germans wanted to forget, or at least they didn't want to talk about what they might otherwise remember. It was guilt no doubt; but it was also a passionate wish to get away into the future, their own future – somehow, anyhow – and to forget the past.

Hannelore's young man – they turned out to have been engaged since 1942, when he joined the army – had simply got left behind in the dark past which everyone wanted to forget. Including Hannelore herself? Evidently not. She had not forgotten, but what would she have done if I had said I wanted to marry her? In the old days in Germany?

I had no idea what her present feelings were, and had no way of finding out. Perhaps she hadn't any? It seemed such a long time since we had met on the sofa together exchanging juvenile kisses while she chattered, as it seemed, about everything under the sun. We had shared a sort of intimacy in those days, of which at the time I had been hardly conscious; but the memory of it, overcoming me in these new circumstances, made me suddenly and passionately desire her. I longed to kiss her red mouth, to force kisses on it, as I had never done before. And now I was a few days too late.

She was going to marry this young man who had come

back from the dead. For they had never heard whether he was dead or whether he might be still alive, somewhere in Siberia. It was known that many thousands of German prisoners were still held in the labour camps.

There were a few moments during the next two days when I made some attempt to ask him about it all. His frank gaze – he had very blue eyes, like Hitler's, under his dark hair – never once met mine. He said nothing; he seemed to know nothing about himself, and what he had undergone. I quickly gave up, feeling guilty myself of some serious indecency; and somehow I felt quite sure that neither his own relatives nor Hannelore and her parents would ever ask him anything, or tell him anything either.

Some of us had known about the concentration camps, and met fellow-soldiers who had liberated them, but we had no real news of the Holocaust itself. The average German knew something; but said nothing. They could not have avoided seeing the packed freight cars which left departure platforms at the main stations, Cologne and Hamburg, Dortmund and Düsseldorf. They did not claim not to know where those freight cars had been bound. They said nothing about it. Like the war itself it was all over and done with, and not to be mentioned again. Least of all to the recent enemies who were now their allies and friends . . .

I found I had conjured myself back into a new country, in which the past had been told not to exist. The German capacity to pass an Act of Oblivion on themselves seemed at that time total and complete.

Hannelore was now as animated as the others. She drank quantities of beer when we all had a meal at the *Gasthaus* together, and made me eat the yolks of several fried eggs, which she neatly extracted from the white part and offered me on the point of a knife. She said in that way one got the maximum benefit from them. I felt she was offering me some sort of compensation for what might have been. Her fiancé she paid hardly any attention to.

Nor did he to her. Feeling in my turn that I must give him some compensation I asked if he would like to drive the Mercedes. It was an absurdly rash thing to do, because I had no idea what the insurance arrangements were, or even if he could drive properly – possibly he hadn't seen a car for ten years. But none of that seemed to matter: his sudden excitement and gratitude at the offer were quite intoxicating. It had been the right thing to do.

He drove us to the *Gasthaus*, he drove us home to Jahnstrasse, dropping various relatives on the way; and then, without being invited, he seemed to think it only natural that he should take the Mercedes back to his own home town.

Without kissing him goodnight Hannelore bade him be punctual in the morning as she wished to go shopping with the car. We drank some more of her father's beer and Hannelore announced that she would take me to the hotel where she had arranged for me to stay. It was a short walk and when we arrived she gave me the intimate kiss her fiancé didn't appear to have had. By that time I was much too tired and bemused to feel anything but desire for bed.

As I entered the hotel I suddenly realised that here was the very same T Force HQ I had once worked in. It must have been bought, rebuilt and done up after the army had left, five years before.

The Mercedes reappeared in the morning, but the fiancé couldn't stay – he was just beginning his new job in the municipal Welfare Office – so I was required to take Hannelore and her mother to Dortmund, for a day's shopping. For them it was a *herrliche Gelegenheit* – heaven-sent opportunity. Hannelore's trousseau was in question, and her wedding-dress and one or two other things, and 'Der John' was so helpful and so kind. At least the Mercedes had a big boot, so I didn't have to wait in it to guard the parcels.

I had intended to stay in Germany a week or ten days, but now I decided that, come what might, I would go home tomorrow. I would arrange to have had an urgent phone call from my brother, who had suddenly found he needed the car. Magic evenings of old, under the lamplight at Jahnstrasse, with Hannelore's huge and shabby old teddybear sitting beside us on the sofa, seemed wholly irrecoverable.

During that time there had been a few subdued lamentations from Hannelore's parents about the terrible scarcity of everything since the end of the war. Now there was brassy abundance everywhere, and loud confident German voices. Even the interior of Jahnstrasse had been redecorated with furry wallpaper in a virulent shade of green.

All of them, including the fiancé, were full of dismay when I said I must go. They urged me please to reconsider, to ring my brother and say it was not convenient, to drive at the weekend with the fiancé and fetch him – the *Oberst* – back among them. I almost feared they might detain me by force. And Hannelore, as I could see with a real pang, was deeply upset and disappointed. I had had my own daydream about what we would do together; but she, and her mother, had been going to make a proper use of me, and I honestly think that they expected I would enjoy it as much as they had been proposing to do.

And so I fled, without shame or dignity, to catch the midnight train from Düsseldorf. After returning the car to the barracks I passed the time at a cinema near the railway station which was showing Clouzeau's masterpiece, *The Wages of Fear*, dubbed into German. Like everyone else I was transfixed by the film, and its title seemed curiously appropriate. Then I sat musing in the quiet station over a glass of Dortmunder beer.

I wondered what Hannelore really felt about this young man who had come back to her. She seemed to take him so wholly for granted. And yet she had not seen him for ten years – he must be a complete stranger to her – while it was only five years since she had seen me.

In spite of everything I had felt that I knew her, and that she knew me. Perhaps that had caused the look of bewilderment – or was it disappointment? – that had sometimes appeared on her rosy face?

I wrote to her of course, with an apology, but I don't think I ever had a reply. And I never saw her again.

PART II

DESIRE

9

The speaker in T.S. Eliot's *The Waste Land* tells us that 'April is the cruellest month . . . mixing memory and desire.' For me those two come separately; and they come most often not in the springtime but in the autumn.

No time for them in the autumn of 1947 – I was young, and it is a long time ago. No time then to reflect on what was past or passing; to look back on the army and Germany and Hannelore.

Desire had hardly played a part in our original Hansel-and-Gretel relationship, and I had no difficulty in putting her out of my mind. I had a shot at desiring her in the abstract when the chance came to go back to Germany; and when I saw her in the flesh, and her fiancé too, I indeed longed, however briefly, to love and embrace her. But she had disappeared into marriage, and I felt no urge to see her again or to revisit the new Germany.

After leaving school in the autumn of 1943 I had gone up to Oxford to try for a scholarship. I was feeling doomed and fatalistic. My call-up summons had come: I had to join the army the day after the exam finished. History was supposed to be my best subject, although I was really only interested in its more picturesque aspects, such as the campaigns of Hannibal or the Duke of Marlborough.

We sat in the hall of one of the oldest colleges – University – and as we toiled away with ink and paper – there were no ballpoints in those days – a form was sent round on which we were required to enter the name of the college at which we would wish to become a scholar, in the event of winning an award. The choice was between four or five, one of which was New College. In the state of mind I was I gave the matter little thought, but it did occur to me that a new college might be easier to get into than an obviously ancient and august one such as University. Each of the four or five was offering a History Award, so I wrote down New College.

It was to prove a fateful choice. In retrospect it seems bizarre that we were all so clueless, and the arrangements so casual, but in the middle of the war Oxford was almost a ghost town, with most of the younger dons away fighting, or working at the great code-breaking centre at Bletchley. There was no one to tell us anything, except for the few broken-down old dons who were supposed to be supervising the exam. I had a perfunctory interview at New College, which I was surprised to find looked much the same age as the one in which I had written my papers.

But by then I had lost all interest in such matters. I could think of nothing but the awful prospect that would be facing me next day.

Possibly that is the right frame of mind in which to do an exam, as I got the award. The telegram announcing my success meant very little, for I was in such a state of bewildered happiness at finding the army so pleasant to be in that I could give no attention to anything else.

And at that moment Iris, whom I have never met or heard of, is giving her whole mental attention inside the Treasury to 'Notional Promotion in Absentia', while falling in love with numerous persons outside it.

Trains of random little memories trail along behind us on our morning walk. One of them amuses me, so that I stop, and try to remind Iris of it. It was in some book about the navy – Marryat? Forester? Patrick O'Brian? The Captain knocks his ship's biscuit on the table during a dinner party, and two weevils emerge. One is a fine plump tough-looking creature, the other wizened and diminutive. 'Which of the two would you rather have, Mr Smith?' enquires the Captain jovially of a shrinking junior midshipman. After a painful pause, 'Why, I suppose the bigger one, Sir.' 'Wrong, Mr Smith, wrong. In the navy you must always choose the lesser of two weevils.' Hearty laughter round the Captain's table.

Iris seems to take it in, but the weevils are obviously too much for her. I move quickly to something else that the weevils have suggested. The 'woolly-headed bastard'. One of her publishers, who had been in the navy, used to tell us about it. A rammer with a lambswool head for cleaning a five-nine, or a six-inch gun.

Iris still seems fully in tune with the woolly-headed bastard, which we often used to laugh at in former days, and it makes her laugh again. We go round the last corner of the block arm in arm, quite animated.

Carers, as I discovered, soon become experts at reading the physical symptoms and choosing a remedy from among the sedatives prescribed. When Iris has a wandering fit at two in the morning Promazine syrup seems the best bet. Pleasant to take and quite easy to get a spoonful down. As indispensable as that old woolly-headed bastard.

'Caring'. The inescapable word today. A postcard this morning from an old army friend whose second wife, much younger than he, developed Alzheimer's. I think he cheers himself up by sending these little offerings. When I knew him he was a spruce and stylish young man. Elderly and retired now he looks after his wife with great devotion.

'We are accompanied into the millennium', said the card, 'not by the Four Horsemen of the Apocalypse, but by the four Cavaliers in White Coats. *Compassion, Caring, Counselling, Compensation*'.

Iris is usually still asleep when I come up to bed after a TV thriller. I crawl in carefully without turning on the light.

Last night there were soft stirrings as in a nestful of birds, and soft cheeping sounds. Opening an eye I saw a shape briefly silhouetted in the faint light from the fifteen-watt bulb in the passage.

Then sounds from below, muffled at first. Iris would be heaping up piles of clothes, or rearranging the cairns of books, stones, cups and shoes that have been assembled on the floor. Sometimes there is the sharp noise of something breaking.

I continue feeling wakeful and preoccupied, as I know Iris does. In this state it is easy to become at one with Dr A's patients. Neither of us now will sleep till morning, and it is no use at the moment giving her a dose of the Promazine. I must gauge the right time for that – about five a.m. probably, when simple tiredness will assert itself, but not enough to calm her down without some chemical help. If I gave it to her now I know from experience that it would be useless. Mania would win.

In spite of the prospect of no sleep I feel calm myself, and professional, morale high. Gone (I hope) are the amateur days of my own tantrums, miseries and irritations, which Iris used to cope with by a kind of matrimonial reflex, a private version of the social one which can still on occasions stand her in good stead.

Undoubtedly one of the compensations, as the Alzheimer's gets worse, is the way in which the carer finds himself becoming two people: one closely identified with the sufferer and her symptoms, as I was with Iris's downstairs: the other in a state of almost enjoyable detachment, much aware of any treat he can save for himself.

Calmness and confidence are what doctors must enjoy: not only displaying them but feeling them too. Their own well-pleased and well-practised resources of calmness and confidence, whose detachment keeps the doctor sane and helps him deal with the anxieties of the patient.

So I feel now, when I lie in bed listening to Iris downstairs.

Is it just another mode of self-protection? Or a symptom of fatigue. The less sleep I get nowadays the more capable I feel of displaying calmness and confidence. Unlike a true professional, a nurse or doctor, I am playing to an audience of one – myself. Iris is indifferent to my performance, and presumably unaware of it. I have to be my own audience; and giving a benefit of an audience of one is part of the solitude of this unchosen profession of carer.

I never minded sentry duty in the army. Two hours, four sometimes, in the middle of the night, gave one the chance to be away in some sense, although the need to keep alert made it hardly possible to daydream. Even when tired I never felt sleepy on those occasions, just as I don't now, when Iris is coming and going in the dim light, and building her mysterious heaps downstairs.

Suggestions that she should come to bed are not exactly ignored but as if put on a file for future reference. Quite courteously, her murmurings seem to imply that there are more important things to do before sleep can be thought of, and that in any case bed is now an unwelcome place, frequented too often and too long.

So Belial takes over, and my mind wanders off. Unlike on sentrygo, daydream seems the most natural state of mind when lying in bed. As a sentry in training one wandered rather as Iris is doing now, investigating shadows and corners but remaining in the open, so that one could be seen to be doing one's job if the officer came round. That at least was how it was at home, at Pirbright or Catterick. At the sharp end it was very different. There the sentry was concerned above all to remain invisible, so that if an enemy scout or raiding party were approaching they wouldn't see him first. The sentry's nightmare was to be stalked by such an enemy, and silently disposed of before he knew what was happening.

On army courses we were told that the Russians were

specially good at such tactics. I wondered idly now whether Hannelore's fiancé had known all about that. I started remembering his cheerful ignorant face, so eerily untouched by what he must have gone through, and his dark unruly hair, so very unGerman, at least for those days.

Impossible somehow, although this must be just self-conceit again, to imagine him and Hannelore behaving like a married or an engaged couple; or talking at least as Hannelore and I used to talk on the sofa in the evenings. In the brief time I had seen them both together they appeared almost to avoid each other. Driving the Mercedes had seemed the peak of his enjoyment at being home after all those awful years.

Had those years been unremittingly so awful? – how could one know, since he said nothing? Or would he have woken up in the night with Hannelore, screaming from a nightmare, sobbing incoherently and beginning to tell her things? Somehow it was impossible to imagine that, which of course didn't mean it mightn't happen.

Another young German whom I met when out in T force and whom I plied with questions about the Russian front when I discovered he had been there, had not been at all reluctant to talk about it. On the contrary he was proud of having got through without a scratch, never anywhere near the enemy. He had been put in charge of some transport behind the lines, and had acquired a local *Bunkermädchen*, as he put it with coy facetiousness. She kept him warm in bed and you needed it with the thermometer at forty below. What had happened to her in the retreat? He had no idea, nor was he in the least interested, but I was struck by the vehemence with which he disowned any idea that during the war he had done his duty for Germany and the *Führer*.

Perhaps Hannelore's fiancé had managed to find a *Bunkermädchen*, even in the Russian camps? Perhaps he, like the other, had good luck, the thing soldiers become aware of after the war, when they find not only that they are still alive but even have agreeable memories of those days. That happened not infrequently. With me he had been so amiable, and so totally incurious – would he be jealous and ask Hannelore about me afterwards; and would she tell him about other possible affairs of hers which I had known nothing of?

But I had, and still have, the feeling that all such things would be irrelevant to him. The past, which means every-thing now to me, was not going to exist for Hannelore and her new husband. Much better not, no doubt.

Back in England I felt too that it would be better to forget all about Germany, and the unsettling thoughts incurred by this brief revisitation. There were lots of other things that I must now try to do; I had my living to earn and my future to consider. Having taken my degree in 1950 at the mature age of twenty-five, I was now doing some teaching, but my position was a humble one and I had no secure job or means of support: the army indeed was still paying for my education.

Well-wishers advised me to embark on serious research for a higher degree. I could think of no one to work on except Sir Walter Scott, whom I liked for his approach to history and the past: I had lately much enjoyed reading him. But it is one thing to enjoy an author, quite another to 'work' on him: my affection for Scott languished when I had to visit libraries, look at manuscripts and read critical books. Like many authors who have to be worked on by students of Eng. Lit., Scott does not lend himself to the process. He should be read for himself, a quiet and mildly soporific turning of pages, at bedtime or teatime.

At this crucial period – the 'Shadow Line' as Conrad thought of it – when one is on the verge of the future and its yet unknown responsibilities, mere indolence is more tempting than any form of dissipation. I privately abandoned Scott as a subject, though I continued to read him as an author, and began to compose, as if in a dream, a novel about the time in Germany which was now over and done with. It came so easily: it was the perfect companion for indolence. It seemed to fill out mornings and evenings perfectly, almost as if I were reading Scott himself. I have never enjoyed doing anything more; and the new little foundation of St Antony's, where I was writing the novel at what seemed a soothing rate of between one and two thousand words a day, was the perfect place to be doing it in.

There were many stories about St Antony's, and much going on there under the counter, so to speak; but I knew nothing about such matters and they never disturbed my own tranquil existence in the little college. I had no duties or responsibilities other than 'helping' with the foreign students as a junior member of what was really an extended house party. St Antony's has since expanded and become a well-respected Centre of International Studies, but I feel it has never been more itself than in those early days, when about a dozen of us lived happily together in this former Anglican convent in the Woodstock Road, spartan within and drably Victorian without, and did our own things in harmonious privacy.

We did them under the command – St Antony's in early days always had a pleasantly if sometimes furtively military air about it – of Colonel Bill Deakin, who during the war had stood at Tito's side in many a tight corner during the guerilla war in Jugoslavia. And given him shrewd advice no doubt. Bill Deakin was small and wiry, very sharp but not frightening. He seemed to invite me to enjoy whatever mysterious game was going on without having to participate in it: he accepted my limitations with amusement and equanimity. It was all a bit like not being expected to play golf when I was a child, except that Bill Deakin was a much more genial figure than my father.

James Joll, his second-in-command, a jovial fair-haired

Wykehamist with a curious bouncing walk, I had known when I was an undergraduate. Taking me aside one day he had said with an air of comic conspiracy, 'John, they are about to found a new college in order that I should be *Vice* Warden. Would you care to join us?'

His blue eyes twinkled in the kindliest way as he emphasised the word 'vice', but my own life at St Antony's was one of almost pastoral innocence. I suppose we did eat and drink rather a lot in the early days, and at a time when Oxford in general was still glumly undergoing the effects of wartime privation. We drank wine at all our meals like Frenchmen, because Antonin Besse, the potent figure who was our patron and founder, was indeed a Frenchman, a captain of commerce who had made his fortune along the Red Sea littoral – partly, it was hinted, by gun-running. He appears in a travel book by Evelyn Waugh, and had himself met Rimbaud when he was a very young man, somewhere in the wilds of Ethiopia. This fabulous figure had made no impression on Monsieur Besse, beyond the fact that he heard Rimbaud's trading ventures never came off. The poet-prodigy, who had abandoned the Muse at eighteen, and longed only to make money, was never much good at it apparently.

Monsieur Besse, who was rumoured to have found Oxford graduates particularly promising material as entrepreneurs in dubious projects, used periodically to descend on his fief to see how things were going. One graduate from the college who was recruited in this way into his business empire also became his son-in-law. Did he know about the other activity of St Antony's in its earliest phase? – recruitment not of spies exactly, but of intellectuals for the fringes of Whitehall security organisations? I know next to nothing about it myself, and knew nothing then, but I used to enjoy talking to David Footman, a sardonic avuncular person who wrote books about Russia and communism and was often away on government business. The higher echelons of St Antony's always had the air of being up to things they did not talk about.

I remained at St Anthony's for three or four years, greatly enjoying both the sociable side of the college and its convent-like seclusion, in which I could happily live while trying to write my novel. In the evenings Dr Zaehner, an expert on oriental religions, taught us to play backgammon, which he called 'tric-trac'. I never understood it properly but I loved to hear Robin Zaehner's manic giggle as he manoeuvred the pieces, chatting the while about Ormuzd and Ahriman and the legendary Zoroaster.

When Monsieur Besse came to visit we were paraded for his inspection. Looking and sounding just like my idea of Napoleon he would examine and address us in turn, barking out *'Et que faites-vous ici?'* with genial ferocity. It was hard to keep any aplomb with him; and when I somehow got out, in bad French, that I taught English literature, he shrugged immensely and turned up his eyes in mock despair. Obviously he expected more enterprise than that. But he did not seem to hold it too much against me, and while he was in the college we all wined and dined in our best country-house-party style.

Naturally enough the novel turned out to be all about Germany, and in a sense about Hannelore too, though there was a good deal else that I made up, including the plot. At the end of it the young hero, demobilised as I had been, and out of a job, has a phone call from the girl – she is called Lise – whom he left in Germany. She has managed to come over to England and is ringing from London, from Harrods. As a child I thought Harrods the most romantic place in the world, which must have been why I chose it for this reunion.

About this time, Michael Jaffé, a brilliant sardonic art critic who looked like an Assyrian monarch on a bas-relief and whom I had known at school, asked me in the kindest and most flattering manner what I was working on. When he heard that it was a novel, and that the hero and heroine were reunited at the end in Harrods, he burst into guffaws of laughter. He was driving me to Cambridge at that moment for a college feast, and his mirth became so uncontrollable that he was compelled to pull into the side of the road and stop the car until it subsided.

I was genuinely puzzled by his response, though gratified too, because it seemed to show that the novel was funnier than I realised. That must be all to the good, no matter how unintentional in this case the humour might be. Why Harrods should have struck him in this context as so hilarious I still cannot fathom, but alas he is dead and I cannot ask him. I told him I thought of calling the novel *In Another Country*. Ah yes, he said knowledgeably. Marlowe – *Jew of Malta* (he was Jewish himself) – '*But that was in another country, and besides, the wench is dead.*'

I recalled the quotation, memorably used by T.S. Eliot as an epigraph for one of his poems, but it hadn't occurred to me when I thought of a title. In my sentimental vision the wench, Lise, was very much alive, and had come to find her lover in England, sure that he still needed her. I felt he did too.

Lise looked a bit like Hannelore of course, but she was much more loving, more mature, more masterful. A day-dream in fact. And yet as I wrote I kept remembering that puzzled lost bewildered look on Hannelore's face when I'd had enough, and told her I must go because my brother needed the car. A look of child-like disappointment, and something more too, as if she had inconveniently found herself committed to an old lover when a more recent one had just come back to her.

The real Hannelore must have been very different. I don't doubt that. But daydreams feed on such sudden unexpected looks on familiar faces, faces with which one can imagine oneself in love.

*   *   *

And scarcely was the novel finished before I had another face to dream about, an image which instantly dispelled my tranquil time in what had once been the nunnery of St Antony's. The new face had come from a nunnery itself, as it happened, but its owner had finally been rejected as a postulant, and had come out again, however reluctantly, into the world. As soon as I saw that face I felt myself to be seriously in love.

It had all come from a poem I had seen in an old-fashioned green-covered monthly called *The Countryman*, which my parents took at home. I liked *The Countryman* anyway, and this poem, 'Evening Primrose', seemed to me then, as it still does, exceptional and charming. In a sort of amateurish footnote, typical of *The Countryman*'s lack of pretension, the editor had mentioned that the author of the poem repaired fine china for a living in a small Cotswold town. I wrote on impulse to the address to say how much I had enjoyed the poem, and a correspondence began. Eventually we met, the town not being far from Oxford.

Mary was a good bit older than I, with hair beginning to be touched with grey at the temples. She was shy in manner and had an enchanting smile, as many nuns or ex-nuns have, which lit up the whole of her face. In repose her face had a resigned and sad look which seemed its natural expression.

In the bus on the way back to Oxford I kept telling myself that if the bus reached a set of traffic lights before they turned red, or if the driver managed to get up a hill without changing gear, then she would marry me. I usually won this game, no doubt because I had subconsciously worked out the odds before making the bet with myself. As the vehicle ground the last few yards into the bus station I put all my winnings on a man who stood on its rear platform with umbrella and briefcase, obviously late for some appointment and impatient to get off. If he did so before the bus came to a stop then I would have scooped the pool, and our marriage was a certainty. Of course he did, sprinting lightly away towards the High Street, but I walked slowly back to St Antony's without any feeling of exultation: only a great and as it seemed a meaningless anxiety.

I had won my bet, and yet in the same moment part of me knew it meant nothing, except – oddly enough – that I was not really in love with Mary at all. I was really just imagining how delightful, how magical, it would be if I were.

And yet during the next few weeks I sincerely wished I had never met this woman. Like Gretchen at her spinning wheel my *Ruhe* was *hin* and my *Herz* was *schwer*. The delightful tranquillity of St Antony days, in which I had seemed to be waiting contentedly and without curiosity for the next thing to happen, was now a thing of the past. I seemed to be writing Mary a continuous love-letter, to which I received disappointingly meagre and politely baffled replies.

Persistence eventually made me at least familiar to her. Though she lived a reclusive life in the Cotswold bedsitter, surrounded by bits of china under repair, she was prepared to come to Oxford now and again. We sat in my cell at St Antony's – it seemed a suitable background for her – drinking wine and eating Marks and Spencer sandwiches. We talked about literature and poetry and that sort of thing, stiltedly and self-consciously as it seemed to me, but I found no way of making our conversation happy and spontaneous.

She seemed painfully unused to talking, but to enjoy it none the less as a new way of coming to terms with secular life. Although she loved discussing books and poems I didn't enjoy it at all: every word seemed to push us apart and make her quite different from the woman I had first seen, as from the woman who had written the Evening Primrose poem.

Our only good moments, as it seemed to me, came in the summer evenings – it was now June – when I went back home with her on the bus. We used to get off it in the country and walk the last mile or two in the summer twilight. Once we saw an owl sitting motionless on a telegraph pole beside the road. Displaying what knowledge I possessed, gratuitously as usual, I told her Hegel's comment about the owl of wisdom, Minerva's bird, only taking its flight in the evening. Presumably because it was by then too late for wise counsels to come to the aid of mankind and to save the world? At such moments Mary had a rather annoying habit of looking indulgent while ignoring what was being said. She continued to gaze at the bird in silence until it grew self-conscious in its turn and drifted away into the dusk like a shadow.

I thought of telling Mary about my owl at the ruined cottage on Romney Marsh. I was about to speak but decided with satisfaction not to. I would keep all such things to and for myself, for I was aware of feeling, with an even greater flood of satisfaction, that I was really beginning to fall out of love with Mary. But I had already started to make the first sounds of confiding my owl story, and to my amazement I heard myself say instead, 'I do wish you would marry me.'

Mary came to an abrupt halt. We stood there on the road in the tepid darkness, gazing at the white blur of each other's face. My unexpected words had filled me with consternation but now I felt calm, almost uninterested. The ball was in Mary's court. I waited with mild curiosity to see how she would play it.

She didn't. She simply walked on in silence, leaving me beginning to feel both silly and tiresome. Also impertinent. In silence we walked on into the little town, and to the point of the street where we usually said goodnight, Mary being unwilling that we should approach together the small house in which she lodged. We stopped, and I was about to say

goodnight and escape when Mary seized me by the arm –
we had no previous physical contact – and started to walk
me rapidly back to the place where we had seen the owl
sitting on the telegraph pole. Arrived there she swung me
towards her and kissed me on the mouth.

If Hannelore's kisses had been like a good ping-pong
player deftly returning the little ball, Mary's was like something she had read about and suddenly received a chance to
try out in action. It was more of a buffet than a kiss, and her
lips were cool and dry like paper. After administering it she
stood back, and dark as it was now growing I could see she
was looking at me intently.

'Do you really mean that?' she asked. 'Because of course,
if you do, I am going to say yes.'

In contrast to the look on her face the voice she spoke in
was low and urgent, although it still had something of the
quiet unworldly sardonic tone which seemed to me to go
with the face for which I loved her. It was capable of such
swift gentleness and intimacy, and yet at the same time
was so austere and far away. Now that I seemed almost
painfully close to the two of them, face and voice together,
I was paralysed and wholly bereft of initiative. I could only
stutter something vaguely, and she paid no attention.

Taking my arm again she said, 'Well let's just walk about
a bit until we've calmed down.'

We did that. As we walked I began to recover something
of my talkativeness. I embraced her and we stopped and
kissed every few yards. I had scarcely been conscious of
her body before, indeed hardly knew she had one, for the
kind of garments she wore seemed to remove from her any
feminine reality. Now I explored her with growing ardour,
though decorously too. She ignored what I was doing and
did not respond to it, but she began to talk with a quite
unusual vivacity. We laughed, still in a rather brittle way,
but with an increasing sense of relaxation between us.

I assured her – what else could I do? – that of course I had meant it. I longed to marry her. I began to talk about what we would do, where we would live. She only half listened, I felt, though she continued to smile almost ecstatically at me as we kissed. I could not make out whether she was simply indulging the antics of her admirer, or whether I had said something for which she had been waiting – could that possibly be it? – but which, now it had come, she did not none the less take quite seriously, or indeed know what to do about.

But between these alternatives I did not feel in the least upset or tantalised. Both seemed to me equally marvellous, equally full of a kind of onrushing and intoxicating promise. What did it matter if she didn't know what line to take, what to think of this new development? I didn't know either. The wonderful thing was that we had achieved a new kind of relationship, and if it had let me in for a permanent future with Mary, then so be it.

Being married to her seemed easily imaginable, delightfully and soberly alluring. I imagined Mary's face beside my own in the church, and friends and relatives looking at us admiringly, and sitting together in our garden when someone, perhaps the vicar, had dropped in to tea. Imagination could do much: all it failed to do was to see what life after marriage would really be like.

That did not matter. The fresh wild pleasure of our nocturnal walk was everything. We patrolled that road, far back out into the country, and when in the silence of the summer night we heard a stream close by we managed to get through a fence and find it. Flowing water glimmered in the obscurity, and we crouched down at the edge and joined hands together under the water. I babbled about this being a pagan or pantheistic betrothal. Mary said nothing, only laughing a little in her old quiet way, but she kissed me again and again.

Now, nearly fifty years later, I have inclination and time – time in my own mind at least – to wonder what she meant, and what she made of it all. Were she as clueless as I was, even though in a different, older, more essentially melancholy way, she must also have been just as confused, just as incapable of knowing or controlling what was happening.

Or was the matter, at least for her that evening, both more trivial and more easily foreseen and taken care of? Had I, almost inadvertently, started a play in which it was a pleasure and even a delight to perform? I remember thinking, with a qualm of depression but also a sneaking sense of relief, that neither of us could be quite serious about the way we were behaving: the only serious thing was our sense of liberation – and clearly we were both feeling that – into the joyfulness of being together, and talking and kissing in the way that we were.

Otherwise? – well. Was Mary herself entranced – liberated too – by the happy way we were both playing our parts while she was receiving, possibly for the first time, a proposal of marriage? In those days such a proposal, no matter how made or by whom, was quite something. Thinking about it all these many years later I can imagine Mary saying to a friend, 'Well, you know, there *was* this young man, in those days, who wanted to marry me' – and she would be saying it with the gentle half-sardonic smile I still remember so well. Perhaps it would be something she had made a poem about, like the one on the Evening Primrose.

In fact I did spot some years later, and not in *The Countryman*, which I no longer saw at my parents' home, but in the much glossier and more prestigious magazine *Country Life*, a poem by Mary about the owl sitting on the telegraph pole. It was a good poem, rather in the manner of Mary Coleridge, the great STC's collateral descendant, and it showed the same art in producing a tension between a natural object closely observed, and an emotional situation which was not specified.

I had not given a thought to Mary for ages and had lost all touch with her, but on reading the poem I at once felt a kind of jealousy and annoyance, as if a possession of my own had been taken and used without leave. Highly unfair, because Mary too had seen the owl just as I had, and yet I felt a grievance none the less, although I did cut out the poem and keep it.

It was above seven in the evening when we had reached the outskirts of the little town after our walk from the bus. By the time Mary disentwined herself from me and said she really must be going in, it was well past midnight. At intervals during our feverishly happy chatter, which came much more from me than from her, I had used phrases like 'When we are married,' 'Where shall we have the wedding?' and 'Where shall we go for our honeymoon?'

To none of this did Mary make any reply; but that did not seem to matter in the least, perhaps not to either of us; although after some hours I think both of us had unconsciously had enough. Mary enquired, rather unromantically I thought, if I was hungry. I discovered that I was, but I said no, of course not, and on that note we parted. I watched Mary turn a key and silently enter the little house where she lived. She turned and waved, and I waved back deliriously before setting out on the two mile walk back to the main road.

The evening's adventures were not yet over. I intended to hitch a lift back to Oxford, something I had often done before and which in those days presented no sort of problem. It was a moonless night but I got up to the big road without difficulty and stood waiting for the headlights of the long-distance lorries that drove by from Wales and from the Bristol docks. One rumbled into view at last and looked like stopping for me, but as I ran up the road to scramble into the cab it accelerated again and its red tail light vanished in the darkness. There was another close behind it which did stop at the sight of my gesticulating figure, and I thanked the driver effusively as he re-engaged the gears of his big Leyland Octopus – I still remember the type of the lorry and the cargo of tobacco it was carrying. It was restful not being able to talk above the roar of the engine housed between driver and passenger, and I was nearly asleep when the lorry stopped with a sudden jerk. Ahead was the lorry that had nearly stopped for me – I recognised the white-painted name on the tailboard – stationary and evidently in collision with another vehicle.

My driver scrambled out and I followed him. There was a great cloud of blue dust in the air, evidently from the cargo of one of the wrecked lorries, and there was already a considerable crowd about, moving and gesticulating agitatedly through a thick blue fog stabbed with headlights. My driver was talking and shouting to some others, and through the pulverised windscreen of the lorry that had been ahead of us I could make out hands, very white, splayed against the ruin as if a part of it.

My driver turned abruptly and went back to his cab, with me following. 'Done for. Fell asleep I reckon,' was all he said as we scrambled in. There were no seat belts in those days. As if still in a sinister dream I jumped off when my driver stopped for me at the Woodstock crossroads – no roundabout then – and remembered to shout up my thanks. He was away without further comment, no doubt keen to get the load to London and be off home, and I began to walk slowly down the dark empty road into Oxford.

Halfway there I made out a tall figure in the gloom on the opposite pavement, who began to cross the road purposefully towards me. One had not the least fear or even an awareness of muggers in those days – in 1952 such things just did not happen – and in any case I soon made out the policeman's helmet. He strolled up to me in leisurely fashion. 'Out a bit late, lad, aren't you?' he observed, without seeming to expect an answer.

I at once felt greatly relieved, not by what he said but by

his general demeanour in the faint light that was beginning to dawn. Everything, I felt, would now be all right, including of course my marriage to Mary, which had become rather lost sight of in the recent events on the road.

I remembered what was supposed to be a chilling moment in one of Sax Rohmer's Fu Manchu stories, which I had been fond of when young. The heroine, escaping and pursued by sinister and silent Chinamen, looks wildly round for help as she runs along a dark road. 'But there was no one in sight, not even a policeman'. Clearly policemen were as common as lamp-posts in those days.

The recollection was interrupted by my own policeman interrupting his air of peaceful scrutiny to ask what I had in that bag. I usually had a book or two which I had lent to Mary, who was scrupulous about returning such things, and I hastened to produce these for the policeman's inspection.

Satisfied, he turned away with a pacific, 'Good morning, Sir,' and I went on my way down to St Antony's, comforted by the encounter, though for the next day or so I often thought about the poor truck-driver's bloodless hands.

Before I went to bed I started to write a love-letter. Although I had thought of the previous ones as love-letters they were really just intended to sparkle and to impress. I found the authentic thing extraordinarily hard to do: and abandoning it at about six in the morning fell immediately and very deeply asleep.

For the next twenty-four hours I knew that something of vital importance had occurred and that my whole life would have to be changed. But I had trouble remembering what the thing was. Another thing in me didn't want to remember. The novel was finished, and so in a sense I was at a loose end; and yet I had never before felt so comfortable in my burrow-like routines at St Antony's. My bit of teaching in the mornings, the cinema perhaps in the afternoon; at night reading in my room, after college dinner and perhaps a game of tric-trac or draughts with Dr Zaehner. How had it happened that all this should have been put under threat? I had some serious disease, and been given only months or weeks to live.

I had lately been reading the philosopher Wittgenstein: everyone was doing it. Along with A.J. Ayer's *Language, Truth and Logic* his *Tractatus* was all the rage. Without understanding much of it I enjoyed the simplicity and confidence of the style. I had been especially struck by one calm observation: something about the different worlds we live in, and the world of the healthy being quite different from that of the sick.

I knew now just what he meant. Something had gone seriously wrong inside me. The events of last night were not going to go away. They meant I was in love, and had entered a different world, one quite unlike the little St Antony's world of my own, which I could so happily control. In the course of the day I finished my love-letter as if I were making a will, and sent it off.

Two mornings later I scrabbled feverishly in my pigeon-hole. If there had been no letter from Mary I should have been desolated, as well as deeply wounded. But there was a letter. Up in my little nun's cell I tore it open. I somehow knew it would be gentle, a bit constrained, considerate for me. It would perhaps be better not to meet, at least not just yet. She would always treasure our talks together and my kindness about her poems – the way I had written about 'Evening Primrose' . . .

The letter, opening with 'Dear John', did indeed begin with thanks. It had been a lovely day, and she did so hope I had got back safely? I put the letter down, with a leaden sense of disappointment, even misery. I looked at the books on the desk and on my bed. None of them held the slightest interest for me now. Neither did the last pages of the novel, laboriously typed, arranged neatly and waiting to be corrected. Listlessly I picked up the letter again. Mary's writing was neat too, without being in any way fancy, and perfectly easy to read. But after a sort of hiatus near the bottom of the first page it started off again in a much wilder script, almost illegible. Sitting down I started to concentrate.

She loved me – she wanted me – she longed to marry me. She wanted me for her very own. No matter for God, the Church, her life, her poems – anything else. She loved me. Would I really marry her? Would I come to her, please?

The letter was quite short – a single page and the reverse not even completed, or signed. My own had of course been much longer.

I was already in a fever of departure, putting on my coat, a tie. I ran down to the bicycle shed – there could be no question of waiting for a bus. Within a few minutes of opening the letter I was bicycling out of Oxford.

It was a hot day and a long way, with a lot of hills. I had plenty of time to reflect on what I was doing, and on my own astonishment at doing it at all. But I knew I must do it. I knew, or at least I had read somewhere, that the fulfilment of sexual obsession is like a dreadful duty. But whatever demon was driving me now it was not sex. I did not really desire Mary: I was still barely aware of her as a woman. Why then?

By now I was so hot and uncomfortable, in imminent danger too from passing lorries whose slipstream nearly knocked me off my bike, that I ceased to feel any interest in why I was doing it. The great thing was to get there.

And eventually I did. I had never been inside the house; it was the first time I had knocked on the door. It was opened by a rather disagreeable-looking woman with a pursed-up mouth. She glowered at me. I explained I wanted to see Mary, and the woman reluctantly let me go up the cramped cottage stairs. I was aware of her standing at the bottom and eyeing me. I knocked on a door.

Mary jumped up awkwardly, almost knocking over a

piece of china under repair. She did not seem pleased to see me. There was no telephone of course; I could not have rung Mary up, but it occurred to me that it might have been wiser as well as more civil to have sent a telegram, a 'wire' as they were known in those days. It also occurred to me, and with a definite pang, that if I had my snug little burrow at St Antony's, so had Mary her own out here, one which she must need and want as much as I did mine.

Mary's face looked pinched, and her mouth as pursed-up as that of her landlady. She also seemed flustered and embarrassed, even frightened. My discomfort was extreme, and before anything was said I realised that others beside myself had daydreams and desires and vague longings which they neither wished nor expected to be implemented and put into action. Mary had written a letter – the second half of it – on the peak of one of those. And now here I was, rudely butting in on her own life, a life which she cherished in her own way as much as I did mine.

I was right of course. Mary became very quiet and calm. She asked me to forget about the letter. A little more experience might have told me that something here was seriously amiss, but I was much too concerned with my own feelings. The things that had charmed me about Mary – a smile, her good sense, her touching interest in everything I talked about and told her – were ways of guarding and protecting something deeply disturbed within. Her poems, her devotions, her meticulous work with china, were doing the same.

She seemed frank about this. She told me she had yielded to some silly irrational impulse, and now she must frighten me off for my own good. So please go.

But I at once determined not to be frightened off. As I bicycled slowly back to Oxford – more than twenty miles and it seemed to take me the rest of the day – I resolved whatever happened to hang on. She had changed her mind

once: why shouldn't she change it again? – and for good
this time?

It was a hope born of ignorance and disregard rather than
of innocence. Not only was my idea of marriage – Mary
beside me in a white wedding-dress, and the vicar coming to
tea – wholly ridiculous, but I was selfish enough to suppose
that Mary must have the same delightful view of it, if indeed
I bothered to think of her having any view at all.

What mattered was that she had said she loved me and
wanted me. *Wanted* me – above all. It was that word, rather
than love, which so deeply moved and flattered me.

I knew every word of that part of her letter by heart, and
repeated them like a charm as I bicycled along in a state
of near exhaustion. I had been so frightened bicycling out
on the main road – this was long before the days of dual
carriageways and cycle-paths – that I returned to Oxford
along a devious route through the country lanes, getting
lost in the process and adding miles to the journey.

The next day I heard from Mary again. It was an affectionate quiet letter, merely saying she did hope we might
go on seeing each other as before. The tone of this letter
annoyed as well as depressed me. So Mary merely wanted
to go on making use of me as a pal, to borrow books and to
chat about poetry and so forth? Well, thank you very much.
Just as I had absolutely believed the words which said she
loved and wanted me, so I now believed a friendly letter
which said couldn't we be friends? It never occurred to me
that Mary, who was after all nearly ten years older than I
was, could be a victim of love's uncertain madness to an
extent which made my own feelings look solipsistic, as well
as jejune. She was the real Gretchen at the spinning wheel,
whose peace and quiet I had in a sense quite thoughtlessly
destroyed.

Looking back, something I have hardly done till now –
this moment when memory has assumed the paramount
place in consciousness – it looks as if I fell in love with

Mary because she was not tough: did not have, that is to say, a normal feminine degree of resilience, of wiry and wary calculation. I may have unconsciously intuited that, and it may have made a strong hidden appeal.

Mary was defenceless. Not in the sense that she could be taken advantage of sexually: I had no idea how to set about that, and no wish to do it either. She had wanted earlier to give herself to God, or to Christ, a need so incomprehensible to me that I could not even begin to imagine it. Had I accidentally given her the impulse to want me instead, or at least want something beyond a quiet life repairing china, going to church and seeing a circle of friends?

Thinking of the owl on the telegraph pole, which Mary was later to write a poem about, reminds me by association how owlish it must always be to write down one's own love experiences. They may seem interesting to me now, but when they happened they were just like everyone else's experiences. Sex may be the ever interesting topic, but love is interesting only to oneself, which is why it seems owlish to expatiate upon it publicly. (Incidentally why should the owl, Minerva's bird, be an emblem of wisdom, when to be owlish is to be merely obtuse, if not downright stupid?)

I was still fixated about Mary. Had she written, 'I'm sorry but I never want to see you again', I should not, I think, have persevered. A dramatic rejection would have satisfied me and set my feelings as much in a proper groove as a joyful acceptance would have done. The awareness of this was what annoyed me, and yet I had the sense to realise that my own best interests – at least as I then saw them – lay in going along with what she had suggested.

So she came to see me again in St Antony's, though I did not now go back home with her to the town where she lived. We sat in my bedsitter as before and had a sandwich and a glass of white wine and talked about books. Should she read Chaucer, *The Faerie Queen*? . . . We debated the question while boredom mounted up in my heart and soul. There were occasional animated moments when Mary seemed to forget herself. Looking suddenly into my eyes she would say, 'John – if only we *could* get married . . .' Like a hunter not daring to move for fear of disturbing shy game, I would remain silent, only returning her look. The next day I would get a brief letter saying, 'Dear John, I am sorry that I am me'.

It turned cold early in December and there was snow even in Oxford. Feeling suddenly resolved I hastened down to the bus station. In the country the snow was thick. I seemed to wade through it to Mary's door. Mary was sitting idly in her tiny room. There were no bits of china under repair. Last time there had been drafts of a poem scattered about, but now there was nothing.

In the bus I had let myself imagine her springing up with a cry, flinging her arms tightly round me and saying, 'Oh, I'm so glad you've come.' I could hear her saying it, and so clearly that when I stood before her I thought for a second she was saying it. But the chilly room remained silent, snow-muffled. Mary's face looked puffy and unusually pale, though in comparison with Hannelore it had never looked exactly rubicund.

When she spoke at last her voice sounded clogged and peevish. 'I warn you I'm getting a cold,' she said. 'So am I,' I replied, which was true enough. 'Don't worry.'

There seemed nothing else to say. She looked away from me towards the window. I had the feeling she was on the verge of tears: also that she was glad I had come, despite appearances; but this feeling gave me neither hope nor pleasure. At the same time I felt I had never loved her more than as she looked now, plain and disreputable, with the grey in her hair much in evidence. For the first time I really desired her. I longed to take her in my arms and make love to her, even though I had very little idea how this should be done when it came to the homely details;

and I knew that Mary had no idea either: I could not expect any help from her.

The fact somehow made me so woebegone that I felt tears coming into my eyes. Then I saw that hers had them too. We began to smile at each other in a way that was almost amused and apologetic. I had never shed tears with anyone before, and the sensation it gave was extraordinarily comforting, even exhilarating. In a minute or two we were chatting quite normally. Mary said she would make some tea. She had to leave the room to do this and I heard a murmur of voices below as if she was continuing her own life, which had been going quietly on before mine, and would continue to do so after I had disappeared and been forgotten.

The thought made me so forlorn again that I could not smile or say anything when Mary reappeared. We seemed to be just on the edge of a wonderful moment which would change our lives but which both of us knew would never happen. We drank the tea in silence, and I still remember how weak and disagreeable it was. Should we always be drinking such nasty tea if we got married? The thought amused and cheered me somewhat; and I was aware, too, that my agonised impression that we were just on the edge of delirious happiness, if we could only nerve ourselves to reach it, was a scene I had picked up from the cinema and from books. Probably a story by Chekhov?

'What are you smiling at?' said Mary, slightly peevish again. I did not tell her, but I think she understood, and was hurt a little. There seemed nothing I could do about that now, nothing to comfort her, though I still longed to do so by some physical means.

'We are rather like a Victorian couple in a novel, aren't we?' I found myself saying instead. Mary seemed to have this effect on me, and I remembered the moment when I had found myself saying, in equally casual terms, something about our getting married.

Mary looked hard and cold now. The emotions of the last few minutes seemed to have vanished away pathetically, knowing they were no use. 'When's your bus?' she asked. I told her the time of the next one back and she said she would come with me to the bus-stop. I besought her not to, with her cold coming on, but she took no notice. Fortunately there was not long to wait and we talked as much as we could. She asked about my plans and my teaching. She seemed like an aunt inquiring about a nephew's future; but I realised she was distrait and not interested in what I said.

The bus came, churning up the unexpected snow which was still dazzling white in its headlights. I got on and sat stiffly at the back. There was an interminable wait while the driver conferred with some unseen person outside his window. Then at my own window Mary's face suddenly appeared, gazing at me, as it seemed imploringly. I got up in haste, but at that moment the driver engaged gear and we lunged heavily away up the hill.

My sore throat was now painful enough to occupy most of my attention. I felt feverish, and the cold was really coming on. But I remembered that a friend who was already a fellow of Lincoln College and Tutor in English had asked me to a party in his rooms that evening, a Saturday. William Empson, a great name and a legendary figure in our Eng. Lit. world at that time, was going to be there.

I went, drank as much as I could, and fell off my bicycle in the snow at two a.m. on my way back to St Antony's. But I had met a couple who knew someone I had known in Gerrards Cross. More important they had been going to bring a friend of theirs whom they said they would have liked me to meet. She had cried off at the last moment because of a former entanglement with our host, whom she did not now wish to encounter. They did not mention her name, but that was the first time I heard of the existence of Iris.

*　　*　　*

I had a letter from Mary the following day saying please, she did not want to see me again. There was silence until nine or ten years later; although I heard from an acquaintance that she had later on been through a bad time, even – the friend thought – an attempted suicide, but was now fully recovered. Then Mary herself wrote out of the blue. She was living in a different place, further from Oxford, but she did so hope that my wife and I might be able to visit them.

The invitation came again and eventually we went to a lunch which I recall as being painfully vegetarian. Mary was living with a woman friend, to whom she seemed to be in a state of total subordination. I suspected this friend might have made Mary ask us out of curiosity. Neither Iris nor I took to her at all. Such instant hostility was rare indeed on the part of Iris, who was never in the least censorious or critical. But the woman's attempts to silence Mary, whom Iris took to at once, and to block off her timid friendliness and her equally timid attempts to ask about Plato and the Christian mystics – all this upset Iris and annoyed her even more. The lunch was not a success, nor was it repeated.

The friend abandoned Mary soon after, and a convent near Worcester took her in for a while. She remained in correspondence with Iris until her death, and in this way became a 'pal for life'. That was how another fan of Iris once expressed it when Iris had replied sympathetically and thoughtfully to her letters.

10

'Thou met'st with things dying, I with things newborn'. It happens to me nowadays to be haunted by Shakespeare's line, which suggests that the two states are not so very different. Sometimes Iris's resemblance to a three-year-old is so uncanny that I find myself expecting her to shrink to an appropriate size.

My own enactment of a parent's role is equally exact, involuntarily faithful. Sometimes when I give her supper with a spoon Iris will eat her creamed rice or baked beans with a sort of negligent greed, like a child pretending it doesn't really want them, is above such things as food. More often she turns her head away, and yet when I proffer a spoonful opens her mouth obediently at once, like a chick on the nest. Being fed is still a pleasure to her.

'Bed now?' I say hopefully but she doesn't care for the idea, or for any other course of action. She sits, and when I smile at her smiles back as if she knows perfectly well what I have in mind.

What I have in mind is my own drink and supper, my own blessed hour when the children are safe in bed, and the parents can relax with each other and resume adult life and its pleasures. At least I would suppose that is what they would do, and would feel like. But I am a lone parent, as they are called today; and I should imagine that a lone parent's evening relaxation, solitary as it may be, provides an even sharper and sweeter relief than those in a communal family.

I don't feel like a father and I don't feel like a mother

either: I'm just going through the joint parental struggles, trials and compensations. Not rewards, because rewards would be seeing the kiddies growing up and saying new words and all the rest of it.

But I do fully appreciate the compensations. And I have that eerie feeling, when Iris smiles back at me as if she knew how much I am going to enjoy my drink when she is in bed, that she is herself cheered and supported by an awareness of the compensations I am getting.

It can hardly be so, yet it certainly feels like it. Three-year-olds don't care whether their parents are enjoying themselves or not. But perhaps they just assume they are, and that is much the same thing?

I don't know how it is with three-year-olds, but Iris's toilet habits, if you can call them that, have become unpredictable. Sometimes she will go to the right place, even though she makes a mess of it. More often she will do it on the carpet outside, or in another room. Then she lays the results, as if with care, on a neighbouring chair or bookshelf. I don't mind a bit cleaning up, an operation which seems mildly to amuse her. I can make a joke of it too, and we can laugh about it together. A small domestic challenge I can easily meet, and Iris seems to enjoy seeing me do it.

Certainly she can now have childish pleasures, presumably undreamt of before. Like the fingernail cutting. I take her arm firmly under mine so that she is behind me, her head laid shrinkingly against my back. She jibs and starts as I carefully cut the nails, with little shrieks and intakes of breath as if she were sure I am going to hurt her. But I can feel she is enjoying it really – the fearful joy of a child.

Time for bed at last. I've given her the sleeping-draught disguised as a 'drink'. Mango and orangeade, a few drops of sweet Cyprus wine. Unlike the Promazine this stuff smells nasty by itself and presumably tastes so too, but Iris drinks it quite happily in its juicy form. All through supper she has been hugging an old summer dress she has found somewhere. Now she goes up the stairs trailing it behind her, looking exactly like E.H. Shepard's illustration to *Winnie the Pooh*. Christopher Robin going up the stairs, dragging Pooh behind him.

I settle Iris down, turn her over, kiss her goodnight. I turn the light off and promise to leave the passage light on. Then I go quietly downstairs, but not yet to my drink. Like every other parent no doubt, I know what may happen. Usually it does. No noise, just a face looking round the door. 'You'll catch cold – back to bed with you at once.' (We used to call it 'mat', from an earlier pretence that we were cats: but now we have reverted to the normal use of bed, the thing that children go up to.)

It may happen again – probably will. Then there is peace at last, total quiet, except for the subdued music of my radio. I pour out my own drink with loving care. But before tasting it I tiptoe upstairs, listen for a few seconds. Still all quiet. I look in very cautiously. Not a sound. Iris's head sideways on the pillow. The light from the door just shows her face, calm and relaxed, as if Dr Alzheimer had sent a friend to soothe away the daytime fears of a consciousness without speech or understanding.

Going down I can almost hear myself saying to an invisible, unknowable co-parent, 'All OK. She's dropped off.'

What would I do without her? Impossible now to imagine any other routine. I certainly cannot imagine enjoying my solitary drink unless Iris was safely in bed and asleep upstairs. When she has to go . . . If I can find somewhere to take her . . . At first only for a few days? But I want the present life, the present stage, to go on for ever.

Do parents feel like that sometimes, about their children? Surely not? Yet to lose a child must be the worst thing of all? Just because they are such a blessed nuisance?

After nearly fifty years I feel far closer to Iris than a parent could be to a child. A child, however loved and doted on, is still 'a little stranger'. Every day the knowledge that Iris and I are one flesh grows more overwhelming. The further the illness takes her away in the spirit, the more she is with me in the flesh.

Were she to be in a home, however 'happy' they would try to make her, the sense of apartness would soon destroy us both. Perhaps me before her, perhaps her before me? At the moment she keeps me sane. The final egoism is it? What would happen to me if she weren't here? Is that my real fear?

When his wife went off her head Macbeth expected the same things from his doctor that we hope for from ours today.

> Can'st thou not minister to a mind diseased?
> Pluck from the memory a rooted sorrow . . .

I fancy that the doctor may have tried on his royal patient all the somnolent potions that were at his command, although he tells Macbeth, perhaps defensively, that the patient must 'minister to himself' when it comes to staying sane and getting a good night's rest.

Sedatives are tricky things. Lady Macbeth's sleepwalking and her hallucinations could easily be the consequence of some too strenuous type of soporific. Chloral used to do it, if regularly taken. Rossetti died of it; and that was what was the matter with Evelyn Waugh when he had the experiences which led him to write that remarkable book, *The Ordeal of Gilbert Pinfold*.

In the early stages of Alzheimer's Iris never needed a sleeping-pill at all. She slept easily, both all night and in the afternoon, sometimes dozing in the morning as well. That lucky gift has now abandoned her. She goes to sleep like a child still, but in the night other things happen. Waking up I know at once she is no longer there. With an uncharacteristically stealthy movement she has gone from beside me, while I still slept. Now I lie tense and listening as on that night when it first occurred. The house is wholly quiet; I can see the light from the weak bulb in the passageway. Not a sound, but then suddenly I hear, and much more often now, the voice which doesn't sound like Iris saying quite clearly, 'Who is it? Who is it?' and then 'Hullo, hullo, are you there?'

It has become just like that Walter de la Mare story of the old man who walks about the house in the small hours, saying with querulous patience, 'Coming, coming.'

I look at my watch. Half-past two. I make a quick calculation: which potion to give her now? Sometimes it is better to wait. Iris may come back, led like a moth by the bedside light I've switched on. She will get quietly into bed, and we will make happy normal noises together as she nestles down.

But if nothing happens for a longish time I have to go in search of her. She is usually standing quietly in a room, having switched the light on. She smiles at me; we greet each other almost like two guests at a party. I take her hand and try to lead her back to the bedroom; but sometimes she resists quietly, turns in the opposite direction, stumbles up or down the stairs, evading me. It may seem best to leave her then. It is no use my going back to bed, but I go through the motions, hoping to lure her to follow me. Sometimes she does, but more often not. The impulses, whatever they are, have to work themselves out, and then she will come back, and sleep when daylight begins to show.

Going about the house after her in the dead of the night makes me also remember Henry James and Rye: that time we were there in his house. For me now Iris is like an elusive Muse, a Muse who has to be coaxed, cosseted, rescued from herself. Why should I think of Henry James doing such a thing, but somehow it seems appropriate. Women did inspire him after all, and then by making much of them he kept them from coming too close. Iris, in this ghostly non-time, can seem concerned I should not come too close to her. She has been calling out in the motionless house for someone else. For whom?

For whom does she cry out *'Are you there?'* and demand *'Who is it?'* Is it her own vanished Muse?

The sadness of it all, the sadness I thought I felt in Lamb House at Rye, when I woke up there in the darkness. The darkness when it was beginning to be light, but it was summer then. In the night, in our house, it is very much winter now.

11

During the summer I longed passionately for winter to come. I imagined it every day. I saw snow falling into the dusty dried-out street.

And now it's come. 'Dark December's bareness everywhere'. I still prefer it; I don't imagine summer being here, or want it to be here. But in the deep night the winter does seem to be a part of our state, too much a part of it.

I try to evade sleeplessness by going up to bed late if there is anything any good on television – excitements, murders, shootings, chasing . . . After those I usually sleep quite well until Iris wakes me. After she is back in bed and all seems calm I find it difficult to go to sleep, and then begins my nocturnal compensation time, an hour or two devoted entirely to Belial's remedy, the thoughts that wander . . .

Although they are not exactly thoughts – more memories again, and, as it were, memory-creations. Much more satisfactory than dreams, even if the two have something in common. They are charms created or invented by the past, charms against the despair of the present.

If only there was some way of sharing such things with Iris. It doesn't seem so long since I used to talk to her about the things we had seen in Wales, when we had been there with Peter and Jim. The blue eyes of Cloudy their sheep dog, the pied flycatchers' nest beside the churchyard. I once reminisced to her about these things; and although she may not have remembered, it gave awareness something to do.

Now it has nothing to do, except to be aware of me. My smiles and jokes still reassure; but as it wears on they begin to be baffled by the sheer bulk of the day. How, at five o'clock of a winter's evening, to get through the three or four hours until her bedtime? Jokes wear thin; tea and biscuits she ignores; TV has become useless, even as another presence in the room, a distraction in the background.

I wonder: can even two- or three-year-old children, end-lessly questing and chattering, be as exhausting as this vacancy? It fills my mind and heart too, paralyses the will, or whatever mechanism it is one uses to plan and overcome the next minute of being. No point in picking things up off the floor: Iris will have them back there in a few minutes. Or other things. Suppose I try to set up a routine? I undo what she does: she undoes what I do? But I haven't got the will for it.

'Please help me,' I say, smiling and trying to make some-thing funny out of this appeal: and to my amazement Iris replies at once, 'Poor doggie!' And she has a smile too.

Thoughts or memories are only free when Iris is asleep. And in a guilty way they depend on disregarding her. They would hardly be free otherwise.

But was that always the case? The happiest marriages are full of alternative lives, lived in the head, unknown to the partner. Or perhaps not so unknown? Iris was leading such lives as she planned each of her novels, and I used to feel an obscure sense of participation. It was very satisfying. The fullness of her hidden life gave me as much daily pleasure as what we did together. In some way it felt as if we were more at one – just in my knowing that things were going on – than if we had been sharing them.

Iris would not have minded if I had asked about them – in fact she would have told me. But I never did ask and we both tacitly preferred it that way. A mutuality in business secrets. But now our daytime contact is so total and so overwhelming that night-thoughts can only be a way of escaping it. Day-thoughts too, when we are outside walking, as we did in the summer. With her hand or arm in mine I moved in a dream. All the convenience and all the vanity of daydreams. Summer walks, and now winter night-time, are the place for them. And they cannot be shared.

That makes them proliferate all the more luxuriantly. And absurdly. Sometimes after a walk, or a sleepless night full of disturbance, satiety makes me feel quite bloated. Like a bird or an animal that eats and eats all it can, knowing that the winter is coming, or the ardours of the spring migration.

Once I was able not exactly to share a daydream with Iris but at least to involve her in it. There were occasions in the summer when she had escape impulses even on our walks, no doubt related to the wish to vanish out of the front door, to wander off somewhere, anywhere.

Nun weiter denn, nur weiter! Once she rushed abruptly up to a young man who happened to be passing. Tall, dark, obviously a foreigner. She caught hold of his sleeve. *'Help me, please, help me.'*

He looked bewildered. The urgency of the appeal not only bothered him but seemed to convince him. 'Please? What?' – addressing me as well, but at me he gave an accusing look. Was I harassing her? It must have looked like that, incongruous as it might seem, when the two parties were so elderly, and apparently so closely connected. Ah, but that was the trouble – the home was the worst place – the media would have taught him all about child abuse and granny-bashing . . .

I gave him a smile and started to drag Iris off by the elbow. Looking back I saw him standing still in doubt, and noted he was big and powerful, built like Bulldog Drummond, one of nature's rescuers and the hero of those stories by 'Sapper' I used to read in childhood.

So I started an instant fantasy along the lines of that Hitchcock film, *The Lady Vanishes*. As we reached home and I deadlocked the door on the inside I was already well into the scenario. Woman abducted in broad daylight. I, the kidnapper, a man of iron nerve, had easily persuaded the bystanders that I was in charge of the poor demented creature. On other occasions when Iris had demanded help from a passer-by I had tapped my head significantly to indicate that I was in charge of a deranged person, a gesture which usually embarrassed the parties concerned into making their own escape.

I got Iris indoors so precipitately that the back of my coat got caught yet again in the slamming door. It's becoming a habit. I had to undo the mortice lock and open the door to free myself, laying a restraining hand on Iris to prevent her blowing away like a plastic bag in the wind. Once off like that she is difficult to catch. I marvel yet again – another of Dr A's almost daily repetitions, like the tail caught in the door – at the contradiction between her instinct to be away – anywhere anywhere out of our world – and her wish to be my shadow. My Water-Buffalo, interposing her bulk so that *I* can't vanish away.

I depend more and more on her dependence, and yet I also need to be exasperated by it. Nowadays I can deliver a volley of obscenities at her and she smiles and nuzzles me as if they constituted the deepest, most loving reassurance. 'Damn your eyes, blast your guts, bugger off can't you!' I shout it with a beaming smile, giving her a not too gentle push or a whack on the behind. Good for both of us, a real relief, and yet is it really so good for me? It's not like the violence she could feel once when she said, 'Don't hit me.' It's formalised, but something feral and fierce is lurking there none the less.

If that sounds portentous, what about that other glib stuff, beloved by romantics, about love and hate being close together? I don't believe that for a moment. Love

is on easy terms with sudden rage, with violent exasperation, but surely not with hatred? Cold hatred? Or is that
complacent?

When freeing myself with what used – how long ago it
seems – to be called filthy words, I sometimes push my
head at Iris, saying, 'I hate you, you know! I REALLY
FUCKING WELL HATE YOU!' To her it all seems to sound
like a comment on the weather. The words fall down disarmed, but could they rise up in the night and mop and
mow before her like malignant ghosts? 'He said that. *Did
he really mean it?*'

But there is no memory involved – within seconds the
waters of oblivion have washed it all away. A child says,
'I hate you I hate you,' and mother takes no notice. It
is no more than a brief disowning of dependency. Iris
now can be like a three-year-old, sometimes an impossible
three-year-old. But it is I who say, 'I hate you,' and she, like
the mother, who takes no notice. Just a happy look for a
moment on her creased little face.

I think this happy look is because I am talking to her in
a serious way, not just inattentively murmuring in reply
to her gabble of unmeaning query. She catches the tone.
More than that, which makes the relation of memory and
understanding so strangely unpredictable, she still seems
able at times to identify an old joke reference.

I used to quote the husband and wife from *Sense and
Sensibility*. Young Mrs Palmer is an infinitely silly, infinitely
good-natured girl who must have charmed dry clever Mr
Palmer, an *homme sérieux*, into making her an offer of
marriage. He puts up with the consequences however
exasperating he finds his wife, who for her part is as
delighted by his displays of bad temper as she is by
everything else. 'Mr Palmer is so droll,' she tells friends
with a fond giggle, after he has just snubbed her mercilessly
in public. 'He is always out of humour.'

Mr Palmer is luckier than he knows. Or did Jane Austen perceive that he secretly loved his wife for her good temper, and because she enjoyed him most when he was at his most disobliging? However that may be I quoted the Palmers to Iris, implying that I was now in the habit of behaving as badly as Mr Palmer did. She understood me; at least her face split into smiles. The Palmers were still somehow there, lodged among the forsaken brain's disused and dusty files.

In actual fact Iris never much troubled herself about consulting those files. She never seemed to need a mental card index of her own, still less a computer. Creation with her was never in the least business-like, and I sometimes wondered how it got done at all. Could it, because so magical, vanish like the ending of a spell, as it did when the dark escort came for her? There was no struggle then, no protest, no fighting retreat. Her powers seemed to vanish between one day and the next. So many times previously she had told me, 'I've finished the novel, now it's only got to be written' – as if when the spell was in place the words would do its bidding obediently.

Her publisher marvelled at, but I think thoroughly appreciated, Iris's unworldliness and her indifference to business matters. All those things Norah Smallwood could take care of herself. Iris rather enjoyed being bossed about by Norah, who had the secret of doing it in a way that reassured and never irritated. For her Iris was like the clever little girl getting on with her own thing in a corner of the nursery, never expecting the attention of the grown-ups, still less their flattery and praise.

I don't think Norah, as effective managing director of Chatto and Windus, ever stood Iris a single meal in the course of their long and happy relationship, and never wasted an ounce of publicity on her.

Not that such practices were normal at that time, as

they are with an important author today. When Aldous Huxley, then the most revered icon on Chatto's list, came over on a visit from California, Norah made the unusually handsome concession of inviting him for supper. But on the firm's premises, a supper she proposed to cook and serve herself. Iris and I were bidden, and told to report to Norah's flat in Vincent Square at seven sharp, bringing our car. There we heard we were to ferry the dinner to Chatto's cramped offices in King William IV Street, where I almost spilt a big bowl of salad when negotiating the narrow stairs.

Aldous Huxley, a man of sense and charm, seemed to regard this arrangement as an admirable one, and to enjoy it in the spirit of old Bloomsbury. But when Iris's New York publisher came over and wished to take her out things were very different. The gentleman from Viking Press regarded her almost as royalty, and took her ceremonially out to lunch at the Connaught Hotel, which is very expensive and where the oysters are out of this world, as my father used to say of Gerda's fish pie. Iris had no interest in oysters but appreciated the bread and butter pudding.

Her host, she told me, sat watching her devour this nursery dish with awed incredulity. But she sharply criticised the lack of drink, regretting the good strong martinis that Norah had served to an appreciative Aldous Huxley and his fellow-guest Leonard Woolf. When I expressed astonishment that the gentleman from Viking had not plied her with booze, she admitted that he had taken a lot of trouble over a bottle of rare burgundy which was, she said, much too good for her. She would rather have drunk the house wine, and plenty of it.

Today, when Iris likes only a few drops of sweet sherry in her orangeade, and is more or less unconscious of it anyway, it seems hardly believable that she was once such a robust drinker, for whom a bottle of wine shared between two was, as she once put it in a phrase she must have picked up in Ireland, no more than 'the sniff of a cork'. She once told me that an old friend, George Lichtheim the political journalist, had taken her to task about this in an avuncular manner, alleging that he had seen many brilliant girls of her sort succumb to the demon drink.

I liked George Lichtheim, a temperate and benevolent man, who killed himself with a drug overdose when he developed cancer. That was many years ago. But I still mildly resent his presumption in advising Iris to go easy on the bottle, even though the advice was given long before I met her. Alcoholic excess in a misspent youth was not Iris's thing at all, however much trouble she may have had with what she had once termed 'the love business'.

Norah herself was no stranger to the love business: she had a close relationship with another director in the firm. Widowed in the war she was the soul of discretion about her authors with whom, in the words of Hilaire Belloc's satire on those who ruled the natives of some backward colony, she was always 'firm but kind'. This suited Iris's own modesty and inherent lack of self-importance. But once when Chatto's asked me to do a book on Tolstoy, and Norah raised some mild objection to the way I proposed to go about it, Iris sprang to my defence like a lioness watching over its cub.

On that occasion Norah backtracked hastily, in some surprise, for Iris was meekness itself when she sent in a novel, as if expecting that it might well be rejected. It was always in her own handwriting – Norah charging a stiff price for it to be typed – and I used to tease Iris by quoting some anonymous rhymester who had himself perhaps at one time experienced rejection by the firm.

> Take it like a trooper
> Your MS missed the bateau.
> Mr Windus thought it super
> But not so Mr Chatto.

It must have been many years since those half-legendary figures had been replaced by other directors, including the redoubtable Norah, but Iris always looked grave if I quoted this little rhyme. I think she really thought it might happen to her, as of course it did happen to poor Barbara Pym in the late '60s (ill-omened decade) when the firm who published her came under dynamic new management.

Pym's story had a happy ending I'm glad to say, and of course Norah received each new offering by Iris with cries of joy, although I suspect she did not read them much herself. Her own tastes were rather different. I once mentioned to her how much I had enjoyed *The Flight of the Heron* when I was at school. Her eyes lit up as she told me that D.K. Broster was a scandalously underrated author. 'So,' she said, 'are Margaret Irwin and Marjorie Bowen. I read *The Glen o'Weeping* every year.' She had once triumphed in the teeth of the Chatto board's more intellectual members by accepting a novel about King Harold by an American lady, Hope Muntz. It was called *The Golden Warrior*, and was in fact a rattling good yarn which sold quite well. I always thought of Norah as the Golden Warrior after that.

Before Norah died she went to the trouble of consigning Iris to the care of Ed Victor, a particular friend of hers and as it turned out the best as well as the most kindly of literary agents. Iris had never had an agent before, and though she had lost her mother publisher she now acquired a father figure who looked after her interests even more shrewdly and devotedly.

Ed rented a medieval cottage in the gardens of Sissinghurst, where he pressed us to stay sometimes in his absence. We used to feel very proprietary when the swarm of day visitors had departed and we had the gardens on a summer's evening to ourselves. Ed also flew over to shepherd Iris round New York when she gave a lecture there, and he showed her with pride the Brooklyn quayside where his father, a newly arrived Jewish immigrant, had once peddled fish.

Iris was not only good at friendship, being deeply interested in the lives of the people she liked, but she even used to extend this interest to professional interviewers, many of whom became 'pals for life' after merely expecting an hour or so of information-gathering for an article on the celebrated author.

I had cause to remember this when an American journalist who did medical articles asked to come for an interview. I made an effort to shepherd Iris into the drawing-room, where the children's programme we still sometimes watch was coming on, but she soon followed us into the kitchen and sat down in her own windsor chair.

Naturally we were talking about her, like two doctors discussing a patient, and the journalist looked a slightly anxious query at me. (She had already said: 'Don't answer any questions you would rather not.') I think I have followed Iris's own example, now that Alzheimer's has removed her from the ordinary decorum of daily life, in ceasing to feel any embarrassment about this sort of thing. The journalist's queries are euphemistic ('Do you have to help her on the loo?') but we both glance appealingly at Iris from time to time, as if for reassurance.

If that's what we are wanting we get it. Iris at least gives the impression of knowing exactly what we are talking about: her face has an expression of courteous but faintly amused interest. If the topic bores her she is too polite to show it – that's the impression – and the lady interviewing me soon looks reassured.

She is a nice woman, a doctor herself, and interested in the duration of the illness. More than four years now, I tell her. A question seems to be imminent – 'Do you still have – er – sexual relations?' I cannot help feeling curious to see when it will come. Feeling like a prostitute with a nervous client I give the lady a look of invitation, but Iris is now getting frankly bored and her air of polite amusement has disappeared. She jumps up, starts to mutter and tug at my coat, and the journalist never does get around to popping the question.

To be honest it wouldn't have been an entirely easy one to answer. It may seem straightforward enough – do you or don't you? – but sex can be vaguer than that, and just as felicitous. No act of the will, no 'What about tonight, darling?' Like many men of his generation the novelist Stendhal saw the Will as all-important. When young Julien in *Le Rouge et le Noir* is alone with Madame de Renal he counts the seconds to zero like a soldier about to go over the top, and then nerves himself to pounce. But the old indeterminacy in our own sexual relations seems to prolong itself naturally into the unending confusion of Iris's present days, in which those long periods of anxiety are followed by brief happinesses, inconclusive moments of peace and close embrace.

What I do have, though I wasn't going to tell the newspaper lady about it, is a fantasy sex-life that has become very much one of Dr A's friends, even boon companions. By proxy a friend of Iris's too.

My fantasies accommodate persons both real and imaginary, the real ones mostly from the past. Characters in novels are not exempt. Young master Holden Caulfield of *The Catcher in the Rye* used to dream about Eustacia Vye in Hardy's *The Return of the Native* – a piquant example of one fictional character having a fantasy about another in a different novel.

I still have a recurrent *tendresse* for one or two of Barbara Pym's female characters. Pym herself, much given to romance but not, it seems, to sex, observes that married couples have no idea of the importance of the *full* hot-water-bottle, an indispensable adjunct to the single bed in that unheated vicarage which features in many of her novels. That full hot-water-bottle could also stand as a kind of symbol for a lot of sexual fantasy during the last few distracted months, even though my own fantasies have been able to grow and blossom in the warmth of a double bed.

I seem to read hardly anything nowadays, but where was it I saw – some review or other – the comment about the murderer West and his wife, who chopped up young women in their cellar. *Lustmord*. They lacked the ability to imagine without enacting. Had they been producing *Macbeth* – an unlikely possibility admittedly – it would have meant nothing to them unless Duncan and Banquo, and Lady Macduff and her children, had really been butchered – and on the stage. For most of us the stage in the head is good enough – in fact what makes the head worth having.

Belial would have agreed, probably with a sly smile. I don't think he would have approved of the Wests' goings-on, devil though he was, but I'm sure he had plenty of sexual fantasies. Or perhaps not? He was in his own way a solitary spirit among that 'hellish crew' who seceded from God's love and abandoned heaven, and it may be that free and solitary spirits don't bother with that kind of thing. Their 'intellectual being' has other things to do. It is those who have become lonely in a relationship who find most release in fantasy.

I am not exactly lonely – how could I be when so close to Iris, every hour of the day and night? And yet that closeness without communication, however loving it may be, is also its own kind of loneliness. That's obvious. What's not so obvious is how much one comes to need both of them: closeness and loneliness alike. I know with certainty – but how? – that if Iris were to have to go from me, into a hospital or home, all these solitary and friendly pleasures, fantasies too, would vanish like a puff of smoke. I should not be lonely then, a happy state now with all Dr A's friends to keep me company. I should be abandoned.

With nothing in the head. I have no illusions about my ability to be a solitary free spirit. The solitariness of a close relationship – and how much closer could we get now? – is for me the fertile ground for fantasy, as it is for memories, the ones that go far far back. When Wordsworth wrote of the memories 'that leap/From hiding-places ten years deep', that was hardly a big deal. Any number of years deep. Sixty-five and more . . .

But such memories predate fantasy. A significant difference. When puberty begins the simplicities of memory disappear. From then on it is mixed with fantasy, almost becomes a part of it. After fourteen or fifteen, or whatever the age of puberty now is, memories must lack their primal truth. The earliest ones come back to me with the new force that is born of the present situation. Later ones have inherited in reverse all the fantasies that come to one's aid at the present time.

Fantasy and enactment are separate, and their co-habitation, to use a word slightly ridiculous in this context, is part of the charm of each. There suddenly comes into my head that absurd story, familiar to all of us in some form, of the sleepy wife murmuring, 'Oh do get on with it, George,' and the husband replying, 'Sorry, dear, I can't think of anyone at the moment.' Did Helen after the fall of Troy think of Paris when her husband Menelaus made love to her? No doubt she did but it's not quite the same thing. George was trying to think of someone he knew and fancied, a girl at the golf club perhaps. Someone he knew, or had seen from afar, but would never get anywhere with. That would be part of her charm, like that of most sex fantasy.

Did Jane Austen ever imagine being in bed with Darcy, or with Mr Knightley? It is possible, but seems unlikely somehow. Fantasy shrinks from the sharp edge of her intelligence, still more from her secret amusement at what people – herself included – might secretly be dreaming.

Such amusement is no enemy to love – on the contrary.

If Anna Karenina had loved her husband she would have delighted in the size of his ears: the sight of them would have fed both love and amusement together. As it is, their all too familiar bigness only reminds her that she doesn't love him.

With fantasy the case is rather different. I am amused by my fantasies, but the fantasies are not, so to speak, amused by me or by the story they tell: they have to get on with it with the necessary concentration, as George would have done had he managed to 'think of someone'.

Love accepts the comic; just as it accepts what is merely sensible. 'An intelligent love'. One of the shrewdest critics of Jane Austen, sometime in the nineteenth century I think, coined that phrase for her own ideal. Was it the same man who quoted the Earl of Shaftesbury? Something about 'the natural free spirits of ingeniose men', who if compelled by circumstances into an imprisoning monotony 'Will find out new motions to relieve themselves in their constraint'. I do not regard myself as particularly 'ingeniose', and in any case Shaftesbury the philosopher and scientist probably had in mind something more intellectually ambitious than the imaginary pictures and possibilities that throng through my head. And the heads of most of us no doubt. But they are friends whom I have special reason to encourage.

One of the most sober and penetrating themes in Iris's novels, the later ones in particular, is the difference, where love is concerned, between fantasy and reality. It's true of course, and she pursues the truth in graphic and illuminating detail as only a great novelist can.

And yet I suspect that in practice the two creatures – love and fantasy – can love and live together in harmony without collision. Why not? You cannot fantasise about the being you love, that's true, and yet the being you love can inadvertently teach you things that will come in very handy on the fantasy side; where, as Shakespeare's Theseus puts it, 'the best in this kind are but shadows'. Love, after all, can even teach you the ability to imagine without enacting.

Milton's Belial must have well understood this, and so incidentally did Shakespeare's Iago. Brilliant as is Shakespeare's portrait of Iago he has the difficulty of suggesting a man who is thoughtful and intelligent but also profoundly stupid; a man who, like those murderers the Wests, is ignorant of the difference between imagination and enactment. Wilfully ignorant one presumes, in Iago's case? For he knows that there are 'meditations lawful' in the human breast which never will and never wish to see the light of day.

There are thousands of potential Iagos, in offices and organisations, in military and political circles, who would dearly love to deceive and betray their bosses as Iago deceived Othello. But the wish remains at the level of fantasy, and probably not only does no harm but may even be beneficial to the psyche, something 'ingeniose' to relieve its constraint?

Much here must depend on the free play of consciousness, which means not only its intelligence but its modesty and humour. Iago was a witty man but not a humorous one. At bottom he was stupid as well as 'knowing'. And he had the mad self-confidence of the deeply conceited man. He should have been content with imagination, but the lure of enactment was too strong for him. It became a duty. A duty owed to the conviction of his own untouchable superiority.

Fortunately for us all, Thurber's Walter Mitty is a much more characteristic fantasist. His constrained homelife under the thumb of a repressive wife bestows on him all sorts of adventures in the world of the mind – lover, fighter pilot, cowboy, intrepid seaman. The film made from Thurber's original little sketch had the bright idea of mingling fantasy with reality. The dream girl, the damsel in distress, really *is* in trouble, pursued by genuine villains, enlisting Mitty's help to save her and the patriotic operation on which she is engaged. It worked because it was funny in the film. Humour came to the rescue, rather than Danny Kaye as real life hero. Fantasy always wants to be real, but never, I'm glad to say, succeeds. Intensities, whether in literature or in life, don't much care for humour.

And yet Dostoevsky – Iris too – are brilliant at combining comic and tragic in the complexities of a plot. In spite of Iris's theoretical warning she *does* mix fantasy with reality, but at the higher level so to speak.

I remember being amused once by an item in the agony column of a magazine, a superior fashion one which our friend the photographer Janet Stone used to read. A rather solemn young lady, a self-declared feminist, had written in some agitation (this was several years ago) to confide that she had the most dreadful daydreams of being seized, subdued and raped by a masterful lover.

What was she to do? – such things were entirely against her true female feelings, her wishes and principles.

A bored but kindly agony aunt replied: 'Don't worry, darling. We all have such desires deep down in us and they're quite harmless. Try laughing at them and carry on with the good work for women's lib!'

Sound advice, I'm sure, for those now old-fashioned times. And for our own. The modern spirit is too insistent on belief and thought kept whole and undivided. One faith, one conviction, one correctness. But surely Belial's 'intellectual being' does not work like that?

Who was it who described post-modernism as 'pre-emptive kitsch'? Not a bad definition. Kitsch is always in good faith: it honestly believes it is dealing with reality. Hence it can appear ludicrous to the latterday viewer, like King Arthur's knights and Victorian nudes. The artist has solemnly and unwittingly mingled fantasy with the reality of painting, or of words. Had he done it deliberately he would have created a new style of art. Like Roy Lichtenstein or Andy Warhol, who *knowingly* transformed the kitsch situation of a comic strip, or the fantasy world of an advertising label.

Knowingness is always total. It never accepts that we live by choice in different worlds. Two of them or more. And one of them at least always has a kind of innocence about it.

12

Musings and ramblings. Through them all I see Iris's face, looking both desolate and impish as it broadens into a smile. She is coming to me now with her arms out for the comfort of a hug, and because she sees I am smiling too. 'Aren't you a bad cat?' She has been banging the locked front door, making her histrionic moaning noise with an occasional 'Help help!' Sometimes a wild cry like an owl.

'Now don't be a bad cat. Be a good cat. Purr, purr.'

Iris seems recovered. So time to have a lie-down. It may be the journalist lady who has accidentally disturbed her. She consents to come to bed, a siesta, and I listen until her breathing is regular, a nice quiet noise that soon sends me off too. Or not quite off. A dream of fair women begins – how many there are these days! Not so fair actually. More fair-to-middling, as Samuel Beckett put it. But then I am asleep, and wake with a jerk. Something is wrong. No it's not. Iris is still beside me. Slipping away again I start to have a fantasy about a Gerrards Cross cocktail party, and a woman I meet there.

Has Iris been listening, just as I listen? She jumps up swiftly and silently and makes for the door. The lady vanishes. I know she can't escape but a siesta now is out of the question. No choice but to follow.

Iris is in the garden, by the padlocked gate. She has been shaking it and shouting; now she is shedding silent tears. She runs to me, buries her face against my body, clutches me as desperately as a three-year-old. As I comfort her I think of my dislike of babies and children, more than dislike

– hatred – when I see them in the supermarket, showing off and screaming.

It makes me start to laugh, and Iris looks up at me, her eyes full of tears, and soon starts laughing too.

To know and see I can comfort her is still the greatest of my own comforts. But the impossible three-year-old will break out again at any moment. Best to go out. Walk therapy. That almost always helps, although Iris doesn't like it, and complains by shuffling along more and more slowly. I go on ahead and turn at intervals to make encouraging gestures. Iris responds and wambles a little more quickly in her endearing duck-like way.

Making quite good progress now. Round the Parks, and I notice with interest for the first time that the cricket pavilion in the middle is quite an elegant structure. Built around 1900. Only fourteen years to go before that innocent world came to an end . . . And what about old people with Alzheimer's then? Would they have been 'inside'? I suppose so.

Getting home is rather a struggle. Iris flags a bit but valiantly keeps going. At the front door she looks glowing, normal, neither her own age nor three years old but a healthy fifty say, a woman who enjoys walking in the country and has just come in from a good long hike.

'You enjoyed that, didn't you?'

She smiles beatifically. 'Oh I did!'

An uncanny sense that all is well. Nothing the matter at all. How long will it last? When we are inside and turn away from the front door together I remember in the nick of time to go back and lock it.

So easy to forget this. To save the appearances I sometimes say to Iris that I have to do it because the Yale lock is broken, as well it might be from the way she shakes and bangs it. Iris looks politely interested and may even believe me; but I don't think she is concerned with the matter at all, or with drawing conclusions. How can she be? All she knows is that when the need to escape overcomes her she cannot get through the door.

The feeling of slightly insane happiness which comes over me at moments of success like these: when we have done something together and it has worked . . . ! But in fact we weren't exactly together. I led the way, like Hermes leading Eurydice back from the underworld, frequently stopping and turning back, as her husband Orpheus was not permitted to do. Orpheus lost her at the last moment by doing it, but I knew Iris would follow doggedly behind me, even if I had paid her no attention at all. I walked ahead to encourage her, and turned back to smile for the same reason. But she has not come from the underworld: she carries it with her, the dark place to which I have no entry.

Now all that is forgotten when we arrive at the front door, like a healthy country couple who have enjoyed their walk.

Enjoyed it, yes, but we weren't together on it; in the curious sense that we are when we stroll round the block together. Then we are together because apart: I am way off in my daydream, all about that Gerrards Cross cocktail party. While we are arm in arm, and Iris is talking in her own way, I replying in mine, nothing is easier than to vanish into a rapturous world of make-believe. It never existed before Dr A came along: now I could not do without it.

And so, this cocktail party, where was I? On that walk through the Parks I lost it entirely, or rather had no need of it, because we were really apart on our walk, and I had other things to do.

It was the Corbins who gave the party – real people. Friends of ours during the war. I was seventeen or eighteen then, but I can allow myself nowadays to be any age I choose – thirties, fifties, sixties, even my present seventy-three. But better at least a few years back?

Plenty of gin there seemed to be in the drinks of those

days. I remember loving the sensation of swimmingness the cocktails induced. It didn't then in the least impair my powers of perception or locomotion, and it made me feel a lot less shy. So what might happen? Who might I meet?

Better make it 1953, the year I met Iris. Well, why not? I might not have met Iris that year: I might have met someone else. As with Poohbah, in *The Mikado*, that lends a touch of verisimilitude to an otherwise bald and unconvincing fantasy. For who is this someone else I meet at the Corbins' cocktail party?

The Perfect Woman of course. The woman who never was, by sea or land. The idea of her is so wonderful, so comic, so grotesque, that I start laughing, and hug Iris's arm. As if obediently she starts laughing too.

'Evil into the mind of God and man may come and go.' Who says that? Is it Iago? Or someone in *Paradise Lost*? Not Belial I think. Perhaps it's Gabriel, the affable archangel? And why would he be saying a thing like that? Coleridge, I remember, lets fall somewhere in passing that moral evil can be explained by the associative processes of the mind. One thing leading to another . . .

Could my Perfect Woman lead me into adultery? I rather think not.

The idea seems so comic that I almost start laughing again. But the associative train is in motion now and I can do nothing to stop it. At least I don't do anything to stop it.

In my head I see the other people at the party, people I don't know. (Do they exist somewhere, and have I seen them without knowing it?) And the woman in the corner, my Perfect Woman, have I seen her before? Of course not, although there are hints and touches of resemblance: for example to the wife of some dignitary whom I once glimpsed at an Oxford lecture.

She stands in the corner, with an uncertain smile on her face. She wears thick-looking glasses. I want just to stand

and look at her, but no one is talking to her at the moment, so social conditioning reminds me of my duty and impels me towards her. To her feet, as it were; for she is immensely tall, and as I approach I find myself gazing further and further up, as if at a lighthouse.

She is not only tall but big. Her huge hands are held lightly clasped in front of her. Very clean they look, and white.

'What a nice party!' I say, gazing upwards, all my bright self. She looks down at me with her kind myopic eyes, as if I were almost too small to be visible.

'Yes, isn't it?' she says. 'Though I'm not really supposed to be here. A friend brought me. After church.'

'And do you live in Gerrards Cross?' (What a silly question, but she happily says yes.)

'So did we once. Not far from the church. Manor Lane.'

'Oh, I know Manor Lane.'

We beam at each other. The hubbub around us has grown more deafening. She leans down to hear what I next have to say, and I can hardly hear it myself. An ordinary woman fights her way through to where my Perfect Woman is standing, and I can just hear her say, 'We really ought to be going . . . in the oven . . . mustn't . . .' I see them smile at each other above my head. They move to the door, but the Perfect Woman turns and looks back at me for a moment with her kind unfocused gaze. Or is she looking at someone else? I shall never see her again.

Nearly home now, and lunch-time, which is never a good time. Iris usually fractious and depressed. She won't eat, but a good moment sometimes comes when I coax a spoonful into her mouth and she makes a happy cooing sound while her face returns to babyhood. I put another spoonful in, just to see it happen again. She is like a baby, but I hate babies. They repel me. And yet she seems herself again for some reason, her own self, when she accepts another spoonful and smiles up at me. Three years old.

And I have been smiling up at the Perfect Woman! The comedy of things! – it is almost too much to bear. Was I three years old myself when I first saw the Perfect Woman?

I don't meet the Perfect Woman again until the evening, when Iris is asleep and I turn out the light and get carefully into bed. Is she coming towards me now, taller than ever? No, the cocktail party is still going on, but has taken a different turn. No ordinary woman comes up to remind her about the roast in the oven. When the Perfect Woman left the party with her friend I knew I should never see her again. But here she is, and I am asking her about books.

Has she read *Georgina and Jane* by any chance?

'No, is it good?'

'I'm sure you'd enjoy it. I've got it in a paperback (were there paperbacks in 1953? Yes but not so many and various – only Penguins I think). May I lend it to you? I could send it. And do keep it. I've read it twice: I don't want it any more.'

Cunning little fellow that I am! The Perfect Woman falls for it. She looks a little bothered, but pleased too. 'If you could let me have the address?' Those great big hands are opening her bag.

'I've got a card somewhere. I use it for church work.' (Apologetically.) 'Here it is. If you really mean it?'

'Oh, I'd love to – I'm sure you'll enjoy it. *Georgina and Jane.*'

And it's done. The card is in my pocket now, like the key which locks our front door on the inside. And not a moment too soon, because the Corbin daughter is fighting her way through the party to me now, and saying Mother thinks we ought to be going. Something in the oven . . .

Memory here can give a solid back-up to fantasy. In 1953

there always was something in the oven on Sunday – the Sunday roast. Every household would gather round it for lunch. Mint sauce, roast potatoes. Queen's pudding to follow.

I eat the Corbin lunch, chat pleasantly I hope. The cocktail party continues to extend its animation over the family lunch table. We discuss hosts and guests. Someone says, 'Who was that great tall woman? Weren't you talking to her, John?'

I am thrilled by hearing her mentioned. So she really *was* tall? On the other hand it gives me acute pain that the others should have been aware of her, talked about her, however perfunctorily. She should have been there only for me. I can see her so clearly now, and I think of nothing else.

After tea I am taken to the station. Twenty minutes to the Oxford train. Corbin *père* has brought me in the Morris 10. A kind act, for petrol is still rationed. Politely I urge him not to stay, and fortunately he needs little urging.

As soon as he has driven off I leave the station at a fast walk. The card is still in my pocket and I have memorised the address. I remember the road perfectly from the time we lived here; I know just where to go. A substantial but modest house, Mock-Tudor front, plumy little conifers in the front garden; probably a bigger garden behind. I can scarcely believe in my own sense of excitement, and yet I long passionately to see this woman again, to gaze up at her glasses, her broad white tranquil face. But my pressing anxiety, tossed over and over in my mind as I hurry down the High Street and into Gaviot Way is, will she be in church?

She was there this morning. Would she attend Evensong? Quite likely, indeed almost certainly.

In which case she would not be at home. Would anyone else be? She had been asked to lunch by her friend who had something in the oven. That suggested she was unmarried, or at least not yet married. Or perhaps her husband was away? There are too many possibilities, and I try to stop them rattling pointlessly too and fro in my head. I must do something, take the bull by the horns.

But she wasn't a bull. It was Iris who had once been described by a mildly malicious friend as looking like a little bull. Coming towards you with its head lowered. Friendly, but formidable too.

I always remembered that description and felt great affection for it, although Iris had not been best pleased. She only liked to be teased by me.

The film stops. There I am, expectant. Full of an excitement I can hardly contain, and which has become almost painful. It would be a relief to break the whole thing off.

So I do. And actually I have no choice. It is just beginning to grow light outside. Can the Perfect Woman have kept me occupied all night? Time goes surprisingly fast when one daydreams in bed, and I have probably been dozing too.

I remember another thing from a magazine, *Woman's Realm*, the one Iris's mother used to enjoy. Once it had a letter from a young woman about to be married who was asking the agony aunt if she would get any sleep at all on her bridal night. The aunt advised her that it probably wouldn't be as bad as all that; but she recommended early hours and a hot milky drink at bedtime for some days before the wedding . . .

Woman's Realm! Oh the innocence of those days, or at least of those magazines.

What about a night with the Perfect Woman? But I am uneasily conscious that Iris, who used to sleep so well in the early morning, is already awake and stirring. A voice comes, not drowsy but muffled. It might be Lazarus, who after a week in the tomb has forgotten the use of language.

'. . . Was a hemp . . . A hemphill, and when . . .'

Uncannily clear but muffled. Impossible not to listen intently, to try to concentrate on what is being said, or meant.

Suddenly Iris sits bolt upright. Old jerseys and towels fall off her like the grave-clothes from Lazarus. With a quick sure movement she is out of bed and out of the room. The front door is locked, the key in my trouser-pocket beside the bed, but I can hear her moving through the house, as if on a systematic search.

Impossible now to turn the light on and read, impossible to stay in bed. What is she looking for? But I need not have worried. When I find her downstairs she looks like an old Russian woman come to market to sell old clothes. She has an orderly pile over her arm and is busily adding to it at every moment. I notice dishcloths in the pile, and a loose armchair cover, nearly worn through where the head would rest.

Poor darling. No rest for that head. And I need its agitations now. If there was peace and silence, if she were not here beside me, my fantasy about the Perfect Woman of Gerrards Cross, together with memories of Littlestone and the golf course and the Mixed Room and my ruined cottage – they would all vanish away together.

Like that puff of smoke. I've thought that before, many times, and it's true, even though I use it to cheer myself up.

At last Iris gets back into bed. Or half in, legs dangling. Her head and shoulders fall over on my side like a puppet's. I stroke her neck and hair. She gurgles happily a little; she is going back to sleep at last. Just when it's time for me to get up. At that moment there's a banging on the door. Mouthing obscenities to myself I descend as I am, see a friendly man with a big parcel through the glass of the front door. Half by signs I ask can't he leave it there? No, with an apologetic grin. Must have a signature. I go back upstairs, get the key out of my pocket, come back, open up and sign. The bulky object is for Iris. Probably six of her novels in Turkish. Or Hungarian. From the foreign publisher.

Trail back upstairs. Iris now beautifully, seraphically asleep, quite undisturbed. As she used to be in the mornings when I was able to sit typing beside her. She liked the noise she used to say when she woke, with a drowsy smile. But that was last year.

I shall stop calling her the Perfect Woman. Her perfection consists in not existing, which is what fantasy requires. And yet she's perfectly real for me. As are Mr Knightley and Mrs Bennet and the Pym heroines and all the rest of them.

Why don't I live in the real world? Does one ever? At the moment, in any case, I have excellent reasons for not doing so. Dr A and his friends all persuade me there is no such thing as the real world. They are good benevolent people, those friends of Dr A's, and well aware that I need all the distraction I can get from mere physiological reality. Escape is all.

I shall think of her as the Woman of Gerrards Cross. That is a more sober title; more, as they say, realistic. The Perfect Woman is a little too fanciful, even facetious. Shall I look at her now in a quite different way, prepare a documentary about her as an 'ordinary person'? Well, that would be quite a different sort of fantasy, like the documentaries and soaps they do on TV.

On our next walk that feeling of almost unbearable excitement returns. By reflex action I hug Iris's arm more firmly. I am in the front garden of the house at Gerrards Cross, between the plumy little conifers, wondering whether or not to ring the bell. No sign of life in the house.

I've done it! The bell sounds appallingly loud. Sensations of panic. Perhaps the door will fly open and I shall be staring into the face of that big barn owl, who once loomed away so soundlessly over my head. Perhaps she is no more than the memory of an owl?

Firm, rather loud footsteps. It must be somebody else. Wrong house? Too late to run away now.

She is even bigger than I remember. Enormous. And she does loom over me, standing in the doorway. Black shoes, such huge ones, her feet must be as big as her hands. Not flat shoes though; three-quarter heels do they call them? My eyes seem unable to travel further up her, not even to her stockings.

How did we get into her sitting-room? But there we are anyway. Fantasy is like the flight of the owl. Let's run it back, as I believe you can do on video – I've never been able to work ours. But I must get further up her than her shoes.

When my eyes finally managed the ascent I saw that she was smiling and that she did not seem surprised to see me. Her kind myopic eyes. I managed to say: 'I thought you would be in church.'

She is telling me that there was no Evening Service this Sunday. The vicar had to take Evensong at Chalfont St Giles. (Is that plausible? – probably not in 1953.) And by that time we are in the sitting-room and she is urging me to sit down. Nice shabby armchairs. Chintz covers. No smell of man.

But . . . I am realistic enough to know that there would then be an awkward pause. Awkward on my side at least, but I am grateful to see that she is smiling on unperturbed. How old is she? A quick calculation going through my mind. The convenience of daydreams means that they must be made inconvenient too. Forty-five? Forty-nine?

The separation now between Iris's world and my own. It did not seem there before the stage the disease has now reached. Even when she no longer spoke coherently she responded to what I was telling her and to all my emotional reactions. To clowning and teasing above all, and the pantomime of love that went with them. I might even have enacted the Woman of Gerrards Cross for her. But no – there would have been no such woman at that time: she has come into existence because of the separation.

The two worlds still co-exist easily enough, in a soundless pathetic harmony. Even when Iris is silently scouring the house, or on the rampage downstairs, drumming on the front door and shouting to the outside world '*Help me – help!*' I have sat tautly in bed at such times, typewriter on knee, awaiting developments. Remembering Byron's lines, 'I don't much like describing someone mad for fear of seeming rather touched myself.'

But it isn't madness, and I can't think of it as such. It is her old familiar self, which means that I cannot remember the self that must once have been. This seems the only familiar one now, indeed the only one.

Reading some letters that Iris's biographer Peter Conradi has unearthed. Letters from Iris written during the war to a lover who became her fiancé. Gay charming letters full of fun and *joie de vivre*. But the hand, though bold and strong, seemed totally unfamiliar, and I could not recognise the person who was writing at all.

Strange. Because I feel I should also not recognise the Iris – my own Iris – of ten, twenty, thirty years ago. The Iris I know, and am so close to, is the one who is with me today.

After their student days Iris and her brief fiancé seem seldom to have met each other. The war kept them apart. They corresponded, a miniature novel in letters, but there is only one side of the correspondence. Iris did not keep his letters, except one, typewritten, saying he had met this other girl, and he was sure Iris would understand. Iris understood; and her next letter is as gay and as mildly teasing as ever.

The other girl was called Clare. She and her husband are

both dead. But if it wasn't for Clare I should never have met Iris. Except as a famous writer she would never have existed for me at all.

And would she have become a famous writer? Virginia Woolf suggested that Shakespeare had a sister, equally a genius, who because she was a woman has never been heard of. Had Iris married her brief fiancé she would have stayed married. I feel fairly sure of that. She would have become yet another woman, one even more unrecognisable than the one whose letters I have been reading.

But what does that signify, as I shouldn't have known her?

How do I know, or think I know, that Iris would have stayed married? Just a hunch: but she is, or was, that sort of person. She would have had children too.

Would I have stayed married to the Woman of Gerrards Cross? But here, steady on, this is becoming absurd. There is, and was, no Woman of Gerrards Cross!

None the less I am sitting on her sofa. It is a dream within a dream, for I cannot get over my astonishment at having acted as I did. She seems less surprised than I am. Can she have fallen as instantly in love with me, in the few moments at that party, as I feel I have fallen in love with her? But come, come – even fantasy must draw the line somewhere. It works best if kept within bounds?

Why bother to try? Already the tape is shooting forward. Already we are chattering away on that sofa, my hand in her enormous hand (cool, soft). Already we are agreed that it had been love at first sight. And now to other matters. When are we going to get married, me and my big sane faultless woman?

Well, she will have to think about that. There are certain practical difficulties: difference in age and so forth.

'But nothing insuperable?'

'Oh no, nothing at all insuperable!'

Simultaneously we burst out laughing. But even in the joy of laughter we are melting slowly towards one another, as in old film romances, for the Kiss . . . At the last second we pause and take off each other's glasses, and start laughing again. And then . . .

13

When I was a tutor and Fellow of New College, already married to Iris, I had a few teaching hours with Dennis Potter, who later became the famous and innovative TV writer, creator of *The Singing Detective*, *Blackeyes*, several others. His reputation at one time stood very high, and I believe the BBC deferred to his lightest word. Potter was reading Philosophy, Politics and Economics, not Eng. Lit., but he asked to come to see me for some talks about authors in whom he was interested.

I liked Potter and got on well with him, but as a student he was a controversial figure in what was in those fairly distant days a conservative and stuffy college, not inclined to welcome or tolerate the defensively aggressive behaviour of this chippy young miner's son from the Forest of Dean. In such an atmosphere Potter longed for some sort of spectacular martyrdom. To be crucified with croquet hoops by sneering young bloods from some dining-club. Or expulsion by the college authorities for obscenity and irreverence, displays of which he hopefully provided. But the more he set out to provoke the gilded aristocrats, or to shock the academic bourgeoisie, the easier he made it for them to display their own sorts of encouraging patronage. His measure was taken, and the young Potter was often a frustrated and disappointed man.

His real moment of glory, however, and the exploit for which he was genuinely admired, was a production in the college cloisters of an early and obscure play of Pirandello, one which has been seldom or never performed either in its own country or abroad. I have forgotten its title, but Potter got his friends in the Languages faculty to produce some sort of translation, to which he added plenty of daring touches and bright ideas of his own. Even as an undergraduate in those dear dead days of the '50s Potter had the foresight to dedicate himself to the pursuit of the bad taste which was later to become the fashion; and Pirandello's youthful *jeu d'esprit*, which Potter had shown considerable enterprise in discovering, gave him plenty of opportunity.

In fact the play was harmless enough, almost quaintly so by modern standards. Potter played the lover of the young wife of a sea-captain, who fears her lover has made her pregnant. At the climax the wife, played by an upper-class student *ingénue*, beautifully unsuited to the part, agrees to put out flowerpots on her window-sill to inform her agitated lover in the street below that her husband, just returned from sea, is unsuspiciously performing his marital office. As the size and number of the flowerpots mounted the audience broke into rapturous applause.

Potter, his bright red locks flopping about and his flaky face glistening with sweat, kept glancing hopefully towards the college Warden, a venerable philosopher who loved to buttonhole reluctant students and show them round the ancestral beauties of the college. With touching naïveté Potter was clearly hoping that the Warden would rise in wrath and disgust and command the play to be stopped – he may even have hoped that he himself, as chief actor and producer, would be summarily cast out of the college.

If so he was to be disappointed. As the play went on, and the audience applauded, the Warden's austere features relaxed more and more into beaming smiles. When play and applause were over he strolled up to the crestfallen young man and congratulated him. 'A slight play perhaps,' twinkled the Warden, 'but a charming one, and your own resource and enterprise helped to give it body.'

Potter as a student had little to complain of. He met

at Oxford people who would be useful to him later in his career, and he was able to try out some of the ideas he would afterwards make use of in his TV career. He did a lot of unusual reading too. Seeing in my room the Diaries of Francis Kilvert, the curate who lived at Clyro near Hay-on-Wye and recorded every day his meetings with his parishioners, his walks over the Welsh hills, and his own private feelings and longings, many of them surprisingly intimate, he asked if he might borrow them. At subsequent meetings we used to discuss Kilvert's daydreams, usually based on some harmless encounter with a young girl in a train, or on one of his walks.

Kilvert the Victorian recorded and wrote with a frank and lyrical innocence; there is nothing salacious about his diaries, although it was clear that they fascinated Potter in the same way that more openly sexual revelations might have done. Potter's TV fantasies, like *Blackeyes* or *The Singing Detective*, are in some sense a distortion or burlesque of the kind of material from which the parson Kilvert made his enchanting diary; but there remains in them too something of the same Victorian innocence. With a dollop of bad taste added of course.

When I first saw a bit of *The Singing Detective* on TV I found it so awful that I at once searched for another channel. Other people's fantasies not only discredit one's own but seem incomprehensible beside them. But I can see that Potter, in his own brilliantly exposed and as it were skinless fashion (almost literally, for the poor man suffered like the hero of his play from psoriasis), was the first to perceive how daydream can turn itself straight into TV script.

The old cinema dealt in public dreams, in some sense shared by everybody, and that gave them a kind of dignity, no matter how ridiculous they were. The Potter-type sex-dream is horribly intimate, and seems deliberately intended to embarrass us as individuals by an intimacy of bad taste. The critics who slated *Blackeyes* for its sickly brand of adolescent fantasy were being both self-righteous and hypocritical, for they could hardly have missed seeing that this was really the whole point and purpose of the charade.

I wonder if Potter, now among the shades where TV is no longer shown (I think he was dead before the age of sixty), might be amused by the daydreams of a septuagenarian who cannot quite decide what his own ideal fantasy age should be; but who firmly prefers, whatever it is, to indulge himself in daydreams not of young girls but of older women. Older, that is to say, than the ages he used to be. Now that I am seventy-three shall I start having daydreams about women of ninety? And so *ad infinitum*?

Well, never mind. It seems unlikely in any case that the Woman of Gerrards Cross would make a suitable fantasy for a Potter-type TV script. But of course I could be wrong.

Naturally I can discuss with the Woman of Gerrards Cross all the things I used once to talk about with Iris. We sit at the kitchen table holding hands and still gazing into each other's eyes (though we have now been married for some time) and we are eating something she has beautifully cooked – tender roast beef, a little underdone, with Yorkshire pudding, or boiled chicken with onions and bread sauce. Things it never occurs to me to eat at home and which in any case I wouldn't know how to cook.

Oh the vanity of daydreams! Their curious bashfulness can be comic too. I never do go to bed with the Woman of Gerrards Cross, even though later on we appear to have got married. As I hold Iris's elbow while she totters uncertainly round the corner of the block I contemplate the intensity with which I envisage this woman, seeing her eyes, her shoes, her big white hands, but nothing more intimate than that. I yearn for her none the less, a yearning whose dream existence has all the greater authenticity because it is never consummated in dream, as it so easily could be. The big Woman is, as it were, there for the taking, but I prefer not to take her.

Instead I stand with an arm round Iris as she rests against the lamp-post. Our short walk round the block is laborious now although she seems to wish to do it – I can't be certain even of that – and I am continually anxious that she may fall, that there won't be anyone about, that I shan't be able to raise her. This anxiety, real enough as it is, in no way diminishes the abstracted busyness with which my daydream is itself continuing.

How sure am I that the Woman of Gerrards Cross loved me at first sight, as I loved her? Oh, quite, quite sure. I see it in her smile. In the depths of her huge being she is secretly and joyfully incredulous that I should have fallen in love with her. But she knows I have. As she has with me . . .

The vanity of daydreams. And the pathos too. I fell in love long ago with Iris, and I was sure she had no awareness of me beyond a mild interest and liking. She fell in love with me much later, at a college dance. We scarcely danced at all.

Now she cannot tell me she loves me, and I cannot tell her that I do. At least not in so many words. The other day in the car she laid a hand on my knee and said with emphasis, '*Susten poujin drom love poujin? Poujin susten?*' I hastened to agree, and one word was clear. As soon as I could stop the car we kissed each other. She knew what she meant even when there is no meaning, and there was in that word . . .

Is my silent communion with the Woman of Gerrards Cross a daydream wish-fulfilment of what I know to be present, in this dreadful deformed state, between Iris and me? The desire to be loved. The desire to be shown that one is loved. In my daydream of the Woman I can feel it, and see it in her face and eyes. She does not have to speak of it, any more than Iris can do as we totter round the block together or drive in the car.

All the same the extent and refuge of my daydreaming has something embarrassing about it, even to me. But it has become part of this new way of life, and though it is so separate from it – hence the relief it brings – it is also closely connected. In the old days, before Iris was ill, daydreaming desire really would have been, and was, separate from our life together. But it was also far more fleeting, less tangible, less greedily to be relied upon.

In those days the agony aunt in the magazine could have given me the same advice that she gave the young feminist who had daydreams of being mastered and enslaved by brutal men. 'Don't worry, dear. It's quite a separate thing, you know.' Nowadays it is not so separate. It is much more pervasive, much more a part of my life, and one on which I am increasingly dependent. It is a true friend of Dr A, and of Iris too.

Communication difficulties. After an impossible night I turn on the light at five and start trying to write this. Iris is asleep. The sleeping draught did not work, but nature seems to have taken over at last. She lies peacefully, her face relaxed. But at half-past six she becomes restless again. The time just before was wonderful, like a pool of clear dark water, the sort of pool we used to dream of finding to swim in. She was asleep and I was tapping my typewriter. Total darkness in the sky outside; friendly darkness with no trace of dawn.

When Iris wakes the daily grind of non-communication begins in full force. But I have never known it as bad as this before. She sits on the edge of the bed, fiddling with the old dress she has picked up from somewhere, trying to put it on like a pair of trousers. I dread her in this position, which can go on for hours, paralysing my freedom of mind. I urge her imperiously and impotently to get back into bed. She does not ignore me, or pay no attention; she seems to be listening to a garbled message. On the Radio-Telephone in the army the operator would have been saying, 'I am not receiving you,' or 'Receiving you Strength One.'

I remember that from the wartime, from yesterday as it seems, as now I try to speak more clearly, more forcefully. It's as if Iris were a very foreign sort of foreigner, but with such a person one might successfully resort to pantomime, exaggerated gestures signifying bed – sleep. Closing eyes, putting a hand under one's head. Such gestures now would only alarm her?

As it is, the more emphatically I try to get over the verbal message the more worried she becomes. I want something from her – what can it be? She gets up, totters round the cluttered bedroom, comes back with a slipper, an old piece of chocolate in silver paper, bits of newspaper off the floor. She offers me these. Rejecting them I make a last appeal: 'Bed! – bed! – get into bed!' I try to have the face and voice of a doctor. It fails. Evidently sad and discouraged, Iris resumes her seat on the side of the bed, her shrunken legs looking so cold.

I know from experience it is useless to lift them up, tuck them in. She would resume her previous position like an obstinate plant, curling itself back to where it has to be. Coercion, however 'firm but kind', never works.

I sit propped upright on the other side of the bed, gazing gloomily at the typewriter. Still with my doctor's face and voice I find myself saying as clearly as I can (Strength Five), 'We're lost, we're lost.' I go on repeating this, forgetting the doctor and saying it more and more histrionically, self-pityingly . . .

Iris looks relieved and collectedly gets back into bed. So that was what I was wanting? Why didn't I say so?

In the wet summer of 1941 I used to walk every day down Hedgerley Lane, inhaling the complex smells of rotting sopping vegetation. Rose Bay Willowherb, drenched through and through, gave off a strange smell like nothing else. It was not exactly a nice smell, but I loved it. As I sniffed it up I used to repeat again and again my favourite lines from a poem by Edith Sitwell.

> The mauve summer rain
> Is falling again.

I wonder now whether the big Woman of Gerrards Cross (why does fantasy insist she should be so big?) ever walked down Hedgerley Lane and inhaled, as I used to do, the rainy scent of rotting willowherb. It would be a moderate walk from where she lived, if she ever existed.

And perhaps she did exist. I mean, I could imagine another kind of existence for her. She might exist not in a fantasy but in a novel. That would be quite a different kind of thing, more free, more capable of true development? If fantasy is developed it becomes not only more improbable, more subject to all the absurdities of wish-fulfilment, but more boring as well. Detail, which is the life of a good novel, may be equally convincing in one's personal fantasies, but has no proper neutrality. It is too much under personal control. Once again I remember Iris's comment, never spoken to me but coming in an essay she wrote, that fantasy and fiction are, and should be, two quite different things.

Essentially true, yes: for art, as it realises itself, must shrivel up the appeal of fantasy, turning its intimacy into openness. But art may begin in fantasy none the less. So what if I take the Woman of Gerrards Cross and turn her into a real person? A person in a true novel?

No. I would rather think of her walking down Hedgerley Lane and smelling the wet willowherb, as I used to do. In that strange scent I could keep her: she would belong only to me, never to any other reader . . .

There is a surreal sense in which Alzheimer's has turned Iris herself into art. She is my Iris no longer, but a person in the public domain. You could say she always was, and yet never so for me. Now even I feel that she has an existence entirely outside my own, conferred upon her by the Dark Lord who is drawing her further and further into his own underworld.

When she has to leave me to be in a home, a beautiful home no doubt, I shall visit her as a stranger. It will be like reading those letters to the man to whom she was briefly engaged, just after the war. I could not recognise the handwriting, or the young woman who had written them.

Those letters have disappeared, gone to Pieland as we used to say. What can have happened to them? Unlike the case of the pie, which remains genuinely mysterious, this is only a rhetorical question. Iris must have found the letters, not with intent or understanding, and left them somewhere else, perhaps dispersed apart, lying anonymous now amongst the innumerable debris of the house.

The same thing happened, comically enough, to my false teeth, and once to my glasses too. The glasses were soon found – Iris had put them carefully inside a vase, fortunately a transparent one; but the teeth were more elusive. The bottom set was under the bed, not tucked in very far. I found them by lying down and surveying the scene beneath there with a torch. It looked like the ocean floor round the wreck of the *Titanic*, littered with indeterminate objects coated with dust, like the ocean ooze.

I had seen the pictures on TV of the real *Titanic* lying unromantically amid her lumber, and buried in what looked like dust. As so often on TV, one look was enough. As the programme ground on I soon lost interest in it, and in the ship too.

But I had part of the teeth back. And before I wanted to eat the next meal I found the upper set too, left carefully by Iris in a little gap amongst the objects on the kitchen table. Those teeth have led a dangerous life, which is rather like saying that a regiment has survived heavy casualties. Twice before

I lost that lower set when swimming and fish-watching. Replacements were necessary. Their comrades remain for ever in the sea's ooze, irrecoverable.

The letters are back. I found Iris wandering with them in her hand, together with a sheaf of other papers, bills, old colour supplements. She parted with them, and the bills and bank statements too, provided I let her keep the Sunday magazines. If I open them and turn the pages for her she closes them carefully, carrying them about like a talisman. Sometimes she sits for a few moments – she never sits for longer – and seems to study the cover picture. One has a particularly disagreeable-looking girl with prickling hair and a snarling expression, wearing a very short skirt of blood-red leather, her legs as far apart as the skirt will stretch.

A far cry to the Woman of Gerrards Cross. Why shouldn't the Woman of Gerrards Cross have come from Sidmouth, or Beaulieu, two places that have become much more recently familiar? Perhaps it's because I have never been back to Gerrards Cross? Fantasy prefers to find a local habitation in the remoter past.

Sidmouth we used to visit quite lately with Janet Stone, who had known the place as a girl and taken Reynolds Stone there when they were first married. The dear artist. Iris was so fond of him, and he returned her affection in his gentle absent-minded way, showing her fossils and telling her by the hour about Victorian printing-presses.

Reynolds was a versatile artist. He engraved on box-wood, painted magically sylvan watercolours, incised lettering on stone so beautifully that he was commissioned to commemorate Winston Churchill on a huge green marble slab set in the floor of Westminster Abbey. His sudden death in 1979 was a desolation for Janet, and a great grief for Iris too.

In the years before Janet died, and well after the time when Iris's Alzheimer's became noticeable, I would drive them for a brief holiday to Sidmouth, staying at a little hotel in a sort of crevasse that ran down to the promenade and the sea. The hotel was an old one and claimed some connection with the Duke of Wellington, which seemed unlikely. But the bar was stocked with an excellent Australian red wine called Long Tom, or maybe Long something else, of which we always drank a bottle at supper, and sometimes two. Although protesting that she must only have half a glass Janet loved red wine, and Long Tom disappeared without any difficulty.

I used to wonder if Jane Austen, reputed to have looked favourably on a young man visiting Sidmouth who never returned the next year to woo her, drank her glass of wine at our hotel. But that wine would certainly not have come from Botany Bay.

Hardy told a friend that when he imagined Tess of the D'Urbervilles he thought of a waitress seen for a few moments through the window of a Weymouth teashop. I had never seen the Woman of Gerrards Cross, I only imagined her; and when we stayed with our friends Diana Avebury and Bill and Lizzie Pease, beside the estuary near Beaulieu, there was no memory for me to keep of the yachting girls who glided past on the brown water down to the Solent.

> To her craft on Beaulieu water
> Clemency the General's daughter
> Pulls across with even strokes.

Such Betjeman girls offered nothing to the imagination, even when they were sunbathing on some expensive vessel, whose sails, folding themselves as neatly as toy blinds in a doll's house, seemed merely for show. An invisible motor was doing the actual propelling, and Betjeman's Clemency would surely have scorned these modern mechanical aids?

In Diana's little marine flat I enjoyed watching some late night horror picture on television, when Iris and our hostess were fast asleep, and red and green lights were moving mysteriously outside on the dark water. I would turn the sitting-room lights off, and a ghostly masthead illumination outside the dark window made a backdrop for whatever Gothic goings-on were illuminating the screen. I sometimes turned off the sound so that the heroine's screams would not disturb the household.

At this silent moment of recollection there is a burst of swallowspeak in the bed beside me. Iris has woken up with the dawn. When we lived at Steeple Aston the swallows would wake us in summer, twittering away on the telephone wire outside our bedroom window. They would break off for a moment, and then one among the row of birds would think of something else to say, and the animated chatter would begin again, always ending abruptly with a word that sounded like 'Weatherby'. We called them the Weatherby family. Now when Iris bursts into a trill of meaningless conversation in the early morning, raising her head slightly and looking up at me, I reply, 'Hullo, Weatherby.' I don't think she knows now why I say this, but she always smiles as if she did.

I cannot *imagine* Iris. But then I never have done. She is not like the Big Woman of Gerrards Cross. Love does not need fantasy, nor imagination either, though I've never been clear what imagination means if it isn't my ordinary Belial activity, grown into a necessary habit now: I couldn't possibly do without it. To imagine women is so easy, and to me now is so necessary, but to imagine them is not to love them.

Shamelessness comes upon me now that Iris herself has gone, or is going. I don't care what I do write or say about her or about anything else. I know I am worshipping her no matter what I say. But these days I find myself proclaiming to others, and to myself as well: 'She seems to want to go to bed about seven,' or 'In this new phase she's very restless in the night.'

Who is this *She* who has made an appearance, and with whom others and myself are so familiar? We are familiar because we are seeing her from the outside. She has indeed become a She.

I feel that at moments with a shudder. It was a strange coincidence that those letters – letters written long ago to the friend who was for a short time her fiancé – should have seemed to be about a different person, and written by someone I had never met. The externalisation of Iris which has begun now, and which will inevitably continue and grow greater, is in a sense a more terrible version of that incredulity I felt when skimming through the letters. Whoever had written them was a She. Not Iris, my Iris.

My Iris is not yet a She, but inevitably she becomes more like one every day, even in my thoughts. 'When she has to go . . . What will it be like when she is gone? . . . What will I do when she is gone, into the home, the hospital?'

Did I write about Iris last year to stop her becoming such a She? It didn't feel like that, but the urge may have been there. And when it came out she loved to see the book, and the picture on the cover. She would once have never believed such a thing would be done, and have known that I couldn't do it, or have done it. Nor would I once. But it comforted me to see her smile in a pleased proprietary way, far away from it all as she now was.

I saw a glimmer of pride, almost of a fond and motherly pride, in the smile she turned on me. I had actually written a book about her! My brother Michael, who is so fond of her, approved the book too, and very warmly, though in his usual military manner. It helped the Alzheimer cause.

That was all the approval I needed, and disapproval there – from Michael or from Iris herself (and I know she would have expressed it somehow had she felt it) – would have been the only kind that I feared.

14

Belial thoughts also played once with a project that would have externalised Iris – at least to me, or for me – and for that reason it would never have been done or even attempted. But it remained a satanic idea, an idea not in the realm of fantasy but of true fiction. Quite a different thing. No friend of Iris, or of Dr A.

Novelists cannot but put 'real' people, or parts of real people, into their novels. Even Iris used to do that. She denied it, and it was true and right that she denied it, because she never did it with any revealing intention, or in any sense to 'portray' an actual person or a friend, no matter in what light. It was a generalised awareness of others that had entered deeply and powerfully into her imagination.

It was easy to see how far it had been transformed in the process, for friends sometimes ventured an opinion, never invited or welcomed, that person Y in a novel by Iris was based on person X in life. When such an opinion was uttered it was invariably wrong or misleading, because resemblances in Iris's novels were, so to speak, metaphysical, never personal.

She was amused once by something she had heard Evelyn Waugh say, and she told me about it, for Iris always appreciated an author who did not talk about his books seriously, no matter how seriously he may have felt about them. Waugh, it seems, had remarked that people never minded being put into a novel, provided the novelist commented somewhere in the text that the person concerned – the He or She – was 'good in bed'.

Iris also discussed this kind of question with a fellow novelist in a more thoughtful vein, at least on one occasion. That was Patrick White, whom we met in the '60s, on a tour of Australia organised by the British Council.

We both found White, with whom we had dinner one evening, a deeply impressive figure. There was something very strange about him, and quite unique, as if he had come from some lost civilisation which had existed long before the present settlement of Australia. He might have belonged to the Minoan or Mycenaean aristocracy, an impression somehow heightened by the dignified and hospitable Greek with whom he lived in a house near Sydney. As usual Iris asked him about himself in a way that never caused offence, and which completely overcame the withdrawn and slightly forbidding manner – very un-Australian – with which he began the evening. They talked about each other's books, and I was surprised by the way in which Iris, who normally never mentioned her own novels, became as forthcoming on the subject as White himself.

They agreed that the great novelists – both admired and cited Henry James and Dostoevsky: both implied a lack of fondness for E.M. Forster and Virginia Woolf – never struck them as making use of the novel form to give their own theories and their own egos an airing. As White put it, they never 'made use of the helpless individual'.

This somewhat Delphic observation appeared to strike an immediate chord in Iris and their discussion grew animated. Art, suggested White, is the very opposite of the capitalist instinct: true art never exploits. Although he admired D.H. Lawrence's writing he deplored the way in which Lawrence, while expressing a lofty contempt for the human ego in art, set up a kind of Punch and Judy show in his novels and stories, in which his own ego could maintain an effortless superiority over the personalities of his friends and the people he met, all of whom were made use of to display their weaknesses and deride their sense of themselves.

White asked if we knew the Australian artist Sydney Nolan, who was then living in England and whom we had once met with Reynolds and Janet Stone. He and White seemed totally different and yet they had something in common – a touch of strangeness. In my memory of that time the pair associate, as wandering memories will do, with our clandestine swim in the Swan river at Perth, and with the flight of black cockatoos in the outback behind the town.

Sydney Nolan's face had lit up when I mentioned those cockatoos to him, and he looked oddly haunted, as if that spectral avian crew, whom I had once seen clamouring through the dead timber, had reminded him of a need to return home.

Dear Reynolds Stone loved birds too, but his own water-colours, painted in the wood behind the Rectory at Litton Cheney where the Stones lived, could hardly have been more different from Nolan's pictures.

When lying beside a sleeping Iris I greedily let these memories slide on, coalesce, drift apart again. Her sleep is doubly precious now, relieving her of the sightless and timeless troubles which perplex her day, troubles of which those dark birds, winging out of the past, can appear in my mind like ominous harbingers. All such memories release me none the less: release me into that inevitably selfish world of sights and sounds I can no longer share with her.

I shudder now when I think of the place where Iris briefly became a *She* in my imagination. It was probably mere coincidence that it should have happened where it did, although things had been getting steadily worse, and particularly if we had to do a long drive. As the miles go on Iris becomes more and more agitated and restless, clamouring beside me in the car like a demented cockatoo. Stopping at intervals does not help, and I have learnt never to undertake such journeys, on whatever pretext. Our car had no childproof locks, and I used to be terrified that at the height of one of these manic fits she would get the door open and jump out into the road.

But there was no escaping such a journey on this occasion. Janet Stone had died at last. During her slow decline we had become much attached, and we tried to see her as often as we could. She was concerned about Iris, giving her the materials for embroidery and trying to teach her the simpler methods, though it was no use.

Janet herself had never got over Reynolds Stone's sudden death. She had tried to make a new life for herself in her Salisbury cottage, devoted like a museum to her husband's paintings and engravings, but she missed him and their life together too much for recovery.

The nightmare drive had worn me out and made it impossible to think about the funeral, at which I had been asked by Janet's children to 'say a few words'. Never an easy assignment, this was likely to be an impossible one in present circumstances. Oppressed by our own troubles I could think of nothing to say. Perhaps something would come to me at the last moment, in the church at Litton Cheney?

Beside me in the car Iris babbled and gestured unceasingly, anxieties rising to a pitch in a weird shrill cry I had never heard before. A word or two came through. 'Wrong! Driving! Not way! Not mother, not house . . . mother house!'

I called on all the friends of Dr A to help me, but for the moment they could do nothing. No desires to conjure up, no fantasy to aid, no memories . . .

Only one friend, and he a terribly dubious one, had the idea of doing something for me: and that was not until we were on the road home. With Iris in this state home itself was not a refuge of promise. Not a 'mother house' as she had so strangely put it. The madness would be there back home to meet us. As death had met the Eastern merchant in Samarra.

At last we were through Dorchester. On the bypass my own agitated gaze had flickered between the road ahead and Iris's hands – none too clean as usual, that was my fault – scrabbling near the door-handle. If only we could have come to the funeral by train. But Oxford to Dorchester by British Rail had seemed an impossible journey, and Iris could be as bad on bus or train as in the car, to the consternation of her fellow-passengers.

In the biography he wrote of himself, and pretended was written by his second wife, Hardy told the story of an American visitor who asked him what was the finest view in Dorset. After some hesitation he opted for the high road above the village of Litton Cheney. The sweep of Lyme Bay below, Portland on the left to be seen on a clear day; to the right Golden Cap and the capes beyond Lyme Regis.

Above the Bride valley the monument to that other Hardy, a distant relation, who had sailed the *Victory* past Portland on her Admiral's last voyage. It looks rather like an old-fashioned telephone receiver, upside down.

A deep relief to turn off the main road at last and dip down the lane towards the village. A sea fog was rolling up over the churchyard. The first snowdrops were showing among the turf on Reynold's grave, with Janet's newly dug and ready beside it. I thought of Reynolds's endearing way of talking to Iris; talking as if to himself, but with his bright eye fixed on hers, its affectionate gaze seeming to make speech unnecessary.

He used to read the Lessons in church. I never heard him, but I wondered how he could have done it, for his voice never rose much above a low murmur, breaking through one's own voice if one had begun speaking, like the sound of the sea. Nobody ever minded being interrupted in this way by Reynolds.

I silently invoked his aid as we walked past the grave

to the west door of the church. He loved taking Iris to the sea, on the long sweep of the Chesil Bank below us. He helped her to find stones. In summer the three of us bathed together, and once Iris nearly drowned, with us two men standing placidly chatting together as we dried ourselves. There was always a slow surge on the steep bank of shingle, but it was easy to judge the moment and let the sea bring one up. Iris had happened to misjudge it, and had been pulled under by the slight undertow. She had not panicked and the next wave brought her in. Reynolds and I, calmly chatting, had noticed nothing, nor did she say anything to us, although she told me what had happened in bed that night. She had used her memory of the moment in one of her novels.

We walked slowly to the church door, Iris fretting sadly beside me, supported on her other side by little Emma Stone, now a mother with three children. Her husband, a wonderful illustrator of children's books, had designed the jackets for my own novels. I had hoped originally that he would do the jacket for Iris's next novel, but the next one never came.

Janet never had flowers inside the Old Rectory, and hardly any in the garden – Reynolds preferred green leaves and bushes and trees. But the church was full of the pure cold scent of snowdrops, for which Janet was prepared to make an exception. Her two daughters had laboriously picked them that morning in the garden of the Old Rectory, with the permission of its new owner. They were massed in jars round the altar and the pulpit.

The sea fog had cleared now, and through the west window I could make out the line of the bay. Could I get by if I were just to give a little commentary on these things, like a radio reporter at a sports event? Sea and snowdrops, and some past events? Placid chats in the hot sun on the Chesil Bank, near drownings . . . ?

I gazed for inspiration at Iris, sitting between the Stone

girls in the front row. She looked like a prisoner under escort and was staring down at the marble floor. It was thick with worn old inscriptions, records of parsons and gentry long departed.

My eye followed her gaze in a bemused way. What *was* I to say when the moment came? And it was just coming . . .

I got out of the pew at the right time and took position on the chancel steps. I opened my mouth. Would I be able to get anything out? The small congregation looked expectant, but also, I thought, a little nervous. They were playing their part, as I would have to be acting mine.

Only Iris, lost now in her own darkness, seemed to have no role to play. There came into my head a line from Auden, from one of his plays. He remarks on the difference 'between the sane who know they are acting and the mad who do not'. Does Iris know the difference? I'm sure she doesn't as she sits there, gazing uncalmly at the floor.

I was able to speak at last thank goodness. I found myself saying that I missed Janet very much. Because I liked to tell her about funny things that had happened. Things, I was about to go on, which I could no longer tell to Iris, but I stopped myself just in time.

Unnerved by this narrow escape I found I had completely dried up. What else was there to say? I must give an example. Things that Janet had liked hearing about. Mind was a blank, but the mourners in front of me were still nobly acting their part and I must go on playing mine. Starting with a jerk I found to my horror that I was telling them the story about Audi and the bath.

Audi Villers, our old friend, now a widow, who lives in a quiet village in the centre of the very unquiet island of Lanzarote, had been staying with us recently. Just for the night. She had to go back next day to see an opera in London.

Soon after she had arrived I found her cleaning the bath. 'Audi,' I said, 'please don't bother. There's no need.'

Audi looked surprised by my words, and also amused. 'Oh yes there is,' she said. 'I want to take a bath.'

Sound logic. But why should it have struck me at the time as so funny? Anyway it did, and we had both burst out laughing. The congregation could hardly do that, but they also looked bewildered. What had this domestic event to do with their departed friend Janet?

To me it was clear as daylight, but to them, naturally enough, it was not. I hastened to explain that since Janet had loved comic things and happenings I was looking forward to telling her this one. Now, alas, I should not be able to . . .

It was too late for my realisation that the funeral audience had not found the story of Audi and the bath comic at all. Perhaps it wasn't? I had to hasten on, but how? Uncertainly I got out once more how sorry I was that I never saw Janet again, and so was unable to tell her the story. Some faces – those of Emma Stone and Phillida her elder sister – did look touched and tearful when I said that.

Greatly encouraged I had, as I thought, a sudden brain-wave, a recollection of the moment towards the end of Tolstoy's *Anna Karenina* when the heroine, on her way to the station to throw herself under a train, sees a shop sign that strikes her as comical. She thinks she will tell her lover Vronsky about it – it will be something to amuse him. Then she remembers she will not be seeing Vronsky again – not ever.

Tolstoy implies that if anything could have deterred Anna from suicide it would have been the realisation of that moment: the joke, the pleasure of telling it to the man she loves, the awareness that their love is over, and that life will soon be over too.

With the madness of those whom the gods wish to destroy I babbled out all this. How very apt it was, and how wonderful and touching was Tolstoy's art! By the time I ran out of steam the audience was looking not only bemused but downright uncomfortable. I still go hot and cold when I think of that moment. How could I have supposed that Anna's suicide would be a suitable topic for 'a few words' at a friend's funeral?

The business was over at last and we were on our way home. Even before we started Iris had become difficult. The kind Stone daughters did their best to soothe her, but her behaviour, normally so subdued in public and smiling, as if she were anxious to show that an Alzheimer sufferer could none the less play the part sweetly, became rude and wild. Like a bad child she wanted to go; and amongst the decorum of the funeral gathering, the sherry glasses and the teacups, she made her wish all too clear.

As I got her away, feeling by that time fairly wild myself, I reflected on the fallacy in Auden's smart epigram. It is the mad, not the sane, who behave as if they knew they were acting, but their parts get mixed up. However strange – 'naturally' strange as it were – Iris may have become in private, carrying odd things about and babbling away to herself downstairs at two in the morning, she had managed to preserve up to now the public part of a deranged person doing her best to conceal and apologise for what was wrong.

The funeral, I saw, had seriously upset her. Over-excited her too. That was why she had become the impossible child, seeming to throw herself with diabolical energy into the part.

Loneliness, as I drove and tried to quieten Iris, seemed overwhelming. I felt I longed for death, like Anna Karenina abandoned as she thought – no, as she knew – by a lover who had become a stranger to her. The person beside me seemed a stranger too. And I should never tell the joke about the bath to Janet Stone who was dead, and who I felt at that moment might have saved me.

All Iris's friends were far away. At the funeral the congregation had the look on their faces of those embarrassed by a mad person. I must have been mad to say what I had. Even now the Stone family must be regretting together their misguided wish that I should 'say a few words'.

The mourners had looked up at me with incomprehension and embarrassment. And Iris had looked down at the floor, with its marble records all worn away. No joke to be shared. I had never felt more hopelessly out of touch with her than at that moment.

Then I saw the house.

The little villages hereabouts were built of grey stone from Portland, nestling in their valleys as naturally as sheep in a field. This house was unexpected and nightmarish. It stood on a hill, proclaiming itself, built in the Olde Worlde redbrick style of the '30s. A long avenue lined with little conifers led up to it from the main road, and where the avenue began a fancy oaken gate stood open.

It was an odious house. And at once, as if despair and loneliness had brought them, things which seem to come from it and to be about it began to crowd into my mind. At that moment, with Iris raving and fretting beside me, the Belial in my head would have greedily welcomed any guest, no matter from where.

What came was like a dream, but it was also a story, a fiction, and it was hateful. My need for it at that moment was hateful too. This was not memory or fantasy, Dr A's faithful and comfortable old friends. This absurd nightmare which I started to tell myself was like a revenge, engendered by the demons of solitude, a revenge taken on the mad stranger screaming and protesting beside me.

In the car we had passed by the gate at the bottom of the avenue. But in my mind we had driven up that avenue. The woman beside me was indeed my wife, whose name now was Priscilla. She was a tiresome girl with whom I was on bad terms. I had a job in London with which I was as dissatisfied as I was with my wife, and my prospects generally.

Priscilla is hissing something at me. 'Why on earth did you do that? You can't just drive up to a private house.' I don't know myself why I did it. Something made me turn off the road, drive up the avenue. Why I don't know.

I ignore the hissing of Priscilla because I have seen something in the mirror. A man has stepped out on to the drive behind us. He has a scythe over his shoulder, and as I watch him he puts this scythe down across the avenue, as if to prevent our turning back.

I stop the car and Priscilla at once jumps out. She shimmies up to the strange man, all apology and London charm. She talks to him, smiles at him. He has a massive face and head, thick black hair. He is squat and sinister.

Where have I seen that man? I know him, I'm sure of it.

Of course! He is Dr Elias Canetti, the distinguished author, Nobel Prizewinner. Why should he be here, of all people? No wonder Priscilla seems to be so taken with him. He is a truly fascinating man.

In the time before Iris and I were married – how long ago it seems! – I was terrified he would carry her off, like Pluto into his own dark underworld. But Iris escaped in time, fortunately for me.

And here he was, back again, growing out of my head in the story I was beginning to make up of the nightmare journey.

I get slowly out of the car. I join my apologies with Priscilla's. Canetti smiles. His smile is that of a crocodile.

We have been invited into the house. Inside the house, sitting vaguely behind a tea-table in the drawing-room, is such a nice-looking woman. Tall, willowy, angular, faded, middle-aged. But so sweet-looking. I feel drawn to her immediately.

If only I could leave Priscilla with Canetti and go off

with this woman! Away and away! I turn politely towards the host, the massive squat saturnine man, who bows and smiles his crocodile smile at me. He knows what I would like to do.

And he wishes me to do it. He always gets what he wants. He is the primal power figure. Iris's one-time lover, tyrant, dominator and master. Teacher too, and inspiration. The great all-knowing *Dichter*.

And now he will take Priscilla, whoever she may be, and give Iris to me. The sweet-looking woman sitting vaguely on the sofa.

Why is he doing that? Of course I know why he is doing it. Because his wife, Iris, who has for so long been his captive, has now for that reason begun to go mad . . .

But he will not tell me that of course. I shall learn of it too late. And Iris will then be taken into the other Dark Lord's domain.

Has Iris really belonged to Dr Canetti, all these years we have been married? Just as she has belonged for the last four years to that other doctor – Dr Alzheimer?

The car swerves violently. Iris has pulled at the wheel as I sat beside her driving, lost in this nightmare.

WE MUST STOP! Anywhere. Anywhere. During my dream, no fantasy but a loathsome scenario for a revenge novel, a hateful novel, we have passed Salisbury. And Hungerford too?

No we haven't – what am I saying? – I have been so lost in that dreadful story. I will not think of it as a fantasy, one of my own. It seemed imposed upon me from outside. An alien threat, as Canetti himself had once been. When I first fell in love with Iris she told me of this strange and wonderful man, with whom she had been and still was in love. When he learned about my existence from some third party he forbade her to see me. Fortunately she ignored that. But the shadow of Canetti seemed in those early days to stretch all the way from Hampstead to Oxford.

Canetti died in Switzerland a few years ago. He was married again, with a young daughter. Year by year he had grown more famous throughout the German-speaking world, until the eventual award of the Nobel Prize. He must then have been over eighty. He and Iris were always on good terms. She advised him about his daughter's education. But they had not met for a long time, more than a generation. I had quite got over my early fear and horror of the great man, a childish fear, as if he were a devouring ogre; and I believe that in some sense he could indeed be that too.

I had enjoyed his books. One about the Jewish community in Morocco I had especially admired, and he was cordial on the rare occasions when we had met. 'I like you,' he once said, confronting me in an amused way with his giant face and squat body. I blushed like a girl and escaped as quickly as I could, for it seemed like a dismissal. Not an unkind one but it made further communication impossible. Canetti was good at doing that.

And here he was, reappearing from the past, in an ugly house on a Dorset hillside. As he had once said, 'I like you,' he said now, 'I give you.' I am giving you this madness, this mad woman . . . To have and to hold, to love and to cherish . . .

Dr A's friends would shake their heads. And I must be going dotty myself, what with the funeral, and the sympathetic eyes, and getting it all wrong like that. And who was this Priscilla anyway, whom the house on the hill had dragged into its story? An awful girl she was – I could still see her quite vividly – and Canetti was welcome to her.

Humour, normality, love. Quite suddenly they seem to come flooding back from beside me, for Iris has gone quiet and I can feel her relax. I reach out a hand and hers finds it and holds it. Instead of stopping the car I feel we can now drive on tranquilly, for we must be on that lonely stretch of high Roman road that runs between Collingbourne Ducis and Wexcombe. A beautiful stretch in summer, when we always have stopped on our drives north and south to wander about for a few moments, contemplate the lofty upland, the clouds over Inkpen, and sometimes the insect dots hovering there which are hang-gliders, soaring and sailing among the huge curves that run down to the plain – the Great Plain as Hardy called it.

Good memories come back again now, like the good warmth that is flowing from hand to hand. In spite of the cold drizzle falling outside.

I remember when we once had the idea of crossing the Great Plain directly. A faint dotted line, I had seen, was marked on the map, leading from the deserted village where the country road comes to an end. All beyond has become an artillery range. I pointed out to Iris that the only truly unspoilt bits left in England are where the army has taken over, and sits growling like a dog in a manger. Growling far off maybe, but scarcely ever present or visible. I reassured Iris that the gunners were never there, and if they should happen to be they were compelled by law to give ample warning of their presence.

And we managed it somehow. The summer was an exceptionally fine one; we spun along over the smooth dry grass. At one point a milestone was embedded in the turf, with elegant incised lettering, probably from the 18th century, which showed the miles to Salisbury. We were on the old high road from London and the north, which once ran direct across the plain.

Iris had the naughty wish to take that milestone home with us. She always felt all stones belonged to her. But fortunately it proved too deeply embedded in the turf.

I wondered then if the deserted village was the one where

Anna was born, the girl in Hardy's story 'On the Western Circuit'. So remote is the village that there is no school and she has never learned to read or write. She becomes a maid in the house of a wine-merchant's wife in Salisbury, where a young barrister working on the Western Circuit sees her riding on the merry-go-round at the town fair. They fall in love, and when she finds she is pregnant she begs her mistress to write letters for her to the young man.

Childless, neglected and lonely as she is, the wine-merchant's wife falls in with the idea, and presently she is herself in love with the young man, by courtesy of the postal service. The young barrister is so charmed by what he thinks are Anna's letters that he determines to marry her, and at the wedding the truth comes out. It is the only moment the real lovers meet, but the barrister finds himself 'chained for life', says Hardy all too predictably, to the wrong woman, an illiterate village girl.

Thinking now of Anna Karenina's last joke, never uttered; and of that other poor Anna, trudging across the wide plain to Salisbury and to her destiny, I remember also the woman I once knew whose husband had Alzheimer's. 'Like being chained to a corpse you know,' she had remarked to me with a cheerful laugh. I saw what she meant, for Iris's own affliction was just beginning to become severe, but no – it was not true. Not true for me then. Or for Iris.

And thinking this now I stop the car at last and put my arms round her. A few miles back I had felt for the first time since we met, nearly fifty years ago, afraid to be alone with her. I had found myself alone with a mad woman. One quite alien and strange, as the Canetti story I had found myself telling myself had suggested.

All that was gone now. She was just Iris, Iris as I had always known her, and loved her.

It was true we were in darkness, but it was a darkness without fear or hope, a darkness in which we were travelling now together again as one. And we could go on together somehow, from day to day, from tea to supper and from supper to bed-time. So long as we went on like that there would be nothing to care about, only the care that was between us. In giving it I received it back, twice blessed.

For by needing me now Iris also sheltered me, nourished me simply by having nothing to give of which she could be conscious. In losing her own, Iris had given me a new life. How could I live without her now, and without her friends, the friends of Dr A?

'Hear what comfortable words . . .' The Bible says that somewhere, or the prayer-book. And it's true. But comfort must have its end, as fear and misery do. Nothing is less predictable than dementia's ups and downs.

And as if to prove the point Iris suddenly wrenches the door open and plunges out, to vanish without a sound into the darkness.

It is so unexpected that for a moment I cannot even stop the car. I saw some miles back that she had got her seatbelt off, as she almost always does. She hates its constriction. And I had not the heart or the will nor the courage either – for that was at the time she was so far away from me, and I myself so lost in that vile Canetti nightmare – to stop the car and to put the seatbelt on again.

We were rounding a corner, going uphill, and I needed both hands on the wheel. There were headlights behind us too, following us up the hill. I had to brake to a stop on a corner and the car behind rushed past, missing us by inches and sounding a furious horn.

Inane thoughts went through my head as I scrabbled at the door-handle to get out, just as Iris had done. We had been to a funeral and done badly – badly then, and now, and in between – in all sorts of ways. And one funeral could so easily lead to another . . . to a couple more at least . . .

The road was quiet now, quiet as the grave, and so

dark that I could see nothing beyond the lights of the car.

'Puss! Puss! My old mouse, my old catmouse! Where are you?'

No sound or reply. A strong cold wind was blowing steadily over the empty down. In the daytime here we had seen the racehorses at exercise, cantering across the downland in long cavalcades.

I groped my way back on the slope, along the side of the road. I shouted again and again. My voice sounded muffled and distracted, and the wind blew it away. The place seemed quite empty.

Has the Dark Lord appeared out of the earth and carried her down with him to his kingdom? Or did she herself deliberately invoke the help of Dr Alzheimer's last and best friend?

Blind terror now as I rushed further and further down the road. How far back could it have been? Another car's headlights approaching, shooting swiftly towards me up the hill, and I peered down the tunnel of light, half hoping half dreading to see Iris standing vacantly in the glare of it, silhouetted against the headlights of the onrushing car. Then I was crouched against the hedge as it tore past me.

And all I thought was: I have lost my Muse. I can do nothing without her. Without her I shall have nothing to write, and nothing to do. Instead of searching for Iris I crouched against the hedge and thought about that sort of thing.

I tried to pull myself together a bit. She must be here somewhere, like all those things that get lost in the house. But many of them are never seen again.

Suddenly there was a sort of noise coming to me in the wind. Not a distress noise, not a cry for help. It was more a sort of chuckling sound, faint but not far away.

Down the road again a few further steps and the shadow

of the hedge lifted: there was a long gap in it. I plunged through and immediately lost my footing. I found myself rolling down a steep grassy slope. As I picked myself up, breathless, I found Iris was beside me. She was lying on her back and laughing, quite unhurt. After jumping out of the car she must have fallen down the slope, just as I had done, and landed up safe at the bottom like a little puffball. Her face now was just visible in the gloom . . .

I start to kiss the face, and I start laughing too, as we embrace one another.

We will get ourselves home somehow and I will not think about what is to come. Short views. Today will soon be over: and then there will be tomorrow, and the next day, and perhaps the day after that . . .

15

Quite suddenly, but some time after that eventful journey, I had a breakdown. Shouting and sobbing and screaming. No reason for it.

Iris at first smiled at me incuriously. She did not seem at all surprised. And not very interested either.

What has happened to me? Why have I suddenly popped off? Iris may not be concerned, but I am. I stare dully at myself and say why, why, why.

Abruptly as it seems I realise. Heart has quietly taken itself off. And courage, and will. I can go on doing all the things I have to do, but none of them seem to help us any more.

As the Germans say, *Mut verloren, alles verloren*. I remember Hannelore saying that. She said it in a slightly smug way, when she thought I ought to be bucked up. Typical of a former member of the *Bund deutscher Mädchen*. It annoyed me at the time, but how true it turns out to be.

Guts gone, all gone. That might be the best translation. And I start thinking about that *Mut*. By thinking about it perhaps I can cheer myself up. I remember the Old English poem we all had to study (do they still? – I'm out of touch now) for the English degree.

The Battle of Maldon. In those days too poets preferred heroic failure to brilliant success. The English commander rashly allowed the Vikings to cross the estuary at Maldon, so that the two armies could fight on equal terms. He was killed. Discouragement set in, but a veteran retainer rallies the ranks with a rousing warcry.

Mod sceal the mara the ure megen lytlath. 'Mood shall be the more as our strength wanes'. Am I remembering it right? We can't say 'mood' in the sense of *Mut* any more. Courage, a French word, must have taken us over with the Normans. (The Germans have it too – Mother Courage.)

But what am I doing, trying to cheer myself up with this stuff? No more *Mod*, or *Mut*, in me. I can feel it's all gone. And the English lost the battle.

That ancient defeat seems the last straw. Suddenly I start crying in earnest, gulping and hiccuping, with my mouth gaping open.

At once Iris takes my hand, pats and strokes it. She hardly seems to feel the hand or to know who I am. And yet out of her own absence is she trying to give me comfort? As she could once do, as if she could do it still?

Iris won't eat, is barely drinking. This is a really alarming development. It drives all frivolous thoughts of *Mod* and *Mut* out of my head. For two days she doesn't seem to have had a pee either. (Later, at the home, the nurse tells me that this phase begins when another circuit shuts down in the brain, stopping even the elementary signals that make us urinate, salivate, feel hungry or thirsty.)

Again and again I try a method which has always worked before. She has always let me put little pieces or spoonfuls in her mouth. A dribble of Complan; tiny morsels of toast and honey.

She does not push them away, but her mouth remains closed, like shops on a Sunday morning. As I fed her, only a fortnight ago, I used to say,

'The King was in the counting-house, counting out his
    money,
The Queen was in the parlour, eating bread and
    honey.'

She would respond to my face then, and smile, and the smile made her mouth open easily.

As I go on trying she moves her head sharply, rolling her eyes like a dangerous horse. Before I can stop myself I start to cry again. This time Iris takes no notice.

Rush out of the house and walk round the block by myself. We used to make it last twenty minutes, now it takes hardly any time. I remembered to lock the door on the outside, although I can feel it is hardly necessary now.

A lost frightened feeling about that. As soon as I got used to them I clung desperately to each stage of the disease. The sleeping and forgetting one, the wandering one, the sleepless and distracted one as well. Each soon became a sort of friend.

But now this last one – feeding Iris with a spoon, kissing her when she consents to take a drink – seems to have abandoned us.

When I get back to the house Iris is still huddled at the kitchen table. Mechanically now and without hope I pick up a morsel of honey and bread and put it in a spoon. Without looking she opens her mouth and takes it in. And then smiles at me and makes her old cooing sound.

Dr Jacoby. A kind man, a scholar and a healer: also the knight-errant who has come to our rescue. He visits every few days.

As I talk to him Iris wanders in and out of the room, murmuring something, dragging an old jersey and a dress behind her. The first time he came she had her smile for him and was almost social.

All that is over now. He says the time has come, no doubt about it.

If we can only get to the right place. Vale House is the best. No doubt about that either. It is strictly for cases of need: there is very seldom a vacancy.

'It's harder to get into than Eton,' says Dr Jacoby.

He pauses as if for reflection, and adds – 'or even Winchester.'

His face splits into a grin and we both laugh.

But I at once feel a terrible anxiety. Will I be able to get my little Iris into this great good place? Will she still miss me, will she hate it, want to escape?

As things are now, surely not? And it would be all kindness and care there. The real sort of care which I cannot give.

Dr Jacoby is back next day to say he thinks we'll manage it. A bit of luck – someone has died.

Sheer relief floods through me and I feel myself give a gasp. His dark eyes twinkle at me in such a kindly humorous way. He tells me more about the home. Too dazed to take it in properly, but he is saying it's such a friendly place. No visiting hours. I can spend all day there if I want. All night too.

At last the taxi comes. We have tried ringing for an ambulance and we tried the Medical Centre. Busy at the moment. So sorry. Try again later. 'Far called, our Navies melt away'. The line from Kipling's 'Recessional', presaging the end of Empire, rattles distractedly through my head. Like *Mod* and *Mut*, whose defection has stopped bothering me for the moment. Farstretched our Health Service does its best.

The taxi man looks unperturbed when we tell him the lady is on the stairs and we can't get her down. He comes in with a pleased benevolent look. Glad to help. Kind Frances had come to help too, but even between us we could not get Iris on her feet. Now the taxi man gives her his arm, calls her my love, and she is soon outside and looking happy. I ask the taxi man about his taxi's doors. Yes, they are locked. Frances waves, and gets into her car.

Suddenly a marvellous peace and quiet. I hold Iris's hand and we smile shyly and happily at each other. The last ride together. Like Anna Karenina's to the railway station.

But it feels more as if we had just got married, or as if we were just going to get married and were going in the taxi together to the Registrar, holding hands.

Trouble getting out. But a nurse takes a gentle hold of Iris's no longer reluctant fingers. The finger-tips of both hands. Walking slowly backwards, Maureen – her name is on her overall – leads Iris to a door. A smile on her face now, and on Iris's too. They process slowly and with a happy concentration, as if treading an informal minuet together.

Through the door and into Vale House. I have lost track of *Mod* and *Mut* and our Navies melting away, and find myself clinging now to another sort of joke, one I cannot share with Iris, with whom I would have shared it once, or with the staff, who are so kind and helpful. It is the memory of Mrs Gamp in Dickens, and her 'Wale', the Vale of Tears in which we are all destined to live. In any age.

But this nice casual house does not look like a 'Wale'. Warmth, brightness, more kind faces, and the lounge where patients are sitting as if in a snug old-fashioned hotel. They pay us no attention, but one or two seem to see us with benign passive incuriosity.

Iris's smile transforms her own face now. She is among fellows and friends, still more of Dr A's friends. She does not look back as she enters the room, and I can see that she is still smiling.

Iris died in Vale House on February the eighth 1999. The reassurance I and all those other friends could not give her had come at last. This was the best of the friends.

She had grown steadily weaker. Without bother or fuss, as if someone she trusted had helped her to come to a decision, she stopped eating and drinking. Gentle pressure from those kind nurses but no insistence. No horror of being put on a drip.

During the last week she took to opening her blue eyes

very wide, as if merrily. Her face was still round and beautiful, although the body I held in my arms was shrunken and light. When she died I closed her eyes and then opened them, as if we could still play together. She had looked and not seen us for days, but now she seemed to see me.

Tricia O'Leary, the head of the home, came in. She was crying, rather to my surprise, as she must have seen this happen a great many times before. But they had all come to love Iris very much.

Dying had been so quiet that I found myself saying to Tricia, 'I wouldn't mind doing that myself.' She smiled and took my hand and Maureen brought me a cup of strong tea.

I thought thankfully of those 'few words' no one was going to have to say at a funeral or a Memorial Service. Iris had told me years back that she didn't want either. She had been firm about that. So there would be a Wake instead, a big party for all her friends.

I don't care for that word 'carer', just because it has become so unavoidable.

And the gap caring leaves when it stops is unavoidable too. A month ago I wrote in my diary: how will I get through the time when I am not looking after Iris?

And as if to cheat emptiness, when it should come, I took care to anticipate. The moments I then looked forward to all day – my drink, my book over supper – would cease to mean anything. They would vanish like a puff of smoke.

And have they vanished? I am still finding out. Remember the Law of the Conservation of Pleasure? Has it become a law of consolation? Not so much a law as a fact.

In this numbed and vacant time our old friend Belial is the first to call with his condolences. He is no more to be avoided than the undertaker. Those thoughts that wander through eternity. And Belial himself, who speaks up for them in *Paradise Lost* with such eloquence, he is still around.

A comic figure but a persistent one. I can't shut him up and tell him to go away.

Iris never knew him personally. He only came into our lives after she became ill. But what he brought to us both we can still share.

Because he resembles another, even older friend. The friend who arrived unexpectedly when we fell in love. It was at that dance in the summer of 1954, when we babbled to each other for hours, upstairs in my little room at St Antony's. Thanks to that friend we had a new language to speak, a language which we spoke together as if by instinct.

I have since thought about what then seemed to come so naturally. I have thought: here I am married to the most intelligent woman in England, and we have never had a serious conversation. We never talk to each other in a way that would be intelligible to anyone else. Or worth listening to if it was.

We are still talking in that way, and I shall never leave home now. Home is Iris and Iris is home. Dr Alzheimer was a friend who never stopped Iris talking to me, nor I to her.

I don't miss her. Perhaps because I don't remember her. Not in the way that I remember things and people in the past. No wonder Iris wanted no Memorial Service. She knew I would not need to remember her. She was not present at the party given in her honour. She stayed at home, and I could not wait to get back to her.

When we left home in former times, before Iris became ill, she was always there to look after me. She enjoyed that. She enjoyed getting the tickets at the station, paying the taxi, steering me through the caverns of the Underground. She kept me safe. And she will still do that at home, the place where in those days I used to look after her.

Bereavement means a tearing away. But we and Belial know it as a comic word. I play with it now, as I used to play with the word 'Alzheimer'. In my mind's eye – Belial's eye – I can see this bereaved person. A grave party, in a smooth furry top-hat. A beaver hat.

I shall linger with him under the benign sky, and wonder how anyone could imagine unquiet slumbers for the sleeper in that quiet bed. The bed where Iris is lying with her martial cloak around her. As she used to do in the evenings when I tucked her up as she was, because I could not persuade her to let me take her clothes off. And so I recited 'The Burial of Sir John Moore' to her instead. And then she always smiled up at me.

I sleep quietly now, with Iris quiet beside me. I drop off in the daytime too, and wake up feeling calm and cheerful as if Iris had been there.

But jokes can show us the truth – too much so – as well as bringing back the past. That last joke, the one Anna Karenina never told.

This morning I caught the tail of my vest again on the windsor chair, coming up with my mug of tea. I wanted to tell Iris about it, and the funny things that had happened in my memory after I had first caught my tail, that morning a year ago. But when I got upstairs I found she was not there, and I could not tell her.

Widower's House

For Audi

PART I

1

Margot at Home

'Now do eat it while it's nice and hot,' ordered Margot, putting a large lump of casserole on to my plate.

I have always disliked casseroles. During our forty-four years of married life Iris and I never made a casserole. Nor did we ever eat one, except under duress, if we were guests at a dinner party.

I was tempted to say rudely that I would rather eat it nice and cold. Instead I found myself rapidly picking the largest lump off the plate – Margot at the stove had her back to me – and stuffing it into my trouser pocket.

I had never done such a thing in forty-four years of happy domestic eating, with myself usually the cook. I felt astonished by my own action: its rapidity, its pointless duplicity. Why was I behaving like this? Was it because I was different now? A different person since Iris died?

That must be it. My instinct now was to escape, to evade, to elude whatever was pressed upon me, whether it was telephone calls or chunks of casserole.

But I could not escape back into my old self, because my old self no longer existed. In widowhood you lose not only your loved one but yourself. And there was no new self to take its place. Only this indistinct creature who put the dinner pressed upon him in his pocket instead of eating it: who was an object of solicitude and a prey to the whims of kindly women.

Widowers are also full of self-pity. Intensified as it had become, this was the only recognisable trait left over from a previous personality. So I reflected in a wild way, as I manipulated the handkerchief in my pocket over the greasy lump of casserole. I used to be a different person, a person who lived with Iris for forty-four years, so different from her and so separate, and yet so completely a part of what she was, of what together we had been.

So instant is thinking that while Margot's back was turned to me as she bent over the stove – not like my stove at home – I had an infinity of time to reflect on the fact that friends, however well you know them, remain unstable and unpredictable creatures. I was wary of Margot; I was wary of her now, because I did not know what she was. She might get cross or irritable, amorous or lachrymose. Whatever she did or was would remain unknown to me. Ill or demented, Iris for me had been always the same, always 'my old cat'. She determined my being.

Well, she was gone now. I could not be the person I had been; the one who was part of her when she died of Alzheimer's disease. She had taken our two selves with her. I could see my old self clearly enough, but only as a fact of history, unrelated to what I seemed to have become.

And what was that? A new person? I did not feel in the least like a new person. Perhaps Margot was trying, even if unconsciously, to make me a new person; perhaps I was unconsciously trying to be one myself. But it didn't seem to be working. My last thought, as Margot turned back again from the stove, was that I was glad it wasn't working.

Yes, I was frightened of Margot. But that was unfair! I had known Margot for years and years. That is to say we, Iris and I, had known Margot for years and years. One of her daughters had been a pupil of Iris's, who was then teaching philosophy at St Anne's College in Oxford. The daughter was not very satisfactory as a pupil but Iris did her best, and the girl scraped a third. She was very fond of Iris, who always kept in touch with her former pupil, and helped to find her a job. Then she got married. Margot always insisted that Iris had somehow saved her daughter.

Margot took to asking us over to her house in Norfolk for the weekend. It was a long and complicated drive, which I hated. I used to try to persuade Iris to beg us out of it with some kind of excuse, but Iris was too honest for that, and besides she felt loyalty as well as friendship for Margot. She could never resist advances, however untimely and unwanted, from people she had once helped, and who insisted on regarding themselves as pals for life. Besides, we were both genuinely fond of the big, awkward, enthusiastic woman, who combined a natural gift of goodness and kindness with being slightly comical in everything she said or did. She could be overpowering and a bit exhausting, but protected by Iris I got on with her well enough.

Her husband Guy was a great help in this. Hospitable, as garrulous as she was but unanxiously genial, he always made the going easy. I seldom got on with men as well as I did with women, but Guy was an exception. He teased and patronised me a little in a way that I enjoyed because he seemed to enjoy it; but he was always attentive and respectful with Iris, and seemed a bit in awe of her.

There was nothing much to do at their big house, and the country round about was unedifying. Their children were grown-up and we hardly knew them, except for Iris's experience of the delinquent daughter, now a model mother. Margot used to drive us to see churches which had immensely high ceilings ornamented with life-size angels. We duly exclaimed and admired; and after each church I would very much hope that we would go home to tea, or to a relaxing drink and chat with Guy. But, laughing heartily at my feeble hints in this direction, Margot used to herd us back into the car and on to the next church. Her enthusiasm had no sense of time or distance, and when we got back at last Guy would have several drinks inside him, and a box or two of Pringles.

In his time Guy had obviously made quite a lot of money, but he retired soon after we got to know them. Then suddenly and unexpectedly he died. Margot was prostrated. One year, two years later she was still a timid and uncertain shadow of herself. That was the time during which she became really close to us, or rather close to Iris. They saw each other in London, and Margot came to us as often as we went to her. Before that, she and Guy had almost always been the hosts.

I found it much easier to deal with Margot after she became a widow. Without Guy she was subdued and clinging, but easy to talk to, and always eager to be told anything that it occurred to one to tell her. We took her abroad once or twice, and that was quite a success. For a time she lost interest in her house and in the household animals to which she had once been so much attached. A cleaning lady from the village came every day to keep things tidy and to talk to her. When we visited her now, or when she came to us, we took her to the pub, where she and Guy never used to go.

After two years of disconsolate grieving she began to get over it. The improvement, I was sure, was as much due to Iris as to her family and her other friends.

When Iris began to be in the bad stages of Alzheimer's Margot was in America, staying with another of her daughters, who had an American husband. Margot got on admirably with both of them, particularly the always-hospitable husband from Virginia, and she was popular with the children too. She stayed in America for a while, and seemed quite recovered when she wrote to us, or in practice to me, for Iris by then could no longer read.

I strongly discouraged Margot from coming to see us, since I intuited that a visit might revive her own depression. Margot for once did not seem to need much discouraging.

Like many naturally hearty and ebullient persons, she overflowed with sympathy for every sort of trouble, and for the trouble-prone, but she shrank from the idea of mental illness.

When Iris died Margot was in touch with me again at once, and the problem of fending her off at least distracted me from my other difficulties. But I could not manage to fend her off for long. Notwithstanding her obvious reluctance to see Iris when she was alive, Margot managed now to sound a little reproachful, however full of forgiveness. Why had I not fully owned up to my situation? Why had I not let her know? I had been a saint to look after Iris for so long and without any help, but why had I not called on her – such an old friend as she was – to come and help me? She would have dropped everything – *everything*! Surely I must have realised that?

Yes, I realised it. And I realised Margot's need for self-deception. She honestly believed – now – that she would have done these things when Iris was alive. Margot spoke more in the warmth of sorrow than with reproach, but she somehow contrived to suggest that Iris's long lapse into mental illness, and even her death, could all have been avoided if she had been on the spot herself. In the old days her busy affection and patronage had always in some way reassured Iris, however much they had flustered and sometimes irritated me. Now I felt indifferent.

But soon Margot was back on the phone. She would come to Oxford, stay as long as I wanted, help me put things in order. There must be so much to do; she knew what it was like, and of course the house had got in such a state . . . In spite of the hens, the horses, the tiresome old vicar, she could leave her own house at a moment's notice.

I was sure she could. And a cold sweat started down my back at the thought of Margot in my house – our house it still was – dealing with its ageless accumulation of dust and dirt, to which, in the old days, Iris and I had both been happily indifferent. Margot would be doing the job on general principles: not censoriously, but as if, in the Duke of Wellington's words, the king's government must be carried on. There was now no one but herself to bear the white man's burden.

I managed to fight her off, but I knew that it was only a question of time before the attack was resumed. The result of the war seemed a foregone conclusion. My widower's house was already under siege. Margot was at the gates.

To continue the metaphor I won a respite by allowing Margot to open a campaign on another front. She quite understood that I might want to be alone in the house, if only for a suitable grieving period; but the weekends in particular must be so bleak and dreary now. A visit to her would make just the right sort of change. If I didn't fancy the drive, which was quite understandable, she would come and pick me up. She could do that easily.

I was sure she could. I didn't fancy the drive. Even with Iris I had always hated it. Now I shrank from travelling anywhere on my own. But I shrank just as much from the thought of having to talk to Margot in the car all the way to Norfolk.

When at length I capitulated, it was to say that I would drive over myself. As the dreaded day came closer I tried to find some of the shabby zip-fastener bags with which Iris and I, long ago, had been accustomed to travel. They all seemed to have disappeared from the house, as if Iris had contrived, in some miraculous way, to take them with her on her last journey.

I threw what I needed into the car, just as it was, wishing that Peter Conradi, or some other congenial friend and colleague made during the final years, would come and bear me off to France, to Africa, to the moon . . . Anything to save me having to go by myself to Norfolk.

Even when Iris was ill and I had to take her on a hazardous car journey – hazardous because of the unavoidable danger of her jumping out, which she had once managed to do – her presence still managed somehow to stiffen my backbone, to lend me support as well as comfort. As a widower my only comfort now must be to stay at home.

I longed to ring Margot and tell her I was ill, unfit, couldn't possibly move. She would only have said, 'All right, I'll come to you, you poor man. Even if you're grieving you must be looked after.'

She would have known that I was not ill; but apart from that, to escape my fate was, as it were, seriously impossible.

A part of my carelessness and my indifference was a belief now in fate. To try to take the initiative from it could only lead to further trouble.

And yet I could already feel my inside beginning to dissolve at the thought of the horrors of the journey. The M25 . . . those endless juggernauts, roaring on their steady note of brutish contempt as they elbowed their way past, their wheels higher than my head as I crouched in my little Fiat Panda, inches away. My stomach gave another squeeze. And the road-works and hold-ups; the confusing maze of sideways lanes on the last stretch – lanes I had travelled so often with Iris. Without her I should need more than a map to find my way there.

The journey was as bad as I had feared. Well, actually not quite as bad. But quite bad enough. It was a Tuesday. Margot had naturally asked me for the weekend – a long weekend she had said – but I had invented a Saturday visitor and a dinner engagement on Sunday. I had hoped in this way to postpone the inevitable to a later weekend at least – and I had devoutly hoped it would be a much later one.

Margot did not sound cross on the phone, as I had feared. Just a little more breezy. Margot could be cross, as I knew from overhearing her with her younger daughter Tamsin, who afterwards married the American, and who, like Iris's former old pupil, was at that time being a bit of a problem. But she had never been cross with Guy. Nor with Iris; nor with me.

Who could ever have been cross with Iris? It would have been undignified. My own occasional tantrums of course had no dignity, but they were part of our private language and understanding and always ended in laughter, almost before they got going. And although Iris was quite unconscious of it – this of course in the old days before she was ill – I was always under her protection. At Margot's and everywhere else.

Now that protection had gone. And without it I had discovered, to my astonishment, that I instinctively feared Margot. A harassed, settled sort of fear, as fated as everything else in my present life.

This makes it sound as if Margot was a termagant, which she most emphatically was not. But just because I now felt so vulnerable I seemed to have a false recollection of moments when her voice had been raised, with a sharp edge of raillery and exasperation in it. Unfair to fear now that I might once have heard it, but so it was. My impression, that is.

'Well, if *that's* the case,' she had said, when I prevaricated with my list of made-up engagements, 'come on Monday or Tuesday, and stay the week, or longer.'

I was relieved when she sounded just breezy, not at all put out. Obviously she didn't believe a word I had said, but that didn't bother her. Or me, come to that. The game was up, however. From her tone I knew that it would be no good trying to invent further, more pressing, yet more improbable engagements. It would be indecent even to try.

As I drove, quaking with what seemed the same kind of anxiety I knew so well from Iris's Alzheimer's, I knew that the Margot situation, for which I was helplessly bound, summed up all my widower's problems. *All old friends were now threats.* They were aimed purposefully at me; sure sources, not of reassurance, but of danger and discomfort. And out of the ground had sprung up, like the dragon's teeth, a fresh and hitherto unknown host of kind good persons, well-intentioned persons, who wanted to make life nicer and less lonely for me.

What a shit I was, or had become! But more and more, these days, I had begun to suspect that I always had been one. Widowerhood just seemed to have brought it out, like nettlerash.

Memories should always be spontaneous. But as I drove fearfully along I tried to cheer myself up by thinking deliberately of a *good* car journey, one long ago with Iris. Even towards the end of Iris's life such journeys could be good to remember, if the memories came of themselves. The best used to come when I was lying in bed in the morning beside Iris, with her tranquilly asleep at last after a busy, Alzheimer-distracted night.

During it she would have been off downstairs at two or three o'clock. I would hear her rattling the front door, always locked on the inside. Sometimes she would cry out in what could sound like indignation, although she was never indignant or in the least angry with me if I groped my way downstairs and tried as gently as I could to make her desist. She used to become quiet then, as if the last thing she wanted was for me to be upset or distressed, but it was always a quiet obstinacy. She would never come back to bed except by herself, and in her own time. And when she did, my thoughts could at last wander off freely, somewhere into the past.

I compelled them to wander off now, in the solitary car: but they failed to obey me or to comfort me. At last I hit on the device, of thinking about that happier and very much earlier journey.

We are sitting in the back of a car, as if with our tails wrapped round each other like the two bad mice. We are

whispering together. In the front are my mother and my
brother Michael, the driver. The car is Michael's, a big
Rover car which even then had an old-fashioned, slightly
grotesque look about it, although it had been a new model
five years before. The road is almost empty, but sometimes
we pass trucks with long bonnets saying LEYLAND on the
side of them (it was that long ago) grinding their way up a
long traverse in the Guadarrama. Occasionally my mother
turns to look at us; not exactly with disapproval, but as if she
would prefer us not to disturb the companionable silence of
the front seats with our chatter.

My father had died the previous February; my mother
and Michael, now very close, must have concluded tacitly
between them that it would be better not to spend this
Christmas at home. Michael must have been on leave. I
fancy he was stationed in Hong Kong at the time. However
it was decided, or whoever decided it, we were to drive
through Spain to Gibraltar, by way of Cadiz and Seville.

We had drunk some excellent young Burgundy at a
tiny and primitive restaurant where we had persuaded
a reluctant mother and brother to stop on the way down
through France; and I had bought a bottle to take away.
At Cordoba I was developing a severe cold, and after a
chilly morning in the Moorish cathedral I remembered the
bottle as we drove out of town. Iris, wise girl, often carried a
corkscrew in her handbag, and crouching down mouselike
in the back of the car we passed the bottle from hand to
hand with smothered and occasionally irrepressible giggles.
But the pair in front never suspected what was going on;
or if they did, they thought it undignified to mention the
matter.

So, buoyed up with Burgundian courage, we persuaded
them to make a lunch stop at Montilla in the sherry district.
Fortunately they were cold and hungry too. We drank dark
golden wine and ate fried sardines fresh from the coast. We
were the only guests, and our host seemed to be inebriated

in a jovial manner well before we left. Removing Michael's hat with a polite flourish, he put it on his own head and executed a sort of fandango. Michael, disarmed for once, produced a smile, and my mother actually clapped and said 'Bravo'. She felt the Spaniards were behaving as she had imagined they might do when she was young.

There was no pleasure in remembering this scene in a solitary car on the roaring motorway. But I remembered it anyway.

> . . . It is truth the poet sings
> That a sorrow's crown of sorrow is remembering
>   happier things.

Not only the motorway but everywhere I went was dangerous now, every person I met constituted a threat. The world was a dangerous place. I didn't believe in other people except as a source of trouble. The world had only made sense when Iris was there and I was looking after her.

And before that. Iris was doing her work, with me there, for more than forty years – real work. It was her own work, it had nothing to do with me: and I loved that. I basked in it. It was like being held in a hand. I was never aware of the supporting hand, and the hand was not aware of me, any more than God may be of his creation.

The horrible great curve going up to Cambridge. Distances and danger, and armies marching. Resolutely, in order to have something in my head, something too that I used to enjoy so much . . . Suppose that young Philip of Macedon had brought an army over to aid Hannibal? Or that the Barca faction had won ascendancy in the Carthaginian council; and instead of their leisurely half-reluctant way of making war the council had supported Hannibal in a *guerre à outrance*?

Why on earth do I go on thinking about things like this?

As if history mattered, as if anything could ever have been done about it.

At the age of seven or eight I read a book called *The Young Carthaginian*. Malchus, the young man's name was, and he went to the wars with Hannibal, like a younger son sent out to fight with the Duke of Wellington in the Peninsula. Hannibal in the book seemed to me rather like Lord Baden-Powell the Chief Scout, about whom we had been given a talk by the games master. But even this was not enough to put me off Hannibal, or to spoil my image of the general who crossed the Alps and beat the Romans in three great battles . . .

G.A. Henty (was it?) must have written that rather uncomfortably bracing book, published in a sturdy embossed binding of dark green cloth. He wrote many others along the same formula – *With Roberts to Kandahar, With Gordon to Khartoum*. Rome was supposed to be the right role model in those days for schoolboys, so it was enterprising of Henty to produce a young Carthaginian instead.

God, I hate driving! Marching would have been preferable. Winning a battle off the march – said to be the great test of generalship. Our English King Harold drove his army (of veteran professionals, mostly Danes) up Watling Street to York, defeated and killed the Norwegian king Haardrada, marched them back southward in four or five days and was ready to meet Duke William on Senlac hill. Two battles off the march. Maybe a mistake? Harold was an impetuous man. His impetuousness was admired and feared by the Welsh, seasoned guerrillas whom he had routed out from among their hills and valleys. If he had had the time to bring a few good South Welsh mercenary archers to the field of Hastings the result might have been different.

Or suppose Stonewall Jackson had not been killed at Chancellorsville? Better still, if John S. Mosby – a former Virginian lawyer and a genius at guerrilla warfare if ever there was one – had won the ear of Jefferson Davis and the

Southern war leaders? A slave-owning millionaire before the war, Mosby was bankrupt when it ended. But he could have husbanded the troops and run rings around the Northern armies, instead of trying to fight them on their own terms, as Robert E. Lee and the rest of the West-Point-trained Southern commanders tried to do. Mosby was an inspired amateur, well aware that war could be too serious a matter to leave to the professionals.

Here – stop it! Why worry about the problems of these people? It's too ridiculous. But what else am I to do? Othello's occupation's gone.

Poor man. As a general, Othello was so good at his job. But then instead of war he embarked on the campaign of matrimony, to be utterly defeated in his very first engagement. He thought he had occupied his bride, as a legion occupies a campsite or an army a surrendered town. And the enemy turfed him out – first go.

Othello, like Hannibal, was quietly confident of his powers. He knew himself to be a good commander, as he would be a good husband to the woman who loved him. But widowers are not required to be good at anything. No qualifications needed. One can imagine that the counsellors at the job centre are most reassuring. You've lost your job – your caring job – but there's no need to find a new one. Previous experience of joblessness is not necessary. We'd rather you started entirely from scratch. You'll soon get the hang of it. Why not hire a new video every day? Or two at a time? Or try some experimental cooking for one?

And a bit later you could always go on an excursion or a cruise. 'Thank you, but I'd rather be in work.' 'Oh, having nothing to do *is* work, you know. That's what we always tell people,' say the counsellors.

Yes, I suppose it is. But looking after Iris wasn't work. It's now that everything is work. Telephoning is work. Facing people and fending them off is work. Living is work. Hard, nasty work.

Not when Iris was around. The world made sense then.
I believed in it. Iris was faith and belief. And reassurance too.

Everybody nowadays is used to being alone in a car.
Commonest of situations, at least in this country. About
the only place you can be alone.

And I was going to be alone with Margot. For three or
four days, perhaps more. The thought filled me with a panic
which had nothing to do with my fear of the road or the
solitude of the car. Once there had been the four of us. Guy
and me, Margot and Iris. Now two of us were left.

There was something worse than that too. Would I, when
it came to the point, *really even want to go home*? The thought
made me too frightened even to start groaning and cursing
the road, and the car, and Norfolk, and Margot. Of *course* I
would want to go home! Home was my one refuge, the one
place where it seemed natural and proper to be. So what
was the matter with me? I must concentrate on getting
through this new 'Margot solo' experience, emerge from it,
get back to my own lair, my own burrow, where I would
be safe again.

'You do the wine. It should be good. It's something Guy
must have had in the cellar for years and years. Ought to
be drunk up I'm sure.'

I had made a hash of opening the bottle of claret. Its label
was foxed with mould and the cork had come to pieces. No
doubt it would be wonderful stuff, but the thought of my
Chilean red at home, and how much I still enjoyed waiting
for it in the evening, and drinking it, getting up from time
to time to see if there was any improvement in the thriller
on TV – that thought prevented me from having any sense
of Guy's wine. It might be very good; it might be dreadful.
I really didn't know. But I sipped it dutifully.

'All right?' asked Margot, eyeing me with what I felt to
be an unnecessary degree of solicitude.

'Superb,' I said faintly. 'Isn't it?'

'Oh, I wouldn't know,' said Margot in comfortable tones. 'I used to leave it all to Guy. He knew about wine.'

I knew what would have been Iris's reaction, although she would have sounded more warmly and more truly pleased about the wine than I had managed to do. But she had once remarked with a twinkle to an American publisher at the Connaught that good wine was completely wasted on her, and could she please just have quite a *large* amount of their House Red instead. I could imagine the publisher's worried look as he wondered whether the hotel would have such a thing as House Red available at all; and how much face he would lose with the wine waiter by asking.

The claret did indeed seem splendid after a couple of glasses – Margot hardly touched it – and I went on to be warmed and comforted by the rest of the bottle. But dinner was hard going. Short silences which would have passed unnoticed in the old days now seemed to extend themselves painfully. We had always found plenty to say in those old days, and in a sense Margot had plenty now, but what we said seemed to come with a lack of spontaneity, even from Margot herself. We were both looking for new ways of dealing with what should have been a nice old familiar situation.

Margot solved the problem by jumping up and down a lot.

'You've let it get cold,' she told me reproachfully, and she put another large lump of casserole on my plate.

2

Mella and the Mermaid

Safe back, after another nightmare journey, I thought about those days I had spent in Norfolk. It had been less bad than I feared, certainly much less strenuous. Margot had made no attempt to take me church-crawling, and there had been no social life. I was even spared the tiresome old vicar. I pottered about the garden and renewed my acquaintance with Margot's hens, to whom I had been much attached in the past. They were magnificent birds of huge size, with bright red combs, sharp yellow beaks and delicately speckled grey plumage. With the cock making unexpectedly deep and melodious noises from time to time to call his ladies around him, they strolled about on their massive legs, sometimes stopping with one claw raised to look me insolently in the eye. I was drawn to them as much as I had been in the old days when I used to tempt Iris away from her work to come and visit them with me, when we used to present them with bits of stale bread.

Margot had been pleased then by our interest in her giant hens, as well as our interest in the horses, the garden, and the conservatory flowers. But the hens had been our favourites, and I lingered in their enclosure now, partly, it must be said, to avoid Margot. Possibly she intuited this.

'I believe you love Mabel and Tim more than me now,' she said with a laugh, referring to her own favourites.

'Well of course I do,' I replied, trying to strike the necessary note of teasing affection. 'I don't presume to look as high as you.'

Margot made a *moue* but did not look best pleased. Presently she was calling me in for another dish that had to be eaten while it was nice and hot. I had the constant feeling that something more was expected of me. It was a dolorous, wearing, apprehensive feeling, which caused me now – back home as I was – to sigh heavily as I sat in Iris's revolving chair.

Why should more be expected of widowers, and what might this 'more' consist of? Hadn't one lost enough without being expected to make it up in some way, make it up to friends and to other people? It seemed highly unfair. I felt now that I was required to be *more* affectionate, *more* outgoing – more this, more that. As a reward for being allowed to stay at home? It felt like that. Here I was back at home anyway, safe and sound, thank God. I had escaped from them all; and as the thought occurred to me in that form I took a deep breath of satisfaction.

But I was doing it deliberately. Playing the part to please myself. I had to realise that. And all the more deliberately because I saw at that moment, and as it seemed between the flicker of an eyelid, the figure at the end of the passage. It was the same as the one I had seen on the drive over to Norfolk, the one who knew what I wouldn't tell myself. That I didn't *really* want to go home. Or to stay at home.

And at that moment the telephone rang.

Before I had sat down in the chair I had remembered that I ought to switch it off. But it wasn't, for once, an anxious thought. Surely I could safely give it another few minutes. All the more enjoyable when I turned it over, pressed the lever, and knew that no one could bother me. No sound. Just a small red light pulsing away almost invisibly on the dial.

There was no need for me to answer it. No reason. But

at once I knew I would have to do so. All my pleasure in being back at home vanished into a vortex of unspecifiable fears and anxieties. Who was it? What did it want? How soon could I get rid of it? To pick up the receiver and answer the phone became an absolute compulsion. That foreboding figure at the end of the passage – a figure who might have come out of one of those cartoons in the *New Yorker* – seemed to nod in agreement, or approval.

I picked up the receiver and made a vaguely helloish noise.

'It's Mella.'

This was extraordinary. Mella had never rung me before. I had a panicky sensation that either this was Margot checking up on me, or that Mella herself was checking to find whether Margot was present, had been present, or could be about to arrive. A 'spoiling manoeuvre' of some sort, as might be said in army circles. But Mella did not know Margot, had never even heard of her!

Long ago, before Iris was ill, Mella's supervisor in another college asked me if I would take her for a few sessions on the Russian authors. She had a particular interest in them, although they only indirectly connected with the subject of her thesis. I saw her. She seemed a nice person, full of enthusiasm but remarkably ignorant, even, so far as I could see, of the English authors she was supposed to be working on. That was not so unusual, however, in students who were studying for their DPhil.

Mella loved the idea of writers and writing, rather as I like the idea of battles in the past and the generals who fought them. Dostoevsky was for her what Hannibal was for me: a glamorous figure she admired from a distance. On the other hand it is possible to find out a great deal about Dostoevsky or Tolstoy, while only very little will ever be known of Hannibal. Mella preferred to know very little of her hero; and I soon gave up trying to enlarge her knowledge.

But she continued to come and see me. She was easy to get on with. She popped her head round my door every two or three weeks, saying, 'Is this a good moment?' She was good at intuiting moments of vacancy in my college office, when I was quite glad to have a chat. At the time I was getting on for retirement anyway, and had not a great deal to do.

She liked to talk about poems or stories I had recommended, short-winded things, which she read slowly, but with great care. (I soon discovered that her real trouble, like that of a lot of students today, was the inability to read reasonably fast while taking in what was read.) She knew no Russian, but flattered me by wanting to hear bits of Pushkin in the original. She listened to these with shining eyes, and it is true that Pushkin does sound wonderful, even if you are not understanding him. But on the whole Mella preferred to talk rather than to listen, and this always suited me.

Although we were getting to know each other I heard very little about her background. I once expressed a mild interest in her name. Even that she seemed reluctant to say much about. She had been christened Melanie because her mother had loved the film *Gone with the Wind*, but her father preferred Melissa, and so she got the nickname Mella, which stuck. She was reticent, and I never asked her anything. I had always found it better in the long run if one did not know much about pupils.

She had flat, straight hair, obviously self-cut; her face was plain but pleasant, and so was her low voice which had a sort of soft wrinkle in it, sounding vaguely foreign. She had a husband or partner, it was not clear which, with whom she was not at present living, and a child with her, a small boy. He seemed of an independent turn, for his presence in her life did not, by inference, greatly discommode her. It remained uncertain whether he had been sired by the husband or partner, or was the result of some previous connection. I had no idea of her age. She might be in her early thirties; she might be older. I became accustomed to her visits. Indeed we got so used to each other that she often got up from her chair and wandered round my college room, peering at the books and talking in her vague way, sometimes stopping to look down at me in my chair.

When Iris's illness was diagnosed I gave up going into college, and I could not manage any more to see the occasional pupils whom I had been taking in retirement. I had a note of awkward condolence from Mella, offering help. I declined as politely as possible, as I had done to most other people. It was not help that was needed for Iris, but little bits of social amusement; and, perhaps mistakenly, I did not see Mella as being much good in this role. I did not like the idea of Mella coming to the house, and perhaps getting into the habit of dropping in as she used to do in college. She might even have brought her little boy, whom I had never seen and was reluctant to meet. This was bad of me, as poor Iris, in the childhood twilight of Alzheimer's, had become quite interested in children, as if they were equals or even friends.

In fact Mella at this time dropped out of mind. Not altogether out of sight, however. Two or three times a week I used to take Iris down in the car to the college to pick up my mail. It gave us something to do. Iris sat in the car and the gardener often stopped and chatted to her. He was a bachelor who kept pet rabbits. She loved hearing about these, and they got along very well together.

I came back from the lodge one day to find Mella talking to Iris, who had got out of the car. For some reason Iris never escaped on these little trips, as she sometimes did from the house if I forgot to lock the door. So I was not perturbed. She was enjoying her chat with Mella, and Mella herself had an animation, a charm even, which I had never witnessed or suspected before. Her sallow face was rather flushed, and she was lifting her hands as if to demonstrate something to Iris, who was as much absorbed in Mella's presence as a child might be who had found an adult with whom speech could be had on equal terms. I heard Mella say, 'You are a darling, Iris, I am so glad to have met you,' and then she turned quickly to me with a look of slightly guilty apology. I hastened to thank her, as a parent might thank a stranger who had shown kindness to his small son or daughter. Mella stooped awkwardly almost to the ground as if she were addressing a real child, and took Iris's hands. Iris bent down and kissed her, putting both hands against her cheeks. Murmuring something and smiling at me, Mella rose and departed as if on cue, and Iris took a few steps after her.

After this I could not but feel that I should thank Mella and ask her to come and see Iris again. But there was a difficulty. I had no idea of Mella's address or how to get in touch with her. In the past she had simply turned up, and it had never occurred to me to ask how or from where. I might have asked the don who had originally asked me to see Mella, but he had gone off to a job at another university – so long had it been since Mella first started coming to see me.

In any case Iris's condition rapidly worsened about this time, and as Mella did not appear again in the college she dropped once more out of mind. But after Iris's death I started to go back into college, where I found a big elaborate card from Mella expressing the usual sympathy and condolence.

But this card also featured a mermaid by John Waterhouse, done in late Pre-Raphaelite style, with great attention paid to the sea person's white shoulders and bosom and her long auburn hair, which she was combing with a piece of coral. She had a pensive faraway look, and the card, as its small print discreetly informed the purchaser, was delicately scented.

It was an odd choice for a condolence card, and yet I found it obscurely satisfactory, even comforting. The mermaid looked thoughtful, sympathetic, kind and good. She was doubtless Waterhouse's favourite model; and, attractive as she was, probably his mistress too. I hoped he had been in a position to be able to reward her adequately. She looked as if she might well have an impoverished family in the background, the proper maintenance of which was her chief concern. Her tail was wrapped neatly around her, and the artist had taken a lot of trouble to suggest realistically the transition of fish scales, in ascending order of size, to just below her waist. Her pubic scales, as one might call them, led the eye pleasantly into an ample and shapely white stomach, ornamented with a neat human navel.

I propped her on the kitchen table and pondered her with a melancholy pleasure, which seemed in keeping with her own subaqueous mood. How solemnly, but how engagingly too, the later Pre-Raphaelites combined sexual fantasy with a meticulous realism! I didn't particularly want to be reminded of Mella by the mermaid, but I remained intrigued by her choice of card. People, women especially, don't choose such things at random. What was the mermaid's significance in terms of Mella's now inevitably changed relationship to myself? Was she preparing to undergo a sea-change for my sake?

In the mood I then was in I didn't bother to excuse to myself the empty vanity of the conceit. Why shouldn't I, at this wretched moment, indulge myself in any comfort, no matter how puerile, that I could get hold of? I felt that the mermaid, pensively drawing the coral comb through her long tresses, would fully understand.

But at this moment, Mella, it seemed, was determined that I should be reminded of her. While she was alive, even in the grip of Alzheimer's, Iris had protected me, just because she was being looked after by me. A firm bulwark, she had stood between me and the people who wanted to help us. Now that I was alone in the world it was more difficult by far to resist encroachment. Could I be surprised from under the sea, drawn down into those new depths? The mermaid might be more comely, but in a curious way her features had a resemblance to Mella's. Had Mella been aware of that?

Mella and her mermaid. They embodied in themselves the condition of being without Iris. I heard Iris's voice from long, long ago, from the time just after we had become 'cats' to ourselves, in our own happy little mythology, saying 'Wow Wow.' Sometimes, if I was feeling low for some reason, it would have a tender note and become 'Nom Nom.'

Iris's voice spoke to me still, but it could not protect me, even from myself. I longed to escape now from Mella and her mermaid – they were a new and alien life from which I instinctively shrank away – but where was I to escape to?

I picked up Mella's card, and with some difficulty, because it was stiffly and expensively made, tore it across and then across again, into four pieces. I dropped them into the overflowing waste-paper basket. Iris's voice sounded upset but unreproachful, as it sometimes used to do if I had been thoughtless and bad. Mella had kissed her and been good to her. She had not tried too hard, and been unnatural, as most strangers unused to it became when coping with mental invalids. Iris and she had responded to one another with perfect simplicity, as if they had been the two children dancing together in that picture by Breughel of the winter *kermesse*. In fact Mella was more like that child than she was like her mermaid.

'I don't want to pester you,' faltered Mella.

There was such a contrast between the way she spoke now, and her voice and manner a few months before when she had talked to Iris beside the car, that I could not help being touched.

'That's all right,' I said, trying not to sound ungracious, and I made a vague movement as if to invite her through the door. Mella had never been to the house before. I had always been careful to avoid that. 'You said you might call in when you rang me up,' I added uninvitingly.

Mella held a done-up paper parcel in both hands, turning it awkwardly from side to side.

'This is for you,' she said.

She stood looking into the inside of the house over my shoulder. Then she gazed at me with an unnerving mixture of proprietorship and humble appeal, as if she owned me now but still looked up to me from afar.

'Come in.'

Mella shook her head slowly, with an air of knowing far more about what was wrong with me and the situation than I did. She held out the parcel again. It was clumsily wrapped, but there was no clue as to what might be in it. I could hardly thank her for it adequately without knowing what was inside, but I was determined not to start the business of unwrapping it. That would be to ask for trouble. I should never get rid of her.

Mella looked at me expectantly, and then at the parcel. She moistened her lips with her tongue.

I started to say thank you again, but she interrupted me.

'It's awful, isn't it? I know . . .'

I was not going to invite explanation. I felt possessed with resolve at last. The more so as Mella had now taken a step forward, and her foot was through the door in the way that debt-collectors are supposed to behave.

'It's extremely good of you to come,' I said. 'But I'm just going out, and I do have rather a lot to do.'

Mella looked horribly understanding and forgiving. Her look was the same as Margot's had been, when she implied that if her own advice had been taken, and her supervision accepted, Iris would still be alive and well.

'I know,' Mella repeated. 'I've been through . . .' and again she broke off.

To a sensitive and understanding person like myself it

should clearly not be necessary to say what she'd been through: nor did I wait to hear more. I joined her over the threshold and pulled the door firmly shut behind me, so that Mella had to step hastily backwards.

Revenge of a widower. Feeling as nasty as Genghis Khan I walked rapidly to the car, unlocked it, started it up with some difficulty, and prepared to back out of the gate. I waved vaguely towards Mella, and then noticed that she was still holding the parcel, which was now looking even more dishevelled. What was I to do? Stop and take it from her? I couldn't bear the thought. I backed hastily out into the road, narrowly missing a pedestrian on the pavement, waved behind me and drove off.

I took the first turning, drove around at random for a bit, and returned the opposite way round the block.

Mella was still standing outside the house, holding the parcel, waiting patiently for me to return. That was what it looked like. She would wait there for ever to give me what she had brought. I drove on down the road without pausing, peering to the left as if trying to identify a house number. I drove to college and spent a long time going through my condolence mail, which was still arriving. I even answered a couple of letters. It must have been well over an hour before I cautiously re-entered my road from the blind end. Mella was gone.

Instead of relieved I felt woebegone, as if I had been abandoned. On the way back I had worried about that wretched parcel. It made a perfect excuse for Mella to return at any moment, to present it to me all over again. Now I felt that I wanted her to come back, as soon as she liked. I had behaved shabbily. I might at least have asked her in for a cup of tea. But at the thought of getting the tea, and finding a biscuit, and making conversation with Mella at the same time, I was glad I hadn't.

I must cling to my conviction – it seemed more than mere experience – that only home was real. Mella and Margot were like phantoms of harassment, Chinese shadows as the Russians call it, flitting to and fro on a backdrop of speeches that I didn't want to hear, and appearances that intimidated instead of relieving me.

But widowers' convictions seemed as light as lovers' vows. How often had I had this same thought, and clung to it, only to realise with a sinking of the heart that I didn't *want* to be at home: that I didn't *want* to be myself, as myself now was . . .

I locked the little Fiat and walked slowly over to the front door. The parcel was humbly nestled on the doorstep, as though trying to get in. That was a relief. At least I needn't expect the imminent arrival of Mella, come back to deliver her present.

I took the parcel indoors, laid it on the kitchen table, and began to undo it. I felt I must get that over as soon as possible, so as to be ready to thank Mella, on the doorstep and not beyond, the next time she came round. For come she would. I was resigned to that; and something inside me, as I very well knew, was positively looking forward to it. I secretly needed her next visit. The disingenuousness of widowers.

The parcel might look insecure and untidy, but it was a long job to get it open. The outside was held by string; inside was a stout layer of newspaper, stuck down with many lengths of Sellotape. I began to swear under my breath as I tore it; finally I fetched the kitchen scissors and treated the whole thing as Alexander did the Gordian Knot.

There was a plastic bag, and inside that, under more layers of greaseproof paper, was a large round pork pie.

I looked with interest at the pages of newspaper. It was the *Independent* of a few days previously. Just the sort of anxious, caring, well-intentioned paper that Mella would read. That started me thinking gloomily about the days, long ago, with Iris at Steeple Aston, when the *Sunday Times* and *Observer* had been delivered outside the door, early every Sunday morning. I had so much enjoyed bringing them in, and looking at the front and the back pages as I got breakfast. Iris would already be working upstairs, and she seldom bothered to look at the papers, although she liked me to read bits to her in the course of the day, or to tell her if there was anything in them about animals or fish or birds. They were a treat, the Sunday papers of those days, because we never ordered a daily paper. I never got them now, I consciously shunned them, but I missed them all the same.

Having finished reading Mella's newspaper wrapping (there was some rubbish in it about the under-fives needing counselling), I turned my attention to the pie. I was relieved it was not a cake or pastry Mella had made herself. Somehow I knew by instinct that she was no cook. This was a fine pie, bought at a thoroughly superior shop, a large and handsome pie. It must have been expensive.

Why, of all other possible things, practical things, had Mella decided to buy it for me? I was not ungrateful. It looked as if I should really enjoy eating that pie, and eating it over several days. But there was something too that Mella's bizarre present reminded me of. What was it?

Then I remembered. And how could I have forgotten? It was the Great Pie – and this one might have been its twin – which Iris and I had once bought and brought home. It had been laid on the kitchen table, and when I went up to Iris, working in her study (it was a Saturday) and suggested some lunch, we came down full of expectation. A slice of that noble pie, crisp yet moist, jellied and rich but homely in texture, was just what we wanted. Perhaps with half a tomato and a leaf of lettuce.

The pie was not on the table. We must have left it in the plastic bag with the other things we had bought. We must have put it somewhere else: in the fridge, in the cupboard; there were so many other places where we might have put it. We were not unduly perturbed. It would be bound to turn up in a minute or two.

But it didn't. We searched everywhere. We began to get quite cross: with the shop, with the pie, with each other. It must have rolled out of our bag somehow; or the shop man must have taken it back by some sleight of hand, and charged us for it while retaining his pie. We would never go to that shop again, but what shop was it? We had already forgotten. In the heat of our disappointment I even accused Iris of removing the pie herself and beginning to eat it surreptitiously upstairs. To this base charge she very properly made no reply beyond a dignified but forgiving look. But she searched harder than ever, peering on her knees again and again into the same crowded frowsty shelves and cupboards, full of nameless bulging cardboard boxes and old frying pans with greasy interiors. In such places the pie might have lurked undiscovered for ever.

And so it must have done. It was never seen again. And here came Mella, months after Iris's death, bearing an identical pie, offering it humbly as a gift. Iris and I had soon recovered, and 'Gone to Pieland' became a myth and a joke, a mode of exorcising the many things that must be some-where or other in the house, but had never reappeared.

The pie had come back at last. Too late. I felt I should not want to eat it. But I did of course – or started on it – the next day. And very good it was.

Mella had certainly come back into my life. And yet she did not reappear. Perhaps she had received the message that I did not want to be called on at home? It had never struck me before that she had a sensitive soul – rather the contrary. In college, when she had wanted to come and see me, she came. When she wanted me to tell her something, when she wanted to bore me with some idea of her own that she fancied, she came and inflicted herself on me without hesitation. In those days I came to quite like being bored by Mella.

The pie lasted me nearly a week and showed no tendency to disappear. Every time I had a slice I wondered where Mella had got it, and where she was. I couldn't write to thank her; I had no idea of her address. Days passed. Sensations of missingness, even of guilt, did not pass. They increased with the simultaneous emptiness and clutter inside the house. And once again the familiar ghost in my head, of Iris's voice and phrase – 'Woof Woof Nom Nom' – became more frequent, and more clear. Iris seemed glad, too, that the Great Pie had come home at last.

In those days the TV reached rock-bottom. Even in late evening there were no good murders, hauntings, shootings, kidnappings, car chases . . . No horror. Only insipid rubbish about disturbed families, rock stars, inane competitions. I never fell asleep over the supper table now; and if I tried drinking more wine than my usual more-than-adequate amount it began to taste disagreeable.

The fact was that I was now missing Mella. I had behaved badly. I had implied all too clearly that I didn't want to see her, and she had received the message. I began to feel quite sorry that she had.

Mella reappeared one afternoon on the doorstep, just as she had done the previous time. I went to the door hoping it would be her and hoping it would not be. When I saw her I realised that I was not disappointed. I welcomed her in quite warmly and suggested a cup of Nescafé. It was easier than tea.

'Oh, that would be a nuisance. It would be a bore for you, and I know you don't like me to bore you. But as you liked the pie I've brought you another one.'

I could scarcely believe my ears. Even more disconcerting than Mella's calm assumption that I had liked the pie was her comment about boring me, and the knowledge that it showed. I could feel my face going red and I blinked rapidly several times. But I managed to speak.

'How did you know I liked the pie? You're quite right,

I did. But I couldn't write to thank you because I didn't know your address.'

'I'll give it to you some time. I was sure you liked the pie, because I could feel you wanting to write and thank me. I'm telepathic that way,' said Mella with a small laugh that seemed to want to give the impression of shyness and timidity, but failed to do so.

I had a vision of the future in which Mella would wing her way to the house from time to time, like one of Elisha's ravens, a pie in her beak.

'You must let me pay,' I said, in an effort to keep matters on a formal basis. 'Those pies must be very expensive. But I really am grateful. They're so very good.'

'No, they're not cheap,' said Mella with pride, as if she had been buying such pies all her life, 'but I think a man needs something meaty. And so easy. No cooking.'

All this was quite unlike Mella's usual way of going on. It was disquieting too. If a man needed a pork pie he probably needed other things, which Mella, in her new proprietary guise, might feel herself well able to supply. Quaint and even touching as this new persona of hers might be, I was not at all sure I liked it. It was like a threat hanging over my head. There seemed something slightly German about it. I remembered the round rosy face of Hannelore, the girl I had known when I was stationed in Germany after the war. She, too, had been shy but proprietary, impregnably respectable, but also giving the impression that she well knew what men liked. '*Mein Mann*, who needs his pork pie.'

These disquieting thoughts and recollections went through my mind as I filled the kettle and put a spoonful of coffee in a mug. Mella looked hungrily on as if she were itching to perform these offices herself.

'Aren't you going to have a cup?' she said.

I told her, untruthfully, that I had just had one before she came. I felt it wiser to isolate Mella's coffee drinking; it shouldn't seem to be mutual, a family affair.

Entering a friend's house they've never been into, some people look round them with frank curiosity, taking in the decor, appraising the pictures and the furniture. Others, the more diffident or better-mannered majority, seem to take no notice until social relations with host or hostess are well under way. Then interest can be shown and compliments paid.

I was relieved to see that Mella belonged to this second group. I had no interest in the house myself nowadays, and I hardly noticed the state it had got into, but I most certainly did not welcome any brisk and disorienting renovation on the part of a female well-wisher. I had a comforting sense that at least Mella was not one of the sweeping and garnishing brigade.

If anything were to be done to the house it would have to be radical, even revolutionary. A series of new times, as Dryden had put it in his poem, would have to begin.

A revolution? Would it start with one of the two women who now seemed to be playing a major part in my life, and if so which one?

As I watched Mella drinking her Nescafé and beginning to chatter away in something like her old style, I thought of Margot, and what her impact on my domestic scene might be like. For some time now she had been ringing up to say she must come and visit me. Drop by, as she put it. I viewed the threat of her arrival with mixed feelings, as I viewed Mella's unheralded arrivals with pork pies. How long would it be before both women had a foot in my door?

And how would I feel about that? A few weeks before I should undoubtedly have viewed the prospect with unmixed dismay. It went clean against my instinctive wish, now that I was alone, for a quiet, solitary, self-centred life-style, with its own official and acknowledged sadness; and its own private pleasures and routines. Boredoms and anxieties too of course; but at least they would be boredoms and anxieties of my own, to be dealt with in my own way, just as the pleasures and rewards would belong only to me, in my new kind of life.

Like all proposals for a way of living that one deliberately puts to oneself, this one was clearly not going to work just like that. I flattered myself that I saw this clearly. It would include all sorts of regrets and yearnings, as well as the plain misery of deprivation. But social engagements and events, including what I had begun to think of as 'Alzheimering', would merely confirm, however tiresome they might be, the placid rhythm of the life I had in mind for myself. I should not be faced with the nightmare of a helpless unpredictable existence, engineered and orchestrated by forces right outside my own control.

Now that both Margot and Mella looked like having a foot in my door, this quiet, sad, untroubled life seemed more than ever difficult to achieve. When I was young, and the war was going on – and in its earlier stages going very badly – my lugubrious elders often observed that if the politicians had only dealt with Hitler in time, nipped the blasted little fellow in the bud so to speak, we should not have had to fight this war. Self-evident, what? I had neither the knowledge nor the wish at the time to remark that a timid and peace-loving electorate would never have stood for such a daring line of action. Dealing with Hitler would have been like arresting a criminal because he was sure some day to commit a crime.

And well now, was there an analogy here with my position *vis à vis* Margot and Mella? A cold, calculating creature inside me was saying that I must expect a great deal of trouble from both of them, unless I nipped their overtures in the bud, dealt with them as Hitler should have been dealt with, however unlike him the two women might be. Someone else inside me, possibly more un-nasty though equally calculating, was saying: 'We are born to trouble anyway, as the sparks fly upward. Why try to avoid it, in this or any other form? You know quite well,' this part of me went on, 'that you are already finding what should be your tranquil and unoppressive widower's life is in practice a harassed, anxious and melancholy one.

'Think of those dreary Sunday evenings at home,' this inner self remorselessly continued, 'with nothing to distract you from your thoughts and memories; the same memories you used to enjoy so much when you looked after Iris, and that amiable fellow Belial brought them to comfort you every afternoon and early morning. Think above all of the Voice. Do you want to go on hearing it whenever you are low and alone?'

Yes, I knew the Voice. It belonged to a being that was not Iris. It was Memory in person, a creature that lived on human flesh and was sucking dry my blood and bones. So both parts of me agreed, like the men of Munich, to do nothing; to hope for the best while waiting to see what would happen. (No doubt vulgar curiosity played its part, too, in my own lack of decision.)

Nipping Mella and Margot in the bud would in practice have proved a far from simple operation; in fact it would have been a highly complex one. I had cause to realise this the very next morning when the phone, which I had reconnected the previous evening to take a call from America, rang at nine o'clock.

'John, I'm coming over to help you.'

'Oh Margot, not just at the moment if you don't mind. I'm rather busy.'

'That doesn't matter. I won't interfere in the least with what you're doing. But someone has just *got* to deal with the state of that house of yours. It really isn't fit for you to live in.'

'But I like living in it as it is,' I said feebly.

'I daresay you do, but it's not good for you. So let me

at least come and *try* to do something. When's convenient for you?'

This was the challenge direct. I knew it. If I was firm now . . . I had only to say, 'Margot, you are very kind. But kindness, even your kindness, is not what I want just at present. I want, if you don't mind, to be left here on my own.'

If I were to say that, even with yet further softening and modification, the thing would be done. All might yet be well.

Margot had always been blunt and rather clumsy about what she said and how she said it. In her it was an engaging, even an endearing characteristic. Besides, she would not take offence. She was too good a soul for that; and even if I had weakened a refusal still further by adding: 'Do come a little later perhaps, when I'm more settled in myself,' she would have obeyed, she would have bowed to *force majeure*. She would have importuned me no further. She would have said something like, 'Of *course* I understand, darling, I know just how you're feeling. Only keep me in touch, won't you, for when things get better?'

All I had to do was to exhibit the stronger will.

But the will and the telephone, in my experience, do not go together. They make bad and treacherous companions. So no doubt that was why I found myself babbling, 'Oh Margot, do come. How wonderful! I was hoping you'd ring. I've so much been looking forward to seeing you . . . And hearing from you . . .'

'I've brought you a small smoked chicken,' said Margot. 'Iris was so fond of them – do you remember?'

Well, of course I remembered. Iris was tactful. She said how good the smoked chicken was while really preferring, as I knew very well, a piece of cheese, or baked beans with tomato ketchup.

'What was the road like?' I asked.

'Perfectly *dreadful*! As usual.'

Margot's voice was exuberant. She always enjoyed her drive. She would have enjoyed driving to hell with her small smoked chicken if the Devil had been in trouble and requiring her services.

As we ate the chicken, which admittedly was very good, I thought uneasily of Mella's last visit. I devoutly hoped she would not take it into her head to come again while Margot was here. After the arrival of the second pie, for which I had insisted on paying her, there had been no sign of Mella during the last week. As she left on that occasion she said, 'You don't mind my coming to see you, do you? You must tell me if I'm being a bore.' She pronounced the word in an odd manner, a combination of 'Boer' and Russian 'Boyar', and she prolonged it as if it were a word she was particularly proud of.

She did not give me her address. Nor did I ask for it.

I felt touched by Mella's wish not to be a bore, which in fact she never was. Besides, I rather like boring women. They are usually quite restful to listen to, whereas boring men are exhausting, and sometimes demanding as well.

I escorted Mella to the front door, which seemed the best way of seeing her off, though she was always good about not outstaying her welcome. As we reached the door she turned to me, as if impulsively, and put her hands on my shoulders, at the same time kissing me a few times on the face.

This seemed not entirely unpremeditated – perhaps spontaneous gestures rarely are. I was very touched all the same, although the moment was a shade comic as well. It seemed as if Mella was demonstrating her understanding of the male need for tangible female affection; something which the simple creatures might themselves be only partly aware of. They were greedy for it, if only unconsciously, just as they were greedy for pork pies. ('*Mein Mann hat immer Hunger.*') Mella's Germanic persona seemed much in evidence at this moment.

None the less her kindly gesture set alarm bells ringing all over my nervous system. I tried to look pleased but also rather wry and sad, as if my widower's status had quite retired me from the arena of the passions. Or the appetites even.

And what would be Mella's next move? Was she methodically coming closer to me by trenches and parallels, like the besiegers of Uncle Toby in *Tristram Shandy*? As an old soldier, Uncle Toby knew all about that.

Tristram Shandy was not a reassuring precedent. Uncle Toby himself was a bachelor, under siege by the widow Wadman, so our positions were in a sense reversed. I was a widower under siege. I recalled that Sterne's old soldier became resigned to the prospect of his matrimonial fate, but could not help feeling wistful when he thought of the pleasure of lying diagonally across the bed, a position he would have to renounce when united with his bride. And it struck me that I, too, was getting quite fond of the experience of having a whole bed to myself with plenty of room to wander about and find a cool patch if one side became too warm.

Now alarm bells of all sorts were certainly ringing. There came back to my mind a comic postcard, which a facetious colleague sent me shortly after I became a professor. A mild little zoologist is examining bugs with a magnifying glass somewhere in the jungle, with his female assistant ready to write down his findings in her notebook. An enormous and very cheerful-looking monkey hangs above her from a tree and places his huge paws over her well-developed bosom, while she, her eyes on the page and unaware of what is going on, remarks good-naturedly, 'Now now, Professor – no monkey business!'

Monkey business of any sort was certainly absent from my life at the moment.

Life none the less seemed to be becoming more and more unpredictable and uncontrollable, and just in those places where it should have been simple, even agreeable, to forecast and to arrange. As Mella went away I made some gesture of farewell, and she returned the wave. I recalled with some relief that she had again said she would give me her address, but that she had forgotten to do so. Unless the forgetting was intentional.

With an effort I brought back my attention to what Margot was saying as she munched the chicken leg held between her fingers. I would have to start thinking now about how best to entertain her during her stay. To my relief she had already said she had to leave on Friday. That meant three clear days. Looking round her with a large gesture while she drank some white wine soon after her arrival, she had announced her intention of setting about the house and making it look a *bit* better anyway. I decided I must postpone this operational plan of hers as long as I could.

As part of the postponing process I suggested after lunch that we might go and look at some of the colleges. She hadn't really seen very much of Oxford, had she? But Margot saw through that at once. It was all very well for her to drive Iris and me, as she used to do, over half of East Anglia to view the magnificent old churches. When it came to sightseeing as a guest Margot's enthusiasm seemed to have quite vanished. No, no, she would start on the house at once.

But she didn't. That was something anyway. She sat and chatted; she strolled in the garden; she spent a long time upstairs in the tiny spare room unpacking her belongings. By then it was time for an early tea, after which I suggested a little walk to Wolfson College to visit the garden and the bridge over the Cherwell. To this Margot agreed, with some appearance of pleasure, and when we came back it was time for drinks. So the day ended, quite pleasantly and without undue trouble.

Lying in bed and still sleepless I considered its events. It was the first time since Iris died that a female guest had stayed in the house, and that was vaguely disquieting; although it was quite normal, after all, and Margot had seemed to take her occupation of the spare room entirely for granted.

There was really no need to feel threatened and disquieted. No doubt widowers' weakness, as it might be called, was a well-known phenomenon in circles which widowers – and perhaps widows too – frequented. The widowers imagined, poor creatures, that women were always running after them. They misunderstood the kindness women bestowed on them in their trouble. They became inordinately vain, as if with an occupational disease. Pathetic really.

I was reassured, as I lay, still sleepless, by the growing conviction that there was really no more to it than that. Mella like Margot, Margot like Mella: the pair of them only wanted to be helpful . . .

And yet at the back of my mind I couldn't help feeling that there was something helpless about their own behaviour, as if they were dismasted ships in a gale, drifting on to a lee shore. Was that too just vanity? There was certainly no evidence for the impression, beyond the sense that we all three wanted something, and that we were none of us sure what it was, or how to get it if we had been.

But naturally we all wanted something! People always did. I thought that I wanted peace and quiet. But that, too, was probably an illusion. As for what the pair themselves wanted, ever since Iris became ill other people, their motives and tastes and wishes, had become a mystery, at once complex and dull, which I had neither time nor patience to try to understand.

I ought to do better now. At least I ought to try. But I lacked any urge to start. For one thing desire, sexual desire, seemed so far away now that I could barely remember what it was like, or how terribly worthwhile and important it had once been. Even when it had only taken the form and the fulfilment of fantasy.

By evening I was feeling the strain of the day. I assembled our supper of tinned spaghetti and tinned spinach, with kipper fillets as a preliminary, and hoped that Margot would not find it too unworthy of her. Iris and I used once to love spaghetti; I made it often, but I had lost the heart to make it now. The art too perhaps.

I had put Margot in the drawing-room with a drink, but of course she kept coming in and asking whether she could do anything; looking all too critically interested, as it seemed to me, in the preparations that were going on. I thought longingly of the happy days – well, the happy if sometimes rather exhausting days – when we had been part of a well-balanced quartet, Guy and Iris absorbing and tempering the impact of Margot's personality upon the group as a whole.

Margot didn't cook in those days. She had an old retainer who had been with her for years, even before she married Guy. Ethel had been taken on by Margot's family as a Barnardo orphan of fifteen or so; and when the parents died and Ethel had been up for sale, as it were, between the three daughters of the family, there had been keen competition to retain and secure her by then invaluable services. Ethel had firmly announced her intention of 'going with Miss Margot', the youngest of the family and at the time a drama student living in Chelsea. Margot was, however, already engaged to Guy, so she was able to bear Ethel off in triumph to her new married home. Ethel stuck firmly to Margot for the rest of her life, never showing any disposition to marry or have children of her own. When she died she was greatly missed by Margot and Guy and their children, and indeed by Iris and me too.

I had sat Margot down on a reasonably clean chair in the drawing-room and got her a Bell's whisky with some tapwater. Naturally I remembered the drink she had always had in the old days. Equally naturally I gave careful thought to our supper, but I doubted that Margot would think much of it, although she would affect to be fascinated by its novelty. Clearly I could not match the shepherd's pie or the steak-and-kidney pudding that Ethel used to make, nor had I anything for afterwards to rival her rice pudding or her treacle tart – a particular favourite of Iris's.

After Ethel died Margot made no attempt to find another 'treasure'; nor did she try to do much cooking herself. But she was the kind of masterful and magnetic woman who has no trouble in getting things done for her and finding people to do them. Persons of both sexes rushed to make cakes and pâté for her, put the car to rights, prune the rose bushes. She had the knack of combining authority with mateyness in just the right proportions.

Even before Guy died Margot barely bothered with cooking. When we were there she sometimes made pasta which was short on cheese, to say nothing of garlic and olive oil. And yet the myth persisted among all her friends that Margot was a wonderful cook. She was careful not to dispel this myth by giving a dinner party. After Guy died she gave up entirely and lived as we did on odds and ends. The casserole she made for me on my first evening in Norfolk was a one-off display of welcome.

Dinner tonight was not too unsuccessful, and afterwards we watched television, to which Margot, strangely enough, was wholly unaccustomed. Although the mildest of men, Guy had always declined with some acerbity to have one in the house, and it may have shown how much she missed him that Margot had neither the heart nor the will to get one after he died.

The channels were all equally wretched that evening, and Margot watched with a kind of sorrowful and incredulous attention, as if barely able to believe that such nonsense was possible in the last year of the millennium.

I did not sleep well – nothing unusual in that these days – and I was glad when morning came, though I now had to wrestle with the problems of Margot's breakfast. Would she want it upstairs, in bed? Formerly I used to assemble toast and honey and her pot of Lapsang, and either Iris or I would take it up to her. But Margot solved the problem by appearing herself only a few minutes after eight, and bustling about the kitchen, demanding where things were kept.

This threw my morning into a state of confusion from which it barely recovered. Immediately after breakfast Margot demanded the whereabouts of the Hoover. I could not remember myself, but it must be somewhere among the confusion of macintoshes, plastic bags and cardboard boxes which filled the cubbyhole under the stairs. I unearthed it eventually and Margot eyed it with disfavour. But when I got it going she seized it at once and pushed it vigorously over the floor, exclaiming unnecessarily about the terrible state the carpets were in, and requesting me to get out of the way as I followed her about.

Quite soon the machine was in grave difficulties, like an old person called upon to perform a feat far beyond his physical strength. It still roared away impotently but it was obvious that it was not doing its job. I switched it gratefully off and Margot advised me to have it seen to properly or, better still, to buy a new one. After that she seemed to lose interest in the state of the house, for which I was equally grateful.

At my suggestion we went out to lunch. After the Hoover debacle it was easy to persuade Margot; and afterwards she showed a surprising and rather touching interest in the local shopping facilities. I was now beginning to feel more at home with her in my role as a comparatively new widower. She seemed so happily oblivious of whatever anxieties and worries I might be feeling about the problem of entertaining her. She was wonderfully unworried and serene, as if she had no sense of what any other person might be thinking and feeling. How restful her husband must have found this trait! And now I, as widower, was getting the benefit of it from his widow!

How restful it would be for me to be with her, once I had grasped this new and elementary point, which had never occurred to me when Iris was alive and we had visited Margot, or been visited by her. Now I realised that she simply didn't notice me, or pay me attention.

Margot's three-day stay went really very well. In any case, any change from the Norfolk house, which would, I realised, feel large and lonely now, must in the nature of things be some sort of relief. What we chiefly did together, without speaking of it, was to organise getting through the day; I had been long enough in the business to know that this simple fact was what mattered most. I was bound to feel a secret comradeship with Margot, just in this matter of passing the time.

To my relief she did not attempt, after that first encounter with the Hoover, to come to grips with the house-cleaning problem. After the first morning she seemed to accept its original state as naturally as I did myself. On the last night we both drank a lot of my red Bulgarian and sat chatting in the kitchen until it was quite late. We went comfortably to bed, and for once nowadays I soon fell asleep.

I woke abruptly, feeling unaccountably displaced. The night was very black, and it felt cold too, so that my impulse was to burrow closer down under the duvet. Something seemed to be there, a large presence in movement; and then a voice close to my ear whispered not to worry: go to sleep.

Sleep was the last thing that seemed possible at such a moment. A bulky form nudged me tentatively, and then settled down against me like a piece of soft cargo released by the derrick and bedding down into its position in a ship's hold. I had just begun to grasp what was going on when Margot gave a heave, and her voice started whispering again in my ear.

'Don't mind my being here, Johnny. I couldn't sleep for some reason, and I thought this might be comforting for both of us. Sleep is the thing now, I feel, don't you?'

I did. But how was it to be arrived at in the present circumstances? I was overwhelmed by conflicting sensations, the main one, I'm sorry to say, being regret that our relations, which seemed to have settled down in such a comfortable way, would now be fatally disturbed. I felt touched by what Margot had said about this being comforting for both of us – she must miss Guy's presence in the bed in the same animal way that I missed Iris's – but just at the moment it was not easy to agree with her. Also I did not care for being called Johnny, although Margot had sometimes called me that affectionately in the past, when the four of us had been together.

Thinking all these things simultaneously I remained as immobile as a spider trapped in an empty bath and uncertain in which direction to run. Margot's ample presence, now that she had settled down, was indeed comfortable rather than the reverse, but not exactly comforting. It had been restful to be with her during the last three days, because she had seemed contented herself, and unaware of me. She continued to whisper in my ear, her voice husky and penetrating; and from what she said, it seemed she had been very far from unaware. She had been thinking about me in relation to herself. And why not, after all?

She was saying now how wonderful the last three days had been; how we must spend more and more – much more – time together. We were both lonely people now, weren't we? We could do so much to help each other. I could do so much to help her; and she hoped, she did hope, that I would let her do the same for me. She knew she could.

All this was so unlike what had seemed our happy obliviousness of each other (for Margot's of me had soon produced a corresponding ability in myself to take her for granted) that I could only reflect despondently on the transformation that seemed to have overtaken us. Margot seemed all too conscious of me now as a body to clutch and a mind to be reconnoitred and invaded. From her, as she now was, I could only want to escape: and this was hardly practicable when it was three in the morning and we were lying in bed together.

There was an even more urgent problem to be considered. Would Margot later on expect me to – well, *do* anything? In fact to make love to her? Lying comfortably against me as she was, and continuing to whisper into my ear, made any such expectancy on her part seem, for some reason, less likely. The question could at least be postponed. And gradually I became aware that the whispering sounds – to which I had hardly been attending, so absorbed was I in my own mental activity – had been replaced by regular breathing, with an occasional mild snore.

What a relief that was! I could only admire her quite passionately for being able to go calmly off to sleep in such tricky circumstances. Or perhaps they were tricky only for me? Perhaps my comfortable relation with Margot could be resumed tomorrow without as much difficulty as I had feared.

I must have been soon asleep myself. And we slept late. I opened my eyes to see I was looking through Margot's hair, with which my face was lavishly entwined. In the daytime Margot's hair was wound up in an artfully copious bundle on top of her head. This must be why I had never noticed it before.

Spread out now on the pillow it presented an arresting spectacle. Most of it was more or less black, some of it dead white, the two shades not combining but contrasting in separate strands and locks.

Margot at this moment gave a little groan and turned her head. The hair on the pillow followed it in a slightly unnerving manner.

'I was just admiring your hair,' I hastened to say, to gain time.

Very adroitly, considering that she was half asleep, Margot seemed to take the hint, and what it implied. In these highly unusual circumstances I was asking for help. I wanted to be given a lead.

'I can't bear dyed hair,' she said. 'Of course it's going white hand over fist, but that's better than having it purple or something.'

I was glad to see that she was wearing a serviceable flannel nightdress, dark blue in colour.

The cue that Margot had so promptly followed had, I now realised, been what she was going to do anyway: that is to say, to be exactly as she had been for the last three days. She got up and went off to the bathroom, and at breakfast-time we were just as easy together as we had been before the night, about which nothing was said.

I had a feeling about her which was new to me, and which in its own way was very cheering, although I don't know why I should have had such a feeling at this point. Margot, I felt, had lots of things going on, people she saw and the problems of such people, with which she helped them cope.

Even a lover maybe? I was one among others. It was hard to say why this realisation should have come to me at the moment it did, but so it was. What had happened in the night had not been so important after all. Margot had only wanted to be kind.

3

Comédie Française

There is nothing like the departure of a guest after a successful visit for making a widower feel happy and tranquil
when left on his own at home. The morning stretched before
me, lazy and angelical. I would sit about for a while, look
at a book, stroll into the garden (it was a balmy sunlit
morning), walk out to the shops, choose my own time
to have a leisurely lunch with a certain amount to drink.
Perhaps a short nap to follow, for sleep last night had been
rather patchy, to say the least . . . A calm tranquil day. A
real widower's day. I contemplated it with satisfaction.

The doorbell rang.

Probably the postman or a special delivery. Tiresome, but
not threatening. I went to the front door.

When Mella saw my face her mouth seemed to turn down
at the corners. Seeing this I readjusted it – my face – and
wondered what line to take; while the delectable, quiet day
I had looked forward to receded like a mirage.

'Isn't this a good moment?' asked Mella anxiously.

If I said no, she would go away, and I would feel unhappy
about it, and the day would be spoilt anyway.

'Of course it is. Come in.'

As if she had been waiting for this invitation to perform
a small but necessary duty Mella made an awkward little
swoop forward to give me a kiss on the cheek. Her right to
do this seemed to have been established by that 'spontaneous'

gesture of affection that she had bestowed on me when we said goodbye last time.

Unable to contemplate the pleasant day I had planned I now contemplated Mella, with rather more objective interest than I had done before. It was something to do with my recent experience of Margot; perhaps, oddly enough, of our having been in bed together.

Shapeless and yet slight, with her sallow skin and straight mouse-coloured hair, Mella always had the air of having been blown to my door like an autumn leaf, rather than by conscious volition. Her appearance was in complete contrast with that of Margot – dark, ample, dynamic – and yet there was a kind of resemblance between them. Both had an uncertainty about them, however little it might be apparent in Margot's case. Both could bother me by their air of looking for something, and not being sure what it was, or how to set about getting it. And both, of course, had a great deal in their lives that I knew nothing about, and wanted to know nothing about. Hadn't I had that very feeling this morning with Margot? And Mella, of course, had her little boy, and other attachments too: a husband or partner, boyfriend, whatever you called them.

And I? Didn't I have attachments? Well no, I didn't, not any longer. And that was the problem, or the danger. I was the vacuum they seemed to be drawn into, however occupied with other matters they might be. I was the lee shore on to which they might be drifting.

Mella was looking at me rather anxiously. I had probably been staring at her without seeing her for quite a little while. I hastened to offer her usual Nescafé and chocolate digestive biscuit.

'Oh, you darling,' said Mella, rather unnecessarily I thought, and she kissed me as if formally on both cheeks.

I was amused by the kiss, and pleased and touched too. I knew that Mella was conscientiously copying what people did nowadays in ordinary social situations, among friends.

The habit wasn't by any means universal. And yet Mella intuited that this was what I did with other people, other friends, and so she wanted to do it to me too. Yet there seemed to be something unnatural about her this morning, which made me feel uneasy in my turn.

Questing about as she often did nowadays, Mella was now well into the main confusion of the house. But then I saw her stop like a bloodhound, stiffen and look about her as if she had scented the presence and the activities of someone else. Another woman? Such a possibility had never occurred to me. Margot after all had done virtually nothing to change the look of the house. Once the Hoover gave up she had abandoned it all to its state of original sin; and I was grateful that she had.

None the less Mella had sensed something from the moment she came in; and it seemed to be the scent of a threat – the subtle atmosphere of another woman's proprietorship. Was this why she had kissed me? As if to make her own formal claim?

Wasn't that really a bit absurd? Surely women nowadays did not feel automatic jealousy about other women who had strayed unknowingly into their territory? It must be just masculine conceit to suppose so. Besides, why should my house be in any sense Mella's own territory? None the less I had the uneasy feeling that this was the way in which Mella was beginning to think of it.

Without a word, after she had finished her coffee, she started to clean the kitchen windows, using some old bits of newspaper dampened in the sink. I remonstrated in vain. I weakened then, and offered her various cloths I found in the kitchen cupboard, but she told me her mother had always used an old newspaper, saying it was the best way to get a window-pane clean. I promptly asked about her mother, not because I wanted to know, but to try to stop her. She blocked that off by asking for a bucket, and things now began to move as if with their own terrifying impetus. Stalking about like an automaton Mella finished the kitchen windows and started on the ones in the drawing-room.

'Why are you doing this?' I asked her in despair, adding, 'I shall have to go out soon. I really must.'

Mella was on her knees by this time, doing something to the floor. Her meagre behind, clad in orthodox student jeans, not very clean ones, stuck out as she pushed her cloths to the full reach of her now bare arms. She had asked me for a mop, and although I told her there wasn't one so far as I knew, she had made an exhaustive search of the house and the cupboards.

'I'll bring one next time,' she said.

By now I was in a daze. How was I to get rid of her? I remembered the time she had brought the first pie, and I had got her out of the house, and she had remained standing patiently by the door, where I found the pie when I came home.

This was a far, far more serious situation. The grim determination with which she was now working seemed to make any form of intervention impossible. I hesitated.

'You go on out,' said Mella, without looking up from the floor.

'But what about you?'

'Oh, I'll just finish up and then let myself out. Don't worry.'

This was a new Mella, one I had never seen before. The sight of her, and all those grimly vigorous movements, gave me a qualm of apprehension. What on earth had happened?

'Well, if you're sure you'll be all right,' I said feebly.

I was giving in to her in the most abject fashion, and I still could not think how it had happened, and why. My one wish now was to get away. To get away from my own house! Suppose she refused to move out when I got back? What would I do then? And what about her little boy, and the girlfriend with whom she seemed to be more or less living? Alison? Angela? Some such name. Mella had told me once.

There was a vigorous, almost violent flopping and sopping sound of wet cloths. Feeling now slightly light-headed, I fled out of the room and got to the front door. There I paused. I still could not make my mind up what to do. That happy anticipation of the day which I had had after Margot left – how many hours and ages ago? – crossed my mind like his past life before the eyes of a drowning man. I had actually shut my eyes, I found. Opening them again I saw Margot's driving gloves, lying in the most conspicuous position possible, on the little ledge by the front door. She had forgotten them.

They were a very elegant pair. Her driving gloves were one of Margot's few affectations. She always wore them, as if they were the outward and visible sign of the good driver she undoubtedly was. They were of black stringlike material, with black leather palms pierced with holes as if for better grip or aeration or something. They looked extremely expensive.

I remembered that we had stood chatting by the front door, and had continued to chat as we walked to the car with me carrying her bag. And they must be almost the first thing Mella had seen as she entered the house. No wonder she had looked round the kitchen in that questing perturbed way, as if she had been almost frightened of finding something more. She had certainly seen those gloves.

While she was here, Margot had two or three enormously long telephone conversations with friends or relations. She apologised for the length of these, and the expense. She even offered to pay for them, an offer which I, of course, dismissed with the usual rather exaggerated emphasis. (Suppose instead of 'Of course not – wouldn't hear of such a thing!' one were to say 'Very well. I calculate you were on the phone for an hour and a half, which would come to about eleven quid – we'll say ten. Give me a cheque if it's more convenient . . .') During one of these conversations I overheard Margot saying, 'Darling, Johnny's house is like those Augean Stables. I'll really have to do something about it.' Then she laughed heartily at something said the other end.

'You know what George said?' she told me afterwards. 'I'm afraid I told him, darling, that your house was worse than the Augean Stables and I should have to do something about it. So he said: "I suppose you had better imitate Hercules, Margot, and divert the river Cherwell through it!" He can be quite witty, old George.'

I had not met old George, whoever he was, nor did I wish to. I felt some resentment against Margot for discussing my house with him in these familiar terms. Margot often surprised me with remarks and references which seemed deliberately designed to show the wide circle of her knowledge and acquaintance.

Well, Margot had not carried out her promise, or threat. She had not done something about it. She had left the Augean Stables to Mella.

I came home at last to find Mella gone. In a cowardly way I had postponed my return to late evening. I had wandered about the town: I had even thought of going to the cinema – something I had not done for years. When I came back I left the car some distance off and approached the house as if casually, but with great caution. All was quiet. It was now twilight, but no lights were on inside. What would I have done if they had been? I could hardly bring myself to think of the horrifying implications, but there passed through my mind the vision of Mella preparing supper, while her little boy sat in a chair turning the pages of a book . . . It might have been one of my picture books, my aeroplane books, as Iris used to call them. I had no idea how old the child was; was he of an age to read? He was probably of an age to poke about and find what he wanted, even in the Augean Stables. I determined on the spot that I would never find out. About him or about anything else in Mella's life.

Heartened by this resolve, though I had no idea how I was going to implement it, I turned my Yale key in the lock. I stood still and sniffed the air. Margot's gloves were still on the ledge where they had been. The house seemed almost unnaturally quiet. Usually I left the wireless slightly on when I left home, and it welcomed me on my return. I turned the lights on and tiptoed towards the kitchen.

Everything looked different. There was a smell of something – could it be furniture polish? I hadn't known I had any.

In the electric light the whole house was strange and staring, like a cat's fur stroked the wrong way. I saw a piece of paper on the corner of the kitchen table, which had otherwise been stripped bare of books, papers, envelopes, breadcrumbs, ballpoints, old letters and picture postcards, including my mermaid. Then I remembered that I had torn the poor mermaid up. Had Mella noticed her absence?

Where had Mella put all these things? Apart from the note the table was ferociously empty.

So was the floor, I noticed. I seized the piece of paper, which was just a scrap torn off something. What would Mella say? 'Now that things are a bit cleaner I'll move in tomorrow. Yours, Mella.' But the note was in the form of a list. It puzzled me for a moment.

Ajax Fairy liquid mop wringing bucket dusters stiff brush.

It was Mella's shopping list. Things she needed for the house – my house. She must have forgotten to take it when she went away. And she might be back at any moment. I looked around me with a hunted feeling. At least she had no key. And she had her little boy to look after. She could hardly be back until tomorrow morning. But tomorrow morning she almost certainly would be back.

And so she was. I awaited her arrival in a fatalistic mood. At first I hardly knew she was there, because there was only a very faint scratching and tapping at the front door. The electric bell had been getting weaker for some reason, and now it hardly functioned at all. I had put a note outside the door for the postman and deliveries saying 'Please knock very hard – bell very weak' – but Mella was too tentative to obey this injunction.

And yet she came in briskly enough. I at once dreaded that briskness; I knew what it portended. She was carrying a large plastic bag, from which the stiff brush protruded. She had not forgotten any of the items she had written on that list. The mop was there too.

'I must pay you for these,' I said faintly.

'If you like,' returned Mella, without interest; and she began at once on a floor that had not yet been 'done'.

I retreated into the front room, although I knew it would be only a temporary refuge. Mella had obviously been in here the day before, because efforts had been made to clear the floor and the top of the big Victorian desk which had once belonged to J.R.R. Tolkien, creator of *The Lord of the Rings*, at which Iris used to write her letters. It had been heaped up with books and papers of every description, lying there undisturbed for the last five years, since Iris had ceased to use it. She had no longer been able to manage any letter-writing. After her death I found innumerable sheets of paper which began 'Dear' or 'Darling', and got no further.

Mella had managed to find other homes for the books by piling them on top of the shelves, and she had arranged the mass of papers in orderly piles. An item at the top of one caught my eye. It was a number of white cards, which Mella had put neatly together. Each card had a Christian name written on it in Iris's firm, bold hand – John, Janet, Eric, Joanna, Angie . . . They were Iris's *'placement'* cards.

In the old days, when we had a dinner party, Iris used to write each guest's name on a card and put it by their allotted place at the table. She took it seriously too, spending a lot of time working out the variations in the way guests could be deployed. She did this with calm concentration, while I was getting agitated over the stove or furiously chopping lettuce and tomatoes to make some sort of salad. It may have struck guests as incongruous that while the cutlery and plates were not exactly clean, and their wine glasses had a rather smeary appearance, so much loving care had none the less been exercised over their positions at the table, and the cards that directed them to it.

If there was a difficult guest present, Iris would always take that guest on herself, refusing to admit to me beforehand that any problem existed. Nor did it, thanks to her. Dinner parties always went well, certainly not by reason of the cooking, nor from the virtues of the wine, although there was always plenty of the stuff on the table. Seeming to negate the traditional concept of an accomplished hostess, Iris took care of the guests in her own way, making them relaxed and the evening a success.

When I saw the cards I felt suddenly angry that Mella had found them and stacked them up tidily like that. She had no business to do it! The feeling of a threat from her made me feel cross instead of just intimidated. I would speak sharply to her, tell her to leave things alone. What a nerve the girl had! Coming here and taking up the business of house-cleaning for me without being asked! I even found myself clenching my fists. If this went on I would have to show her what was what. *If* it went on? I would stop it at once! I would go back into the kitchen and tell her thank you very much but you can go now, and if you don't mind I don't want to see you again for the present.

For the present? Who was I kidding? The thought of a Mella-less future suddenly seemed curiously bleak. To that extend had she somehow climbed inside my life, my life as a widower. It put me in quite a panic to realise it.

But panic dulled into a sort of resignation, even apathy. I started idly to turn over the old cards – pretty grubby most of them – which Mella had stacked up. Those old dinner parties, before Iris became ill, seemed very far away. I remembered the animation and the pleasant intimacy of *tête-à-têtes*, eating bits of cheese, smoking Gauloises, drinking too much wine. How long ago it all seemed.

I was abruptly tugged from my reveries by a name on one of the cards. Margot! I looked for Guy but his name was not there. Had Iris taken the card away when Guy died? It seemed unlikely, but she might have done. Margot had come to us more often after that. Her name was still there.

Another thought – Mella had probably seen it? But it couldn't have meant anything to her? No possible reason to connect it with the driving gloves beside the front door. Mella couldn't possibly have started feeling jealous of all the female names she had found on the cards.

Then I remembered something else. The last letter I had got from Margot must have been lying on the kitchen table, amongst all the rest of the junk. Had Mella seen that, and read it? It was, so far as I could recall, a jolly, affectionate sort of letter, with nothing specifically embarrassing about it. To a stranger it could mean much or little. But it certainly mentioned that she was coming, and when.

Was that why Mella had appeared yesterday, and had seemed so conscious of another female presence in the house?

I became aware at this point that the sounds of banging and brushing, which had been so audible in the background, had now ceased. How still it was in this part of the house. I had noticed it before. It seemed even stiller now. I stood motionless, as alert as a hunted animal. I noticed I was still holding Iris's *placement* card, with 'Margot' on it, in my hand, and hastily put it back in the pile.

Then I called out, 'Mella, don't do too much, will you!' in what I hoped were placatory tones.

There was no reply. Could she have gone? Impossible, I would have heard her going. Besides, I realised, I didn't want her to go. I should have felt worried and unhappy, and there would have been a void, with nothing to do. I stole to the kitchen door and peered round it. Mella was sitting on a chair, with her hands hanging down on either side. Her eyes were closed. Her face was extremely pale.

Good heavens! Had the girl had a heart attack or a fit? Through my mind went the memorable words of Lady Macbeth when the news of Duncan's murder, which of course she knows all about, is brought. She makes the most unsuitable exclamation possible in the circumstances, but a very natural one. *'Woe, alas! What, in our house?'*

No, not in my house! Mella could not be allowed to have a heart attack here! Besides, the girl was far too young for one. It was much more likely to happen to me.

To me – in my house? I put aside the thought. But Mella had no right to be ill here! My indignation was absurd, but it was as natural as Lady Macbeth's exclamation (to which Macduff makes the dry rejoinder: 'Too cruel anywhere').

Mella must have heard me. She opened her eyes and stood up, quite briskly.

'Are you all right, Mella?' I said, as solicitously as I could manage.

'Of course I'm all right.' Mella spoke in her new 'positive' voice, with a strong hint of impatience in it.

'But what happened?'

'Nothing happened. I sometimes feel a bit faint, that's all. It passes quite quickly. I've done it since I was a child. It's nothing, really.'

'But can I bring you anything? A glass of water? Milk, or something?'

'No, no, I'm quite all right. What I'll do is just lie down a little. D'you mind if I go upstairs?'

I suspected that Mella knew all about upstairs. She'd had plenty of time to find out yesterday.

'Of course not.'

'I can find my way, I'll be better quite soon, I promise.'

She promised. I felt rather touched by that, and by the way she said it. And I'd thought I'd never be touched or interested by anything that Mella said or did. Well, now she had 'promised' and had proved me wrong.

I wondered what to do. The bed which Margot and I had slept in had been untouched after we got up. I wondered if she'd remembered to take her night-dress away or if she'd forgotten it, like the gloves. Margot had always had a habit of leaving things behind.

Parts of the floor were still wet from Mella's ministrations. There was a bucket of water on the floor, and the new mop was propped against the fridge. When Mella had arrived this morning with her plastic bag of cleaning substances, she had been carrying the mop like a spear.

I went quietly up the stairs. They, too, had been brushed and cleaned, I noticed. I supposed, not very hopefully, that Mella might be lying down in the little spare room where Margot had slept, at least where she had slept for most of the time. That too would bear ample traces of her occupation. A good thing if it did.

On my bed – our bed? *My* bed – Mella was lying flat on her back, her arms spread out as they had been in the chair downstairs. Her eyes were again closed and I could see no sign of breathing. I approached the bed, fascinated.

Mella sprang up, threw her arms round my neck and gave me several kisses at random. She continued to hug me, and

I did my best to detach myself. She pulled me down beside her on the bed.

At least we were both fully clothed.

A couple of hours later we were not. Quite how this had come about was still uncertain to me.

After what had seemed a suitable lapse of time I had got up from beside Mella, asking how she felt now and making some remark, pleasant I hoped, about our having something to eat. Mella, after all, had never eaten in the house before. I had a vague hope that if she partook of bread and salt, as it were, in the way that Margot had, she might be propitiated, and feel herself to be on more or less even terms with that as yet unknown female presence.

But that was not how things turned out. Mella had jumped up when I moved and detained me by force. She was extremely strong, too. Suddenly she released me and said, 'I'm going to the bathroom. I won't be a minute.'

It was an extremely long minute. It was more like twenty minutes. I contemplated getting out of the house, or at least out of the bedroom. It was ridiculous to have been manhandled as I had been by a slip of a girl like Mella. But there, I was an old gentleman who had never been particularly strong at the best of times. None the less, I felt determined now, come what might, to stand my ground and stick up to Mella. Just like the hero of an old-fashioned school story, except that Mella, the school bully as it were, happened to be a girl. It would be a poor show, unsporting too, to run away. I would stand my ground, as much out of defiance of Mella, even resentment of her, as out of acquiescence in what she presumably had in mind.

She came back eventually, and of course she came back with nothing on. Her body was scrawny and unattractive, and it was somehow not a very nice colour either – no pink or white about it. But once more I felt touched, as when she had said in her suddenly shy confiding way, 'I promise'. There was a kind of mystery about her too, as she came, timidly now, across the room. I suppose there is about all women who unexpectedly appear naked, although there was nothing exactly unexpected about Mella's absence of clothes. She had, in a sense, given me plenty of warning.

She came up and kissed me, and then got straight into bed and pulled the duvet up over her head. It was obvious what I had to do, nor, on the whole, did I mind doing it. It was handing the situation over to Mella of course, rather as an admiral in the days of sail used sometimes to allow his opponent 'the weather gauge' in order to gain some other advantage than having the wind in his favour. I forget what the advantages were in the admiral's case, but in mine they seemed clear enough. If my relations with Mella were on this footing she would cease to persecute me with mops and brushes. Honour would be satisfied, and the house-cleaning need go no further. It seemed a crude bargain, but that was the way I saw it.

I thought about Iris. She did not seem so very far off now; not so far off as the dinner parties of those distant days. And she seemed to be smiling at me in her old way. I could almost hear her saying our old private recognition sign. 'Nom Nom.' And I loved hearing her say it. I felt she was agreeing that I had made the correct move.

The day was not yet over – far from it. I was feeling extremely hungry, and with a sudden movement I got out of bed before Mella could stop me. If, indeed, she had had a mind to do so.

It has often struck me that the worst thing about love is the business of getting dressed and undressed. Undressing had been quite easy because Mella's head had been well under the duvet, and her eyes presumably closed. But putting on my odd assortment of raggedy vests, my socks and my support stocking, under Mella's calm and – it has to be said – now placidly affectionate scrutiny, was quite an ordeal. I could feel her deciding to do something about my underwear, and as for my socks – well, I really ought to have washed them myself, some time ago.

Murmuring words to her about getting us something to eat I went slowly downstairs, pulling on my jersey. At that moment there came a robust knocking on the door, very different from the scratching sounds that Mella had produced that morning. I stopped in dismay. Whatever it was, probably nothing worse than the gas man or a charity or the local neighbourhood magazine, it came at an inconvenient moment. But I had better get it over with. I went to the front door.

It was Margot.

'Hullo, Johnny,' she said, walking straight in. 'I thought when I left you I'd call on Peggy and Mike, over at Kingston Bagpuize you know, and they persuaded me to stay the night. Look here, did I leave my gloves? Ah, thank goodness, there they are,' and Margot scooped them up in mid-sentence. 'I won't keep you,' she said. 'I expect you're busy.'

'Look here' was a favourite locution of Margot's. In someone else – a man with a moustache say – the old-fashioned turn of speech might have sounded a little abrupt, even hectoring. But with Margot it just sounded jolly.

I gazed at her with stupefaction. Somehow this classic situation, staple of so many French farces, was completely unexpected, wholly out of place in a widower's house, and its setting.

I had no leisure to reflect on this fact. Mella must have approached very quietly round the corner at the bottom of the stairs. Seeing Margot's face I turned quickly round and there Mella was, wearing my old dressing-gown which had obviously been just put on. Mella was still trying to tie the cord round herself.

I have never seen anyone look more delighted than

Margot did at that moment. Sheer spontaneous joy shone on her face and sparkled in her eyes. I thought she was going to burst out giggling. And in fact, she was overcome by laughter as she seized both of Mella's hands.

'Hullo, my dear, *hullo*, my dear,' she chortled. 'I'm so glad to meet you! And what's your name?'

She said this exactly as she might have asked the same question of a little girl in a school. Mella didn't seem to mind in the least. In fact she looked almost as delighted as Margot. Her little face was wreathed in smiles, and she played rather provocatively with the cord of my old school-type dressing-gown.

Seeing them both look so delighted with the situation and with each other was, very naturally, a great relief to me. I saw at once that Mella must have heard Margot's voice, and known at once who it was likely to be. She may have come down with the intention of wiping her rival's eye: but the sight of Margot, and her face, must have removed any such impulse forthwith.

All the same, it was scarcely puzzling that Mella should have looked so pleased with the situation; and indeed with herself. In a sense it did her credit. Here she was, ensconced as it were, at the heart of what she must have thought of as Margot's territory; and her rival, so far from being cross, was being so charmingly gracious about it. In fact their response did credit to both of them.

Both women were now ignoring me completely. Mella was already telling Margot about her little boy, and her work, and her thesis, and all the difficulties she suffered under.

I looked at my watch. It was half-past three. Margot must have had lunch with Peggy and Mike, whoever they were, and come to me on the way home. I myself was hungrier than ever. I didn't bother to consider whether Mella was hungry or not. I felt that the two women had taken their affairs off my hands. And that was a relief. My own requirements I could look after myself. We drifted into the kitchen, with Mella and Margot still talking away nineteen to the dozen. They were a mother and daughter, reunited after a long and eventful separation. I was neither the father nor the son. Nor a husband either. I was just an old widower whose house had been taken over on behalf of a newly-formed, younger, more dynamic relationship, a sisterhood.

That was certainly what the situation began to look like. Where Mella was concerned I welcomed what I hoped would be a return to our previous placid and comparatively undemanding relationship, with its regular conversations and routines. Mella had found a new focus of interest, a new object in her life. It was ironic that this should be my old friend Margot, whom for only one exhausting day – exhausting for me that is – Mella had clearly regarded as a threat and a rival. For the first time it occurred to me how good Iris would have been with Mella; how much Iris would have helped her with whatever invisible and indefinable furies she felt herself to be pursued by.

But there was no point in my having that realisation now. Maybe Margot, who was still so very much alive and dedicated to whatever goal of the moment she could triumphantly score, would be able to sort out Mella's problems for her.

But if I supposed that I could now return to my old, simple, though undeniable need for Mella's company, and on the old terms, I was in for a rude awakening. True, she soon abandoned her house-cleaning activities, not with the uncompromising insouciance displayed by Margot, but enough to show that her heart and her emotions were no longer in it. Where were they then? I very sincerely hoped they might be with Margot, provided that left for me my former Mella, the old sleep-walking waif who had drifted to my door once or twice a week; who had been, I now recognised, so soothing to get on with, and so easy to entertain.

John Sparrow, the Warden of All Souls College, who had always been a cynophobe, if that is the correct term for a sincere detester of dogs, had once encountered at a tea party a quiet lady with a small dog, so very subdued that it was virtually unnoticeable.

'Your dog is almost as good as no dog at all, Madam,' he told her approvingly as he said goodbye.

I don't know whether the lady grasped how rare a compliment she and her dog had been paid; but the philosopher in Iris was amused by the notion, and it became one of our own useful categories. Children ('No man can be wholly bad if he hates dogs and children'), restaurants, students, parties, even marriages like our own – all could find an occasional place in the area of response suggested by Sparrow; and indeed already implicit in W.C. Fields' use of the original Oscar Wilde joke. ('A man must have a heart of stone not to laugh at the death of Little Nell.')

In any case, Mella's visits, and Mella as a visitor, had been for me almost as good as no visit and no visitor at all. Which is not to say that I would not have seriously missed them had they been discontinued. Where would Sparrow and Fields have been, after all, in a world in which there were no dogs to dislike, and no children?

The meeting with Margot that morning had for some reason made me feel that I ought really to make further enquiries about Mella's little boy. She had once told me his name: at least she had once told me that she sometimes called him Damian and sometimes Darren; he liked both these names and so did she. To me they seemed a good deal worse than no name at all, but that was Mella's affair. At the time, it struck me as just another of those inexplicable things about Mella which one took for granted. Besides, when Mella's personality had abruptly become so alarming, projecting itself into mops and brushes and house-cleaning gear, I had sworn in silent retaliation to find out nothing else from her ever again, and never to ask another question.

Margot drove off home in her rescued gloves; Mella disappeared to wherever Damian (or Darren) and Alison (or Angela?) awaited her.

But next day Mella was back, and at the same disconcerting hour of ten in the morning. I was sitting in one of the two office chairs in the kitchen, and she promptly took the other one. Lips parted and her voice hushed as if with religious awe, she began to ask me questions about Margot. Where had I met her? Where did she live?

Her interest surprised me a little. I had supposed that all such matters must have revealed themselves during those torrents of intimacy in which the two women had indulged yesterday; but I now saw that Margot had probably heard everything about Mella, but that Mella was by no means in the same position with regard to Margot. To my dismay the temperature of intensity appeared to be rising. I made an offer of Nescafé and the biscuit, but it was ignored. Instead Mella pulled herself closer to me, the oversized castors of the office chair rumbling over the wooden floor like the gun-trucks of a man-of-war. 'Showing her teeth', I remembered, was the phrase used of a warship running out its guns. I hoped Mella was not going to show hers.

'John, I don't want to upset you. You've been through such a bad time . . . I know, because . . .'

Although I had invited Mella long ago to call me John, she had only used the name very rarely and tentatively, as if she feared to be taking a liberty.

'You're going through one too?' I supplied helpfully.

Mella looked rather annoyed at that. Her speech this morning was full of those moments which writers indicate by three dots . . . Her eyes now had a faraway look, as if she were pining for Margot in distant Norfolk.

'It's worse in the night of course,' she said.

This last observation seriously alarmed me. Margot was safely away in distant Norfolk, but if Mella took to proposing nocturnal visits to me the circuit would be closed. My house, I felt wildly, would no longer be mine, but hers as well. And what about Damian/ Darren and the obliging Alison/Angela? No doubt they would be quite happy together if Mella took to spending nights with me. I was in something very near panic. Perhaps Mella saw this: perhaps she misunderstood it.

'*I* know what it's like,' she emphasised again, in an unexpectedly high, crowing voice. The castors rumbled; the chair, like an eighteen-pounder on the gun-deck, moved even closer to me, and Mella seized my hand in a grip which, as I knew from yesterday, was something very like iron. She drew my own chair towards herself, and now we seemed more like a pair of invalids in a nursing home, beginning what might become, if things prospered, a passionate relationship.

One thing led to another but, thank goodness, our relationship showed no signs of being like that. We went to bed, certainly, as we had done the day before; but I think it was probably just because we had done it the day before that we now must have felt something like a mutual obligation to do it again. Politeness, really. Each felt the other must be expecting it.

Mella was usually a reliable conversationalist, but she seemed to believe in silence in bed, as if she were in church, and if I ventured some more or less light-hearted comment her reply took a physical form, accompanied by some heavy breathing. Yet carried away by passion we certainly were not, although Mella's nakedness continued for me to have something unexpectedly and mysteriously touching about it.

Soon it became a ritual like our other routines; the Nescafé, the biscuit, and our always relaxed and undemanding talk. We added yet another routine: a short walk round the block after we got out of bed. This was almost the same walk that I used to take many times a day with Iris, when she was ill.

I had heard nothing from Margot, and disliking the telephone as I did, I never attempted to ring her. Relations with Mella seemed to have settled down quite comfortably. And yet I always felt a slight reluctance, when she turned up, usually at ten in the morning or half-past, to engage in the first and most strenuous part of our routines of meeting. It was not a good time of the day to be going back to bed. I sometimes felt tempted to beg off it, but I could not see how that could be done without causing offence.

There was nothing to be done about it, any more than there was when, as a child in London, I used to be taken by my mother to a weekly gymnasium class, somewhere near the back of Sloane Square Underground station. My weekly apprehensions about this were greatly enhanced by my fear of the station itself, at which we arrived by train after the short journey from Gloucester Road. I loved the Underground and its stations, but I dreaded arriving at Sloane Square which, no doubt because of its proximity to the gymnasium, always struck me as an evil and sinister place, inhabited by hirsute ogres and fairies with bad taste, for the passages leading to the exit were in those days rough brickwork, slapped over with paint of a peculiarly sickly green.

By the time we got to the gym I would be feeling thoroughly depressed, nor were my fears allayed by the sight of Mr Macpherson and his cherubic assistant. But they were friendly enough; and by the time the hour was over I had quite enjoyed the gym class, just as, about sixty-five years later, I found myself quite enjoying my encounters in bed with Mella.

Mella seemed to like them too, but one could never be quite sure; indeed with her one could never be quite sure of anything. I sometimes had the feeling that we were both engaged in what Iris and I used to call a 'Gore'. Some friend had told us about a Mr Gore who had isolated a particular social situation, and named it after himself. It occurred when he was staying with a friend. This friend had suggested visiting a church. Mr Gore had no great wish to see this church, and neither, as he intuited, had his friend; but politeness required a show of enthusiasm on both sides, and, after all, the period of the visit had to be got through somehow . . . With Mella I felt that our love-making rather resembled a 'Gore'. Neither of us were all that keen, but neither of us liked to say so. And it was as good a way as any of passing the time.

Iris and I were partial to terms and phrases like the 'Gore'. Another one we used was 'barnacling'. The great whales, as I had read somewhere, lesser cetaceans too, as well as huge fishes like the whale shark (memorably encountered by Thor Heyerdahl during the voyage of the Kon-Tiki) have the habit of rubbing off the barnacles on their backs against some convenient large object: a ship, a pier, even another whale.

The analogy explains itself, and yet I was in two minds about it. Did I want to rub Mella off against Margot? Did I at least want to attempt it? The widower part of me, the part that wanted a quiet life and no further trouble, was certainly attracted by the idea. But did I really want to lose Mella, despite the rather more exacting form which her society had recently been taking?

After my first reaction, which had been one of relief, I had begun to feel rather less than pleased by Margot's unalloyed delight in the relation between Mella and myself, on which she had so unexpectedly stumbled. A little resentment – even a touch of jealousy – would surely not have been out of place? Margot's fascination with the newcomer, as apparently revealed in the sheer ebullience of that meeting, had seemed to reveal uncompromisingly that her fondness for myself had no trace of possessiveness about it.

Of course no widower wants his close friends to be tiresomely possessive. That went without saying. But equally no widower wants to feel that he is a bit of a burden, whom his friends would be thankful to transfer to other shoulders, if a willing pair of these happened to present themselves.

All of us, and not just widowers, might wish on occasion to barnacle an inconvenient friend. But to be barnacled oneself is quite another matter.

The barnacling business was in its nature a kind of comedy. But I was not inclined to find anything comic in the letter I received from Margot a few weeks later.

My Darling Johnny,

(Not having yet read the letter I was touched by the 'My Darling', although I could have done without the Johnny.)

You'll never guess what's been happening here! Wot larks! On Wednesday your Mella turned up out of the blue! When I saw you together I thought she was a nice little thing, and I was so pleased for you both. You *needed* something like that, you know. I still think she's nice – in fact I'm becoming very fond of her – but what a business, good heavens! I can't help wondering if you had any idea!

To begin with, of course, the girl is a consummate liar. But one can't blame her a bit. It's so pathetic, and her story is so sad. I don't suppose you've heard it, except for the special items she wanted to make you believe. No little boy of course, as she told you, and indeed as she told me when I called in at your place to pick up my gloves. All that came out when she'd been crying on my bosom for about two hours, after she showed up here. She really is a waif and stray, you know. I expect she wanted you to feel that there was nothing for you to worry about – that she had not only her child but a great friend, even an ex-husband, was it? – supporting her in the background. So you wouldn't have to feel you need do anything.

Well, that all disappeared with me of course. No child, no husband, no girlfriend. Did she ever tell you how and where she had been living? Probably not. A wretched half a room over a shop run by some Indians, and they made her pay thirty quid a week. She wouldn't have wanted to let you know about that – you might have thought you ought to help her with money – and so she invented the child and the girlfriend. To reassure you I really think. She's not a natural liar. By nature, I think, she's as honest as the day. But what a time she's had! And no one, absolutely no one, in the University of Oxford to give her a helping hand. She's quite alone in the world.

She can stay here with me of course as long as she likes, and I really think that's the best thing. Oxford's no good to her, although she's a brainy little thing too, and there was some work she was doing for you wasn't there? Best forgotten about, I should think – for the moment anyway. What she needs is a complete rest. I can give her that here. Peace and quiet, and proper food at last. I gather she didn't even like to ask you for anything to eat when she came to see you!

Well, no point in going on. I'll keep you in touch with her if you like, although I really think it's best for her to be quite on her own for a while – and that she can be here with me. She's a dear creature. As I said, I'm getting very fond of her.

Now look after yourself. I don't think you feed yourself properly, so of course you couldn't be expected to
do Mella.

So much love to you XXX
Margot

I read the whole letter, and then I read it again. As I finished
it, I decided that the subtlest insult in the whole thing was
the sting in the tail. Margot wouldn't have known it was
an insult of course, or have used the word in any way
deliberately. She wouldn't have thought that anything in her
letter was at all insulting. Why should it be? The facts about
poor Mella and her travails spoke for themselves. Nobody's
fault. Except, of course, for the villainous Indian grocer, who
was charging her thirty quid a week. If he really was.

Why couldn't Margot have written at the end, 'So of
course you couldn't be expected to *feed* Mella?' More natural
surely? Whatever the wounding implications of that too
might be. But no, through some quirk of her own Margot
had preferred to write that I 'couldn't be expected to *do*
Mella.' It sounded as if sex-wise, too, the poor old gentleman
was obviously not up to it, just as he couldn't be expected
to care for Mella; to cherish her problems; to cope with her
and, if need be, to control her. Even to find out anything
about her.

As I pondered all that I began to laugh. Margot's letter
was comic, after all. And the odd verb she had made use of
at the end was probably fully justified. I just couldn't 'do'
Mella in any sense. As Margot obviously could.

When Mella's daily visits stopped I had been rather
relieved. I hoped we might have reverted, with some minor
differences, to our previous undemanding itinerary, on a
weekly or fortnightly basis. I hoped so. But I had missed
her. And of course I couldn't stop thinking about her.

I was genuinely surprised to hear that she had no child.

The very fact that she had not talked about her little boy, knowing that I would not be interested, had always seemed to me – now that I came to think about it – an implicit proof of the child's existence. Because I knew no more of little Damian, or little Darren, than the name, it had never occurred to me to doubt that he must be running about somewhere, attended, when she could manage it, by the faithful Alison, or Angela.

There was no reason either why Mella should have told me of the grocer problem. She had never given the slightest sign of being short of money. Of course I should have asked her; and yet why should I? She had a college where someone was responsible for her. She must have had enough money to continue with her studies, taking her own time. I wasn't even her supervisor. I had just been asked to see her a few times on topics in which she was said to be especially interested; and I had certainly done that. In fact I had been seeing her once or twice a week now for at least a year. Longer.

And yet Margot was right. Of course she was right. I had never wanted to find out about Mella, or to help her, come to that. I had just gone along with what she seemed to want; and it looked now as if she had hardly known herself what she did want. Except, when the chance offered, to flee to someone like Margot, to weep on her bosom, to confess and confide her troubles, to be fed and comforted, to stay as long as she wanted . . .

Well, I had at least done that for Mella, however accidentally. I had put her in touch with the right person; and she, leaping out of my bed, had shown the initiative to do the rest.

And now I was missing her. I was very much missing her. Nor did there seem to be any prospect of seeing her for a long time. Comfortably settled with Margot in Norfolk (and how had she got there? Train or bus, I supposed) there seemed no reason why she should ever leave. I paused to consider Margot's own motives in the matter. I brushed aside the vulgar idea that she might be a bit lesbian. And so might Mella herself, come to that. But to suppose such a thing was a typically glib masculine reaction to the natural kindness of women to other women. Their fellow-feeling, their desire to rush in and rescue a lame duck. Iris herself had been always prepared to help and counsel and comfort, although naturally she couldn't provide the amenities, in the way of house and hospitality, which Margot could easily manage.

All the same, there might be some possibility that Margot had a *tendresse* at times for persons of her own sex. Or that Mella had. Why not? Perhaps Margot had fallen in love with her? Or each with the other? What seemed certain was that I should not be seeing Mella for a long time. If at all. The thought caused me annoyance rather than sadness. I should miss the simplicity of our relationship, the undemandingness. Taking each other for granted . . .

For Mella Margot's arrival had perhaps been a turning-point? The big chance in life, an offer of salvation? Who could say? They would certainly not be taking each other for granted.

Another annoying thing was that the invisible presence of Margot had clearly galvanised Mella into going to bed with me. I doubted that she would have wanted to do it otherwise. Nor would I. The idea had never occurred to me before. And if it had done so, I would have rejected it as quite unsuitable. Mella was not exactly my pupil, but our relationship was still a formalised one: that of student and teacher. It was entirely because of Margot, the outsider, that a sudden change had been precipitated.

And Margot and I had neither made love nor, so far as I could remember, had we intended to do so. Just one, or two, of life's little ironies, as poet and novelist Thomas Hardy would say. I loved almost all Hardy's books; but I didn't greatly care for the way he overworked his little ironies.

4

The Falling Snow

All these things being so, what happened next was the last thing I expected. But that was how it was, anyway. Mella appeared at the door at ten o'clock the next morning.

It was early December now. Iris had died at the beginning of the previous February. Another winter was well under way. The weather had suddenly changed and gone very cold. In the night it had started to snow, and though there was very little left on the ground, small, damp flakes were still falling. In the snow light Mella looked more than ever insubstantial and waif-like. I gaped at her.

'Mella! I thought you were with Margot!'

She stumbled across the doorstep like the orphan of the storm who has come home at last to a safe place to die. I retreated before her. In a second we were in the kitchen, and Mella was seated on one of the office chairs.

'Nescafé? Your biscuit?'

Mella smiled wanly. She said nothing. I put the kettle on for the coffee and opened the biscuit tin. As I turned to fill her mug, Mella was suddenly on me. Her arms went tightly round my neck. The mug which I had been about to fill went flying across the room. Mella's face was against my nose. I had difficulty in breathing. I wondered with some annoyance if the mug was broken – I was rather fond of that mug – and I made efforts to wriggle out of Mella's grasp.

'Please, John,' she was saying. 'Let me come to you. I'll

look after you, I promise. I won't bother you. I'll go out. I'll clean the house and everything.'

If she hadn't mentioned the house, and cleaning it, she would have had a better case. That was a caddish thing to think, but I did think it. The idea of the house, my house, a house which had been cleaned by Mella, was instantly and totally insupportable.

'But what about your little boy?'

'All right, I don't have a little boy. I made that up. And about my husband. Why shouldn't I? I thought that if I said about those things you wouldn't be worrying about me.'

I wouldn't be worrying about her, as a woman on her own. So it was all done for my sake, really. That might have been touching. Perhaps it was intended to be. But I failed to be touched. She was studying my face, or at least looking at it closely. It must have looked full of dismay, guilt, embarrassment: all sorts of things like that. But chiefly my face felt as if it belonged to a small boy at school, who has been made some outrageous proposition by a school chum – climbing the chapel roof, pinching the master's gown – and who doesn't know how to get out of it without losing too much face.

In the midst of these horrors a thought struck me. Mella had made up the child, the husband and so forth, just as Margot had written. But how much else might she have made up? Margot had contradicted herself. She had said Mella was a consummate liar, but also that she was not a natural liar, and was as honest as the day.

Maybe she was. I was not exactly a gem of truthfulness myself. I had certainly been taken in about the child, but I began to wonder now about some of the other things Mella had 'confessed' to Margot. Was it a question of owning up to one lie, and after that everyone will start believing you?

I said boldly: 'I'm worried now about how you live, darling, and where you live. I don't think it would be a good idea being here, but what about your digs? Can't we get you better ones? Can I help?'

I put the darling in a bit self-consciously. I had never called her darling before. When I was together with Mella, as I now realised more and more, we had our own thing, our own way, of being ourselves. We were not in darling circles. I was glad we weren't, but none the less I had made a mistake, a fatal mistake. Mella's eyes narrowed, and her lips compressed. I felt like the captain of a seventy-four who has unavoidably allowed his opponent to cross his stern, so that he is about to receive the blast of a thirty-seven gun broadside.

'For what we are about to receive . . .' was supposed to have been the chant on deck in the terrible slow seconds before the enemy ship opened fire.

But Mella, gazing at me with a frightening air of devotion (I don't suppose the captains of rival ships ever did that), merely said, 'Where do you think I live, then?'

This was it. Devoted she might look, but there was a faint air of amusement too on Mella's face as she awaited my reply.

'I seem to remember you once mentioned the little shop you lived over? Handy in a way, I suppose.'

How could I have thought that was going to work? I was making one bloomer after another. Mella's mild little face now looked stern, like Portia's in the seat of judgement.

'Of course I never told you anything of the sort. You've been talking on the phone to Margot, haven't you? That skunk. That female bastard. She's been telling you all sorts of rotten things about me, hasn't she?'

'No, no,' I protested in alarm. 'I haven't spoken to her. She just wrote.'

Too late again, I realised my mistake. Mella had risen to her feet and was glaring down at me.

'Show me. Show me what she wrote.'

'No. I can't do that, Mella,' I said, with a feeble attempt at dignity.

Quite out of the question of course. But then I suddenly thought: why not? Margot had, after all, been so nice about Mella in the letter. I wouldn't mind reading those things about myself; indeed I would rather enjoy it. And to read about oneself in a letter is always, surely, irresistibly interesting. If I tried to keep the letter back, Mella would only grow more and more angry. And it was no use denying that I felt frightened of her now, when she showed signs of getting angry. Just as I had once found in my solitary state, that I could be a little frightened of Margot.

So I gave her the letter. Unable to bear looking at her while she read it, I picked up the broken mug and busied myself with making a fresh cup of coffee. Then I darted a fearful glance sideways at Mella's face. It was very pale. I thought she might be going to faint again. And apart from the pallor the face looked old. As old as Margot's. Almost as old as mine. How old was this girl, anyway?

I gave her the cup of coffee and she started to drink it without expression. I handed her the biscuit. That gave me a twinge too. I had handed Mella so many biscuits in our time. A nice simple heart-warming thing to do – giving people biscuits. People with whom one had a special relationship.

Too late, as usual, I knew that my real reason for showing Mella the letter, apart from sheer funk about how she might carry on, was to induce her to realise what a happy home she had presumably left in Norfolk; how sensible it would be to go back there to all the warmth and interest of Margot's hospitality.

Had she already quarrelled with Margot? Had they had a 'blood row', as it was called? But I couldn't believe it. Margot was kind, good-natured, easy-going. She loved to chatter away. And Mella talked enough when she was with me, for God's sake. I could see she might, on getting to know her at home, have felt a bit inhibited with Margot and her style of action, but surely she would get over that very soon. What could have gone wrong? I asked the question directly. Mella promptly dissolved in tears.

'How could you have read that letter she sent you,' she blubbered. 'How *could* you, how *could* you? I didn't want you to know that I was going, that I was there. Of course I didn't! It's ruined everything . . . It'll never be the same again, never.'

She had just been crying before, but now her face seemed to dissolve itself, like a baby's, into a single contortion of misery. I tried to put my arm round her shoulder. I even tried to kiss her. I had no experience of what to do in cases of such extreme emotion, of which I took this to be one. My Iris had never done anything of this kind. With other people perhaps, at some earlier stage of her life, but never with me.

In some strange way, Mella seemed to realise all this. She straightened up and blew her nose.

'Sorry,' she said coldly.

'That's all right.'

It was borne in upon me somehow that they hadn't had a quarrel at all. Being over there with Margot had somehow given Mella the nerve and the resolution to come back straight to Oxford, and make me the proposition that she had just made. And the whole thing had been ruined, as she may have seen it, by that letter I had received from Margot. Why on earth had I been such a fool as to show it to her, and to let her know that I had heard about her from Margot? But really, I knew I was glad that I had shown it. And suffered the consequences: which is another way of saying that I had escaped them.

Outside, I noticed, the small flakes of wet snow were still falling. It looked thoroughly miserable. Not a day to travel on. Not a day to do anything but keep snug and warm at home. In one's house. My widower's house.

But, on the other hand, it was not a day on which to be by oneself either. Much better, if one could, to be at home with somebody else? I looked at Mella. Mella looked at me. I said nothing. Then she got up and adjusted herself and took her bag. She was never without that.

'Shall you go back to Norfolk now?' I quavered.

She did not reply. I dithered after her to the front door. She opened it herself and turned back for a moment.

'I *hate* Margot.'

She ran through the snow to the garden gate, turned the corner and disappeared.

I stood gazing stupidly at the falling snow. But only for a few moments. Then I ran back to the kitchen, got my cap and coat, and followed her out into the garden. If she had disappeared I might have run after her, tried to find her. But there she still was, a small figure, trudging up the straight street in the snow. I had an impulse to shout after her, but I didn't. I gazed until she was lost to sight round a corner and then went back into my house and shut the door.

I wrote to Margot, but there did not seem much to say, for I was disinclined to tell her what had really taken place. The worst of the trouble seemed to have been caused by my own stupidity, if it was no worse than that, in letting Mella know that I had heard from Margot, and then letting her see the letter. It was obvious to me now why I had done this. A few days with Margot had been enough to make Mella decide to come back to Oxford, and to move in on me and my house. For that was what it came to. It was even possible that Margot had encouraged her to try taking this course. In spite of what she had written, Margot had no doubt had enough of Mella's company after not many days.

It was also possible, it was even likely, that the two had held a council of war, at which Margot had urged bold measures on the younger woman. Nothing venture, nothing win. I shrank from the odious complacency entailed on me by that supposition. It was hateful to see oneself as pursued by designing women; but more hateful still to envisage the determined selfishness with which one would plan counter-moves, measures with which to fight them off.

And I knew quite well that it was not only hateful, it was also misleading. Only in silly plays and soap operas, or novels like Mrs Gaskell's *Cranford*, do plots to inveigle men into marriage get hatched. They are a literary device, not a true reflection of human nature. Human nature deals in impulses, often conflicting or irrational, which besiege the consciousness, storming and abandoning it again from day to day. One never knows what it might do, or feel, next.

Why had Margot come to my bed in the night? Why had Mella become so different so suddenly when she knew that another woman had been in the house? Surely no deep strategy was involved in these actions; they were just a part of human behaviour, its diversions as one might say, bringing about both troubles and rewards.

Well, it was all very well to say that, and even to feel it. Was I myself a good example of this Law of Impulsive Behaviour? I might think not, when I considered how selfish I was about my house and about the kind of life I thought I wanted to live in it. And yet, just think of the dangers to that way of life which I seemed to have been deliberately letting myself in for lately!

I could easily have got in a real mess with Mella. Not marrying her of course, nothing so antique as that, but sharing my house with her. For not only did I feel sorry for her, at least by fits and starts, but I also wanted her company. I needed it, on my own terms of course; but until lately Mella had always seemed perfectly happy to accept those terms. Assuming, of course, that she was aware of them; and I myself was well aware that one could not always make such an assumption.

But why had I not run after her through the snow and asked her to come back to the house, to be there, if she wanted, for a day or two, so that we could begin to get to know each other? And all that. Which we hadn't done before. Because I had not wanted us to get to know each other?

Iris died a year ago.

I had wanted this to be an especially quiet time. It was not. And no doubt it's better that it should not have been. I think of the way she used to laugh as she quoted a song, or hymn, sung at school.

> Come, we must be up and doing,
> With a heart for any fate!

She always did have a heart. And perhaps one for any fate, too. I only wanted one kind of fate: being in my house and living to myself and for myself. Not much to ask? But other people seemed to think it was. Much too much. Look at all the trouble I'd lately been having. Did I want that trouble? I thought I didn't, but one could never be sure. People like trouble. I thought suddenly of Margot's face, looking over my shoulder on the doorstep, looking at Mella. Margot's large well-wishing features had been absolutely transformed. She might have been told she was going to give birth to the Saviour or something, instead of meeting the girl with whom I had just been in bed, the bed to which Margot herself had paid a nocturnal visit the night before. It had been *exciting* for Margot; it seemed to me to be as simple as that. And so, old as I was and set in my ways, like a hermit crab in its adopted shell, hadn't I better try to find ways myself of finding life exciting?

Suppose, for a start, that I said to Mella when I next saw her – she was bound to come back in a day or two – supposing I said: 'Mella, I'm really very fond of you, you know.' I would say it in firm tones, indicating exactly what I meant. 'I'm very fond of you.' I remembered from school, or from something I'd read, that there is a fatal French phrase, *'je t'aime bien'* – fatal because it reveals, with unforgiving French logic, the difference between saying 'I'm fond of you' and 'I love you' – *'je t'aime'*. The English try to soften the blow. The French will have none of that. They may not have many words, but they know how to use them incisively. *'Je t'aime bien'* *should* be able to mean 'I love you well – I love you even more than loving you.' But it doesn't. Because of the fatal *bien* it can only mean 'I like you a lot,' or, with the blow slightly softened, 'I'm really very fond of you.'

But what's the point of that? What it comes to is that I can't say to Mella: 'I love you.' Why not? There would be no harm in saying it, but I can't. I never said it to Iris – at least I don't think I did. There was no need to, and it never occurred to me. But I wouldn't say it to Mella, or to anyone else, on principle.

So it's principles now, is it? What about the Law of Impulsive Behaviour? If you can cheer the lady up by suddenly saying, 'I love you', why not do it? She may not believe you, but that's not the point. She'll be pleased, anyhow. Even comforted.

I should have run after Mella in the snow and said, 'I love you.' What would she have done? Turned around and trudged on? Alternatively, she might have flown like a bird into my arms (but I am seventy-four and slightly built) and said, 'I love you too.'

A fortnight later I was no longer interested in the question of whether or not to say 'I love you' to Mella. I just wanted to see her. I wanted to see her badly, and I was deeply upset and disturbed by her absence. If she returned I should not bother about 'I love you' . . . I should say . . . What should I say? 'Come and try living in my house for a bit if you like.'

Mella did not reappear. And I got very low. I wondered whether she could possibly be back with Margot. I rang Margot. Margot sounded no longer very interested in Mella. She had a daughter there, with her children.

'Don't worry,' said Margot. 'I expect she'll turn up in a day or two.'

She did not. I meditated unhappily. I had spoilt her life. Perhaps she would end up as a drug addict or a prostitute? And it had been so pleasant to be together, in terms of a biscuit and a cup of Nescafé . . . After a few more days I decided to ring her college. I still remembered which it was. After a bit of trouble I got through to the Tuition Secretary. She was a helpful woman, but she knew nothing about the whereabouts of Mella, who had long since ceased to have an official college connection.

'The lodge may know something about her,' she suggested.

I tried ringing the college lodge, but they were always busy, so I decided to walk down there. I was nervous of buses, and parking a car had become quite impossible. The lodge was full of students, but a young woman (what had happened to college porters?) who had been busy on the phone was free at last and looked at me enquiringly. I asked if they had seen Mella Handley lately.

'Mella's gone away, hasn't she, Mr Pratt?' asked the lady of some invisible colleague in the inner office.

Mr Pratt couldn't say.

'Well, there's nothing in the pigeon-hole for her,' said the lady porter. 'She used to come in for her mail.'

I started wondering who the people were who had once written to Mella. Had they given up writing? It was hard to imagine Mella as a correspondent. Had they not received replies?

I hung about in the quad, at a loss for what to do next. Then I saw the lady porter emerge with a bag and the satisfied air of one who has finished their tour of duty. She saw me too, and her features became friendly.

'Little Mella, wasn't it, you were asking for? We're sorry she's gone,' indicating her colleagues behind her in the lodge with a wave of the hand. 'We all liked her.'

'Where did she live, d'you know?' I asked.

The lady porter was obviously reluctant to return to the scene of her labours to find out the address, and I did not press the point.

'Oh, she had a lovely flat,' she said instead. 'It was up Parktown way. I used to visit there you see, because Mella loved my kids – two little boys they are – Damian and Darren. And she was that kind, I could leave them with her sometimes. Thought the world of her, the children did. Always giving them presents.'

'Did you meet her friends at all, a boyfriend perhaps? Someone told me she was married.'

'Oh no, she certainly wasn't married. Very much on her own, she was. I never saw any friends at her flat.'

I thanked the lady porter and we parted company. I remembered to ask if Mella had left any address behind her, for forwarding of mail. She had not done so.

'But,' said the lady, whom I now began to think of as my friend and ally, 'I've known her take herself off for a week or two, longer sometimes, and be back when I next gave her a call or dropped in with the boys. You never quite know where you are with Mella; but we've been so fond of her, you know. We'd miss her if she went for good, but I don't think she has done, not now. She'll be back again one of these days. Did you want to leave a message?'

I said no, thank you very much, and I thanked the lady porter profusely. It occurred to me that she should really be called the portress. Didn't Milton have such a person, on duty at Hell's Gate?

'We're here to help others, that's what I always say,' my own particular portress was going on in her comfortable manner.

I wondered if or how I could give her a tip, which would have been a commonplace in the old times of college porters. I decided that in our changed circumstances today it could only be inappropriate.

*   *   *

I can't say I missed Mella for long, or, indeed, Margot. I didn't in any case have to miss Margot because I went on seeing her from time to time. We sometimes talked about Mella; Margot asked if I missed her, and how important the relationship had been to me. I returned a vague reply because I didn't know myself. I had missed her; but what the lady porter had said about Mella had somehow deprived her in my eyes of the being she had possessed when she used to visit my widower's house, and have a mug of coffee and a biscuit. The things revealed by Margot's letter had also made a difference. Mella in bed, or Mella violently mopping the floor, had seemed perfectly normal extensions of the Mella who had come periodically scratching at the door. But after hearing about her flat, and her kindness to the lady porter's little boys (and they *were* called Damian and Darren) I found it hard to believe in Mella at all. Her disappearance seemed a natural thing, like that of someone seen on the tube, who gets out and walks away down the platform, leaving you thinking for a moment or two how nice it might have been to meet them.

5

Limbo

The most unexpected aspect of bereavement, and the one hardest for a bereft person to identify, turned out, when I started thinking about it, to be the simplest of all. Everyone, even the very young, unconsciously grasps that daily life is founded on the principle of Sam and his brick wall; with age we become increasingly conscious of that principle, and learn to use it purposefully. Perhaps it's more a Law than a Principle. In any case, if you spend some time, like the proverbial Sam, banging your head against the wall, you know that the ensuing period, before the cycle starts up again, will be agreeable. Margot and Mella had made a fine wall to bang my head up against – Sam himself could have done no better.

In a more general way, bereavement, to my surprise, had at first removed the brick wall. By its nature bereavement entitled me to unlimited wall remission. Or so I supposed. I could concentrate on enjoying myself, my own life, my own time and routine. No wall appeared to be in the way. But that, it soon appeared, was just the trouble.

Walls have ears; they soon divined my intentions and set out to put things right. These obliging structures crowded on me from all sides, and when my head instinctively avoided them they peremptorily banged it for me.

What was I to do now without Margot looming up on one side, Mella on the other? I soon found out, for with Mella gone and Margot no longer so intent on suggesting a visit from me to her, or from her to me, I was thrown back on my own resources.

After the trouble I felt I had had with the two ladies, this should have been just what I wanted. A remission from the natural Law of Sam and his wall. And indeed, it was very agreeable at first to live, as I thought of it, to myself and for myself. Agreeable to think about Margot and Mella, and to be grateful for their absence.

But after a few days I was not so sure. The two women and their – in some ways – equally vigorous personalities had given me willy-nilly a new personality of my own. A negative one no doubt, because evolved under stress for a special purpose. A personality specialising in self-protection.

Now I must try to develop into someone more like my old self, as I thought of it; a self more like the one who had been looking after Iris. I would wake up early and read or write in bed. I would walk regularly around the block, as I used to do with Iris. I would shop in a leisurely fashion. And all the time I would be looking forward to the evening, and the dark coming on; looking forward also, with the poor remains of an old pleasure, to my drink. Two drinks. More than that I knew by now to be a mistake. I would have a long vague supper over a book, with music on the radio. And maybe the TV a little later in the evening. I would cruise the five channels, each more idiotic than the last, and then switch it thankfully off, unless there happened to be a good car chase, some brisk shooting, a promising creature from outer space. I had really enjoyed such things once, and with Iris peacefully asleep upstairs they had all fitted cosily into the evening's routine. Now it was a relief to turn the box off and go to bed. With a pill.

Memory again began to take me over. Margot and Mella between them had distracted it, chopped it into pieces which lay writhing in the dust like severed dragons' heads;

and at the time it seemed as if it would not grow again. But it was growing now, the pieces slithering swiftly together and reassembling themselves like those old, green, viscid beings from some horror movie who used to amuse and comfort me on the TV.

At first I welcomed the memories. Then I did not. But there was something at the back of my mind which came with them, and which seemed a familiar but invisible accompaniment. What was it? The thing irritated me because it seemed so real. Not like memory, whose reality was oppressive and overbearing, sweetly and insidiously compulsive, but without life.

Then it came back to me, and how could I have forgotten? It showed at least that my short-term memory was seriously impaired; so seriously that I at once began to wonder with apprehension whether that total recall of the last few months and years would, before I knew it, be gone the same way.

But at least I *had* remembered. Or rather it had come back to me. And what had come back was very simple: the fact that in those early mornings after Iris died, I had lain in bed and written about it all. (That was well before the arrival in my life of Margot and of Mella.)

Where had it gone, the stuff I had written? Had it gone to Pieland, to join the Original Great Pie, never refound? Mella's pies had replaced that legendary Pie, but now Mella's pies had themselves vanished. Into the limbo of things eaten or not eaten. Into the limbo of things equally lost, whether forgotten or recalled.

I began to search. I remembered Margot's apt reference to the Augean Stables. Mella's subsequent activities with pan and brush, mop and Ajax, had seemed dreadfully effective at the time, but time itself had gone on to mock them – scarcely a trace of those levellings and excavations now remained.

After opening and closing the same drawers and folders

many times, and turning over the piles of old papers on
the floor, as foxes turn cowpats over in pursuit of the
beetles that lurk beneath, I gave it up. Why should I
bother anyway? What I had scribbled down had given me
something to do at the time, and might even have cheered
me up, but that was all there was to it. I abandoned the
search.

But a lingering curiosity remained. What sort of things
had I put down then, and presumably thought it worthwhile
to put down during that period of trance, when I seemed to
live with the dead and not with the living? I had written
things down. And I had agreed with what seemed now
an almost pathetic relish to talk at a number of 'carers''
meetings and medical conferences, at which we had all
seemed to be dementia sufferers, fans even, joined together
in a fellowship of mutual comfort and interest.

I had a lot of letters from that time, which were still in
a cardboard box on the kitchen table. I still received them,
and still went quite often to the meetings, although Mella
and Margot had made something of a temporary disruption.
The letters were there, even though Pieland had claimed so
many others, and I started idly to look through them. There
was a dishevelled sheaf of paper underneath, twisted up
athwart the bottom of the box.

I pulled a piece out, and instantly recognised what I had
once written. It must have been less than a week after Iris
died. It began quite abruptly; and I at once sat down to read
it. I couldn't think at first what I had been talking about,
but then it all began to make sense, of a kind. I was still
amazed, as I read, by the way I had forgotten all about it,
as if memory had lost all function and purpose now that Iris
was dead, and could refer only to the time she had been ill,
and we had been together.

During the night [so it began] I heard the voice of the lady at
the supper table the evening before. 'Just beside him in the

garden . . . such a suitable arrangement, don't you think? And they were both such keen gardeners . . .'

She was not talking to me but to her neighbour at the end of the table about some devoted couple, now deceased. As insomnia wore on and it began to get light I lay and pondered the advantages of the arrangement. I couldn't see any, I finally decided. Between listening to what my own neighbour was saying, and replying suitably, I tried to hear whether there had been any memorial to the couple. A small stone, as on a dog's grave, or perhaps just a patch of their favourite flowers? But if any detail had been given about this I had missed it.

I wished that I had sought out the woman in the drawing-room after dinner and gone into the matter thoroughly. But such a show of interest from one recently bereaved might not have seemed in the best of taste. My curiosity was natural, yet it could have been embarrassing for a fellow guest to satisfy. I had never met the woman before, and I scarcely knew the kind persons who had asked me to dinner.

I was well aware that they had thought I ought to be asked, to be 'brought out'. Brought out of whatever state of aloneness one should not be left in. But the couple buried in the garden, or rather under the garden, would not be alone.

That seemed to be the crucial point. They would have each other for company, as in life. What I was thinking about in the night, since I couldn't think of anything better to think about, was whether the friends supposed that the buried couple had enjoyed, before they died, the prospect of being together under the garden. Had they looked forward to it? Were they still enjoying it?

Perhaps it had been her idea, after he died, to put him in the garden. In which case had it been a surprise, and perhaps not an altogether welcome one, to find that his wife was being installed there beside him? By the time she arrived he might have settled down to the pleasures of being alone. And for some reason I liked the idea that he hadn't really been a keen gardener at all, but that in the interest of marital solidarity he had gone along with the version of himself that his wife had put about.

Endless possibilities. And all that really mattered was they had vanished from the world, into total existlessness. Speculation about their hypothetical feelings could none the less go on, in the same way that information could be exchanged about their physical whereabouts. There they were, in the garden; so must they in some sense not be aware of this comforting fact? It was certainly a comfort for others to suppose so.

The couple interred under the rosebed in their garden continued to exist in the consciousness of the living. In what Milton called the 'thoughts that wander through eternity'. And eternity is not in the afterlife but in our own minds. Communing with the dead in this way must be one of the oldest of all human indulgences. The Russian poet Tyutchev, a near contemporary of Pushkin, wrote a moving poem with the refrain: 'My Dear One, do you see me?' Better to be seen by one's dead wife than by God; but Tyutchev, a devout Orthodox believer, would be sure to have included the Deity along with his wife in this hope of living under perpetual observation.

To all this Thomas Hardy provides an illogical contrast. In Hardy's view of the matter God didn't actually exist, but He none the less contrived to keep Mr Hardy under close observation, just as Hardy's dead wife did, and his dog, and various other animals. True, Hardy only required their continued existence for the purpose of writing poems about them; but that, after all, is the best use a writer can possibly make of the dear departed – or of God himself, come to that. As poets who were able to make good use of their material, the devout believer Tyutchev and the wistful atheist Hardy are a long way from being far apart.

As I was lying in bed the next night, I started wondering about the obvious fact that people today who have no belief either in God or in an afterlife should none the less continue to feel that their loved ones are still there, still aware of their situation, whether reposing in the garden, or the churchyard, or as a handful of ashes in an urn. The dead expect the attentions the living bestow on them; and almost unconsciously the living assume that this must be so. Certainly a beliefless Hardy clung to the notion of, as it were, poetic survival. In his verses the dead continue to converse with the living, quarrel with them, patronise them for still being above ground, become satirical at their expense. They can be downright nasty sometimes too.

Well, and why not? Sometimes Hardy comes clean. In one poem 'a dead man's finer part' is kept alive in the hearts of those who loved him, like human tissue under a slide or in a bell jar, until the moment when memory and mortality fail, and one feeble spark is left in no other heart but that of the poet – where it is 'dying amid the dark'.

Writing about the dead is not only a way of continuing to feel in touch with them, but also of expiating guilt. As soon as his wife Emma died, Hardy visited the village in North Cornwall where he met her, and poured out a stream of the most wonderful poems about that first magical meeting time, alleging that he was just the same as when

Our day were a joy and our paths through flowers.

No wonder wife number two – Florence – used, privately and rather sourly, to refer to her predecessor as 'the late espoused saint'.

She had much to put up with, including the fact that although Hardy referred to himself, in one of his most haunting poems, as 'a man who used to notice such things', he turned the blindest possible eye to his own domestic situation, preferring not to notice how it functioned, and at what cost and what sacrifice to whom. In that respect, no doubt, he was not a unique and original poet, who saw the hedgehog in the warm and mothy summer darkness travelling 'furtively over the lawn', but a man who resembled – and outwardly at least preferred to resemble – all the many other deliberately unseeing men of his age.

Hardy's poetry flourished alike on his lack of belief and on his devotion to the uses of poetic survival. In one poem to the dead Emma he acknowledges her 'existlessness'. But when he came to revise the poem he substituted the phrase 'wan wistlessness'. A beautiful Hardy coinage, very Old-English in feeling. It should mean, literally, not being in a position to have thoughts or consciousness, although in Hardy's own poetic mind the dead Emma goes on having plenty of both. The phrase is wistful as well as wistless, but 'wan', which in Old English meant dark or gloomy, weakens the effect; for by Hardy's time it had become a washed-out little word, suitable for a state of non-awareness. 'Existlessness' is much better, more uncompromising, even though it is contradicted by everything else about the continued existence of Emma, in this poem and in many others.

It cheers one up, in a way, to brood about such matters. I see why Hardy wrote those poems about Emma immediately after his wife died. Not only was she still very much there for him, but she carried him back, as in 'After a Journey', to the days and the places where he first met her. To write about her made him feel just the same as when their 'days were a joy and their paths through flowers.'

With me the effect is the opposite. I can write about Iris again now, as I used to before she died ten days ago. But I am writing about her the other way round. Hardy kept Emma alive, at least for a while, by writing about her. I felt that Iris was alive with me until this morning. Now I feel, quite suddenly, that she really has ceased to exist, and that is why I must write about her as if she were still alive.

I feel that she has gone. But there seems rather more to it than that. I *know* that she has gone. She was here yesterday, and the day before, and the day before that. But not now. This morning I went down to the kitchen at six o'clock, as I always used to do when she was in the final stages of Alzheimer's disease. I made myself a cup of tea, weak green tea, to which I first became addicted in the early hours of the morning when Iris used to wander about downstairs, talking to herself, piling up rubbish, cutlery, cushions, bits of clothing.

She was never difficult or ungentle with me, even then, but it was no use trying to persuade her back to bed until some invisible natural process seemed to summon her to go back there. I used to follow her cautiously upstairs, and when I found her lying in bed and smiling up at me I used to turn her gently on her side, which I knew she liked, tuck her up and kiss her goodnight, although by then it was often four or five in the morning. That was a blessed moment. I did not try to go to sleep then. I felt too wide awake. So I made the tea and wandered about a bit myself, and then went upstairs and lay down beside her, now sweetly and tranquilly asleep. This was my day-dreaming and remembering time, the best time of the day, apart from the happy hour in the evening when I got Iris into bed and kissed her goodnight, and then came down and had two strong drinks and read some old favourite like *Hornblower* or Barbara Pym.

Remembering those days, wishing they weren't over, I went down this morning, ten days after she died, to make my cup of green tea, and I hooked the back of my vest over the arm of the Windsor chair. Surprisingly difficult to put the mug down carefully, turn round and unhook myself. As I did so there fell like a chord of music on my mind the knowledge that I'd done it before, almost exactly a year ago; and that I had meant to tell Iris about it. If I could have made her understand, and even at that stage she could usually understand funny things, I was sure that she would have been amused. But I never told her, because she was asleep, and later on other more pressing matters had driven the incident out of my head.

This time I was determined to tell her. I would carry my mug upstairs and show her how the hole at the back of my vest had got itself hooked on the chair. I was sure she would find it funny when I explained that I had felt like a dog pulling at the lead. At all stages of Alzheimer's, getting jokes across seems of great importance.

I had honestly forgotten for the moment that Iris was dead, and that I shouldn't be able to tell her.

It must have been because the original moment when I had hooked my vest on the chair, a year ago, was still so vivid in my mind.

I could see myself going rather quickly up the stairs, though carrying the mug carefully, and saying, 'Darling, guess what happened.'

I saw myself doing it, and I saw Iris in bed, and beginning to sit up with a smile to hear what I was going to tell her. But she had disappeared before I reached our bedroom.

She wasn't there. She had died in the Home ten days before; yet she seemed to have been with me, at our house, until this moment. My wish to tell her this comic incident of the morning, the thing that had also happened to me a year ago, seemed abruptly to have deprived her of the life which, up to that moment, she had been living in my mind. The joke had vanished with her. There were no more jokes. Because jokes were things that I shared with her.

So I sat down on the bed, drinking my tea, and wondering what I was going to do with the rest of my life.

There is a play by Bernard Shaw called *Widowers' Houses*. I have never seen or read it and have very little idea what it's about. Possibly it's about respectable people who get their income from slum properties; some issue that was then festering away under the skirts of polite society. I recall that he wrote a series called *Plays Pleasant and Unpleasant*. This must have been one of the unpleasant ones.

The title intrigues me, though I shall take no steps to find out more about the play. For me, *Widowers' Houses* are houses with widowers living in them. Like my house. It used to be our house. It is still our bedroom, our garden, our fig-tree, Iris's chair in the garden, over which Virginia creeper has been stealthily growing all last summer. In the autumn the plant would go scarlet, and how passionately I longed for that autumn, and for an end to the long, stale summer days. I think Iris longed for them to be over too. Autumn and winter were our time, and grey days without sun. I hate the sun especially.

For some reason it is not 'our house' any more, but we still seem to have 'our friends' and even 'our Home'. That is Vale House, where Iris died. Tricia O'Leary, who runs it, is very much 'our friend'. The Home is a safe, good, happy place, which Iris loved at once. But when we arrived she wouldn't get out of the taxi until the nurse gently took her fingers. Smiling at her, and walking backwards, she led Iris unresisting to the door, as if they were having a little dance together. In a moment Iris, too, was smiling; and she never looked back.

Vale House was far from being a Vale of Tears. But as I sat in the taxi holding Iris's hand and telling the driver where to go I remembered Mrs Gamp's philosophical observation. 'He were born in a Wale and he lived in a Wale, and he must accept the consequences of his sitiwation.'

I must accept them now too, as Iris did.

Although it may be a widower's house, it feels just the same as it was when it was our house. It's not that I haven't 'had the heart' to do anything; it's more that I can't see the point of doing it. Iris's things stay heaped up on the floor, undisturbed. Her dusty spectacles, unworn for several years, lie on the window-ledge, coiled about with the black cord I got for her to hang them round her neck, which she never did. There is a vague drift of objects in the corners of rooms, piled up sometimes to a depth of a foot or more, so that one has to climb over them. Five, six weeks have now gone by, but nothing has been cleared away.

Some day, I suppose, I shall get rid of them all. Some day the house will become a new sort of house, a house for me to occupy.

Iris wrote in the little upstairs room. I don't know what I shall do with that. She wrote six or seven of her novels there, and most of her long philosophical study, *Metaphysics as a Guide to Morals*. I can't remember which novel she was in the middle of when we arrived here, back in 1989.

I have a sudden premonition that the widowed state must ripen and fatten as the months and years go by. Does the past then eat the present, becoming even more powerful, more unruly and seductive? As I try to find new things to do, will the past just smile at me like a big cat, and creep all the closer?

Well, anyway, I remember our arrival here as an exciting moment. I had been fond of our little house in Hartley Road, where we had moved from the country when our old home at Steeple Aston – shabby but rather grand in its way – had begun to feel as if it could tolerate us no longer. The Hartley Road house was on a corner and noisy, but Iris was loyal to it because she knew I had fallen sentimentally in love with the idea of such a house, if not the reality. It was a relief to us both, however, when we had the unexpected chance of moving again.

Our new house was no bigger than Hartley Road and the rooms were pokier, but the little back and front gardens were full of big trees. Brickwalled on two sides, the back garden soon began to show, under our ownership, a fine mass of weeds and undergrowth. Elder, bramble, sapling hazel, chestnut and forsythia, growing thickly up to the back fence, gave an impression of sylvan endlessness. Bluebells had probably always been there, but Queen Anne's Lace now arrived, together with bindweed and dog's mercury, ground elder and deadly nightshade. Two blue cedars that I put in keep state in one corner, and grow a couple of feet every year.

Our small patch of lawn contrasts sprucely with the wilderness. A Russian vine canopies the garage, in which there is everything except a car. Four ornamental conifers, which we used to call the king, the queen and the two princesses, came with us in their tubs from Hartley Road. Replanted in the garden they have shot up like the others. The queen has outgrown her consort and now overtops him by five or six feet. A handsome family.

Iris did sit now and again in the garden chair I got for her, but not very often. I once had a slight qualm when I saw her sitting outside with her exercise book and fountain pen. She looked thoughtful, but not in a good sense. She seemed to be wondering what was happening to her, and finding it something quite outside her experience.

When the chair goes red with the Virginia creeper next autumn and then dulls away into winter, I shall have forgotten how she looked when she sat there. Perhaps I'll take the chair away, because the green plastic chairs I got later at a supermarket are much more practical. More comfortable too. The creeper grew on top of the matted ivy that was making our neighbour's wall so damp, and both had to go. It then grew along the ground and began to entwine itself round the king and queen. I thought it best to pull it off their majesties, but I let it continue to flourish on the teak chair, its only chance of growing upwards. So I'll leave the chair there to turn red next autumn. It's not spring yet, and I hope autumn comes early this year.

At the moment the house – my house – is a refuge rather than a home. A lair. I think of it with longing if I'm forced to go out, and I can't wait to get back again into safety. Once I'm back I at once feel its emptiness, so I go out for one of our little walks – those are still 'ours'. Round the familiar block, and perhaps down to Wolfson College garden and to the middle of the Cherwell bridge where we often used to stand, and sometimes played poohsticks. We never went any further than the middle of the bridge.

Our very old friend Audi, who speaks excellent Spanish having lived in the Canaries for so many years, was once standing there with Iris and a Spanish friend when a punt came under the bridge, creeping sideways and very unadroitly propelled. The friend said to Audi in Spanish, so that he shouldn't be understood by the puntsman: 'That chap's no good. Can't do it for toffee.'

Whereupon the young fellow in the boat looked up and barked back in Spanish, 'It's not so bloody simple as it looks.'

It turned out he came from the Asturias, and he and his fellow-countryman on the bridge exchanged jocular insults as the punt receded crabwise into the distance.

Iris was scornful of the Oxford school of punting. She had learnt to do it at Cambridge when she was a research student at Newnham. She had been refused a visa for America, where she had been awarded a Commonwealth Fellowship, because of her one-time membership of the Communist Party. (Because she had owned up to it, which her former friends, many now in senior government positions, did not, she was automatically debarred from entry to the USA.)

In Cambridge, an Arab philosopher taught her to punt, and she was proud of being able to do it in the Cambridge style. The puntsman stands precariously on the slippery end, instead of on the more safely recessed stern. But I never saw her punt, and I have never done it myself, nor wished to. I liked looking at the young women in punts, as I stood there with Iris, but few of them looked at all ladylike, or were dressed for the part. They wore grubby jeans and many of them were doing the work themselves, often with a fixed sneer of contempt or concentration while the boyfriend lolled on the cushions.

Back to the house again, with the usual feeling of relief and release. Into safety, where I don't have to catch trains, go into college where everyone looks so sympathetic, or be invited out to supper. I don't even have to answer the phone, I can switch it off.

Overgrown as the front garden is, you would hardly guess from the outside of the house what a mass of debris lurks within. When I go to have a pee I notice that even the soap by the bath is dirty. How does it get like that? Disuse? Overuse? Hardly the latter.

It was some time before she died that I gave up trying to get Iris's clothes off, let alone wash her. Like a timid animal to whom it is natural to be as it is, she had begun to shy nervously away from Audi or me, but when she was in the Home, for less than a month as it turned out, she loved being washed, and would sit smiling blissfully as Tricia or Maureen soaped and towelled her. Our friend Peter's angelic partner Jim had this natural gift too, very much like that of a good keeper at a zoo, and Iris loved having him shampoo her hair. Sometimes she uttered eldritch shrieks as he did so, whereupon Jim, with a beaming smile, would shriek back at her, and then both of them would go off together into fits of hearty laughter. But in the last days even Jim could not help her.

Nothing has changed in the bedroom, which is still 'ours'. I am still on my side of the bed, naturally enough. Hotel beds are like this when you arrive: no sign of any previous occupant. But hotel beds get made.

A friend sends a photo taken last year. It's in the kitchen. Like all photographs of house interiors (pictures too, including Vermeer) the room looks more mysterious and more attractive than it really is. Can a photograph show dust, even in the quantities we have it? Hardly. But the walls I painted a warm red nine years ago look warmer and redder in the photo, less faded than they are, and the hugger-mugger of half-full mugs and unwashed plates and saucers appear as positively picturesque, with the look, as T.S. Eliot wrote in a poem, of things 'that are looked at'. On their best behaviour.

Shadowy through the doorway looms the book-mountain. Row upon row of piled-up books have accumulated for years in the narrow passage – review copies, reprints, proof copies, or new novels in their once spotless jackets sent by publishers, or sometimes by the authors themselves. All seem to reproach me, saying they might have been brilliant and wonderful, or at least profoundly interesting and informative, if they had been given their chance. And now they know it's too late. They peer wistfully into the kitchen; they even give me guilt feelings. Now and again I open one, read a few sentences, can't make head or tail of them, put the book back.

Sometimes I have managed to give one away to a visitor. But mostly they sit there hopelessly, the ones towards the bottom with the least hope of all. I should take them to Oxfam, I know, but still they sit there, and still they accrete. Who would want to read them now?

The photo makes the dried marguerite daisies in the Korean vase seem strange, outlandish, almost beautiful. The vase comes from a pottery in Seoul. When we were there once on a cultural visit we were invited to draw on a newly-made vase which was brown and unglazed. I drew a big Russian Ж (*Zh*) – a letter I loved at the time. I was trying to learn some Russian in the cause of my passion for Pushkin's poems.

The vases came to us glazed next day with an exquisite grey sheen; the markings with a dark brown pencil had come out Vermeer blue. Iris preferred to leave her own vase unmarked. It should be in a cupboard somewhere, but where?

Iris faces the camera, her hands on the back of her chair. She looks alert and happy, and is wearing the purple T-shirt Jim once gave her. The logo of a Canadian sports club is stencilled ornately on the front. On her shoulder sits the little yellow Teletubby someone else gave her. Members of a savage tribe, if savage tribes still exist, would assume at once that the little creature is the Alzheimer demon. A palpable emanation, surprised here by the camera.

Looking at the photo, I think of the last page of Iris's last novel, *Jackson's Dilemma*. Jackson is sitting on the grass feeling that life is over. 'He thought, my power has left me, will it ever return? . . . At the end of what is necessary I have come to a place where there is no road.' Jackson haunts me. So does the picture of him on the jacket. He looms there in a shadowy half-transparent way, concerned, unhappy, but always well-wishing, and as if about to disappear for good. I see from the note that it was drawn by a lady called Liz Cooke. I feel a momentary urge to get in touch with Liz Cooke, wherever she is, and ask what she thought about Jackson, and why she drew him like that.

Jackson is a baffling character. Also a strangely successful one. The reader believes in his powers, his benevolence, his capacity to help others without, apparently, needing to do more to help himself. He is good rather than nice or potent or wonderful. An Irish monk, who came once or twice to visit Iris, courteously disagreed when I suggested that Jackson might be Iris's own inner sense of what was beginning to happen to her. Did Jackson embody 'the end of what is necessary', death, that cannot but be good? We all share in it. The monk, however, would have none of this. For him, Jackson was the Holy Spirit, *tout court*, which Iris's genius as a writer had found and served, even though she was never a conscious believer.

None the less at the end of the book Jackson has lost his powers, but his obscure serenity remains. On the last page he rescues a spider. Iris would have done that, at any stage of her illness.

In the last sentence he smiles, as Iris smiled on the day she died.

I don't like going into the room she wrote in. It is still 'her' room. But it doesn't look as if she could ever have been in 'her room'. Or anybody else for that matter. Her room looks now as if it had already been abandoned long before we came here.

There is a copy of *Jackson's Dilemma* on the floor, which I pick up. The floor is thick with single shoes, and socks, and pieces of the *Evening Standard*, which she used to bring home after she had been up to London. I pick a bit off the floor – already the paper is turning a brownish colour – and find the date. 5 February 1994. About a year before the Alzheimer's started unmistakably to declare itself. No, not so much as a year; more like five or six months.

Iris was always fond of the *Evening Standard*, particularly the comic strips – Modesty Blaise being her favourite. I don't think she ever identified with the exploits of that redoubtable female, but, unconsciously perhaps, she liked to see a woman who was really very 'womanly' (not a word Iris at all cared for) behaving with such supermasculine vigour and resolution. Up to the time she ceased reading altogether she looked at the paper for Modesty's sake. I managed to get it for her most days by going down to the railway station, the only place it was available in Oxford. I would make a little routine of our driving down together, and she would sit in the car while I nipped in to buy it at the bookstall. I, too, followed the adventures of Modesty, although I could not see her as a woman at all and she had no part in my sex daydreams. Iris said she liked the absence of sex. 'Same as in *Treasure Island*?' I asked, and Iris emphatically agreed. Stevenson was a favourite of her father's, and *Treasure Island* was read to her when she was five or six.

Writing about his father, John Mortimer records that his last words were 'I'm always angry when I'm dying', and adds that these seemed like words that his father – a barrister in the Probate, Divorce and Admiralty Division

– might have been preparing to say for some time. In any case they are just right; and yet they are the words of an actor, which all barristers have, to some extent, to be. Iris had no last words, which was natural in her circumstances, but also she didn't have to be any sort of an actor.

In fact we both much disliked the theatre, though my dislike of it was more vocal than that of Iris, who without pretending was always polite and deferential about theatre business, as she was to her actor acquaintances and friends. But if we had to go to the theatre, she had, just as I did, that awful mixture of boredom and embarrassment that natural non-theatre-goers feel about the whole thing. It is like being tone-deaf.

Shakespeare is not exempt from this tone-deaf reaction in Iris and me: in fact he is, quite involuntarily of course, the prime offender. To read him, to recall the words of his beings in the mind's eye – that is one thing. To see the poor man 'acted' is, for us, quite another. We would rather pay a large sum than have to sit through *King Lear*; and we would do anything to avoid a 'sparkling performance' of Rosalind in *As You Like It*, or Beatrice in *Much Ado*.

For more than thirty years we managed to avoid Stratford altogether, except for one occasion when we were staying with the Priestleys, who lived nearby. Most uncharacteristically, for although a playwright he was no great devotee of the theatre, the Bard least of all, Priestley had taken seats for us to see Peter O'Toole as Shylock. After that experience we recovered over dinner in the sumptuous atmosphere of Kissing-Tree House, where Jack's expert staff had been devoted to him for many years.

By no means an untalkative man, Jack made no comment on the performance or play, but as he poured us out a bottle to go with the smoked salmon, he remarked: 'The quality of Meursault is not strained.'

It was indeed delicious Meursault, but I couldn't help

wondering if, as in the case of Mortimer's father, the jest mightn't have been some time in preparation.

No more than actors are playwrights spontaneous people, but whereas actors have to pretend to be, writers and their audience are well aware how much midnight oil has been burnt, and can savour the results accordingly, like connoisseurs of a fine wine. Shakespeare's happiest things can *seem* to come off the cuff – to the envy of Dryden and Ben Jonson – but as with all verbal art, appearances can be misleading.

Jack was much attached to Iris; he called her 'Ducky' and advised her in a fatherly way when she tried turning some of her novels into plays. He co-wrote with her the play *A Severed Head*, producing a number of new jokes, all of which, as even I had to admit, came off delightfully in the theatre. I remarked as much to Jack, who told me that things that are not funny at all when you merely say them, like 'Did you find a parking space?' could, by means of context and timing, become hilarious on the lips of a really good actor. For us theatrically-challenged persons that is the only thing an actor is really good for.

To my surprise I was not in the least embarrassed by Iris's plays, and in fact rather enjoyed them, particularly *The Servants and the Snow*, which was turned into an opera by William Matthias. One of its sad little arias still haunts my ear. Although not tone-deaf about music, Iris and I had no more inner sense and true grasp of it than we had of the theatre. Although Jack did such a brilliant job on *A Severed Head*, Iris's other plays are all rather lacking in excitement, a fact she was well aware of herself, and quite unbothered about. She knew the theatre wasn't her thing, but why shouldn't she have a try occasionally? It interested and amused her, and did no one any harm.

For me this introduces one of life's little ironies, only discoverable after a death. Bereavement has to be acted. Living now in my widower's house it is no use saying

I'm tone-deaf theatrically, for widowers are compelled to be actors; they have no choice. Naturally all of us are always acting a bit, acting the part of ourselves; but when we acquire a new profession – still more a new status – a new kind of role is required. At first I played a teacher of English, then a retired teacher of English. Not difficult to get the hang of that sort of part.

Playing a relict, or bereaved husband, is rather more demanding, but in an absurd sense more rewarding too. That acute, if tiresome, old theologian Von Hügel remarked that one kissed one's child not only because one loved it, but *in order that* one might love it. Does that sound like Teutonic overkill, or to put it in more Anglo-Saxon terms, a belt-and-braces policy? Going through the motions in order to feel the right emotions.

Getting a letter from anyone who has written good – as opposed to those merely conventional – words of condolence, such as 'our thoughts are with you at this difficult time', I find a helpless and involuntary spasm of tears prickling at my eyelids, while my face contracts like that of a disappointed baby. These symptoms have to be sternly repressed in public, and a properly controlled portion of restrained lachrymosity put in their place. At this stage I remember how the young David Copperfield, all of eight or nine years old, learned his own part as a bereaved child. He stood on a chair in the schoolroom to see with satisfaction how red his eyes were; and this in a sense had nothing to do directly with the depth and desolation of his grief at his mother's death. It was a way of revealing it, and so of coming to terms with it. Crafty old Von Hügel may have detested his offspring, if indeed he had any, but he perceived that by playing his part correctly he would come to feel the right thing about them. No hypocrisy in that. 'Being is acting,' says one of Iris's characters.

So I play my part. And really, it is hard to distinguish at moments between playing the part of one who is bereft,

and one who suffers all the inward misery of bereavement.

None of this acting business applied when I was a 'carer'.
There was no one then before whom to play the part. Not
even myself. For the first time in my life I suppose, and it
must apply to all the rest of us 'carers' too, I found myself
in what seemed the truly natural state of man, doing not
what I wanted to do but what had to be done: sinking into
daily depression; flying into rages; knowing wild moments
of the purest relief and elation when I loved Iris more than
I had ever done before, and felt closer to her than I had
ever felt before . . .

That was the end of what I wrote down just after Iris died,
and apparently forgot about in the days that followed. The
two women and the time I had had with them had driven
it out of my head.

I sat at the kitchen table and pondered the pages. I
decided it must have cheered me up to write them. I decided
it would do me good now to go on writing. I realised, in
an indifferent way, how extremely self-centred I seemed
to have become. With Iris gone there was no other centre.
Anything I wrote would just be about myself now. That
could not be helped: or at least I was not going to do
anything to help it.

Margot and Mella had certainly been a distraction. To
start writing again now would at least be a substitute for
Mella's departure. Should I write now about the time I had
had with the pair of them, and the drama – for surely it was
no less than that? – of their meeting?

I decided not to. Perhaps I had the feeling, even the wish,
that the drama might not yet be over. Mella might return.
Perhaps I half hoped she would.

I might as well start again from the point – more or less –
where I had left off: that morning quite soon after Iris died.
Probably now that Mella had disappeared, and there was

little news of Margot, nothing much more would happen. Part of me – most of me – hoped it would not. That must be, surely, the way I still wanted my new life to become? And to remain.

PART II

6

Back to Words and Books

I still have a sensation – no doubt all widows and widowers know it? – of being dead and buried. In the grave beside the loved one, like the deceased who might or might not have been a keen gardener. A rather grotesque sensation, putting one in the same place too as Hardy's wife, or his dog, or the other denizens of that buried world that he liked in his poems to imagine as still capable of being in touch with the living. They recall us at moments, and wave to us, and it is a satisfaction for them to think of us there, under the ground, separated but together. And not unseparated, even if we are in the form of ashes – the ashes of incinerated bones weigh quite a bit apparently – and scattered over the fields, or in the sea . . .

Suppose one were to become the unknown skeleton, hanging in a dusty corner of the anatomy department? Odd how difficult it would be to feel 'together yet separated' from a skeleton, even that of a loved one whose identity was known. At this point matters become too Gothic. In *The Revenger's Tragedy*, a Jacobean play now thought to be by Middleton, if I remember rightly, and not by Tourneur as was once supposed, the hero carried his fiancée's skull about with him. He does this to remind him to avenge her murder, but it would be a bit like knowing whose skeleton it was in the corner of the lab.

Since I've left myself to science in my will, as Iris did, I could easily end up as such a skeleton. Half of me might belong to some medical student. Peter Conradi told me that when he started off in medicine (he gave it up later) he temporarily owned such a half, bargaining it from a needy fellow student for whisky and cigarettes.

Hardy might easily have written a poem – perhaps not one of his best – about such a skeleton, hanging in a corner of the anatomy department, and lamenting to the poet that in the pride of enlightened middle age, when death is unimaginable, he had left himself to science. How bitterly he now regrets it as he hangs in his dusty corner!

I remembered asking the undertaker about coffins. I already knew from an official on the phone that Iris would have to be cremated or buried. After taking samples of her brain they were, for some reason, not permitted to make the rest of her over to the anatomy department.

Was it necessary to have a coffin, I asked. The undertaker looked unsurprised and a little weary, as if this was just one of the ways by which his customers hoped to reduce the bill, and he had heard them all many times.

'Coffin? Not for the interment, sir.'

I must have looked surprised, because he went on to explain that, strictly speaking, all that was technically necessary for an interment was a shroud. Cremation, on the other hand, required a coffin. This seemed to me illogical, but there was no point in saying so. Instead I was tempted to ask what difference it made to the price. But I didn't feel up to trying to tease him. It was clear, in any case, that he was impervious to being teased. He anticipated any query I might have raised.

'Expenses, sir, are very similar, unless you should be requiring something quite out of the ordinary.'

I wondered what sort of thing I could suggest: perhaps a silver birch or a gingko (Iris's favourite tree) planted on the site of the grave or ashes. But again, in his slightly uncanny fashion, the undertaker seemed to anticipate the direction in which my mind was working. Should I have ecology in mind, he assured me, the plain wooden coffin was kinder to nature than the composition substitute. He did not explain why, and again I did not feel up to asking him. I wanted now to end the interview as soon as possible. But something about it made me suddenly determined to change my will. Previously I had been convinced that I couldn't care less about my own disposal, but something about the undertaker now made me think again. I felt relieved and grateful that Iris, apart from the samples of her brain in various places of learning, was to be safely incinerated. I determined to follow her example.

Nor need I be present, as the undertaker was now reassuring me, when Iris was cremated. The job would be done at the quiet time in the early morning; before the rush, so to speak. I was glad of that. And I was glad I had decided not to be an official skeleton. I must remember to change my will.

I thought of the skeleton I would escape becoming, its bony arms and legs manipulated expertly by a demonstrator, or jocosely by idle students. The thought of it brought me back to the moment on that Monday afternoon in Vale House. Iris had seemed a little uncomfortable on her back, and I settled her on her side where she lay quietly at ease, her eyes open. She reached her arms out and began to move them to and fro as if playing. Perhaps she was indeed playing a game, the rules of which would never be explained. Patting her hands I tried to play with her, but her arms were like well-designed mechanical devices, which did not resist my hand, but as soon as released resumed their purposeful continuity, to and fro, to and fro.

There began to be something perturbing about these movements, which bore no relation to the games we used to play together. Remembering now their strange softness and gentleness I thought of Dr Jacoby, that kind scholar and brain specialist, who used to drop in on us from time to time when the Alzheimer's was entering its final stages. After Iris died he told me that our brains are made of a very soft, almost jelly-like, material. To be studied under the microscope they must first be 'fixed' in formalin, a delicate and complex process which takes weeks, perhaps months, to complete in the pathology lab.

Through this softness in the head all the infinite complexity of physical and mental behaviour is transmitted and controlled. Was this movement of Iris's arms all that was left of the mysteries within a once brilliant brain? 'I intend to make my mark,' the young Iris had once said, long before I met her.

Her genius lives in her books, but that brilliant brain will continue, strangely enough, to have its own sort of physical existence.

I remembered turning Iris gently on to her other side, and as I moved her I realised that she was no longer there. She had stopped breathing. And she had done it as naturally as the rest of us carry on breathing. I held her hands now and they remained, as if trustfully, in mine. I closed her eyes and then opened them again as if I were myself playing a little game with her; and when I opened them she looked at me, as if merrily, and as if she were glad that I was still there.

I was glad too. I should always have been sorry if I had not been there. I would have felt like a bird-watcher who had been absent, or looking the wrong way, and had missed the brief appearance of a rare and wonderful bird.

That sense of exaltation soon disappeared. And soon, too, there were all the 'arrangements' to be made. It was perhaps because I was still feeling the effects of being exalted that I had the idea of teasing the professionally unteasable undertaker. A big, solidly-built man, who looked like my idea of a Victorian archdeacon. He wore a curious sleeveless waistcoat of black padded nylon, which seemed thoroughly suitable as a kind of 'undress' style for calling on clients on a cold day, although not, of course, for the pomp and circumstance of the funeral. His manner was equally calm and reassuring. We will take care of everything; all you have to do is pay the bill. Which I had done, on the spot, and without a murmur.

A widower after forty-four years, or however much more it is. I don't feel strong enough at the moment to tot the months up. I only feel strong enough to go on writing about Iris, which means writing about ourselves – myself. G.K. Chesterton said that if a man ceases to believe in God he doesn't believe in nothing – he believes in anything. I cling to writing as a form of belief. I don't believe in anything else, but I believe in Iris, and believing in her is a belief in her survival, both for me in my own way, and for her survival in everyone who reads her work. How could I not believe that?

I'm like Hardy believing in his wife, Emma, surviving on the wild North Cornish shore and on the cliff-top where she used to ride her pony. Emma surviving and talking to him, telling him she was not as she was . . . But Iris for me is just as she was, whether before or after the Alzheimer's; although I know that her survival for me depends on me, that we shall soon pass into 'existlessness' together, and that Iris will then remain alive only for her readers down the years and the ages.

> It shall not last for ever,
> No more than earth or skies . . .

as Housman says; but at least it will last as long as there are books to read.

I thought of Jake in Iris's first novel, *Under the Net*, riding on top of a bus and thinking of death. Thoughts come and go; they are used and they are enjoyed, and they vanish with the last chop which ends them. 'So I meditated, and was reluctant to get off the bus.' Had Iris lost all thoughts before she died? Again I can't stop thinking of that once active, fertile brain darkening, emptying, going dim and void . . . And as so often when she was alive, I don't know whether or not to hope that through that dark time there was nothing there.

What can one mean by a brain with nothing there? It sounds peaceful, even merciful, and yet of course it isn't. There was the unending anxiety of Alzheimer's. During the last few months, when the incoherence that goes with anxiety began to dissipate at last, Iris could not think. But she could feel, act on impulse, even plan. Anxiety as a state of mind was replaced by an occasional, but purposeful, impulse to escape. To try the door until the moment came when I had forgotten to relock it after we had come in together, and then to run out and disappear from the oppressions of the mind and its emptiness, and the house and its emptiness. She could no longer fill it with her love and purpose and all their activities. Love had lost its purpose and remained only as itself, the impulse that still made her throw herself into my arms, but could shed no tears for us, nor look into my eyes.

To escape. Anywhere, anywhere out of the world. Not into death, for clearly death as an idea no longer existed. Iris no longer had any awareness of it.

Or had she? At Vale House in the last month she was happy. No need for escape now. Her body seemed to know that death was coming and became glad; her smiles in reply to the nurses' smiles more rapturous. She smiled at us all as if she were giving a party. That she did not, or could not, eat or drink was for her a bit of a joke, about which she was half apologetic, and a little mischievous too. Yet no one in Vale House thought she was going to die so soon.

Her body wished to be finished with itself. Those reachings out of her arms seemed like a rite of departure. And then she was gone. Broncho-pneumonia, said the death certificate: the standard conventional formula. But an elderly body cannot last long without food or water, and the body seems to know this well.

I keep coming back to it all and mixing up experiences in a chaotic way. But I must become coherent; settle down in my new widower's house, put the rooms and myself in order. In several places, on the floors of rooms or in a pile of miscellaneous objects, I see Jackson's beautiful haunting face, the face on the jacket of Iris's last novel.

'My powers have left me, will they return? At the end of what is necessary I have come to a place where there is no road.'

Jackson is there; but so many things that used to be in the house seem to have disappeared. Suddenly remembering the Korean vase, one of the pair we were given in Seoul, I started the other day to search for it compulsively. She said she liked the plain grey. But perhaps if I could only find it there would be a message on it for me, some tranquil blue letters which would speak to me alone?

It was no use. I looked everywhere. But the vase had gone.

All right, let all the things in the house disappear, unremembered and unrecorded, without my having to do anything further about them. Let them all vanish and be no more seen, so that I can start again. But for the bereft, remembering becomes as much of an obsession as first love once was.

I loved Iris when she was writing, and far off from me. As a writer she was always spare, quiet, intent. A very private writer, who seldom showed me anything at the time she was writing. And I never asked her. All that was outside ourselves, and our own life together. Now I read her books the whole time; and writing of her – with her as it seems – is the only way of communicating I still have.

No wonder Hardy held those dialogues in poetry with

his dead wife Emma. They drifted apart – really apart, not closer apart. He didn't talk to her much when she was alive, and he seems not to have talked to his second wife Florence either. Communication for him was his poetry, the mode through which he learnt – after her death – to talk to Emma. For a reticent man, too, it was a way of communing with himself.

I never felt that that was true of Iris. The self she was with me was not the self who wrote, but she never seemed to commune with any other self in her own writing either. One odd reason why the characters in Hardy's novels are often unsatisfactory is that they are outside himself. Iris's were all inside her. Hardy's own inside being comes out only in his poetry; he always regarded himself as a poet who wrote novels for the money. In poetry he leads his own life, and talks with himself as he wishes. His own little fantasies, which often come out in poems, are quite ordinary. He might have married someone else; he might have been a swell gent, or a landowner, or a beautiful woman or a singing bird. But for him as for Yeats, a very different kind of poet, words themselves are the true good, the certain comforter.

Much more so, I myself find nowadays, than fantasies are. Nowadays, I have fantasies with words. They get nowhere, and would have very little public appeal, but they absorb me in some familial way, for I find myself explaining them to Iris, who lends an indulgent ear. I wouldn't, of course, have bothered her with them when she was alive and well and busy.

As the poet Auden wisely observed, 'Memorable Words' is the only good definition of poetry. He himself when he was young loved geological terms like 'iron pyrites'.

I have learnt a few words of Spanish, mostly of the useful kind, which for that reason are the ones that are hardest to remember. The only one of these that has really stuck means our plain and humble little 'too', which no one could consider putting in any category of memorableness.

But the Spanish *demasiado* – there is a lordly 'too', with a fine full distinction, a word under full sail! *'Demasiado caliente!'* I imagine myself observing tersely but graciously to some chambermaid, as I step into the high hot bath she has prepared for me. She will hasten to run in some cold water, giving me occasion to tell her a few moments later, *'Ahora demasiado frio!'* It would make my day.

This kind of fantasy has no linguistic boundaries, particularly if one knows very few of the words in a language, and none of the grammar. In 1993, Iris and I were conveyed in a ramshackle Russian van from the city to Moscow airport, in company with Sir Michael Caine, promoter of the Russian Booker Prize; an enterprising venture which was having its first trial that year. Although she had once studied Russian, Iris in her modest way declined to take part, but she was warmly pressed by Sir Michael, who had become very fond of her, to come along anyway to grace the judging ceremony. Like many incompetent linguists, including, by his own claim, Edward Lear, I can read – up to a point – without properly understanding a language or being able to speak it. This is true of my Russian. I love the words, but learnt them only from Pushkin's poems, bits of which I know by heart. This hardly constituted a reason for being a junior member of the Booker jury committee, but Sir Michael seemed to think it enough; and I struggled with the (fortunately meagre) number of novels offered by sceptical Russian publishers for our attention. The list had already been weeded out by native critics. We duly made an award, which seemed reasonably just as well as popular, letting ourselves be guided by the masterful Chairwoman, a former high-up in the Communist Party educational system. One of the books on offer she had viewed with great severity, pronouncing it a novel too disgusting even to read. This verdict mildly surprised the American juror as well as myself, as both of us were well accustomed to much worse things in our perusal of contemporary Western fiction. But Russian novelists had recently drunk the uncensored draught of sexual liberty, and had become touchingly determined to demonstrate that today in the former Soviet Union anything goes. With the usual results.

The ceremony that followed was not without some tricky moments. The assembled guests, having drunk a good quantity of vodka, seemed unaware that Sir Michael was making a rather good speech to them in English; they paid no attention to the translation which followed, but continued to dispute the award among themselves with some heat, and at the tops of their voices.

Next morning we set off for the airport in a van which seemed about to break down at any moment. The only thing that worked well was the heating, which was super-efficient, but as it happened the early November weather was uncommonly warm. On our first visit, more than a month before, it had snowed and frozen so hard that the planes on the runway had had to be de-iced. We were appropriately clad for an arctic Moscow, not for this unexpected and overpowering heatwave.

After we had endured it for a few minutes, Sir Michael turned to me and said, 'John, tell him to open the window and switch the bloody heating off. I'm being boiled.'

There was no Russian in the van, or an interpreter to help me out. I had a moment of utter blankness, and then two words from Pushkin popped into my head as if by magic, as magically indeed as the wonderful events in his poem *Ruslan and Lyudmila*. I turned to the driver and said in what I hoped was a lofty and authoritative tone:

'Slishkom teplo.'

The sallow woebegone face of the young driver, who looked like an old-fashioned English spiv and was dressed for the part, turned its gaze on me in some surprise. I had a moment of panic. Were Pushkin's words wholly obsolete, poetical, old-fashioned, entirely devoid of contemporary meaning? . . . But then with suddenly respectful haste, the driver fiddled with something on his antique dashboard. An irregular roaring, which we had hardly heard above the noise of the van traversing the ravines and crevasses in the Moscow suburban boulevard, ceased abruptly. With a sweep of his arm the driver forced down the window, and within seconds the temperature was back to normal, indeed rather below it.

Pushkin had saved the day. I had a quick mental picture of his dark good-natured face and his famous flashing white teeth, smiling at me with puckish amusement. But anxieties instantly returned. Suppose Sir Michael now felt too cold and asked me to have the window closed, and the heating restored? I searched my mind for a word-spell that might do this, but nothing came. Iris gave me a comforting smile and a squeeze, but I remained on tenterhooks until we bumped past the last of the scraggy birches and into Sheremetyev airport. After uttering my majestic announcement I was further distracted by the young driver, who kept up a one-sided conversation, presumably taking for granted that 'too hot' was not the only Russian phrase I knew. He seemed to have taken quite a fancy to me. I laughed heartily at what he said to try to show I was in the picture, and occasionally uttered a '*Da*' or a '*Horosho*', but I hadn't the faintest idea what he was talking about, and I was relieved to get to the airport without too much loss of face.

Slishkom teplo! Demasiado caliente! These lordly phrases seem to speak to one another from opposite ends of Europe, almost unattached to their meanings, but sharing that ring of zestful exactness which goes with the words of which poetry can be made.

When in Pushkin's heroic poem *Poltava* the young Cossacks dismiss the wily old Mazeppa as being too old to lead them – *on slishkom star!* – the words give the feeling of poetry springing freshly from the page, uncreated before. It seems as scornfully *slishkom* as it is possible to be. Pushkin only uses simple words in his poems; but he uses them as if such words had never been used before, and had never before possessed the force and magic of meaning which his poetry now gives them.

Since Iris died poems and bits of poems float into my head at all hours, in place of those little 'soap fantasies' that used to run there, sometimes rewinding themselves and reappearing in a slightly different version. But now pieces of poem come when I get out of bed, or when the disturbed and disturbing emptiness of mid-morning seems all that the day offers. These poem-words not only console more than my soap fantasies ever did, but seem to wander about in the head and out of it, like the thoughts which Belial in *Paradise Lost* says are the chief consolation of consciousness, of being alive.

> For who would lose
> Though full of pain, this intellectual being,
> These thoughts that wander through eternity,
> To perish rather, swallowed up and lost
> In the wide womb of uncreated night,
> Devoid of sense and motion.

When Iris was alive I often thought of Belial's words, and of the horror in her poor head, where thoughts no longer hovered about like dust motes in the mind's sunlight.

Or did they? How could we be sure, who could say? Was it just that she had no means of letting me know? Is the expression of our experience inseparable from experience itself, as I think we unconsciously assume and take for granted? If we feel or think something we cannot help but express it in some form, in our heads or to other people: the one following from the other.

Critics have suggested the possibility that Milton, writing that passage in *Paradise Lost*, had in mind, or at least in his unconscious memory, the speech in Shakespeare's *Measure for Measure* in which Lucio, under sentence of death, expresses so dramatically the terror of losing all that comes to us with our consciousness.

> Aye, but to die and go we know not where,
> To lie in cold obstruction and to rot . . .
> This sensible warm motion to become
> A kneaded clod, and the delighted spirit
> To bathe in fiery floods, or to reside
> In thrilling region of thick-ribbed ice . . .

Never mind the fire and ice that once went with hell and purgatory. What strikes home now in the passage is our precarious possession of a 'delighted spirit', and its 'sensible warm motion'. No: we can't leave that, whatever happens. Not until we absolutely have to.

It seems likely that both passages may derive, perhaps independently, from that little poem supposed to have been written by the Emperor Hadrian; perhaps written when he was himself near death.

> *animula vagula blandula*
> *hospes comesque corporis*
> *quo nunc abibis? in loca*
> *pallidula rigida nubila*
> *nec ut soles dabis iocos*

> little mind, tender little wanderer,
> body's guest and companion,
> where must you be off to now? into a place
> dark enough, and rigid and gloomy,
> nor will you exchange familiar jokes.

Translation, however inadequate, at least shows the similarity with those other examples. The mind, like the body, is warm and tender, but until it dies and disappears with the body it can wander about as the body cannot, cherishing itself, and its thoughts, and its joke-pleasures.

If examples like this are anything to go by, the Roman sense of humour remains quite familiar to us. Those customary or habitual jokes and comic rituals must go on in most homes, now as then. Their usualness can become wearisome, but is also a part of their power to comfort, like those 'situation' jokes which recur week by week in the *New Yorker*; the cowled figure with a scythe over his shoulder who appears at the door of the matrimonial apartment, or (as used to be) the Charles Addams family spreading their own peculiar forms of sweetness and light.

A truly new joke is the greatest of rarities, but possibly the Emperor Vespasian, one of Hadrian's predecessors, made such a joke when by accident or design he exclaimed on his deathbed *'ut puto deus fio'* – 'I rather think I'm becoming a god.' Deification after death was a normal part of the imperial procedure, but Vespasian, toughest of tough eggs – and with his son Titus the destroyer of Jerusalem – might seem on the face of it the last person not to take himself quite seriously, even as he lay dying. His remark might of course have been made in all seriousness, but it doesn't sound like it. It is disconcerting to think that ogres and tyrants (and possibly Vespasian was neither) may have just as much ability to see a joke, or to make one at their own expense, as we would wish to think we had ourselves. That said, it is none the less hard to imagine Hitler or Stalin making or enjoying a merry quip about their failing powers, or their ultimate destiny.

As it happens A.E. Housman the poet and Adolf Hitler the monster had the same sort of sense of humour – crude, vulgar, scatological and unfunny. But there don't seem to be any conclusions to be drawn from that. Iris disliked sex jokes except the really elegant and witty ones. Sex is a subject about which the humorist is well advised to go carefully and to tread delicately – not usually a recipe for successful joke-making, nor for the sudden burst of quaint inspiration which caused the emperor Vespasian to observe that he felt he might be on the verge of becoming a god.

Thinking about the Russian Booker Prize (now alas defunct) and those fine old muscular words *slishkom* and *demasiado*, led me back to the following year, 1994, and the English Booker Prize. The five of us on the panel had four or five hundred novels to get through – perhaps more, memory does not recall the exact amount – and there was no question of their numbers being weeded out for us; we had to do the whole job ourselves, with three or four months to do it in. I found myself in a state of dazed enjoyment, as book after book, all fresh and optimistic in their gleaming jackets, abode their destined hours in my company, and went their way. A select few were retained beside me for further consultation.

It was books, books, books from morning to night. I asked one or two friends if they would mind reading a few about which I was both interested and doubtful; but with one exception I did not inflict any on Iris, who was just completing *Jackson's Dilemma*. (This was a year or so before the first signs of Alzheimer's disease became fully apparent.) Iris had herself been on the shortlist for the Booker many times, and she won it in 1978 with *The Sea! The Sea! Jackson's Dilemma*, her last offering, appeared in 1995. Its predecessor, *The Green Knight*, had come out at the end of 1993 and was eligible for the 1994 prize. My colleagues were enthusiastic about it, but we all agreed, sensibly I think, that a previous winner should be considered ineligible, at least unofficially. (This sound *ad hoc* convention was not observed when J.M. Coetzee – or was it some other novelist like Salman Rushdie? – was given the prize a second time.)

I had no need to declare an interest in *The Green Knight*; my relation to Iris was obvious. But it happened that my own novel, *Alice*, my first for many years, appeared in June 1994. The publisher said he would have liked to put it in for the prize, but agreed that in the circumstances this was hardly possible. *Alice* was a small *jeu d'esprit* which I had much enjoyed writing; and Colin Haycraft, kindest of men, who ran Duckworth on a shoe-string, said he would be delighted to publish it, provided I did not expect to get paid.

Another colleague, James Wood, caused a slight hitch in our deliberations, upon which the press descended with their usual glee. His wife, like mine, had a novel in for the prize, and he had had the good idea of keeping quiet about this until he had heard the candid comments, arrived at all unawares, from his fellow-members of the jury; for at our joint sessions we briefly discussed each offering. At that crucial point he was planning to modestly observe that the lady whose novel we were talking about happened to be his wife.

But unfortunately another juror got wind of the connection, and taxed James with it before we came to discuss the book, which as it turned out we had all enjoyed, although no one suggested putting it on the shortlist. It was a small matter, although the press inevitably made as much of it as they could. For some reason these Booker goings-on are always newsworthy, and the journalists were delighted when we got ourselves into another muddle over the final selection, ending up with a winner – James Kelman's *How Late It Was, How Late* – which none of us particularly wanted. I was unable to press very hard for my own favourite, Alan Hollinghurst's *The Folding Star*, because that delightful writer had been a pupil of mine when he was doing his thesis at Oxford. Our most spirited juror, Rabbi Julia Neuberger, protested vigorously against our eventual award, taking much the same stand against an 'obscene' novel that our Russian Chairwoman had taken in Moscow the previous year.

Obscenity apart – and the obscenity certainly became monotonous and even ritualised – James Kelman's offering was in its own way a remarkable book, and I do not think we were so wrong in thinking well of it, even though not to the point of wanting it to win. One of our number was strongly in favour of a curious work whose name I cannot now recall, which the author had published herself. It was a religious allegory, set in an imaginary rather than a historical past, and I asked Iris if she would like to have a look at it, since the book certainly made an impression. Iris was impressed too, reading it with characteristic care (the reason why I did not inflict more than this unusual one of my bunch upon her) and making some shrewd comments and criticism. It was less than a year before the early symptoms of Alzheimer's were bad enough to make reading all but impossible for her.

The Booker Prize gives good service to the reading public, and the publicity that surrounds it is not necessarily a bad thing. Martin Goff, the humorous and extremely competent Director who used to run the show, told me that the Board were delighted by the amount of dissension and controversy that went on that year.

'They all agreed, John, that you were the most incompetent Chairman ever, and that this had been a most *excellent* thing.'

On the more serious side, Booker judges can point to uniquely good writers, like Anita Brookner and Penelope Fitzgerald, who won the prize in their uncertain early days, and went on to produce many mature masterpieces. Such an award can give a promising and original writer the best kind of practical encouragement.

I keep remembering the day, ages ago now, when I repeated the mantrap episode, catching my tail on the windsor chair. The way in which the repetition made me forget that Iris was dead was certainly remarkable. I really did think I should be able to tell her what had happened. And it was a bit later that day that I had my first real explosion of tears, as unexpected as a sudden cloudburst or a flash flood. I felt myself borne along on top of it, as one might be on fast flowing water, but the sensation of helplessness was compellingly comforting and engrossing. I couldn't help thinking that it must be rather like the female orgasm, which has been compared to a waterfall. Perhaps it's the only occasion when a male gets some notion of what female experience can be like.

But weeping itself is a solitary experience. Men do it as much as women, but both sexes are secretly indifferent to the other's tears. To be 'a good cry' it must be done on one's own. Otherwise it cannot avoid looking done for a purpose. Tennyson's Princess had no choice but to weep in public, but being used to that she could also be spontaneous. Tennyson the Victorian certainly knew all about it. Home they bring her warrior dead, and she remains expressionless and dry-eyed. What can her maidens do to make her weep?

> Rose a nurse of ninety years,
> Set her babe upon her knee.
> Like summer tempests came her tears.
> 'Sweet my child, I live for thee.'

A fairly accurate account, minus the child in my case of course. But perhaps that mantrap story I so much wanted to tell Iris was a kind of substitute for that cathartic nurse and child?

A quotation from that song in the poem was used by Kenneth Grahame, rather oddly but successfully, as almost everything in *The Wind in the Willows* is successful. 'Like summer tempests came his tears' became the heading for the last chapter. They are Toad's tears of remorse. Toad – so terminally if so very improbably – has turned over a

new leaf. 'He was indeed an altered Toad.' It is as good
a way to end the immortal fantasy as any other could be.
But summer tempest tears do not herald a new beginning.
They hold only belated recognition of what is past.

Iris used to hum her own kind of Toad songs, and she
continued to do this after she became ill.

Wow-wer-wer-wow-wow-wow
Wow-wowo-wer-wow-wow-wow

Sometimes, when she could no longer speak at all coherently, she would hum her tune as we lay in bed together
in the early morning. In earlier days I used to play our
record of the ballet music of *Petrushka*, and Iris loved the
bit near the beginning, which we imagined must be the
puppet ballerina dancing her *pas seul* for the Moor. We
used to hum it together.

WOW-wowo-wow-wow
Wow-wowo-wer-wow-wow-wow

trying to end on that little note of hesitancy and interroga-
tion which is interrupted by new and threatening chords.
Together with the later tune from the fairground, which
I always thought of as 'Sorochintsy Fair', though that is
a tale by Gogol – Stravinsky's is the big annual fair at St
Petersburg – we liked it the best of the music in *Petrushka*.

I remember now reading somewhere, or perhaps I heard
it on a Radio 3 programme, that Stravinsky 'borrowed'
what we thought of as the tune of the little ballerina from
a barrel organ which was playing outside his hotel in Paris.
To his surprise and annoyance, the composer of this tune –
a popular cabaret song – turned out to be very much alive,
and recognised it at once when the music of *Petrushka* was
publicly recorded. His agent promptly sued Stravinsky for
infringement of copyright, and the great composer had to
pay up.

With Iris's little tune often in my head, I recognise it for the first time as her own memory of *Petrushka*. Emphasised and simplified, her wow-wows approximate to the tune we used to try to hum together.

I think Iris never tried to compose music, though she had a few piano lessons when she was small, and at the age of seven or so she wrote a fairy play for performance by her school class. It had a chorus of rabbits. So far as I could gather, the rabbits didn't have much to do except caper about in their furry costumes, but the star part of the Fairy Princess was written for a big girl about to leave school. Iris told me she was always kind and encouraging to the young ones. Her name was June Duprez. Her father was an impresario of some kind, and later on managed to get his daughter, who was exceedingly pretty, the star part of the Persian Princess in a wartime Korda film called *The Thief of Baghdad*.

Done in sumptuous Technicolor, *The Thief of Baghdad* was deservedly successful, and June Duprez was absolutely sweet as well as beautiful. She couldn't act for toffee, however much of a success she may have been with Iris and the rabbits, and I believe her subsequent career in films faded painlessly out. This film had a lot of stunning special effects – the genie emerging out of his bottle in a great black cloud, and the 'child' star Sabu, known as the 'Elephant Boy', riding on his magic carpet over spectacular Arabian mountains and ravines, no doubt borrowed from some Californian footage the studio happened to have around. It was all shot in Pinewood, during the war.

I remember the shock of coming out of the small cinema where these wonders had taken place into the grey winter afternoon in Gerrards Cross; and in my memory now June Duprez and the young Caliph and the villainous Vizier Conrad Veidt, with his green eyes and sinister German accent, have somehow got mixed up with Iris's rabbit play, her early morning wow-wer-wows, and the haunting little jingle from *Petrushka*, which Stravinsky first heard on the barrel organ. Wow-wows had in any case been our recognition signal from early days. If I came back to the house and couldn't find Iris at once I used to give a wow or two and hear a distant wow-wow in response, and more of them as we came closer to each other.

Even today my pulses would quicken a little at the sight of June Duprez in that film. In her elocution school accent she repelled the advances of Conrad Veidt until he got the young Caliph in his power and threatened to blind him and throw him in a dungeon. Then: 'Take me in your arms,' she told the villainous Veidt with icy disdain, sounding as if she had just come back from helping with the school treat at whatever academy young Sabu attended. I forget how she was rescued, but I still vividly recall the moment earlier on when the young Caliph climbed a tree overlooking the harem garden in order to see her. Sitting with her ladies at the edge of a pool – fully clothed of course – she sees his face reflected in the water, and hears his disembodied voice swearing that he loves her.

'Now that you have found me, O genie of the pool, will you love me to the end of the world?'

I sometimes used to imitate that speech for Iris when we spoke of her early schooldays, and she always shed a tear or two, and told me how nice June had been to the little ones, which I could well believe, and how the school had idolised her. Probably some of the mistresses too, I should imagine.

I once suggested to Iris that we write together an academic version of the rabbit play, with a chorus of inebriated dons chanting:

> We don't care for the thinky girls
> What we want are slinky girls,
> Minky girls, kinky girls, winky girls,
> And most of all the drinky girls . . .

So far as I can recall no more was done, but we used to chant something like that in the car sometimes. It became a part of our mythology.

So did two other songs we used to play: 'Yellow Bird' and 'Yellow Submarine'.

'Yellow bird, you seem all alone like me,' Iris would hum, looking at me with a fond look, which seemed to imply that I was never to be alone like the bird; even though, as we both knew, being married was the best possible way of being alone. I used to tell Iris that I was annoyed with the lyrics of 'Yellow Submarine'. The chorus should have taken up the words of the grizzled mariner who supposedly tells them about his life in the land of submarines. 'We all lived in a yellow submarine' it should go, I thought: not 'live' in a yellow submarine. I preferred the notion of past dangers and wartime patrols, to the distasteful idea of a contemporary rave, in which the old salt's tale is forgotten. To the young, in any case, the song itself must now seem antediluvian.

If I got too pedantic about such things Iris sometimes said 'Woof Woof', like a dog, impatient for its owner to stop talking and take it for a walk. She herself was a stickler for accuracy in her novels, and she enjoyed any procedure that was intent on getting things right. A Canadian friend of hers, a philosopher who had taught at a military academy, once fascinated her by explaining how important it was to get right the exact proportions of the new Canadian flag: the maple leaf just the right size and in the middle of the white centre section, the red borders neither too big nor too small. I had a fondness for flags myself. Iris bought me a handbook called *Flags of the World* or some such title, and while she was away with a delegation in China for three or four weeks – the longest time we were ever separated – I made some Valentine flags for her return. By coincidence she came back on 14 February. The flags were of Catland, as we called our own imaginary country.

Today I found the big card, quite unexpectedly; it was preserved carefully at the bottom of a cluttered drawer in Iris's study, or rather the room upstairs where she wrote. 'Study' sounds like an organised methodical place, and the room where Iris wrote was anything but that. The quantity of papers and books and sea-stones and shoes and bits of clothing, to say nothing of less identifiable rubbish, is so great that I have done nothing about it; I didn't want even to go in there. This morning I tried just to drift in absently, determined not to make it seem like an act of the will, but I realised as I poked about that I had been almost frightened to go in before.

Was this because of the concentration of now derelict or indefinable things that had once meant something to Iris, even if briefly? Of the scraps of letters, some half-finished, or hardly begun, I felt an almost superstitious horror. But I was glad anyway to find my valentine for that year, 'The Flags of Old Catland', although it had faded almost out of recognition. My crimson and dark-blue designs had turned pink and grey over the years; the chalks, or whatever it was I had used, had certainly not been colour-fast.

But the one I remembered having been proudest of and had given pride of place in the centre of the design, 'The Banner of the Fighting Mouse', still looked bold and black. The mouse's belligerent whiskers, done in Indian ink, were still as spruce and sharply defined as they were all those years ago, when 'How's that catmouse?' was a greeting between us.

The Chinese expedition, I recall, was quite a grand one, headed by Richard Attenborough. Iris was one of the distinguished female delegates, presumably representing art and letters. They had an audience with Deng Xiaoping, the Party boss and head of the government. They travelled mostly by train, staying in vast and gloomy hotels. In one of these a party of Rolls-Royce engineers was rumoured to be billeted. Iris and a couple of others set out to walk the long corridors in search of these fellow-countrymen, and Iris made the ingenious suggestion that they should chant 'Rule Britannia' as they went. It worked like a charm. Doors flew open and lonely engineers swarmed out, eager in their solitude to meet up with compatriots.

On another occasion Iris found herself talking in a general way to some Chinese peasant women. As they all relaxed – audiences always did that with Iris – the women began to ply the interpreter with questions. The interpreter, an efficient and sophisticated lady from Beijing who was minding the delegation, looked rather embarrassed. Iris made enquiry.

'Well, you must excuse please, Miss Murdoch. They are simple people, and they are asking if Western women are the same as Chinese, or different.'

The interpreter made matters clear by sketching in the air below her waist with a delicate forefinger. Iris assured the peasant ladies, rather to their disappointment she felt, that those arrangements were the same throughout the world, at least so far as she knew. The story grew in the telling. Another female member of the delegation swore that Iris had promptly dropped her skirt and pants and given a practical demonstration, which met with hearty acclaim. That seems most unlikely; Iris said nothing about it to me. She had a great deal of natural modesty, and in spite of their curiosity I imagine that the Chinese ladies would have understood that.

Do all widows and widowers go through a time of hearing the voice? Or perhaps it's more a question of listening involuntarily to what the voice suggests? Inflections, pet words, scraps of song? At moments the 'Yellow Submarine'; then the little theme from *Petrushka*. That is the most insistent of all. Iris always took it up if I started to try to hum it and we made a hash of it together. We loved trying to put that last 'wow' in the right place.

I began to hum it this morning, almost masochistically, as I sought a footing amongst all the varied junk that covered the floor of Iris's room. And as I hummed, an unfamiliar name popped into my head. Maud Bigge. Who was she and where had she come from? Was there an association with *Petrushka*? Yes, indeed there was. I hummed again, hearing Iris hum too, and the title came to me. *My Secret London*, by Maud Bigge. She must have been a journalist of the Twenties or Thirties, who probably wrote for the *Evening News* or *Standard*. She must have assembled her pieces into a book; now I remember its colour, and that it was published by Methuen.

I was six or seven. My godmother had given it to my mother as a birthday present. I was bidden to write a birthday greeting on the flyleaf, which I accomplished laboriously in pencil.

I doubt if my mother ever read the book. I rediscovered it, tucked away on the shelf in a corner of her bedroom, when I was just about to go back to boarding school. It was going to be my second term and I felt apprehensive and miserable. On an impulse I asked if I could take the book back with me; anything about London could only be comforting. My mother let me do that, and I was not wrong: the book *was* cheering.

Hard now to imagine why. The unpretentious, quietly amusing, sometimes sentimental little book became a part of my imaginative life. And *Petrushka* came into it. Miss Bigge (or Mrs, but I still like to think Miss) had attended a performance of Stravinsky's ballet in London, and the clown Petrushka had touched her heart. She wrote a whole piece about him.

I remember finding the book years and years ago – it must have been some time after we got married. But then I felt not the smallest revival of interest in it and so it dropped out of sight again. Now I've spent two days searching for it – all over the house. Quite uselessly. It has gone back into the shadowy old London of those days, together with its unknown author.

Could she be still alive? Hardly. But it feels as if both of us are in the widowed state. Maud Bigge and her book have disappeared as definitively as Iris has. But Iris's books live on. I hope Maud Bigge's do too, somewhere, and are still read by some old lady or gent like myself, who has taken them from the bookcase in the same fit of nostalgia.

I imagine Maud Bigge as a jolly, spirited young woman, with dark hair and a decisive manner. The sort of woman whom a boy at the age of twelve or so would get on with. And I was touched by her tenderness for poor Petrushka, whom I had never heard of before.

Iris had never heard of Maud Bigge, nor seen the book, and her interest in *Petrushka* was limited to the little hum which pleased her even after she became ill, because we used to hum it together. In happier times she loved more robust affairs, like the Irish songs of Percy French, who wrote 'Abdul the Bul-Bul Emir' and sold it to a Dublin publisher for five shillings. Had he retained the copyright it would have made him many thousands of pounds.

Iris also knew all the words of 'The Old Orange Flute' and in the days before she was ill would sing it with great *brio*.

In the midst of the flames there was heard a great noise,
'Twas the old flute still playing 'The Protestant Boys'.

'The Protestant Boys' was originally sung to the tune of 'Liliburlero', the defiantly ironic little ditty with words invented by Protestant singers to suggest the sort of gibberish that they thought of the native Irish as speaking. The BBC World Service has now adopted it for a signature tune. Probably the tune was already old when Purcell used it in a harmonious suite. A few politically-correct PR men suggested to the Corporation that the Irish might not like it, but one hopes the Irish have more sense than that, as well as more sense of humour.

I sometimes teased Iris about her staunch Irish Protestantism, whereupon she would purse up her lips and smile forgivingly, implying that although I might know something of history I none the less knew nothing about Ireland. That may well be true; but I used to remind her of my Irish grandfather, name of Heenan, a promising engineer who came over to England to seek his fortune. He found it, and ceased to be an Irishman; or at least he preferred to forget that he was one. That was common enough at the time, but things today are very different. The English now fall over themselves to claim Irish or Scottish ancestry; but it is an odd fact that no Scot or Irishman has ever been known to claim that he is partly English.

7

Canary

There was a time, after Iris died, when things got better, or at least different. My fortnight with our old friend Audi in the Canary Isles.

Although seldom able to be in England, Audi was immensely helpful to Iris when she came. Iris loved her. In the days when she was well they had a very special relationship. Friends used to say, what do they talk about all the time?

Audi has been many years a widow, a veteran in the trade. She said, and says, nothing about it, but I know now how much and how continually she misses her husband. We were friends for so long, the four of us: Borys and Audi and Iris and I. Every summer we did a bit of travelling together, and we often stayed in the little house they had built on the island of Lanzarote, partly on account of Audi's severe asthma. The climate relieved it.

Their house was right in the middle of the rocky volcanic island, far away from the crowded beaches. In the days when they built the house, the beaches were not crowded. There was no telephone, uncertain electricity. Very little water, for rain hardly ever fell. Very few people. Now the island has been 'developed'. With the usual results.

The island grows on me none the less. I detested it at first. The Sunset Strips along the beaches, full of discos and Irish pubs and Viking wine bars. They look like all such places,

only even more so. But once we are away from the coast all
this disappears; and although the island is not much more
than fifty miles long there is a good deal of quiet country
inland. Tourist buses go to the Fire Mountain, a mass of
coagulated lava with one or two small bits of permanent
volcanic activity; but the real character of the place is not in
these outlandish and comparatively recent manifestations
of subterranean inferno. It is in the round hills that swell
up from the tawny landscape in conical, almost pyramidal
shapes, with a strange and slightly uncanny lightness and
grace about them. They are smooth and bare, untrodden
by tourists, and in the evening their silhouettes cut the
lucid sky into shapes that can look both razor-sharp and
voluptuously tender. The strange world they come from,
silent and distant and long extinct, has nothing to do with
the ever-growing pullulation on the island shores. Nor with
the reddish contortions of the Fire Mountain, that volcanic
parvenu whose ungainly bulk, like a noisome and decaying
monster, reveals at a distance the tourist buses on their
perpetual scenic round, crawling over it like maggots.

This unquiet effect is even presented by the low island
cliffs, the only alternative to the beaches on the sheltered
eastern coast line. At a distance they relieve the eye by
seeming bare and unpopulated, but as you come closer
you see that every fissure and cranny contains human
figures. Heavy-looking topless girls bask awkwardly in
each sunny niche, while their German boyfriends cling
and crawl indefatigably, vying with each other to get to
the cliff top, or in finding ways down to the obedient sea
at its base.

Lanzarote is not an island to give you any illusion of
wide open spaces. It is claustrophobic in the extreme. But
although the flat white houses between and at the foot of
the hills are constantly multiplying, as if they too were
maggots, there are still inland corners by the conical hills
where there is no movement, no sound but the steady

trade-wind blowing and the occasional call of a hoopoe.
When flying, those bizarre birds resemble giant moths, so
sharply contrasted on their wings is the patterning of black
and white and cinnamon brown.

Audi's house is in one of these still secluded places. It is
white, like all the island houses, with a lot of bougainvillaea
in striking shades of mauve, orange and maroon and a
garden of pepper trees and little palms like pineapples,
growing in semi-circular compounds made of the black lava
stone. To give it further protection from the wind, each tree
stands in a shallow dimple scooped out of the black sand-
like *picon*, velvety-looking ground-up lava which holds
the strong fall of dew. There is usually no rain at all on
the island, and this soft dimple of *picon* helps the trees
survive.

It keeps vines going too. In the remote parts of the island
there are whole slopes and acres of such dimpled depres-
sions, each with a few wizened shoots at the bottom. They
run up the sides of the smooth hills, making them sleek and
black to a certain height instead of the strange golden-brown
which is always changing under cloud shadows in the pure,
brilliant light. The wine produced in this way is expensive,
naturally enough, and not specially good, although it is
drunk by some of the residents and a few tourists, out of
a sense of loyalty.

The English residents, of whom there are not very many,
rarely speak more than a few words of Spanish, and see
comparatively little of one another. Nor do they hob-nob
with the natives or with the tourists. It is a bit of a mystery
what residents find to do, since they do not engage in tourist
activities. They probably watch TV and videos, just as they
would at home.

One resident I met said confidentially as we drank some
of the local wine: 'You know, there are people who come to
Lanzarote and never leave again.' He paused for a moment's
rumination and added: 'Others leave at once.'

But the place does grow on one, no doubt about that. The coast of Africa is not far off; the flat-roofed houses with thick white walls that look as if they were made of adobe have a Moorish look. Audi's has no staircase, but it is built on different levels and the roomy interior is paved with Spanish and Italian tiles, which the warm wind sprinkles with black *picon* from the garden. Audi is often out there, watering the Teresita and Plumbago flowers on the terrace, or grooming the soft cup-shaped black hollows in which lemon and olive and fig-trees do their best to grow.

In the evenings Audi played Patience and I sat reading, looking up from time to time to ask her something. In the daytime it was a relief not to have to do anything much except go to the shop. The time passed very well.

Iris used to love it here, and Audi used to drive us to the sea so that Iris could swim. Afterwards she took us to a small fishy place where she and I sometimes had a scarce local delicacy unknown to the tourists; Iris, who distrusted fish, stuck to an egg and salad. Our strange creatures, known as *clacas*, came from a part of the rough western coast facing the Atlantic, where the shoreline is a mass of jagged black lava boulders left over from the last eruption. The locals lower themselves on ropes to prise off these giant barnacles, which are then boiled in sea-water. To eat them you fish them out one at a time with a bit of wire; the scrap tastes like very tender lobster. You then drink the warm liquid from the aperture, a delicate marine soup which might have been used to baptise Venus.

Audi knew all the quieter places where it was possible to bathe, including one frequented by brown and naked German grandmothers. They seemed to resent our clothed state, but smiled forgivingly at us none the less. As her illness increased Iris became afraid to bathe, and Audi used to take her into the shower at home. She loved that.

Evening on the island is the best time. Although the

Canaries are well above the tropics, night here comes on at a run.

> The sun's rim dips, the stars rush out,
> With one stride comes the dark . . .

So Coleridge put it in *The Ancient Mariner*. Malta was the furthest south he went, and that was long after he had written the poem. He was secretary to the governor, Sir Alexander Ball, who had been one of Nelson's captains at the great Nile victory. How on earth did Coleridge get the job? How did he hold it down? Possibly through being such a wonderful talker – people really loved conversation in those days.

From Richard Holmes's biography I remember a touching detail. Because of his opium habit Coleridge suffered so severely from constipation on the way out to Malta that the fleet surgeon had to be rowed across to put things right. But once arrived the poet was the life and soul of the local dinner parties. Perhaps he was really just employed to talk, and to keep the English garrison entertained and amused. He seems to have been no use as a secretary, but Sir Alexander tolerated him manfully. How would he have got on in Lanzarote today? Not too well probably.

And yet he would so much have enjoyed the dinner party we had during my holiday. Prawns, *osso bucco*, lots of red wine. (From the mainland, although we loyally drank some Lanzarote white wine as an aperitif.) Dinner ended in laughter and good cheer, which would have pleased Coleridge and his contemporaries.

An English guest told what he said was not an old Spanish joke but a true story he had heard from the local barman, who was a character. A man once asked him for a drink compounded of kümmel, aniseed, vermouth, crème de menthe, grappa and a few other things. He drank and made a face.

'Excuse me, sir,' said the barman, 'but do you really like that stuff?'

'No,' the man said. 'I drink it because it reminds me of the taste of a woman.'

The barman, intrigued, asked to try the drink. He tasted it and shook his head. '*Ne parecido*,' he said. 'Not a bit like.'

Laughter anyway, especially from the ladies, who must feel it important not to seem stuffy or feminist. I suspected the point of the story had been watered down a bit; but many Spanish sayings have an enigmatic air about them.

'With St Joseph, a beard, without, the Virgin Mary.'

What can that one mean? It teases you with a suggestion of something louche but obscure. You must be in the know to get the point, if indeed there is one. Coleridge might have enjoyed the barman's story, but not have told it in mixed company? His parson father, who sounds rather like him, was once keeping the table in a roar when he glanced down and saw his shirt front was coming out. He tucked it in and went on talking, but in a minute or two he noticed it was out again. This went on until the ladies got up to leave, when it was found that his neighbour had the long white skirt of her dress securely tucked into the parson's waistband.

I remember and tell the story, which has its moment of amusement. A tall Norwegian with a charming voice begins without preamble on a Scandinavian joke, the equivalent of our laborious old ones about the Englishman, Irishman and Scotsman. A Norwegian, a Swede and a Dane, revolutionaries in South America, are caught by government troops. 'Alas, gentlemen,' says the general, 'we shall have to shoot you, but you shall each have a last wish.' The Dane chooses a steak, a bottle of wine and a cigar. The Norwegian wants to make a speech. That leaves the Swede, who says would they mind shooting him before the Norwegian makes his speech.

Much laughter and applause. Audi has told me of her

countrymen'sfondnessformakingafter-dinnerspeeches;and this story, needless to say, was invented by a Norwegian.

The birds of Lanzarote give great pleasure, although there are not many of them. Just before dusk falls the hoopoes sometimes come, flittering among the diminutive pepper and acacia trees. Striped alternately in black and white, their moth-like wings show up boldly against their drab body plumage. On the ground they are almost invisible, but the agitated movement of wings shows where the little group are until they settle among the trees and disappear. They are small birds, hardly bigger than the thrush, and they grow in size and presence when they spread their great crests, rufous colour tipped with black and white, like the head-dress of an Indian chief. They nest among the low stone walls, built of black lava and left full of holes so that the wind won't blow them down.

As we watched the hoopoes through the window, settling themselves for the night, they reminded me of a fussy group of maiden ladies quarrelling politely over the rooms allocated them in a crowded hotel. Their profile, as the birdwatchers say, suggests a kind of faded Edwardian femininity.

Another bird that has almost disappeared in England used to visit round the house in Lanzarote – the Great Grey Shrike. Despite his majestic name and his very definite masculinity compared to the feminine hoopoes, he was not very big either. But he was very assertive. He perched at the top of a tall cactus or euphorbia, keeping watch for the lizards and beetles he preyed upon, and uttering a harsh note, almost a bark, like an irate colonel. His Latin name is *excubitor*, the sentinel: literally, I suppose, the one who has to stay out of bed. In Spanish he is 'Alcairon', which Audi thought had a Moorish sound; it may mean the same sort of thing in that language. Candellaria, Audi's cleaning lady, told us a rhyme in the local Canary dialect.

Alcairon, Alcairon, que noticias traes?
Si es para mi
Deja lo aqui
Si es para otro que te vaya.

'Shrike, shrike, what news do you bring? If it's for me leave it here, if it's for someone else, go away.'

Audi was very knowledgeable about local and many other matters. Useless but fascinating information has always cheered me up, and here at last I found my old appetite for it returning. But only for things that were safely and entrancingly in the past, a point even explaining my fondness for the hoopoes, with their air not only of bizarre and gigantic moths but of string and calico aircraft from the dawn of human flight. All my 'aeroplane books', as Iris called them, were about obsolete aircraft, ships and weaponry, never the modern ones.

Bereavement too can seem old-fashioned and obsolete; perhaps I embraced the idea of it for that reason. The Victorians were good at it, so to speak – the period seems to have been full of widows and widowers in becoming black clothes. But at the same time as I feel nostalgia and affection for the bereaved who are past and gone, I feel an equal urge to analyse the state of bereavement, in the modern clinical manner.

Shall I be the shrink or the patient? It hardly matters. The canny shrink (he sounds like the shrike – does he too bring news?) obviously perceives this indifference; and makes a note of it? But I'm tired of the shrink already. His eyes have noted a loss of weight, otherwise no marked physical deterioration.

'Bereaved persons have a tendency to idealise the dead loved one,' he says blandly.

Do I do that? I wouldn't have thought so. True, I found myself thinking the other day, in the context of our mutual acquaintance, that I had never heard Iris speak ill of anyone, or say anything sharp about any of our friends. But that wasn't idealising her. It was no more than the truth. And it sometimes irritated me when I would have liked a good malicious gossip about some tiresome acquaintance recently endured. Iris had her own brand of wholly private political correctness. She didn't disapprove of gossip and backbiting; she just never indulged in them herself.

So I don't idealise her. I am remembering her as she was, as she was for me.

But the bereaved soon discover that there are two sorts of memories involved. There are deliberate memories, of what we did and what we said. I summon her up: walking, talking, sitting down, washing the dishes. But after a few moments of deliberate recollection this person loses outline; she becomes not just shadowy, but unreal. She will not stay in place. I cannot even be sure she is the right person.

Then sometimes, without warning, involuntary memory can still ambush me, like a ruffian on the stairs. That is authentic, the real thing, staying for no more than a second or two. There she is suddenly, the vision that makes me cry with grief just because it is so true; because I have not created it. It came in Lanzarote, just as it had done at home. Or I opened a door, in either place, and heard the real Iris say 'Wow Wow' as she looked up with a smile from her work.

On our last trip together to Lanzarote, Iris and I saw again the one or two places which had begun to have their own sort of private importance for us. We looked at each other with a smile when Audi drove us past viewpoints with which we had developed our own brand of intimacy. A white speck on the brown flank of a conical mountain had intrigued us, visible at a great distance in the glass-clear air. It turned out to be a rusty white car panel, abandoned – heaven knows why – far up, and far from any road.

Then there was a kind of house beside the huge lava

rocks on the wild western shore, a small rectangular hotel, abandoned and derelict, like a building in the background of a Magritte painting. We were fascinated by it; it was the only really lonely place on the island. The Swedish owner had hoped to make an artificial beach among the sea-buffeted rocks, but it came to nothing. Audi said that the locals had stripped and carried off all the fittings, including windows and doors. I spotted the white car panel again, but I no longer felt the fascination of old when we passed by the derelict hotel the other evening. This again seemed the index of a more general lack of interest in things.

I felt half tempted to ask Audi if she had felt the same sort of lack of interest after Borys died, but I said nothing, which seemed easier. I knew how much she had missed him, still missed him. In terms of missingness I had a long way to go before I was up to her level.

Back in Oxford, alone in my house, I found that the freedom and the solitude, which I had once wistfully supposed to be the positive side of bereavement, still showed no signs of arriving. Doing things that should have occupied and consoled me made me feel as miserably anxious as poor Iris had been when she first began to suffer from Alzheimer's. I felt busier and more bothered than ever, and the distractions that are supposed to keep the mind off things seemed quite unable to do that job.

And I missed kind, learned Audi, who knows about the birds of the Canaries, and the volcanoes and the cochineal plantations, and about sailing and sailing-ships and the discovery of longitude. She even knows all about the Guanchos, the mysterious people who lived on the Canary Islands before the Spaniards arrived. They must have originally come over from Africa. Having arrived, they or their descendants forgot how to use or to make boats, so that they could not even move from one island to another. Guanchos in Lanzarote lived mostly in remote caves at the northern end of the island.

Margot and Mella have passed like a dream, but I keep remembering those earlier days in Lanzarote.

Iris and Audi used to meet on their own in London and chatter happily away together over lunch or supper. Iris had a natural seriousness and rarely laughed, but she would go into fits of laughter over things that Borys and Audi said and told her.

I say that now, and I know it's true; and yet I can't really remember. Was Iris fond of laughing and joking? She must have been, but it doesn't sound right, like so many of the things that one says about people after they have gone, or indeed before they go. Personality never really survives reminiscence and discussion. But voices do.

Watching Audi playing her game and occasionally making some remark, I used to concentrate my own attention on the theme of Forgotten Wars. That helped to stop the voices coming back into my head, both the one I had heard and the one I could not hear.

I was reading a novel recommended by Audi called *The Blue Afternoon*, by William Boyd. It is set in the Philippines during the Spanish-American war – 1900 or so – when many Filipinos were all for independence, and the Americans had decided in paternal fashion that they weren't yet ready for it. A gripping love story about a surgeon and an officer's wife vividly suggests the background of the place and period. The war began in 1899 after the liberation of the Philippines from Spanish rule, raged until 1903, and dragged on in some of the islands until 1914. It was full of incidents which make the My Lai massacre in Vietnam seem mild and insignificant.

I remember reading in Louis Untermeyer's long outdated anthology a few high-minded and suitably agonised poems which American women poets wrote about this wicked war

– the equivalent, in those days, of campus protests and peace marches against Vietnam.

Shame-faced victors and gallant losers are alike forgotten today. Many American soldiers, as in Vietnam, came from the Southern states, and some must have recalled their own struggle against the Union, not much more than thirty years before. The difference is that this Philippines war is forgotten, by common consent as it seems, while the Civil War is consecrated for ever in American folk memory and legend.

Rudyard Kipling was highly gratified by the Philippines conflict and wrote a poem about it, which Americans thought in the worst of taste.

> Take up the White Man's burden,
> The savage wars of peace . . .

That brilliant bit of self-congratulation, self-exculpation too, has certainly survived. It was only a short time since our own Zulu War and the war in the Sudan against the Mahdi, both accompanied by the usual massacres. The British Army was keeping busy, and was about to embark on a conflict with the Boers – a 'Sahibs' War', as Kipling called it – but more significant for him was the heartening spectacle of the Land of the Free joining the British Empire in its perennial police actions against primitive people, who had to be civilised, one way or another.

All forgotten now. Except by the historians, a novelist maybe, and a few politicians as and if it suits them. For them – for me too – it has all become part of the comfort of history. Wordsworth himself wrote a memorable line or two when he spoke of 'old unhappy far-off things and battles long ago'. But he was wrong. They are not really unhappy. Time always has enough distance to cheer us up. The great healer. But only across the centuries, not in terms of one year.

*   *   *

And the first year of bereavement is probably the best. Not the worst. That is a thought to make me feel uneasy, but nothing can be done about it. That is why I cling as tightly as I can to thoughts about the past. Wars, battles, things that were: and things that might have been. The wars of Hannibal and Belisarius. The wars of Jenkins's Ear and the Spanish succession . . .

Memories, daydreams, associations. All useful for the comfort process. Reading Boyd's excellent novel reminded me of the museum at Tromsø in North Norway. I asked Audi, who is Norwegian after all, if she'd ever been there, but she hadn't. I remember it well. Iris and I were giving a talk there once, arranged by the British Council and the local university. I don't remember much of what we said, or whom we met, but I vividly remember the little museum, which was devoted to the history of Norwegian settlers in Spitzbergen and the Arctic. It had life-size models of Arctic huts in the snow, and dummies dressed in white furs. I was especially fascinated by the model of a polar bear trap. These bears were a deadly danger to the settlers, who often had to spend a solitary winter in a snowhouse. To kill the bear you arranged a large piece of seal meat on a stand outside a hide. Inside it was a rifle, carefully aligned on a point just above the bait, from which a string was attached to its trigger. When the bear seized the bait it pulled the string and the rifle went off. With luck all round, instant end of bear.

I recognised the rifle – a genuine article – in the museum tableau. After the war I was in Norway with the army, and I saw a good deal of the celebrated Krag-Jörgensen rifle, still used then by Norwegian troops, as it had been used by the American army more than forty years before in the Philippines. It was a simple gun, but it had earned an international reputation for its phenomenal accuracy at long range. The Norwegians were justly proud of this weapon – even Audi knew about it – and it was often mentioned in *The Blue Afternoon*.

Thinking about the Krag-Jörgensen – known to American soldiers simply as 'the Krag' – and watching Audi tranquilly playing out her Patience, seemed like a phantom replay of Iris and myself. Years ago, when we lived at Steeple Aston, Iris would soon be asleep when we went to bed, tired with a long day's writing, and I would lie browsing in one of my 'aeroplane' books. For a surprise present she once ordered a series called the *Phoebus History of Two World Wars*, which featured not so much the wars themselves as the weapons employed in them. I used to browse over machine-guns, tanks and Messerschmitts, while Iris slept tranquilly beside me. Very often she would wake up in the small hours and pad round to my side of the bed to turn off the light and remove my spectacles. The Krag-Jörgensen – a resounding name like my other favourites – had revived the memory, together with Audi's quiet concentration while I dreamily read my book.

Two people, each doing their own separate thing. It is a situation that is always happening. In offices or in families. No doubt also in ships and aeroplanes. The steersman motionless at the wheel, while the officer of the watch paces calmly up and down the bridge. Or is all that obsolete? But the idea of a pair, in the communion of a mutual non-awareness – that has its own significance. Widows and widowers must often brood about it, as they find out what it once meant to them.

I dreamed over that *Phoebus History* as I used to dream, between the wars at the age of eight, over the historical drawings in Warne's *Pictorial Knowledge*. Pictures of Hannibal and his men, sword in hand, gazing down from the Alps; Napoleon at the battle of Lodi, or on the island of St Helena . . . I don't think I would have enjoyed the aeroplane books as I did without the presence of those old memories, and of Iris asleep beside me.

For the bereaved the worst – or the best? – moment is remembering those times together, each unconscious of the other. But when Iris was ill with Alzheimer's, I only enjoyed my daydreaming when we were together, on one of our endless little walks round the block, or when I lay beside her in bed and she was gently snoring, released for a few hours from the perpetual restlessness and anxiety which compelled her to wander round the house in the small hours, collecting her oddments together.

During those days and nights, when Iris was ill, and in a weird way all the more companionable for being ill, my usual dreams were narrative fantasies, long-running soap operas of imagined lives, which I conjured into existence and changed at will. The most persistent, as venerable as one of Iris's comic strips in the *Evening Standard*, concerned the Big Woman of Gerrards Cross.

The Big Woman was just that: a lady of immense height and size, who lived in a nice house left her by her father, whom she had looked after devotedly for many years. She lived alone now, and was much involved in good works and church activities.

My own relations with the Big Woman were equivocal and varied a good deal. Sometimes I preferred, as it were, not to know her but only to think about her. Sometimes, in my imagination, the Big Woman had a female friend staying with her, and the Vicar had brought them both along to a party. I can hear his breezy tones, 'apologising' to the hostess, in the way the clergy do, for having 'inflicted' two extra guests on her. 'But Miss' (I fail to catch her name) 'is such a blessing, such a help to me. A real pillar of strength, a *tower*, you know.' His unctuous tones waver for a moment, as if it has just occurred to him, as it must have done to everyone else within earshot, that he has chosen his metaphors not quite fortunately, in view of the lady's remarkable height and size. She and her friend look predictably embarrassed; not by his words but by the fact that they are at the party at all.

Filled, in my daydream, with sudden inspiration I go

boldly up to the Big Woman. I smile up at her – my very best smile. Warm, friendly, reassuring, conveying a certainty that she and I understand one another, are two of a kind. Her own smile, remote as a lighthouse but not distant, beams down gratefully upon me.

The scenario had many variations. Sometimes it stopped altogether, and then restarted itself at some other point in the saga. It was important that nothing very dramatic should happen. No love, no kisses. The Big Woman was not exactly intended for that sort of thing. Our relationship is secret, innocent . . . We understand each other wholly, and the feeling of unspoken intimacy between us is at times almost overpowering . . .

Meanwhile I would be walking hand in hand with Iris, round the block. Often she would drop my hand and fumble on the pavement for a bit of silver paper that had caught her eye, a plastic top, even a cigarette end. She examined them carefully. Did they hold some message for her? Hard not to imagine that these fragments were becoming the properties of some scene with which she was inwardly preoccupied.

It soothed me to believe what I felt, even knew, to be unbelievable: that Iris still had an inner life to match my own. *Far* greater than my own. Could that brain, once creating so many fantasies, stories, situations for novels which had become true masterpieces – could that brain really be closing down completely, paralysed and trapped in the lesions and irregular plaques that had developed on its unseen but mysterious, once symmetric, surface? I wanted to believe that just as we had once lain in bed together – me reading my aeroplane books, she tranquilly asleep, or me pottering in the house and garden, doing some absorbing little thing, and she waving from the window and continuing her writing – so, even at the worst, some unknown harmonious mutual activity between us must be still going on.

*   *   *

Those moments in the street came back to me as I turned the page of the book, and looked up at Audi, quietly working away at her Patience. Audi and the Krag-Jörgensen rifle, and the Big Woman of Gerrards Cross – all mixed up . . .

This must be all part of being a widower. I used to be good at marshalling thoughts and sentences, getting what I wanted to say into some kind of order. Now I slip and slide. From one thing to another, without knowing whether it's memory, fantasy, something old or something new. Typical bereavement syndrome?

I realise, or think I realise, what is happening. Something inside is putting things together, laboriously stitching a presence together out of an absence. A presence involves two people. Separate from one another, unconscious of each other's presence, and, because unconscious, all the closer together. Closer and closer apart.

That phrase used to comfort me a great deal because I only read it, and the poem of which it's a part, after Iris had started to be ill with Alzheimer's. It described so well our former relationship, of which I only became aware after the illness had virtually taken it away. The poem is by A.D. Hope, a mysterious Australian about whom I know nothing at all except for that line from one of his poems.

When Iris was ill we could still communicate – we seemed to do so just as much as ever – but those moments of tranquil apartness, togetherness in apartness, were no longer there. I was no longer reading my aeroplane books while Iris was writing quietly away, or waving to me from the window with one hand while writing with the other. But as I dreamily watched Audi playing Patience, and then looked at my book, the same pattern seemed to be forming again.

But, like all patterns, it was different. Iris didn't read novels. Audi does, and she had read this one, which was why I was reading it; and every so often I asked her something about it. With her eyes on the Patience cards she replied, sensibly but abstractedly, and I forgot what she had said and dipped back quietly into the book again. There is a lot about obscure illnesses in the book, for its hero is a surgeon; and Audi, who has had severe asthma attacks all her life, and allergies since she was born, knows a very great deal about illnesses and about being ill.

When staying with her I really enjoyed reading books – new and old, familiar and unfamiliar – for the first time since Iris became ill. In addition to *The Blue Afternoon* I found Audi's paperback of *A Handful of Dust* and re-read it, for the third or fourth time, with even greater enjoyment. It is the sort of masterpiece which, like Jane Austen's, presents a subtly different picture and a different emphasis with each re-reading. I had always had the impression before that the characters were too much made use of by the author, who had his own decidedly unartistic axe to grind: namely, revenge against the wife who had left him, and the man she had gone off with. Through the imaginary characters, Brenda Last and John Beaver, Waugh portrayed these two real persons, at least for his own satisfaction, in as disagreeable a light as possible.

But however familiar one may be with Evelyn Waugh's life and the unlucky history of his first marriage, the art of the novel wins hands down. I used to think that the reaction of Brenda Last to the news of her little boy's death in the hunting field was dramatically effective but psychologically implausible. Now it seems to me all of a part with Waugh's understanding of the social world he both inhabited and created. Brenda is not a monster of cold egoism; she has the extreme inner carelessness involuntarily nurtured by her set, and by the society she moves in. Life as she finds herself living it, in an ugly great country house with her adoring husband and her little boy, is simply not real to her, not to be cared about. She is not just bored; she has no sense of life's true necessities, their promise and design. John Beaver, the vulgar nonentity whom no one else wants, represents for her a reality she can seize and own for herself, a reality that brings her her first awareness of love. By throwing herself at him she can make both him and herself real. Almost 'caring', in fact.

I very much sympathise with Brenda. In fact, since Iris died I have been feeling rather like a Brenda myself, but a Brenda whose sense of reality has gone, rather than one who has suddenly found it. Widowers are not necessarily monsters of egoism, but perhaps they may suddenly find in themselves that same inner carelessness. I feel I am doing a Brenda all the time. I have lost my Beaver. I have suffered bereavement.

John Beaver, as drawn by Waugh, is a perfect mate for Brenda. Neither have anything inside them. I feel an affinity now with him too. No more inner life, no more Belial thoughts that wander through eternity . . .

The life of the couple is supplied entirely by what they can get from society. But Brenda unexpectedly finds herself capable of love, although she does not recognise it as such, while Beaver sees her only as a means of getting on in smart society. In the eyes of their friends they both become interesting because of the improbability of their relationship, and both are gratified by the fact. A lesser artist might have portrayed Beaver as a mother's boy, but Waugh's Beaver is not even that. He uses his mother so far as he can, just as he uses any contact that will aid his social advancement. This is the man for whom Brenda bursts out 'Oh, thank God,' when she finds that it is not he who has been killed in an aeroplane accident, as she feared, but only her little boy in the hunting field.

Brenda cannot bear the thought of the one *real* object that is her own being taken from her; Beaver is merely gratified that society gossip is so enthralled by their unlikely and unexpected walk-out. There must be more to him, society concludes, than meets the eye. But there is nothing, nothing at all, and Brenda loves him just for that. With him at last there is no need for her to deceive, or to play a part.

Would Brenda have married her Beaver if he would have had her? Would the marriage have lasted if he had? Hard to say. Perhaps it would, in its own way; she might have stuck to him like a leech. Her own. But that's outside the particular heart of this novel, the circle in which, as Henry James said, the relations of life which end nowhere must happily *appear* to do so. Brenda ends up marrying Jock, her husband's oldest friend. She may well feel at ease with him, too, in a rather different way, for he heard what she said when her little boy was killed, and she thought for a moment that it was her lover. They were both called John.

Things were very different, naturally enough, in real life. Anthony Powell in his memoirs gives an excellent sketch of John Heygate, the man with whom Waugh's wife actually went off. In terms of Waugh's world nobody could have been more different from John Beaver. Heygate was good-looking, talented and popular, from an old family and with all the right schools and clubs. He seems to have had, too, just the right sort of dashing high spirits and fecklessness of which his social set would approve; for when news of the affair came out he was not with the wife he had removed from her husband, but travelling with Powell on the continent in his touring car.

A peremptory telegram from Waugh, who could be highly formidable in his own style, summoned him home to face the music. Heygate and Waugh's wife got married subsequently and the marriage was quite a success although it did not last. To earn money Heygate wrote a school novel which sold well, and he was also successful in the film world; but in later life he suffered breakdowns and fits of mental disturbance. That might have interested Waugh as the author of *The Ordeal of Gilbert Pinfold*; but in general Heygate was not a promising character for a novel, especially not a novel by Waugh. One can see why Waugh was inspired to create John Beaver, one of his best characters, and one to whom he could transfer the contemptible qualities which he would no doubt have liked to find in Heygate, but could not.

Tony Last's Victorian Gothic hall is obviously based on Madresfield House near Malvern, which Waugh knew well and felt as much affection for as Tony Last did for his own Gothic pile. Tony's presumed end in the Amazon jungles, captive of the dreadful Mr Todd, was suggested by Waugh's own experiences in Guyana, where he had gone exploring in an effort to forget about his failed marriage. The best of Waugh's excellent travel books is *Ninety-Two Days*, which he wrote about his South American experiences. Even the fictional Mr Todd is not as vivid as his counterpart in real life, the old hermit whom Waugh encountered in the jungle, who distracted his guest with theological speculation, and roamed around Waugh's hammock as he lay in the rain getting steadily drunk on rum. (This strange old man also rejected a medallion of the Virgin which Waugh offered him, saying 'Why should I require a picture of someone I see so frequently? Besides,' he added contemptuously, 'it is not in the least like her.')

When his wife leaves him and insists on a divorce Tony Last finds himself living 'in a world suddenly bereft of order', in which 'no outrageous circumstance he found himself in could add a jot to the all-encompassing chaos.' What ordinary widowers discover is a world not so intense and dramatic as that, and yet it is essentially similar. Even such books as I now read seem to reflect this. I can't manage Barbara Pym any more, whom I used to read with such pleasure. But I now feel as completely at home in Waugh's world as I used to do with Pym's spinsters and curates, and eccentrics of quite a different kind.

During a sleepless night after my return from Lanzarote I try to contrive a different kind of ending to Waugh's novel. Suppose Tony Last had woken up prematurely, after being drugged by Mr Todd to conceal him from the rescue party? It is essential to keep Mr Todd in the story: he is one of

Waugh's most memorable creations. But if Tony Last had escaped from him what might have happened? The next scene would be back in England at Hetton, with Brenda now making much of the returned hero. As happy days go by she might have blandished Tony into settling some sort of capital sum or jointure on her. Tony is now eating out of her hand, but Brenda is still secretly in touch with John Beaver, and still loves him. Beaver is at a loose end, again ignored by the smart world who took him up as an object of interest after Brenda made him her young man.

When Brenda secures her jointure she invites him to marry her after she gets her divorce. Beaver is tempted. Her money is not much, but together and married they will get a place in the London smart set; they will be talked about. He agrees to do it after he gets back from an American trip with his mother. And over there he meets an heiress, very rich, very suitable, very easily taken in. Bully for Beaver. His bride-to-be rejoices at the prospect of life in Mayfair with an upper-class young Englishman. Mrs Beaver is delighted. She will keep her son; she will have the heiress in hand as part of her own show.

And what of Brenda? Deep down poor Brenda is a stoic; she knows when she is beaten. She cannot stop wanting her Beaver; perhaps she can still have him on the side? She thinks of him when she lets Tony make love to her and then she is pregnant again. On that note the alternative novel ends?

And about time too – daylight is showing outside. Waugh himself could never have written such a novel of course. His genius as an artist went quite another way and revelled in the grotesque horror of the conclusion he created. Tony Last, last of his kind, rescued from death by this jungle hermit with an insatiable lust to listen to the novels of Dickens, which he cannot read. And so while life back in England goes on, Tony is kept a prisoner by his terrible host and made to read novel after Dickens novel. For ever and ever.

Masterly. Waugh's inimitably cool manner makes it all plausible, as well as frightening. But with Waugh, character is at the disposition of dramatic effect. Had Henry James written *A Handful of Dust* he would have been more interested in the people themselves. He would have pondered the inwardness of Brenda and Beaver, of Tony too, as the last representative of a type and a tradition. He would have stifled any sensational denouement in the interest of human relations, 'which stop nowhere'.

Jamesian scrupulosity is of course not suited to the bitterness that Waugh felt at the time, in the pursuit of which he contrived a black outcome. But however superb an artist he could be, Waugh was a cynic as well. He was quite prepared to accommodate his American publisher and compose a different ending for an American readership who, as Scott Fitzgerald said, must always have a tragedy with a happy ending.

Waugh made his alternative solution absurdly snug. Tony Last, rather like Waugh himself in *Ninety-Two Days*, looks forward to catching the boat home, and to his first dinner at Wheeler's or the Savoy; perhaps, too, a reconciliation with Brenda. In London, in response to his telegram, he does indeed meet a repentant Brenda, more than anxious to escape the poor and solitary life-style to which she has been reduced. They travel back to Hetton together and are last seen eating muffins in the dining-car. Not like Brenda? Of course not; and Waugh has already made it abundantly clear how far the iron of her faithlessness had eaten into Tony's soul.

But the author has obviously decided that the snugger the scene the greater the underlying irony. And did he consider that the irony would be safely lost on his American readers? The fact that he misjudged them was shown by the great success in America of his much later satire, *The Loved One*, a black comedy about Californian funeral customs. And of course by that time the success of *A Handful of Dust* on both sides of the Atlantic had led to the restoration of the original ending.

8

Belial and his Friends

I cling with possessive loyalty to the Iris who had Alzheimer's disease, and whom I looked after during those years. The disease itself seems to belong to me, and I don't like other people having it, although when I go to those Alzheimer gatherings I enjoy the comradeship and the togetherness, and I feel like a veteran at an Old Soldiers' Reunion. I have given up trying to remember Iris as she was before she was ill. (She would sometimes say 'Here's Ginger' even when she could barely say anything else.) Walking round the block with Iris, and afterwards with Mella, I always looked at one house in particular, where my old teacher David Cecil used to live.

Other people's houses may be untidy, but they have an air of knowing what's what, of being house-wise, knowing what they can get away with. David's house was like that. It was a rented house, pseudo-Georgian, quite large enough for a family of five, six or seven including nanny and cook. Rachel Cecil liked going out on her bicycle to buy food but hated cooking it; she had a particular horror of onions. One result was that eating at Linton Road was hardly an exciting experience, although talking and drinking there was such fun. The standard tipple favoured by David was mixed dry and sweet vermouth, with as much gin as one could surreptitiously pour in for oneself during one of his rhapsodical flights. Not that he was a monologuist; he had a habit of suddenly shouting out 'What do you think?' and listening with an almost embarrassing intentness to what one thought, which was seldom of much interest. But as well as being the most comfortable person imaginable to talk with, he raised and inspired the spirits like champagne, or at least as champagne is supposed to do, though I have never found that it does.

Just as he required you to put in more gin yourself if you wanted it, conferring his approval, if he happened to notice, with an absent wave of the hand, so he was the reason why wit was in you: if it happened to be so it came from him, although it was yourself you thought was being so clever. He was like Falstaff, not only funny and delightful in himself but the reason why fun and delight were in others. Like the Duke in *Measure for Measure* too, who said he enjoyed seeing other people laugh and rejoice more than doing so himself. Possibly Shakespeare too was a bit like that, although it may be significant that it is the Duke in disguise who makes the claim. The Duke may really have been a rather priggish fellow, concerned only with his image in his own eyes, and in those of his subjects.

Iris was certainly and honestly more concerned to see other people happy then than to be happy herself. But the two went together, as they should. Iris loved to ask people what they did, and what they thought, and they were never slow to tell her.

I remember that; of course I do; but I can't remember *her*, as she did it. I can remember David Cecil perfectly: how he looked, how he turned his head like a bird, his every inflection and gesture. But the Iris of those days has gone from me.

Do others remember her better than I do? Much better? Probably. For me will she now always remain my Iris of the Alzheimer's? I don't know. There seems such a long way to go. And I've no idea whether the former Iris will ever come back, or how, or even if I want her to. Existlessness can't change much, even for the bereaved. The bereaved only become more and more obsessed with themselves, and with how they are taking it. And with their own image of the dead.

Perhaps that's the main reason why I can't now remember Iris, as she once was.

Memories are obsessions too, I suppose; but I like to think of David Cecil, and the things he said, and the stories he told. He was fond of Christopher Woodforde, the sardonic Chaplain of New College, who was sometimes displeased with him about something or other, and then addressed him, disapprovingly, as 'Lord David'. Christopher's great-however-many-times-grandfather was the Parson Woodforde who wrote the Diaries, which are chiefly concerned with what the Parson had every day for dinner.

The Parson's latter-day relative was not altogether a popular figure in the college, having an extremely sharp tongue; but he and David Cecil got on very well. Christopher's wife, who had the same tongue although she was both nice and kind, once amused David very much by her remark about Dr Cooke, the Fellow in Chemistry. David said to her how much he liked Dr Cooke, who was indeed a most amiable and estimable man.

'So do I,' replied Mrs Woodforde. 'But do you know, whenever I see him I imagine him wearing a white coat and wrapping me a bottle of cough mixture.'

Christopher Woodforde hated the College Warden, in a manner altogether disproportionate to that unfortunate man's capacity to be a nuisance, although indeed he could be one. When the Warden died Christopher gave an eloquent and touching address at the funeral – like many sardonic clergymen he was an excellent preacher – and afterwards he was congratulated on it by Alan Bullock (now Lord Bullock), the History Fellow. Giving him a venomous glance the Chaplain hissed: 'I hope the bastard is frying in hell.'

Bullock, a robust atheist of enlightened views, was deeply shocked by this unlooked-for depth of clerical ill-feeling, although it did not lessen his respect for the Chaplain as a man of what Hardy calls 'sound parish views'.

It was soon after this episode that David Cecil fell from grace in the eyes of Christopher Woodforde, never afterwards retrieving himself but becoming 'Lord David' from then on, although his habitual insouciance made him sublimely unconscious of the fact. It arose when he and his wife Rachel asked the Chaplain to dinner. Christopher knew very well that this would be a sparse and unattractive meal compared to the dinner he would get in college; but he was fond of the Cecils and prepared to renounce for once the solid comforts of his usual college evening. He was touched too, because his wife had recently died, and it was clear that the Cecils were anxious to help, and solicitous that he should not mope alone in his college rooms.

Christopher arrived punctually in Linton Road at the hour of invitation. As he opened the garden gate the front door was flung open and David and Rachel came out, obviously in a hurry. They swept past Christopher with a word of hasty apology, Rachel pausing for a moment to thank him for calling, and saying that he must come again soon.

'I didn't mind their forgetting so much,' the Chaplain explained to me later. 'What I really resented was that I had missed dinner in Hall. I didn't get my usual dinner, and I didn't even get whatever concoction would have been served up by the Cecils.'

He bore no malice for the incident, beyond reverting to that formal style of address when addressing David Cecil. But there was certainly no doubt that Christopher could be a champion hater if he wanted. Later, when he had retired from New College and become Dean of Wells, he sometimes asked Iris and me to stay with him and his son Giles at the

Deanery. Giles was an odd but likeable boy whose hobby – it was more like a vocation – was to visit and make a record of every cinema which had a teashop attached. Once almost universal, the cinema tea-lounge was then a vanishing amenity, and Giles's passion was to draw up an exhaustive list of them for the sake of posterity, and before they had all disappeared, carefully noting what kind of buns were served, and whether the waitresses wore a uniform.

His father meanwhile waged a ferocious war against the doddery old Canons in the Close, singling out one who was especially harmless and amiable for bouts of intensive persecution.

'I hate that man,' he confided to Iris and me when his enemy was seen toddling along before us in the Close. 'I'm going to have him *shot out*.'

Christopher never specified how this dire deed – pronounced with an explosive hiss – was to be accomplished; and I imagine that the old Canon remained happily oblivious of the fate that was allegedly hanging over him. Christopher was not exactly kind-hearted at bottom, but one could be sure that threats and imprecations, alarming as they might sound in the mouth of a distinguished churchman (he had written the definitive work on ecclesiastical stained glass), would never in practice produce any serious consequences.

I thought of Christopher Woodforde, and the aborted dinner party, when I had myself begun to suffer the well-meaning persecution to which widowers appeared to be subject. Many times in these weeks, as I presented myself at some hospitable front door, I remembered what had happened to Christopher, and thought how lucky in one sense at least he had been. He might have missed his dinner, but he had escaped the evening; and what a relief it would often be for me if my putative hosts had left as I arrived, with the hasty wish that they might see me again soon. I should have wandered thankfully home, and enjoyed my usual supper of sardines or scrambled eggs . . .

And now the burglars have been.

Their visit was like a tonic. It seemed, too, absolutely the right thing to happen in a widower's house. Part of a ritual, like the interment, or the wake, or the memorial service. And wasn't there a time when they read the will?

I can almost imagine responsible burglars saying to one another in a concerned sort of way: 'It's high time we paid that call on Mr Bayley. It's quite a while now since his good lady died. Don't want to leave it too long. You free tonight, George? Good. In that case . . .'

We never had the burglars before, even when there were the two of us here. Several houses round about were burgled – we knew all about it – and on one occasion I found traces of a not very convincing attempt to break in. Our neighbours had burglar alarms, but I shrank from the technology involved, the tedium of setting it and at least partly understanding it, the annoyance to everybody when it went off by mistake. Someone suggested, not altogether seriously, that we get a dummy burglar alarm. This seemed to me a good idea. I have always been attracted by pretence. A successful fraud; something, in this case, just as good as the real thing. Besides, in those days it would have given us something to do; probably for the whole of one morning.

That was two years ago. Iris had not yet reached the stage of incoherence and unpredictability. It had not yet occurred to me to keep the doors locked on the inside; up to that point there had been no need to do so. She still enjoyed going out in the car and for both of us it was better than staying at home.

We went to a huge Do-It-Yourself store in the outskirts of the town. The place, I had been advised, to buy these funny things, which were made in Korea, or perhaps in

Singapore. When, after endless wanderings among forests of lampshades and electrical fixtures we chanced on an assistant preoccupied with some papers but prepared to lend us an ear, I found him at first baffled, but then disapproving. He was clearly disposed to find the whole notion improper and irregular. Such a low-down idea discredited the mystery of the do-it-yourself trade.

I saw his point, and began to feel it was bad form to make such a request. But at last the assistant relented and indicated a row of cardboard cartons on a shelf. He asked me to refrain from opening the thing in the shop. I wondered if this was to avoid compromising the security of my house; but it seemed more likely that the man wanted no further part in what he considered an under-the-counter transaction, alien to the clean-living ethos of the store. Feeling shamefaced I paid, and we took the box home.

When I got the dummy alarm out I saw at once what the objection was. No one, let alone a burglar, could possibly be taken in by this. Even the gadgets and the lettering which attempted to give it a semblance of reality were flashy and overdone. 'Spyder Alarms' it said; and the spider portrayed was a spirited, even a threatening creature. And yet no burglar could possibly have felt threatened by it.

The burglars probably never even bothered to look at it. They came when I was away for a day or two with my brother Michael and a friend. Some days earlier a nice old man had been trimming off the ivy from a neighbouring wall. He rang the bell and suggested that a huge bush which was straggling up the side of the house might also be profitably trimmed a little. I had to agree with him, and he did a good and unobtrusive job, not bothering me at all. The height of the bush required him to use a ladder. He removed the debris in an ancient van. A nice job, tidy and not expensive.

When I got back from my two-day absence I didn't notice anything different at first. Widowers' houses probably get to have a look inside as if nothing has ever changed, or could change. Then I went to turn a standard lamp on and found it wasn't there.

Well, natural enough. 'Pieland' had got it. Probably wouldn't be back, but I could do without it. In fact it got in the way rather. I only used it when I had to telephone. A bit odd though. In fact, come to think of it, distinctly odd.

Only when I went upstairs to the bedroom – our bedroom – did I get a real shock. The big oak chest which stood by the window and prevented one looking out and was layers and layers deep with books and old *London Reviews* and socks and things – the chest wasn't there either. Where had we got it? Many years ago, in some half antique, half junk shop. Cheap. Probably the reason why we got it; Iris could never resist something like that.

What was inside it? No idea, haven't looked in it for years. Always far too much lying on the top. But there must have been something inside it, indeed quite a lot, because my eye now takes in a new mass of stuff – the usual sorts of stuff, quite tidily disposed all round about; everywhere, in fact, except on the more than usually dirty patch where the great chest once stood. With a feeling of liberation – nice to be able to move about freely – I went to the window to open it. No, it was already open. That's funny. The security lock was dangling rather elegantly by one screw. No other damage.

At this moment I remembered Mr Sullivan, the nice old gentleman who had been clearing the bush off the wall. Surely not. And how on earth? Well, it certainly looked like it. Moving more alertly now around the house I began to realise how much had gone. Two large oak chests, one of which had contained our collection of old 78 and 33 records, which had now been neatly stacked on the ragged drawing-room carpet. The French tapestry armchair which Iris had bought for me ten years ago, on my sixty-fourth birthday Even that old friend, the windsor chair in the kitchen on which I had twice caught my tail when coming down to make tea in the morning. I began to notice numerous other gaps – small tables, vases, ornaments, a few pictures.

The TV and the video, which I had never managed to work, were still sitting in their corner. Untouched and unwanted.

But what a relief that Iris was not here to see that her treasures had gone! She would have been *so* upset. More than upset. Indignant, sad, miserable, even furious for a while. The fury she would have concealed, knowing that it would upset me; but she would have felt it inside all the more. I mean of course if the burglary had happened before she was ill. Towards the end she would not have seen nor noticed anything. And I should not have told her.

I began to realise now how dismayed I felt that I didn't feel anything. Not only dismayed but frightened as well. I didn't care. The things were gone; I wasn't interested in them. Was I interested in *anything* any more? The disappearance of the things made the question abruptly and alarmingly meaningful.

I pushed it aside and began to think about the things themselves. Wasn't it a relief that so much had gone, particularly those two great chests? But think of the labour of getting them out of the house! And why on earth should they have wanted them? I was told afterwards that antique oak furniture, even semi-antique oak furniture, is extremely valuable today. Well, so much the better for that nice Mr Sullivan.

Could one be sure that it had been Mr Sullivan? He might well have tipped off his friends, supplied the van and the local knowledge. And I remembered now that I had given him the key to the padlock of the side gate, so that he could come and go. He had apologised that he had lost the padlock – must have dropped it somewhere – and he had brought another padlock and given me the key. One key, I now realised; the other one he must have kept.

When the police came a day or two later, and asked me whether I had any ideas, I enquired rather diffidently if it was all right to mention a possible suspect. By all means, they said. And when I explained about the bush being trimmed off the wall, and who had performed this service, they chuckled, and one of them remarked wearily: 'Oh, we know Mr Sullivan.'

I felt inclined to ask why, in that case, they didn't do something about him; but then I remembered that in England suspicion, no matter how overwhelming, is not enough. Besides, the policemen gave me the decided impression that they would much rather not do anything about Mr Sullivan. It would involve too much work, as well as being rather unsporting. Instead they suggested that I should have the services of a counsellor, which they would be more than happy to arrange. A counsellor for what, I asked? The shock, they explained.

After they had gone I started to wonder about that. Was I feeling any shock? The answer seemed to be no – absolutely none at all. What had happened seemed an entirely natural – even inevitable – part of my new existence. One could hardly call it my new life-style. Anything that happened from now on, good, bad and indifferent, cancer, a car smash, a gigantic legacy, a best-selling novel, months and years of quiet total boredom – somehow it would all be the same.

And for some reason it was not a depressing prospect. Like the disappearance of the furniture, I faced it with a mild sense of relief. There were other things that had happened in the course of bereavement about which I was far from feeling the same sort of equanimity. For instance, the gradual vanishing of that old desire for my evening drink. And the looking forward to it. Now I pour something out with languor and lack of appetite. Might as well have a drink as anything else. That's not the way to go about it.

The drink had been part of my old routine. The routine of looking after Iris, which had blessed existence with reality.

Now it was just existence. One thing or one person was now as real or as unreal as the next.

If only I could be thoroughly independent, free from all these daily fidgets and anxieties and exasperations which have suddenly got so bad . . . Why didn't I have them before, when Iris was ill? Why couldn't I settle down to the *propriety* of bereavement, which should surely have its own spare and dignified emptiness of routine? Like being a monk, even a Trappist monk.

Being bereaved is not a career, like teaching or acting. I can see that. But I wish it were. How much more comfortable if it were a recognised profession, one of those

> in which men engage –
> The army, the navy, the church or the stage . . .

Isn't life happily like that in one of those Gilbert and Sullivan operas? I would like to be *engaged* in bereavement. An exacting job but a rewarding one, after the arduous period of preliminary training.

Or even if it isn't a career there must be some ideal way of doing it. A way of living I could aspire to, a Platonic vision of the widowed state?

Iris, who was such a deep and wise student of Plato, would be amused by that. But, I suppose, as things are, this is just the untidy, scuffling, scuttling way of living that bereavement must be for everybody.

How would I set about finding out? I don't want to find out.

Now I am missing the attacks of grief, which once came on with the suddenness of asthma or toothache. With the difference that each had an indescribable and physical happiness about it. More like sex in a way than misery; and yet so sharp and so agonising that each felt as if it would have been impossible to bear without the rush of tears and hiccups that accompanied it. I am sure that some people suffer the agony without those relieving symptoms: but I don't see how they do it.

As with most other things in life it is impossible to imagine or to be sure how other people are taking it. All experience is private, however universal, yet this one must in its own way be a special case. Between attacks, as it were, I remember thinking that all widows and widowers must undergo the same sort of symptoms, just as patients who have the same disease must do.

The condition of bereavement is well-defined. Less well-defined, possibly, is the wonderful sense of being alive that grief confers on its patient. Now, a year after Iris died, I miss that aliveness more than anything.

I miss other symptoms of aliveness too. The frenzies of rage and despair which came on sometimes before Iris died, in the same way that the fits of grief came on afterwards. And the fits of love too, during the months before her death, as wonderful and as physical as any experience in life could be.

Life – that's it. I haven't lived since the grief began to go away, and that is why I miss it so much.

And yet talking about 'life' in this way always sounds bogus. D.H. Lawrence was apt to do it, and his disciples and admirers were always talking about being 'on the side of life', whatever that means. Lawrence *was* alive, oh yes, and one can feel it as if not only in his words and his style but in his actual sensations, as if the two were the same. But talking about 'life' in that reverent way is another matter. It takes away the thing itself.

I feel not only that I have not been living since grief, now so much missed, started to go away, but that I haven't wanted to live. I preferred the other thing: just waiting to die. But the tranquillity of death, which I hoped to get into my daily experience, has proved to be something of an illusion. A nice, quiet, settled existence of routines, and little things presenting themselves throughout the day; that was what I was always harping on to myself. And nothing came of it. Naturally enough perhaps. Nothing except trouble, as it now seems, in various forms. Trouble like Margot and Mella. And did I, without knowing it, need that trouble? As a man in the desert needs water?

The chief comfort of my imagined way of being a widower had been quietly to look forward to each thing, each minute *being over*, while it was still actually going on. Anticipation as an end in itself, a goal and centre for consciousness? But what about that fallen but persuasive archangel, Belial? He wanted a quiet time too, but a quiet time for simple intellectual indulgence, for those 'thoughts that wander through eternity'. These, like those outbursts of grief, seem to me now no longer a part of daily existence. Why this should be so is not easy to say. Perhaps because they were an involuntary indulgence, like grief itself? My vision of the ideal widower's regime is that nothing should be involuntary. It should all have been arranged beforehand, by myself, for myself.

The chief danger to such a regime is its vulnerability. I had known Margot and Mella for years! Well – for a long time anyway. How could I have known that they would start to behave in the way they did? My own behaviour, in response to theirs, was, I like to think, far more predictable. Predictable, yes – but also extremely shabby? And yet could I really have behaved in any other way? I don't see that I could. My desire, at all costs, was to keep my widower's house intact. Granted that wish, all the rest follows.

During the last year I have become in my own eyes a more unattractive character, and, what is worse, a more boring one. Boring to myself, un-nice in my own interior being. ('Un-nice' is a coinage of Audi's, from the days of we four [or we three] being together. It is also possible to be 'un-nasty' in the same spirit.)

Iris and I used to be 'bad' with great pleasure and

frequency. She or I would say: 'Bad animal!' to the other, and this was a reassurance and a compliment, although Iris would often say as if in protest 'I am *not* a bad animal!' and I would reply: 'Course you're not a bad animal!' Good and bad naturally meant more to Iris, as a philosopher, than they did to me.

'It's a bit wonkmouse,' I used to say to Iris, who took the point of the word for my sake. Words with the suffix 'mouse' were OK words, which pleased us more for themselves than for what they signified. 'Wonkmouse' indicated something one was trying to do, and not succeeding, and deciding in consequence that it probably wasn't worth doing anyway. I was very definitely a wonkmouse man, whereas for Iris wonkmousery was only acceptable for the pair of us together, and for our joint activities. The more 'mouse' these were the better, for 'mouse' meant everything we took for granted and did together, without even being conscious of the fact that we did.

Iris, however, without ever being 'un-mouse', was in her own world completely separated from mouse activities. Her work was as much shut off from ordinary mouse activities as it was in itself deliberate and mysterious. This sense of her wholly separate being was to me the greatest source of pleasure and relaxation that our marriage afforded. On the Sparrow and Dog principle, it was almost as good as not being married at all.

I once teased Iris by telling her that she must have taken her own sort of vows when we got married.

'You're right,' she said. 'It was such a nice moment. Getting married to you meant I could give up living, and all that love business, and start doing my work.'

An exaggeration of course, but it was true that Iris's sense of life, however different from that of Dostoevsky or D.H. Lawrence, was in its own way an equally positive affair, which included loving, suffering, pitying, tormenting and being tormented – all the standard ingredients of passion and ecstasy, guilt and misery and desire. What she had called 'love business' most of all. She had lived life, as the saying is, to the full: and now she was going to write about it.

Which she did, and had done. For me, living with Iris, as she was with me and for me, was quite enough. Year by happy year, as it had been for me, while we had grown ever 'closer and closer apart'. I had no conscious desire for life in any fuller or more absolute sense. But while she was very ill, and after she died, the aliveness began. The rage, the suffering and the grief. I was not exactly surprised by it, but without conscious reflection I decided I must get rid of it somehow. I must achieve that patterned existence of quiet, empty, solitary routines.

I never had. And while all the business with Mella and Margot was going on I had those frequent moments of panic and emptiness that made it clear to me that I didn't, after all, really want to be left on my own.

What was I to do then? To be a widower in my own house, with my own routines and thoughts, had been my ideal. I had behaved ingloriously where Mella and Margot were concerned, in order to retain that way of being, and to keep it safe. And now it seemed that I didn't want it after all.

But I *must* do! For what else was there? Even those thoughts, the thoughts that wander through eternity, taking in on their way such interesting objects of speculation as the Krag-Jörgensen rifle, and the historic battle of Svold, which I had once or twice discussed with Audi – even these thoughts had lately begun to pall. It was a pity, because I was genuinely interested in the battle of Svold. It was fought in the year 1000, a thousand years before our own tedious millennium.

That rash and glorious Viking Olaf Tryggvason, who in his youth had beaten the English army at Maldon on the Essex marshes, had then won his way to his kingdom in

Norway. Now he was throwing it away in a mad expedition to extract a great dowry from the Danish king, Svein Forkbeard, for his wife, the king's daughter, whom Olaf had married against the king's will. He knew that Svein Forkbeard had allied himself with the king of Sweden, and with malcontents from his own Norway, but he did not care. He did not care even when it was clear that they had ambushed him off the island of Svold, or when he saw the size of their fleet . . .

What matter? In his great ship, the *Long Serpent*, the biggest longship in the north, he would fight them off. And if he failed? Well, he failed, and went down to Valhalla fighting gloriously as a Viking should. (He remembered now and then that he was supposed to have been converted to Christianity; he had given up raiding England because it was a Christian country; but in this last fight he would have put all that out of his mind.)

His comrade Einar Tamberskelver was beside him on the poop of the *Long Serpent*, which towered above the remainder of his little flotilla. Einar was a crack archer, and had been picking off the opposition with his deadly arrows. But a Finn in the Swedish fleet, a skilled warlock like all Finns, contrived to pierce Einar's bowstring with a magic arrow. Between blows at Swedish and Danish heads Olaf asked what had caused the resounding twang he had just heard.

> Einar then, the arrow taking
> From the loosened string,
> Answered 'That was Norway breaking
> 'Neath thy hand, O king.'

Longfellow, the American poet, does that part of the old chronicle in his poem very well. As the greatest warship in the north was systematically boarded and overwhelmed by the enemy, Olaf struck down a last opponent, jumped from the stern with his sword in his hand and in all his armour, and was never seen again. He was long looked for and prayed for. After the battle Norway was overrun by Swedes and Danes, but although his countrymen prayed to Christ and Odin for his return 'Olaf Tryggvason never came back to his kingdom.'

Suddenly that seems to me overwhelmingly sad. Why? I don't care a curse about others – kings, princes, pretenders – who never came back to their countries. When he drowned at Svold was Olaf's father still alive? The cunning old fox, Trygve of the Vik, the Vik being the fjord that led to the town of Oslo. That may be the reason why Vikings are called Vikings, though the point is disputed.

'Is it now?' as Iris would say. She would have looked and listened to me with smiling indulgence. And now what should I care? But if I give up caring about thoughts like that, where should I be? I wish Olaf had won his last battle. He was only trying, for himself of course, to get a queen's dowry for his new wife. Her father must have been that Svein Forkbeard who became king of York, and whose son, the great Knut (Canute to us) made himself king of England. King of Denmark too of course. Who was it told me that a verse in the Danish National Anthem still celebrates that fact? 'Once we ruled England . . .'?

How I wish I could tell Iris all this! Talk about it to her, as I would have done once, many years ago. She never minded my rambling on to her about something of absolutely no importance at all. She used to say she liked it. She used to sit looking at me with a smile on her face, and I could see she was herself thinking of something important. Something worthwhile. That used to give me such pleasure.

Curious that when Iris was ill these Belial thoughts that wander about were my great solace, indeed my greatest pleasure. Did I think that I was still sharing them with Iris? I don't think so. It's only now, when she's not here, that I want her to be here, so that I could share them with her.

Olaf's new wife, the Danish princess, was his third. I fancy his first was a Wend. No doubt a Wendish princess. They thought a lot about royal blood in those days; took its importance for granted, if they happened to have it themselves. The Viking aristocracy bled to death in civil wars . . .

This is becoming a nightmare. Never mind the Viking aristocracy, I feel as if I were bleeding to death myself. What is wrong with me nowadays? I wouldn't want to ask Mella or Margot, those ghost figures from a more recent past. From a past that is more distant to me than Iris. I seem to be losing all sense of the past; and with it all the thoughts that cocooned me round when I was looking after Iris, and which I thought I could still depend upon, now that she is gone. It seems I can't. And I can't now even remember how long she has been gone for.

Head spinning round and round, I must stop it. There must be something left, something to hold on to? That last Christmas, for instance? No, it had better not be that last Christmas. What about the one before? And now, of course, I am vividly remembering both of them, but particularly the one which I didn't want to remember.

Michael comes to fetch us in his car. On Christmas morning, when he goes off as usual to Chelsea Old Church, I hope that Iris and I could do our usual walk to Kensington Gardens. But Iris is so much weaker. We get as far as Kensington Gardens, and it was not far, but once there we have to sit down. No question of the Serpentine. We sit down, and lean ourselves together, and twine our hands. I say to Iris: *'Poujin?'*

I am smiling at her, hoping she will reply. It is a word she invented herself, or seemed to invent, about three months earlier. It was in the car; she turned and put her hand on my knee, and said, with some emphasis, sounds or words, two of which sounded like 'Poujin'. She seemed to think the word an important one, and she looked happy while she said it.

But now, however many times I hopefully repeat 'Poujin', Iris's eye and face gives no flicker of recognition. The word-sound has gone, and will not return. She looks vacantly into the distance. But then in a moment or two she seems to be looking at something.

She is. It is the Albert Memorial, newly washed and cleaned and painted and gilded, so that it shines like an eastern temple in the weak winter sunshine. It was foggy when we got to the park and found our seat, which faced down Queen's Gate. We did not notice the Memorial; in any case, I have quite given up thinking that Iris might notice things. I take it for granted that she cannot.

But she has. She has seen the sun-gilt back of the Prince Consort, vast and cloaked in his scrubbed new imperial majesty. He is looking away from London, sitting on his chair or throne or whatever it is, and gazing placidly over the green stretches of the park, as if they were his own German fields.

I wonder what it was like, that Christmas at Windsor. There was probably a big and boring dinner party going on, when Albert felt the first feverish symptoms of typhoid. If typhoid gives you feverish symptoms. All I had to go on was Virginia Woolf's first and best novel, *The Voyage Out*, in which the heroine, Rachel, dies of typhoid. She has just become engaged to be married and is very happy but rather giddy and distracted. She has a headache. For coolness she puts her hand on the metal globe which ornaments her bed, and soon finds that it has become uncomfortably hot . . .

Virginia Woolf knew all about it, because her brother Thoby had died of typhoid. In their house somewhere just across the park there.

Iris has no further interest in the Prince Consort. Probably it was only his gilded back that caught her attention. I hug her and say 'Poujin!' once more, but for her it is only some incomprehensible word-sound. Her face puckers, and the anxious look, so far absent this Christmas morning, comes back over it, like clouds beginning to come back over the sun.

As indeed they are. I shiver, but Iris doesn't seem aware of the cold.

I smile at her, reassuringly, I hope. She was always young, and still looks youthful enough to live for ever. This dreadful childhood has come upon her as if she were Peter Pan himself. Peter Pan is eternally youthful; and here broods the still comely Prince Consort, looking as if he had never been young. Marriage to a queen robbed him of that chance, poor man. The irony of it seems worse this year than last year, when I could talk away to Iris beside the Serpentine statue, not indeed in the hope that she could join in, but with the feeling, given confidence by her own eyes and smile – however timid and uncertain these had become – that my chatter still reassured her, as it had always done in the past.

Not now: not any longer. As we walk along together I talk absently to myself, without even turning my head to see if the words have any effect on Iris. But then I pull myself together and ask if she enjoyed seeing Albert? All done up in his new gilt cloak?

'Albert, darling?' I say hopefully.

Iris waves her head, still smiling. Two big tears peer out under her eyelids and then slide down her cheeks. The sight is extraordinarily reassuring, as satisfying as if it were some much more intimate bodily process of my own. I seize her round the waist and dance a few steps with her, kissing both her cheeks. We go along together arm in arm.

But why Albert? 'Peter Pan?' I say hopefully. And then 'Poujin?' To neither of these does Iris make any response. Albert is the one she fancies. A dashing name? At one time it could have had the glow and the sweet nostalgia of a first remembered love . . .

But not for Iris surely? Only if she had lived in those old Victorian days, for which she would now have to be about a hundred and something instead of a mere seventy-nine.

Being a 'carer' is in one sense a wholly incurious business. Curiosity about the behaviour of the person you look after seems to dry up and die, as if it was as much as you could do to look after them as they appear to be, and attend to their needs mechanically and without attention. I was fascinated for a moment, none the less, by Iris's Albert response. It was like operating the machine cluelessly and at random, and suddenly making it disgorge a mass of coins or tokens. At one time I had hoped 'Poujin' – Iris's own word – would prove similarly rewarding, but no.

I clung to Poujin all the same. Iris had given it to me, even if she didn't want it herself. I felt, quite arbitrarily of course, that she had intended to convey something about our present relations to each other. I was her Poujin, as it might be a husband or a 'carer', even, as it might have been in the days of Albert, her 'young man', or with a change of sex a 'best girl'. It was, at least, a more vigorous and somehow a more expressive word than the deadly dull and null 'carer', with its whiff of Welfare State correctness. I mentioned Poujin once at an Alzheimer meeting, and Dr Jacoby suggested we should all become Poujins, instead of carers.

It was our last Christmas. And Albert must have had his last Christmas too. At Windsor, where the drains were so bad. The Queen wouldn't have cared or noticed. She could have stood any amount of infection from drains.

Our last Christmas. And Iris, although I had no idea of it, had less than two months to live. Did she wish to live? Or was she content, all unconsciously as Albert may have been, to let life slip away?

About the middle of January she stopped eating or drinking. Nothing I could do would persuade her to take in as much as even a teaspoonful of milk. And she was very merry about it. She smiled at me in an almost roguish way as I coaxed and cajoled. It could hardly have been a death-wish, because Iris had long since passed the point where any wish or desire could come into her head, or into her voice. She was not wanting to die. But she seemed to have received secret orders, which at once filled her with a secret joy. She could do what they suggested; she could fulfil their requirements to the letter.

So I took her to Vale House, that wonderful Home. It was always full up, and I was extremely lucky to get her in; only someone dying there made it possible. There seemed nothing else to do, but I was in terror none the less in case she should be so miserable, perhaps even violent (which she never had been), that I should have to find something else, some other way of dealing with the situation.

But Iris was happy. Her face lit up like an angel's when I appeared every morning, but this seemed not because of me but because she was so happy that she showed her happiness to me like a child. She even permitted herself to relax a little those invisible orders she had received. Not officially as it were. She still refused anything we tried to give her. But if I and the Irish nurse sat beside her she would wait until we were deep in talk and paying her no attention, and then suddenly swoop on the spoon we were holding and suck a little milk from it. Then she would look inimitably sly. She wanted us not to have noticed, but at the same time to admire what she had done, and the clever way she had done it.

But after a while, a short while, she seemed to think she had amused us long enough. She was as merry and courteous as ever, but there could be no further compromise, even for our pleasure. It was time to go.

And so she went. No death-wish – how could there have been? But terminal illness may at moments give the impression of one. Alzheimer's most of all. The brain and body seem so far apart, and the body seems to issue its own orders, as if saying, 'I am perfectly capable of carrying on. But why should I?'

Nobody *really* wants what they want. Or, to put it another way, everyone unconsciously rejects the image of themselves and their doings which they know to be most desirable and proper for them. I knew, all those years and years ago, that I was making a great mistake in marrying Iris. Every instinct about myself that I recognised and valued told me not to do it.

But it seems that I did do it. I jumped. I jumped where I should have stayed still, and I was sure, quite sure, that doing nothing was the thing for me to do.

So the forty-four years that mostly constituted my adult life had been determined by doing the very thing I was sure I didn't want to do? Good. And of course it is a familiar and indeed a banal story. Lots and lots of people have done, or are doing, just the same thing. And with the same wholly satisfactory results. A life lived and in no way regretted can only be satisfactory: both for those who lived it, and in the eyes of anyone who has happened to notice them.

Now, as a widower, I again found myself in the position of being able to do what I wanted. And this time I didn't have to make a choice. I could do what I knew I wanted to do without being confronted or threatened with an alternative. There was no alternative. Even Mella and Margot, distracting as their ministrations had been, had only deflected at a superficial level my wish to lead my own widower's life.

But widowers, as I was finding out, don't lead lives. They wait for something to happen: and when something does happen it becomes a muddle from which they at once have to try to escape.

That at least was my experience. I had tried to make a life – almost a 'Life' – out of being a widower, and it had led into this vertigo of anxiety, a state which I found myself comparing more and more with the state of anxiety to which Iris had first succumbed with the onset of Alzheimer's.

However blasphemous the comparison might be I couldn't help making it. Day and night now I was haunted by the sound of things we had said together in earlier times; by the smile she wore in her last days, by the way she lay in her bed on that last afternoon. Her last afternoon as herself. Since then she had been memories, images in the mind, words in books.

And those memories were pressing upon me with a greater and greater urgency. For the first time I longed to ask another widow or widower whether it was, or had been, the same for them. But as it happened I didn't know any recently bereaved persons: a surprising fact, it occurred to me, considering my age, and that of my contemporaries. Why was nobody dying at the moment? But it didn't matter, because I knew quite well that if I had known someone in my own position, the last thing I should have done would be to ask questions of this kind. Or of any kind. The bereaved should maintain the privacy and, in their own eyes, the singularity of their status. A privilege not to be transgressed.

I might be feeling more and more desperate but I was also getting more and more pompous. Was it because I had no one to think of but myself? No doubt. I actually needed now *more* harassment from other people, even from people like Mella and Margot. In my nice quiet widower's regime, which I had been so sure I wanted, depression was rising every day, as stealthily as floodwater.

I answered the phone now whenever it rang. I sat hoping for a call. And at last there was one! A nice foreign female voice which said something about Brussels. At once I felt harassed again, but almost happily harassed. I could not make out, however, what she was saying or what she wanted.

After we had rung off, with what must have been mutual relief, I felt I had had my adventure for the day, enough indeed for several days. I rather hoped to hear more, none the less, and I was not disappointed. Next morning there was a letter, with a Belgian stamp and a Brussels postmark. Thank goodness for the post!

The letter inside was headed 'Saint Amour'. Who was Saint Amour? Perhaps, with that ironical name, he was going to come and cure all my widower's problems.

In fact it turned out to be some kind of theatrical enterprise which was inviting me to take part in a series of performances 'on the theme of Love'. These would consist of authors, mainly Flemish, reading from their work. It was suggested that I should read some extracts from my memoir of Iris.

Of course I would give them a polite refusal. No other possibility entered my head. So certain was I of this decision that harassment and vertigo disappeared and left me feeling quite calm. This unnatural state of calm had unforeseen consequences. It must have had; because a week later I found myself walking into the Hotel Metropole in Brussels.

How had I got there? I seemed hardly to know myself. But I recalled that I had picked up the telephone and got through to Saint Amour in Brussels with dream-like ease. Before I knew what had happened, they had arranged the journey, and it was so simple.

The train slid under the Channel. Northern France looked as huge and desolate as Siberia, and I contemplated it with approval as I drank some wine and ate one of those long crusty 'sandwichs' which I had always, but apparently mistakenly, supposed that the French called 'tartines'. The landscape suited my mood, and so did the sandwich and the wine.

But how had it happened? I had thought that I would never again leave the widower's house; at least not voluntarily. And here I sat on a train in France. Feeling quite happy about it. Perhaps Iris had arranged the whole thing? I clung to that notion.

However my heart sank as I entered the Metropole. It was like coming back to school, and that was more than sixty years ago. It made me shed my widowerhood instantly. Here was all the awkwardness of the first day of term, after the unhappy arrival by train. True, the Hotel Metropole itself was not like school. It was vast and highly ornamented and full of *art nouveau* and monotonous great mirrors. But it must have been the experience of going back to school – coming back rather – which had suddenly exorcised widowerhood.

Images of school persisted. When I crept out to find somewhere to eat, for it was now past eight o'clock, I obtained a simple but satisfying meal at a café called The Rugbyman. My dish was a large quantity of tiny brown shrimps in their shells. As I crunched them with appetite they gave off a delicious aroma of saltmarsh and sandy northern beaches – the odours of my childhood. They were accompanied by Belgian 'white beer', a pallid but delicious brew, with a slice of lemon stuck tastefully on the rim of the big glass. It looked like ginger beer and was perfectly in keeping with the school tuckshop image; but it was very much stronger, as I soon found out.

On the following morning we answered our names to the Saint Amour 'schoolmasters' in the lounge of the Metropole. The name of the enterprise now seemed wonderfully well suited to the new school I had been sent to, in my new adolescent and unwidowed persona. It must be one of those fictional establishments about which boys and girls used to read in school stories. 'The end of term play at Saint Amour' – there was always fierce competition to be one of the cast, perhaps even to shine as a star. I remembered from long ago reading about the exploits of 'the worst girl at St Chad's', and all those gripping doings which took place at St Dominic's.

The role of school matron was taken at our performances during the week by a dark-featured, strikingly tall girl, whom I privately christened the Angel of Death. Apart from nurse-maiding and feeding us and driving the minibus to the towns where the show was to take place, it was her duty, and by no means an unarduous one, to flush out delinquent performers from some adjacent bar or café when their number on the programme was imminent.

As the week went on, and the author-readers became more accustomed to their roles in the production, the Angel of Death had to work harder than ever, sometimes appearing as I was about to raise a glass to my lips to march me back rapidly into the tartaric sub-regions of the theatre. But once I had become accustomed to her slightly sinister appearance and her imperious forefinger I became quite fond of the Angel of Death; and her smile for me grew more indulgent as the week went by, probably because my number was the last on the list, and signalled the end of our labours for the evening. My attachment seemed all the more suitable by reason of the boarding school atmosphere in which we moved; no doubt I had unknown rivals among the rest of the cast. We were all on very jolly terms together, and like a busload of schoolboys we always chorused a fond farewell to the Angel as she dropped us off at the Metropole, well after midnight.

The show itself remained largely incomprehensible to me, partly because none of us saw much of it outside our own particular acts. Undertaken in the furtherance of Flemish culture it was entitled *Behoude de Begeerte*, a sonorous and harmonious phrase which meant something like 'Hold on to the Passions'. For love, in its various obsessions and diversities, was the theme. A lively young Flemish author started us off by reading an extract from his book about the affection – perhaps more than affection – between a grandfather and granddaughter. The evening continued with another author's passion for his car, went on to examine crushes between girls, and those between younger and older men, culminating in a best-selling French writer's account of the joys of sex in a jacuzzi. I followed him as the last number on the bill, and was kindly described in a newspaper review as the 'Nestor of the company'.

As we read, our words appeared translated into Flemish on a giant screen behind our heads. Our invisible audience must have been bemused and not infrequently bored, but they remained kindly disposed, and gave us all a vigorous clap towards the end, when it dawned on them that the interminable evening – the show lasted more than three hours – was nearly over. It was strange to sit on a deck-chair in the darkness, the Angel of Death hovering nearby in the eerie light of a blue bulb, waiting for my cue. The measured French tones from the stage would cease and I would prepare to read to an audience I never saw about the joys and woes of looking after Iris, the Alzheimer patient whom I had, indeed, so much loved.

Back in England, I could scarcely believe that this strange interlude had taken place. I hoped, vainly as it turned out, that my widower's house would now seem real, and interruptions to my Platonic regime of widowerhood, the idea of which I still clung to in my mind, would vanish like the dance of those Chinese shadows. Mella, Margot, Saint Amour and *Behoude de Begeerte* – none of them *were* real, surely? The only real thing was an immense great hard sausage, or salami, that I had not been able to resist buying on my last day in Brussels. Its sheer size and weight made it an object of comfort. Caressing it sadly in the kitchen at home I remembered Audi poking knowledgeably about among the charcuterie in her local supermarket.

'I want something strong enough to kill a Swede,' she had observed with her angelic smile.

This, it seemed, was an ancient and neighbourly Norwegian proverb.

*   *   *

Apart from the sausage one other thing seemed weighty and worthwhile – even true. I had managed to visit a gallery before leaving Belgium, and I had seen the Virgin on her deathbed, in the picture by Van der Goes. It was like Iris on her deathbed. Perhaps it was like all of us on our deathbeds, but I thought only of Iris then. I failed to buy a postcard of that picture, but at the time it filled me with comfort.

There was a moment long ago on our honeymoon when we discovered, almost by accident, the little Italian town of Borgo St Sepolcro, and saw in its original setting in the town hall the fresco of the Resurrection by Piero della Francesca. Gazing vacantly at Van der Goes's Virgin I recalled that very different moment of her son's triumph over death. The muscular figure climbing effortlessly out of the grave, with his round dark eyes fixed on nothingness: filled with a fathomless vacancy and yet piercing the beholder with uncanny force.

He lives, but his mother dies. That was what it looked like. Her friends around her in Van der Goes's picture only emphasise the solitude of the central figure, lost in her blue-grey mantle of existlessness.

W.H. Auden had been to Belgium, and he wrote a memorable poem, *Musée des Beaux Arts*. I remembered that now too. Auden must have seen Breughel's painting of the Fall of Icarus. From this picture he drew the conclusion that 'they were never wrong, the Old Masters.' They understood the solitude and separation in which we all live, engrossed in our own lives. The soldiers around the grave are asleep when Christ steps from his tomb. The ship that must have seen the boy Icarus falling from the sky sails calmly on. The dying Virgin seems indifferent to her friends, and at a great distance from them.

For all their beauty and memorability all these pictures went out of my head when I was in my house again. Iris, too, was not there; neither as she once was nor as she had become. Not even Iris on her deathbed, whom I saw in my mind's eye so many times every day, and whom I had felt I was seeing in the picture. They had all gone, and with them had gone the memory of love.

There remained that Belgian sausage, long, hard and weighty. It brought to mind Mella's pie. And our Great Pie of long ago, the first that had gone to Pieland.

There was a sudden loud knocking on the door. The bell had still not been fixed. It was quite early, just after eight in the morning.

It was three weeks now since I had got home. My state of agitated vulnerability had again become normal. I had taken to locking the doors as I had locked them in Iris's time. Now I locked them to try to feel secure in my own house.

Memory, like a cancer, had returned to eat me up. I welcomed it too. Where should I be without it?

I hated even looking out of the window. What calamity was I expecting? There was nothing, good or bad, to expect.

Brussels had been a dream. But I still saw so clearly the Angel of Death and her smile – although now there was only the certainty of tiresomeness, in all its leaden forms. The widower's curse. Trouble would come. It would probably come in the predictable form of a helping hand. Trouble was a friendly knock on the door. So was fear.

How exciting and yet how full of fear the cinema had once been! The explorers or the soldiers were tiptoeing through the jungle. I used to feel a kind of despair on their behalf. Both excitement and hopelessness. In spite of all the precautions they took, the dreadful thing was bound to happen. Indians would ambush them; the bearded tribesmen would rush out. I always knew the good guys would win in the end, but that was not the point. Far, far worse was the dreadful certainty that they would soon be in bad trouble.

Those joys and terrors were long ago. Meanwhile the house was decaying around me; in a terminal state, as if it, too, suffered from the cancer of recall.

And then there came the knocking again, like the knocking on the gate in *Macbeth*. Trouble from somebody. Not likely to be Indians or tribesmen. Something worse than that.

9

The Return of Mella and Margot

And yet probably just a parcel. Most likely six of Iris's novels in Turkish. Or Japanese. They arrived regularly, adding to the confusion of objects on the floor – no room for them anywhere else – but I welcomed their arrival none the less, and even looked inside them with curiosity; as if Iris's words might have taken on another meaning in this unknown tongue, and reveal to me something new and wonderful. Not about the incomprehensible language in which they now found themselves, but about Iris herself.

I remembered the moment, about three months before she died, when the same thing happened. The banging on the door had come at about the same time. Iris was asleep, and I was reading in bed beside her. I had the typewriter on my lap, but at that good time of the morning I used to indulge myself in a page or two of a familiar book, some old favourite which I could then look forward to reading more of over supper.

It was the peaceful time, from about six till nine in the morning, before I had to get up and try to persuade her to drink tea, eat porridge . . . Then the day's troubles began. How much I missed them now.

Through the glass in the front door I saw, on that occasion, the delivery man with his big parcel. I made signs for him to leave it on the step outside. That was because the door was locked on the inside. It had to be.

Miming his regrets the delivery man indicated through the glass that he had to have a signature. I had already realised I had forgotten to bring the key down; that was why I had signed to him to leave the parcel. The key was in my trouser pocket, but I had not got my trousers on. Only shirt and dressing-gown.

I stole upstairs, got the key without waking Iris, and let the parcel in. He was a nice man, I remembered, and we had a moment or two's chat about the weather, although I was rather conscious at the open door of my trouserless state. When I got upstairs again Iris had woken up and the peaceful part of the morning was over.

These former things were vivid in my head as I went to the front door to let in what at that time of the morning – barely eight o'clock – could only be the post or a parcel. So vivid was my memory of that earlier occasion that I found myself wondering, as I had often done at the time, why it was that Iris so much preferred to be left as she was: always dressed, always unwashed. Could it have been because I *really preferred it too*, in my own case, I mean; and Iris was expressing, in some strange way, a kind of sympathy and solidarity with me? Was it an aspect of our closeness, one that had now come fully out, fully into its own?

However that was, I felt sure that Iris was pleased not to be bothered and cared for when it came to clothes and hygiene. She could do as she wished, and as she preferred, just as if she had not been an invalid and a patient but a normal person. At the time I really felt that she was happy and pleased about that. She seemed to show it sometimes by smiling, as if understandingly, by stroking and caressing me. And as I went to the door at that moment I could feel her presence, as if I were still holding her hand.

At Alzheimer meetings since then I had made the point that it might be better for the patient, and for the carer too, just to let things go in this same way. Better all round in fact. And I had felt pleased and honoured when Dr

Jacoby summed up at one of these meetings by agreeing that it could be a good solution. He had seen so many cases, in families looking after an Alzheimer patient, of over-insistence on cleanliness and tidiness. It could cause stress and exhaustion all round. Family friction as well, in a situation that was already quite bad enough.

I was lost among these thoughts – quite bemused. I saw the kindly face of Dr Jacoby when he used to visit us, and Iris rushed to meet him like a child, smiling all over her face.

Lost in the past, I stooped down to undo the bolt on the front door. It must be the parcel man, with six novels in Turkish, Hungarian, or Japanese. I should have to sign for them. I hadn't even looked through the glass to see who was there.

It was not six of Iris's novels in Turkish or in Japanese. It was Mella. And it was Margot. Both together.

They stood shoulder to shoulder, smiling at me.

Mella looked rather well. Hair tidy, almost shining. Face perhaps more eager and expectant than happy, but cheerful anyway. Margot, as usual, a big, calm, smiling presence.

I gaped at them. They looked solid enough, like the great Belgian sausage, which by now I had successfully eaten. But were they really just phantoms of my brain? A brain distracted by living in this house, among all its fears and fancies and anxieties?

As I gazed at them, with my mouth no doubt hanging foolishly open, I had the grotesque thought, certainly born of the Alzheimer meetings and our discussions there, that Mella might be expecting me to wash her, as Iris had not done. It had been pleasant and peaceful not to bother Iris with fuss about hygiene. But perhaps Mella would be more demanding now? She might *insist* on being washed?

'Oh, do come in,' I heard myself saying.

As I uttered the words I had a vision of escape. I would go back to Brussels. I would seek out the Angel of Death. Together we would fly to a distant, tropical country. The

Angel would occupy herself with some theatrical enterprise. I would support and assist her. In the warm evenings we would sit together, our work done, listening to the tree-frogs and smelling the heavy scent of dark petals and Zambezi mud . . .

We would be calm. We would be happy.

'We've just this moment got here from Heathrow,' announced Margot.

There was something gushing and unfamiliar about the way she spoke, as if her relationship with Mella, whatever it was or had become, had changed her whole personality. Perhaps mine had changed too? Other people were said to notice such a thing more than one did oneself.

Margot was now babbling something about Barcelona. Why Barcelona?

I was locked eye to eye with Margot. As we gazed tautly at each other, revelation came to me abruptly. Margot was afraid of Mella. That was why they were here. Wherever they had been together, Barcelona or somewhere, Margot had managed to bring her here now in order to get rid of her. She was afraid of Mella. Indeed it looked as if she had come positively to hate her. And to think I had once found myself afraid of Margot!

How confusing it all was. I remembered in a benumbed way, and hardly even with astonishment, that it was Mella who had said she hated Margot. How could one know where one was with them? My own part in the trio, such as it was, seemed to have shrunk away to nothing. That should have given me relief and satisfaction, and yet I realised gloomily that it did not. I might think I wanted to get away from both of them; but that did not mean I wanted now to be left out of whatever was going on between them.

'Well, I must be getting along,' said Margot. Her voice had a ghastly jauntiness; her eyes met mine and looked quickly away. Easy for her to talk, but would the gangster let her go?

'Goodness knows what's been happening at home,' Margot went on. 'My precious animals must feel awfully neglected. Jimmy and George and the poor little donkey, and those hens you're so fond of, Johnny . . .'

Her voice trailed away and she seized her bag. Mella glanced incuriously from one of us to the other.

Should I try to get away, not with the Angel of Death, but with Margot? It was a terrible prospect, fond as I might be not only of Margot but of her hens, those great speckly monsters. And the poor little donkey, come to that. And even Jimmy and George, that clapped-out couple who wandered all day about the paddock with sad equine patience. No, I couldn't face it. Besides, there was no indication at all that Margot needed a companion in her getaway.

Voluble in her goodbyes and good wishes, 'You *must* come! – both of you – *any* time,' Margot was out of the door. She waved vigorously without turning round. A moment later a car started.

'Well, that's a relief,' said Mella. 'Bloody woman.'

Was she coming out in her true colours now? Did anyone have any true colours? The bloody woman had been of great service to her – she had wanted to be. Mella had none the less exploited her. Said once that she hated her. Had been all over Margot before that, and presumably after it too. Free trip to Barcelona? Why had they wanted to go to Barcelona, of all places?

With a timing that seemed uncanny Mella answered that question. 'I have this thing about Gaudí,' she remarked airily. 'Margot likes him too, or says she does. I really couldn't go on living without seeing the Sagrada Familia.'

What was all this then? But Mella no longer surprised me; she just depressed and exhausted me. She made me feel I never wanted to see anybody ever again.

Had I ever really known anybody, except Iris? Had I ever really known her? *Yes, of course I had.*

But perhaps Mella was unusually unknowable. Even Margot's behaviour had begun to startle me. Was it just that I had no idea nowadays, in my solitary state, how people could be expected to behave? Or what they wanted, or how they lived? None of these things had seemed to matter before, or even to exist. When there had been just the two of us – Iris and me – everything and everybody made sense. Or if they didn't do so, it wasn't any business of mine.

I noticed an efficient-looking holdall, fat and well zipped, which had appeared beside the kitchen door. In the confusion all round it looked trim and determined. It looked as if it had come to stay.

How long ago it seemed since Mella had run away into the snow. And vanished.

Paying her bag no attention, Mella sauntered out of the kitchen. I heard her on the stairs. Probably she needed a pee, which was natural enough. Margot had been too precipitate to stop for one. All she had thought about was getting away. We had no lavatory on the ground floor, possibly the consequence, as Iris and I had sometimes speculated, of the house having been built by and for a pair of maiden ladies. We had no other evidence of the existence of those ladies – a gentle, retiring sort of couple? – but in those days we liked to imagine them.

Mella's voice floated down from upstairs, but I couldn't hear what she was saying. My house had suddenly become dreadfully, overpoweringly domesticated. All around me, in addition to the usual mess were faint but discernible traces of Mella's previous attempts at clearing things up, attempts so much more effective than Margot's. The latter, I remembered, had scarcely got going at all.

I continued to stand motionless, as if paralysed. Mella's voice was again audible from upstairs, with a rather more demanding note in it. She seemed to require my presence.

She was standing in the bedroom, holding a single sock in her hand. Her voice when she spoke was mild and explanatory, as if she were telling me something I ought to know about for my own good.

'Seventy per cent nylon thirty per cent wool is better, you know,' she said. 'This is a woollen sock, and look at the hole! The moths are in it too.'

This was yet another side to Mella. I preferred it. A dangerous, if not fatal, preference, as I quickly saw. She seemed relaxed and peace-loving, as if she had recently won a great victory. Against Margot no doubt? After that I was a simple assignment. She would have no trouble with me.

She was all kindness and benevolence now, prepared to let me off the delinquent sock. Men couldn't be expected to manage such things. They needed pork pies too, and other feminine favours.

I wondered vacantly what lies, or even truths, she had told Margot about our relations. And yet why should she bother? None the less I felt a little hurt at the idea of being left out. No doubt their own relationship, whatever it was, had absorbed them completely.

Then what had gone wrong? Something had. There was nothing 'feminist' about either of them, no suggestion of solidarity or a sisterhood that excluded men. Had that been why they quarrelled? If they had? Or was I just being inept and patronising? Whatever the truth of the matter it looked as if Margot was not prepared to tolerate Mella and her company a moment longer. She was desperate to get rid of her. Had that sudden trip to Spain, undertaken with an almost honeymoon gaiety, ended in a row? Was Margot through with Holy Families, and with Lame Ducks as well?

Was she longing now to get back to her real animals, to the hens, the ancient horses and the donkey?

With an effort I brought back my attention to Mella. She was a phenomenon not to be got rid of, at least not by me, and certainly not at this moment. How much I envied Margot! But there was nowhere I could escape to as she had just done.

'What about your flat?' I asked. 'Have you been back there yet?'

I knew she hadn't. Margot had said that they had this minute arrived from Heathrow, and Margot was a woman whose word could be trusted. Unlike me? Unlike Mella? Perhaps Mella and I were soulmates really? Two of a kind?

What about the lady porter, who had told me about Mella's flat? She had seemed a trustworthy woman, like Margot. It seemed certain that the flat existed, and that Mella occupied it. Then why hadn't the pair of them gone straight round there, instead of coming straight to me?

Grimly I thought I saw the reason. Margot wanted the job to be done properly. A handing-over ceremony, just as I remembered from the army, in which responsibility was formally transferred from one person to another. Margot was making sure that I didn't miss the point. Mella was going to be my problem from now on.

Margot might be honest, at least compared to Mella and me, but I could hardly believe that after a few days in Mella's company she could have continued to believe the waif-and-stray story. As an orphan of the storm she had been authentic enough, so that was indeed a sense in which I, too, had been deceived. What had she done then? Conquered Margot? Or rather reconquered her and bewitched her? In the end Margot had the sense to run for it, flee away home in her car.

But I *was* in my home. Or rather in my house. What was I to do now?

'Let me give you a lift,' I said. 'Back to your place.'

Mella said nothing and we continued to stand in the

bedroom. Was it to be the centre of our lives from now on? I cast a despairing glance at the dishevelled bed, the books, my typewriter, the worn old rubber cushion that propped my back when I sat typing in bed. How purposeful and happy they all looked! How much I loved them and yearned to be back among them! The things of the house, which had always been there, and which I could rely on as I had once relied on Iris's presence. They were just as they had been early this morning, when I sat in bed reading. Should I ever be able to read there again?

Hypnotised by their familiar presence I hardly noticed that Mella had not replied to my suggestion. When she did so her words filled me with a renewal of all my alarms. And not just alarm. Despair.

'Oh,' she said, 'you mean my flat? I've given that up. I only had it by the month, and they were always bothering me about the rent. The landlord was terribly tiresome.' She dropped my sock on the floor.

'But what about all your things?' I cried, trying to keep the panic out of my voice.

'My things?' Mella said patiently. 'My things are all in my little bag. Downstairs. The flat was rented furnished, of course.'

She picked up the sock again and looked at it critically, sniffed at it, turned it inside out or right way round – I couldn't see which – and dropped it on the floor again.

'Not worth washing,' she said, comfortably, as if there were lots of things here that might be worth it, and which she would soon be giving herself the pleasure of attending to.

'I must have a pee,' she went on. 'Forgot about it when we landed.'

She wandered off in the direction of the bathroom.

Had I come to a decision without knowing it, ever since the pair of them appeared at the door? However that might be, this moment now was a revelation.

I must leave the house. I must leave it at once.

The mistake had been to cling on so desperately to my life there. It was the house itself, my widower's house, that was causing the trouble, however much I felt that I loved it, needed it, filled it with the consolations of the past. For Iris was no longer in it; Iris was no longer there, as she had been after her first death. She did not exist now except in my own mind, and even in my own mind her existence was purely notional.

I remembered – what a moment to remember it – the important concept on which she had made herself an expert when she worked at the Treasury during the war. 'Notional promotion *in absentia*.' Soldiers from the peacetime Civil Service were metaphysically promoted, in terms of their future pay and prospects, as if they were still doing their old jobs at home.

Now Iris was *in absentia*, and her notional existence was fading, dying, disappearing out of my head. Except at those moments of joy and grief, when involuntary memory released the real Iris to leap out and surprise me . . .

But she was not in the house. That was certain. Unanticipated moments of grief and joy, if they continued to come to me, could come anywhere.

The house had become like a fortification, as in the old days of military science. A dangerous place, because it attracted enemy shellfire. *I must leave the house.* If I stayed I should never know the peace and quiet I thought I wanted. If I did want them. Whether I did or not, the solution was so obvious now that I felt exalted. As if I had been suddenly told I could fly.

My old terror of leaving the house since Iris died – my fear of going anywhere. How absurd those terrors and fears now seemed!

I must escape from my own house, just as Iris used to try to escape. And sometimes, if I had been careless, Iris had succeeded. In the unknown wilderness of dementia she, too, had felt that she must leave home. Somehow. Anyhow . . .

So the thing now, the only thing, was to get away. To imitate Iris. To follow in her footsteps.

I went quickly and quietly downstairs and picked up my coat, with my wallet in the pocket. I squeezed the front door shut behind me. How many times Iris and I had started out like this on our little walks together, except that in those days I had had to unlock the door before we could get out.

Should I lock it now, on the outside? Better not. Mella might hear me.

I closed the door carefully and quietly, and ran away.

10

Leaving Home

And so, in one sense, that was the end of it. The end of the story.

But the tale of the widower's house is not quite over.

I decided to take the train to London. Even the simple business of getting a ticket – simple maybe, but absurdly slow and tiresome – had been a purgatory since I had been on my own and compelled to go to London for some reason. Now it all paraded along with fabulous ease, as if I were indeed flying.

I had a credit card and money in my wallet. I had left home. I could do as I pleased.

But most of my fears came back as the little train rattled on its way to Reading. Where was I to go? Where could I stay? I might be able to fly, but somehow I couldn't face the thought of going to a London hotel.

In the old days Iris had a tiny flat, more of a 'pad' really, at the top of a very tall but rather gimcrack house in a Kensington square. Innumerable stairs. No lift. The floors at the top were so flimsy they creaked at the lightest tread, and Iris used to creep about in her socks for fear of disturbing the tenants below. But she loved it. It was useful for seeing her friends, and essential early on, when her mother was still alive. I loved it too on the occasions I went there, particularly at Christmas time, and on our periodic jaunts, when we bought food and wine in the Gloucester Road and had a long picnic.

Tall as the house was the plane trees in the square outside were even taller, and in summer their broad leaves, pale green against the black and yellow pattern of the trunk, looked in at our window.

After Iris died the pad was got rid of. I couldn't bear to go there; it was the reverse of my house. It was Iris's flat, and there she had lived her own life, seeing her friends all day, creeping back upstairs to bed in the evening. In the morning at seven or so I used to ring her, acting as an alarm clock, and I loved her sleepy, happy 'Wow Wow' as she answered the phone.

It would have been useful now as a jumping-off place. Now that I had left home. I felt about my house now as I had felt about the flat after Iris died.

But what should I do now? I had no idea.

And then suddenly I had. It was obvious: it stared me in the face, just as the need to escape had done.

I would ring up Audi and ask if I could come and stay for a bit in Lanzarote. She had said, very kindly, that I could come and stay if I wanted, but she had never pressed or bothered me about it.

I clutched at my coat pocket, the opposite side to my wallet. Her long phone number was written in my diary, along with others which I could not possibly have remembered, and, thank goodness, my diary was there. So why shouldn't I go now straight to Gatwick instead of to London, which I instinctively feared, and get a ticket and get on the first available flight? I knew there was an airport hotel; I had seen it the last time I had been away – ages ago it seemed.

I caught the train from Reading to Gatwick, and as I sat down a sort of jerk jumped up into my mouth.

Oh heavens! My passport!

My passport must be sitting back in the house. With Mella. Perhaps she had already found it. And confiscated it.

The train was crawling steadily towards Gatwick, towards

freedom. But of what use was freedom without a passport? I sat there hopelessly. When it arrived I should have to get in another train and go back home. If Mella was still there, still occupying my house, and I was sure she would be, how was I to get at my passport?

Then I had another inspiration. The passport was a new one, a flimsy little red thing which had replaced the old stout blue-bound document 'requesting and requiring' all foreigners whatsoever to assist and befriend me as a subject of Her Majesty. Those fine resonant sentences had probably been dropped.

But what had happened, as I now recollected, was that at the time of our last visit to France, to Natasha Spender's cottage in Provence – Iris and I and Peter Conradi looking after us – I had travelled with a passport already out of date. We had sailed past the control in all innocence. The passport photo was glanced at and the document politely returned. But Peter had spotted the date on the way home; and this time we slunk guiltily past the official, who again hardly bothered with us.

But soon after that, and in the midst of all my other troubles, with Iris's condition getting worse every day, I had none the less remembered to apply for a new passport.

When the burglars came they had taken what money there was from the kitchen drawer, but not the new passport. Providentially: because I knew from hearsay that a stolen passport had considerable value. I felt deeply grateful to the burglars for not taking it. But in case they came again, or in case another lot of burglars visited me, I had taken the precaution of tucking the little passport into my wallet, where it fitted quite comfortably.

But was it still there?

Thank God, it was! It was still there because I had forgotten all about it. I felt I could face anything now. And to think that I might have gone tamely home, with the passport all the time in my wallet!

My luck held. The charter flight to Lanzarote turned out to be full that day, but there were two or three the day after. I was on the waiting list with a good chance of catching one of them. I managed to ring Audi.

It was still only three in the afternoon. The day dragged. I prowled restlessly about the little hotel room, lying on the bed and trying to relax, but then almost immediately getting up again. I felt sober now, with all the exaltation of leaving home quite gone.

Had it been a mean thing to leave Mella like that? Of course it had been a mean thing, but something had had to be done; I even felt a sneaking gratitude to Mella for forcing me to make up my mind. Thanks to her I had had no choice. Deliberately or unconsciously she must have thought that I would acquiesce in her annexation of the house, and of me too. I would helplessly accept a *fait accompli* and let her live with me, at least for the moment.

But no! Whatever she was, Mella wasn't like that. She wasn't a schemer, an adventuress, a woman who lived by the wits and the will. True, in that tense three-cornered situation with Margot I had seen her briefly as a gangster, holding a pistol to our heads. But come, the poor girl was more like an autumn leaf, fluttering from place to place, person to person, moment to moment. If I could have done more for her I might have felt more sorry for her – sorry, not guilty. But I knew I could only go on doing the same sort of thing – her coffee and biscuit, the tepid time in bed, the walk round the block.

Perhaps that would have been doing more for her? – all the 'more' of which I was capable? I actually felt now a twinge of nostalgia, of homesickness even, for what we used to do together. Was that the routine, and the kind of 'peace and quiet', which I had really wanted?

But was it what Mella wanted? It came over me again, as so often since I had been alone, that I seemed to know nothing about anybody. What about Margot? Her behaviour with Mella had surely been far from sensible. Had she, too, been blindly in search of a friend, a companion, a helpmate of some sort? Against all the loneliness and fear, the anxieties of being on one's own? She had been wrong about Mella, but how could she have been right? How could I have been right? I was still sure that Mella was not a bad person, not even a scheming person. But how did that help? It was not Mella's fault that she had this effect on the people she met, or rather on the people who found that they had met her.

I got up, wandered about, lay down again. I didn't even want a drink, let alone any dinner. I had begun to feel a more acute anxiety about Mella's activities. What was she doing now? Had she given up and gone away? Somehow that seemed too much to hope for.

As I prowled about my unresponsive little room at the airport hotel I tried to imagine what might be going on back in my house. I felt sure that Mella was still there, but what would she be up to? After all the agitations of the day, I couldn't remember my own phone number, but I had had the forethought to write that down too, at the front of my diary.

The phone in the house rang and rang, and nobody answered it. But that did not reassure me. Obviously Mella, if Mella was lying there in wait, would not answer the phone. She would not wish to alert a caller, who might be a friend of mine, to what was going on in the house.

I stopped ringing, waited for an interval, and tried again. Still no reply.

Then it occurred to me to try my neighbour, who had the spare keys. Her number, too, was in my diary. She was a helpful, good-natured lady. I said that I was very sorry to bother her but I thought I might have left the back door unlocked, and I would be away for a day or two. I mentioned the visit of the burglars. Could she very kindly check that back door?

How would she deal with Mella, if Mella were still there? I told myself, and I was not being disingenuous, that my neighbour was the sort of person who enjoyed a challenge. She would enjoy, too, making a sensible and brisk response. I need not worry too much on her behalf, I thought, even though it was quite possible that Mella would find some way of attaching herself to my neighbour as she had initially done to Margot. Or was it more likely that my neighbour would accept Mella's presence sensibly and briskly, even if with some tacit disapproval? It was no business of hers if I kept a mistress in my house, who preferred not to answer the phone.

At last it was time to ring back. My neighbour sounded unsurprised. Yes, the back door had been open. She had locked it.

Another piece of undeserved good fortune. But relief was soon tempered by anxiety. For one thing, I should not have behaved as I had done towards Mella. I should have asked her firmly to leave, and softened firmness by offering to help her, although short of giving her money, which she did not seem to need, and would possibly have refused with indignation, I saw no material way in which I could be of use.

But another possibility was much more alarming. Suppose she had just popped out for a while to buy food? And perhaps arrange with a locksmith to change the keys of the house? Such reckless daring and bold initiative did not seem like Mella, but what did I know about Mella after all? I only knew that Margot, warm, sensible, open-hearted woman as she was, had decided that enough was enough where she and Mella were concerned, and had barnacled the girl back on to me.

During the night, which was interminable, I tried to do some of what used to be called 'straight thinking'. All my timidities and illusions now seemed crystal clear. But – thank goodness – by four in the morning it began to go all fuzzy in my mind. Dream images and objects came instead, although I knew that I was still awake. Mella entered the room. She looked like an owl, with a sharp beak and round accusing eyes. She brought with her, like a parcel, a piece of poetry – it must be from *Paradise Lost*.

As when a Gryphon through the wilderness
Pursues the Arimaspian . . .

Who was this Arimaspian? I tried to ask Mella but she did not reply. She just looked at me with big, clear, yellow eyes.

'How's the Arimaspian this morning?'

Audi looked and sounded amused. I had told her the night before about the Arimaspian, and Mella, and leaving the house. I had been tired, and had talked a lot, and drunk a lot of red *rioja* wine. The flight to Lanzarote is never easy and always crowded, and it had been delayed.

But Audi looked as if something else was amusing her too; something about which I had not told her, something she must have deduced for herself.

It was a calm, tranquil morning. No wind for once. We could hear a hoopoe calling somewhere far off, and the neat cone of the mountain, pale in the sunlight, had a delicate cinnamon flush which spread into darker colours down its barren flanks.

Audi had listened with patient indulgence to the tale of my leaving home. Through the mistiness of a mild headache I thought over and over how Iris had sometimes escaped too; leaving dementia behind by leaving the house when I forgot to lock the door. When I found her, or when she came back, she wore a mysteriously mischievous but satisfied expression: as if she had found something, or seen some spectacle, about which she could not tell me, or anyone else.

Audi brought out our breakfast to the terrace, where

I was contemplating the mountain and listening for the distant hoopoe. Though a good bit less than a thousand feet its shape somehow made it a mountain rather than a mere hill. It was restful to contemplate, while from time to time laying a hand on my brow. It must have been this that occasioned Audi's amusement at the appearance and demeanour of the Arimaspian. Had he also, I wondered, taken refuge in the bottle from thoughts of his pursuer?

After I had told her about him the previous evening, and about my dream, Audi had gone to find her copy of Milton – an annotated one. I had no idea where the Arimaspian was, although I felt that he was somewhere in *Paradise Lost*. With quiet persistence Audi, one of nature's scholars, tracked him down as we continued to sit chatting and drinking our wine. There he was, in Book II, a one-eyed Scythian tribesman who stole the Gryphon's gold, and was implacably pursued over hill and dale, through plains and deserts, by that fabulous beast, half eagle and half lion.

Was Mella like a Gryphon? Poor Mella – I could hardly believe in her existence now, whether as a real girl or as a legendary monster who might still be pursuing me. And yet Mella, unlike the fabulous Gryphon, did exist, and I had escaped from her. Or was it rather that I had abandoned her? In any case it was unfair to turn her into a monster. But dreams are unfair, as much as are the lives and habits they reflect.

Should I not have reasoned with Mella, compromised and discussed, above all made some attempt to find out about her? She had never seemed to want to talk about herself; but then, I had never given her any encouragement to do so. I had thought only of my own state, and what I had seen as my own needs. Being a widower had indeed turned me into a monster of egoism, just as I had once suspected.

Of course it was open to me to feel, if I felt like it, that widowers had a natural right to be monsters of egoism. Widows too, come to that. But what about Margot? Had she not done her best for Mella, out of kindness as well as out of her own needs, whatever they were? Mella, it was true, had told her a lot of lies, many more than she had bothered to tell me.

I could tell myself now that I had had to abandon Mella – nothing else would have worked. It might well be true, though I didn't like the taste of it. Was I developing a conscience at long last? Was that the trouble? In any case I poured it all out to Audi.

She had listened patiently, and finally said that without knowing either of these two ladies she could hardly give an opinion. But that was reassurance enough, and a great and somehow comic restfulness seemed to come over us while we talked. Perhaps all my problems and troubles as a widower were not so serious after all?

Perhaps it was just the red Spanish wine, but it really did seem as if anxieties and loss had miraculously taken their departure.

One night a week later we went out into the garden after supper. Audi was going to show me the night-flowering cactus, which she hoped might just have come into bloom. There was a crescent moon, but it was very dark, and she took my hand to steer us through the *picon*, velvet black in the darkness, which rose and fell in miniature dunes among the acacias and the wizened lemon trees.

Then Audi switched on her torch, revealing a ghost-like apparition, a dark pillar twelve feet high and covered in spectral white flowers. They blossomed, she said, for a single night: by morning they would have disappeared.

We stood hand in hand in silence while the light from Audi's torch stole about among the gigantic ghost-blooms, bowing and shaking in the night wind. Gazing at them, spellbound, I was back at the beginning of the year. The flowers were like a dance of the blessed spirits. I didn't believe in blessed spirits; but I believed that Iris was with me once more, joining us and making three with us in the warm breath of the night.

A moment later she seemed still closer. A huge moth from Africa flew out of the darkness above our heads and hovered in the torchlight round the flowers. I remembered Iris's strange genius for summoning to her those frail creatures of the night, succouring them and setting them on the way they should go. Once in a hotel at dinner-time the waiters had been trying to knock such a moth down with their napkins, as it flitted to and fro over the heads of the diners. But it flew down straight to Iris's hand, and she carried it to a window, and we watched it fly safely away into the darkness.

Audi and I talked for a long time that night, and on the days that followed, and as we talked Iris came always closer to both of us. Grief may have been difficult to live with, but much worse had been its aftermath, and all the new problems and difficulties it had brought. Now all these had vanished, and Iris was here, the three of us together as we had so often been together in the past.

Audi knew this, I realised. And it soon became clear that she knew – as well as I had begun to do – the real reason why I had come to her, and why I had abandoned the widower's house.

GOOD COMPANIONS

An Anthology to Inspire, Amuse or Console

John Bayley

'A good book is the best of friends, the same today
and for ever'

John Bayley takes us through over seventy years of
extensive reading, judiciously selecting extracts from novels,
poems, letters and diaries that have long been his good
companions, inspiring or amusing him or curing his spirits
in times of adversity.

Unlike many standard anthologies, *Good Companions* is
highly personal and full of Bayley's wit and wisdom:
from Lord Rochester's earthy, but touching 'A Song of a
Young Lady to her Ancient Lover' to Raymond Chandler's
classic, *The Big Sleep*, and from Philip Larkin's little-known
'Marriages' to gems such as Dorothy Fields' 'A Fine
Romance' – which Bayley's wife, Iris Murdoch, 'used to sing
with great brio'.

Whether welcoming back a long-forgotten favourite or being
introduced to a new and unfamiliar face, *Good Companions*
always provides something to move and to delight.

Abacus
0 349 11496 X

FATHER & I

A Memoir

Carlo Gébler

You cannot change the past but, with understanding, you
can sometimes draw the poison out of it.' *Father & I* is Carlo
Gébler's powerful personal testimony to that: the memoir of his
almost impossible relationship with his father Ernest, a man in
later life he would learn to love and understand.

'The literary world has hardly been short of writers'
recollections of their parents in recent years, but they
don't come much better than Carlo Gébler's account of his
relationship with his father . . . This is a marvellous book,
beautifully capturing the bewilderment and betrayals of
childhood, as well as the shifting perspectives of adulthood.
At times unbearably sad, at others ludicrously funny, it is
written with great honesty and charm'
Sunday Telegraph

'A spare, lean, haunting account . . . Written with Gébler's
trademark no-frills prose, and relentless attention to the detail
of a child's life as it is lived, this memoir also provides a vivid
evocation of Britain and Ireland in the 1960s and 1970s'
Will Self, *New Statesman Books of the Year*

'*Father & I* is more than worthy to share shelf space with such
acknowledged masterpieces of the genre as Edmund Gosse's
Father and Son and J. R. Ackerley's *My Father and Myself*'
Times Literary Supplement

'A book of great merit . . . Gébler's is a strong authorial voice,
unsentimental and unabashed. The humanity of the author
comes through and we begin to share his compassion for his
father . . . highly recommendable'
Literary Review

Abacus
0 349 11293 2

PICASSO

Portrait of Picasso as a Young Man

Norman Mailer

Pablo Picasso is arguably the most brilliant and influential artist of the twentieth century, but his confrontational demeanour and stylistic versatility seem forever designed to frustrate critics seeking to achieve an intimate sense of this genius.

In *Portrait of Picasso as a Young Man*, Norman Mailer portrays the monumental artist in the vital, intimate and formative days of his youth. At the heart of Mailer's interpretation is Picasso's relationship with his first great love, Fernande Olivier, conducted over a seven-year period that included revolutionary works such as *Les Demoiselles d'Avignon*, the mysteries of Cubism and Picasso's friendships with Apollinaire and Gertrude Stein.

Written with a clarity far removed from the accepted abstractions of art critics, *Portrait of Picasso as a Young Man* brilliantly demonstrates Norman Mailer's genius for understanding the most enigmatic and protean of minds.

'It has great qualities . . . Mailer has an intuitive understanding of Picasso's machismo and Shamanism that the average art critic lacks'
Andrew Marr, *Independent*

'Sparky and enjoyable'
Val Hennessy, *Daily Mail*

'Possesses the intimacy of a novel and the opulence of an art book'
Boston Globe

Abacus
0 349 10832 3

LETTERS BETWEEN A FATHER AND SON

V. S. Naipaul

'What makes the letters between Vidia Naipaul and members of his close-knit family, especially Seepersad, his father, and his sister Kamla, so remarkable . . . is their literary beauty, and indeed their literary intent . . . what is already clear in these letters is that Naipaul always cared about the bigger things. What is also clear is that he had the literary talent to write about them. All that was still lacking was the books themselves, without which we would never have read these beautiful letters in the first place'
Ian Buruma, *Literary Review*

'You do not even need to open the covers of this handsome book to know that it is a rare and precious one . . . if any modern writer was going to breathe a last gasp into the epistolary tradition, it was always likely to be V. S. Naipaul'
Robert Winder, *New Statesman*

'A very moving book . . . what is delightful about the father who lives in these pages, however, is that unlike most ambitious parents, he does not squeeze his son for guilt'
James Wood, *London Review of Books*

'A fascinating psychological narrative'
Jason Cowley, *The Times*

Abacus
0 349 11313 0

Now you can order superb titles directly from Abacus

☐ Good Companions	John Bayley	£7.99
☐ Father & I	Carlo Gébler	£7.99
☐ Picasso	Norman Mailer	£14.99
☐ Letters Between a Father and Son	V. S. Naipaul	£9.99

The prices shown above are correct at time of going to press. However, the publishers reserve the right to increase prices on covers from those previously advertised, without further notice.

——————————— ⬭ABACUS⬭ ———————————

Please allow for postage and packing: **Free UK delivery**.
Europe; add 25% of retail price; Rest of World; 45% of retail price.

To order any of the above or any other Abacus titles, please call our credit card orderline or fill in this coupon and send/fax it to:

Abacus, PO Box 121, Kettering, Northants NN14 4ZQ
Fax: 01832 733076   Tel: 01832 737527
Email: aspenhouse@FSBDial.co.uk

☐ I enclose a UK bank cheque made payable to Abacus for £...........

☐ Please charge £........... to my Visa/Access/Mastercard/Eurocard

Expiry date ☐☐☐☐   Switch Issue No. ☐☐

NAME (BLOCK LETTERS please) _____

ADDRESS _____

_____

_____

Postcode: _____   Telephone _____

Signature _____

Please allow 28 days for delivery within the UK. Offer subject to price and availability.
Please do not send any further mailings from companies carefully selected by Abacus ☐